Pro MySQL NDB Cluster

Jesper Wisborg Krogh
Mikiya Okuno

Apress®

Pro MySQL NDB Cluster

Jesper Wisborg Krogh
Sydney, New South Wales, Australia

Mikiya Okuno
Tochigi, Japan

ISBN-13 (pbk): 978-1-4842-2981-1
https://doi.org/10.1007/978-1-4842-2982-8

ISBN-13 (electronic): 978-1-4842-2982-8

Library of Congress Control Number: 2017958958

Managing Director: Welmoed Spahr
Editorial Director: Todd Green
Acquisitions Editor: Jonathan Gennick
Development Editor: Laura Berendson
Technical Reviewer: Charles Bell
Coordinating Editor: Jill Balzano
Copy Editor: Kezia Endsley
Compositor: SPi Global
Indexer: SPi Global
Artist: SPi Global

Distributed to the book trade worldwide by Springer Science+Business Media New York, 233 Spring Street, 6th Floor, New York, NY 10013. Phone 1-800-SPRINGER, fax (201) 348-4505, e-mail orders-ny@springer-sbm.com, or visit www.springeronline.com. Apress Media, LLC is a California LLC and the sole member (owner) is Springer Science + Business Media Finance Inc (SSBM Finance Inc). SSBM Finance Inc is a **Delaware** corporation.

For information on translations, please e-mail rights@apress.com, or visit http://www.apress.com/rights-permissions.

Apress titles may be purchased in bulk for academic, corporate, or promotional use. eBook versions and licenses are also available for most titles. For more information, reference our Print and eBook Bulk Sales web page at http://www.apress.com/bulk-sales.

Any source code or other supplementary material referenced by the author in this book is available to readers on GitHub via the book's product page, located at www.apress.com/9781484229811. For more detailed information, please visit http://www.apress.com/source-code.

Printed on acid-free paper

Contents at a Glance

Contents

About the Authors

Jesper Wisborg Krogh is a member of the Oracle MySQL Support team and has spoken on several occasions at Oracle OpenWorld. He has a background with a Ph.D. in computational chemistry before changing to work with MySQL and other software development in 2006. Jesper lives in Sydney, Australia and enjoys spending time outdoors walking, traveling, and reading. His areas of expertise include MySQL Cluster, MySQL Enterprise Backup, and the Performance and sys schemas. He is an active author in the Oracle Knowledge Base and regularly blogs on MySQL topics.

Mikiya Okuno is a member of the Oracle MySQL Support team based in Japan and has written four database-related books in Japanese. He joined the MySQL support team in 2007 when MySQL AB was an independent company. Before joining MySQL, he worked at Sun Microsystems (which acquired MySQL AB, then was acquired by Oracle) as a technical support engineer. He has over 16 years of technical support experience in the computer industry. Mikiya is a self-confessed computer geek and loves Gentoo Linux OS and ErgoDox keyboard for his desktop. Emacs is his preference.

About the Technical Reviewer

Dr. Charles Bell conducts research in emerging technologies. He is a member of the Oracle MySQL Development team as a senior developer working on a variety of database administration and high availability projects. He lives in a small town in rural Virginia with his loving wife. He received his Ph.D. in engineering from Virginia Commonwealth University in 2005. His research interests include database systems, software engineering, sensor networks, and 3D printing. He spends his limited free time as a practicing Maker focusing on microcontroller and 3D printers and printing projects.

Acknowledgments

We would like to thank all of the people who made this book possible. First of all, Jonathan Gennick, Jill Balzano, and Laura Berendson ensured its progress. Jonathan and Jill, your guidance has been invaluable. However, the rest of the team at Apress should not be forgotten either: thank you.

A special thanks to our technical reviewer, Charles Bell. It has been great to get your feedback and learn from your experience as an author. Our colleagues at Oracle also deserve credit for this book becoming a reality. The discussions with the MySQL NDB Cluster developers and our direct colleagues in the MySQL Support team were key to becoming an expert on MySQL NDB Cluster. It is hard to start mentioning names while not forgetting any, but a definite thanks to our manager Adam Dixon for the support. Thanks to the developers Frazer Clement and Mikael Ronström for, time and time again, explaining technical matters of MySQL NDB Cluster, as well as Pekka Nousiainen for his feedback on the index statistics implementation. Of course, Jon Stephens must not be forgotten for his work on the MySQL NDB Cluster chapter in the MySQL Reference Manual.

Last but not least, a warm-hearted thanks to our wives, Ann-Margrete and Junko, as well as Mikiya's children, who put up with us while we were busy writing this book.

Introduction

MySQL NDB Cluster is part of the MySQL family of products. There are few databases matching as many buzzwords as MySQL NDB Cluster: high availability, SQL, NoSQL, in-memory database, automatic failure handling, sharding, etc. This book discusses how these properties are integrated into MySQL NDB Cluster and how they are not just buzzwords, but real features.

Whom This Book Is For

The book has been written for database administrators who are looking into deploying MySQL NDB Cluster or already have a cluster in production and want to increase their knowledge to be able to handle routine administrative tasks and troubleshooting. While we have attempted to write the book assuming as little existing knowledge as possible, it is an advantage to have at least some SQL database background.

How This Book Is Structured

The chapters have been divided into five parts, with each part covering related topics. The journey starts with some background knowledge of how MySQL NDB Cluster works, then moves on to installation and configuration, daily tasks and maintenance, monitoring and troubleshooting, and completes with development and performance tuning.

Part I

The first part consists of two chapters and discusses how MySQL NDB Cluster works from a technical point of view. There is not a lot of focus on practical tasks, but some of the theory is exemplified through case studies. The two chapters are:

- Chapter 1: Architecture and Core Concepts. The first chapter goes into how the cluster works at a high level as well as more specific details for two of the nodes types: management and API nodes.

- Chapter 2: The Data Nodes. The second chapter exclusively focuses on the data nodes, which are where the data is stored and queries are executed.

Part II

The second part explains how to deploy MySQL NDB Cluster, starting with system considerations, then discusses configuration, installation, and replication. The four chapters are:

- Chapter 3: System Planning. This chapter discusses what to consider when choosing hardware and how to plan for network partitioning and scalability. There are also several examples of typical topologies.

- Chapter 4: Configuration. This chapter shows how MySQL NDB Cluster is configured and goes through the most important configuration options.

- Chapter 5: Installation. It is finally time to install MySQL NDB Cluster. The chapter has installation instructions for Linux, Microsoft Windows, and MacOS.

- Chapter 6: Replication. Replication allows the data from one cluster to be replicated to another cluster, or an InnoDB database. MySQL NDB Cluster's conflict resolution features for active-active replication between two clusters are also included.

Part III

The cluster is up and running, so this third part moves on to a series of practical focused chapters describing how day-to-day tasks and maintenance are performed. There are seven chapters in this part:

- Chapter 7: The NDB Management Client and Other NDB Utilities. This chapter discusses the utilities available in the MySQL NDB Cluster installation. Most of the focus is on the NDB management client, which can be used to perform a range of tasks such as starting, stopping, and restarting nodes as well as creating backups, getting the cluster status, etc.

- Chapter 8: Backups and Restores. The data is worth no more than its ability to be recovered in the event of a disaster. This chapter discusses the ins and outs of backups and restores.

- Chapter 9: Table Maintenance. This chapter goes through the online and offline schema change features, defragmentation, and index statistics.

- Chapter 10: Restarts. In a product that aims at making itself highly available, online restarts are important. This chapter goes through the concepts of rolling restarts and system restarts. There are also several detailed examples of tasks requiring a restart.

- Chapter 11: Upgrades and Downgrades. This chapter discusses and gives practical examples of how it is possible to perform upgrades and downgrades, both online and offline.

- Chapter 12: Security Considerations. Security must be a primary part of the design decisions, starting from the initial planning and continuing through the lifetime of the cluster. This chapter goes through the most important security aspects for MySQL NDB Cluster.

- Chapter 13: MySQL Cluster Manager. This chapter provides a tutorial for the MySQL Enterprise offering MySQL Cluster Manager (MCM), which provides an easier way to manage a cluster. The chapter includes the main steps, from the initial installation through an upgrade.

Part IV

A special part of a database's daily routines is monitoring and troubleshooting. That is the topic of Part IV. There are four chapters in this part:

- Chapter 14: Monitoring Solutions and the Operating System. This chapter goes through how monitoring solutions, particularly MySQL Enterprise Monitor, can be used to prevent and solve issues, and ends with considerations of what to monitor at the operating system level.

- Chapter 15: Sources for Monitoring Data. This chapter goes through the traditional sources in MySQL for collecting and monitoring data, including the Information Schema, the Performance Schema, the sys schema, the SHOW statements, and the MySQL error log.

- Chapter 16: Monitoring MySQL NDB Cluster. MySQL NDB Cluster provides some additional monitoring sources: The ndbinfo schema and the logs on the management and data nodes.

- Chapter 17: Typical Troubles and Solutions. No matter how careful a database is managed, there will be times when something goes wrong. This chapter goes through some general troubleshooting techniques for MySQL NDB Cluster and some typical issues.

Part V

The last part moves on to the development part of MySQL NDB Cluster. Developing using SQL and NoSQL and performance tuning are all discussed. The three chapters in Part V are:

- Chapter 18: Developing Application Using SQL with MySQL NDB Cluster. This chapter goes through table and index creation and other considerations, such as error handling when using SQL statements in the development.

- Chapter 19: MySQL NDB Cluster as NoSQL Database. MySQL NDB Cluster supports several NoSQL APIs. This chapter discusses NDB-memcached, the C++ NDB API, and ClusterJ. The chapter also includes several code examples.

- Chapter 20: MySQL NDB Cluster and Application Performance Tuning. The final chapter of the book covers performance tuning at the system and SQL levels. The system level, for example, includes binding data node threads to CPUs and disk types. The SQL level includes optimizing joins and partitioning, mixing NoSQL and SQL, and more.

Downloading the Code

The code for the examples shown in this book is available on the Apress web site, *www.apress.com*. A link can be found on the book's information page.

PART I

▪ ▪ ▪

The Basics

CHAPTER 1

■ ■ ■

Architecture and Core Concepts

MySQL NDB Cluster is a distributed real-time database management system using a *shared nothing architecture*. It excels at workloads with a high volume of small transactions, and it aims at providing high availability with no single point of failure and duplication of data through *two-phase commits* and *synchronous replication*. Part of the high availability implementation also includes a real-time promise; that is, MySQL NDB Cluster looks to provide consistent response times. To avoid problems on one node causing delays in the rest of the cluster, MySQL NDB Cluster employs a *fail early strategy,* which affects particularly the data nodes and is something that users should have in mind.

The communication within the cluster is performed using the NDB API (a NoSQL API), which was originally developed together with the rest of NDB Cluster in the 1990s. However, since NDB Cluster became part of MySQL in 2003, a storage engine that plugs into MySQL Server using the pluggable storage engine API has been developed. So nowadays the most commonly used method of interacting with NDB Cluster is through SQL statements similar to other storage engines in MySQL, such as InnoDB.

■ **Note** For MySQL NDB Cluster, the term NoSQL API means an application programming interface that allows communication with the backend storage engine while bypassing the SQL layer. The underlying storage is identical irrespective of the API used, and the same data can be accessed concurrently using different APIs, including the SQL API. Chapters 18 and 19 discuss the APIs in more detail.

With the ongoing development, MySQL NDB Cluster is today a general-purpose storage engine that supports a wide range of features, including features not supported by any other storage engine in MySQL.

This chapter provides the big picture of MySQL NDB Cluster by looking at the general characteristics and features of MySQL NDB Cluster, limitations, the various node types, and the built-in high availability. Chapter 2 continues the discussion by focusing on the backend storage, the data nodes. First up though, a quick overview of the terminology in MySQL NDB Cluster.

Terminology

One of the aspects that can be difficult when studying a new subject is the terminology. Each product has its own way of naming and describing features. This section provides an overview of the most important terms used in MySQL NDB Cluster. More details of what these terms mean will become apparent as the features are discussed throughout this book.

Table 1-1 contains a list of several of the terms used in the description of MySQL NDB Cluster and all of its features. The list is ordered alphabetically.

© Jesper Wisborg Krogh and Mikiya Okuno 2017

J. W. Krogh and M. Okuno, *Pro MySQL NDB Cluster*, https://doi.org/10.1007/978-1-4842-2982-8_1

Table 1-1. *Terminology of MySQL NDB Cluster*

Term	Description
Angel	The angel process monitors the actual ndbd/ndbmtd process (data node) and handles node failures.
Arbitration	The process of determining which data nodes can continue after the failure of a data node.
API node	A process communicating with the data nodes. This can, for example, be part of the application, an SQL node, or a utility program.
Asynchronous replication	The replication used to replicate between two clusters or MySQL Server instances. The replication is asynchronous because it is performed after the control is returned to the application. Thus, only the master side is guaranteed to apply the change.
Binary log	A log used to record all schema and data changes. Primarily used for replication and *point-in-time recoveries* (PITR).
Cluster	In this book, used for a collection of data, management, and API nodes in MySQL NDB Cluster.
Data node	The backend storage for MySQL NDB Cluster. Also known as ndbd or ndbmtd.
High availability	The ability to provide the service with "very little downtime". What "very little" is and what constitutes "downtime" depends on the system and product. For MySQL NDB Cluster being available means being able to execute transactions with consistent response times.
Kernel block	The building blocks that make up the data nodes.
InnoDB	The main storage engine in MySQL Server.
ndb_mgmd	The binary used to start the management nodes.
ndbd	The binary used to start the single threaded data nodes. See also data node.
ndbmtd	The binary used to start the multi-threaded (mt) data nodes. See also data node.
OLAP	Online analytical processing: A typical OLAP workload can be used to generate reports.
OLTP	Online transaction processing: Mostly small, quick transactions.
Management node	The MySQL NDB Cluster nodes handling, for example, configuration, connections, and arbitration.
mysqld	The daemon process used for MySQL Server and the SQL nodes. See also SQL node and API node.
MySQL Server	The standard MySQL database product not including data nodes and management nodes.
Node group	A group of data nodes sharing the same data. Each node group has as many members as there are replicas of the data. When a cluster has more than one node group, the data is automatically sharded between the node groups, so each node group only stores a subset of the data.

(continued)

Table 1-1. (*continued*)

Term	Description
Partition	A table may be logically split into several partitions. MySQL NDB Cluster can use this to process data in parallel for some queries. Sharding is performed in units of a partition (the entire partition is always in only one shard).
NDBCluster	The name of the storage engine providing the link between SQL nodes and the data nodes.
Replica	Copy of the data in the data node. It is recommended to have two replicas.
Replication	The method to keep multiple copies of the data up to data. Replication happens at two levels in MySQL NDB Cluster. There is synchronous replication between the data nodes in the same cluster, and asynchronous replication between two or more instances (an instance can be either be MySQL NDB Cluster or MySQL Server). See also replication master and replication slave.
Replication master	The "active" side of an asynchronous replication setup. The replication master can be used for writes and reads. The writes are copied to the binary log, which is streamed to the replication slave. It is possible for a cluster to be both a replication master and a replication slave.
Replication slave	The "passive" side of an asynchronous replication setup. The replication slave receives the updates from the replication master's binary log.
Rolling restart	The process of restarting several or all of the nodes in a cluster while being able to process transactions while the restarts are ongoing.
Sharding	Dividing data into multiple groups, so each node does not need to store all data.
SQL node	A MySQL NDB Cluster API node using mysqld from MySQL Server as the API node. See also API node.
Storage engine	MySQL supports a range of different engines to handle the underlying storage. These are called storage engines. Examples are InnoDB and NDBCluster.
Synchronous replication	The replication used between data nodes in the same cluster. That the replication is synchronous means the changes take effect on all affected nodes at the same time, and that either all nodes or none accept the change.
Transporter	The connection between two nodes in a cluster. This is usually a TCP/IP connection.
Two-phase commit	Committing through a *prepare* phase followed by the actual commit. After the prepare has succeeded, it is guaranteed that all participating parties (data nodes in a cluster) can commit the change. Another use of two-phase commit is in XA transactions (which are not supported in MySQL NDB Cluster).

Characteristics and Features

MySQL NDB Cluster is a technology that expands the traditional standalone MySQL Server to provide a high availability storage engine. The characteristics and feature set of a storage engine set one storage engine apart from others. This section goes through some of the high-level characteristics, features, limitations, and use cases.

Architecture

Some of the important architectural characteristics of MySQL NDB Cluster are:

- **Primarily an in-memory database:** In-memory data provides fast and consistent access. On-disk data is also supported for non-indexed columns.

- **On-disk data:** On disk tablespaces can be used to allow for large volumes of data.

- **Distributed system:** The cluster is created by having nodes on one or several hosts. This includes splitting the data across multiple processes.

- **Shared nothing architecture:** As discussed in the section entitled "Built-In High Availability," MySQL NDB Cluster uses a shared nothing architecture to ensure no *single point of failure* (SPOF).

- **Commodity hardware:** MySQL NDB Cluster runs on commodity hardware, making it relatively inexpensive in hardware costs.

- **Duplication of data:** The data can be duplicated to ensure that the failure of one node does not stop access to the data. Duplication of the data is performed through synchronous replication and two-phase commits.

Features

MySQL NDB Cluster inherits many of its features from MySQL Server, but there are also several features that are specific to MySQL NDB Cluster. This subsection provides an overview of the most important features. The rest of the book will go into more detail with each of these features.

ACID Compliant Transactions

ACID stands for (Atomicity, Consistency, Isolation, Durability) and is an important feature of transactional databases. Atomicity means that a change is either fully applied or not at all, and all changes within a transaction will be seen as one change. Consistency means that the content is always correct from a database point of view (for example, with respect to constraints). Isolation ensures that two concurrent transactions can only make changes that are isolated from each other (i.e., the result is the same as if they were executed in sequence). Durability is the property that a committed transaction will not be lost if there is a subsequent crash. How durability is ensured while storing the data in-memory is discussed in Chapter 2.

Foreign Keys

The NDBCluster storage engine supports foreign keys, including for partitioned tables. This makes NDBCluster the only storage engine in MySQL supporting foreign keys on partitioned tables. Both tables included in the foreign key must be NDBCluster tables and there must be an index for the referenced columns in both the parent and child tables.

High Availability Is Built-In

There are several meanings of the term "high availability". In MySQL NDB Cluster, it means that the cluster can execute queries and the response times are predictable. MySQL NDB Cluster has been designed from the beginning to provide high availability instead of adding high availability on top of an existing product.

The ability to answer queries is a result of the shared nothing architecture together with support for multiple replicas of the data and each node type. This allows the cluster to continue operating even if one node (or in some cases several nodes) is unavailable. The consistent response times are ensured through several means, such as storing the data in memory, not allowing the internal job processing in the data nodes to block for more than 10 milliseconds at a time, and shutting down nodes that are too slow.

Overall this means that no special software is required to use the high availability features in MySQL NDB Cluster. High availability is discussed in more detail later in this chapter.

Auto-Failover

When a node shuts down, the remaining nodes automatically handle any tasks related to the node failure. Network partitioning is solved through arbitration and, if necessary, by *shooting the other node in the head* (STONITH). Once the failover is completed, the remaining nodes can continue operating.

SQL and NoSQL Access

There is a choice between several APIs to access the data in the cluster: *SQL nodes*, the *NDB API, ClusterJ, Node.js,* and *NDB-memcached.* (NDB-memcached is special in this context as it requires a daemon between the client/application and the data nodes.) It is possible for an application to mix the use of several APIs, for example to execute complex queries through SQL nodes and use ClusterJ for simpler queries. This provides flexibility for the developer to use the API that provides the best features for each task.

Auto Partitioning and Auto Sharding

Distribution of the data happens automatically based on the cluster configuration. The more data nodes, and the higher parallelism (number of threads) configured for the data nodes, the more partitions will be chosen for the tables. The sharding is done across the data nodes, so each data node only stores a part of the data. The automation means that the application does not need to know how the partitioning and sharding have been done.

Horizontal Scalability

When a system is scaled horizontally, it is done by adding more nodes to the system. (On the other hand, vertical scalability is achieved by improving the hardware of each node.) It is possible to add data nodes, management nodes, and API nodes while the cluster is online. Additional data nodes particularly improve the storage capacity of the cluster, but can also improve the performance for some workloads (see Chapters 3 and 20). More API/SQL nodes can be added as the requirements change to help distribute the load among the nodes, which can improve the throughput.

Online Operations

There is wide support for performing operations online, which is also part of the high availability story. As already mentioned, all three node types (data nodes, management nodes, and API nodes) can be added while the cluster is online. There is also support for making schema changes online—in fact, MySQL NDB Cluster was the first storage engine in MySQL to support online schema changes. Finally, both upgrades and downgrades can be performed with the cluster online. This includes both changing the patch release version (for example, 7.5.4 to 7.5.5) and moving between major versions (for example, 7.4.14 to 7.5.5).

Geographical Replication

Geographical replication makes it possible to set up another cluster or MySQL Server instance with a copy of the data. This is based on the standard (asynchronous) replication in MySQL Server. When a change is made in the replication master, it is send to the replication slave using the binary log. The replication slave can be located in the same data center, but also as far away as another continent.

There are several uses for replication slaves. They allow the application to scale out reads, which can be used to improve the overall throughput of the system. Another use is to have a standby cluster that can be used if the replication master is shut down—this improves the availability. Finally, some workloads are not optimal for MySQL NDB Cluster, so the replication slave can use the InnoDB storage engine for use with, for example, OLAP workloads.

Replication is a big topic and there are several changes for the replication to support the distributed nature of MySQL NDB Cluster. Chapter 6 is dedicated to discussing how replication works.

Conflict Resolution in Master-Master Replication

In a geographical replication setup, it is possible to enable writes on more than one cluster. Since the replication is asynchronous, this presents a problem that writes to different clusters may conflict. Since there is a delay after the transaction commit until the changes have replicated, this conflict will not be detected until after both transactions have been committed. Traditionally, it has required manual intervention to resolve such conflicts—often requiring rebuilding one of the sides in the replication setup.

MySQL NDB Cluster has support for handling the conflicts automatically, either by making a decision which updates win and/or log details about the conflicting updates to make it easier for the database administrator to decide how to proceed.

Limitations

Like all other database implementations, MySQL NDB Cluster has limitations. It is important to be familiar with both the strengths and the limitations, so it can be ensured the application is designed to take advantage of the strengths and minimize exposure to the limitations. There are several reasons for limitations to exist. A common reason is that it is necessary to make a choice between two features, for example performance or a functionality. This also comes down to the design decisions made, in some cases, two decades ago. The limitations will change over time as new development is completed and advances in hardware and software become available. The limitations of the NDBCluster storage engine can be divided into two categories: schema limitations and everything else.

■ **Note**   The MySQL NDB Cluster limitations are well documented in the Reference Manual at
https://dev.mysql.com/doc/refman/5.7/en/mysql-cluster-limitations.html.

Schema Limitations

Schema limitations have to do with tables, indexes, and other objects that are created by a database user. Notable schema limitations include the following:

- All tables must have a primary key. If none is provided, MySQL NDB Cluster will add a hidden auto-increment column as the primary key. However, this hidden primary key introduces restrictions on the table. The hidden primary key cannot be used for filtering, including on a replication slave for replicated statements; tables with a hidden primary key do not have support for online schema changes; and if the table has one or more BLOB, TEXT, or JSON columns, the table will not be included in the binary log.

- No index can be wider than 3072 bytes.

- The only index types supported are T-Tree indexes (like B-Tree indexes but optimized for in-memory use) for ordered indexes and hash indexes for unique indexes. The index types are also discussed in more detail in Chapter 18.

- Indexes cannot be added to BLOB, TEXT, and BIT columns. BLOB and TEXT data is stored using a secondary table (details follow in the next chapter) and several BIT columns are combined into one storage location. This design prevents indexes on the columns using one of these data types.

- There is no support for prefix indexes (that is, it indexes the first N characters/bytes of a column).

- Indexed columns cannot be stored on disk; they are always stored in memory to allow the best performance. The index implementation with T-Tree indexes for ordered indexes assumes the indexes are stored in memory, and hash indexes are partly stored in a dedicated memory segment (index memory).

- A foreign key cannot be `ON DELETE CASCADE` if it is a reference to the primary key in the parent table.

- The maximum row size is 14000 bytes. The row size is calculated as the width of each column with a BLOB, TEXT, and JSON data type contributing 264 bytes. Each column's contribution is 4-byte aligned; that is, a `VARCHAR(12)` using UTF8 requires 12 * 3 bytes for the content and 1 byte for storing the length, so 37 bytes. However, the column contributes 40 bytes to the row size due to the 4-byte alignment.

- The sum of the number of databases, tables, and indexes in MySQL NDB Cluster is limited to 20320.

- `NDBCluster` cannot be used for temporary tables (`CREATE TEMPORARY TABLE …` statements).

Other Limitations

There are a few other limitations spread across various categories, such as transactional support and binary logging. The most important limitations are:

- Only the `READ COMMITTED` transaction isolation level is supported. This is similar to Oracle DB, but unlike the `InnoDB` storage engine.

- There is no support for savepoints.

- Binary log events for changes to data in NDBCluster are always logged using the ROW based format.

- There is no support for global transaction identifiers (GTIDs).

- No schema changes (DDL) can be made while a data node is restarting.

Use Cases

While historically, the main usage for MySQL NDB Cluster was for telecommunication companies, today, particularly thanks to the improvements made over the last five years, the number of use cases has increased significantly. The following list includes examples of use cases and actual users of MySQL NDB Cluster.

- Phone call routing for telecommunication companies. If you make a phone call, it is likely that MySQL NDB Cluster is involved. Examples of users include Alcatel-Lucent (now part of Nokia) and Telenor.

- Session management for web sites.

- Authentication services, for example FreeRADIUS and for VoIP systems.

- For online gaming. Examples are Big Fish and Playful Play.

- Metadata management for the HopsFS file system, which is for example used by Spotify.

- Real-time fraud detection. An example is PayPal.

- Flight planning, for example for the US Navy.

■ **Note** If you are interested, *https://www.mysql.com/customers/cluster/* contains more information about the use cases as well as a list of some of the MySQL NDB Cluster users, including all of those mentioned in the use case list.

The list of use case examples shows several workloads that consist of relatively simple queries, such as authentication services and phone call routing. This is indeed the biggest strength of MySQL NDB Cluster. The optimal workload is one consisting of queries that all use the primary key to access the data, and where only a few rows are used in each transaction. While this may in general be true for databases, it is particularly true for MySQL NDB Cluster because of the design.

The data is distributed, so accessing large amounts of data also increases the load of the network, and all records of the current activity must be kept in memory to fulfill the real-time promise. On the other hand, a single row picked using the primary key will allow the API node to request the row directly from the data node storing it, and small transactions mean a small overhead of storing transactional metadata. This may seem abstract and difficult to understand with the information available at this point, but rest assured, throughout this book the required background will be built up to make it easier to see this relationship. Particularly this chapter as well as Chapters 2, 3, 18, 19, and 20 will be useful in this respect, as they describe the fundamentals, configuration, development, and performance tuning of MySQL NDB Cluster.

In short, it can be said that MySQL NDB Cluster excels at *online transaction processing* (OLTP) workloads, but is less suited for *online analytical processing* (OLAP) workloads. Figure 1-1 shows a graph where the workloads with the most optimal workloads are at the origin, which signifies a transaction only accessing a single row through the primary key. The least optimal workloads are for large transactions and large scans.

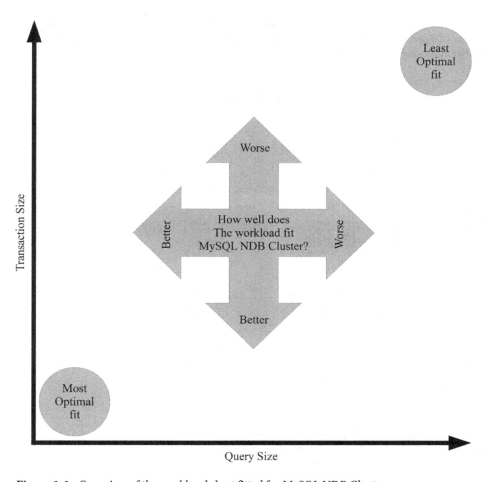

Figure 1-1. *Overview of the workloads best fitted for MySQL NDB Cluster*

In the real world, most workloads are not exclusively at one end of the spectrum, and it is not a requirement that all queries be in the optimal part of the graph. However, if most transactions are in the least optimal part, MySQL NDB Cluster may not be the best fit—in that case, MySQL Server with the InnoDB storage engine is likely to provide a better experience. A possibility that is discussed in Chapter 6 is to have NDBCluster as the storage engine on a replication master and to use the InnoDB storage engine in the replication slave. This will allow writes and small transactions to take advantage of NDBCluster's features, while larger read transactions such as reports use the more flexible InnoDB storage engine.

Node Types

MySQL NDB Cluster has three types of nodes, all serving their special roles. The node types are:

- Management nodes
- Data nodes
- API/SQL nodes

11

The relationship between the various node types is displayed in Figure 1-2, and each node type will be discussed in more detail following the figure. For simplicity, NDB-memcached is just listed with the daemon process and not the clients connecting to memcached.

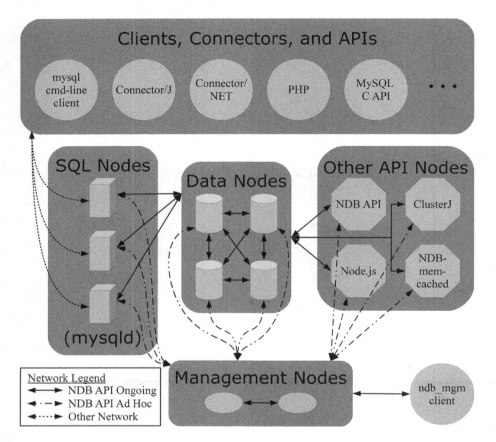

Figure 1-2. *Overview of the various nodes participating in a cluster and the relationship between them*

Management Nodes

The management nodes are the most lightweight nodes of the cluster. They have five roles in a cluster and are only required at a few specific times during the lifetime of the cluster:

- To handle the configuration.

- To allow other nodes to connect to the cluster.

- To maintain the *cluster log* with messages from all nodes.

- For arbitration in case of a potential *split-brain* scenario.

- For administrative tasks initiated by the database administrator, such as starting a backup or restarting a data node.

In a high availability setup, it is common to have two management nodes, so there is one remaining in case the other is shut down.

Handling the Configuration

The management nodes are responsible for taking care of the configuration. The configuration is created in an INI style formatted configuration file typically named *config.ini*. The configuration file includes the configuration for all nodes in the cluster, though the API/SQL nodes may additionally have their own local configuration file. For example, SQL nodes also read the usual *my.cnf* or *my.ini* configuration file known from a standalone MySQL Server installations. If there are multiple management nodes in the cluster, each management node has its own configuration file, but they must be identical. When the management node is started, it can optionally read the configuration file and apply it. The parsed configuration is then stored in a local cache.

Listing 1-1 shows an example of an INI style formatted *config.ini* file. In production systems, the configuration will typically include more options and configuration sections than in the example, but the overall structure will be the same. Chapter 4 goes into detail about the MySQL NDB Cluster configuration.

Listing 1-1. Example Cluster Configuration File (*config.ini*)

```
[ndb_mgmd default]
DataDir                       = /cluster/

[ndbd default]
NoOfReplicas                  = 2
DataMemory                    = 20G
IndexMemory                   = 2G
MaxNoOfConcurrentTransactions = 400K
DataDir                       = /cluster/

[ndbd]
NodeId                        = 1
HostName                      = 192.168.56.103

[ndbd]
NodeId                        = 2
HostName                      = 192.168.56.104

[ndb_mgmd]
NodeId                        = 49
HostName                      = 192.168.56.101

[ndb_mgmd]
NodeId                        = 50
HostName                      = 192.168.56.102

[mysqld]
NodeId                        = 51
HostName                      = 192.168.56.103

[mysqld]
NodeId                        = 52
HostName                      = 192.168.56.104
```

```
[api]
NodeId                       = 53
HostName                     = 192.168.56.101

[api]
NodeId                       = 54
HostName                     = 192.168.56.102
```

Connection Handling

Whenever a node wants to join the cluster, it must first contact a management node. The management node will check whether the node is allowed to join the cluster; if the joining node is allowed to connect, the management node provides the configuration to the joining node. This also means that no nodes can join the cluster if there are no management nodes online or reachable.

Logging

The management nodes maintain the cluster log that receives messages from the whole cluster. The messages range from informational messages about the memory usage to critical errors of unintended node shutdowns. This means the cluster log is a good place to look for the initial overview of the status of the cluster.

Arbitration

Arbitration is the task of deciding which data nodes should stay online in case of a split-brain scenario where at most half of the data nodes can see each other. All other data nodes will be instructed to shut down. The arbitration process is discussed in more detail in the section on "Built-In High Availability".

Administrative Tasks

Using the ndb_mgm management client to connect to the data nodes, it is possible to perform several administrative tasks such as creating backups, starting and stopping nodes, controlling log levels, etc. For more details, see Chapter 7.

Data Nodes

The data nodes comprise the very core of MySQL NDB Cluster, as they are where the actual data is stored. There are two types of data nodes:

- **ndbd**: The original single-threaded version of the data node
- **ndbmtd**: The multi-threaded version for modern hardware

From a functional perspective, the two are the same, but there are differences in terms of performance. In most cases, a production system should be using the multi-threaded binary.

Since data nodes play a very important role in a cluster, Chapter 2 is dedicated to discussing data nodes in greater detail.

API and SQL Nodes

The API nodes are where queries are submitted. Each API node is connected to all the data nodes and has access to all of the data without any extra consideration. For instance, even though the data is sharded, it is not necessary for the application or user to know anything about the sharding, which allows for simpler logic in the application.

It is also possible to execute one query through one API node and the next through another node, as long as they are not in the same transaction. Due to MySQL NDB Cluster's exclusive use of the READ COMMITTED transaction isolation level and the synchronous replication between the data nodes, as soon as a transaction is committed, all the API nodes can use the committed data.

MySQL NDB Cluster supports several APIs:

- **NDB API:** This is the original API and what all other APIs use under the hood to talk to the data nodes. It is only supported in C++.

- **SQL Node:** This is a MySQL Server (mysqld) instance. This is the most common API node. Since this is the most common API node type, API nodes are also commonly known as SQL nodes. SQL nodes can also optionally be used for arbitration. The application connects to the SQL node using any of the available connectors or APIs that also can be used to connect to MySQL Server and InnoDB tables.

- **ClusterJ:** Java applications can use the ClusterJ API to bypass the SQL nodes.

- **Node.js:** For Node.js (JavaScript) applications, there is an API that can be used directly as well.

- **NDB-memcached:** Using the NDB-memcached API allows an application to access the data using memcached, which is a distributed in-memory caching system. NDB-memcached is a special build that can use the data nodes for its backend storage. The homepage of memcached is *https://memcached.org/*.

When using mysqld as an API node, a special version compiled with support for MySQL NDB Cluster must be used. Even though SQL nodes can store data on their own by using other storage engines such as InnoDB, no SQL node stores any data where the table is created using the NDBCluster storage engine. Every time data is changed in the table, the data is sent to the data nodes, and every time data is fetched from the table, the data is sent from the data nodes to the SQL nodes and then back to the application. Thus, an SQL node not only needs to perform relatively expensive parsing of the query, there is also an extra hop between the application and the data nodes.

This means it can be an advantage to use an API that talks directly with the data nodes, as that will reduce the overhead on two fronts:

- The parsing of the SQL statements is avoided.

- One level of network communication is removed.

For this reason, the general performance of the API types in order of best performing to the least performing is:

- NDB API: This is the only API that can communicate directly with the data nodes. All the other API node types eventually use the NDB API, although it is hidden from the developer.

- Other NoSQL APIs: ClusterJ, Node.js, NDB-memcached.

- SQL nodes.

Several of the APIs are discussed in more detail in Chapters 18 and 19.

Built-In High Availability

One of the main reasons MySQL NDB Cluster is chosen over other database systems is its built-in design for high availability. You may have seen that MySQL NDB Cluster can get 99.999% (five nines) uptime (or at most around 5 minutes 15 seconds of downtime each year). Five nines is a classical threshold for considering a system highly available and this has become a bit of the magic number that high availability databases strive to achieve.

High availability can mean a number of things. For MySQL NDB Cluster, the emphasis is on being able to avoid a total cluster outage and being able to provide consistent response times to the queries. High availability is achieved by means of:

- The shared nothing architecture.

- Support for no single point of failure. It is possible to have redundancy of all node types and multiple replicas of all data.

- Automatic detection and handling of node failures.

- The fail early strategy to avoid a slow or failed node causing slow response times.

The fact that MySQL NDB Cluster is designed from the start for high availability does not mean that high availability and particularly the five nines uptime comes for free. When you deploy a cluster, it is important to have this in mind, or you may inadvertently reduce the availability compared to a more traditional MySQL Server deployment using the InnoDB storage engine. Important things to keep in mind are:

- MySQL NDB Cluster supports no single point of failure, but the database administrator and system administrator must ensure it is implemented. For example, the network must be designed to ensure that the failure of a switch does not prevent at least half the data nodes from communicating.

- The fail early strategy means it is important not to overload the cluster. Overloading can happen at several levels, including the SQL nodes trying to write all data changes to the binary logs (replication and point in time recovery logs), the network becoming a bottleneck, the disk or CPUs or the memory not being able to keep up, etc. One key task for the database developers and administrator is to ensure that the queries executed on the production system are well tested to ensure they do not contribute to an overload.

- While the cluster as a whole can survive single node failures, transactions executing at the time may fail with a temporary error. Likewise, transactions may fail due to resource exhaustion. So, the application should always be ready to retry temporary failures.

These are things that are also discussed in more detail in Part II.

Shared Nothing Architecture

The shared nothing architecture of MySQL NDB Cluster is one of the most significant aspects of the architecture. A shared nothing architecture means that each node shares neither disk, memory, nor any other resource with the other nodes in the cluster. This influences how most aspects of the cluster work, for example:

- Communication between the nodes

- Detection of whether the other nodes are online

- Failover

■ **Note**   Failover is the process of resolving a state where one or more nodes have become unavailable. This is handled automatically in MySQL NDB Cluster and is discussed in more detail later in the chapter.

Figure 1-3 shows how the data nodes have their own hardware resources, and no component is shared between the nodes. The same is true for the other nodes in the cluster, but to keep focus on the important part these are not depicted explicitly in the figure. This means that should a hard disk fail in one node, the node can be taken offline and the rest of the cluster can continue. The advantage of this choice is that it makes it possible to avoid single point of failure, which is the cornerstone in the strategy to achieve high availability.

■ **Note**   Each hardware component may itself be redundant. For example, the disks may be forming a RAID array, so one or more disks can fail without losing the storage altogether. This will provide an extra layer of protection.

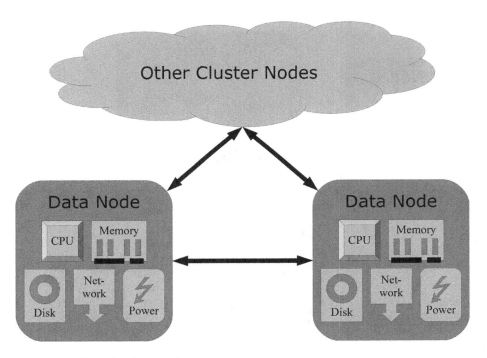

Figure 1-3. *Shared nothing architecture*

Heartbeats

An essential mechanism for the cluster to be able to auto-detect node failures of one or more of the other nodes in the cluster is heartbeats. There are essentially three kinds of heartbeats for a cluster:

- **Between data nodes:** These heartbeats are sent in circular fashion so each data node only receives heartbeats from one other data node and only sends to one data node. It is said that a data node receives heartbeats from the data node to the left of itself, and it sends to the data node to the right. Some of the messages in the logs use this left-right terminology. A data node is responsible for detecting whether the data node to the left of itself is still alive.

- **Between data nodes and non-data nodes:** These heartbeats are sent for all possible combinations, i.e. a given data node sends and receives heartbeats to/from all non-data nodes. Non-data nodes include management nodes and all types of API nodes.

- **Between management nodes:** These heartbeats are sent between the management nodes, so a management node knows whether its peer(s) are online.

These heartbeats are also depicted in Figure 1-4.

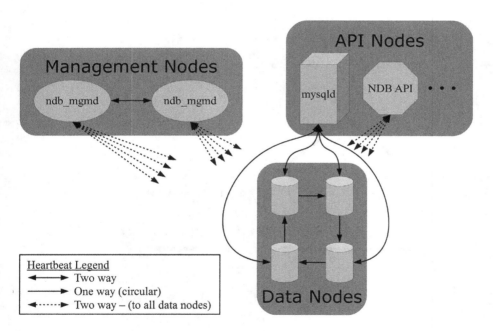

***Figure 1-4.** The heartbeats between the various nodes in a cluster*

Data Node Failure Handling and Arbitration

A data node may fail for several reasons such as missing too many heartbeats due to overload or network failure, hardware problems, bugs, or other reasons. Irrespective of the reason, the remaining nodes must determine whether they can continue or they must shut down. If the surviving data nodes as a group holds all the data, and more than half of the data nodes are in the group, it is easy to determine the data nodes can continue. If the group does not have all the data, it is equally easy to determine they must shut down.

A more complicated scenario occurs in the case when one or more groups of data nodes have access to all the data, but do not have a majority of the data nodes. In this case, it is impossible for the data nodes to know on their own whether it is safe to continue, and arbitration is required. For example, if the cluster is split into two halves by a network failure, and both halves on their own have all the data, it is known as a split-brain scenario. That is, in principle both halves can continue on their own. However, if the split-brain state is allowed to stay and updates occur on both halves, the data in the two halves will start to diverge, and API nodes will get different results depending on which half of the data nodes it happens to query. This is something that under no circumstances is allowed to happen, so the cluster will automatically perform arbitration to determine what should happen.

In case of a potential split brain, the data nodes will therefore only be allowed to continue operation if they can contact the arbitrator. Most commonly one of the management nodes will act as the arbitrator, and the arbitration is decided by letting the part of the cluster that first contacts the arbitrator win. The other part(s) of the data nodes will then be forced to shut down to avoid the data diverging.

In short, data nodes are allowed to continue if the following conditions are true:

- The group of data nodes holds all the data.

- Either more than half the data nodes are in the group or the group has won the arbitration process.

The process to determine whether a group of data nodes can continue after a failure of one or more of the other data nodes is outlined in Figure 1-5.

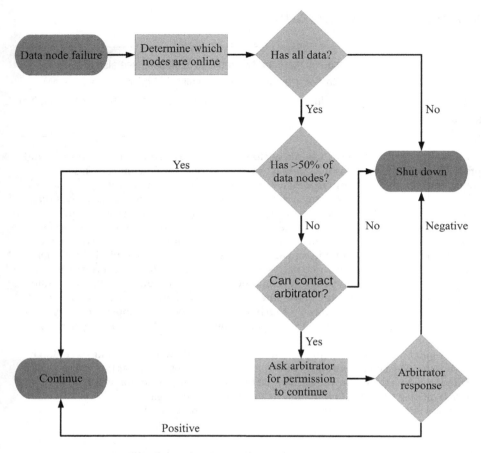

Figure 1-5. *The data node failure handling process in case of two replicas of the data*

The arbitrator can be a management node or an SQL node. By default, management nodes are configured to be available as an arbitrator, whereas SQL nodes are not. At any given time, there will be at most one arbitrator. It is the data nodes that elect which of the eligible nodes will be the current arbitrator.

■ **Caution**   The arbitrator can never be changed while handling a node failure. For this reason, it is very important that the nodes that are allowed to become the arbitrator are accessible by all data nodes. Particularly, do not allow a node installed on the same host as a data node to become the arbitrator. If the whole host shuts down, the cluster can only remain online if the arbitrator is not required to determine whether the group of surviving nodes can safely continue operations!

Summary

This first chapter has provided an overview of MySQL NDB Cluster. Among the topics discussed were:

- The terminology

- Characteristics and features

- Limitations

- Use cases

- The three node types: data nodes, management nodes, and API/SQL nodes

- How high availability works in MySQL NDB Cluster

In the discussion of the node types, the data nodes had little coverage. This is because they are so central to MySQL NDB Cluster that the next chapter is dedicated to discussing the data nodes.

CHAPTER 2

■ ■ ■

The Data Nodes

The data nodes are in many ways the heart and soul of MySQL NDB Cluster. This is where the data is stored, the bulk of the high availability is focused, and where most of what requires special considerations is located. There can be between 1 and 48 data nodes in a cluster, and each data node is built from 23 different kernel blocks and can have between 1 and 98 threads. This chapter introduces the specifics of the data nodes to give you a solid background for the later chapters that focus on the usage of the cluster.

Single-Threaded Versus Multi-Threaded Data Nodes

The data nodes come in two flavors, depending on the internal organization: single-threaded and multi-threaded. The single-threaded binary, ndbd, is the original architecture. As the name suggests, everything is executed within the same process thread. The multi-threaded binary, ndbmtd, was introduced in MySQL NDB Cluster 7.0. ndbmtd allows specific parts of the data node kernel to be split into their own threads and, in that way, takes better advantage of modern hardware. The section entitled "Performance Considerations" covers when to use ndbd and ndbmtd.

■ **Note** Unless you use MySQL Cluster Manager (see Chapter 13), the choice of whether to use ndbd or ndbmtd is not part of the configuration. Which one you are using is simply decided by which binary you invoke when you start the data node.

The two data node binaries are compatible, so you can change between them with the same limitations that apply to changing the thread configuration for the multi-threaded data nodes: it is always possible to scale up to use more threads, but scaling down may require an initial restart and possibly restoring the data from a backup. The default thread configuration for the ndbmtd binary is roughly equivalent to using ndbd.

Thread Types

The multi-threaded binaries can execute a number of different thread types. Each thread type has specific tasks it performs and there can be a varying number of each type. Table 2-1 summarizes the eight thread types available in MySQL NDB Cluster 7.5. The column *number of threads* specifies the range of allowed values for that thread type. A value of 1 means the number of threads cannot be changed and there will always be exactly one thread or pool of threads (for the I/O and watchdog threads). The thread type is listed in lowercase as it is used with the ThreadConfig option; however, the convention when discussing the thread type is to use uppercase. So, for example the local data manager is called ldm when specifying it in the ThreadConfig option, but *LDM* when discussing the thread.

J. W. Krogh and M. Okuno, *Pro MySQL NDB Cluster*, https://doi.org/10.1007/978-1-4842-2982-8_2

Table 2-1. *The Thread Types Supported by MySQL NDB Cluster 7.5*

Type	Name	Number of Threads	Description
main	Main thread	1	Handles the data dictionary and has a transaction coordinator.
ldm	Local Data Manager	1, 2, 4, 6, 8, 12, 16, 24, 32	The threads contain the local query handler (LQH). The number of *LDM* threads directly affects the number of partitions each table can have, as each *LDM* thread is responsible for its own set of partitions. It also affects the parallelism queries are executed with.
tc	Transaction coordinator	0-32	The threads that contain the state of each ongoing transaction.
recv	Receive thread	1-16	The receive threads handle the receiving end of the socket that communicates with the other nodes in the cluster.
send	Send thread	0-16	The send thread is similar to the receive thread, but it is at the sending end of the sockets communicating with the other nodes in the cluster. Setting the number of send threads to zero causes each thread to handle its own sending. Having multiple send threads can greatly improve throughput, but having each thread handling its own communication reduces latency provided the thread is not getting overloaded.
rep	Replication thread	1	The replication thread is used for asynchronously communicating with the SQL nodes for schema changes and binary logging.
io	I/O thread	1	The I/O thread is special (together with the watchdog thread) that it is for a pool of threads. The thread count of 1 is used to indicate that the number of I/O threads cannot be specified directly. Instead there will be one I/O thread per open file. The "I/O thread" is usually lightweight, but is also used when compression is enabled for local checkpoints (see the "D for Durability" section later in the chapter) or backups.
watchdog	Watchdog thread	1	The watchdog thread, like the I/O thread, covers a pool of threads. The watchdogs are responsible for checking that threads are progressing. This is part of the strategy to detect whether a node is slowing down the rest of the cluster, i.e. the fail early strategy discussed in Chapter 1 is used.

In older versions of MySQL NDB Cluster, the thread types available and the supported number of threads may be more restricted.

■ **Note** See the documentation of the `ThreadConfig` option in the Reference Manual for details: *https://dev. mysql.com/doc/refman/5.7/en/mysql-cluster-ndbd-definition.html#ndbparam-ndbmtd-threadconfig.*

It can seem overwhelming having to consider all the thread types and determine the optimal number of each thread for your workload. Fortunately, there is an option to let MySQL NDB Cluster automatically distribute the threads, and all you have to do is specify the maximum number of threads you want. The automatic distribution supports up to 72 threads according to a predetermined table and can be very useful initially, but it will not be able to provide the optimal performance.

■ **Note** See *https://dev.mysql.com/doc/refman/5.7/en/mysql-cluster-ndbd-definition.html#ndbparam-ndbmtd-maxnoofexecutionthreads* for the distribution table.

The advantage, on the other hand, of manually specifying the number for each thread type explicitly is that it allows you to tailor it for your workload. For example, if you do not need a high send throughput, you can disable the send threads. Furthermore, when you manually configure the threads, additional options for each thread type are available:

- The CPUs the threads can use. This combined with excluding other processes/ threads from the CPUs can avoid contention at the CPU level.

- The wait time before the thread goes to sleep[1].

- Whether the thread should run with real-time priority (mutually exclusive with the thread priority).

- The thread priority (mutually exclusive enabling real-time priority). The exact effect of the thread priority is system dependent; for example, on Linux increasing the thread priority lowers the *niceness* of the thread (how likely the thread is to give up the CPU to another process), and on Microsoft Windows, it sets one of the *THREAD_PRIORITY_** priorities (depending on the thread priority chosen).

The actual configuration of these options is covered in Chapters 4 and 20.

It is generally safe to change the number of each thread type during the lifetime of a cluster. However, there is one exception: the *LDM* threads. The number of partitions supported depends on the number of *LDM* threads (see the "Partitions" section later), and the memory available for hash indexes is divided between the *LDM* threads. So, changing the *LDM* threads may on one side improve the performance. However, if care is not taken, it can also cause an unbalanced use of memory and in the worst case may prevent the data node from starting.

■ **Caution** If you change the number of *LDM* threads, you may be necessary to re-initialize the cluster (performing an *initial system restart*). See also "Data Memory and Index Memory" in the section "Data and Indexes" later in the chapter. For an example, see the "Initial System Restart" case study in Chapter 10.

---

[1] When a process thread becomes idle, it can do one of two things. It can start spinning, which means it can very quickly resume work again, but it blocks the CPU for other processes. Alternatively, it can go to sleep and allow the CPU to do work for other processes, but this means it will take much longer for the thread to wake up again.

Performance Considerations

There are several considerations when choosing whether to use the single-threaded or multi-threaded binaries and, if the latter, what the optimal configuration is.

The first thing to consider is your hardware. If you only have a couple of CPU cores available, you may be best off using the single-threaded binaries as effectively the multi-threaded data nodes require at least five threads. This comes on top of the CPUs required by the operating system and other processes on the host.

Otherwise, the tradeoff is as a rule of thumb that the single-threaded binary will provide lower latency as there is less overhead communicating between the various parts of the data nodes; however, since everything is running in a single thread, the throughput will be severely limited.

For the multi-threaded data nodes, having dedicated send threads can add latency compared to each thread handling the send side of communicating with the other nodes on its own. However, the maximum throughput will be reduced. In the end, the decision greatly varies depending on the actual workload.

In practice for most production systems, the multi-threaded data nodes should be used. On modern hardware, the limitation in throughput of the single-threaded data node is just too restrictive. For many workloads specifying the maximum number of threads is good enough; as a bonus, you avoid the risk of micromanaging to the extent that you may end up hurting the stability of the cluster. When you choose the maximum number of threads, make sure you leave room for the operating system and the other processes on the host.

■ **Caution**   If you have an API/SQL node or other CPU intensive on the same host as a data node, it is particularly important to take that into consideration when you configure the threads of the data node. In cases like this, it is often worth binding the threads to specific CPUs and excluding the API/SQL node from using those CPUs.

To summarize in a typical production environment, make your choice as follows:

- Use the multi-threaded data nodes unless you're using a virtual machine with very limited CPU resources.

- On a host dedicated to a single data node, set the maximum number of threads so around two to four CPUs are left for the operating system.

- For high performance clusters, workloads not fitting the automated thread distribution, or when other CPU-intensive processes such as API/SQL nodes are executing on the same host, specifically choose the number of each thread type and bind each thread to its dedicated CPU and exclude that from use by other processes.

Replicas

In InnoDB, all data is stored locally in a single copy. This makes a simple solution, but has the disadvantage that if you have to shut down the instance, or it for some other reason becomes inaccessible, the data is offline. This constitutes a single point of failure, which MySQL NDB Cluster is designed to avoid.

Primary and Backup Replicas

To avoid having just a single copy of the data, MySQL NDB Cluster supports storing all data in up to four copies (the NoOfReplicas configuration option; see also Chapter 4). By copying the data across multiple data nodes, it is safe to shut down one node, as the data can still be read and written to in the remaining copies.

> ■ **Note** It is recommended to use NoOfReplicas = 2. This is the most well tested configuration, including the one most commonly used in production. The arbitration process as described in Chapter 1 is also optimized for at most two replicas.

If the cluster has been configured to have two replicas of the data, each data node has one primary replica and one backup replica. The backup replica is kept up to date with synchronous replication and a two-phase commit process. This relationship between the primary and backup replicas is shown in Figure 2-1.

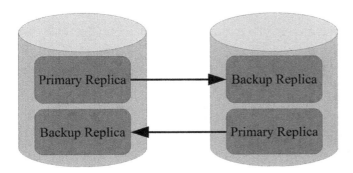

Figure 2-1. *Two-replica configuration*

> ■ **Note** The synchronous replication internally between the data nodes should not be confused with the asynchronous replication (MySQL Server replication) supported between SQL nodes or for a standard MySQL Server instance. While named similarly, the two types of replication are completely different, and MySQL NDB Cluster supports both. For asynchronous replication between SQL nodes, see Chapter 6 for details.

MySQL NDB Cluster 7.5: Read from Backup Replica

Until MySQL NDB Cluster 7.5, the backup replica has only been used to select data when the primary replica was offline. This is still the default behavior as it allows control to return to an API/SQL node that performs a write as soon as the transaction has committed. The implementation details are beyond the scope of this book, but the result is that the locks on the primary replica can be released a little earlier than for the backup replica—at the commit stage of the transaction versus the completed stage. This means it is not safe to attempt to read from the backup replica, as you may not see the data just written.

If you want to allow reads from the backup replica, a transaction commit cannot return until the changes have been unlocked on the backup replica as well. This will increase the latency of commits, but has the advantage that it can reduce the need to read from multiple data nodes and thus reduce the amount of network traffic.

If you are migrating an existing InnoDB database to MySQL NDB Cluster, you likely will get a performance characteristic that is closer to what you expect, if you allow reads from the backup replica. This is particularly the case when you have two data nodes, two replicas, and two API/SQL nodes with the API/SQL nodes located on the same hosts as the data nodes, as shown in Figure 2-2.

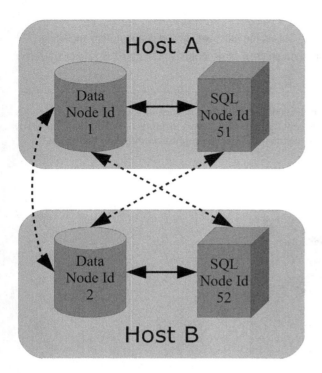

Figure 2-2. *Using the read from replica feature*

In Figure 2-2, the solid lines are the communication links used to read from the local data node. The dashed lines are the communication links used for reads when the local data node is offline and for the synchronous replication between the data nodes.

As part of the new feature is an option to tell the API/SQL node which is the preferred data node to contact. Since two data nodes means each data node has a copy of all data, the two API/SQL nodes will only communicate with the data node on the same host as itself unless the data node is offline. Similarly, there will be reduced network traffic between the data nodes, as it is not necessary to ask for the data from the peer data node. Should one of the data nodes go offline, the API/SQL nodes can still connect to the remaining online data node to access all the data.

To summarize whether to use the read from backup feature:

- The default behavior is optimized for write latency.

- The read from backup behavior is optimized for read latency.

Whether the read from backup replica feature should be enabled depends on whether the application should be optimized for write or read latency. The effect of enabling the read from replica feature will be reduced as more data nodes are added; this is due to the sharding, which makes each data node only have part of the data, so it will in all cases be necessary with some network traffic.

Node Groups

The number of replicas discussed in the previous section specified the number of copies of the data that exist in the cluster. Related are the node groups. Each node group is a group of data nodes, where each data node holds the same data. The only difference is what is considered the primary replica and what are the backup replica(s). Looking at Figure 2-3, it depicts the same setup as discussed when primary and backup replicas were introduced. However, it also depicts one node group consisting of two data nodes.

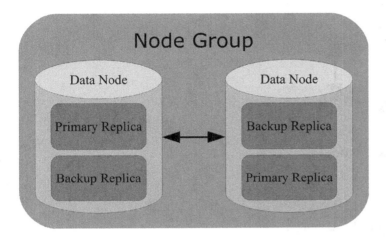

Figure 2-3. *A node group*

The number of node groups in a cluster is the total number of data nodes divided by the number of replicas. For a typical cluster with two replicas, it means if there are eight data nodes, there will be four node groups:

$$\# \text{ Node Groups} = \frac{\# \text{ Data nodes}}{\# \text{ Replicas}}.$$

Except for tables that are fully replicated (see later in the next section about partitions), the data is sharded between the node groups. Sharding means that the data is divided among the node groups in such a way that is there is no overlap between the data stored in two different node groups. In MySQL NDB Cluster, the sharding happens automatically based on the partitions. In case of a perfectly even data distribution, each node group will have exactly 1/N of the data where N is the number of node groups. For example, suppose there is a total of 10GB of data and there are four node groups, then each node group will store 2.5GB of data.

It is a requirement that each data node must belong to exactly one node group and that all node groups have the same number of data nodes. This means you cannot create a cluster with two replicas and three data nodes. Similarly, if you want to add data nodes to an existing cluster, you must always add a whole node group at a time.

By default, the data nodes are distributed among the node groups automatically using the node IDs set with the NodeId option, so the lowest node IDs go into the first node group, the next data nodes by node ID go into the next node group, and so on. The numbering of the node groups starts with zero. Figure 2-4 shows the two node groups arising from a typical configuration with two replicas and four data nodes.

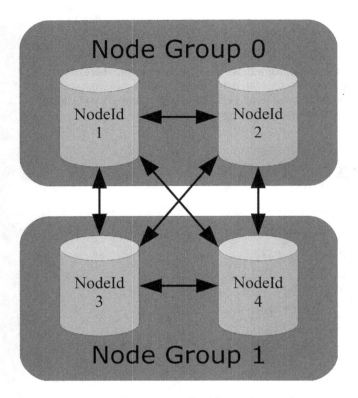

Figure 2-4. *Two node groups, each with two data nodes*

New node groups can be added to the cluster without downtime (see also Chapter 10). However, moving existing data nodes between the node groups requires a re-initialization of the cluster (and thus restoring all data from a backup).

Partitions

Partitioning is the smallest unit in the division of the data between the data nodes. All tables storing data in NDB Cluster are partitioned by default and will have the number of partitions optimized for the size and configuration of the cluster. MySQL NDB Cluster supports two types of partitioning:

- Partitioning by key
- Partitioning by linear key

For both partitioning schemes, MD5() is used for the hashing[2]. The difference between partitioning by key and by linear key is that partitioning by key uses modulo arithmetic whereas partitioning by linear key uses a power of two algorithm.

---

[2]This is different than for InnoDB, which uses a hashing function internal to MySQL Server based on the same algorithm as the PASSWORD() function.

The modulo arithmetic is simple:

$$Partition\ \# = MOD\big(MD5(key),N\big)$$

In the formula *key* is the column value used for the partitioning and *N* is the number of partitions. The advantage of this algorithm is that, it in most cases, it gives an even data distribution.

The power of two algorithm is more complex:

$$V = POWER\big(2,\ CEILING\big(LOG(2,N)\big)\big)$$
$$Partition\ \# = MD5(key)\ \&\ (V-1)$$

V is a constant based on the number of partitions. If the resulting partition number is larger than the number of partitions (N) for the table, the result is reduced in a loop until the partition number is less than the number of partitions using:

$$V = \frac{V}{2}$$
$$Partition\ \# = Partition\ \#\ \&\ (V-1)$$

The main benefit of linear key is that it makes partition management such as adding, dropping, splitting, and merging partitions faster. However, these operations are not supported for MySQL NDB Cluster, so it is better to use partition by key, which usually gives a more even distribution of the data.

While the automatic partitioning usually works great, it is possible to override it using a custom partitioning. Additionally, MySQL NDB Cluster 7.5 supports a greater level of fine-tuning the partition balancing for each table as well as the option to have fully replicated tables. The following sections go into details with the partitioning features.

Automatic Partitioning

Automatic partitioning is the default and will be used unless explicitly overwritten. The primary key will be used as the partition key using partitioning by key. The number of partitions will be scaled according to the number of data nodes and the number of *LDM* threads, i.e., the number of partitions is: # of partitions = # of data nodes * # of *LDM* threads. Some examples of the number of partitions can be found in Table 2-2.

Table 2-2. *Examples of the Automatically Determined Number of Partitions*

Number of Data Nodes	Number of LDM Threads	Number of Partitions
2	1	2
2	2	4
2	8	16
2	32	64
4	8	32
6	8	48
8	8	64
48	32	1536

User-Defined Partitioning

With user-defined partitioning, it is possible to overwrite the automatic partitioning. The advantage exists particularly for tables with multiple columns in the primary key, as the partitioning key can be chosen to optimize the data access. By choosing the partitioning key to match the column(s) mostly used for selecting rows in queries, it is possible to achieve improved performance as it increases the use of local access to the data.

One example is a foreign key relationship where it is expected to perform joins between the parent and child tables. If the child table has its data partitioned according to the foreign key column, it is possible to perform the join locally without having to access other data nodes and thus improve the performance. Listing 2-1 shows an example using the album and album_artist tables from a database with music albums. The primary key of the album_artist table contains both the album_id and artist_name columns. In this case, partitioning by just the album_id column allows for an optimized join between the two tables.

Listing 2-1. User-Defined Partitioning Example

```
CREATE TABLE album (
  album_id INT UNSIGNED NOT NULL,
  album_name VARCHAR(50) NOT NULL,
  PRIMARY KEY (album_id)
) ENGINE=ndbcluster;

CREATE TABLE album_artist (
  album_id INT UNSIGNED NOT NULL,
  artist_name VARCHAR(100) NOT NULL,
  PRIMARY KEY (album_id, artist_name)
) ENGINE=ndbcluster
  PARTITION BY KEY (album_id)
  PARTITIONS 4;

SELECT *
  FROM album
       INNER JOIN album_artist USING (album_id);
```

The following limitations apply to user-defined partitioning:

- The partitioning key must be part of the primary key.

- Only partitioning by key or linear key is supported.

- The maximum number of partitions supported for a table is: 8 * # LDM threads * # Node Groups

See also Chapter 20 for more information on using user-defined partitions.

MySQL NDB Cluster 7.5: Partition Balancing

One of the new features in MySQL NDB Cluster 7.5 is the ability to specify in more details how the partition balancing should be done for a table. Previously there was always one primary replica for each *LDM* thread in each node, unless user-defined partitioning was used. The partition balancing names follows the schema *FOR_<read option>_BY_<distribution>* where the read option is either *RP* for "read primary" or *RA* for "read any".

The distribution can either be *LDM* or *NODE*, depending on which level the partition distribution is done. With the new options, there are now four different partition balancing schemes:

- **FOR_RP_BY_LDM:** The default and the partitioning scheme used exclusively in previous versions of MySQL NDB Cluster. One primary partition for each *LDM* thread on each node. With two replicas, this also means one backup replica for each *LDM* thread. Reads are done from the primary replica.

- **FOR_RA_BY_LDM:** One primary or backup partition per *LDM* thread. Reads can be made from any of the replicas.

- **FOR_RP_BY_NODE:** One primary partition is stored in each data node. Reads are done from the primary replica.

- **FOR_RA_BY_NODE:** Each node group has a combined single partition. That is, each node will have one primary or one backup replica. Reads can be from any replica.

Choosing a non-default partition balance is only needed in rare cases and can only be done by setting the table comment. For example:

```
mysql> CREATE TABLE t1 (
          id int unsigned NOT NULL,
          val char(36),
          PRIMARY KEY (id)
       ) ENGINE=NDBCluster
         COMMENT='NDB_TABLE=PARTITION_BALANCE=FOR_RA_BY_LDM';
```

Examples of the partition balances will be shown in the case study after the following section.

■ **Note** For more information about using table comments to set table options for `NDBCluster` tables, see *https://dev.mysql.com/doc/refman/5.7/en/create-table-ndb-table-comment-options.html*.

MySQL NDB Cluster 7.5: Fully Replicated Tables

Another new feature in MySQL NDB Cluster 7.5 is the possibility to choose a table fully replicated to all data nodes even in clusters with more than one node group. That is, all data nodes have all the data for the table. The use case is primarily relatively small tables that are often used in joins, for example lookup tables. A side effect of enabling the fully replicated feature is that reads from backup replicas are also allowed, so the same write overhead as for the read from replica feature exists.

Fully replicated tables will use more memory than normal tables. Consider a case with two node groups. In this case with a table that is distributed as per default, each node group will on average have half the data. With a fully replicated table, both node groups have all the data, meaning the total memory usage has doubled.

Case Study: Partition Distribution

The best way to understand the effect of the four partition balancing options as well as the read from backup (any replica) and fully replicated tables features is to look at how the partitions are distributed in each case. The case study considers a cluster with two replicas and four data nodes in two node groups. Each data node has four *LDM* threads.

Figures 2-5 through 2-8 show the distribution of partitions for each of the four partition balancing schemes. Additionally, Figures 2-9 and 2-10 show the default partitioning scheme *FOR_RP_BY_LDM* with the read from backup and fully replicated features enabled, respectively. In the figures, a P means the partitions in that half are primary partitions; a B means partitions in that half are backup partitions. Each figure is discussed in turn.

The actual distribution for a table may differ from table to table, but the overall distribution will be similar. A good source for studying the distribution of the partitions and which node has the primary replica is the ndbinfo.table_fragments table (the ndbinfo schema is discussed in Chapter 16), which is new in MySQL NDB Cluster 7.5. Another information table that is new in version 7.5 is ndbinfo.table_info, which, for example, includes details about the partition balancing used and which other features are enabled for the table. Alternatively, the ndb_desc utility (see also the case studies later in this chapter) can provide information about the partitions of the table.

Figure 2-5 is an example using the *FOR_RP_BY_LDM* partition balancing, which is the default distribution. With four data nodes and four *LDM* threads there are 16 partitions, with one primary and one backup partition allocated for each *LDM* thread. The partitions are numbered 0 through 15. The primary replicas on node 1 are backup replicas on node 2 and vice versa; likewise for nodes 3 and 4.

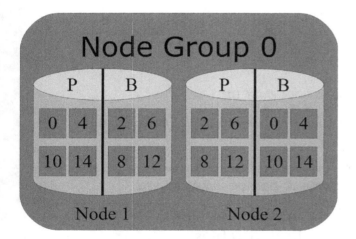

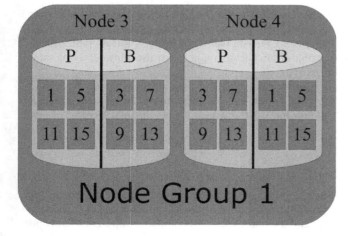

Figure 2-5. *The FOR_RP_BY_LDM partition balancing scheme*

Figure 2-6 shows the balancing using *FOR_RA_BY_LDM*. The *RA* (read any) part of the scheme causes the number of partitions to be halved compared to *FOR_RP_BY_LDM*. With this distribution, there is either one primary or one backup replica per *LDM* thread.

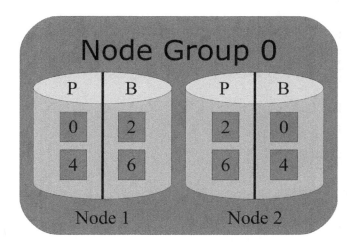

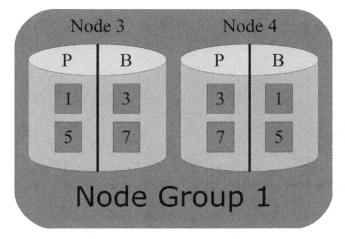

Figure 2-6. *The FOR_RA_BY_LDM partition balancing scheme*

Figure 2-7 moves on to *FOR_RP_BY_NODE*, which has one primary partition and one backup partition per data node. This leaves half the *LDM* threads without any partitions, which makes it likely that the load will become unbalanced with one *LDM* thread being busy and the other idle. Use this partition balancing with care and primarily for tables with only a few rows.

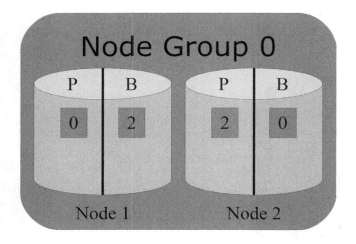

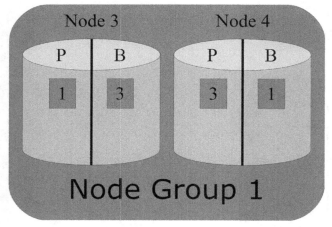

Figure 2-7. *The FOR_RP_BY_NODE partition balancing scheme*

Even fewer partitions exist for *FOR_RA_BY_NODE*, where each node group only has one partition, with the primary partition on one node and the backup partition on the other. This is shown in Figure 2-8. Since *FOR_RA_BY_NODE* allows reading from the backup partition, there is less difference in practice between a primary and backup replica than for the *RP* balancing schemes. Like for *FOR_RP_BY_NODE*, this scheme is mostly useful for small tables.

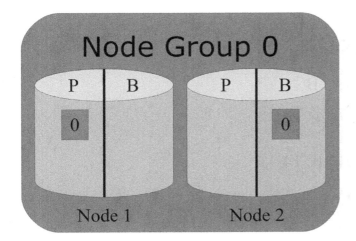

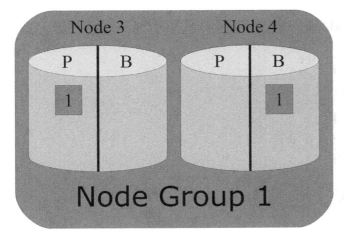

Figure 2-8. *The FOR_RA_BY_NODE partition balancing scheme*

The final two cases examine the default partition balancing, *FOR_RP_BY_LDM*, with each of the two features, read from backup and fully replicated table. Figure 2-9 shows that partition distribution does not change when reading from the backup replicas is enabled. The distribution is the same as for the regular *FOR_RP_BY_LDM* case.

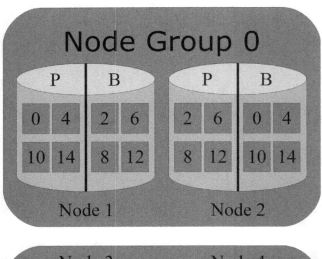

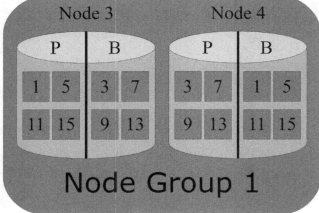

Figure 2-9. *The FOR_RP_BY_LDM partition balancing scheme with read from backup enabled*

Enabling the fully replicated table feature, however, does change the partition distribution, as shown in Figure 2-10. The biggest change is that the replicas are the same between the two node groups. Having fully replicated table enabled is also the one case where *partition* and *fragment* are not synonyms (not visible from the figure).

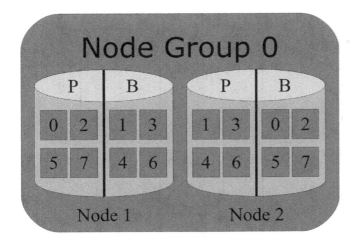

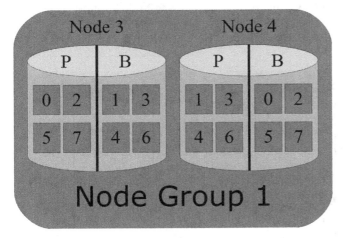

Figure 2-10. *The FOR_RP_BY_LDM partition balancing scheme with fully replicated table enabled*

To make it easier to compare the six distributions, Figures 2-5 through 2-10 are displayed side by side in Figure 2-11. The labels below each example show the partition balancing used and whether the read from backup or fully replicated tables feature is used. The read from any backup (any partition) feature is indicated with + *Any* in the label, and the fully replicated table feature is indicated with + *Full* in the label.

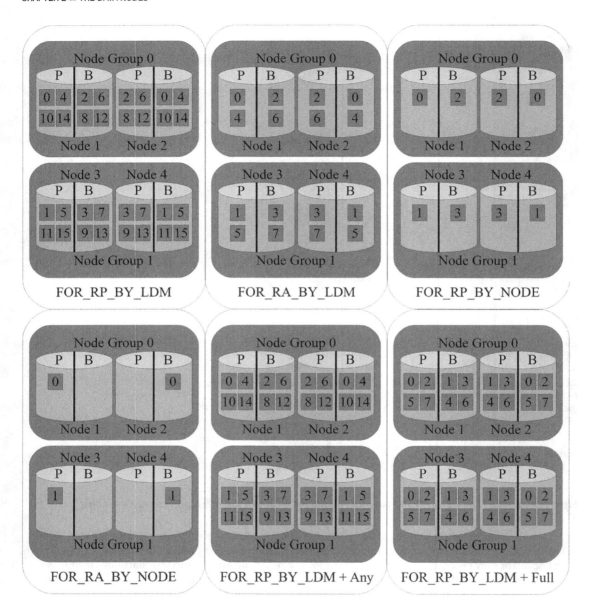

***Figure 2-11.** Six examples of partition distributions*

D for Durability

MySQL NDB Cluster is primarily an in-memory database, but still it aims at being fully ACID compliant. How is durability (the D in ACID) delivered while also providing real-time performance? There are several elements to this:

- Duplication of the data through synchronous replication and two-phase commits

- Local checkpoints (LCPs)

- Redo logs

- Global checkpoints (GCPs)

The relationship between the data, local checkpoints, redo logs, and global checkpoints is shown in Figure 2-12. The data memory (excluding the ordered indexes) is written to a local checkpoint. In the meantime, all writes are written to the redo log buffer, which in turn is flushed to the redo log for every global checkpoint. It is worth referring to the figure again, as the four elements are discussed in the rest of this section.

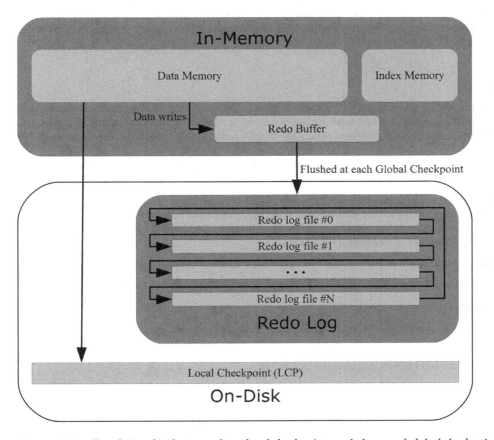

Figure 2-12. *The relationship between data, local checkpoints, redo logs, and global checkpoints*

Duplication of Data

The first important part of duplicating data is to enable multiple replicas (see also the section "Replicas" earlier). MySQL NDB Cluster uses synchronous replication as well as a two-phase commit to ensure that the replicas and nodes in other node groups that also are affected by the transaction will either all commit or all fail the transaction.

This means when a transaction is committed, the data is safe even if one of the data nodes crashes. However, the data is not safe in case of a catastrophic issue that brings down the whole cluster. For the data to survive a cluster shutdown, the data must also be on disk, which is done through a feature called *local checkpoints* (LCPs).

Local Checkpoints (LCPs)

The LCPs are MySQL NDB Cluster's solution to keep the data safe even if the cluster shuts down as a whole. An LCP is essentially an online backup that reads the data from end to end while writing it to disk. In fact, the code module handling LCPs is called *BACKUP* (see the section "Kernel Blocks" later in the chapter) and the same code also handles backups.

The process of creating an LCP can be compared to how MySQL Enterprise Backup (MEB) and Percona XtraBackup copy the InnoDB tablespace files online. An LCP copies the data (but not indexes) from the data memory as well as schema information from the data dictionary. MySQL Enterprise Backup copies the data files from disk (the *.ibd* files for InnoDB tables) as well as the data dictionary files (*.frm* files). Because the process is online, i.e., data changes will happen while the LCP is written, it is necessary to keep track of the changes. This is the task of the redo logs.

The Redo Logs

The redo logs keep track of all the changes that occur while the LCPs are created. If it becomes necessary to restore an LCP, the redo log is applied, and together the two create a consistent view of the data. This is again similar to how InnoDB online backup programs collect the InnoDB redo log to be able to create a consistent backup.

The redo logs are in several contexts, called fragment log files. This includes all the related configuration options related to the size of the redo logs:

- **NoOfFragmentLogParts:** The number of sets of files per data node that together constitute the redo log for the data node. It is a requirement that there are at least as many fragment log parts as there are *LDM* threads. The default—and minimum—number of fragment log parts is 4.

- **NoOfFragmentLogFiles:** The number of files in each fragment log part. The default is 16.

- **FragmentLogFileSize:** The size of each fragment log file. The default is 16MB.

The total amount of redo log created is:

Total redo log created = NoOfFragmentLogParts * NoOfFragmentLogFiles * FragmentLogFileSize

However, the total amount of redo log that can be used is:

Total of usable redo log = # LDM threads * NoOfFragmentLogFiles * FragmentLogFileSize

With the default settings for the redo log and two *LDM* threads, this gives:

Total redo log created = $4 * 16 * 16MB = 1024MB = 1GB$

Total of usable redo log = $2 * 16 * 16MB = 512MB$

At a minimum, the redo logs must be able to hold the changes occurring during the time it takes to write two local checkpoints. However, to be able to handle an increased load, it is recommended to set the total size so it can hold the changes for six local checkpoints. If one of the redo log parts become full, the cluster will be in a read-only state until enough local checkpoints have been written to free up some redo log again.

The fact that at least four fragment log parts are created can seem like wasted disk space. The reason for four parts minimum is that originally ndbmtd supported at most four *LDM* threads. With four fragment logs parts, it would be possible to choose any of the supported number of *LDM* threads. However, the disk is by default not used, as the redo log files are created *sparse*, i.e., they are basically created as empty shells with the requested size. The section entitled "The NDB File System" at the end of the chapter gives an example of this.

Within each set of redo log, the log is written in a circular fashion:

1. The *LDM* thread will start writing to the first file.

2. When the first file has been written to the end, the *LDM* thread will switch to the next file and write to that.

3. When reaching the end of the last file, the *LDM* thread will move back to the start of the first file.

To improve performance of the redo log, the data changes are first written into an in-memory buffer, then flushed to disk. This is where the global checkpoints come into play.

Global Checkpoints (GCPs)

Since MySQL NDB Cluster in general will have multiple data nodes in a cluster and it is a shared nothing architecture, some mechanism is required to ensure all data nodes agree on how to restore the data. This mechanism is the GCPs.

When the data nodes flush the redo buffer to disk, the transactions are safe even in the case of a total cluster outage. The GCP occurs when the data nodes synchronize the flushing of the redo logs. This means all data nodes are always able to restore the data to a given GCP.

By default, a GCP occurs every 2000 milliseconds (the `TimeBetweenGlobalCheckpoints` configuration option). This means that in case of a catastrophic crash, up to two seconds of committed transactions may be lost. Going back to the start of the section and the discussion of the D for durability in ACID, the premise that MySQL NDB Cluster is ACID compliant only holds to the extent that there never is an event that causes the cluster as a whole to crash.

Restarts and Processes

MySQL NDB Cluster has several ways of restarting the data nodes depending on what the status of the cluster is and what you are trying to achieve. Other than initially starting the cluster, the most common reason to perform a restart is to change the configuration or to recover from a node outage.

There are four main types of restart types:

- **Node restart:** The most common restart type where all of the data remains available for the application throughout the restart.

- **Initial node restart:** This is similar to a *node restart* with the addition that each node deletes all of its data as part of the restart.

- **System restart:** Like a *node restart*, but all data nodes are started together. The cluster is offline during the restart.

- **Initial system restart:** Like a *system restart*, but all data nodes also delete their data. Except for logfile groups and tablespaces, everything in the NDB file system (see also "On-Disk Data" later in the chapter) is deleted, i.e., all data must be restored from a backup.

The two *node restart* types allow you to restart a data node while the cluster as a whole remains online. A restart where eventually the whole cluster is restarted using node restarts is also known as a *rolling restart*. The opposite is a *system restart,* where all data nodes can be started at the same time. Restarts are discussed in detail in Chapter 10.

When a data node is started, by default there will be two processes, both using the ndbd or ndbmtd binary: the *angel* process and the data node process itself. This is similar to starting MySQL Server using the mysqld_safe script on Linux and UNIX, except the angel process is using the data node binary itself, and by default the angel process will not automatically restart a failed data node. The role of the angel process is to monitor and (if configured to do so) restart the data node if it has not been shut down cleanly. An example from Linux shows the angel process as the parent of the actual data node process (see the two ndbmtd processes):

```
shell$ ps axf | grep nodeid=1
 3391 pts/3    S+     0:00 |                \_ grep --color=auto nodeid=1
 2421 ?        Ss     0:00 ndbmtd -c 192.168.0.101 --ndb-nodeid=1
 2422 ?        Sl     0:14  \_ ndbmtd -c 192.168.0.101 --ndb-nodeid=1
```

Data Node Internals

The data nodes themselves have an internal architecture that is not entirely different from the architecture of the cluster as a whole. As the cluster has different nodes types, a data node thread is built from kernel blocks; and as the cluster has *transporters* (network connections, MySQL NDB Cluster supports several types of transporters, but for the purpose of this discussion, the connections can be assumed to be using TCP/IP) to allow the different nodes to talk to each other, there are signals between the kernel blocks.

Understanding the internal structure is one of the more advanced topics of MySQL NDB Cluster, and the details are beyond the scope of this book. However, the remainder of this section gives an overview of the memory usage, kernel blocks, signals, and related topics, as understanding the internal data node architecture at a high level helps you understand the philosophy used in MySQL NDB Cluster and can also help with day-to-day operations such as configuration and troubleshooting.

Memory Usage

As a primarily in-memory database, the data nodes are obviously a big user of memory. However, it is even more so as memory is also used to reduce the fluctuations in response times, i.e., for the real-time promise that is part of the high availability implementation. Currently there is no pooling of memory implemented except for send buffers, so each use of memory has its own specific allocation. An important aspect is that all memory is allocated and *touched* as the first thing during a restart. That the memory is touched means it is not only requested from the operating system but also taken into use; on Linux, this means the memory will show up as resident memory instead of only as virtual memory.

The following list includes some of the areas that require memory. The related options are noted in parentheses; increasing the values of the options will increase the memory usage and vice versa. If the setting is reduced, then the memory is also reduced.

- In-memory data and ordered indexes (DataMemory)

- Unique hash indexes (IndexMemory)

- Buffering of on-disk data (DiskPageBufferMemory)

- Transaction records for coordinating transactions between the data nodes (MaxNoOfConcurrentTransactions)

- Transaction operations on data (MaxNoOfConcurrentOperations, MaxNoOfLocalOperations)

- The internal triggers; see also the "Triggers" subsection (MaxNoOfTriggers)

- The redo buffer (RedoBuffer)

- Send and receive buffers (TotalSendBufferMemory, SendBufferMemory, ReceiveBufferMemory)

Chapter 4 goes into how to configure these uses of memory, and some of the areas are also discussed later in this chapter. The important points here are that it is important to plan ahead, for example with load tests, and consider how the cluster is used, and that the memory usage is higher (in some cases much higher) than the memory directly allocated to data and indexes.

Kernel Blocks

The kernel blocks are the building blocks on which the data node is made. Each thread inside the ndbd and ndbmtd binaries includes one or more kernel blocks. A little simplified, a kernel block can be compared to a Lego block. Each kernel block is largely self-contained and is responsible for specific tasks. For example, the *BACKUP* block is responsible for creating backups and local checkpoints. There are currently a total of 23 different kernel blocks, summarized in Table 2-3.

Table 2-3. *The 23 Kernel Blocks*

Kernel Block	Name	Description
BACKUP	Backup	Creates backups and local checkpoints (LCPs).
CMVMI	Cluster Manager Virtual Machine Interface	Handles the configuration management between the kernel blocks and is responsible for the job queue (see the "Job Buffers" subsection later) and the transporters.
DBACC	Access Control	Manages access to the data and is responsible for storing the primary keys and the unique hash indexes. Works together with the *DBTUP* block: The *DBTUP* block physically stores data. It returns a pointer to the data which *DBACC* stores together with the primary key. Implements part of the checkpoint protocol. *DBACC* also performs undo logging.
DBDICT	Data Dictionary	The definition of tables, columns, indexes, etc. The only block other than *DBTC* that applications can talk to directly.
DBDIH	Distribution Handler	Has a range of responsibilities: data distribution management service, local and global checkpoints, and restarts.
DBINFO	Information Database	Responsible for the ndbinfo schema. See also Chapter 16.
DBLQH	Local Query Handler	The main part of the *LDM* threads (which are sometimes referred to as *LQH* threads for this reason). Manages data: each *LDM* thread owns specific partitions. Coordinates the two-phase commit.
DBSPJ	Select Project Join	Handles push down joins.
DBTC	Transaction Coordinator	The global counterpart to the *DBLQH* block.
DBTUP	Tuple Manager	Responsible for the physical storage of data. Implements part of the checkpoint protocol. See also the *DBACC* block.

(continued)

Table 2-3. (*continued*)

Kernel Block	Name	Description
DBTUX	Tuple Index	Local management of ordered indexes.
DBUTIL	Utilities	Various internal utilities, for example for transaction and data operations.
LGMAN	Log Manager	Handles the undo logs for disk data tables.
NDBCNTR	NDB Controller	Handles initialization and configuration when starting a data node. Also involved in clean shutdowns.
NDBFS	NDB File System	Abstraction layer for the NDB file system and handles the actual I/O and supports asynchronous I/O. See also the section "The NDB File System" later.
PGMAN	Page Manager	Buffer management for disk data tables.
QMGR	Logical Cluster Management	Handles the heartbeats and node membership of the cluster. Additionally, it is involved in the early phases of starting a node.
RESTORE	Restore	Handles restoring data from backups through the ndb_restore utility or local checkpoints.
SUMA	Subscription Manager	Used for event logging, reporting functions, and replication (via the binary log on one or more SQL nodes).
THRMAN	Thread Manager	The thread management block. Included in all threads.
TRPMAN	Transport Manager	Handles signal transport. See also the next subsection.
TSMAN	Tablespace Manager	Manages the tablespace files for disk data tables.
TRIX	Transactions and Indexes	Handles internal triggers and unique indexes. Provides utilities for index rebuilds and handling signals between nodes.

■ **Note** The kernel blocks are described in more detail, including references to the source code, in the MySQL NDB Cluster Internals Manual: *https://dev.mysql.com/doc/ndb-internals/en/ndb-internals-kernel-blocks.html*.

The relationship between several of the kernel blocks is shown in Figure 2-13. The large shaded area represents the NDB kernel. Notice that in order to keep the diagram reasonably simple, not all the connections between blocks are included.

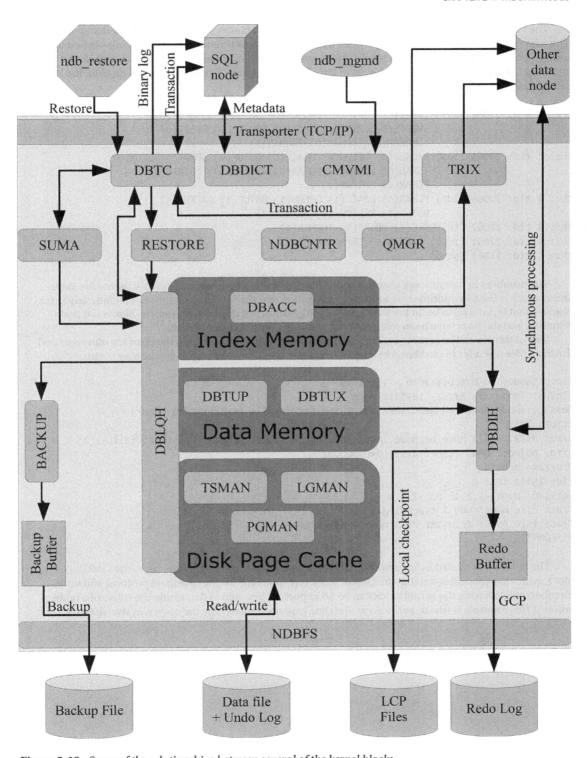

Figure 2-13. *Some of the relationships between several of the kernel blocks*

The various thread types use different kernel blocks. Some blocks may be part of more than one thread type—for example, *THRMAN* being the thread management block is required for all threads—whereas other kernel blocks may be used only for a single thread type. Which blocks are used for each thread can be seen in the *out log* of the data node near the start of the output of a restart. The following excerpt from the log of data nodes provides an example:

```
thr: 0 tid: 22064 (main) DBTC(0) DBDIH(0) DBDICT(0) NDBCNTR(0) QMGR(0)
                         NDBFS(0) CMVMI(0) TRIX(0) DBUTIL(0) DBSPJ(0)
                         THRMAN(0) TRPMAN(0) THRMAN(1) ...
thr: 1 tid: 22065 (rep) BACKUP(0) DBLQH(0) DBACC(0) DBTUP(0) SUMA(0) DBTUX(0)
                         TSMAN(0) LGMAN(0) PGMAN(0) RESTORE(0) DBINFO(0)
                         PGMAN(2) THRMAN(2) ...
thr: 2 tid: 22066 (ldm) PGMAN(1) DBACC(1) DBLQH(1) DBTUP(1) BACKUP(1)
                         DBTUX(1) RESTORE(1) THRMAN(3) ...
thr: 3 tid: 22067 (tc) DBTC(1) DBSPJ(1) THRMAN(4) ...
thr: 4 tid: 22051 (recv) THRMAN(5) TRPMAN(1) ...
thr: 5 tid: 22063 (send)
```

The numbers in parentheses after the kernel block name is a counter to distinguish when the same kernel block is used in multiple threads. It is worth noting that the send thread does not include any kernel blocks—that is not a mistake. In the listing, some information not related to the kernel blocks has been removed, and the lines have been reformatted to make the output easier to read.

One of the places the kernel blocks show up is for data node failures. Both the error log messages and the trace files will refer to the kernel blocks. For example, the following error message may occur:

```
Time: Sunday 30 October 2016 - 13:12:19
Status: Temporary error, restart node
Message: Node declared dead. See error log for details (Arbitration error)
Error: 2315
Error data: We(2) have been declared dead by 1 (via 1) reason: Heartbeat failure(4)
Error object: QMGR (Line: 4213) 0x00000002
Program: ndbmtd
Pid: 25141 thr: 0
Version: mysql-5.7.16 ndb-7.5.4
Trace file name: ndb_2_trace.log.3
Trace file path: /cluster/data/node_2/ndb_2_trace.log.3 [t1..t4]
***EOM***
```

The failure was caused by too many missed heartbeats. The *Error object* references the *QMGR* block, which is expected given that the *QMGR* block is responsible for the heartbeat protocol and node membership. Knowing the kernel block can be an important first step to determine the cause of a node failure. (This example is trivial, as the *Error data* line explains exactly why the node was shut down.)

Signals

The kernel blocks need to communicate with each other; for example, an API node may tell the *DBTC* block it needs a transaction where a row with a given primary key is required. This request triggers the *DBTC* block to ask for the data from the *DBLQH* block. The communication between the kernel blocks is done using signals. There are two types of signals for the data nodes:

- **Synchronous:** The synchronous signals block until they have been processed. An example of a synchronous signal is a heartbeat.

- **Asynchronous:** The asynchronous signals can be sent to:

    - Another block in the same thread; the recipient block may be the same as the sending block

    - A block in another thread in the same data node

    - A block in a thread on another data node

The asynchronous signals are the most common and can have one of two priorities: 0 or 1, where 0 is the highest priority. There is a job buffer (see the next subsection) for each of the two priorities where the signals are queued.

When a data node crashes, it will create a trace file for each thread. These trace files each have two parts: a trace through specific points in the source code and a signal trace. The signals included in the signal trace are the last received asynchronous signals. (Synchronous signals are not included in the trace as they do not pass through the job buffer.)

Job Buffer

A job buffer in MySQL NDB Cluster is essentially a queue of signals. When a signal arrives, it is placed into one of two job buffers, depending on the signal priority:

- Priority 0 signals go into job buffer A

- Priority 1 signals go into job buffer B

Signals are processed in the order they arrive into the job buffer—first in, first out (FIFO).

Additionally, there are job buffers C and D. Job buffer C is used exclusively during restarts and job buffer D is used for the time queue. As the C and D job buffers are special purpose, they will not be discussed more.

For the single-threaded data nodes, each data node has one set of job buffers. For the multi-threaded data nodes, each thread—except the send threads—has a set of job buffers. The reason send threads do not have a job buffer is that they do not contain any kernel blocks and thus cannot receive and execute signals. The job of the send threads is exclusively to send signals directed at other nodes.

The job buffers are a fixed size. If they get full, it is not possible to receive any more signals, which will cause a node failure. For this reason, it is very important that the job buffers never become full. One measure to avoid this is that no job is supposed to block for more than 10 milliseconds. (Warnings are printed in the data node's log when an operation blocks for more than 100 milliseconds.) If a task requires more time, it should pause and send a signal (called *CONTINUEB* as in "continue a job from the B job buffer") to itself to continue the paused operation. The continue signal will be placed at the end of the queue, meaning the other signals get a chance to be processed. To keep track of the time, the signal *TIME_SIGNAL* is sent every 10 milliseconds.

The use of the job buffers is illustrated in Figure 2-14. A signal arrives from the same thread, the same node, or another node, and then is inserted into job buffer A or B per the signal's priority. Then it is processed for at most 10 milliseconds.

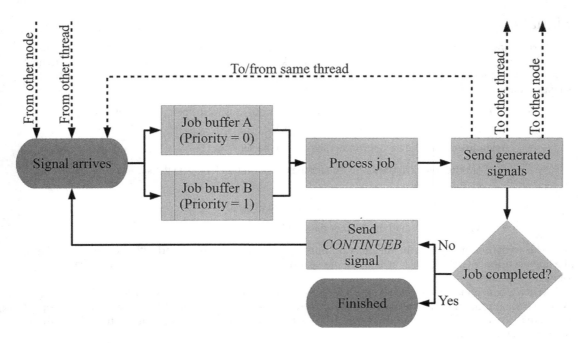

Figure 2-14. *The flow of signals through the job buffers*

Send and Receive Buffers

As MySQL NDB Cluster is a distributed system, it is necessary to incorporate support for communication between the various parts of the cluster. By far the most commonly used mechanism is TCP/IP. There are other options, but they are beyond the scope of this book. To ensure stable operations even during a temporary overload of the network and to handle bursts of messages, all nodes have send and receive buffers. As the data nodes have the most network traffic, the buffers are most important for these nodes.

Both the send and the receive buffers are always created for every possible transporter for a node. Data nodes and management nodes will have a transporter to all other online nodes; API/SQL nodes will have a transporter to all online management and data nodes. An important point is that the send and receive buffers are created whether or not the transporter currently exists.

The send buffers are the ones that most likely require explicit configuration. Each node has a memory pool reserved for send buffers, and each transporter from the node has a dedicated send buffer. By default, the memory pool is large enough so all send buffers can grow to their maximum size. However, it is common that at any given time some transporters are busier than others, so particularly for large clusters, it makes sense to have the memory pool smaller than the default, as it is rare that all send buffers will require their maximum size at the same time.

Figure 2-15 shows an example of the send buffers for the data node with NodeId = 1 in a cluster with two data nodes (NodeIds 1 and 2), two management nodes (NodeIds 49 and 50), and five API/SQL nodes (NodeIds 51-55). This setup gives a total of eight transporters for the node (one for each of the eight other nodes in the cluster). There is one send buffer for each of the transporters, and each send buffer uses memory out of the total send buffer pool.

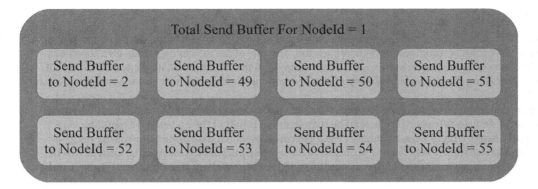

Figure 2-15. *The total send buffer pool with eight send buffers*

The receive buffers are similar to the send buffers, but are on the receiving end of the TCP connections. Unlike the send buffers, which are taken out of a global pool for the node, each receive buffer is always allocated in full. This is important to have in mind when configuring extra nodes or the default size of the receive buffers is changed.

Triggers

There are two types of triggers: the normal MySQL Server triggers and MySQL NDB Cluster triggers that are internal to the data nodes. In MySQL Server, triggers are something that can be added to perform an action when a row is inserted, updated, or deleted. Triggers inside the data nodes are similar; however there is one important difference: the MySQL NDB Clusters triggers are entirely internal. The DBA should not create, drop, or maintain these internal triggers manually. (The MySQL Server triggers can still be used.) MySQL NDB Cluster uses triggers to monitor for changes. They are used in several places, such as for unique hash indexes, ordered indexes, foreign keys, backups, and replication.

While the data nodes automatically handle creating, removing, and updating the triggers as needed, the DBA should still be aware of them as the triggers can show up in the configuration, monitoring, and for example, the output of the ndb_show_tables utility program, as shown in the case study later in the chapter.

Epochs

The epochs in MySQL NDB Cluster are not the same as those known from the UNIX and Linux operating systems; however, it is somewhat similar in the sense that it measures time. MySQL NDB Cluster uses epochs to track time and for grouping. The default duration for an epoch in MySQL NDB Cluster is 100 milliseconds (the TimeBetweenEpochs configuration option) and the epoch for a cluster will never decrease during the lifetime (between complete initializations) of the cluster.

This means, given two events and the epochs in which they occurred, it is possible to determine the order of the two events. The conflict resolution for master-master replication (see also Chapter 6) for example uses this fact. In general, replication is using epochs not only for conflict resolution; it also groups all transactions in one epoch into one transaction in the binary log (for performance reasons), and the epochs are used to correlate the binary log file and position between the SQL nodes with the binary log enabled.

The internal implementation of counting epochs depends on the platform. If you look at the epoch number reported for example in replication, it will not be the number of 100 milliseconds periods the cluster has been online. The main point is that the epoch number must always be increasing, and the grouping of events will by default be in 100 millisecond periods.

Master Node

The cluster will choose one of the data nodes as the master node. This should in no way be compared to the master/slave roles of traditional MySQL replication. The role of the master data node is to coordinate some of the internal management tasks, such as the changes to the distributed data dictionary from DDL statements, handling the joining and leaving of management nodes, etc. The master node is also known as the president.

The master role is always assigned to one of the data nodes and reassignment only occurs when the current master date node leaves the cluster. The reassignment is part of the node failure handling. As a MySQL NDB Cluster DBA or user, it is not necessary to consider which data node is the master node. It is all handled automatically and the role is only used for internal purposes. However, the term occurs in some contexts such as viewing the cluster status through the ndb_mgm client (see Chapter 7) and in some log messages.

Data and Indexes

Everything discussed this far in the chapter has provided the framework to store the data, which after all is the main purpose of a database. It is now time to look at how data is handled in MySQL NDB Cluster.

There are three main parts to data storage in the data nodes:

- **Data memory:** This is where all in-memory data as well as all ordered indexes are stored.

- **Index memory:** Used for the unique hash indexes.

- **On-disk tablespaces:** On-disk data is stored in tablespace files. Columns that are part of an index are still stored in memory.

The decision whether data is stored in-memory or on disk is done on a per-column basis. That means it is possible to keep the most frequently used parts of a table in-memory but store rarely used data or large data objects in an on-disk tablespace. The only limitation in this respect is that all indexed columns must be stored in-memory.

Data Memory and Index Memory

The data memory and index memory are always present in a cluster, and originally this was the only place to store data. The data memory is used not only for storing data, but also the ordered indexes, while the unique hash indexes are stored in the index memory.

The data memory is organized as one large pool that is available for all the *LDM* threads in the data node. During a restart, the data is loaded from a local checkpoint, the redo log, and/or another data node in the same node group. The indexes are recreated on each restart.

The index memory works a little different. The unique hash indexes are stored in a separate table (not directly accessible) as a key-value store:

- The unique index is the primary key.

- The primary key of the parent (user created table) is the value.

That the unique index is used as the primary key in the hash index table has the consequence that NULL for the indexed column cannot be stored. This again means that the unique hash index cannot be used to look for NULL values, instead a full ordered index scan or table scan is performed. Chapter 18 has some considerations about table design and creating indexes in MySQL NDB Cluster.

The internal organization of the index memory is also different from the data memory, as it is divided evenly between the *LDM* threads. That is, if the data node has 20MB of index memory and four *LDM* threads, each *LDM* thread will have 5MB of index memory. This may not at first sound like big difference, but the consequences are big. If the number of *LDM* threads is doubled, the memory per *LDM* thread is halved, but the number of partitions for existing tables is unchanged. As each partition is associated with a specific *LDM* thread (per replica), the cluster may run out of index memory for some *LDM* threads while other *LDM* threads have not used any.

■ **Note** This is the reason for the caution—that changing the number of *LDM* threads may require a system initial restart—in the section Single-Threaded Versus Multi-Threaded Data Nodes earlier in the chapter. In MySQL NDB Cluster version 7.6 (available as a preview in a milestone release at the time of writing), the index memory has been removed and this limitation lifted.

On-Disk Data

Data that is stored on-disk has different requirements than the data stored in-memory. The architecture is such that writes first go to the disk page buffer. From the *disk page buffer*, the data goes into *tablespaces* and undo data goes into a *logfile group*. The tablespace files and undo log files are organized as follows:

- **Logfile group:** A logfile group contains one or more undo log files.

- **Tablespaces:** A tablespace is associated with a logfile group and contains one or more tablespace files.

Figure 2-16 summarizes this flow of the data and shows how the on-disk data updates fit in with the in-memory data. Notice how the writes also go to the redo buffer and redo log. The parts in the figure that are new will be introduced in this subsection, and the process is discussed in more detail in Chapter 18.

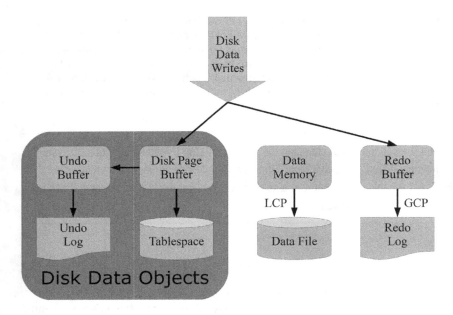

Figure 2-16. *Overview of the disk data write flow*

To take advantage of storing data on disk, it is necessary first to create a logfile group to store the undo log, and to create one or more tablespaces to store the on-disk data. The undo logs are required if a transaction is rolled back. This task is performed through an SQL node. The SQL node will automatically tell all the data nodes to create the files. If you have multiple data nodes on the same host, it is important that the nodes will not share tablespace or undo log files.

The logfile group and the tablespaces each consists of one or more files. It is possible to add files to an existing logfile group or tablespace, and it is possible to remove tablespace files. One special behavior of the on-disk data related files is that they are not removed during an initial restart (neither node nor system restart); only the data within the on-disk tablespaces is removed.

There are a few restrictions on the creation of logfile groups and tablespaces in MySQL NDB Cluster:

- There can be at most one logfile group.

- There can be multiple tablespaces, but all must use the same logfile group.

- The namespace for logfile group names and tablespace names is the same. So, you cannot for example create a tablespace with the same name as a logfile group.

The on-disk storage is on a per-column basis, though it is possible to set a default for the table. If the table default is on-disk storage, all non-indexed columns created will be using on-disk storage. The default for the table can be changed using the ALTER TABLE statement; however, to change the storage type for existing columns, it must be done on a per-column basis. Chapter 18 gives examples of creating logfile groups, tablespaces, and tables using on-disk storage.

It is easy to get started using on-disk storage. However, it is important to be aware of some of the implementation details to avoid surprises:

- As mentioned earlier, only columns without indexes can be stored on disk.

- Each column stored on disk has an eight-byte pointer that is stored in-memory. The pointer is used to locate the data in the tablespace.

- TEXT, BLOB, and JSON columns (irrespective of the maximum length) store the first 256 bytes in memory (plus the eight-byte pointer).

- Variable length columns are stored as a fixed-width column using the space required for the largest value possible. (BLOB, TEXT, and JSON columns are as discussed in the next subsection stored in fixed-width chunks, so a LONGBLOB column does not require 4GB of tablespace.)

Additionally, if the on-disk files are stored on the same disks that are used for local checkpoints and redo logs, it can severely impact the performance and stability of the cluster. These details mean it is not always a win to store data on disk rather than keeping it in-memory, and when using on-disk storage, it is important to consider the data types very carefully.

Similar to the InnoDB buffer pool, on-disk tables in a cluster use a buffer (called the *Disk Page Buffer*). This buffer is used to cache the data from the on-disk tablespaces to avoid re-reading frequently accessed data. The effectiveness of the disk page buffer can be monitored through the ndbinfo schema in the diskpagebuffer table (see also Chapter 16). Additionally, there is a buffer for the logfile group called the *undo buffer*. The memory for the undo buffer is taken from a memory pool called the *Shared Global Memory*.

BLOB, TEXT, and JSON Columns

The BLOB and TEXT data types are treated special in the data nodes. As the JSON data type internally is stored as a BLOB, it is also included. For all columns using one of these data types, only the first 256 bytes are stored in the table itself. The remainder of the values is stored in an internal complementary BLOB table.

■ **Note**   The complementary table is called a BLOB table irrespective of whether the column data type is BLOB, TEXT, or JSON.

The complementary table is named *NDB$BLOB_<table id>_<column number>*, where the table ID is the internal table ID of the main table, and the column number is numbered zero through N, with N being the total number columns in the table minus 1. The table definition of the complementary table consists of columns to identify and order the chunks (see the next paragraph) as well as a column to store chunks of the data. The primary key of the main table is the partition key to ensure the data in the main table and the data in the complementary table that belongs to the same row is located on the same data node. The implementation is transparent for the application.

When data is inserted into the complementary table, it is split into chunks. The maximum size of each chunk depends on the exact data type; for example, for BLOB or TEXT, the maximum is 2000 bytes, for JSON, it is 8100 bytes, and for LONGBLOB or LONGTEXT, it is 13948 bytes. Consider a 6000 byte long BLOB value; in that case the value is stored as follows:

- 256 bytes with the row in the table itself

- Bytes 257 to 2256 in the first row of the complementary table

- Bytes 2257 to 4256 in the second row of the complementary table

- Bytes 4257 to 6000 in the third row of the complementary table

The way that BLOB, TEXT, and JSON values are implemented has a couple of side effects:

- Operations on BLOB, TEXT, and JSON values involve joins and multiple rows in the complementary table for each row in the main table. This affects performance and locking.

- The link between the complementary table and the main table is the primary key of the main table. This means that if there is no explicit primary key on the main table, it will for example not be possible to match the rows in the complementary table with the rows in the main table on a replication slave. The reason is that the hidden primary key will not in general have the same values on a replication master and a replication slave. For this reason, tables without an explicit primary key and with BLOB, TEXT, or JSON columns cannot be logged to the binary log.

Cases Studies: Investigating the Schema Objects

To get a better understanding of the objects and organization in the data nodes, it can be useful to use the two utilities ndb_show_tables and ndb_desc to get information about the schema objects, table definitions, and partitions directly from the data nodes. The two utilities are included with the MySQL NDB Cluster downloads; if you use a packaging format that organizes the binaries into multiple packages, the utilities will be in the client package.

The two case studies use a freshly initialized cluster with the logfile group, tablespace, and table and data shown in Listing 2-2.

Listing 2-2. The Example Disk Data Objects, Table and Data Used for the Two Case Studies

```
CREATE LOGFILE GROUP loggroup_1
  ADD UNDOFILE 'undo_1.log'
  INITIAL_SIZE 128M
  UNDO_BUFFER_SIZE 8M
  ENGINE ndbcluster;

ALTER LOGFILE GROUP loggroup_1
  ADD UNDOFILE 'undo_2.log'
  INITIAL_SIZE 64M
  ENGINE ndbcluster;

CREATE TABLESPACE tblspc_1
  ADD DATAFILE 'datafile_1.dat'
  USE LOGFILE GROUP loggroup_1
  INITIAL_SIZE 128M
  ENGINE ndbcluster;

ALTER TABLESPACE tblspc_1
  ADD DATAFILE 'datafile_2.dat'
  INITIAL_SIZE 64M
  ENGINE ndbcluster;

CREATE TABLE db1.t1 (
  id INT UNSIGNED NOT NULL,
  name VARCHAR(20) NOT NULL,
  birthday date NOT NULL,
  comment TEXT STORAGE DISK,
```

```
  PRIMARY KEY (id),
  UNIQUE INDEX (name),
  INDEX (birthday)
) ENGINE=ndbcluster TABLESPACE tblspc_1;

INSERT INTO db1.t1
VALUES (1, 'Bob'  , '1980-03-21', REPEAT('a', 10000)),
       (2, 'Alice', '1977-08-08', REPEAT('b', 4400)),
       (3, 'Hanna', '1982-05-30', REPEAT('c', 2400)),
       (4, 'Mike' , '1973-11-17', REPEAT('d', 400));
```

The ndb_show_tables Utility

The ndb_show_tables utility can be used to list all tables, indexes, and some other objects in the data nodes. An example output is included in Listing 2-3. The sample output has two columns—state and schema—removed.

Listing 2-3. Example Output of the ndb_show_tables Utility

```
shell$ ndb_show_tables
id  type            logging database  name
2   IndexTrigger    -                 NDB$INDEX_19_CUSTOM
14  Datafile        -                 datafile_1.dat
8   UserTable       Yes     mysql     ndb_index_stat_sample
13  Tablespace      -                 tblspc_1
11  Undofile        -                 undo_1.log
15  Datafile        -                 datafile_2.dat
18  OrderedIndex    No      sys       PRIMARY
3   SystemTable     Yes     sys       NDB$EVENTS_0
5   IndexTrigger    -                 NDB$INDEX_21_CUSTOM
6   UserTable       Yes     mysql     ndb_apply_status
7   UserTable       Yes     mysql     ndb_index_stat_head
12  Undofile        -                 undo_2.log
20  UniqueHashIndex Yes     sys       name$unique
10  LogfileGroup    -                 loggroup_1
16  UserTable       Yes     db1       t1
1   0               -                 DEFAULT-HASHMAP-3840-2
0   IndexTrigger    -                 NDB$INDEX_9_CUSTOM
5   UserTable       Yes     mysql     NDB$BLOB_4_3
1   IndexTrigger    -                 NDB$INDEX_18_CUSTOM
17  UserTable       Yes     db1       NDB$BLOB_16_3
19  OrderedIndex    No      sys       name
9   OrderedIndex    No      sys       ndb_index_stat_sample_x1
3   HashIndexTrigger -                NDB$INDEX_20_UI
21  OrderedIndex    No      sys       birthday
2   SystemTable     Yes     sys       SYSTAB_0
4   UserTable       Yes     mysql     ndb_schema
1   TableEvent      -                 REPL$mysql/ndb_schema
2   TableEvent      -                 NDB$BLOBEVENT_REPL$mysql/ndb_schema_3
5   TableEvent      -                 REPL$db1/t1
3   TableEvent      -                 REPL$mysql/ndb_apply_status
```

```
6   TableEvent      -            NDB$BLOBEVENT_REPL$db1/t1_3
4   TableEvent      -            ndb_index_stat_head_event

NDBT_ProgramExit: 0 - OK
```

The example output shows how there are several "table" types ("table" should not be taken too literally in this case, as it for example also includes the internal triggers):

- **UserTable:** These are tables that use the NDBCluster storage engine and can be accessed through the API/SQL nodes. From the output, it can also be seen that several user tables were created as part of the installation. Some of these will be discussed later; for example, ndb_apply_status is part of the replication implementation discussed in Chapter 6. Additionally, the complementary BLOB tables are also considered user tables even though they are accessed through their parent tables.

- **SystemTable:** These are internal system tables that cannot be accessed directly.

- **UniqueHashIndex:** The hash index used for a unique index.

- **OrderedIndex:** An ordered index. Note how there is both a unique hash index and an ordered index for the index that was added to the name column.

- **IndexTrigger:** This is an internal trigger (see Triggers in the "Data Node Internals" section) for an ordered index. It can be determined from the name which index the trigger belongs to. For example, for NDB$INDEX_19_CUSTOM the 19 is a reference to the ID for the index. Looking through the list, the ordered index with id = 19 can be seen to be the one on the name column; however, there is no clear way from the output to link the index to the table.

- **HashIndexTrigger:** This is an internal trigger for a unique hash index. The trigger can be associated with the index in the same way as for an index trigger.

- **Undofile:** These are the undo files that have been added to the cluster.

- **Datafile:** These are the tablespace files for the cluster.

- **TableEvent:** Internal events used for the replication streams.

The logging column shows whether a "table" will be logged as part of the local checkpoints. In general, user and system tables are logged whereas everything else is not. For user tables, it is possible to specify whether it should be logged or not when the table is created. An advantage of not logging a table is that the local checkpoints become smaller, but the table will be empty after a system restart. In this sense, non-logging tables can be compared with tables using the MEMORY storage engine in a traditional MySQL Server instance.

■ **Tip** Don't confuse the *sys* database listed in the output with the sys schema that is installed as part of MySQL Server 5.7 and MySQL NDB Cluster 7.5. The *sys* database referenced in the output in Listing 2-3 is an internal database to NDBCluster.

The ndb_desc Utility

MySQL DBAs will be familiar with the SHOW CREATE TABLE command to get the table definition of a table. In MySQL NDB Cluster, there is also another way to get information about the NDBCluster tables, the ndb_desc utility. The advantage of ndb_desc is that it not only works as an NDB API client, so it can be used independently of SQL nodes. It also provides more details.

As an example, consider the table db1.t1 from Listing 2-2:

```
CREATE TABLE db1.t1 (
  id INT UNSIGNED NOT NULL,
  name VARCHAR(20) NOT NULL,
  birthday date NOT NULL,
  comment TEXT STORAGE DISK,
  PRIMARY KEY (id),
  UNIQUE INDEX (name),
  INDEX (birthday)
) ENGINE=ndbcluster TABLESPACE tblspc_1;

INSERT INTO db1.t1
VALUES (1, 'Bob'  , '1980-03-21', REPEAT('a', 10000)),
       (2, 'Alice', '1977-08-08', REPEAT('b', 4400)),
       (3, 'Hanna', '1982-05-30', REPEAT('c', 2400)),
       (4, 'Mike' , '1973-11-17', REPEAT('d', 400));
```

The default output of ndb_desc contains the information in Listing 2-4.

Listing 2-4. The Output of the ndb_desc Utility for the db1.t1 Table

```
shell$ ndb_desc --database=db1 t1
-- t1 --
Version: 1
Fragment type: HashMapPartition
K Value: 6
Min load factor: 78
Max load factor: 80
Temporary table: no
Number of attributes: 4
Number of primary keys: 1
Length of frm data: 373
Max Rows: 0
Row Checksum: 1
Row GCI: 1
SingleUserMode: 0
ForceVarPart: 1
PartitionCount: 2
FragmentCount: 2
PartitionBalance: FOR_RP_BY_LDM
ExtraRowGciBits: 0
ExtraRowAuthorBits: 0
TableStatus: Retrieved
Table options:
HashMap: DEFAULT-HASHMAP-3840-2
-- Attributes --
id Unsigned PRIMARY KEY DISTRIBUTION KEY AT=FIXED ST=MEMORY
name Varchar(20;latin1_swedish_ci) NOT NULL AT=SHORT_VAR ST=MEMORY
birthday Date NOT NULL AT=FIXED ST=MEMORY
comment Text(256,2000,0;latin1_swedish_ci) NULL AT=MEDIUM_VAR ST=DISK BV=2 BT=NDB$BLOB_16_3
```

```
-- Indexes --
PRIMARY KEY(id) - UniqueHashIndex
PRIMARY(id) - OrderedIndex
name(name) - OrderedIndex
name$unique(name) - UniqueHashIndex
birthday(birthday) - OrderedIndex

NDBT_ProgramExit: 0 - OK
```

The first part of the output is general table information such as the version, which is updated each time the table definition is changed. Some of the interesting details available are:

- **PartitionCount:** The number of partitions available for the table.

- **FragmentCount:** The number of fragments available for the table. For all other tables than fully replicated tables, the fragment count will be identical to the partition count.

- **PartitionBalance:** This is the partition balance discussed earlier in the chapter. In this case, the default *FOR_RP_BY_LDM* is used.

- **HashMap:** MySQL NDB Cluster supports two hash maps for the partitioning function. The current default of using the large (3840) hash maps is the preferred. The smaller (240) hash map is only provided for backward compatibility, but as all releases since MySQL NDB Cluster 7.2.7 supports the larger hash maps, backward compatibility is no longer an issue. The -2 at the end of the HashMap value refers to the number of partitions.

After the general table properties, there is the Attributes section. In MySQL NDB Cluster, the columns are called attributes. For each column, the various properties for the column are listed. Some of the more interesting properties are:

- For the id column, it is the primary key and the distribution key.

- The *AT* property tells whether the column is stored using the fixed or dynamic (the *%_VAR* values of the *AT* property) column format.

- The *ST* property tells whether the column is stored in-memory or on disk.

- For the comment column, one interesting property is *BT*. Because the comment column is a TEXT column, it has a complementary BLOB table, as discussed in the BLOB, TEXT, and JSON Columns subsection of the previous section. The *BT* property tells the name of this BLOB table. Additional information can also be seen from the data type *Text(256,2000,0;latin1_swedish_ci)*. The 256 means the first 256 bytes are stored in-memory, and the 2000 means that the rest of the data is stored in chunks of up to 2000 bytes.

As mentioned for the *AT* property, MySQL NDB Cluster supports two columns formats: fixed and dynamic. Fixed is, as the name suggests, used for fixed-width storage. In MySQL NDB Cluster 7.4 and earlier the limit for fixed-width storage was 16GB per partition, but in version 7.5 this has been increased to 128TB. The dynamic column format uses variable-width storage. The dynamic format is more flexible than the fixed, for example it is only columns using the dynamic format that can be added online. The advantage of the fixed format columns is that they use less memory for data that is fixed length in nature (such as integers). The two column formats can be mixed within the same table.

Finally, the indexes are listed. Note here how there are two indexes for the primary key and the unique key on the name column: a unique hash index and an ordered index. This is the default for all unique indexes in MySQL NDB Cluster. The unique hash index (stored in the index memory except in the case of the primary key) is used for matching single rows and the uniqueness check. The ordered indexes are used for example for range comparisons.

ndb_desc supports additional options. One commonly used option is --extra-partition-info (or -p), which as the name suggests provides information about the partitions for the table. This option can be combined with the --extra-node-info (-n) option to also include node information. An example is given in Listing 2-5. The part of the output that is the same as in Listing 2-4 has been replaced with ... Some columns of the partition info have been removed.

Listing 2-5. The Output of ndb_desc -p for the db1.t1 Table

```
shell$ ndb_desc --database=db1 t1 -p
...
-- Per partition info --
Partition  Row count  Commit count  Frag fixed memory  Frag varsized memory
0          1          2             32768              32768
1          3          6             32768              32768
```

The partition information in Listing 2-5 has one row per partition. The row count and commit counts are self-explanatory. More interesting are the *Frag fixed memory* and *Frag varsized memory* values. As discussed, the column format can either be fixed or dynamic. This is what is reflected here as the data in the id (INT data type) and birthday (DATE) columns are contributing to the *Frag fixed memory* value, and the data in the comment column (TEXT) contributes to the *Frag varsized memory* value. The reason the usage is 32KB for each partition and storage type is due to the small amount of data in the table. The page size used for the data is 32KB, so this shows that one page is currently used for each column format in each partition.

Another option that can provide details of the table is the --blob-info (-b) option, which as the name suggests provides information about the complementary BLOB table. In MySQL NDB Cluster 7.4 and earlier, it adds per partition information for the BLOB table and must be used together with the -p option; in MySQL NDB Cluster 7.5, it displays the full details of the BLOB table like for the parent table. Listing 2-6 includes an example of part of the output. Some output, including some columns of the partition info, has been removed. The *Frag fixed memory* and *Frag varsized memory* columns have been truncated to *Frag fixed* and *Frag vars*, respectively.

Listing 2-6. The Output of ndb_desc -pb

```
shell$ ndb_desc --database=db1 t1 -pb
...

-- NDB$BLOB_16_3 -
...
-- Attributes --
id Unsigned PRIMARY KEY DISTRIBUTION KEY AT=FIXED ST=MEMORY
NDB$PART Unsigned PRIMARY KEY AT=FIXED ST=MEMORY
NDB$PKID Unsigned NOT NULL AT=FIXED ST=MEMORY
NDB$DATA Char(2000;binary) NOT NULL AT=FIXED ST=DISK
-- Indexes --
PRIMARY KEY(id, NDB$PART) - UniqueHashIndex
-- Per partition info for NDB$BLOB_16_3 --
Partition  Row count  Frag fixed  Frag var  Extent_space  Free extent_space
0          2          32768       0         1048576       1026120
1          9          32768       0         1048576       1012036
```

From the `Attributes` section, there are four columns in the BLOB table:

- **id:** The primary key of the parent table. This is also part of the primary key of the BLOB table and it is the distribution key. That is, the rows in the BLOB table will be stored in the same partition as the row in the parent table they belong to.

- **NDB$PART:** The BLOB part. This is the second part of the primary key and is basically a counter for each row that builds up the one BLOB value. The counter ensures the BLOB data can be put together in the correct order.

- **NDB$PKID:** This is reserved for future use.

- **NDB$DATA:** The actual data. It's a fixed width `CHAR(2000)` column.

The fixed width property of the data column can also be seen from the partition info, where only *Frag fixed memory* has data. Since the column is stored on disk, the partition information also includes details of the use of tablespace extents. Each extent is 1MB and each partition uses one of these with most of the space free.

The NDB File System

The final thing to discuss about data nodes is the NDB file system, which is where the data nodes store their files. The top level of the data directory contains various log and trace files as well as the NDB file system directory, as shown in the following directory listing:

```
shell$ ls -lh
total 3.8M
-rw-r--r--. 1 mysql mysql 1.1K Nov  3 18:25 ndb_1_error.log
drwxr-x---. 9 mysql mysql 4.0K Nov  3 16:57 ndb_1_fs
-rw-r--r--. 1 mysql mysql  48K Nov  3 18:26 ndb_1_out.log
-rw-r--r--. 1 mysql mysql    5 Nov  3 18:25 ndb_1.pid
-rw-r--r--. 1 mysql mysql 974K Nov  3 18:25 ndb_1_trace.log.1
-rw-r--r--. 1 mysql mysql 997K Nov  3 18:25 ndb_1_trace.log.1_t1
-rw-r--r--. 1 mysql mysql 948K Nov  3 18:25 ndb_1_trace.log.1_t2
-rw-r--r--. 1 mysql mysql 881K Nov  3 18:25 ndb_1_trace.log.1_t3
-rw-r--r--. 1 mysql mysql    1 Nov  3 18:25 ndb_1_trace.log.next
```

Note how all the file and directory names are prefixed with *ndb_* followed by a number. The number is the node ID of the data node. The logs and trace files are discussed in Chapter 16. The file *ndb_1.pid* stores the process ID of the data node. The directory *ndb_1_fs* (the *d* in the first column to the left tells it is a directory) is where the redo logs and other files are stored. This is what the remainder of this section will look at.

The content of the *ndb_1_fs* directory includes several directories and possibly several files. In this example, there are seven subdirectories and four files:

```
shell$ ls -lh
total 385M
drwxr-x---. 4 mysql mysql  31 Nov  3 16:51 D1
drwxr-x---. 3 mysql mysql  18 Nov  3 16:50 D10
drwxr-x---. 3 mysql mysql  18 Nov  3 16:50 D11
drwxr-x---. 4 mysql mysql  31 Nov  3 16:51 D2
drwxr-x---. 3 mysql mysql  18 Nov  3 16:50 D8
drwxr-x---. 3 mysql mysql  18 Nov  3 16:50 D9
-rw-r--r--. 1 mysql mysql 129M Nov  3 18:25 datafile_1.dat
```

```
-rw-r--r--. 1 mysql mysql  65M Nov  3 18:25 datafile_2.dat
drwxr-x---. 4 mysql mysql   22 Nov  3 18:25 LCP
-rw-r--r--. 1 mysql mysql 128M Nov  3 18:25 undo_1.log
-rw-r--r--. 1 mysql mysql  64M Nov  3 16:56 undo_2.log
```

The four files are tablespace date files and logfile group files. These files were all created with relative paths, so they have been placed in the *ndb_1_fs* directory and the corresponding directory for the other data nodes.

The seven directories always exist for a data node, but there may be more depending on the configuration. The directories can be divided into three groups:

- **Metadata:** The *D1* and *D2* directories store metadata about the tables and the cluster.

- **Redo log:** The *D8*, *D9*, *D10*, and *D11* directories contain the redo log. There is one directory for each part of the redo log (see also the subsection earlier in the chapter entitled "The Redo Log"). In this case, there are four parts.

- **Local checkpoints:** The *LCP* directory stores two local checkpoints.

The most interesting of these groups are the redo log directories. Each of these contains the number of files configured by *NoOfFragmentLogFiles* and each file of size *FragmentLogFileSize*. Listing 2-7 shows this for the *D8* directory.

Listing 2-7. The Contents of the *ndb_1_ fs/D8* Directory

```
shell$ ls -lRh D8
D8:
total 4.0K
drwxr-x---. 2 mysql mysql 4.0K Nov  3 16:51 DBLQH

D8/DBLQH:
total 8.8M
-rw-r--r--. 1 mysql mysql 16M Nov  3 20:39 S0.FragLog
-rw-r--r--. 1 mysql mysql 16M Nov  3 16:50 S10.FragLog
-rw-r--r--. 1 mysql mysql 16M Nov  3 16:50 S11.FragLog
-rw-r--r--. 1 mysql mysql 16M Nov  3 16:50 S12.FragLog
-rw-r--r--. 1 mysql mysql 16M Nov  3 16:51 S13.FragLog
-rw-r--r--. 1 mysql mysql 16M Nov  3 16:51 S14.FragLog
-rw-r--r--. 1 mysql mysql 16M Nov  3 16:51 S15.FragLog
-rw-r--r--. 1 mysql mysql 16M Nov  3 16:50 S1.FragLog
-rw-r--r--. 1 mysql mysql 16M Nov  3 16:50 S2.FragLog
-rw-r--r--. 1 mysql mysql 16M Nov  3 16:50 S3.FragLog
-rw-r--r--. 1 mysql mysql 16M Nov  3 16:50 S4.FragLog
-rw-r--r--. 1 mysql mysql 16M Nov  3 16:50 S5.FragLog
-rw-r--r--. 1 mysql mysql 16M Nov  3 16:50 S6.FragLog
-rw-r--r--. 1 mysql mysql 16M Nov  3 16:50 S7.FragLog
-rw-r--r--. 1 mysql mysql 16M Nov  3 16:50 S8.FragLog
-rw-r--r--. 1 mysql mysql 16M Nov  3 16:50 S9.FragLog
```

First in the *D8* directory, there is the *DBLQH* subdirectory. This shows that the files are used by the *DBLQH* kernel block, which is the main part of the *LDM* threads. Inside the *DBLQH* subdirectory there are 16 (the default) files, each 16MB large (also the default). At face value, this would suggest that the total size of the directory is 256MB, but as shown in Listing 2-8, this is not the case.

Listing 2-8. The Actual Disk Usage of the Redo Log Files

```
shell$ du -shc *
1.9M    S0.FragLog
548K    S10.FragLog
548K    S11.FragLog
548K    S12.FragLog
548K    S13.FragLog
548K    S14.FragLog
548K    S15.FragLog
548K    S1.FragLog
548K    S2.FragLog
548K    S3.FragLog
548K    S4.FragLog
548K    S5.FragLog
548K    S6.FragLog
548K    S7.FragLog
548K    S8.FragLog
548K    S9.FragLog
9.9M    total
```

Instead, each file only contributes 548KB, except *S0.FragLog,* which has had a few writes. This is an example of the files being created *sparse* by default.

Summary

The topic of this chapter was the data nodes, which are at the heart of the cluster. The data nodes are where the data is stored and where the bulk of the data processing is done. The topics discussed were:

- The single-threaded (ndbd) and multi-threaded (ndbmtd) binaries.

- Which thread types make up the multi-threaded binary.

- Replicas, which are the number of copies MySQL NDB Cluster has of the data.

- Node groups and partitions, which are the building blocks of horizontal scalability and sharding.

- Local and global checkpoints and how they are used to ensure that the data changes are durable.

- A brief overview of restart types.

- The internals of the data nodes, including how there are kernel blocks that use signals to communicate with each other.

- Data and indexes and how they are stored and used in the data nodes.

- Case studies looking at database objects and the ndb_show_tables and ndb_desc utilities.

- The NDB file system.

This concludes Part I, which provided an overview of what MySQL NDB Cluster is and went into some detail of how it works. Part II goes through installation and configuration, with system planning the first area discussed.

Installation and Configuration

■ ■ ■

System Planning

In this chapter, we discuss key points for planning MySQL NDB Cluster system architecture design and briefly discuss configuration. Since NDB Cluster has a built-in *High Availability (HA)* functionality, it does not require additional clustering software. However, there are several limitations on its built-in HA functionality, as nothing can be perfect, so the planning phase is very important for system reliability. We should choose the proper topology, network, server machine, *Operating System (OS)* and so forth. It's not too much to say that whether the system is successfully stable or not is dependent on the planning phase.

Determine Your Priorities

The most important point upon planning NDB Cluster setup is to clarify why you want to use it. NDB Cluster can be used for different purposes:

- **High availability:** It is important to make the entire system accessible even when some components go offline. To achieve this ability, all components within the system must be redundant.

- **Scalability for access increase:** One of the most important challenges for recent database systems is to handle workload increase.

- **Disaster recovery:** A very important system may be required to be running even when the data center experiences disruption due to a disaster.

Which factor is the most important for your application? Please consider carefully and determine your goal. If you make a wrong choice here, you will employ the wrong configuration too.

High Availability Requirements

While NDB Cluster consists of three types of nodes—data node, SQL node, and management node—it doesn't have a *Single Point of Failure (SPOF)* on every type of node. Each type of node can be configured so that it has fault tolerance against node failure. To make each type of node fault tolerant, the following conditions should be met.

Data Node

The first parameter that you need to decide for data node is the number of replicas, and more than one replica is required as spares in the event of failures. The number of replicas should be identical among all node groups. So, the number of replicas must be a common divisor of the total number of data nodes. NDB Cluster supports one to four replicas. Databases can survive unless all replicas within one node group fail. One replica means each node group has only a single copy at most, so there is no fault tolerance against node failure, because there is no spare. Thus, configuration with one replica is not practical in production systems.

How many replicas should be configured then? In most cases, two replicas are sufficient and recommended. In fact, configuration with three and four replicas is not officially supported at this moment. So, configuration with two replicas is the only choice.

Theoretically, three or four replicas will provide more redundancy and improve system availability. If you need extra availability against node failures and are ready for self-support, consider having three or four replicas.

Please carefully choose the number of replicas. This cannot be changed after the cluster has started. To change the number of replicas, a system initial restart (initializing the whole data) is required.

SQL Node

While SQL nodes don't have any user data, one SQL node failure doesn't affect other SQL nodes. SQL nodes can be easily configured as high available. Having multiple SQL nodes is sufficient for this purpose. In the event of failure, an application can continue its operation by simply reconnecting to another SQL node. See Chapter 18 for more details about how an application reconnects to another SQL node.

SQL nodes don't communicate directly each other. All communications between SQL nodes goes through the data nodes. For example, a schema change triggered by one SQL node will be propagated as an event via data nodes. So, clients will see identical data regardless of which SQL node they connect.

It is also a good idea to have one SQL node on every host where an application is running. In that case, an application will connect directly to local SQL node, and that connection is very fast. In the event of machine failure, an application and SQL node on the same machine will go down together. If application servers are redundant (and such configuration is very common), failure of one machine isn't a problem.

The more SQL nodes are installed, the more the cluster gets highly available. However, be careful not to have too many SQL nodes with binary logging enabled. On NDB Cluster, binary log is generated using data sent from data nodes. The more SQL nodes with binary logging enabled are configured, the more data is transferred over the network, which may cause network congestion.

Management Node

Management nodes are not involved in data access at all. Management nodes are required in the following situations:

- **Configuration handling:** Management nodes read the cluster configuration from the configuration file and deploy the cluster configuration to other nodes when the other nodes start.

- **User operations:** Management nodes handle various operations, such as starting and stopping data nodes, starting backups, etc.

- **Logging:** Management nodes collect events from all data nodes and write to a centralized log file called the *cluster log*.

- **Arbitration:** When network partitioning happens, MySQL NDB Cluster must decide which operational cluster should survive. MySQL NDB Cluster employs a technique called *arbitration* for this purpose.

- **Status monitoring:** Management nodes have several commands to display the status of running nodes.

It is not necessarily required to configure multiple management nodes for high availability purposes. If you prefer extra safety, having two management nodes is sufficient.

Prepare for Network Partitioning

Network partitioning is a well-known problem for cluster systems, and it may happen on NDB Cluster, too. Network partitioning is also known as *split brain*. Network partitioning is a situation whereby a network between data nodes is disconnected evenly so that one data node within each node group is running and connected. That way, more than one working cluster is formed by chance. Figure 3-1 depicts a typical network partitioning situation on four data nodes.

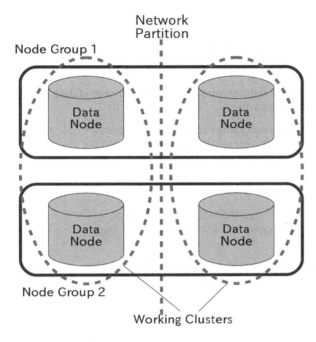

Figure 3-1. *Network partitioning*

Arbitration is a mechanism implemented on NDB Cluster to resolve network partitioning. An arbitrator is picked from candidates (management nodes or SQL nodes) by a representative data node called the *president*. At any time, only the arbitrator is configured and running. When the network partition happens, all data nodes try to access an arbitrator to get approval to carry on its operation. Only one partition will win on every arbitration process. If a data node is "lost" or timed out on arbitration, it is forcibly shut down. This type of shutdown operation, done by the other surviving cluster, is called *STONITH* (*Shoot The Other Node In The Head*). Refer to Chapter 1 for more details on the arbitration process.

■ **Caution**   Do not place an arbitrator and a data node on the same server machine. If they are placed on the same machine, an arbitrator and a data node can be lost at the same time when the server machine faces an unplanned outage. So, an arbitrator should be placed on a separate machine from any data nodes.

From the nature of arbitration, it is desirable to configure separate network paths; one is to interconnect the data nodes, the other is to communicate between data nodes and arbitrators. Network partitioning happens upon network problems between data nodes, but at least one surviving cluster should reach the arbitrator to avoid whole system shutdown. Because both of the surviving clusters will be shut down if both clusters lose arbitration.

Arbitration is required on the data nodes only. SQL node and management node don't require arbitration, because they don't store any data.

Scalability

One big reason to use NDB Cluster is to achieve high performance. NDB Cluster is good at gaining better performance by processing data access requests using computer machines in parallel. This strategy is called *scaling out*.

It is important to know what types of data access are scalable in proportion to the number of data nodes. For example, the following types of data access are scalable.

- **Lookup reads:** Row lookup in equality comparison using primary key or secondary unique hash index. Only the data node where the row resides will be involved in the lookup operation.

- **Insert:** Also known as write scale-out where a high number of writes is spread over several nodes.

- **Range scan using user defined partition:** With user defined partitioning, only a specific data node will be involved in the scan operation when partition pruning is possible.

- **Range scan which returns a lot of rows:** Since the scan is done in parallel, the time taken to scan will be reduced in proportion to the number of data nodes.

- **Join with pushdown algorithm:** When a join is pushed down to the data nodes, it is done in parallel.

In contrast, the following types of data access are not scalable against the number of data nodes.

- **Range scan that returns a few rows:** When data nodes return only a few rows, overhead to involve data nodes will dominate over the advantage of parallelism.

- **Join without using pushdown algorithm:** When join is not pushed down to the data nodes, lots of network round-trips are required to access inner tables.

Scalability is not a silver bullet and it does not solve all performance problems. For example, a range scan query that returns a lot of rows is inefficient anyway even if many data nodes can handle range scanning in parallel. In fact, resource consumption per data node caused by a such query will be reduced in inverse proportion to the number of data nodes, and total throughput will be increased in proportion to the number of data nodes. So, it scales automatically. However, it remains inefficient anyway. If the system has throughput that can execute an inefficient query X 4 times per second, after increasing data nodes twice, it will be able to execute the same query X 8 times per second. The number of queries per seconds remains small anyway. So, such queries cannot be executed frequently, even though execution of such queries is parallelized among data nodes. Otherwise, the entire cluster will easily slow down.

Disaster Recovery

MySQL NDB Cluster has a functionality to replicate data from one cluster to another, which is called *NDB Cluster Replication* or *Geographic Replication*. NDB Cluster Replication is done via the SQL node just like standard MySQL replication. All modifications are written to the binary log on the master SQL node. The master SQL node sends events in the binary log to the slave, and the slave SQL node applies events in the binary log. This way, the whole data is synchronized from the master cluster to the slave cluster.

Since standard MySQL replication is very efficient, it is possible to configure NDB Cluster Replication so that the master cluster and the slave cluster are located at geographically separated sites. With this setup, the slave cluster can be used as a stand-by for disaster recovery. When the site of the master cluster faces outage, but the site of the slave cluster is alive, the slave can take over the data service.

See Chapter 6 for more details about NDB Cluster Replication.

Typical Topologies

In this section, we describe the typical topology of NDB Cluster. Although the topology of NDB Cluster is flexible, there are some restrictions and considerations discussed in the following subsections.

Number of Replicas

As described earlier in this chapter, the number of replicas is the first thing to consider. Since copies of data also consume memory for data storage (and disk for *LCP*; see Chapter 1 for more details about LCP), the more replicas you have, the smaller the total data size. The following formula calculates the total amount of data size.

```
(Number_of_data_nodes × Memory_per_node) ÷ Number_of_replicas
```

Do not choose one replica in a production system, because there is no redundancy. One replica configuration is valid only for benchmarking purposes, etc. Choose two in most cases.

Maximum Number of Data Nodes

NDB Cluster can have up to 48 data nodes in total per cluster. If you plan to set up a huge cluster, be careful not to exceed this limit. When you need a huge capacity, you may consider a huge cluster like 40+ data nodes. However, using many server machines will increase the probability of machine failures. Consider using server machines with larger memory size over increasing data nodes to avoid increasing the probability of machine failures, if you need only more capacity.

Maximum Number of Total Nodes

NDB Cluster can have up to 255 nodes per cluster, including all types of nodes. We can configure 48 data nodes at most, and we do not need many management nodes in general. So, this limitation practically affects the maximum number of SQL nodes only. For example, if you have 20 data nodes and 2 management nodes, you can have at most 233 SQL nodes.

The SQL node is often placed on the same machine as the application server. Such configuration is not a bad idea, because an application will connect to the local SQL node via a UNIX domain socket except for Windows machines, where the connection is very fast. However, this configuration is likely to hit an upper limit for maximum number of total SQL nodes, when you want to increase the number of application servers for scale-out purposes, because the number of SQL nodes is same as the number of application servers in this configuration. For example, if you have 20 data nodes and 2 management nodes, you can have at most 233 SQL nodes and 233 application servers.

Arbitration Rank

By default, only the management node is configured to be an arbitrator. But an SQL node can be an alternative arbitrator by configuring the `ArbitrationRank` option. The `ArbitrationRank` option specifies the likelihood of being an arbitrator. The range for this parameter is 0, 1, and 2. Setting it to 1 means it's most likely to be an arbitrator, which is a management node default. 2 is less likely than 1. 0 disables the arbitrator, which is an SQL node default.

If you want to make an arbitrator highly available, making some of SQL nodes candidates instead of adding management nodes is a good option. If an SQL node is configured as a candidate arbitrator, management nodes are not required in the event of network partitioning. It will save one node slot for the total number of nodes limitation and one host machine.

Placing the SQL Node and the Data Node on the Same Machine

If the SQL node is not placed on the same server machine as an application server, it can be placed on the same machine as the data node. However, such a topology is not optimal, thus we do not encourage you to do so. Here are several reasons why:

- SQL node also consumes a certain amount of CPU and memory resources. Parsing SQL and optimizing an execution plan often consume more resources than expected.

- Resource consumption may not be even among SQL nodes. This will cause a bottleneck on data nodes, because the available resource per data node is not even.

- The distance between an SQL node and each data node (the network hops) is not even. This will also cause a bottleneck on the data nodes.

If performance is not your top priority and a certain amount of performance degradation is acceptable, you may place the SQL node and data node on the same machine. Otherwise, do not do this.

Typical Topology Examples

This section describes several example topologies from minimum to large configurations. Note that this section shows just examples. You do not need to follow the identical configurations here, but can employ any configuration as you see fit.

Minimum Configuration: Three Hosts

To run NDB Cluster as a highly available database system, at least three server machines are needed. Two server machines are needed for data node redundancy. It is possible to place an SQL node and a data node on a same host if performance isn't the highest priority. An additional host computer is needed for the management node, because it should be placed on a separate host computer from the data nodes. This constraint is required because the arbitrator will go offline together with the data node if it is placed on the same host as the data node. Since the management node doesn't require lots of computer resources, using an inexpensive machine for the management node is fine and recommended.

Figure 3-2 depicts the minimum configuration for three hosts. In this case, the system has a dedicated network or subnet for NDB Cluster, separated from the applications.

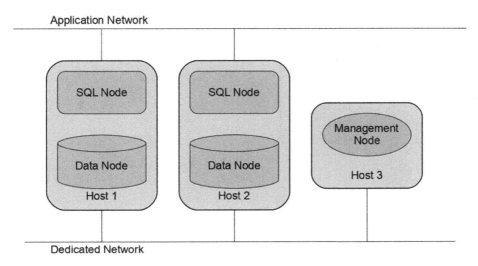

Figure 3-2. *Minimum configuration (three hosts)*

Alternative Minimum Configuration: Four Hosts

As it is not recommended to place the SQL node and the data node on the same server machine, we often need to place them on separate machines. In such cases, the minimum number of required host computers is four, as SQL node also requires redundancy. Figure 3-3 depicts an alternative minimum configuration with four hosts. This setup is far more practical compared to the three-node setup, because placing the SQL node and the data node on separate hosts will avoid contention of computer resources between them.

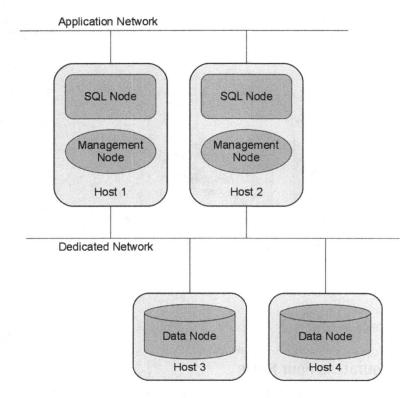

Figure 3-3. *Alternative minimum configuration (four hosts)*

Aside: Cluster Using Minimum Computer

In this chapter, we have shown the minimum topology in the sense of the number of host computers. What about the minimum computer hardware then? There is no definition for the minimum requirements for computer resources. Of course, less powerful computer hardware cannot provide good performance. So, you need to choose the appropriate computer hardware to achieve the required performance.

Figure 3-4 shows a mobile NDB Cluster concept on a demo machine. It houses six *Beagle Bone Black Single Board Computers (SBC)* for the cluster nodes and one *Raspberry Pi* for the console.

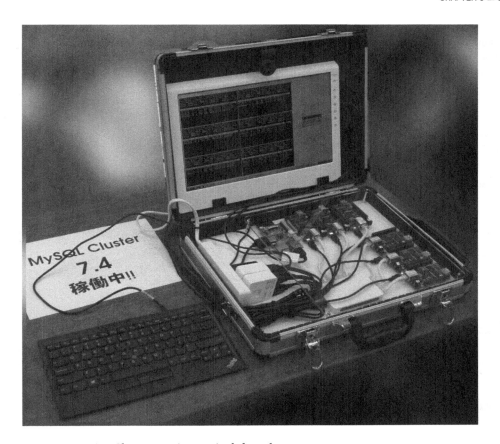

Figure 3-4. *NDB Cluster running on single board computers*

One can carry this machine by housing all the components inside the case. To use this machine, all you need to do is to open the case and connect the power plug. Unfortunately, it does not have batteries for mobile use.

Each computer has 512MB RAM, a single core ARM® Cortex®-A8 32-Bit RISC processor, and a 16GB micro-SD card. You see that these computers have very poor resources. NDB Cluster can run on small computers like this for experimentation and demonstration purposes.

■ **Tip** When it comes to the *sysbench* benchmark, it reveals the best score when four SQL nodes and two data nodes are configured. The benchmark score is the sum of scores on all SQL nodes. This means that the parsing SQL statement and the optimizing execution plan are very resource-intensive processes.

Medium Configuration: 10 Hosts

One of the most significant features of NDB Cluster is its outstanding scalability. It is not very often that NDB Cluster is configured as its minimum possible configuration. Instead, a large number of cluster nodes are often configured for better performance.

Figure 3-5 depicts a typical topology of an NDB Cluster system, which involves 10 computer hosts. In this case, the application servers are placed on the same hosts as the SQL nodes. In addition, the management nodes are placed on the same hosts as the SQL node. Placing the management node and the SQL node on a same host is not a problem, because SQL nodes don't require arbitration.

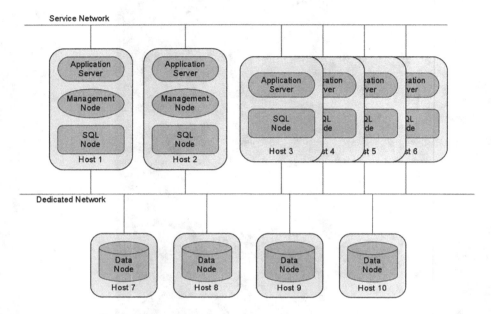

Figure 3-5. *Medium 10 hosts configuration*

Large Configuration: 50 Hosts

Of course, you can configure larger configurations until you reach the node number limitation. If you need extra capacity and/or performance, you can configure many nodes until your requirements are satisfied. Capacity increases and write performance scales in proportion to the number of data nodes.

Figure 3-6 depicts a 50 hosts configuration, which is very large. Note that MGM in Figure 3-6 indicates management node.

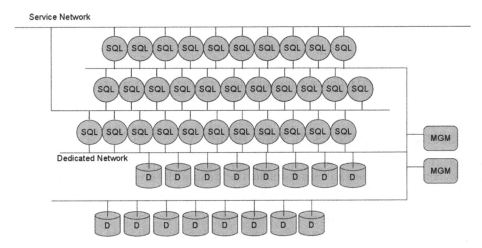

Figure 3-6. *Large 50 hosts configuration*

Platform Considerations

So far, the chapter has discussed the high-level perspective of MySQL NDB Cluster topologies. It's now time to discuss details for each computer machine in this section.

Processor Type and Operating System

You can use any type of processor and operating system for your MySQL NDB Cluster installation if they are supported by Oracle. You can verify whether the desired combination of processor and operating system is supported or not on the following page:

https://www.mysql.com/support/supportedplatforms/cluster.html

Even if your platform is not supported and binary packages are not provided for the platform, it could be technically possible to run MySQL NDB Cluster on those platforms by compiling MySQL NDB Cluster from source, because MySQL NDB Cluster is designed so that it runs on commonly used POSIX systems, which is why we were able to run it on the BBB. This would be a good choice if you don't need official support and you need to run MySQL NDB Cluster on a specific platform.

CPU Performance and Characteristics

CPU performance is important for MySQL NDB Cluster, because CPU is the most important resource for in-memory database systems in general. (One of other important resources for MySQL NDB Cluster is network throughput, because it is a distributed system.) What characteristics of CPU are the most important then? CPU has many characteristics, such as:

- Clock speed
- Number of cores
- Number of threads per core

- L2/L3 cache size

- Memory type

- NUMA vs. UMA

This section covers what type of CPU resource is important for each type of node in order to achieve optimal performance.

Desirable Processor Characteristics for Data Nodes

The most important thing for CPU selection is to use identical CPUs among all data nodes. Due to its shared-nothing architecture, workload against data nodes is distributed to all data nodes evenly. In other words, all data nodes will handle approximately the same volume of workloads. So, if one data node can handle less workload than the others, that data node will be a bottleneck of the entire cluster, because other data nodes cannot handle more workloads than that data node.

CPU is the most important component for the performance of a data node. Choose the right CPU according to the following criteria:

- High clock speed CPUs for minimizing response time

- Many core CPUs for maximizing throughput

If your application doesn't issue many queries in parallel, but response time is important, choose a CPU model with a very high clock speed. If your application needs very high throughput, choose a CPU model with many cores. However, there is a limitation to the maximum number of CPU cores that a data node can use. Table 3-1 shows the maximum number of threads that every data node process can spawn, configured by the MaxNoOfExecutionThreads option.

Table 3-1. *MaxNoOfExecutionThreads by Version*

MySQL NDB Cluster Versions	Range of MaxNoOfExecutionThreads
7.2.0	2 – 8
7.2.5, 7.3.0	2 – 36
7.3.3, 7.4.1, 7.5.0	2 – 72

Having more than 72 CPU cores on one machine (not within one CPU chip) doesn't make sense at this moment, because no versions of MySQL NDB Cluster can utilize so many cores unless you are using the MaxNoOfExecutionThreads option. The ThreadConfig option, introduced in 7.2.3, allows you to use more CPU cores. (Up to 100 threads. See Chapter 4 for more details about these options.) Anyway, you need to increase the number of data nodes if throughput is not sufficient.

Desirable Processor Characteristics for SQL Nodes

If your application accesses the database via SQL nodes, CPU performance on the SQL node is also important. Since SQL nodes do not store any data, they don't require much memory or a fast disk, but they need fast CPU. All of the activities done by SQL nodes, such as parsing SQL statements and optimizing execution plans, are CPU-intensive workloads. SQL nodes require more CPU performance than data nodes in total. If your cluster has sufficient data nodes with powerful CPUs, but has insufficient CPU resources for SQL nodes, it is not possible to utilize the CPU resources fully on the data nodes even when the SQL nodes are 100% busy.

Desirable Processor Characteristics for Management Node

Since management nodes do very few tasks, they don't require fast CPU. The less powerful CPU model is just fine.

Key Points When Choosing the Most Suitable CPU

To increase total memory size and the total number of CPU cores, server machines may have more than one CPU chip (sockets). Recent x86_64 CPUs have memory controllers inside, and each memory controller has a maximum memory capacity. So, the server machine must have multiple CPU chips to increase memory size.

This approach is good for memory size and CPU processing power, but not very good for memory access speed. Memory access speed isn't homogeneous on such server machines. Memory access speed varies depending on to which CPU the target memory is connected. If the target memory is connected to the same CPU as the one trying to accesses the target memory, then access speed is optimal. Otherwise, memory access speed gets slow because data is transferred to the CPU that has the target memory under the memory controller.

Systems that don't have homogeneous memory access speed are called *Non-Uniform Memory Access (NUMA)* machines. Since NUMA machines have small disadvantages on memory access speed, choose non-NUMA machines if possible. Having many CPU cores within a single CPU chip is preferable to having multiple CPU chips with a few cores within each CPU chip. Likewise, having a large memory capacity under a single CPU chip is preferable to having multiple CPUs with smaller memory capacity per CPU chip.

L2/L3 cache memory is yet another important factor when selecting a good CPU. The larger the L2/L3 cache memory size, the better its memory access performance. NUMA systems also have a disadvantage on L2/L3 memory access, because content of cache memory should be synchronized on all CPU chips to ensure data integrity. The cost of cache synchronization isn't negligible.

As a rule of thumb, follow this criteria:

- If performance is the highest priority, choose a server machine with a single CPU that has many cores and large memory.

- If capacity is the highest priority, choose a server machine with several CPUs with large memory.

■ **Caution**   While it is possible to mix different CPU architectures or OSs in the same cluster, CPU endianness should be same. The NDB API protocol, which is used for communication between SQL nodes and data nodes, is a raw binary protocol and not portable between machines with different endian. If you use little endian machines for SQL nodes, you should use little endian machines for data nodes, too. So, for example, it is not possible to employ x86_64 (little endian) machines for SQL nodes and SPARC (big endian) machines for data nodes. By contrast, MySQL protocol, which is used for communication between client applications and SQL nodes, is an endian-aware protocol. You can employ any types of CPU or OSs for application servers regardless of the CPU types employed for the MySQL NDB Cluster.

Memory Consumption

RAM modules are getting cheaper and cheaper; however, they are still expensive components nevertheless. So, it is not a good idea to install more memory than required.

Data nodes require lots of memory. Prepare sufficient memory modules according to the required data capacity. Other node types don't require much memory. Management nodes require only several dozen megabytes of memory. Several gigabytes of memory are sufficient for SQL nodes in most cases, if you don't use InnoDB on it.

Disk Performance

Even though MySQL NDB Cluster is mainly used as an in-memory database, disk performance is still important for data nodes. On the data node, disk performance is required in the following situations:

- **Storing checkpoint data on disk:** The data node continuously writes its data in DataMemory to disk as a local checkpoint (LCP). If LCP delays, the redo log is filled up and cannot write more data.

- **Redo logging:** The data node writes modifications to the redo log for persistence of data. Redo log entries are generated upon transaction commits.

- **Taking a backup:** The back up is saved on disk.

- **Reading data on restart:** Whole data for the in-memory table is read from disk upon restart of the data node.

- **Reading/writing disk data tables:** Disk speed is critical for performance of disk data tables.

Except for disk data tables, reads and writes are handled sequentially. So, you can use inexpensive *Hard Disk Drive (HDD)* for systems that are not too busy. If your application requires maximum write performance, consider using *Solid State Drive (SSD)*. When using SSD, it's best to avoid models that employ *Triple-Level Cell (TLC)* NAND flash memory. TLC has much less lifecycle compared to other types of NAND flash memory, such as *Single-Level Cell (SLC)* or *Multi-Level Cell (MLC)*.

Management nodes and SQL nodes don't require high disk performance. Inexpensive disks are just fine unless you use InnoDB on the SQL node.

Virtual Machines

Compared to physical machines, virtual machines have inferior performance to run MySQL NDB Cluster. If you need a database system with maximum performance, do not employ virtual machines such as cloud services. Certainly, virtual machines are handy in general, but they fall behind physical machines in terms of performance.

Network Design

Network is one of the most important components for MySQL NDB Cluster, because it is a distributed system that exchanges lots of data across the network. So, network tends to be a bottleneck if it doesn't have sufficient bandwidth compared to computer hardware.

Network Devices

Ethernet is the most commonly used because it has good cost performance ratio. However, in most cases, *Gigabit Ethernet (GbE)* is not sufficient for interconnect between cluster nodes. At the least, consider employing 10GbE network cards and switches. Otherwise, network will be a bottleneck and sufficient throughput cannot be achieved.

MySQL NDB Cluster supported *Scalable Coherent Interface (SCI)* protocol in versions prior to MySQL NDB Cluster 7.2, but has not supported this in recent releases. However, it is possible to use SCI devices as the interconnect, because SCI devices also support TCP/IP connection over the SCI protocol, called *SuperSockets*. SuperSockets is handy because it doesn't require recompiling the cluster binaries. SCI devices have up to 20 Gbps throughput, which is twice 10GbE. Since SCI has lower latency than 10GbE, it might be possible to achieve higher performance than the MySQL NDB Cluster setup with 10GbE. The most significant drawback of SCI is that the SCI switch supports up to eight computers only; it is much less than the maximum number of total cluster nodes.

InfiniBand is a good alternative to Ethernet and SCI. Even though MySQL NDB Cluster doesn't support InfiniBand native API called *InfiniBand Verbs*, it is possible for cluster nodes to communicate using InfiniBand using the *IP over InfiniBand (IPoIB)* protocol, which cluster nodes see as usual TCP/IP sockets regardless of the underlying layers.

Network Redundancy

MySQL NDB Cluster is not fault tolerant against network failures. In the worst case, an entire cluster shutdown may happen due to a network failure. To improve the availability of the MySQL NDB Cluster system, it is important to make the network redundant beforehand.

On Linux systems, a *bonding* driver is widely used. The bonding driver defines a pseudo-network interface over multiple physical network interfaces for redundancy. In the event of failure of one network route, traffic is redirected to other network interfaces.

Other OSs have similar functionalities. For example, Solaris has *IP Multi-Pathing (IPMP)* and Windows has *NIC Teaming*.

Direct Connection

To minimize network latency and maximum network bandwidth, direct connection using Ethernet cross-cable is useful. Even when connecting directly via Ethernet cross-cable, network redundancy is required. Each host machine needs to have multiple network interface cards to connect to each other. To connect four data nodes redundantly to each other, six network interface ports are required.

Direct connection is a good choice when the number of nodes is small. It does not require a network switch device in between, so you can save a certain amount of money. However, separate network interface cards are still required for direct connection even if there are no network switches between the host machines.

Security Considerations

NDB API protocol cannot be secured by encryption. So, network between SQL nodes and data nodes should be physically secured to prevent unauthorized data access. Do not allow unauthorized people to access computer hardware that runs cluster nodes.

If you must use a cloud environment for some reason, you need to connect virtual computers using *Virtual Private Cloud (VPC)*. Otherwise, your cluster will be at some risk of data interception.

See Chapter 12 for more information about security.

Extending Capacity Using Disk Objects

The last thing discussed in this chapter is whether to use disk data tables or not. MySQL NDB Cluster supports disk data tables as of version MySQL 5.1.6 (MySQL Server and MySQL NDB Cluster were not separate products at that time).

Disk data tables need additional file and buffer memories—data files, undo log files, disk page buffers, and undo buffers. These objects have a big impact on the MySQL NDB Cluster configuration. It is important to decide whether to use disk data tables or not at the planning phase.

See Chapter 2 for more details of disk data tables.

Performance Considerations

Disk data tables get a bigger capacity by storing data on relatively cheap disks (file system) instead of expensive memory. So, disk access speed could be a potential bottleneck, because disks are slower than memory. If rows on disk data tables are often accessed, consider using high-speed storage such as SSD with a high-speed interface like PCI Express and Non-Volatile Memory Express (NVMe).

Using many data nodes is a good alternative strategy. Since MySQL NDB Cluster employs shared nothing architecture, disk access workloads are split and distributed to data nodes evenly. Theoretically, total I/O throughput for disk data tables on the cluster would be increased in proportion to the number of data nodes. Increasing the data nodes will also increase capacity. Consider using many data nodes by way of performance and capacity.

Storage Requirements

Unfortunately, disk data tables don't support variable length columns, so all the columns have a fixed length that can store the maximum data size for that column. For example, the VARCHAR(10) column with the utf8 character set will always require 30 bytes, which is not efficient. For this reason, the data size on the file system will be much larger than the actual data size.

When using a variable length size column with in-memory tables, actual data (rounded to four bytes alignment), headers, and fragmentation all consume storage. So, the required storage size is proportional to the average data size of the column. On the other hand, when using disk data tables, where only fixed size column format is supported, the largest possible space is always allocated for each column per row. As a result, the disk data tables usually consume several times more storage than in-memory tables.

Memory Consumption

Despite storing data on disk, disk data table also requires a certain amount of cache memory for speeding up data access, just like InnoDB requires a large buffer pool memory. So, you need to allocate sufficient memory to the disk page buffer and the undo buffer. This means you need to reduce memory for DataMemory and IndexMemory instead. So, take extra care when planning the memory size of the server machine when you use disk data tables.

Summary

This chapter discussed the strategy to determine the big picture of cluster setup, according to your application needs. The main aspects be considered when planning the cluster are:

- **Priority of application needs:** MySQL NDB Cluster is a highly available but scalable database management system. It also provides disaster recovery. Determine which aspects of the product are most important for your application.

- **Topology:** MySQL NDB Cluster is flexible and can configure various topologies. Determine which type of topology is suitable for your application needs.

- **Platform:** Determine which type of server machine is suitable for each node according to your application needs.

- **Network design:** Network design is important to maximize performance and availability of the cluster. Since MySQL NDB Cluster is a distributed database management system, lots of packets are exchanged over the network.

- **Whether to use disk data tables for capacity:** Disk data table can provide far more capacity than in-memory tables because the disk storage medium is less expensive than memory. However, when using disk data tables, extra care must be taken due to limitations and resource consumption.

The planning phase is very important, because characteristics of the system are decided. It is possible to adjust the details later, but the overall direction cannot be changed easily.

In the next chapter, we discuss the detailed configuration of the MySQL NDB Cluster. Detailed configuration is as important as an overview, discussed in this chapter. The former is a top-down approach, whereas the latter is a bottom-up approach.

CHAPTER 4

Configuration

Before installing MySQL NDB Cluster software packages on your system, this chapter discusses the configuration of MySQL NDB Cluster. You can perform the configuration or package installation first, as you like. However, the configuration must be done before starting the cluster the first time. Although most options can be changed later using a rolling restart, the initial configuration must be at least practical enough. Since a rolling restart is a time-consuming operation, it is a good idea to mitigate the necessity of a configuration change by reviewing the options carefully as much as possible.

Configuration Overview

On MySQL NDB Cluster, there are two types of configurations:

- **config.ini:** Mainly used to define installation layout and resource allocation. This file is read by management node and distributed to other types of nodes. This configuration file defines the topology of the cluster.

- **Command-line options and my.cnf:** Mainly used to define the startup behavior of each process and fine-tune the SQL node. All types of processes have their own command-line options and read options from my.cnf. SQL node has variety of command-line options to customize various aspects of SQL.

When using the *MySQL Cluster Manager (MCM)*, the way to configure the cluster is different and these files are not edited directly. See Chapter 13 for more information about MCM.

Defining a big picture of cluster installation is an important process, because it's not changed easily afterward. Fine-tuning the SQL node and startup options is less important than *config.ini*, because changes on *my.cnf* can be applied by restarting the SQL node, so they can be changed casually.

The following sections explain details about the major configuration options. Since this chapter is a bit long, you can skip the details now and then return to this chapter later, when you need a one-stop reference for the major options.

Formatting config.ini

Before discussing the details of each configuration option, we cover the content of *config.ini*; how it's are organized and how to write options correctly. *config.ini* consists of sections starting with the section name enclosed in square brackets. There are two types of sections:

- *Configuration for individual node or connection.* Typically, one section corresponds to one node. The section name is the same as the node type, e.g., NDBD. Table 4-1 shows the available section names.

- *Default configuration for one node type.* This type of section must precede all individual node sections. The section name is the node type plus the DEFAULT string, e.g., NDBD DEFAULT.

Table 4-1. *Section Names in config.ini*

Section Name	Description
MGM or NDB_MGMD	Configuration of management node.
NDBD	Configuration of data node.
API or MYSQLD	Configuration of SQL node or NDB API client application.
TCP	Configuration of node interconnect.
SCI	Configuration of SCI connection.
COMPUTER	Naming each node different than its hostname or IP address.
SHM	Configuration of shared memory connection.

In this book, we do not discuss the following sections.

- **SCI:** Support for SCI is outdated. In addition, this section is not required when using *SuperSockets*.

- **COMPUTER:** Not often used.

- **SHM:** Shared memory connection is experimental at this time.

Typically, *config.ini* begins with several default sections followed by individual sections. Each section consists of the option name and value. In contrast to *my.cnf*, *config.ini* cannot include duplicate options. Each option should be specified only once.

Listing 4-1 shows an example of config.ini for a small system.

Listing 4-1. An *config.ini* example for a Small System

```
[MGM]
NodeId = 255
HostName = mgmhost
DataDir = /var/lib/mysql-cluster

[NDBD DEFAULT]
NoOfReplicas = 2
DataDir = /var/lib/mysql-cluster
DataMemory = 4G
IndexMemory = 512M

[NDBD]
NodeId = 1
HostName = host1

[NDBD]
NodeId = 2
HostName = host2
```

```
[MYSQLD]
NodeId = 49
HostName = host1

[MYSQLD]
NodeId = 50
HostName = host2
```

In this example, only five nodes are configured—one management node, two data nodes, and two SQL nodes. Hostnames for data nodes and SQL nodes overlap, so they are placed on the same hosts (host1, host2). A management node is placed on a separate host (mgmnost), so three hosts are involved in total.

The configuration is distributed to each data node and each SQL node when it connects to the management server. When a node connects to the management node, the management node identifies which slot is matched for the connecting node by comparing the hostname of the connecting node and the HostName option under each section. For example, if ndbmtd connects to the management node from host2, its node ID is identified as 2, because there is one NDBD section that has configuration with NodeId = 2 and HostName = host2. If one more ndbmtd attempts to connect to the management node from host2, the connection will fail because there is no available free slot for data node that connects from host2. However, mysqld can connect to the management node from host2 even if the slot for the data node is occupied, because there is one available slot for SQL node on host2.

Restart Types

To apply the configuration after starting the cluster, node restarts are required. In the following sections, every option is explained with *restart types*, which is how the target node is restarted. On MySQL NDB Cluster, four restart types are defined:

- **Node Restart (N):** One node is restarted at a time, without specifying additional instructions. In order to apply configuration changes to an entire cluster, every node should be restarted in turn. This operation is also known as a *rolling restart*. During a rolling restart, the cluster is running and applications can access data. It is not possible to perform a node restart when NoOfReplicas = 1, because no surviving data nodes exist within the same node group.

- **System Restart (S):** All nodes are stopped (the cluster is entirely shutdown), then the cluster starts again. During system restart, applications cannot access data because the cluster completely stops.

- **Initial Node Restart (IN):** This is a similar restart type to the node restart, but each data node is restarted with the --initial option. This option instructs the target data node to wipe its data, then copy the whole data from another node within the same node group. This restart type is required when file related options are changed, for example.

- **Initial System Restart (IS):** This is a similar restart type to the system restart, but all data nodes are restarted using the --initial option. This results in the all the data being cleared and lost. If you need existing data after restart, take a full backup before performing a system initial restart.

Details of restart types and operations are discussed in Chapter 10.

Management Node Options

This section covers the management node options. There are not many options for management node. In this section, only the major options are listed.

Major Options for Management Node

NodeId

Default	Automatic
Range	1 – 255
Section	[MGM]
Restart Type	Node restart

Identifier for each node. In previous versions, the Id option had the same meanings as NodeId, but it has been removed in MySQL NDB Cluster 7.5. It is possible to configure each section without specifying NodeId, because its value is automatically assigned if it's not specified explicitly. However, it is not a good idea to omit this parameter, because it causes ambiguity of configuration.

HostName

Default	None (accept connection from any host)
Range	Arbitrary hostname or IP address
Section	[MGM]
Restart Type	System restart

Hostname or IP address where the node resides. You may wonder "why management nodes should know management node's hostname by itself?" The hostname is required when multiple management nodes are installed.

DataDir

Default	Current directory where the process is started
Range	Arbitrary directory pathname
Section	[MGM] or [MGM DEFAULT]
Restart Type	Node restart

In this directory, data generated by management node is stored, such as log files and PID file.

PortNumber

Default	1186
Range	Arbitrary port number
Section	[MGM] or [MGM DEFAULT]
Restart Type	Node restart

This is the port number where the management node listens. In most cases, it is not necessary to change this value. When the default port number (1186) is occupied by another program, you should change it to a different value to avoid port collision. For example, if you installed more than one cluster inside your local network, you may want to consolidate management nodes to a single host to save on the number of hosts. Such configuration is practical because management node requires very few computer resources. Be careful not to mistake the port number on the *connectstring* for each node. If the wrong connectstring is specified, the node will connect to a different management node.

ArbitrationRank

Default	1
Range	0 – 2
Section	[MGM] or [MGM DEFAULT]
Restart Type	Node restart

This option specifies the likelihood of being an arbitrator. The range for this parameter is 0, 1, and 2. Each value has the following meanings:

- **0:** The node will never be used as an arbitrator.

- **1:** The node has high priority; that is, it will be preferred as an arbitrator over low-priority nodes.

- **2:** Indicates a low-priority node that will be used as an arbitrator only if all nodes with a higher priority are not available.

If you have multiple management nodes and you have some preference for which node should be an arbitrator, set this option to 2 against less preferable management nodes. Note that not only management node, but also SQL node can become an arbitrator. Even if you have only one management node available, arbitrator can be fault tolerant using SQL nodes as additional arbitrators. Be careful not to use an SQL node that resides on the same host as the data node, because the arbitrator should reside in a separate host as any data node.

LogDestination

Default	FILE:filename=ndb_node_id_cluster.log,maxsize=1000000,maxfiles=6
Range	CONSOLE|SYSLOG|FILE with additional parameters
Section	[MGM] or [MGM DEFAULT]
Restart Type	Node restart

This option specifies the output destination of the *cluster log*. The cluster log is the centralized event log file for MySQL NDB Cluster, whereby all event reports are aggregated as a single continuous log. Destination has the following three types:

- CONSOLE: Log entries are directed to the standard output ndb_mgmd process.
- SYSLOG: Log entries are sent to a syslog facility.
- FILE: Log entries are written to a log file. Log files are reused in a circular fashion.

SYSLOG and FILE need additional parameters to specify the details of log specification.

For SYSLOG output, the facility should be specified. Facility indicates what component generated the log message. Facility is not an arbitrary string, but is defined as part of *syslog protocol* in RFC 3164. Defined facilities are listed in Table 4-2. Facility is specified using a keyword as in Listing 4-2.

Table 4-2. *Syslog Facilities*

Numerical Code	Keyword	Facility
0	kern	Kernel messages
1	user	User level messages
2	mail	Mail system
3	daemon	System daemons
4	auth	Security/authorization messages
5	syslog	Messages generated internally by syslogd
6	lpr	Line printer subsystem
7	news	Network news subsystem
8	uucp	UUCP subsystem
9		Clock daemon
10	authpriv	Security/authorization messages
11	ftp	FTP daemon
12		NTP subsystem
13		Log audit
14		Log alert
15	cron	Clock daemon (scheduling daemon)
16 ~ 23	local0 ~ local7	Local use 0 ~ 7

Listing 4-2. LogDestination Using SYSLOG

```
LogDestination = SYSLOG:facility=local0
```

Facility is commonly used for log filtering. It is a good practice to specify a facility that does not overlap with other applications, system programs, or the kernel. local0 ~ local7 are suitable for that purpose. They are so called custom log messages and not used by the operating system. The default facility is user.

It is possible to store log messages with a specific facility to a separate log file. In that case, you can customize log filename, log rotation, and so forth, as you like.

It is even possible to direct the cluster log to a remote host (log server) using the syslog capability. Such configuration is useful when you have multiple cluster installations. You can monitor all clusters using a single log entity. For more information, refer to the syslog manual. There are several implementations of syslog. Configuration depends on implementation.

For FILE output, the following three parameters exist:

- filename: Log filename

- maxsize: Maximum size for each log file

- maxfiles: Maximum number of log files kept

Default values for the FILE output are shown in Listing 4-3.

Listing 4-3. LogDestination Using FILE

```
LogDestination = FILE:filename=ndb_{node_id}_cluster.log,maxsize=1024000,maxfiles=6
```

{node_id} in Listing 4-2 indicates the Node ID for the management server. You do not necessarily specify all parameters, but you specify every combination of parameters. For example, you can specify only maxsize, and leave filename and maxfiles unchanged.

I recommend that you increase the size of cluster log about 10 times. The default size is too small and logs are rotated too quickly.

Vital Point for Management Node Configuration

Management node doesn't have many options. The vast majority of options can be omitted in the config.ini file. However, I recommend setting at least the following three options for a robust setup:

- NodeId: Node ID is automatically assigned by default; however, it will result in assigning different identifier afterward.

- HostName: If the hostname is not specified explicitly, the management node can be connected from any host.

- DataDir: The default data directory is the current directory where the management node is started. It is subject to change when the management node process is started from a shell.

Explicitly setting these options will eliminate ambiguity of management node configuration.

Data Node Options

We begin to discuss the data node options. As discussed in Chapter 2, data node is the very core of MySQL NDB Cluster. Configuring data node is one of the most difficult phases when setting up MySQL NDB Cluster, because lots of options exist. However, if you change your perspective, configuration of data node is one of the most challenging and exciting tasks during MySQL NDB Cluster lifecycle.

Since data node options are very actively developed, they are subject to change or be newly introduced frequently. The sections indicate the effective version numbers if they have changed or were introduced in version 7.2 or newer.

Basic Options

The following options are mandatory in the configuration of data node. Set these options explicitly for a robust installation.

NodeId

Default	Automatic
Range	1 – 48
Section	[NDBD]
Restart Type	Node restart

This is the identifier for the node, which has the same meaning as NodeId for other node types. However, the possible range of values is 1 – 48, because the maximum number of data nodes should be less than or equal to 48. So, it is good practice to let other node types have a NodeId greater than 48.

HostName

Default	None (accept connection from any host)
Range	Arbitrary hostname or IP address
Section	[NDBD]
Restart Type	System restart

Hostname or IP address where the node resides. You can leave this option unset, but I do not recommend you do so. To make the data node configuration robust, you need to set this option and make the hostname exclusive to the slot.

HostName and NodeId are used for identifying the slot when a node connects. So, these options are unique for each slot and cannot be written in the [NDBD DEFAULT] section, because they cannot be shared among more than one slot.

ServerPort

Default	None (automatically assigned)
Range	1 – 64K
Section	[NDBD] or [NDBD DEFAULT]
Restart Type	System restart

This option is specified by the port number to accept connections from other nodes. By default, data the node asks the OS to assign the port number to ephemeral port numbers. For example, the bind(2) system call does it on POSIX systems.

DataDir

Default	Current directory where the process is started
Range	Arbitrary directory pathname
Section	[NDBD] or [NDBD DEFAULT]
Restart Type	Initial node restart

This option specifies the directory where the data resides.

Since data node handles various kinds of data, it is possible to specify separate directories depending on data type. DataDir is treated as a default value for specific directory path options such as FileSystemPath.

Log files (not transaction log files, but log files for the ndbd or ndbmtd process) are also stored under DataDir and cannot be specified separately.

DataDir is not necessarily identical for all data nodes.

NoOfReplicas

Default	2
Range	1 – 4 (practically, 2 is the only choice)
Section	[NDBD DEFAULT]
Restart Type	Initial system restart

This option specifies the number of copies of data. Theoretically, the more replicas there are, the more robust the cluster is. However, three or four replicas are not officially tested and supported yet. One replica means no redundancy; a single node failure immediately results in system failure. You should choose two for the time being. Future releases may support three or four replicas, but it's not certain at this time.

Refer to Chapters 2 and 3 for more information about replicas.

Memory Data Storage Options

The following options are related to memory sizing. Strategy for memory sizing is not difficult; allocate memory as much as the system has unless the system causes memory swapping. Note that objects for schema and transaction processing also consume a certain amount of memory. It is important not to allocate memory to buffers in this section too much. Leave a margin for them.

DataMemory

Default	80M
Range	1M – 1024M (bytes)
Section	[NDBD DEFAULT]
Restart Type	Node restart

This option specifies the size of the memory area that stores row data and ordered index data. This option decides the upper limit of data size. It is often misunderstood that ordered indexes are stored in IndexMemory, but they are actually stored in DataMemory. Technically speaking, it is possible to write this option under [NDBD] section, however, it doesn't make sense. Data is split evenly across all data nodes and every data node has approximately the same amount of data. Similar reasoning applies to the following options in this chapter to which only the [NDB DEFAULT] section is written in the list.

The total available memory size for the entire cluster is calculated as in the following formula:

```
DataMemory × number_of_node_group
```

The number of the node group is the number of data nodes divided by NoOfReplicas. So, the theoretical maximum available data memory for the entire cluster without SPOF is 24TB (48 data nodes, 1TB per data node, and 2 replicas). The amount of DataMemory also has an impact on the size of LCP, GCP, and backup. Memory size has a big impact on storage requirements, too.

IndexMemory

Default	18M
Range	1M – 1024M (bytes)
Section	[NDBD DEFAULT]
Restart Type	Node restart

This option specifies the memory size for hash indexes, which is used for primary key and unique hash indexes. Key data and extra overhead (including pointer to row data) is stored on IndexMemory. The amount of required IndexMemory size approximately depends on the number of rows. Some other overhead exists, but they are negligible unless you have tons of small tables. Data size per row is approximated using the following formula:

```
Number_of_Rows * 18 * NoOfReplicas
```

The calculated value indicates the total amount of required memory for the entire cluster. So, the required memory per one node is calculated by dividing it by the number of data nodes. For example, if the table has 1,000,000,000 rows, the cluster has 10 data nodes and NoOfReplicas = 2, required IndexMemory size per data node for this table is as follows:

```
1000000000 * 18 * 2 / 10 = 3.6GB
```

This formula is only an approximation, and the real amount of allocated memory is likely to be less than the calculated value. On MySQL NDB Cluster 7.5 series or later, you can query the exact allocated memory size using ndbinfo.memory_per_fragment table. Refer to Chapter 16 for more information about ndbinfo schema.

StringMemory

Default	25
Range	1 – 100 (percent) or 101 – 4294967039 (bytes)
Section	[NDBD DEFAULT]
Restart Type	System restart

This option specifies memory for object names. When the value is less than 100, it means percentage against theoretical maximum required memory size calculated by options indicating the number of objects that require names, such as MaxNoOfTables, MaxNoOfAtrributes, MaxNoOfOrderedIndexes, MaxNoOfUniqueHashIndexes, and MaxNoOfTriggers. These options are described later in this chapter. In most cases, the default is sufficient.

When StringMemory is short, you will see the following message when you create new tables or add columns:

```
Got error 773 'Out of string memory, please modify StringMemory config parameter' from
NDBCLUSTER
```

In this case, you need to increase StringMemory.

SharedGlobalMemory

Default	128M
Range	0 – 64T
Section	[NDBD DEFAULT]
Restart Type	Node restart

This option specifies the size of the *shared global memory*, which is used for various purposes:

- Undo log buffer for disk data tables
- Metadata for logfile group and tablespaces
- Pushdown joins
- Schema transactions

Increase this option when you use disk data tables and/or lots of pushdown joins in parallel. The actual required size of SharedGlobalmemory is often larger than expected.

LockPagesInMainMemory

Default	0
Range	0 – 2
Section	[NDBD DEFAULT]
Restart Type	Node restart

This option controls whether memory is locked using mlock(2) or not. When memory is locked, the data node process is unlikely to be swapped out when system memory is short. Memory shortage is likely to happen when lots of files are copied and large file system cache is consumed, for example.

This option takes one of these values:

- **0:** Do not lock memory.
- **1:** Lock memory after required memory areas are allocated.
- **2:** Set locking mode before allocating memory.

The difference between 1 and 2 is trivial. Sufficient system memory is required anyway.

Numa

Default	1 (True)
Range	0, 1 (Boolean)
Section	[NDBD DEFAULT]
Restart Type	Node restart

This option causes memory allocation interleaved on Linux systems.

As stated in Chapter 3, recent x86_64 CPUs have memory controller inside, and each memory controller owns memory. If the server has more than one CPU chip, each CPU has it has non-uniform memory access speed depending on which CPU has target memory. Such architecture is called *Non-Uniform Memory Access (NUMA)*. By default, Linux tries to allocate memory in the same CPU where the thread is running. This strategy works well for small programs because local memory access is faster than remote memory access, which program runs in single threaded requires small memory. However, it will cause problems on the server program, which requires many threads and huge memory, because memory is allocated non-uniform among NUMA nodes.

This option causes memory allocation interleaved, which means memory is allocated from all NUMA nodes evenly. The default value enables NUMA interleave, and you usually don't have to change it. An unusual case would be if you run more than one data nodes on single NUMA machine and bind each data node to separate NUMA node.

Schema Object Options

On MySQL NDB Cluster, metadata of schema objects is stored in fixed size arrays that are allocated at the startup of the data node. The maximum allowable number of various objects is configured by the following options. It is important to allocate a required size for each schema objects beforehand. Schema object design is covered in Chapter 18.

MaxNoOfTables

Default	128
Range	8 – 20320
Section	[NDBD DEFAULT]
Restart Type	Node restart

This option specifies the maximum number of tables allowed in the cluster. Note that it includes system tables such as ndb_schema, ndb_apply_status, and so forth. The unique hash index creates an internal support table, so it consumes one table object and determines the optimal number of tables from application needs.

MaxNoOfAttributes

Default	1000
Range	32 – 4294967039
Section	[NDBD DEFAULT]
Restart Type	Node restart

This option specifies the number of *attributes*. An attribute is an element that belongs to a table, such as a column or index. The number of attributes consumed per object varies depending on the type of object, as described:

- **Non-BLOB column:** 1

- **BLOB (TEXT) column:** 5

- **Hash index in PRIMARY key:** 0

- **Unique hash index:** 1 plus the number of columns in the index

- **Ordered index:** 1 plus the number of columns in the index

You may wonder why hash index in PRIMARY key doesn't consume an attribute. It doesn't consume MaxNoOfAttributes; it consumes MaxNoOfTables instead.

Note that the ordered index is created along with primary key and unique hash index unless USING HASH keyword is specified in the DDL statement.

Since the attribute data should be shared among all data nodes, it is not divided by node groups like row data. The MaxNoOfAttributes value should be decided according to the total amount of schema objects.

The number of attributes actually consumed by each table can be shown using the ndb_desc command. However, information about BLOB columns and the unique hash index is not included in output of ndb_desc command by default. You need to specify the --blob-info option to see information about BLOB columns. Rows for a BLOB column are stored in a separate support table, which consumes four attributes. Unique hash indexes are also stored in a separate support table, but there's no way to see the number of attributes assigned to unique hash indexes.

MaxNoOfOrderedIndexes

Default	128
Range	0 - 4294967039
Section	[NDBD DEFAULT]
Restart Type	Node restart

This option specifies the number of *ordered indexes*, which are used for secondary indexes, primary keys, and unique keys. As the name suggests, an ordered index is used for ordered index scans. Practically, everything but full table scans and primary or unique key lookups are handled as an ordered index scan. Ordered index is a key object for various types of queries.

The number of required ordered indexes are dependent on the schema design. You can determine the number of ordered indexes using the following rule:

- Non-unique secondary index: 1

- Unique secondary index without USING HASH clause: 1

- Primary key without USING HASH clause: 1

Each ordered index also consumes one MaxNoOfAttributes.

MaxNoOfUniqueHashIndexes

Default	64
Range	0 - 4294967039
Section	[NDBD DEFAULT]
Restart Type	Node restart

This option specifies the number of *unique hash indexes*. As the name suggests, every unique index consumes this object by 1. Increase this option according to your application needs.

Each unique hash index also consumes one MaxNoOfTables and several MaxNoOfAttributes according to the number of columns that make up the index.

MaxNoOfTriggers

Default	768
Range	0 - 4294967039
Section	[NDBD DEFAULT]
Restart Type	Node restart

This option specifies the number of *internal triggers* used inside data node. Note that *trigger* in this context isn't the same one as the one in SQL. In the data node, an internal trigger is used in various processes:

- Updating ordered index entries

- Updating unique hash index entries

- Updating BLOB columns

- Foreign key checks and updates for parents and children

- Backing up

- Replication (binary log generation)

- Table reorganization

During normal operations, it is not necessary to modify this value, because it's automatically adjusted if it is too small. The number of required triggers is calculated internally using the following options: MaxNoOfTables, MaxNoOfOrderedIndexes, and MaxNoOfUniqueHashIndexes.

Transaction Options

Since MySQL NDB Cluster is a real-time database system, it doesn't allocate memory on the fly. Instead, it allocates memory at startup. It includes various types of buffers used by transactions and data operations.

MaxNoOfConcurrentTransactions

Default	**4096**
Range	32 - 4294967039
Section	[NDBD DEFAULT]
Restart Type	Node restart

This option specifies the number of *transaction records* allocated in each data node. A transaction record is a memory buffer used by *Transaction Coordinator (TC)*. As stated in Chapter 2, one TC on a certain data node takes care of each transaction throughout its lifecycle. Every data node has TC on it. So, the entire cluster has (MaxNoOfConcurrentTransactions * number_of_data_nodes) transaction records in total.

Despite its name, MaxNoOfConcurrentTransactions doesn't represent the number of transactions. It represents the number of transaction records instead. They are logically different. A transaction record is an object consumed in TC to process transactions. TC consumes transaction records according to the following rule:

- One per each active transaction

- One per table accessed by the transaction

So the number of required transaction records for the entire cluster would be calculated using the following formula:

```
max_connections *
    (average_number_of_tables_accessed_per_transaction + 1) *
    number_of_sql_nodes
```

The average number of tables accessed per transaction varies depending on the queries used in the application. So it is not possible to estimate it without examining the application.

MaxNoOfConcurrentTransactions specifies the number of transaction records per data node. Its value should be a value calculated by the formula divided by the number of data nodes. However, in the event of node failure, surviving node(s) in the same node group must handle transactions instead of a failed node. It is a good practice to divide the value by the number of node groups instead of by the number of data nodes:

```
MaxNoOfTransactions =
    max_connections *
    (average_number_of_tables_accessed_per_transaction + 1) *
    number_of_sql_nodes / number_of_node_groups
```

MaxNoOfConcurrentOperations

Default	32K
Range	32 - 4294967039
Section	[NDBD DEFAULT]
Restart Type	Node restart

This option specifies the number of *operation records*. One operation record is required per one row updated, deleted, inserted, or locked within a transaction. This option puts an upper limit on the number of rows operated per data node. So, it is possible to operate (MaxNoOfConcurrentOperations * number_of_data_nodes) rows on the entire cluster. Just like MaxNoOfTransactions, use the number of node groups instead of the number of data nodes to estimate the value for this option with consideration for node failures.

Note that rows in the support tables created with unique hash indexes and BLOB columns also consume operation records. For example, when a non-key value for a row in a main table with unique hash index is updated, then a row in its support table is shared-locked.

MaxNoOfConcurrentScans

Default	256
Range	2 – 500
Section	[NDBD DEFAULT]
Restart Type	Node restart

This option specifies the number of *scan records* per data node. A scan record is required for each scan operation. As discussed in the section of MaxNoOfOrderedIndexes, all operations but primary or unique key lookups are scan operations. In addition, a scan record is also required for full table scans. For the entire cluster, it can handle the number of scans calculated by the following formula:

```
MaxNoOfConcurrentScans * number_of_data_nodes
```

Of course, estimates of this option should take node failure into account.

In most cases, more scan record is required than expected. So, I recommend you increase it to the maximum value from the beginning. Even if you increased it to 500 and get "Too many active scans" errors frequently, consider adding more data nodes.

MaxNoOfLocalScans

Default	Automatic
Range	32 - 4294967039
Section	[NDBD DEFAULT]
Restart Type	Node restart

This option specifies the number of local scan records. In contrast to scan record, which is used for taking care of scan accessing the entire cluster, local scan record is responsible for accessing data in its own data node.

By default, this option is calculated automatically using the following formula:

```
MaxNoOfCuncurrentScans * number_of_data_nodes * 4 + 2
```

In most cases, the default automatic value is sufficient and you don't have to change it. However, in old versions (< 7.2), the formula is different and the calculated value is much less than the current version. Increase this option when "Too many active scans" errors are observed in old versions.

MaxParallelScansPerFragment

Default	256
Range	1 - 4294967039
Section	[NDBD DEFAULT]
Restart Type	Node restart

This option specifies the maximum number of scans per fragment. If scan accesses from applications are concentrated in certain tables, consider increasing this value for more efficient CPU utilization.

TransactionDeadlockDetectionTimeout

Default	1200
Range	50 – 4294967039 (milliseconds)
Section	[NDBD DEFAULT]
Restart Type	Node restart

This option specifies periods in milliseconds that elapses from when a given transaction is blocked and when it's determined as timed out. Despite its name, it doesn't indicate a timeout for deadlock, but lock wait timeout. So, this option is equivalent to the innodb_lock_wait_timeout option for the InnoDB storage engine.

However, MySQL NDB Cluster doesn't have a deadlock detection functionality. So, deadlocks are detected as lock wait timeouts instead, because transactions under deadlock cannot proceed anyway.

By increasing this option, transactions become less likely to be aborted due to lock wait timeout. However, an overly large value is not recommended, because transactions under deadlock will also last very long time as well. Transactions under deadlock may block other innocent transactions, which may result in degrading the system throughput badly. On a very busy system, consider shortening timeout to avoid performance degradation due to deadlocks.

RedoBuffer

Default	32M
Range	1M - 4294967039 (bytes)
Section	[NDBD DEFAULT]
Restart Type	Node restart

This option specifies the size of the *redo buffer*, which is used to temporarily store the redo log content before committing the transaction. All changes should be held on the redo buffer before writing to the redo log. So, the size of the redo buffer should be calculated from size of the data changes by concurrent transactions. If you increased MaxNoOfConcurrentOperations, you need to increase the size of the redo buffer too.

Note that the redo buffer is allocated for each LDM thread with the size of RedoBuffer. So, the total size of the redo buffers is RedoBuffer * number_of_ldm_threads.

RedoOverCommitLimit

Default	20
Range	0 – 4294967039 (seconds)
Section	[NDBD DEFAULT]
Restart Type	Node restart

MySQL NDB Cluster has a mechanism to allow certain delay for write and sync operations against the redo log. It prevents performance degradation in the event of disk I/O delays.

Of course, redo logging is crucial for MySQL NDB Cluster not to lose committed transactions, so it should not delay. If redo logging is slower than updates done by transactions, the volume of unflushed the redo log data would increase continuously. The transaction cannot proceed faster than the redo logging speed. However, disk I/O speed caps the redo logging speed. So, disk I/O can be a bottleneck in the event of sudden load spikes.

To solve this problem, MySQL NDB Cluster implements overcommitting against the redo log. It allows unfinished disk flush operations to proceed. Since MySQL NDB Cluster is fault tolerant against a node failure, data included in the unflushed redo log will not be lost upon node failure, because the other node in the same node group has the same data.

Even though redo logging is fault tolerant, it is not a good idea to allow unlimited delays of the flush operation, because the longer value increases the chance of losing data while the other data node is unavailable. RedoOverCommitLimit defines the timeout in seconds against the disk flush operation for the redo log. This option is used conjunction with RedoOverCommitCounter. If the redo log flush operation takes longer than RedoOverCommitLimit seconds RedoOverCommitCounter times, the pending transactions will be aborted. Upon redo logging timeout, the API node will take an action as defined by DefaultOperationRedoProblemAction, which is described later in this chapter.

RedoOverCommitCounter

Default	3
Range	0 – 4294967039
Section	[NDBD DEFAULT]
Restart Type	Node restart

This option specifies the number of timeouts for the redo log flush operation. See the explanation of RedoOverCommitLimit for more information.

Estimate for Total Memory Consumption

It is an important that a DBA be able to estimate total memory size allocated to the database server. On the MySQL NDB Cluster data node process, the following types of memory are allocated:

- Memory for program image
- Global buffers
- Array of schema objects and transaction objects
- Various buffers

The next sections explain the details of each type of memory area.

Memory for Program Image

As usual, ndbd and ndbmtd allocate memory for program executable file, shared libraries, and stack memory. The total memory size for program image is typically less than 20MB, which is negligible. You can confirm the memory size for this purpose using the /proc file system on Linux. See VmExe, VmLib, and VmStk.

Global Buffers

Global buffers are large chunks of memory allocated for specific purposes. The types of global memory buffers and allocated memory sizes are listed in Table 4-3.

Table 4-3. *Global Memory Buffer Types and Memory Sizes*

Buffer Type	Memory Size	Over Allocate
Data buffer	DataMemory + IndexMemory	No
Job buffer	(number_of_threads)^2 + 1MB	No
Transporter buffer	SendBufferMemory * (number_of_ nodes -1) or TotalSendBufferMemory + ExtraSendBufferMemory	Yes
File buffer	RedoBuffer + 1MB per each log part	No
Disk page buffer	DiskPageBufferMemory	No
Undo buffer	Defined in the CREATE LOGFILE GROUP statement	Yes
Schema transaction memory	2MB	Yes
Shared global memory	SharedGlobalMemory	No

Some of the global buffer memory might be over-allocated when more memory is required. As allocation is done from the shared global memory, the total memory size of the data node process will not increase during normal operation.

Be sure that the *job buffer* is a large memory area when lots of threads are configured. It consumes approximately 5GB when the maximum number of threads (72) is configured.

Array of Schema and Transaction Objects

MySQL NDB Cluster has a fixed sized memory area for various purposes. Sizes of those buffers are not trivial, so you should take those memory sizes into account to avoid memory over-allocation. Table 4-4 shows list of fixed size arrays and memory size per unit (memory size increase for one increment of each option).

Table 4-4. *Memory Size Increase by Option*

Option	Memory Size Per Unit
MaxNoOfConcurrentTransactions	1.6KB
MaxNoOfConcurrentOperations	873 bytes
MaxNoOfConcurrentIndexOperations	160 bytes
MaxNoOfTriggers	381 bytes
MaxNoOfFiredTriggers	68 bytes
MaxNoOfConcurrentScans	70KB
MaxNoOfAttributes	4.3KB
MaxNoOfTables	11KB
MaxNoOfOrderedIndexes	11KB
MaxNoOfUniqueHashIndexes	11KB

Memory sizes in Table 4-4 are actual measured values from running the ndbd process and changing the option values step-by-step. The observed version is 7.5.4.

Various Buffers

Some more buffers exist, such as LongMessageBuffer, UndoDataBuffer, and so forth. It is messy to sum up those buffers for estimation. It's better to determine the actual memory size from the running process as a starting point. You can estimate memory sizes from options to be modified.

Checkpoint Options

Checkpointing is a very important process for MySQL NDB Cluster, because it makes data durable against entire system shutdown regardless of whether the shutdown is planned. It is also important from a performance point of view, because it caps throughput against write transactions. Clients cannot commit transactions faster than checkpointing. So, options for checkpointing are very important for write-intensive clusters.

As discussed in Chapter 2, there are two types of checkpoints:

- **LCP (Local Checkpoint)**: Entire cluster data at certain point of time.

- **GCP (Global Checkpoint)**: History of all changes.

See Chapter 2 for more information about the checkpoints done in MySQL Cluster. This chapter covers how to tune options for checkpoints later.

FileSystemPath

Default	DataDir
Range	Arbitrary directory pathname
Section	[NDBD] or [NDBD DEFAULT]
Restart Type	Initial node restart

This option specifies a directory where checkpoints, backups, and disk data table files are stored. Except for checkpoints, additional options exist for fine-tuning the directory layout.

NoOfFragmentLogFiles

Default	16
Range	3 – 4294967039
Section	[NDBD DEFAULT]
Restart Type	Initial node restart

This option specifies the number of redo log files. The redo log is written in a circular fashion. See Chapter 2 for more information about the redo log.

The total file size of the redo log is calculated using the following formula:

```
NoOfFragmentLogFiles * NoOfFragmentLogParts * FragmentLogFileSize
```

The default values for these options are 16, 4, and 16M. 16 * 4 * 16M = 1G is the default for total size of the redo log.

FragmentLogFileSize

Default	**16M**
Range	4M – 1G (bytes)
Section	[NDBD DEFAULT]
Restart Type	Initial node restart

This option specifies size of each redo log file. See NoOfFragmentLogFiles for more information. If you need more redo log space, consider increasing this option first, because each log file needs a memory buffer.

NoOfFragmentLogParts

Default	4
Range	4 – 32 (only multiples of 4 are allowed)
Section	[NDBD DEFAULT]
Restart Type	Initial node restart

This option specifies the number of redo log files within a group. See NoOfFragmentLogFiles for more information.

InitFragmentLogFiles

Default	SPARSE
Range	SPARSE, FULL
Section	[NDBD] or [NDBD DEFAULT]
Restart Type	Initial node restart

This option specifies how the redo log files are initialized. The default is SPARSE, which means the redo log files are created as a *sparse file*. A sparse file is a mechanism to save unnecessary I/O operations and file spaces. If redo logs are created as a sparse file, each file size looks the same as FragmentLogFileSize, but data blocks aren't actually allocated. If a program reads from a sparse area, data padded with zeroes is read up to the length of the file. Data blocks are allocated when data is written to a sparse area.

The main drawback to the sparse file is that size of file system free space decreases only when data is actually written to it. So, you might notice file system shortage during normal operation, not initialization time. Be 100% sure that your file system has sufficient free space.

FULL means the redo log files are really initialized and data blocks are actually allocated. You will not see a "file system full" error for the redo logging afterward.

This option does have any effect on the first startup of the data node. Changing the value for this option upon restart doesn't make sense.

CompressedLCP

Default	0
Range	0, 1 (Boolean)
Section	[NDBD DEFAULT]
Restart Type	Node restart

When this option is true, it causes LCP to be stored in compressed format. It saves certain disk space, but consumes more CPU time upon LCP and restart. It is better not to compress LCP on a busy system. CPU resources should be reserved for transaction processing.

It is not recommended to set this option different per data node. Available resources should be the same among all data nodes to avoid bottlenecks.

ODirect

Default	0
Range	0, 1 (Boolean)
Section	[NDBD DEFAULT]
Restart Type	Node restart

When this option is true, it causes write operations for checkpoints to be done in O_DIRECT mode, which means *direct I/O*. As the name suggests, direct I/O is an I/O operation done directly without routing file system cache. It may save certain CPU resources. It is best to set this option to true on Linux systems using kernel 2.6 or later.

DiskCheckpointSpeed

Default	10M
Range	1M – 4294967039 (bytes)
Section	[NDBD DEFAULT]
Restart Type	Node restart
Effective Versions	7.2.0 – 7.4.0

This option determines the speed of the write operation for checkpoints in amount of data written per seconds. This option is deprecated on 7.4.1 and removed in the 7.5 series. Use MinDiskWriteSpeed and MaxDiskWriteSpeed instead on the 7.4.1 or newer series. On the 7.4 series, which is newer than or equal to 7.4.1, this option can be set, but it has no effect.

DiskCheckpointSpeedInRestart

Default	100M
Range	1M – 4294967039 (bytes)
Section	[NDBD DEFAULT]
Restart Type	Node restart
Effective Versions	7.2.0 – 7.4.0

This option determines the speed of write operation for checkpoints in the amount of data written per second during a local checkpoint as part of a restart operation. This option is deprecated on 7.4.1 and removed on the 7.5 series. Use MaxDiskWriteSpeedOtherNodeRestart and MaxDiskWriteSpeedOwnRestart instead on the 7.4.1 or newer series. On the 7.4 series, which is newer than or equal to 7.4.1, this option can be set but it has no effect.

MinDiskWriteSpeed

Default	10M
Range	1M – 4294967039 (bytes)
Section	[NDBD DEFAULT]
Restart Type	Node restart
Effective Versions	7.4.1 and 7.5.0 or newer

This option is added in MySQL NDB Cluster 7.4.1. This option determines the lower bound of I/O speed of LCP and backup. The I/O speed of redo logging is not affected by this option.

Data node adjusts I/O speed of LCP and backup under the following conditions:

- Slows down if the redo logging delays (> 2 seconds)

- Speeds up if CPU usage is lower than 90%

- Slows down if CPU usage is higher than 95%

- Slows down even more if CPU usage is higher than 97% or 99%

Adjustment of speed is done gradually every cycle (approximately 1 second). LCP will not be slower than MinDiskWriteSpeed and will not be faster than MaxDiskWriteSpeed. Within this range, a backup may take up to BackupDiskWriteSpeedPct percent of I/O speed.

MaxDiskWriteSpeed

Default	20M
Range	1M – 4294967039 (bytes)
Section	[NDBD DEFAULT]
Restart Type	Node restart
Effective Versions	7.4.1 and 7.5.0 or newer

This option determines the upper bound of I/O speed of LCP and backup. See MinDiskWriteSpeed for more information.

MaxDiskWriteSpeedOtherNodeRestart

Default	50M
Range	1M – 4294967039 (bytes)
Section	[NDBD DEFAULT]
Restart Type	Node restart
Effective Versions	7.4.1 and 7.5.0 or newer

This option determines the I/O speed when another data node is restarting. The I/O for LCP must have higher priority when other data nodes are restarting, because the data node performs LCP as part of restart process. LCP on restarting data node will not start until the ongoing LCP is completed. So, ongoing LCP on surviving node must be urged and have more I/O speed than usual.

MaxDiskWriteSpeedOwnRestart

Default	200M
Range	1M – 4294967039 (bytes)
Section	[NDBD DEFAULT]
Restart Type	Node restart
Effective Versions	7.4.1 and 7.5.0 or newer

This option determines the I/O speed for LCP done as part of the restart process. Since the data node does not need to do GCP during restart, all I/O bandwidth can be allocated to LCP. Thus, this option will have a higher value than other MaxDiskWriteSpeed options.

TimeBetweenLocalCheckpoints

Default	20
Range	0 – 31 (words of data written in base-2 logarithm)
Section	[NDBD DEFAULT]
Restart Type	Node restart

This option determines the minimum size of data written between LCPs. Despite its name, this option doesn't specify time between LCPs.

The size of data in this option is specified in a base-2 logarithm of the number of words. The size of each word is four bytes. So, the default value 20 means $4 * 2^{20}$ bytes = 4MB. This means new LCP won't start if very few updates are done on the cluster after the previous LCP and written data size is less than 4MB.

Setting large value to this option will prevent unnecessary LCPs when the cluster is not busy. It is preferable, especially when SSD is used as its data disk, because SSD has a smaller write limit compared to HDD. If you set this option very large, you must accommodate sufficient redo log space. On busy systems, a new LCP will start right after the previous LCP anyway.

TimeBetweenGlobalCheckpoints

Default	2000
Range	20 – 32000 (milliseconds)
Section	[NDBD DEFAULT]
Restart Type	Node restart

This option specifies the time between one GCP and another. Unlike `TimeBetweenLocalCheckpoints`, this option specifies the time in milliseconds. During GCP, the redo log is written and synchronized to disk so it becomes durable.

TimeBetweenEpochs

Default	100
Range	0 – 32000 (milliseconds)
Section	[NDBD DEFAULT]
Restart Type	Node restart

This option specifies the time between *micro-GCPs*. Micro-GCP is a unit of the redo log written to a file at a time, which is committed simultaneously at a certain period. A set of transactions included in one micro-GCP is called an *epoch*. In other words, epochs are generated every `TimeBetweeEpochs` milliseconds. Content of every epoch is ensured to be synchronized among all data nodes. So, they call micro-GCP as data synchronization process in alias. Since epoch is synchronized among all data nodes, it's safe to write to the redo log and can be used for crash recovery.

As the name suggests, micro-GCP is done more frequently than GCP. Micro-GCP is used for binary log generation on SQL nodes. This makes the data node send data for binary log generation to SQL nodes more frequently and more quickly than GCP. It results in less replication lag.

Micro-GCP is kept on the redo buffer until GCP is done, so it's not durable upon node failure. The content of the redo buffer that's not written to disk by GCP will be lost after a crash. Although micro-GCP is not durable, it's fault tolerant if `NoOfReplicas` is 2 or more. Even if one data node crashes, and any node within a node group where a crashed node belongs survives, no committed transactions will be lost. However, micro-GCP will be truly lost during an entire cluster failure if it's not flushed to disk by GCP.

TimeBetweenEpochsTimeout

Default	0
Range	0 – 256000 (milliseconds)
Section	[NDBD DEFAULT]
Restart Type	Node restart

This option specifies the timeout in milliseconds between one micro-GCP and another. 0, the default value, means that timeout is disabled. Once micro-GCP starts, new transactions cannot be committed until ongoing micro-GCP completes. So, the stuck micro-GCP will slow down system write throughput badly.

Since micro-GCP may get stuck for various reasons (faulty NIC), MySQL NDB Cluster has functionality to prevent slowness due to micro-GCP lag by cutting a data node that cannot complete the micro-GCP on time. A data node that misses this timeout will be forcibly shut down.

If your application need a good response time, consider setting this option to a non-zero value. However, do not set this option too small. If it's too small, it causes unnecessary data node shutdown upon incidental slowness. Do not set this option to a non-zero value for a cluster running on virtual machines, because the response frequently lags on virtual machines due to limitation of CPU schedulers.

In previous releases (7.1 series or older), the default value was 4000.

Estimating Redo Log Size

Choosing an optimal redo log file size is an important task for MySQL NDB Cluster, because new transactions cannot commit when the redo log is running out. The bigger redo log is, the less likely it will run out. However, it is not a good idea to have an unnecessarily big redo log, because wasting valuable file system space should be avoided. So, you need to determine an optimal redo log size. When determining an optimal redo log size, consider the following factors.

- Data size
- I/O speed

The redo log is required for crash recovery, which is applied against LCP. LCP shows a full data snapshot at a certain time, and the redo log shows incremental differences in time series. So, all redo log entries after the latest LCP are flawlessly required. So, existing redo log entries cannot be freed until the next LCP completes. This means the maximum size of the required redo log file is equal to the total size of the redo log entries generated between one LCP and another. To calculate it, the following instructions are needed.

Calculate Theoretical Maximum Time Between Two LCPs

The time between two LCPs approximately equals the time taken to complete one LCP. It can be calculated using the following formula:

```
data_size / average_disk_write_speed_for_lcp
```

Average disk I/O speed will be a value intermediate between `MinDiskWriteSpeed` and `MaxDiskWriteSpeed`, unless disk speed is insufficient. As you need to prepare for the worst-case scenario, you should take `MinDiskWriteSpeed` for calculation. Since I/O speed is shared among LCP and backup, LCP can consume up to `BackupDiskWriteSpeedPct` percent of the bandwidth. Data size is capped by `DataMemory`. So, the time taken to complete LCP is:

```
DataMemory / (MinDiskWriteSpeed * BackupDiskWriteSpeedPct / 100)
```

Calculate Theoretical Maximum Size of Redo Log Entries

There is no upper limit for I/O speed when writing the redo log. The amount of data written by GCP depends on the volume of write requests. You can determine the amount data written by GCP using the `disk_write_speed_aggregate` table under the `ndbinfo` schema, which was added in 7.4.1. It is best to run some write benchmark and monitor this `ndbinfo` table to see the I/O speed of the redo logging.

Once you determine the speed of redo logging, then you can calculate the theoretical maximum size of the redo log entries using this formula:

```
time_taken_to_complete_lcp * io_speed_of_redo_logging
```

Alternatively, amount of data written per second can be assumed as physical disk I/O speed as the worst case. However, physical disk speed is often too fast and unrealistic. Actual values retrieved from the live system is preferable after all.

Calculate Redo Log Size Options

As discussed in earlier in this chapter, the total size of the redo log is calculated using the following formula. How do you determine the value of these options?

```
NoOfFragmentLogFiles * NoOfFragmentLogParts * FragmentLogFileSize
```

Theoretical maximum size of the redo log entries calculated in the previous section must match this total size of the redo log. It is best to have some margin of safety. If this condition is met, you can choose an arbitrary value for these options.

Calculation Example

For example, assume DataMemory is 18GB and MinDiskWriteSpeed is 32M. The time taken to complete one LCP is 10 minutes in the worst case. If the redo logging speed is 80M/sec, 48GB of the redo log entries will be generated during one LCP. With 33% margin, the required size of the redo log is approximately 64GB. Assume that NoOfFragmentLogParts is set to 32, which is required to run as many as LDM threads. Then, the following combination of option values meet the requirement.

```
FragmentLogFileSize = 500M
NoOfFragmentLogFiles = 4
NoOfFragmentLogParts = 32
```

Multi-Threading Options

By Moore's Law, the number of transistors within a single CPU chip is still increasing. However, performance per CPU core isn't being improved recently because:

- Clock speed is not increasing
- Single core performance does not improve by increasing the number of transistors

Thus, recent high-end CPU chips have many cores per chip. To achieve high performance, software must utilize many CPU cores. So, a program must run in parallel. From a parallel programming point of view, there are two choices—multi-threading or multi-processing. MySQL NDB Cluster employs the former, multi-threading. To achieve high performance as much as possible, optimizing multi-threading options is key.

MaxNoOfExecutionThreads

Default	2
Range	2 – 8 (7.2.0 – 7.2.4)
	2 – 36 (7.2.5 – 7.3.2)
	2 – 72 (7.3.3 – latest)
Section	[NDBD DEFAULT]
Restart Type	Initial system restart

This option specifies the number of threads used for data processing for the multithreaded version of data node, ndbmtd. Multithreaded data node has the following types of threads.

- **LDM thread:** A thread for actual data access, such as key look up and scan.

- **TC thread:** A thread for transaction handling.

- **Send thread:** Sending signals to other data nodes.

- **Receive thread:** Receiving signals from other data nodes.

- **Main thread:** This thread handles various tasks such as checkpointing, arbitration, failover, etc.

- **Rep thread:** This thread sends changes from micro-GCP to specific SQL nodes for binary log generation.

- **I/O thread:** This thread handles file I/O requests.

- **Watchdog thread:** This thread determines if each thread is running well.

This option specifies the total number of these types of threads, and the number of each thread is automatically adjusted. Of course, the automatic value might be suboptimal while it is handy for DBA. If you want to achieve the highest possible performance, use `ThreadConfig` instead.

Note that `NoOfFragmentLogParts` must be increased altogether if a big value is set to this option. The number of LDM threads must not be larger than `NoOfFragmentLogParts`. Table 4-5 shows acceptable `NoOfFragmentLogParts` values against `MaxNoOfExecutionThreads`. Note that Table 4-5 has several variations for `MaxNoOfExecutionThreads` values, because thread assignment has changed as of 7.4.2.

Table 4-5. *NoOfFragmentLogParts Required for MaxNoOfExecutionThreads*

MaxNoOfExecutionThreads	NoOfFragmentLogParts
2 – 8	4
9 – 23 (< 7.4.2) 9 – 19 (>= 7.4.2)	8
24 – 32 (< 7.4.2) 20 – 31 (>= 7.4.2)	12
32 – 47 (< 7.4.2) 32 – 39 (>= 7.4.2)	16
40 – 47 (>= 7.4.2)	20
48 – 63	24
64 – 72	32

LockExecuteThreadToCPU

Default	None
Range	Comma-separated list of CPUs Each CPU has an identifier from 0 – 64K
Section	[NDBD] or [NDBD DEFAULT]
Restart Type	Node restart

This option specifies the CPUs to bind execution threads in a comma-separated list of CPUs. The target thread types are all but I/O thread and watchdog thread.

You can specify several CPUs to bind in range using dashes when the target CPUs have sequence identifiers without missing numbers. For example, 2-5 is identical to 2,3,4,5. It is not possible to fine-tune using this option. For example, you cannot specify which thread is bound to which CPU. If you want to specify things like that, use ThreadConfig instead.

It is not a good idea to bind threads to CPUs on virtual environments, because CPUs seen from virtual machines are virtual cores and are subject to change anyway.

LockMaintThreadsToCPU

Default	None
Range	Comma-separated list of CPUs Each CPU has an identifier from 0 – 64K
Section	[NDBD] or [NDBD DEFAULT]
Restart Type	Node restart

This option specifies CPUs to bind the I/O thread and watchdog thread in a comma-separated list format. It is not possible to fine-tune using this option. If you want to specify which thread is bound to which CPU, use ThreadConfig instead.

ThreadConfig

Default	None
Range	See below
Section	[NDBD] or [NDBD DEFAULT]
Restart Type	Initial system restart
Affected Versions	7.3.0 – latest

This option allows fine-tuning of thread configurations. You can specify the number of threads and their CPU affinity altogether for each thread type. Values of this option consist of a comma-separated list of attributes with thread_type={property=val[,property=val...]} format. Defined thread types are ldm, tc, recv, send, io, watchdog, main, and rep. Thread types are the same ones as described in MaxNoOfExecutionThreads. Properties in Table 4-6 can be set for each thread type.

Table 4-6. *Thread Properties in ThreadConfig*

Property Name	Range	Description
count	Number	Number of threads for each type of thread. See Table 4-7 for more information.
cpubind, cpuset, cpubind_exclusive, cpuset_exclusive	List of CPUs	List of CPUs in comma-separated list, the same as LockExecuteThreadToCPU and LockMaintThreadsToCPU. cpubind causes each thread is bound to one CPU. cpuset causes each thread is bound to set of CPUs. Exclusive variation, which is available on Solaris only, disallows other threads or processes to be bound to the same CPUs.
spintime	Time in microseconds	Time to spin before sleep when there's no signal to handle. Once the thread sleeps, it cannot respond quickly. Spin can improve response in exchange of CPU time.
realtime	0 or 1	When set to 1, a real-time scheduler is used. It may improve performance.
thread_prio	0 – 10	10 is the highest priority. This property makes sense when more than one thread shares the same CPUs.

By default, the number of threads is minimal, no threads are bound to any CPUs, no thread doesn't spin, and all threads have the same priorities. The default value for the reatime property is the value set to the RealTimeScheduler option.

Table 4-7 shows the range of threads per each type. You can adjust the number of threads within this range. Take care not to assign threads in an imbalanced way. Too many of one type of threaad compared to others will cause some threads to be idle while others are very busy. Ideally, threads must be configured so that the CPU cores are evenly loaded.

Table 4-7. *Number of Threads Per Each Type*

Thread Type	Range
ldm	1, 2, 4, 6, 8, 12, 16 (< 7.3.3) 1, 2, 4, 6, 8, 12, 16, 24, 32 (>= 7.3.3)
tc	1 – 16 (< 7.3.3) 1 – 32 (>= 7.3.3)
send	0 – 8 (< 7.3.3) 0 – 16 (>= 7.3.3)
recv	1 – 8 (< 7.3.3) 1 – 16 (>= 7.3.3)
main	1 only
rep	1 only
io	1 only
watchdog	1 only

Listing 4-4 shows a sample configuration on a 32 core system. Assume that the system has two CPU chips with 16 cores each and hyperthreading is disabled.

115

Listing 4-4. Sample ThreadConfig Configuration on a 32 Core System

```
ThreadConfig = ldm={count=16,cpubind=1-4,9-12,17-20,25-28,realtime=1,spintime=1},tc={count=6,
cpubind=5,6,13,21,22,29,realtime=1,},send={count=2,cpubind=7,23},recv={count=4,cpubind=8,15,
24,31},main={cpubind=14},io={cpubind=14},watchdog={cpubind=16,realtime=1},rep={cpubind=30}
NoOfFragmentLogParts = 16
```

In the example of Listing 4-4, CPU 0 is not bound to any thread. It is intended to make some room for tasks executed by OS and other system processes. Note that `ThreadConfig` in Listing 2-2 is written in one line without the newline character, while it looks like multiple lines. It is not possible to write this very long line in a single page of a book.

It is very difficult to determine the optimal setting. You may need to do benchmarking repeatedly and determine the best setting by trial and error. As a rule of thumb, the following configuration is a good starting point:

1.   Assign half the available CPU cores to the `ldm` threads.

2.   Assign a quarter of the `ldm` threads to `tc` threads.

3.   Assign a quarter of the `ldm` threads to `recv` and `send` threads. If the number of available threads is odd, assign more to `recv` thread.

4.   Assign other CPU cores to other types of threads respectively.

5.   Leave at least one CPU core unused for system use.

6.   Bind each thread to a certain CPU, which enables it to monitor how busy each thread is by determining CPU usage.

Consideration for CPU Properties

Since the CPU must respond to a variety of requests, some tuning is required to use its potential performance. For MySQL NDB Cluster, performance is the most significant requirement.

Power Saving

It is best to turn power saving facilities off, such as *cpuspeed* on Linux systems. With power saving features, the OS will drop CPU frequency depending on the workload. It is reasonable for systems that have hubby workloads, such as desktop computers. However, it has a negative impact for busy server machines. When CPU frequency is low, it is not possible to handle sudden workloads quickly, because there is a lag until the CPU frequency goes back to the original. It harms data access responsiveness.

On Windows, choose the *High Performance* power plan from the *Power Options* settings.

Interrupts

Interrupts from devices are nonnegligible in most cases. For example, network interface cards will cause lots of interrupts when there is a lot of data traffic. By default, on most operating systems, interrupts are handled on specific CPUs. It makes some CPUs busy compared to others. This is a good choice in terms of power saving. However, it can cause performance bottlenecks. In the worst case, a single CPU core will be 100% busy due to interrupts. If the system has many devices, then that CPU core cannot do any other tasks.

One option to prevent this issue is to spread workloads due to interrupts to all CPUs evenly. The capability to reassign interrupts to other CPUs is so called *interrupt affinity*. To achieve this, *irqbalance* for Linux systems is the choice. It reassigns interrupt requests to other CPUs if interrupts are concentrated to only specific CPUs. This prevents specific CPUs from being a bottleneck.

Another option is to reassign interrupt requests to specific, but more than one CPUs. This strategy is good especially when threads are bound to specific CPUs using `ThreadConfig`, `LockExecuteThreadToCPU`, or `LockMaintThreadsToCPU` options. Assign interrupts to CPUs that are not bound by threads in data node, so that interrupts do not drain CPU resources from the data node threads. In this case, *irqbalance* is the choice for Linux. It can rebalance interruption workloads within specific CPUs.

On Windows, it is necessary to edit the *Registry* to configure interrupt affinity. On Solaris, `pcitool` is the tool to configure it. See the manuals for the given OSs for more information.

Hyperthreading

In general, hyperthreading increases overall throughput in exchange for responsiveness. When it is enabled, more than one logical core shares the same physical core. If hyperthreading is not available, some CPU cycles will be wasted in the following scenario, for example:

1. A thread issues load (read data from memory) instruction.

2. Data is mandatory for following instructions.

3. CPU cannot execute more instructions until memory responds and load instruction completes.

Hyperthreading aims to improve performance under such scenarios. With hyperthreading, it might be possible to execute instructions for another thread that's running on another logical core, then the CPU core is fully utilized.

There are several main drawbacks to hyperthreading:

- **Single thread performance may degrade:** As more logical cores share the same physical core, one thread cannot execute new instructions while the other thread is executing instructions.

- **Efficiency of CPU cache memory may be decayed:** One instance of physical cache memory must store data from multiple threads. This is the same problem as when multiple threads are running on one CPU core using context switches. However, the data node doesn't rely on context switches. It is preferable for each thread on the data node to have a monopoly on a bound CPU core.

- **CPU usage indicator is fooled:** While OS doesn't see usage of physical cores, capacity of the CPU resource is likely to be shorter than expected.

So, should you use hyperthreading after all? The answer is "it depends." It depends on various factors such as type of application load and hardware specs. So, it is best to run benchmarks while changing the hyperthreading setting. You can turn it on or off from the BIOS setup.

If you feel that turning it off is bothersome, don't use more than one logical core per physical core. In that case, it is possible to configure thread assignment so that some types of thread use hyperthreading and others don't. For example, the `ldm` thread tends to perform better without hyperthreading, but the `recv` and `send` threads perform better with hyperthreading.

Backup Options

It is needless to say that backing up is one of the most important tasks for database management systems. Any storage medium can fail. Even without hardware failures, important data could be lost due to operation mistake or bugs in the application. To protect important data, it is necessary to take a backup frequently. MySQL NDB Cluster has native backup functionality, which is the only way to take online backups. However, online backups are resource-consuming processes, because they handle lots of data. The default settings are just fine, but sometimes you need to fine-tune them for better performance. See Chapter 8 for more information about backups.

BackupDataDir

Default	FileSystemPath
Range	Arbitrary directory pathname
Section	[NDBD] or [NDBD DEFAULT]
Restart Type	Initial node restart

This option specifies the directory to store the backup data. Backups are large, so they are often stored on separate non-expensive disks from the primary data. Separate disks are preferable in terms of I/O bandwidth, too.

BackupDiskWriteSpeedPct

Default	50
Range	0 – 90 (percent)
Section	[NDBD DEFAULT]
Restart Type	Node restart
Effective Versions	7.4.8 – latest

This option specifies the rate of I/O bandwidth for LCP and backup. They share the same I/O bandwidth specified by MinDiskWriteSpeed and MaxDiskWriteSpeed. This means that speed of LCP will be throttled during backup. A smaller value should be specified for this option on busy systems.

See the sections covering these options described earlier in this chapter for more information.

CompressedBackup

Default	0
Range	0, 1 (Boolean)
Section	[NDBD DEFAULT]
Restart Type	Node restart

When this option is true, backup is stored in compressed format. It saves disk space, but consumes more CPU resources. Do not enable this option on busy systems.

BackupWriteSize

Default	256K
Range	2K – 4294967039 (bytes) (< 7.4.8) 32K – 4294967039 (bytes) (>= 7.4.8)
Section	[NDBD DEFAULT]
Restart Type	Node restart

This option specifies the default size of the write unit for the backup data and log. A larger write unit size reduces I/O operations. The write size will be expanded automatically up to BackupMaxWriteSize when more room is needed.

BackupMaxWriteSize

Default	1M
Range	2K – 4294967039 (bytes) (< 7.4.8)
	256K – 4294967039 (bytes) (>= 7.4.8)
Section	[NDBD DEFAULT]
Restart Type	Node restart

This option specifies the maximum size of the write unit for the backup data and log.

BackupDataBufferSize

Default	16M
Range	0 – 4294967039 (bytes) (< 7.4.8)
	2M – 4294967039 (bytes) (7.4.8 – 7.4.10, 7.5.0)
	512K – 4294967039 (bytes) (7.4.11 – latest, 7.5.1 – latest)
Section	[NDBD DEFAULT]
Restart Type	Node restart

This option specifies the buffer size of the backup data. The data node uses two types of backup buffers. One is for data and the other is for the log. The ldm thread sends data for backing up this buffer. Once the buffer is filled larger than BackupWriteSize, data is written to file. A backup process can continue while writing to file, and it continues to fill the buffer in parallel.

BackupLogBufferSize

Default	16M
Range	0 – 4294967039 (bytes) (< 7.4.8)
	2M – 4294967039 (bytes) (>= 7.4.8)
Section	[NDBD DEFAULT]
Restart Type	Node restart

This option specifies the buffer size of the backup log. The backup log keeps track of all changes made to the data during backup.

BackupMemory

Default	32M
Range	0 – 4294967039 (bytes)
Section	[NDBD DEFAULT]
Restart Type	Node restart
Effective Versions	– 7.2 series Deprecated on 7.3

This option is deprecated on the 7.3 series and removed on the 7.5 series. This option is just a sum of BackupDataBufferSize and BackupLogBufferSize. In older versions, this option must be adjusted when one of these options changes.

BackupReportFrequency

Default	0
Range	0 – 4294967039 (seconds)
Section	[NDBD DEFAULT]
Restart Type	Node restart

This option specifies how often the backup progress is reported to the cluster log. The default value 0 means no backup reports are made. Don't set it to be too frequent, because the cluster log will be filled with backup reports. If you want to check just whether there are backup delays or not, the ALL REPORT BACKUP command from the ndb_mgm client can be used as an alternative.

Transporter Options

Basically, properties of transporter are configured per the individual transporter. However, there are a few options set per data node. Note that the data node usually has multiple transporters.

TotalSendBufferMemory

Default	0
Range	0, 256K – 4294967039 (bytes)
Section	[NDBD DEFAULT]
Restart Type	Node restart

This option specifies the total memory size of the send buffer for all transporters. One transporter is required per one node regardless of node type. The send buffer is allocated for each transporter, by default. So, the total memory size required for the send buffer increases in proportion to (number_of_nodes - 1). It results in large memory consumption when many nodes are configured.

This option caps memory consumption and causes the send buffer memory to be allocated on demand. Consider setting this option when lots of non-busy API nodes or SQL nodes are connected.

ExtraSendBufferMemory

Default	0
Range	0, 32G (bytes)
Section	[NDBD DEFAULT]
Restart Type	Node restart

This option specifies the size of memory additionally allocated when transporter send buffers are running out. Having extra send buffer memory makes the data node stable. Currently, there is no difference in how memory is used by TotalSendBufferMemory and ExtraSendBufferMemory. The sum of these options is allocated to one buffer.

Disk Object Options

If you decide to use disk data tables, it is important to set options for objects used by disk data tables. For more information about disk data tables, see Chapter 2.

FileSystemPathDD

Default	FileSystemPath
Range	Arbitrary directory pathname
Section	[NDBD] or [NDBD DEFAULT]
Restart Type	Initial node restart

This option specifies default values for the FileSystemPathDataFiles and FileSystemPathUndoFiles options.

FileSystemPathDataFiles

Default	FileSystemPathDD
Range	Arbitrary directory pathname
Section	[NDBD] or [NDBD DEFAULT]
Restart Type	Initial node restart

This option specifies the directory path where data files for disk data tables are stored. This option enables you to place disk data tables and checkpoint data on separate disks. It is a good practice to use separate disks so that checkpoint is performed smoothly without interference by disk data tables.

It is highly recommended to use disks with good random I/O performance. Do not use hard disk drives for this purpose, because they are bad at random I/O.

FileSystemPathUndoFiles

Default	FileSystemPathDD
Range	Arbitrary directory pathname
Section	[NDBD] or [NDBD DEFAULT]
Restart Type	Initial node restart

This option specifies the directory path where undo log files for disk data tables are stored. It is even possible to use separate disks for data files and undo log files for disk data tables. Of course, it has the benefit to use separate disks because it increases the total disk I/O bandwidth.

InitialLogFileGroup

Default	None
Range	String to specify logfile group
Section	[NDBD DEFAULT]
Restart Type	Initial system restart

This option specifies properties of logfile group that are automatically created upon system startup. The option consists of three or more parts separated by semicolon. In the following example, the logfile group named LG1 is configured with two 5GB undo log files and 1GB undo log buffer. These undo log files are created under FileSystemPathUndoFiles.

InitialLogFileGroup = name=LG1; undo_buffer_size=1G; undo1.log:5G; undo2.log:5G

The name and undo_log_buffer properties are optional. Their default values are DEFAULT-LG and 64M. Undo log files can be listed using semicolon, if more than one undo log files are configured. The number of undo log files doesn't matter as long as sufficient capacity is allocated. So, you do not need to list the small files.

This option is a handy way to set up a logfile group needed for disk data tables. This option affects only when the cluster is started the first time. You can set up logfile groups using DDL statements such as CREATE LOGFILE GROUP. See Chapter 18 for more information.

InitialTableSpace

Default	None
Range	String to specify logfile group
Section	[NDBD DEFAULT]
Restart Type	Initial system restart

This option specifies the properties of tablespace for disk data tables automatically created upon system startup. The option consists of two or more parts separated by semicolons. In the following example, the tablespace named TS1 is configured with four 16GB data files. These data files are created under FileSystemPathDataFiles.

```
InitialTablespace = name=TS1; data1.dat:16G; data2.dat:16G; data3.dat:16G; data4.dat:16G
```

While tablespace must be associated with the logfile group, the tablespace created by this option needs the logfile group created by the InitialLogFileGroup option.

This option is a handy way to set up tablespaces needed for disk data tables. This option must be used together with InitialLogFileGroup. This option affects only when the cluster is started the first time. You can set up the logfile group using DDL statements such as CREATE TABLESLACE. See Chapter 18 for more information.

DiskPageBufferMemory

Default	64M
Range	4M – 1T
Section	[NDBD DEFAULT]
Restart Type	Node restart

This option specifies memory size allocated for the *disk page buffer*. This buffer is used for caching row data on disk data tables. If you use disk data tables heavily, you need to allocate a large amount of memory for this buffer. On the other hand, if you do not use disk data tables, you can reduce this option to its minimum value to save memory.

DiskIOThreadPool

Default	2
Range	0 – 4294967039
Section	[NDBD DEFAULT]
Restart Type	Node restart

This option specifies the number of threads used for disk I/O against tablespace and undo log files. The main reason you should use many threads is that disk I/O is very time consuming task and file operation system calls will not respond immediately. When a thread is waiting for a response from a system call, it cannot process other tasks. Thus, a thread cannot issue file operation system calls when it's working on other tasks. This wastes CPU time.

Accessing files using the proper number of threads may ease this problem. If more than one I/O request is issued from a user process, requests are queued within the kernel and/or disk controller. I/O requests are processed in the order decided by I/O scheduler in the kernel and/or disk controller. This maximizes disk I/O performance.

This option may have to be increased in the following scenarios:

- **Spreading I/O loads among separate disks:** Tablespace and undo log files are placed on multiple disks. In this case, more threads can be utilized to increase I/O parallelism.

- **Using high performance disks:** High performance disks are used as underlying storage. More I/O parallelism will be required to fill up I/O bandwidth.

You may know that this kind of problem can be solved using *asynchronous I/O* such as *epoll* on Linux. But there is no option associated with asynchronous I/O, because MySQL NDB Cluster has not implemented it yet. It uses many numbers of threads for disk I/O.

Heartbeat and Watchdog Options

As described in Chapter 1, MySQL NDB Cluster employs a *fail-early* strategy, which forcibly stops an unresponsive data node to avoid slowdown of the entire cluster. To detect unresponsive data nodes, MySQL NDB Cluster utilizes heartbeat and watchdog.

HeartbeatIntervalDbDb

Default	5000
Range	10 – 4294967039 (milliseconds)
Section	[NDBD DEFAULT]
Restart Type	Node restart

This option specifies the time between heartbeats. The data node sends heartbeat signal (CM_HEARTBEAT) to another data node and checks if the heartbeat signal has arrived every HeartbeatIntevalDbDb milliseconds. The data node has two separate timers for heartbeat signal send and check, but their intervals are the same. If a data node detects that heartbeat signals from another data node have been missed four times consecutively, the other data node is marked as dead, and it will cause failover or system shutdown depending on whether there are sufficient surviving nodes to continue cluster operation.

Increase this option slightly when your cluster is running on freaky network. If your application needs the best response time and it uses dedicated high-speed network, consider decreasing this option to 1500, which is a default value in older versions (< 7.2.0).

HeartbeatIntervalDbApi

Default	1500
Range	100 – 4294967039 (milliseconds)
Section	[NDBD DEFAULT]
Restart Type	Node restart

This option specifies time between heartbeat checks sent from API (SQL) nodes. All API nodes send heartbeat (API_REGREQ) signals every 100 milliseconds. The data node checks if heartbeat signals have arrived every HeartbeatIntervalDbApi milliseconds. If an API node misses four heartbeat signals consecutively, the API node is marked as dead. Then, the API node will be disconnected and all ongoing transactions will be aborted.

Increase this option slightly when your cluster is running on freaky network.

HeartbeatOrder

Default	0
Range	100 – 4294967039
Section	[NDBD]
Restart Type	System restart

This option defines the order in which heartbeat signals are sent. Heartbeat signals are sent in circular fashion. This means each data node receives heartbeat signals from only one node, and at the same time, a data node sends heartbeat signals to only one node. When the number of data nodes is more than two, the source node (left node) and destination node (right node) of heartbeat signals are different. Otherwise, they are the same.

The order of heartbeat signals is specified as an integer value in each [NDBD] section, not just [NDBD DEFAULT] section. Heartbeat signals are sent from one node to the other data node which has the next big number of this option. The data node with the highest HeartbeatOrder value sends heartbeat signals to the data node with the lowest value.

In most cases, you don't need to change this option. When the network topology is asymmetric and there is some difference of stability for each transporter, the unstable network is more likely to miss a heartbeat. In such cases, configure the heartbeat order so that at least one data node within every node group must have a stable heartbeat source to avoid entire system shutdown due to node group failure.

TimeBetweenWatchDogCheck

Default	6000
Range	70 – 4294967039 (milliseconds)
Section	[NDBD DEFAULT]
Restart Type	Node restart

This option specifies the time between every watchdog check. Watchdog is a mechanism to check if the data node is frozen. If the watchdog thread observes a job thread that remains in the same state during three consecutive check periods, it shuts down the node immediately.

ArbitrationTimeout

Default	7500
Range	10 – 4294967039 (milliseconds)
Section	[NDBD DEFAULT]
Restart Type	Node restart

This option specifies timeout in milliseconds for arbitration. As described in Chapters 1 and 3, arbitration is performed when the cluster gets into network partitioning. If data node cannot get a reply from the arbitrator for more than `ArbitrationTimeout` milliseconds, it terminates immediately.

StartPartialTimeout

Default	30000
Range	0 – 4294967039 (milliseconds)
Section	[NDBD DEFAULT]
Restart Type	Node restart

This option specifies the number of seconds to wait until all other nodes become ready. 0 means it waits indefinately. Once `StartPartialTimeout` milliseconds have passed while one or more data nodes are missing, the cluster forcibly continues the startup process without waiting for the missing nodes.

StartPartitionedTimeout

Default	60000
Range	0 – 4294967039 (milliseconds)
Section	[NDBD DEFAULT]
Restart Type	Node restart

This option specifies the number of seconds to wait until the network partition is resolved. 0 means it waits indefinately. Once `StartPartitionedTimeout` milliseconds have passed while any data nodes are missing and the cluster gets into network partitioning, the cluster forcibly continues the startup process even if the potential network partitioning issue is not resolved.

I recommend setting this option to 0 or to a very large value. Starting with a potential network partitioning is very dangerous. It is very likely to cause network partitioning, because arbitration isn't performed upon this timeout. Thus, two separate clusters can start at the same time when timeout occurs. This must be avoided to protect data from corruption.

Logging Options

While the management node records the cluster log, the source of its content (such as its events) is generated on the data nodes. There are several options related to event reporting on the data node. For more information about log levels, refer to Chapter 16.

MemReportFrequency

Default	0
Range	0 – 4294967039 (seconds)
Section	[NDBD DEFAULT]
Restart Type	System restart

When this option is set to a non-zero value, the cluster log records memory usage periodically. If periodical usage is not activated, the cluster log reports when memory usage reaches 80%, 90%, and 100%.

StartupStatusReportFrequency

Default	0
Range	0 – 4294967039 (seconds)
Section	[NDBD DEFAULT]
Restart Type	System restart

When this option is set to a non-zero value, the cluster log records the progress of the *Startup Phase 4* of the initial start. This phase can take very long if the size of the redo log is large, because the redo logs must be initialized during this phase.

Recommended Configuration Strategy

The most important thing when configuring the cluster is that you should choose appropriate server machines based on requirements. Don't determine your requirements based on server machine specs. Application needs are roughly classified into the following categories—capacity, performance, responsiveness, and availability.

For example, in terms of capacity, it is not possible to set DataMemory larger than the physical memory size of the server machine. You shouldn't choose a server machine before determining how much memory is required.

Configuration of the data node should follow these steps:

1. Estimate required computer resources such as memory size, disk space for the redo logs, I/O speed, network speed, and CPU speed.

2. Choose an appropriate computer hardware within certain margins.

3. Fine tune data node configuration so that data node can fully utilize computer resources.

4. Get ready for data node addition upon future capacity expansion.

When estimating memory size, the number of threads is very important, because it's the most significant indirect factor to increase the required memory size. Multi-threading is mandatory for modern computer hardware. Well-defined TheadConfig may double performance compared to handy MaxNoOfExecutionThreads.

Carefully estimate the LCP speed and the redo log file size. They are the main factors to define the upper limit of overall write speed done by transactions.

Configuration and system planning are not disjointed processes. I recommend reading through Chapters 3 and 4.

SQL Node Options

This section discusses the major options for SQL nodes and API nodes. The section name can be either of MYSQLD or API. Sections are identified as identical node types, whichever section name is specified. In the following descriptions, MYSQLD is used for convenience.

Major Options for SQL Node

NodeId

Default	Automatic
Range	1 – 255
Section	[MYSQLD]
Restart Type	Node restart

Identifier for the node, which has the same meaning of NodeId as the other node types.

HostName

Default	None (accept connection from any host)
Range	Arbitrary hostname or IP address
Section	[MYSQLD]
Restart Type	System restart

Hostname or IP address where the node resides. You can leave this option unset, which means the slot allows connecting from any host. If you don't want unprivileged node to connect, set this option explicitly.

ArbitrationRank

Default	0
Range	0 – 2
Section	[MYSQLD] or [MYSQLD DEFAULT]
Restart Type	Node restart

ArbitrationRank option specifies the likelihood of being an arbitrator. The range for this parameter is 0, 1 and 2. The default value for SQL node is 0, which means SQL node will not be an arbitrator by default. To make SQL node an additional arbitrator, set a non-zero value. 1 has higher priority than 2. Note that the arbitrator should not be placed on the same host as the data node. Refer to the explanation of ArbitrationRank earlier in this chapter, as well as to Chapters 1 and 3, for more information.

DefaultOperationRedoProblemAction

Default	QUEUE
Range	ABORT or QUEUE
Section	[MYSQLD] or [MYSQLD DEFAULT]
Restart Type	System restart
Effective Versions	7.2.10 or newer

This option defines how aborted transactions are handled due to the redo overcommit limit exceedance. Each value has the following meaning:

- ABORT: Any pending operations from aborted transactions are also aborted. This is suitable when you want to handle retries in your application.

- QUEUE: Pending operations from aborted transactions are queued for retry.

See the explanation of RedoOverommitLimit and RedoOvercommitCounter earlier in this chapter.

BatchSize

Default	64 (7.2.0)
	256 (>= 7.2.1)
Range	1 – 992 (records)
Section	[MYSQLD] or [MYSQLD DEFAULT]
Restart Type	Node restart

This option specifies the batch size for a scan operation in the number of records. Since the scan operation returns many rows, it is important to pack records into properly sized batches in terms of performance. Batch size is capped by this option and BatchByteSize, which is described next.

BatchByteSize

Default	32K (7.2.0)
	16K (>= 7.2.1)
Range	1K – 1M (bytes)
Section	[MYSQLD] or [MYSQLD DEFAULT]
Restart Type	Node restart

This option specifies the batch size for the scan operation in bytes.

MaxScanBatchSize

Default	256K
Range	32K – 16M (bytes)
Section	[MYSQLD] or [MYSQLD DEFAULT]
Restart Type	Node restart

This option specifies total data size that one SQL node can receive from the data nodes at a time. It is possible that SQL node receives too many records from the data nodes at a time and consumes excessive memory. This option is aimed to protect the SQL node from such excessive memory consumption.

TotalSendBufferMemory

Default	0
Range	0, 256K – 4294967039 (bytes)
Section	[MYSQLD] or [MYSQLD DEFAULT]
Restart Type	Node restart

This option specifies the total memory size of the send buffer for all transporters. One transporter is required per one node regardless of the node type. The send buffer is allocated for each transporter, by default. So, the total memory size required for the send buffer increases in proportion to (number_of_nodes - 1). Note that the SQL nodes don't connect to each other. However, even though the SQL node connects to data nodes and management nodes, it results in large memory consumption when a large number of data nodes are configured. See the explanation of TotalSendBufferMemory earlier in this chapter.

ExtraSendBufferMemory is also defined for SQL node. Memory configured by these options is allocated to the identical buffer, and the buffer usage is not distinguished by option.

Vital Point for SQL Node Configuration

In most cases, default values for SQL node options are just fine. It is not necessary to change them very often. If the server machine for SQL node has high-speed CPU and large memory, consider increasing batch sizes to maximize performance. While there aren't many options for SQL node in config.ini, lots of options exist on mysqld.

Note that SQL node will have more than one NDB API connection when the --ndb-cluster-connection-pool option is set to more than 1. In such cases, the total size of buffers also increases in proportion to the number of connections.

TCP Transporter Options

On MySQL NDB Cluster, it is possible to fine-tune an individual transporter, a network path between two nodes. The following pattern of transporters can be configured:

- Two data nodes

- Data node and SQL (API) node

Note that the SQL (API) node doesn't connect each other. The transporter for the management node cannot be configured.

In most cases, individual transporters are configured when they connect using dedicated network paths, such as a direct connection using a cross-over Ethernet cable.

The total number of transporters will increase drastically with an increase in the number of nodes. Transporter exists per each combination of arbitrary two data nodes or each combination of data node and SQL node. The number of transporters between two data nodes can be calculated by $_nC_2$, where n stands for the number of data nodes. The maximum number of data nodes is 48, so the maximum number of transporters is $_{48}C_2$ = 1128. The maximum number of transporters between the data node and the SQL node is 48 * (255 - 48 - 1) = 9888. (In this case, there are 48 data nodes, one management node, and 206 SQL nodes.) So, the maximum number of transporters is 1128 + 9888 = 11016, which is a lot. You can see that defining individual transporters is a tough task on a large cluster installation.

Major Options for Transporter

NodeId1, NodeId2

Default	None
Range	1 – 255
Section	[TCP]
Restart Type	Node restart

These two options identify the transporter using node IDs. There is exactly one transporter per arbitrary combination of two nodes. In other words, you need to list the [TCP] sections for each combination of two nodes.

HostName1, HostName2

Default	None
Range	Hostname or IP address appearing in NDBD, API, or MYSQLD sections
Section	[TCP]
Restart Type	Node restart

These options specify the hostname or IP address to be used. If a server machine has more than one network interface, they should have more than two IP addresses along with hostnames. So, it is possible to separate the network path with respect to each node type, for example. Such configuration is discussed later this section.

SendBufferMemory

Default	2M
Range	256K – 4294967039 (bytes)
Section	[TCP] or [TCP DEFAULT]
Restart Type	Node restart

This option specifies the size of memory to buffer data for each transporter. Signal data is stored in this buffer before sending to other nodes, thus this buffer is called the *send buffer*. When the send buffer becomes full, the data node fails to write signals onto the buffer and the signals are lost. That situation is critical for data nodes, so the node will shut down.

In most cases, the default value is sufficient.

ReceiveBufferMemory

Default	2M
Range	16K – 4294967039 (bytes)
Section	[TCP] or [TCP DEFAULT]
Restart Type	Node restart

This option specifies the size of memory to receive data for each transporter. Signal data received from other data nodes is stored in this buffer before dispatching to NDB kernel blocks. This buffer is called *receive buffer*.

In most cases, the default value is sufficient.

OverloadLimit

Default	0
Range	0 – 4294967039 (bytes)
Section	[TCP] or [TCP DEFAULT]he
Restart Type	Node restart

When there are unsent signals in send buffer more than this option, DBLQH kernel block will abort more requests with error 1218. It is a reasonable implementation to reject more requests when the send buffer is almost full. Setting this option to approximately 80% of the send buffer size will reduce tprobability of shutdown due to a send buffer shortage. The default value is 0, which means DBLQH doesn't check the overload status. I recommend setting this option appropriately in the [TCP DEFAULT] section.

Transporter via Separate Network Path

Without explicit configurations, nodes communicate with each other using the network interface specified on the HostName option. However, it is possible to specify other network interfaces in the [TCP] section than HostName. Then, you can achieve following scenarios:

- Separate network allows the data node to access an arbitrator in the event of a network failure. It may avoid entire system shutdown.

- Spread workload among low-cost switches for better throughput and low cost.

- Redirect communication between data nodes that belong to the same node group to direct connection of physical servers for a quicker response.

- Redirect communication between all data nodes to dedicated fast network switch.

Although defining lots of [TCP] sections is a messy task, it's worth it, because the network is most likely to be a source of failures and performance bottlenecks.

Program Startup Options (my.cnf)

This section describes the major startup options for each program, and which options are specified as command-line options. Just like with conventional MySQL programs, MySQL NDB Cluster programs also read options in *my.cnf*.

Options in the *my.cnf* file and command line are the same thing except for their format. The former doesn't have dashes. Another difference is that it is not possible to use the abbreviation in *my.cnf*.

It is possible to have more than one *my.cnf* file in different directories. You can see which files are read by the programs using these --help --verbose options:

```
shell$ ndbmtd --help --verbose | grep /my.cnf
/etc/my.cnf /etc/mysql/my.cnf /usr/local/mysql/etc/my.cnf ~/.my.cnf
```

Common Options

There are several options commonly used on NDB programs, including mysqld. Table 4-8 shows these common options.

Table 4-8. *Common Options for NDB Programs*

Option Name	Abbrev	Default	Description
--ndb-connectstring=string **--connect-string=string**	-c	localhost:1186	Specify connect string, which is used to connect the management node(s).
--ndb-nodeid=num		0 (Automatic)	Node ID for this node. When more than one node is running on the same host, node ID must be explicitly specified.
--connect-retries=num		12	Number of retries when connection to management server fails.
--connect-retry-delay=seconds		5	Interval between retries in seconds.
--ndb-mgmd-host=host[:port]		localhost:1186	Specify management server host and port.
--ndb-optimized-node-selection=num		3 for mysqld TRUE for others	Determines how to choose the data node that works as TC upon data access.
--character-sets-dir=path		None	Directory that contains character set information. This option is practically valid on mysqld only.
--core-file		FALSE	When it's true, the core file is written upon crash.
--debug=options		d:t:0,/tmp/*.trace	This option is available on the debug version only.
--help	-?	FALSE	Print the help message.
--version	-V	FALSE	Print the version.

Connect String

Except for offline utilities such as ndb_print_file, all NDB programs connect to the management server at startup. So, the *connect string* is a crucial, common option.

When a node attempts to connect, the management server compares the client's hostname and HostName option on each slot. If any matching slot is available, the connection is accepted. To connect to the cluster, you specify the connect string that matches at least one available slot. No authentication or other things are required.

■ **Note**   A slot that doesn't have HostName option will accept connection from any host.

Connect string is a string that represents the location of the management node(s). The option to specify the connect string is --ndb-connectstring (or --connect-strong). Although it is possible to specify the hostname of management server using --ndb-mgmd-host, I don't recommend you use it. Because it has bad limitations, the option cannot specify a port number, for example. I recommend using --ndb-connectstring. The format of the connect string is as follows:

[nodeid=#,]{hostname_or_ipaddr[:port][hostname_or_ipaddr[:port], ...]}

Note that parameters enclosed in brackets are optional and can be omitted. For example, if management server runs on a host named mgm1 with the default port and without the desired node ID, connect string is:

mgm1

If management servers run on hosts named mgm1 and mgm2 with network port 1188 and the desired node ID is 20, the connect string is:

nodeid=20,mgm1:1188,mgm2:1188

Major Options for ndb_mgmd

There are several options to control the startup behavior of the ndb_mgmd daemon. Table 4-9 shows the frequently used options for ndb_mgmd.

Table 4-9. *Major Options for ndb_mgmd*

Option Name	Abbrev	Default	Description
--config-file=file	-f	*./config.ini*	Path to configuration file.
--configdir=dir **--config-dir=dir**		Installation directory	Directory to store configuration cache.
--initial		No arguments	When this option is specified, all configuration cache entries are cleared and a new cache entry is created.
--reload		No arguments	When this option is specified, config.ini is read and a new cache entry is created.
--config-cache[=TRUE|FALSE] **or --skip-config-cache**		TRUE	This option specifies whether configuration cache is used or not.
--bind-address=host[:port]		None	This option limits hosts where management client to connect from.
--print-full-config	-P	FALSE	Prints effective configuration and exits.

Configuration Cache

The management node has a mechanism to cache configuration data in binary format instead of reading and parsing the *config.ini* file. This feature is called a *configuration cache*. It stabilizes the configuration of cluster against changes. It is convenient feature, but requires some attention.

Configuration cache is enabled by default. Upon startup, ndb_mgmd reads the latest configuration cache entry without reading *config.ini*, even if *config.ini* is updated. To let *config.ini* be read, the --reload option must be specified. This option causes ndb_mgmd to read the *config.ini* file and compare the content with the latest configuration cache entry. If there are any changes, a new cache entry is created from the content of *config.ini*.

Configuration cache entry has the following filename format:

```
ndb_node-id_config.bin.seq-number
```

For example, the third configuration cache entry on management node with node ID 255 is ndb_255_config.bin.3. Since the files have sequence numbers, it is easy to identify the latest cache entry. If you face a problem after changing the configuration, you can revert to the previous configuration by deleting the latest cache entry file and restarting the management node.

The --initial option will erase all cache entries. It is handy when you migrate cluster installation to another environment and you want to refresh the configuration from beginning.

Note that the configuration cache entry is read if one exists, even though --skip-configuration-cache is specified. To disable to configuration cache completely, you must delete all cache entries and specify the --skip-configuration-cache option.

Reading New Configuration with Multiple Management Nodes

When there is more than one management node, a special procedure is required upon restart with configuration changes, because the management server reads the configuration from a running management node if one exists. A simple rolling restart will fail, which restarts management nodes one by one. Restart of ndb_mgmd must be done using the following steps:

1. Modify *config.ini*.

2. Stop all management nodes, one at a time.

3. Start one ndb_mgmd with the --initial or --reload option.

4. If you started the first ndb_mgmd with the --initial option, start the remaining ndb_mgmd processes using --initial.

5. If you started the first ndb_mgmd with the --reload option, start the remaining ndb_mgmd processes without specifying the --initial or --reload options. They will read the configuration from the first ndb_mgmd.

Options for ndbd/ndbmtd

Options for the data node control the behavior of startup processes. Table 4-10 lists the frequently used options for ndbd and ndbmtd.

Table 4-10. *Major Options for ndbd and ndbmtd*

Option Name	Abbrev	Default	Description
--initial	-i	FALSE	This option causes an initial start when specified.
--nostart	-n	FALSE	When this option is TRUE, the data node will not start after connecting to management server.
--nowait-nodes=list		None	This option specifies missing data nodes and lets the data node perform a partial restart.
--initial-start		FALSE	This option causes the data node to perform initial partial restart. This option is used with the -nowait-nodes option.

Initial Start

As described in Chapter 2, data node has a start type called *initial start*. Upon initial start, the data node wipes all the data at startup. Initial start the following types: *initial node restart* and *initial system restart*. The difference between these two initial restart types is whether data nodes are restarted in turn (the former) or the cluster is restarted after whole system shutdown (the latter). See the explanation of restart types described earlier in this chapter.

Partial Start

Sometimes it is necessary to start the cluster with some missing data nodes due to hardware failures and so forth. Even if some data nodes are missing, it is possible to start the cluster as long as every node group has at least one available data node. This kind of start is called a *partial start*.

When performing a partial start, the --nowait-nodes option must be specified. Its argument is a comma-separated list of node IDs for missing nodes. For example, if data nodes with node ID 3, 5, and 7 are missing and the cluster is runnable using remaining data nodes, you start all the remaining data nodes using the --nowait-nodes=3,5,7 option. If it is initial system restart, the --initial-start option is also required.

No Automatic Start

Personally, I recommend this feature. When the --nostart option is specified, the data node pauses its execution after connecting to management node. To resume startup process, the START command must be issued from the ndb_mgm client.

By default, data node automatically starts after connecting to the data node. Upon system start, all data nodes must be started at a time. If some data nodes are missing and are not ready to start, all starting data nodes wait for the missing ones. Starting data nodes will continue the startup process when all data nodes (except for data nodes specified by the --nowait-nodes option) are ready or when StartPartialTimeout milliseconds has passed. If the missing data nodes can form a runnable cluster, in other words, if at least one data node is missing from each node group, it is possible that the cluster might get into *network partitioning*. In such cases, the starting data node will wait for the StartPartitionedTimeout milliseconds.

Taking care of all the data nodes that started after automatic start is a waste of effort. I recommend disabling auto start using the --nostart option, then seeing if all data nodes are connected and startting them one at a time using the following command from the ndb_mgm client.

```
ndb_mgm> ALL START
```

Options for mysqld

SQL node, mysqld, has lots of options, because its functionality is complex. For example, since it executes a query, it needs performance options to tune up query execution time. Table 4-11 shows options for mysqld, except for replication related options, which are discussed in Chapter 6. Many options in Table 4-11 are also discussed in Chapters 10, 18, and 20.

Table 4-11. *Major NDB Related Options for mysqld*

Option Name	Default	Description
--ndbcluster	TRUE	Enable or disable NDB Cluster storage engine. Don't change from default.
--ndb-cluster-connection-pool=#	1	Number of NDB API connections to data nodes. One connection consumes one MYSQLD slot. Range is 1 – 63.
--ndb-cluster-connection-pool-nodeids=#	None	Comma-separated list of node IDs for connection pool. This option is introduced in the 7.5 series.
--ndb-optimized-node-selection=#	3	Strategy to choose data node as TC. Range is 0 – 3.
--ndb-data-node-neighbor=#	0	Defines nearest data node from the given SQL node. Used with optimized node selection. Range is 0 – 255. This option is introduced in the 7.5 series.
--ndb-autoincrement-prefetch-sz=#	32	Auto-increment column values are reserved for the given SQL node in a batch to reduce access to data node. Range is 1 – 256.
--ndb-batch-size=bytes	32K	Transaction batch size.
--ndb-force-send=[0|1]	TRUE	If set to true, requests to data nodes are sent immediately.
--ndb-blob-read-batch-bytes=bytes	64K	Batch size of blob data read from data nodes.
--ndb-blob-write-batch-bytes=bytes	64K	Batch size of blob data written to data nodes.
--ndb-default-column-format=name	FIXED	Default column format upon table creation.
--engine-condition-pushdown	TRUE	Enable or disable engine condition pushdown optimization.
--ndb-join-pushdown	TRUE	Enable or disable join pushdown optimization.
--ndb-index-stat-enable=[0|1]	FALSE	Enable or disable table statistics functionality.
--ndb-index-stat-option=string	None	Comma-separated list of parameters of index statistics functionality.
--ndb-allow-copying-alter-table=[0|1]	TRUE	If true, COPY algorithm of ALTER TABLE is allowed. This option is introduced in the 7.5 series.
--ndb-deferred-constraints=[0|1]	FALSE	Whether unique key constraint check is deferred until commit instead of each statement.
--ndb-distribution=method	KEYHASH	Distribution method of tables. Acceptable values are KEYHASH and LINEARHASH.
--ndb-optimization-delay=milliseconds	10	Time delay inserted between every round of operation during OPTIMIZE TABLE.

(continued)

Table 4-11. (*continued*)

Option Name	Default	Description
--ndb-fully-replicated=[0|1]	FALSE	If true, new tables without explicit specifications are created as fully replicated style. This option is introduced in the 7.5 series.
--ndb-read-backup=[0|1]	FALSE	If true, new tables without explicit specifications are created as read from any replica style. This option is introduced in the 7.5 series.
--ndb-extra-logging=level	0	The lager this option is, the more information is logged. Range is 0 – 20.

Location of Option Files

Conventionally, MySQL programs may read more than one option file if they exist. It can specify the same option multiple times on separate option files. If the same option is specified more than once, the last-read value is accepted. So, the order of how programs read option files is important.

Locations and order of option files read by MySQL program vary depending on compilation time configuration. You can confirm locations and order of option files using the program binary on your system with the --help option regardless of whether the program is a client or server. The following command output is an example of mysql CLI on UNIX-like systems.

```
shell$ mysql --help | grep /my.cnf
/etc/my.cnf /etc/mysql/my.cnf /usr/local/mysql/etc/my.cnf ~/.my.cnf
```

On Windows PowerShell, you can do the same thing.

```
PS C:\Program Files\MySQL\MySQL Cluster 7.5\bin> ./mysql --help –verbose | Select-String
"my.ini"

C:\WINDOWS\my.ini C:\WINDOWS\my.cnf C:\my.ini C:\my.cnf C:\Program Files\MySQL\MySQL Cluster
7.5\my.ini C:\Program Files\MySQL\MySQL Cluster 7.5\my.cnf
```

The MySQL programs accept two types of configuration filenames on Windows—*my.cnf* and *my.ini*. You can choose the filename as you like.

In addition to the configuration file, MySQL programs read options from command line after reading all option files. So, commandline options, which are specified as arguments of the command line, have the highest precedence.

Additionally, there are several options that influence how option files are read, as described:

- --no-defaults: No option files are read and only command-line options are accepted.

- --defaults-file: Only the option file given as an argument of this option is read. Any other option files are ignored.

- --defaults-extra-file: The option file given as an argument is read in addition to option files.

These options are mutually exclusive, so you can specify only one of them at a time. These options must be specified as the first command-line options. No other options can precede these options.

On UNIX-like systems, MySQL Server also reads an option file under a directory specified by an environment variable $MYSQL_HOME. If the variable is not set, mysqld --help --verbose will not show it. The rule of reading option file is rather complicated. Table 4-12 shows list of option file locations. Option files are read in the order from top to bottom. I intentionally omit the *.cnf* files for Windows from Table 4-12, because they are redundant and have similar precedence (.cnf files are read just after *.ini* files). The exception is *.mylogin.cnf*, because there is no *.ini* variant.

Table 4-12. *Option Files for MySQL Programs*

Windows	UNIX-Like
%PROGRAMDATA%\MySQL\MySQL Server 5.7\my.ini	/etc/my.cnf
%WINDIR%\my.ini	/etc/mysql/my.cnf
C:\my.ini	SYSCONFDIR/my.cnf
BASEDIR\my.ini	$MYSQL_HOME/my.cnf (MySQL Server only)
--defaults-extra-file	--defaults-extra-file
%APPDATA%\MySQL\.mylogin.cnf (client only)	~/.my.cnf
	~/.mylogin.cnf (client only)

SYSCONFDIR in Table 4-12 is a compile-time option. By default, it is the same as CMAKE_INSTALL_PREFIX option for *CMake*, which default value is */usr/local/mysql*. *.my.cnf* and *.mylogin.cnf* are only applicable for the current user who is going to execute the program. Other option files are read by any users, if ones exist.

Summary

This chapter discussed major options for management node, data node, and SQL node. This chapter can be used as a reference when you're reviewing the configuration of your cluster.

MySQL NDB Cluster has many options, as you saw in this chapter. It is a hard task to configure that many options. The data node especially has many options and configuration of the data node is very important. Not all data node options are necessarily configured in a production system. There are several vital categories in data node configurations, as discussed in this chapter:

- **Memory consumption:** It is important to cleverly use up to the available memory on the server machine. Memory is used for storage as well as to buffer the processing data during operations on MySQL NDB Cluster. Memory sizing is the most crucial configuration for MySQL NDB Cluster.

- **Redo log sizing:** MySQL NDB Cluster requires relatively large redo logs on busy systems, because it has to hold all modifications done during two consecutive local checkpoints. If redo log space runs out, clients cannot commit new transactions until the ongoing local checkpoint completes.

- **Checkpoint speed:** Checkpoint speed is important to finish a local checkpoint in a reasonable time. Speeding up the checkpoint will save space required for redo logs.

- **Multi-threading:** Without properly configuring multi-threading on data nodes, it is not possible to achieve good performance no matter how many CPU cores the server machine has.

Generally, configuration must be done in top-down manner. Fine-tuning can be done later, but the right direction must be chosen at first.

In the next chapter, we discuss the architecture of NDB Cluster Replication and how to use it. NDB Cluster Replication involves more than one clusters and they both must be well configured, as shown in this chapter.

CHAPTER 5

Installation

In this chapter, we discuss the installation process of MySQL NDB Cluster. This discussion assumes that you have acquired target machines and completed the initial configuration for the hardware. If you have not done this, review Chapters 3 and 4 for the system planning and configuration tasks.

Package Installation

The installation process of MySQL NDB Cluster is not difficult. It is a straightforward process. It consists of two steps for all types of nodes, plus one step for the SQL node, described here:

1. Obtain package files

2. Install packages

3. Initialize data directory for only SQL node

Obtaining Packages

To install packages, you must first obtain the package files. Oracle Corporation distributes MySQL NDB Cluster binary packages for officially supported platforms. You can verify if your platform is supported or not on the supported platforms page, as described in Chapter 3.

https://www.mysql.com/support/supportedplatforms/cluster.html

There are two types of packages depending on the license—free software/open source license and the commercial license. They are called *Community Edition* and *Carrier Grade Edition,* respectively. They are distributed on separate sites, as described next.

Community Edition

The *Community Edition* is a free software/open source version of MySQL NDB Cluster. Everyone can download, install, execute, and redistribute the program per its license, *GNU General Public License Version 2 (GPLv2)*. It is distributed on the MySQL download site:

http://dev.mysql.com/downloads/cluster/

© Jesper Wisborg Krogh and Mikiya Okuno 2017

J. W. Krogh and M. Okuno, *Pro MySQL NDB Cluster*, https://doi.org/10.1007/978-1-4842-2982-8_5

The download site shows the download page in Figure 5-1.

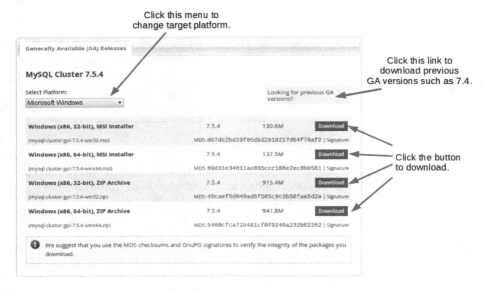

Figure 5-1. *Community downloads screen*

By default, the download page automatically detects the platform from information sent by the browser, which you use to access the page, and shows packages for that platform. Click the Download button to download the desired package. If you want to change the target platform, click the pull-down menu at the left-top side of the download menu.

If you want to install previous GA versions such as 7.4, click the link at the top-right of the download menu. By default, the previous GA versions page shows 7.4 packages. You can download even older versions by selecting the desired version from the pull-down menu at the top-left of the download menu.

If you have signed in to the MySQL developer site using an Oracle account, the download will begin right after you click the Download button. Otherwise, you will see a screen that prompts you to sign in to the site or create a new Oracle account. I personally recommend that you create an account if you don't have the one, because you must to sign in to the MySQL developer site to achieve some tasks such as filing a new bug. If you are in a hurry and just want to download the package files, click the No Thanks, Just Start My Download link, as shown in Figure 5-2.

Begin Your Download - mysql-cluster-gpl-7.5.4-winx64.ms

Login Now or Sign Up for a free account.

An Oracle Web Account provides you with the following advantages:

- Fast access to MySQL software downloads
- Download technical White Papers and Presentations
- Post messages in the MySQL Discussion Forums
- Report and track bugs in the MySQL bug system
- Comment in the MySQL Documentation

Login » using my Oracle Web account   **Sign Up »** for an Oracle Web account

MySQL.com is using Oracle SSO for authentication. If you already have an Oracle Web account, click the Login link. Otherwise, you can signup for a free account by clicking the Sign Up link and following the instructions.

No thanks, just start my download. ◄─────── Click this link to start download immediately

Figure 5-2. *Additional download page when you are not logged in*

Carrier Grade Edition (CGE)

The *MySQL Cluster Carrier Grade Edition (CGE)* is a commercial licensed version of MySQL NDB Cluster. You need to purchase the license to use this version of the software. CGE includes some additional features compared to the Community Edition. You can see features of CGE at a glance on the following page:

http://www.mysql.com/products/

CGE package files can be obtained from *My Oracle Support (MOS)* or from the *Oracle Software Delivery Cloud*. On both sites, you need an Oracle account to sign in. So, you can use a common account on the MySQL community download site, My Oracle Support, and the Oracle Software Delivery Cloud.

On My Oracle Support, you can obtain all versions of MySQL NDB Cluster except for very old versions. If your desired version of the package is missing from the site, contact Oracle support service. Figure 5-3 shows the tab menu at the top of MOS after signing in.

Figure 5-3. *Top tab menu on MOS*

To obtain CGE packages, click the Patches & Updates tab. Then, you will see the Patch Search screen shown in Figure 5-4.

Figure 5-4. *Patch search screen on MOS*

Enter MySQL Cluster into the Product textbox. Then, check the Include All Products in a Family checkbox, select a desired version from the Release dropdown menu, and select a desired platform. Finally, click the Search button and you will see list of packages to download. If you choose Linux x86-64 as the platform, several package files per version are listed because there are various Linux distributions that officially support MySQL NDB Cluster. Take care to select the appropriate package.

On the Oracle Software Delivery Cloud, only the latest versions of the packages are available. Once signing in to the Oracle Software Delivery Cloud, you will see the package search menu shown in Figure 5-5. Enter MySQL Cluster into the textbox. Then, several candidates are shown in a pull-down menu. MySQL Cluster Carrier Grade Edition is a product name, and it includes not only MySQL NDB Cluster packages, but also auxiliary packages such as drivers. If you need only the server package, select the software name with the version number, such as "MySQL Cluster 7.5.5". The next step is to select an appropriate platform. Once a platform is selected, the software is added to the download queue. Finally, click the Continue button and proceed to the download screen.

Filter Products by ▣ Programs ▣ Linux/OVM/VMs ☐ Self-Study Courseware ☐ 1-Click Offerings

Search by [All ▾] [Start typing…] (Select Platform ∨)

Download Queue	Continue
Selected Item	**Platform**
Release: MySQL Cluster 7.5.4 ✖	Linux x86-64
Remove All	Continue

Figure 5-5. *Software search screen on the Oracle Software Delivery Cloud*

On the download screen, you will see a software license notification. The license notification indicates that the trial license is applicable to packages on the Oracle Software Delivery Cloud, in addition to commercial license. The trial license is limited to 30 days for evaluation purposes. The body of the agreement is found in the license notification. If you don't have a commercial license and want to evaluate the commercial version of MySQL NDB Cluster, read the license notification carefully before you download the software. If you don't need commercial features and/or support, the Community Edition is a good alternative because it's licensed under GPLv2, which will not expire.

If you want to obtain an old version, you need to access MOS instead of the Oracle Software Delivery Cloud.

Installation on Linux

On Linux systems, two types of packages are available. One is the *compressed tar ball (tar.gz)* package, and the other is the installer package for *package managers* such as the *RPM package* and *Debian package*. Although many other types of packages exist, only the RPM and Debian packages are officially distributed.

Tar.gz Archive Package Installation

Tar.gz is a compressed file format that's archived using *tar (tape archive)*, then compressed by *gzip (GNU zip)*. In the tar.gz archive package, all MySQL NDB Cluster programs and related files are included in a single file. Installation of the package is very easy; you just extract the archive. The typical target directory is */usr/local* or */opt*, but you can extract the tar.gz file to anywhere as you need. Listing 5-1 shows example of tar.gz archive installation command.

Listing 5-1. Installing the tar.gz Archive to the */opt* Directory

```
shell$ su
shell# mv mysql-cluster-gpl-7.5.5-linux-glibc2.5-x86_64.tar.gz /opt
shell# cd /opt && tar xf mysql-cluster*tar.gz
shell# ln -s mysql-cluster*64 mysql-cluster
```

In this example, the last command creates a symbolic link to the extracted directory for easy access. When upgrading or downgrading the cluster, it is necessary to install more than one version on the same host. Making a symbolic link to the extracted directory is preferable over renaming the installation directory itself. Extracted directory entries are described in Listing 5-2.

Listing 5-2. Contents of the tar.gz Archive Package

```
shell# ls -lh
total 56K
drwxr-xr-x  2 root root  4.0K Jan 13 22:18 bin
-rw-r--r--  1 7161 31415  18K Oct 13 19:59 COPYING
drwxr-xr-x  2 root root  4.0K Jan 13 22:18 docs
drwxr-xr-x  4 root root  4.0K Jan 13 22:18 include
drwxr-xr-x  4 root root  4.0K Jan 13 22:18 lib
drwxr-xr-x  4 root root  4.0K Jan 13 22:18 man
drwxr-xr-x 10 root root  4.0K Jan 13 22:18 mysql-test
-rw-r--r--  1 7161 31415 2.5K Oct 13 19:59 README
drwxr-xr-x 31 root root  4.0K Jan 13 22:18 share
drwxr-xr-x  2 root root  4.0K Jan 13 22:18 support-files
```

All programs are installed in the bin subdirectory. You can add */opt/mysql-cluster/bin* to your PATH environment variable (*the executable search path*) for easy access.

On typical setup, you need to create a dedicated user account to run the server daemons. Although it is possible to run server daemons using the root user, it is not preferable from a security point of view, because the root user has extra privileges that are unnecessary to run NDB Cluster programs and will harm the system if the account is hijacked by attackers. Listing 5-3 shows a command example of creating an OS user account for MySQL Server.

Listing 5-3. Creating a User Account

```
Shell$ su
shell# mkdir /var/lib/mysql
shell# groupadd mysql
shell# useradd -g mysql -s /bin/false -d /var/lib/mysql mysql
shell# chown mysql:mysql /var/lib/mysql && chmod 700 /var/lib/mysql
shell# passwd mysql
```

In Listing 5-3, the login shell for mysql user is set to /bin/false. This prohibits the mysql user from logging in to the system, but mysql can still be used as the effective user for server processes.

In addition to creating a user account, you need to initialize the data directory by hand on the SQL node. On MySQL NDB Cluster 7.5, which is combined with MySQL Server 5.7, the data directory is initialized using mysqld --initialize. On older MySQL NDB Cluster versions, which are combined with older MySQL versions, the data directory is initialized using the mysql_install_db command. Although mysql_install_db is still available for MySQL Server 5.7, it's been deprecated and will be removed in future releases.

Listing 5-4 shows a typical command example of initializing the data directory on MySQL NDB Cluster 7.5. All you need to do is start mysqld, the MySQL Server daemon program, with the --initialize option. This will create necessary system tables with the user account, which is set to the --user option for mysqld. The default username for this option is mysql. You don't have to change the owner of the generated files.

Listing 5-4. Initializing the Data Directory on MySQL NDB Cluster 7.5

```
shell$ su
shell# mysqld --initialize
```

On MySQL NDB Cluster 7.4 or older, you need to initialize using the mysql_install_db script. Listing 5-5 shows a typical command example of this script. The script doesn't change the owner automatically, so you need to change the file owner manually after initializing the data directory.

Listing 5-5. Initializing the Data Directory on MySQL NDB Cluster 7.4 or Older

```
shell$ su
shell# cd /opt/mysql-cluster
shell# bin/mysql_install_db --defaults-file=/etc/my.cnf
shell# chown -R mysql:mysql /var/lib/mysql
```

Whether mysqld --initialize or mysql_install_db is used, it is recommended that you complete the MySQL Server configuration file, such as */etc/my.cnf*, before initializing the data directory, because several options for InnoDB cannot be changed after initialization is done. For example, the innodb_undo_tablespaces and innodb_undo_directory options for separate undo tablespace cannot be changed after initialization of the data directory.

Optionally, you can configure your system so that MySQL Server starts or stops automatically upon system startup and shutdown. There are two choices for MySQL Server—*SysV style init* and *systemd*. Check your operating system manual to see which init system is used. It is even possible to set up automatic start and shutdown on other init systems, such as *OpenRC* and *upstart*, but only SysV style init and systemd are officially supported. The procedures for other init systems are beyond the scope of this book.

To set up automatic startup and shutdown using *SysV style init*, you copy the *mysql.server* script to */etc/init.d* and register it to each run level. Listing 5-6 shows the procedure of setting up the init script for *SysV style init*, which uses the chkconfig command.

Listing 5-6. Setting Up Automatic Startup and Shutdown Using SysV Style Init

```
shell$ su
shell# cp mysql.server /etc/init.d/mysqld
shell# chmod +x /etc/init.d/mysqld
shell# chkconfig --add mysqld
```

For further details of the chkconfig command, consult with the manual of your operating system.

To set up automatic startup and shutdown using *systemd*, you need to create the *systemd* configuration file by hand or copy it from elsewhere. The easiest way to obtain the *systemd* configuration file is to copy it from the RPM package. You can extract the RPM file using the rpm2cpio and cpio commands. The RPM package also includes an auxiliary script called mysqld_pre_systemd. This script initializes the data directory, if it was not initialized before starting MySQL Server. This script is optional. It is not required if the data directory has been initialized. These configuration files and auxiliary script assume that the installation target is the */usr* directory. If you extract files under a different directory, such as */opt/mysql-cluster*, paths in these files must be adjusted. You also need to create the */var/run/mysqld* directory, which is owned by the user, to run MySQL Server. The procedure to set up automatic startup and shutdown using *systemd* is shown in Listing 5-7.

Listing 5-7. Setting Up Automatic Startup and Shutdown Using Systemd

```
shell$ rpm2cpio mysql-cluster-community-server-7.5.5-1.el7.x86_64.rpm\
> | cpio -id
shell$ sed -i -e 's#/usr/s\?bin/my#/opt/mysql-cluster/bin/my#'\
> usr/lib/systemd/system/mysqld.service
shell$ sed -i -e 's#/usr/s\?bin/my#/opt/mysql-cluster/bin/my#'\
> usr/bin/mysqld_pre_systemd
shell$ su
shell# cp usr/lib/systemd/system/mysqld.service /usr/lib/systemd/system
shell# cp usr/bin/mysqld_pre_systemd /opt/mysql-cluster/bin
shell# mkdir /var/run/mysqld && chown mysql:mysql /var/run/mysqld
shell# systemctl start mysqld.service
shell# systemctl enable mysqld.service
```

This example assumes that the RPM and tar.gz packages have been downloaded into the current working directory. The rpm2cpio command and piped cpio command extract files under the current working directory with the directory structure intact. For example, the program binaries are extracted to the *usr/bin* directory, which is relative to the current working directory. The sed command is invoked using the non-standard character # as field delimiter to avoid escape characters for the path delimiter /.

RPM Package Installation

RPM is used by Red Hat Enterprise Linux and its variants, including Oracle Enterprise Linux and SUSE and its variants. Installation of the RPM package is straightforward; it can be achieved using the rpm command. The overall MySQL NDB Cluster distribution is separated into several RPM packages by component. So, you need to install the appropriate package(s) into the target host.

On MySQL NDB Cluster 7.4 or older, types of RPM packages are the same as the standard (non-NDB) MySQL Server, as described in Listing 5-8. NDB Cluster related files are included in the *server, devel,* and *test* packages.

Listing 5-8. List of RPM Packages for MySQL NDB Cluster 7.4

```
shell$ tar tf MySQL-Cluster-gpl-7.4.13-1.el7.x86_64.rpm-bundle.tar
MySQL-Cluster-shared-gpl-7.4.13-1.el7.x86_64.rpm
MySQL-Cluster-devel-gpl-7.4.13-1.el7.x86_64.rpm
MySQL-Cluster-test-gpl-7.4.13-1.el7.x86_64.rpm
MySQL-Cluster-shared-compat-gpl-7.4.13-1.el7.x86_64.rpm
MySQL-Cluster-embedded-gpl-7.4.13-1.el7.x86_64.rpm
MySQL-Cluster-client-gpl-7.4.13-1.el7.x86_64.rpm
MySQL-Cluster-server-gpl-7.4.13-1.el7.x86_64.rpm
```

The *server* package includes all the programs, shared libraries, and data files required to run NDB Cluster. Auto installer is also included in this package. Server daemon programs are installed into */usr/sbin*, client programs are installed into */usr/bin*, and libraries are installed into */usr/lib*. So, you need to install the *server* package to run data node, management node, and NDB client programs such as ndb_restore. The *server* package is also required when you want to run your NDB API client application, which links libndbclient.

The *devel* package includes header files and static libraries required to build MySQL C API and NDB API programs. So, you need to install it on your development machine, if applicable.

The *test* package includes additional test cases for MySQL NDB Cluster. The *test* package is required for debugging MySQL programs created by MySQL developers. So, it's usually unnecessary in a production system.

In short, for MySQL NDB Cluster 7.4 or older, you need to install the *server* package to run NDB Cluster daemons and link the NDB API shared library, the *devel* package to develop NDB API programs as well as MySQL C API programs, and other packages just like with the standard MySQL Server.

On MySQL NDB Cluster 7.5, packages are split into smaller pieces, as listed in Table 5-1.

Table 5-1. *List of RPM Packages for MySQL NDB Cluster 7.5*

Component	Description
auto-installer	The Auto Installer package. Discussed later in this chapter.
client	NDB client programs for MySQL Server and MySQL NDB Cluster, such as mysql, mysqldump, ndb_mgm, ndb_restore and so forth.
common	Common package for MySQL Server (not MySQL NDB Cluster). The package includes character set information and error messages.
data-node	ndbd and ndbmtd program executables.
devel	Header files, static libraries, and shared libraries required to develop MySQL client C/C++ programs.
embedded	Embedded (library) version of MySQL Server (libmysqld). This package includes a shared library version of libmysqld.
embedded-compat	Backward compatible libmysqld.
embedded-devel	Header files, static libraries, and shared libraries required to develop embedded MySQL Server application programs.
java	JAR (Java Archive) files required for ClusterJ applications.
libs	MySQL C API client library (libmysqlclient). This package includes a shared library version of libmysqlclient.
libs-compat	Backward compatible libmysqlclient.
management-server	This package includes ndb_mgmd.
memcached	Memcached related binaries.
ndbclient	NDB API shared library (libndbclient).
ndbclient-devel	Header files and libraries required to develop NDB API client programs.
nodejs	A driver for Node.js application.
server	MySQL Server and related programs. This version of MySQL Server includes NDBCluster storage engine support.
server-minimal	Minimal installation of the database server and related tools. Available as of MySQL NDB Cluster 7.5.7.
test	MySQL Test Suite package.

Package division for MySQL NDB Cluster 7.5 has precedence over one for 7.4 or older. On MySQL NDB Cluster 7.4 or older, it often becomes a problem that all MySQL NDB Cluster related programs are included in the server package. This means all of management server, data node, and SQL node programs are installed or removed at the same time. This makes difficult to roll upgrades or downgrades when more than one type of nodes is installed in one host. For more details about upgrade and downgrade operations, see Chapter 11.

Unfortunately, the *Yum (Yellowdog Updater Modified)* repository is not available for MySQL NDB Cluster for the time being. You need to install, upgrade, or downgrade packages without using the Yum repository.

Unlike the tar.gz package, some RPM packages modify your system and perform administrative tasks for you. The *server* package does the following tasks upon installation (not upgrade):

- Creates the mysql user and group

- Creates a data directory

- Initializes the data directory (MySQL NDB Cluster 7.3 and 7.4 only)

- Sets up automatic startup and shutdown for mysqld (for *systemd* or *SysV style init*)

The shared package invokes the ldconfig command to set up symbolic links, which are necessary to link the installed shared library. See the man page of ldconfig for more information.

The *server* RPM package also sets up automatic startup and shutdown. On old systems, which use *SysV style init*, automatic startup and shutdown is enabled by just installing the *server* RPM package. You can verify this using the chkconfig command. For further details of this command, refer to the man page. MySQL Server will be started automatically upon the next restart of the system. To start the service immediately, execute the service command as root:

```
shell$ su
shell# service mysqld start
```

The service name may differ depending on the OS; it might be mysqld or mysql. The service name can be confirmed by inspecting the contents of the */etc/init.d* directory.

On recent systems, which have *systemd*, the configuration file for the *systemd* is also installed with the *server* RPM package. However, the service is not enabled by default. You need to explicitly enable it using systemctl:

```
shell$ sudo systemctl enable mysqld.service
```

This command lets MySQL Server start automatically upon the next OS restart. However, the MySQL Server has not started at this stage. If you want to start it immediately, execute systemctl:

```
shell$ sudo systemctl start mysqld.service
```

The Tar.gz Package vs. the RPM Package

Which type of package should be used for your system? This depends. Package Manager actually eases some operational tasks. It is useful especially on SQL nodes. So, I generally recommend RPM package.

However, there are some reasons not to use RPM package. For example, RPM packages for MySQL NDB Cluster 7.4 or older have some drawbacks; the package is not separated per node type. It is not possible to install more than two versions for one RPM package. So, RPM package may not be suitable when more than one type of node is installed on a single host, because it might be a problem upon rolling upgrades or downgrades.

DEB Package Installation

DEB is a package format used by *Debian* and its variants, such as *Ubuntu*, *KNOPPIX*, and *LMDE*. However, Debian and Ubuntu are the only Linux distributions supported by MySQL NDB Cluster. See the supported platforms page for more information about supported Linux distributions.

MySQL NDB Cluster 7.5.5 or older including series older than 7.5, the DEB package for MySQL NDB Cluster is all in one type, and available only for Debian. All program binaries and related files are included in a single package. All that you need to do is run the dpkg command with the -i option:

```
shell# dpkg -i mysql-cluster-gpl-7.5.5-debian8-x86_64.deb
```

This all in one package doesn't run a script upon installation. So, you need to set up a user account, initialize the data directory, and run automatic startup and shutdown just like with the tar.gz package. So, the benefit of using the all in one type DEB package is just that it's managed by the package manager.

As of MySQL NDB Cluster 7.5.6, the DEB package organization has been changed and Ubuntu is also supported. It has been changed to identical to RPM package of MySQL NDB Cluster 7.5 series. Refer to Table 5-1 for more details of the RPM package organization of MySQL NDB Cluster 7.5 series. So, you can install only required packages for the host like the 7.5 RPM package.

There are several differences the RPM package organization and the new DEB package organization.

- **The server DEB package has systemd related files:** It is possible to configure automatic start of SQL node upon system restart. The service name is mysql.service.

- **MySQL NDB Cluster dedicated packages for some functionalities are not available:** You need to install packages derived from MySQL Server for mysql-common, mysql-client, and libmysqlclient. I recommend you to download DEB Bundle tar file.

- **Debugging symbols are stored in separate package:** For Debian packages, debugging symbols are stored in separate package with -dbgsym suffix in its name. No debugging symbols are available for Ubuntu.

- **Minimal server package is not available:** It might be added in the future release, but it's currently unavailable.

Installation on Windows

On Windows systems, two types of packages are available. One is the *ZIP archive* package, and the other is the *Windows Installer (MSI) package*. Since there are no other distributions than those released by Microsoft Corporation, the installer package format is Windows Installer only.

The Zip Archive Package Installation

Zip is a well-known file compression format. Recent versions of Windows include compress and decompress functionality for Zip files. The process for installing a Zip archive on Windows is similar to the process for installing the tar.gz archive on Linux systems. Installation can be done by extracting the archive anywhere on the system. For example, you can extract it into *C:\MySQL*. You can use Explorer to extract the archive.

Create an option file and put it in a directory where MySQL Server reads option files, such as *C:\Windows\my.ini*. You can place an option file in an arbitrary directory if you start the server with the --defaults-file option.

Create data directories for installed node(s). For management and data nodes, the data directory can be left empty. The installation process ends here.

For an SQL node, the data directory must be initialized after completing an option file. On Windows, the mysql_install_db script doesn't work. So, the data directory should be initialized using other methods. As of MySQL 5.7 and MySQL NDB Cluster 7.5, it is possible to initialize the data directory using mysqld --initialize:

```
PS C:\> C:\mysql-cluster-gpl-7.5.5-winx64\bin\mysqld.exe --defaults-file=C:\MySQL\my.ini
--initialize
```

On MySQL NDB Cluster 7.4 or older, it is not possible to initialize the data directory on Windows, because mysqld doesn't have the --initialize option and mysqld_install_db doesn't work on Windows. The Zip archive package includes a directory named data. Copy the contents of this directory to the target data directory, or you can copy the directory itself so that the name of the directory is the same as the target data directory.

Finally, you can start the SQL node. If the data nodes are not ready yet, temporarily disable the NDBCluster storage engine (e.g., comment out the NDB related options), and start SQL node to verify installation. When you start the SQL node the first time on Windows, specify the --console option to see

151

if any problems are reported. The `--console` option lets error logs be printed on the console. You can see errors followed by the command execution, if any errors are reported. Listing 5-9 shows example output of the first startup on Windows systems.

Listing 5-9. Starting MySQL NDB Cluster on Windows the First Time

```
PS C:\> C:\mysql-cluster-gpl-7.5.5-winx64\bin\mysqld.exe --defaults-file=C:\MySQL\my.ini
--console
2017-02-09T11:53:37.224242Z 0 [Warning] TIMESTAMP with implicit DEFAULT value is deprecated.
Please use --explicit_defaults_for_timestamp server option (see documentation for more
details).
2017-02-09T11:53:37.224242Z 0 [Note] --secure-file-priv is set to NULL. Operations related
to importing and exporting data are disabled
2017-02-09T11:53:37.224242Z 0 [Note] C:\mysql-cluster-gpl-7.5.5-winx64\bin\mysqld.exe
(mysqld 5.7.17-ndb-7.5.5-cluster-gpl) starting as process 1184 ...
... snip ...
2017-02-09T11:53:37.640424Z 0 [Note] C:\mysql-cluster-gpl-7.5.5-winx64\bin\mysqld.exe: ready
for connections.
Version: '5.7.17-ndb-7.5.5-cluster-gpl'  socket: ''  port: 3306  MySQL Cluster Community
Server (GPL)
2017-02-09T11:53:37.640424Z 0 [Note] Executing 'SELECT * FROM INFORMATION_SCHEMA.TABLES;' to
get a list of tables using the deprecated partition engine. You may use the startup option
'--disable-partition-engine-check' to skip this check.
2017-02-09T11:53:37.640424Z 0 [Note] Beginning of list of non-natively partitioned tables
2017-02-09T11:53:37.702924Z 0 [Note] End of list of non-natively partitioned tables
```

Optionally, you can configure installed server daemon programs, MySQL Server, data nodes, and management nodes, as *Windows Services*, which start up and shut down processes automatically upon system startup and shutdown. To install a daemon program as a Windows service, run it with the `--install` option. This option needs *Administrator* privilege to manipulate a Windows service. The way to specify options for MySQL Server and NDB daemons (ndbd, ndbmtd, ndb_mgmd) differ. We discuss the MySQL Server installation first.

To install MySQL Server as a service, if you want to use an option file that's placed in a non-standard location, use the `--defaults-file` option with the `--install` option:

```
PS C:\> C:\mysql-cluster-gpl-7.5.5-winx64\bin\mysqld.exe --install NDB75 --defaults-file=C:\
MySQL\my.ini
Service successfully installed.
```

Unlike normal MySQL program invocation, the `--install` option must be specified as the first argument. It even precedes standard first options; `--no-defaults`, `--defaults-file`, and `--defaults-extra-file`. The second argument, NDB75 in the example, is a service name to register. Note that an equals sign is not required between `--install` and the service name. The command results in an error if an equals sign exists. Take care so that the service name doesn't collide with other services. The service name can be omitted if no additional options are specified. If it's omitted, the service name will be MySQL. The following option after the service name is used as a command line option when the mysqld is invoked as the service. Only one additional option is allowed. So, you usually need to specify `--defaults-file` here. This is required when installing more than one service with different configurations on a single host.

MySQL Server does not automatically start after the service is installed. If you want, you can start the installed MySQL Server using the *Services* interface of Windows. It can be accessed via *Computer Management* or by entering `services.msc` at the *Start menu*. The way to open *Computer Management* varies depending on Windows versions. Figure 5-6 shows a popup menu when right-clicking the Windows *Start menu*. You can see *Computer Management* in the middle of the menu.

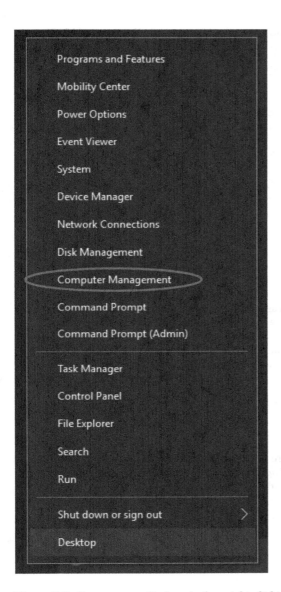

Figure 5-6. *Popup menu displayed when right-clicking the Windows Start menu*

Figure 5-7 is a screenshot of the *Services* screen within *Computer Management*. You can find NDB75 there. The service is not running.

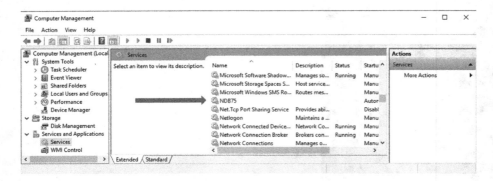

Figure 5-7. *Windows Services management interface*

You can start, stop, disable, or configure the service just like with other standard Windows services. To configure it, right-click the target service (NDB75 in this case) and select Properties from the popup menu.

For NDB daemon programs—ndbd, ndbmtd, and ndb_mgmd—although you need to specify --install first, the way to specify the --install option differs from mysqld. An equals sign is required between --install and the service name. If it's missing, the command will result in an error. The default service names are "ndbd" for ndbd and ndbmtd, and "ndb_mgmd" for ndb_mgmd. You can remove the service using the --remove option just like mysqld. An equals sign is also required when uninstalling the service with the --remove option.

Windows Installer Package Installation

On Windows, packages for *Microsoft Windows Installer* are available. Its file extension is *.msi*, so a package for *Microsoft Windows Installer* is also called an *MSI package* or *MSI file*. Installation using *MSI* is very easy. You can install MySQL NDB Cluster using the GUI installation wizard.

To begin installation, double-click the saved *MSI package* in *Windows Explorer*. Figure 5-8 show the welcome screen of the installation wizard. Click Next to proceed with the installation.

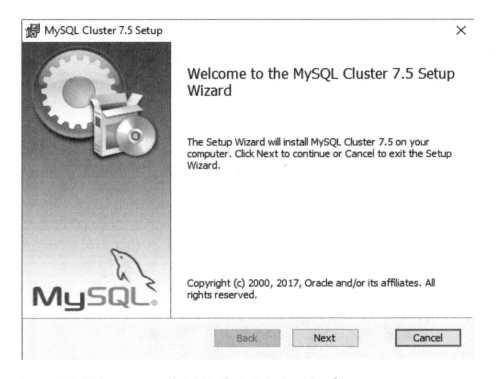

Figure 5-8. *Welcome screen of MySQL Cluster 7.5 setup wizard*

Then, you will see the license agreement screen, as shown in Figure 5-9. Read the license agreement, and if you can accept them, check the agreement checkbox. Click Next to proceed.

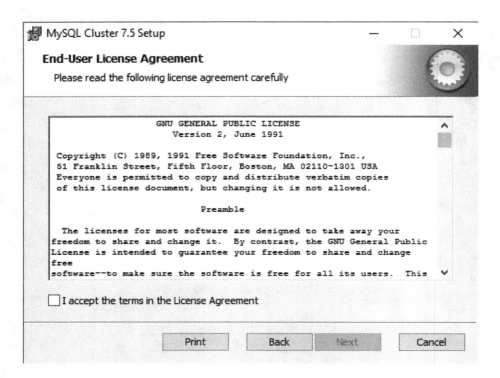

Figure 5-9. *License agreement during MSI package installation*

Then, choose a setup type from the three choices. Figure 5-10 is a setup type selection screen. When you choose Typical, everything but the documentation will be installed. When you choose Complete, everything will be installed. You can choose what to install by choosing Custom.

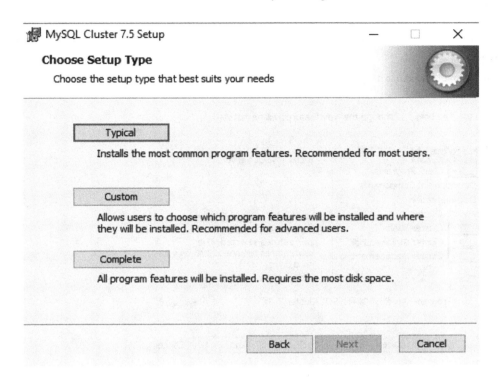

Figure 5-10. *Setup Type selection screen*

Figure 5-11 shows a custom setup screen to choose components to be installed. You can omit unnecessary components to save disk space. For example, if you need to install only a data node, make all but the Cluster Storage Engine component under the MySQL Cluster menu unavailable.

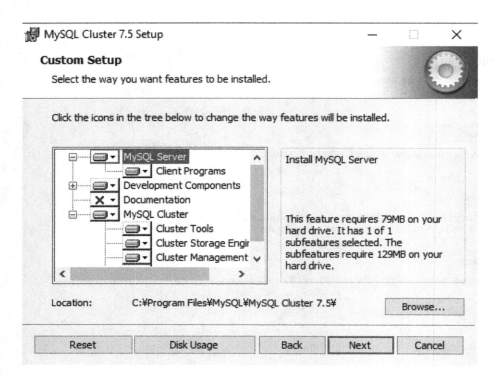

Figure 5-11. *Choosing components to install*

Click Next to proceed. You will see the *UAC (User Account Control)* screen after completing the wizard choices. Click Yes on the UAC screen.

Program binaries are installed into directory under *C:\Program Files\MySQL*; e.g., *C:\Program Files\ MySQL\MySQL Cluster 7.5*. If you like, add the `bin` subdirectory under the installation directory to the `Path` environment variable, which is your program search path so that the MySQL programs can be started easily from the *command prompt* or the *Windows PowerShell*. You can change the environment variables on *System Properties*, which can be accessed from the *System* submenu in the System and Security menu in the *Control Panel*. Figure 5-12 shows the *System* submenu in the *Control Panel*.

Figure 5-12. System submenu in the Control Panel

Click Advanced System Settings. You will see the System Properties screen, as shown in Figure 5-13.

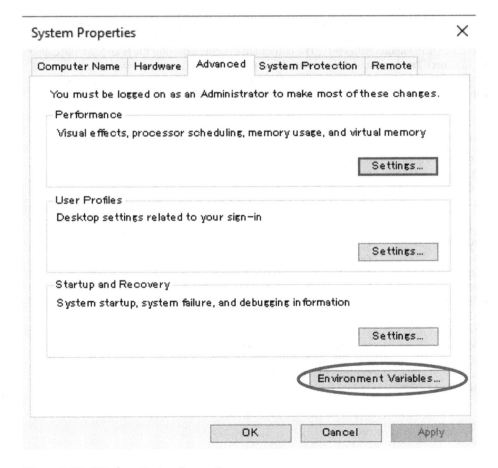

Figure 5-13. Windows System Properties screen

Click the Environment Variables button at the bottom-side of the window. Then, you will see a list of environment variables for the current user and the system wide settings. Edit the Path environment variables and add *C:\Program Files\MySQL\MySQL Cluster 7.5\bin*, for example.

The MSI package doesn't set up Windows Service for MySQL NDB Cluster daemons. So, you need to do this by hand, just like with the Zip package installation. As of MySQL NDB Cluster 7.5, the MSI package doesn't initialize the data directory for an SQL node either. On the other hand, the initial data directory is included in older versions.

Installation on macOS

On *macOS* (also known as *OS X* or *mac OS X*), two types of packages are available. One is the *compressed tar ball (tar.gz)* package, just like on Linux. The other is the *native installer package* installation.

The Tar.gz Archive Package Installation

Installing the tar.gz package on macOS is just like the Linux process. See the section "Tar.gz Archive Package Installation" described earlier in this chapter.

However, the way to set up automatic startup and shutdown for MySQL Server as a service differs. macOS employs launchd for this purpose. To set up a service on launchd, place the service configuration file under the */Library/LaunchDaemons* directory. The content of the configuration file is an XML file called *property list* (or *plist* in short). The format of the property list is pre-defined. The easiest way to make a desired launchd configuration file is to copy the one from the native package, described in the next section. Listing 5-10 is a property list file included in the macOS native package (com.oracle.oss.mysql.mysqld. plist).

Listing 5-10. Contents of MySQL Property List for Launchd on macOS

```
<?xml version="1.0" encoding="UTF-8"?>
<!DOCTYPE plist PUBLIC "-//Apple Computer//DTD PLIST 1.0//EN" "http://www.apple.com/DTDs/
PropertyList-1.0.dtd">
<plist version="1.0">
<dict>
    <key>Label</key>              <string>com.oracle.oss.mysql.mysqld</string>
    <key>ProcessType</key>        <string>Interactive</string>
    <key>Disabled</key>           <false/>
    <key>RunAtLoad</key>          <true/>
    <key>KeepAlive</key>          <true/>
    <key>SessionCreate</key>      <true/>
    <key>LaunchOnlyOnce</key>     <false/>
    <key>UserName</key>           <string>_mysql</string>
    <key>GroupName</key>          <string>_mysql</string>
    <key>ExitTimeOut</key>        <integer>600</integer>
    <key>Program</key>            <string>/usr/local/mysql/bin/mysqld</string>
    <key>ProgramArguments</key>
```

```
    <array>
        <string>/usr/local/mysql/bin/mysqld</string>
        <string>--user=_mysql</string>
        <string>--basedir=/usr/local/mysql</string>
        <string>--datadir=/usr/local/mysql/data</string>
        <string>--plugin-dir=/usr/local/mysql/lib/plugin</string>
        <string>--log-error=/usr/local/mysql/data/mysqld.local.err</string>
        <string>--pid-file=/usr/local/mysql/data/mysqld.local.pid</string>
    </array>
    <key>WorkingDirectory</key>  <string>/usr/local/mysql</string>
</dict>
</plist>
```

If required, fix the program path and arguments written in the plist file. Automatic startup and shutdown is enabled at this stage. The OS reads every configuration file for a *launch daemon* if the configuration file exists. While the server will start MySQL Server upon the next OS restart, it has not started yet. To start the server immediately, run launchctl:

```
shell$ su
shell# launchctl load /Library/LaunchDaemons/com.oracle.oss.mysql.mysqld.plist
```

You can stop MySQL Server by running launchctl unload, instead of launchctl load. To disable automatic startup and shutdown, modify the plist file and set the value of RunAtLoad to false.

macOS Native Package Installation

The native package for macOS has a suffix of .pkg. Installation using the native (.pkg) package is very simple and easy and completed using the GUI wizard. The package is distributed in the *Apple Disk Image*, which has the .dmg suffix and can be mounted as a file system as if it were an ordinal disk. To mount it, double-click the DMG file. Figure 5-14 shows the Finder, which mounts the MySQL NDB Cluster package.

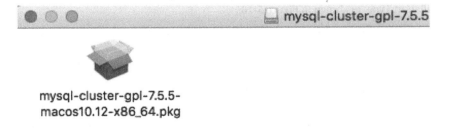

Figure 5-14. *MySQL NDB Cluster DMG file is mounted*

To begin installation, double-click the .pkg file. The installer wizard is displayed, as shown in Figure 5-15. Click Continue to proceed.

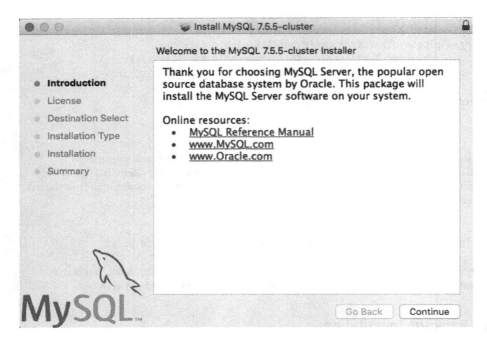

Figure 5-15. *Introduction page of MySQL NDB Cluster installer on macOS*

The next screen is a license agreement. If you're using the Community version, the license is GPLv2. Otherwise, it will be Oracle Corporation's proprietary license. When you click Continue on the license agreement screen, a dialog box is displayed. If you agree to the license, click Agree to proceed.

The next screen is Installation Type, as shown in Figure 5-16.

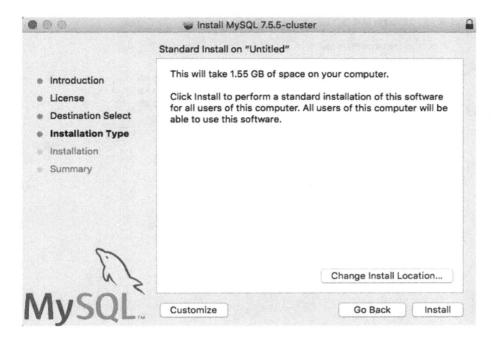

Figure 5-16. Installation type on MySQL NDB Cluster installer on macOS

Initially, Destination Select is skipped. When you click the Change Install Location button, the wizard goes back to Destination Select, but you cannot change it from the default.

When you click Customize, you will see the screen like the one in Figure 5-17. On this screen, you can select or deselect the installed components. Each component includes the following contents:

- **MySQL Server:** Main body of the MySQL NDB Cluster program, including all types of server daemons and client programs. At the least, you need to install this package.

- **Preference Pane:** This package adds the MySQL preference pane in the *System Preferences* in macOS.

- **Launchd Support:** Configuration information for *launchd*, which manages automatic startup and shutdown on macOS.

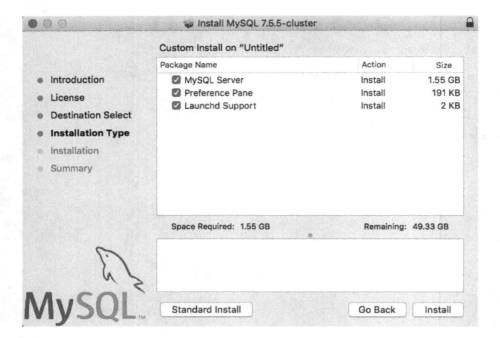

Figure 5-17. Component selection screen on MySQL NDB Cluster installer on macOS

By default, all components are installed, and I recommend installing all of them. Click Install to proceed.

At the beginning of the installation process, a dialog to input the current OS user password is displayed. It is required to gain superuser (root) privilege to write files into the file system. Once installation completes, a password for root@localhost for the installed MySQL Server is displayed, as shown in Figure 5-18. The password is generated randomly. So, you will see a different password on this screen. (Don't worry that the actual password is displayed in Figure 5-18. I don't use this password anymore.) Do not close the window until you copy your password elsewhere. If you like, press *Command+Shift+3* to take a screenshot. The screenshot will be saved onto your desktop.

Figure 5-18. *Summary screen on MySQL NDB Cluster installer on macOS*

The server is installed in a subdirectory under the */usr/local* directory, and the installer creates a symbolic link called */usr/local/mysql* to the installation directory. Add */usr/local/mysql/bin* to your PATH environment variable for easy access to MySQL programs.

On the macOS native package setup, it is very easy to configure automatic startup and shutdown. To configure that, open *System Preferences* and find *MySQL* at the bottom. When you click the *MySQL* icon, you will see a configuration dialog like the one in Figure 5-19. You can stop or start the server and enable or disable automatic startup and shutdown.

■ **Note**   Once configuration is changed using the MySQL Preferences pane, the launch daemon configuration file under */Library/LaunchDaemons* is converted to the binary plist format. To revert back to the XML format, run `plutil -convert xml1 com.oracle.oss.mysql.mysqld.plist` against the plist file.

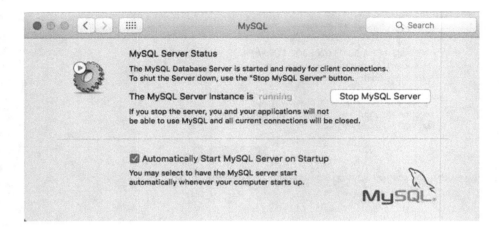

Figure 5-19. *MySQL preference pane on macOS*

Installing MySQL NDB Cluster Instances Using Auto Installer

MySQL NDB Cluster Auto Installer (*Auto Installer*, in short) is a supplemental tool to set up MySQL NDB Cluster instances from the Web GUI interface. Auto Installer isn't a package installation tool, but a tool to set up node instances easily. This means that packages should be installed in advance.

To start Auto Installer, run ndb_setup.py installed together with the MySQL NDB Cluster package. As the filename suggests, ndb_setup.py is a Python program. So, you need Python interpreter installed on your target system. The required Python interpreter version is 2.6 or higher. In addition, two Python libraries— *Paramko* 1.7.7.1 or higher and *Pycypto* 2.6 or higher—are required. Install these programs in your target system preliminarily.

Since ndb_setup.py executes commands on remote hosts via SSH protocol, the SSH server must be running on remote hosts. It is also necessary to set up users to log in to remote servers. Remote logins via SSH are made using the user who executes ndb_setup.py unless the username is explicitly specified in the username/password pair, as described later in this section. So, basically you need to create remote users with the same name as the local user. Instances will be initialized and started using that user. If you want to run MySQL NDB Cluster programs using the mysql user, allow the user to log in. (Usually, mysql user login is disabled for security reasons.) Listing 5-11 is example output when ndb_setup.py runs from command line.

Listing 5-11. Running ndb_setup.py from the Command Line

```
shell$ ./ndb_setup.py
Running out of install dir: /opt/mysql-cluster/bin
Starting web server on port 8081
deathkey=787953
Press CTRL+C to stop web server.
The application should now be running in your browser.
(Alternatively you can navigate to http://localhost:8081/welcome.html to start it)
```

See that the program listens to TCP/IP port 8081 as a default port. You can change it by specifying the --port option in the command line. The command automatically opens your browser and shows the screen in Figure 5-20.

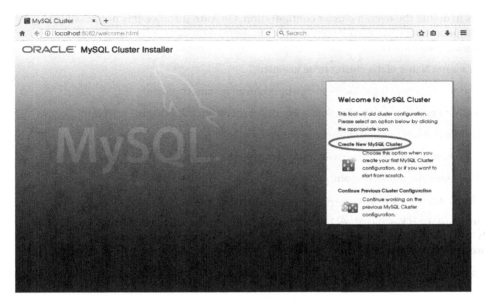

Figure 5-20. *Initial screen of MySQL Cluster Auto Installer*

Click Create New MySQL Cluster to set up the new installation. A wizard style setup screen is displayed, as shown in Figure 5-21.

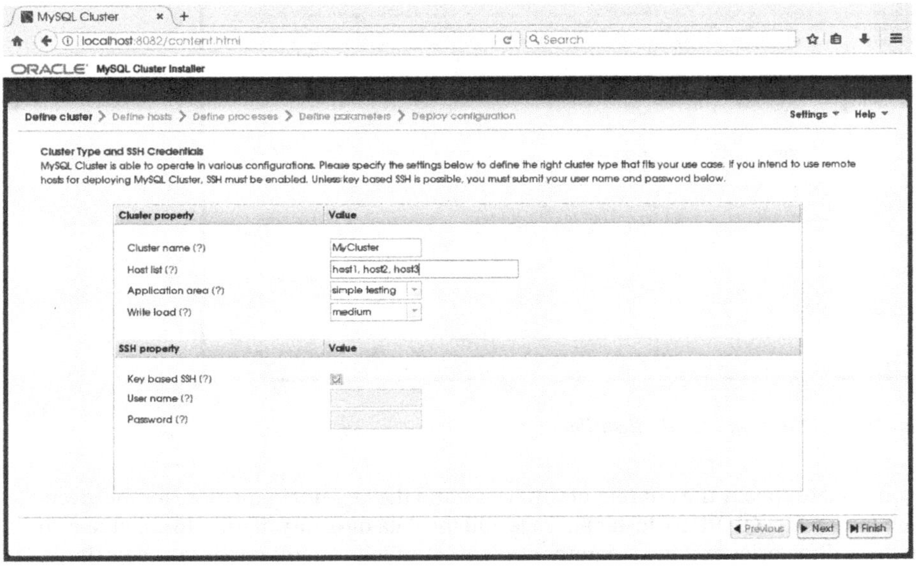

Figure 5-21. *The Define Cluster screen on Auto Installer*

The first task is to define the overall cluster configuration. On Auto Installer, it is not possible to fine-tune individual parameters, but a brief configuration is defined on this screen. Each input box stands for the following parameters:

- **Cluster name:** Name of the cluster to be installed.

- **Host list:** Comma-separated list of hosts where cluster instances reside.

- **Application area:** Type of application to use the cluster from the following selection:

  - **Simple testing:** Minimum resource configuration for testing

  - **Web:** Maximum resource configuration for given hardware

  - **Real-time:** Minimize response time

- **Write load:** Amount of write transactions (choose one from Low, Medium, and High).

- **SSH credentials:** If Key Based SSH is checked, SSH authentication is made using a public key, which is registered beforehand. Otherwise, specify the username and password for authentication.

Click Next to proceed. The next screen is a configuration screen for host details, as shown in Figure 5-22.

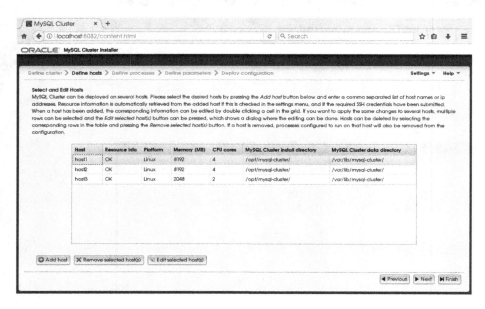

Figure 5-22. *Details of host definition in Auto Installer*

In this screen, you need to specify the number of CPU cores and the amount of memory for the given hosts, as well as a path for the MySQL NDB Cluster package and the data directory. If Auto Installer fails to find the programs in these directories or if the programs don't have sufficient permissions to access these data directories, the installation will fail later. Make sure that the package installation directory is correct and that the owner, group, and permission of data directories are correct. Click Next to proceed.

The next screen is a process definition, as shown in Figure 5-23.

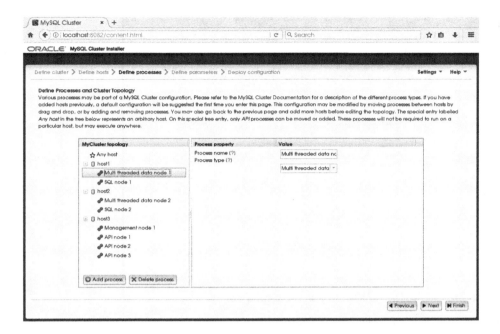

Figure 5-23. *Process definition in Auto Installer*

On this screen, you define which host will have which types of nodes. Click Add Process to add a new node to the host. You can move a node by drag and drop it onto another host. Click Next to proceed. The next step is to define the parameters, as shown in Figure 5-24.

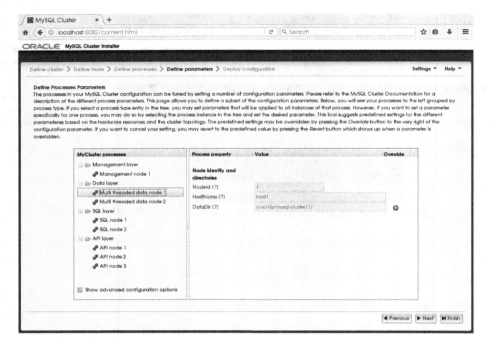

Figure 5-24. *Defining the process parameters in Auto Installer*

You can change basic parameters such as the data directory, the socket, and the port number for SQL node. Again, it is not possible to fine-tune detailed parameters on Auto Installer. Click Next to proceed. The next screen is the final installation step, as shown in Figure 5-25.

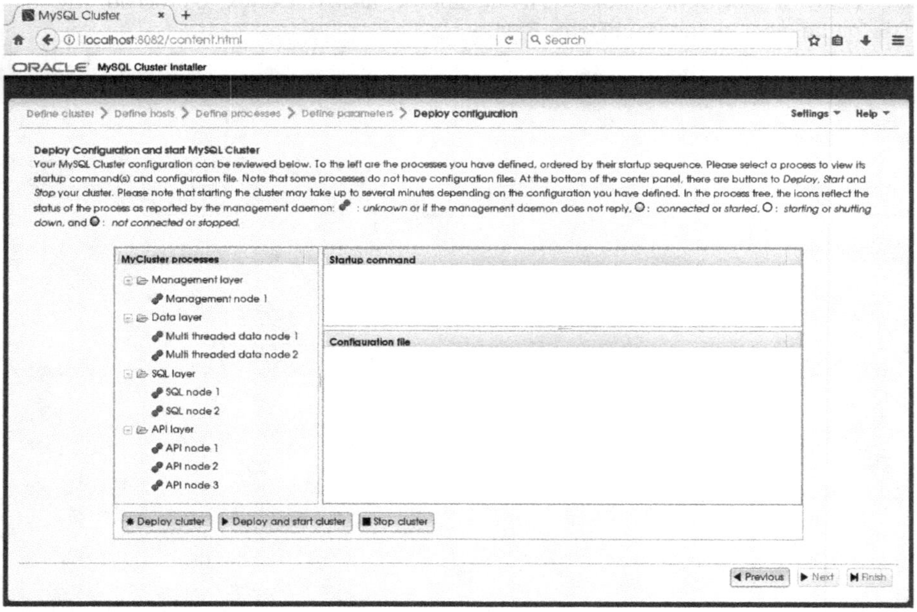

Figure 5-25. *Deploy, start, and stop a cluster in Auto Installer*

As you can see, Auto Installer's functionality is very limited. It is not feasible for daily use. For example, it is possible to start and stop the entire cluster, but it's not possible to stop or start an individual node. Rolling restarts are not possible, either. Try Auto Installer if you want to set up MySQL NDB Cluster quickly for evaluation purposes. It might still be a good starting point for further fine-tuning as well.

Verifying Installation

Once all the installation steps have finished, verify that the installation was successful.

Configuration Files

Before starting the cluster, make sure that the configuration files, such as *config.ini* and *my.cnf,* are completed and the intended options are set. For the MySQL Server daemon mysqld (and other non-NDB programs), you can easily verify if the options are read and set to their desired values. Run mysqld with the --print-defaults option:

```
shell$ mysqld --print-defaults
mysqld would have been started with the following arguments:
--character-set-server=utf8 --user=mysql --port=3306 ...
```

It lists all the options specified in the command line or the option file (*my.cnf*).

For NDB programs, --print-defaults doesn't work. The management server daemon, ndb_mgmd, requires a path to the configuration file as a command line option. You don't need to worry about which option files are actually read by the program. While ndb_mgmd has an option named --print-full-config, it prints all the options, including the unchanged ones for all available slots. It is not handy to check quickly whether the option values are set correctly. Instead, it is useful to check if the configuration file is formed properly. When --print-full-config is specified, ndb_mgmd parses the given configuration file as if it were a usual startup, so it ensures that the option names are correct and that the values are in range.

Initial Startup

Once the configuration has completed, the next step is to start the cluster. At the very first startup, the cluster initializes its data directory and creates data files on the management node and data node. So, some configurations, such as FragmentLogFileSize, cannot be changed without re-initializing the data once initialization has been done. In other words, before you store any data on your cluster, you can wipe the whole data and restart the cluster as many times as you need.

Listing 5-12 shows an example command to start the management node. While it is an initial startup, the --initial option can be omitted.

Listing 5-12. Starting Management Node at the First Time

```
shell$ /opt/mysql-cluster/bin/ndb_mgmd -f /etc/mysql-cluster/config.ini\
        --configdir=/var/lib/mysql-cluster
MySQL Cluster Management Server mysql-5.7.17 ndb-7.5.5
```

Once all the management nodes have been started, the next step is starting the data nodes. Listing 5-13 is a typical command to start a data node. Start all the data nodes using the command shown in Listing 5-13. In this example, a multi-threaded version of the data node (ndbmtd) is employed.

Listing 5-13. Starting a Data Node the First Time

```
shell$ /opt/mysql-cluster/bin/ndbd -c nodeid=1,host3:1186
2017-01-30 16:56:09 [ndbd] INFO     -- Angel connected to host3:1186'
2017-01-30 16:56:09 [ndbd] INFO     -- Angel allocated nodeid: 1
```

It will take some time to complete the startup of the data nodes. To verify if the data nodes have started, issue an ALL STATUS command from the ndb_mgm CLI, as shown in Listing 5-14.

Listing 5-14. Checking the Data Node Status from ndb_mgm CLI

```
shell$ ndb_mgm
-- NDB Cluster -- Management Client --
Connected to Management Server at: 127.0.0.1:1186
ndb_mgm> all status
Node 1: started (mysql-5.7.17 ndb-7.5.5)
Node 2: started (mysql-5.7.17 ndb-7.5.5)
```

The final step is to start the SQL nodes. The command to start the SQL node is the same as the standard MySQL Server. For example, if the server package is installed using RPM on the RHEL7 system, you can start the SQL node using the systemctl command like so:

```
shell$ sudo systemctl start mysqld.service
```

Checking the Status

The most basic operation to verify if the cluster is running properly is to see its status. First, connect the cluster using ndb_mgm CLI and issue the SHOW command, as shown in Listing 5-15. Check if all the nodes are connected and their status is okay.

Listing 5-15. Sample SHOW Command Output

```
shell$ ndb_mgm
-- NDB Cluster -- Management Client --
ndb_mgm> SHOW
Connected to Management Server at: 127.0.0.1:1186
Cluster Configuration
---------------------
[ndbd(NDB)]     2 node(s)
id=1    @host1  (mysql-5.7.17 ndb-7.5.5, Nodegroup: 0, *)
id=2    @host2  (mysql-5.7.17 ndb-7.5.5, Nodegroup: 0)

[ndb_mgmd(MGM)] 1 node(s)
id=255 @host3  (mysql-5.7.17 ndb-7.5.5)

[mysqld(API)]   7 node(s)
id=50   @host1  (mysql-5.7.17 ndb-7.5.5)
id=51   @host1  (mysql-5.7.17 ndb-7.5.5)
id=52   @host2  (mysql-5.7.17 ndb-7.5.5)
id=53   @host2  (mysql-5.7.17 ndb-7.5.5)
```

For more details about the procedure to start or stop the cluster, refer to Chapter 10.

After all the nodes are ready, run the queries against on the SQL node to check if the cluster is running properly. Create a test database and a test table using the NDBCluster storage engine, then insert some rows and query the table. If the commands work without any problems, your installation is successful.

Uninstalling Packages

If you have stopped using MySQL NDB Cluster and you do not need the packages anymore, you should uninstall them from your system. To uninstall MySQL NDB Cluster, first shut down the cluster. Optionally, remove data files and configuration files if you don't need them anymore.

The uninstallation steps vary depending on package type, as described in the following sections.

Tar.gz and Zip Archive Package

These types of packages can be uninstalled by removing installed files. If you installed the package into */opt/mysql-cluster* on Linux, for example, just run the rm command as follows:

```
shell$ su
shell# rm -rf /opt/mysql-cluster
```

On Windows, remove the installation directory using Windows Explorer.

Make sure that the installed services are removed, too.

On Linux, services are removed using chkconfig --del or systemctl disable. Both commands require a service name as the last argument. Consult with the operating system manuals for more details. You also need to remove the installed script file, such as /etc/init.d/mysql, and the systemd configuration file such as */usr/lib/systemd/system/mysql.service*.

On Windows, run daemon programs using the --remove option. This should be done before removing the package files. Alternatively, you can remove the service using sc.exe. This can be done after uninstalling the package.

```
PS C:\> sc.exe delete NDB75
[SC] DeleteService SUCCESS
```

Note that sc is aliased for Set-Content on *Windows PowerShell*. So, sc.exe should be executed with the *.exe* suffix. Otherwise, a file named delete with content NDB75 is created under the current working directory.

On macOS, run launchctl unload to stop the server. This command requires a plist file as the last argument. Then, delete the plist file.

RPM Package

You can uninstall the package using the rpm command with the -e option. No extra steps are needed.

Windows Installer Package

You can delete a Windows Installer package from the *Windows Settings*. Click *System*, then *Apps & Features* to open list of installed application packages. Choose *MySQL Cluster* from the list of applications, which is sorted alphabetically. Click *Uninstall* to uninstall the package.

macOS Native Package

Before you begin, make sure that the service has stopped. You can stop the service from the system preferences or using the `launchctl unload` command.

Unfortunately, macOS doesn't have command to uninstall a native package. This surely is very inconvenient. This means that installed files must be removed manually. The first step is to inspect which packages are installed on your system, like so:

```
shell$ pkgutil --pkgs | grep mysql
com.mysql.launchd
com.mysql.mysql
com.mysql.prefpane
```

You can see three MySQL related packages. These are the MySQL launch daemon, MySQL NDB Cluster main package, and MySQL System Preference Pane. The following commands remove all files included in these packages as the root user:

```
shell# rm -rf /usr/local/mysql*
shell# rm -rf /Library/LaunchDaemons/com.oracle.*.mysqld.plist
shell# rm -rf /Library/PreferencePanes/MySQL.prefPane
```

■ **Note**   You can identify the location where the files are installed using `pkgutil --info`, and which files are installed using `pkgutil --files`.

Then, remove the package information from the package manager.

```
shell# pkgutil --forget com.mysql.launchd
shell# pkgutil --forget com.mysql.mysql
shell# pkgutil --forget com.mysql.prefpane
```

Summary

This chapter discussed the installation types available for each platform and how to install MySQL NDB Cluster packages on each system. Installation is not a difficult process, but it's very important. Installation must be always perfect in the production system. Without appropriate installation, your system will not function correctly.

Each installation type has its pros and cons. Determine which installation type is most suitable for your system and perform the installation smoothly. Care must be taken, especially when installing non-installer packages.

CHAPTER 6

Replication

Replication is one of the most popular features of MySQL. It allows one or more slaves to have an identical data copy of the master. It is a very useful feature; thus, it has a variety of applications. MySQL NDB Cluster also has a replication facility, called *NDB Cluster Replication*. This chapter explains how to use it and what it can be used for.

NDB Cluster Replication Overview

Before discussing how to use NDB Cluster replication, this section contains an overview of NDB Cluster replication.

Replication Architecture Overview

On standard MySQL replications, the master records all modifications into a special log file called the *binary log*, and the log contents are sent to the slave immediately after each event is ready. Binary log contents are written when a transaction is committed for transactional storage engine, and after each query for non-transactional storage engine. Each content of the binary log is a unit of modification against the database in a "replayable" format. Binary log content can be executed so that it causes the identical modification as the originating transaction or query. Thus, it is possible to replay identical data changes as on the master by applying a series of binary log contents continuously.

Figure 6-1 is a schematic view of standard MySQL replication. On the master, the *master thread* sends contents of binary log to the slave. This thread is also known as the *binlog sender thread*. The binlog sender thread is just a normal connection thread, but the command being executed is different from the norm. The command is COM_BINLOG_DUMP, which continuously sends binlog contents to the slave connected as a client.

© Jesper Wisborg Krogh and Mikiya Okuno 2017

J. W. Krogh and M. Okuno, *Pro MySQL NDB Cluster*, https://doi.org/10.1007/978-1-4842-2982-8_6

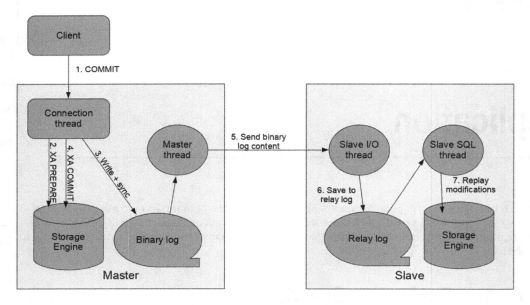

Figure 6-1. *Standard MySQL replication (with InnoDB) architecture overview*

The slave has two types of threads. One for receiving binary log contents and writing them into *relay log*, the other for replaying relay log contents. The former is called the *slave I/O thread* and the latter is called the *slave SQL thread*.

The slave I/O thread receives binary log contents continuously, then stores them into an intermediate log called the *relay log*. Once writes to the relay log are completed, the slave SQL thread executes the content and apply the modification to its underlying database. In Figure 6-1, database is depicted as the storage engine, as the true entity holding data is the storage engine.

All relevant threads in Figure 6-1 are not synchronized by default. Since the master doesn't wait until the slaves applies the modifications, the slave data will in general lag slightly compared to the master data. This type of replication is called *asynchronous replication*. However, the slave data is catching up on master data closely all the time, because every step depicted in Figure 6-1 is performed very quickly.

■ **Note**   MySQL replication has a special mode called *semi-synchronous replication*, which lets the connection thread on the master wait until the slave I/O thread has written the binlog content to its relay log and synced to disk. Semi-synchronous replication ensures that there is not data loss on the slave in the event of the master crashing. This feature is useful when implementing failover topology on *1:N replication* setup. On standard MySQL replication, it is possible to connect multiple slaves for one master. With 1:N replication setup, one slave is promoted to the master when existing master crashes. Since MySQL replication is asynchronous, there is a small chance you'll lose the latest modifications when the master crashes. Semi-synchronous replication solves this problem. However, semi-synchronous replication is not supported on MySQL NDB Cluster, thus it's out of the scope of this book.

MySQL NDB Cluster implements asynchronous replication over standard MySQL replication. An SQL node collects all modifications done on the cluster and records them into its local binary log. Such an SQL node can work as a master to send modifications to slaves. Figure 6-2 shows an overview of NDB Cluster Replication.

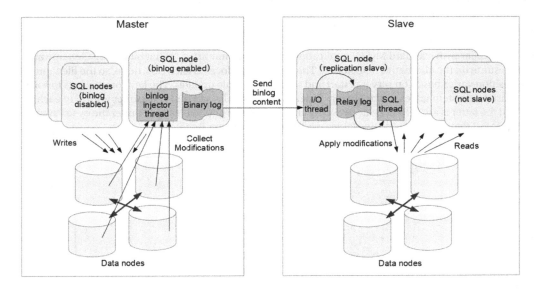

Figure 6-2. *NDB Cluster Replication architecture overview*

The key architecture of NDB Cluster Replication is that modifications done on data nodes are sent to an SQL node where binary log is enabled. Without this mechanism, the master SQL node cannot keep track of modifications done on other SQL nodes. On a standard MySQL Server, all modifications done within the server can be tracked by the server, then serialized and written to the binary log. On an SQL node of MySQL NDB Cluster, such implementation is impossible because changes will be made on other SQL nodes and other types of API nodes as well. On MySQL NDB Cluster, the actual data modification is made in the data nodes. Thus, data nodes continuously send all modifications to SQL nodes where the binary log is enabled. Modification data is sent upon every *micro-GCP*.

Although the micro-GCP is a data source of the redo log on the data node, the micro-GCP is not written to disk unlike usual the *GCP (Global checkpoint)*. Micro-GCP is a mechanism to synchronize data among data nodes. A set of transactions included in one micro-GCP is called an *epoch*, which are committed simultaneously at a certain period. So, the contents of every epoch, called *events*, is ensured to be synchronized among all data nodes. Micro-GCP is executed more often than GCP. By default, micro-GCP is done every 100 milliseconds and GCP is done every two seconds. This allows a data node to send the events to the SQL node much quicker than if the data node had been sending the events every GCP.

On the SQL node, events from the data nodes are handled by a dedicated thread called *binlog injector thread*. It receives all events and serializes them, then writes them to the binary log. Thus, the binary log is a serialized history of all modifications made on the cluster, just like standard MySQL replication.

■ **Note**   Since binlog injector receives all events from data nodes, the SQL node becomes very busy especially when the cluster has many data nodes. This is one of the reasons we recommend having dedicated SQL nodes to handle the binary logging.

Replication Channel Failover

Since the data node can send events and the source of binary log content to an arbitrary SQL node, more than one SQL node can have the binary log at the same time, and we strongly recommend you do this. Since the SQL node cannot receive events while it's offline, we need spare SQL nodes with binary logging enabled for redundancy. When the active master SQL node crashes or is shut down, the replication must be resumed using an alternative SQL node, because the binary log contents are completely lost while the SQL node is offline. This is a very important concept for NDB Cluster Replication.

If you are familiar with standard MySQL replication, a question may arise. "What binary log filename and position will resume on the alternative SQL node?" The binary log is local to each SQL node, so the filename and binlog position varies based on server restart and server local table updates. The key components to solve this problem are two system tables—ndb_binlog_index and ndb_apply_status. The former is local to each SQL node, and the latter is an NDB table accessed by all SQL nodes. These tables exist under the mysql system database. Figure 6-3 depicts how these two tables work with NDB Cluster Replication.

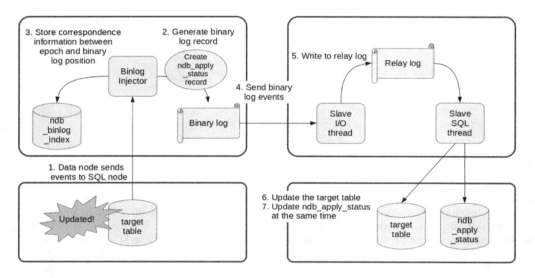

Figure 6-3. *Function of ndb_binlog_index and ndb_apply_status system tables*

The binlog injector thread records the correspondence between epochs and binary log positions into the ndb_binlog_index table. Since the unit of modification on MySQL NDB Cluster is an epoch, the unit of binary log events is an epoch as well. This means that the slave can apply an epoch as if it were a single inseparable chunk of modification, that is a transaction. So, the binlog injector records the beginning of each epoch within the binary log.

Then, the binlog injector thread generates an original record within each binlog event, which updates ndb_apply_status table. The event keeps track of which epoch is included in the binary log event. Since the modification of the ndb_apply_status table is included in the same event, the slave SQL thread updates ndb_apply_status along with the original modification for target tables within the same transaction. Thus, you can find the very latest epoch applied to the slave cluster in the ndb_apply_status table.

So, when you switch to an alternative replication channel, you need to read the latest epoch from the ndb_apply_status table on a slave SQL node, then find the corresponding binary log filename and position based on the retrieved epoch. We'll discuss details of the failover procedure later in this chapter.

NDB Cluster Replication Tables

Table 6-1 summarizes system tables related to NDB Cluster Replication. Note that all the tables in Table 6-1 reside in the mysql system database.

Table 6-1. *List of NDB Cluster Replication Tables*

Name	Used On	Description
ndb_binlog_index	Master	Binlog injector records correspondence between binary log position and epoch into this table.
ndb_apply_status	Slave	Binlog injector generates a dummy event to update of this table even though update is not really done on master cluster. On the slave side, slave SQL thread updates this table as part of replication. The content of this table indicates the latest epoch on the master cluster where the slave cluster catches up.
ndb_schema	Both	Synchronize schema information among SQL nodes using this table.
ndb_replication	Depends	Configuration table for conflict detection and resolution.

The ndb_schema table isn't involved in NDB Cluster Replication itself; however, the table is monitored using the same mechanism of NDB Cluster Replication.

You might notice that this table cannot be found on the mysql system database using the SHOW TABLES command and information schema. The table is hidden, but it exists. You can query the content of ndb_schema table using the SELECT statement. This table stores the definition of all tables, tablespaces, and logfile groups for NDBCluster storage engine. This table is updated upon DDL statements on the SQL node where the statement is issued. On all SQL nodes, binlog injector monitors this table. So, other SQL nodes can detect if any changes are detected on this table. Then, an SQL node updates local data dictionary, as we say the *.frm* file, according to the definition in ndb_schema table. Even if binary logging is disabled, the binlog injector thread runs and monitors only the ndb_schema table, because the schema changes cannot be detected without monitoring this table. The ndb_schema table is also described in Chapter 9.

The ndb_replication table is used to configure conflict detection and resolution. This table doesn't exist initially. So, the table must be created in order to configure conflict detection and resolution. Details of the table are covered later in this chapter.

Use Cases and Advantages of NDB Cluster Replication

The way NDB Cluster Replication is implemented, in that it uses the same mechanism as standard MySQL replication, is a great decision in my opinion. As discussed in the previous section, data is synchronized without using a special communication channel, but synchronized using the binary log and the MySQL protocol. It has definitive advantages like these:

- It is possible to configure NDB Cluster Replication between two MySQL NDB Clusters as well as between MySQL NDB Cluster and a standard MySQL server (InnoDB).

- For existing MySQL users, it is possible to manage NDB Cluster Replication in a familiar way. This reduces learning costs for new NDB Cluster Replication users.

- It is possible to configure NDB Cluster Replication in various topologies just like standard MySQL replication.

NDB Cluster replication is very flexible. There are thousands of ways to use it. The following use cases are well known:

- **Disaster recovery:** Make the data service available on alternative sites even when a disaster occurred, and the whole data center becomes unusable, as depicted in Figure 6-4. Data is transferred over the Internet using secure connection (TSL) or via a private network.

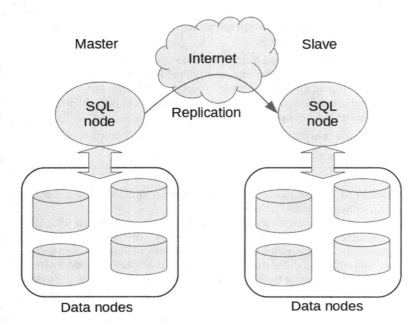

Figure 6-4. *Disaster recovery configuration using NDB Cluster Replication*

- **Stand-by cluster for maintenance:** Used for various maintenance tasks such as taking a backup to avoid workload on primary cluster, planned switch over for heavy maintenance tasks like redistributing partitions for adding data nodes, and copying schema changes.

- **Read scaling:** 1:N topology for scaling purposes just like standard MySQL replication is also applicable for MySQL NDB Cluster. Although MySQL NDB Cluster has good scalability, it is not good at some types of queries. Replicating from MySQL NDB Cluster to InnoDB will solve such read scalability problems, as depicted in Figure 6-5.

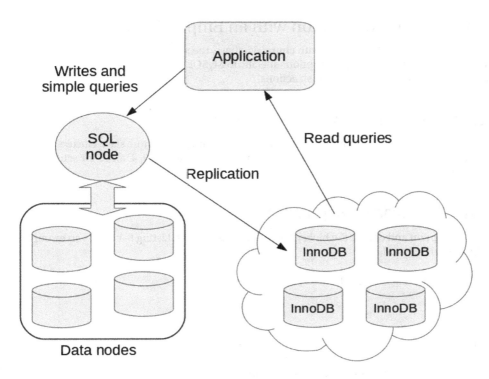

Figure 6-5. *Read scaling by replicating from MySQL NDB Cluster to InnoDB*

To make your NDB Cluster Replication setup productive, make it clear what the replication is used for. In other words, clarify the application needs and recognize why NDB Cluster Replication is required. Without such a definitive purpose, your system will not be utilized well.

Setting Up NDB Cluster Replication

In this section, we discuss how to set up NDB Cluster Replication. As the architecture of NDB Cluster Replication is close to the standard MySQL replication, the setup procedure is close as well. While they are close, they are somewhat different.

When it comes to setting up NDB Cluster Replication, consider the following scenarios:

- Set up fresh cluster instances with replication. As instances are newly installed, clusters don't have any data in advance.

- Install a new cluster instance as a replication slave for an existing cluster instance.

- Set up alternative replication channel upon replication failure.

Let's see detailed procedures of these scenarios.

Setting Up NDB Cluster Replication with an Empty Database

In the scenario to set up NDB Cluster Replication with empty database, the procedure to set up replication is identical to standard MySQL servers, except for options specific to MySQL NDB Cluster. To complete the NDB Cluster Replication setup, use the following instructions.

Set Up Master and Slave Clusters

You need at least two clusters to set up replication—one master cluster and one or more slave clusters. Set up the clusters with required configuration per application needs. See Chapters 3, 4, and 5 for setup procedures and configurations.

Configure Master SQL Node for Replication

Configure the `server_id` option and enable the binary log with the ROW format. Listing 6-1 shows an example configuration for the master SQL node.

Listing 6-1. Example Configuration for the Master SQL Node

```
[mysqld]
server_id = 1
log_bin = mysql-bin
binlog_format = ROW
```

Since NDB Cluster Replication only supports the ROW binary log format, the `binlog_format` option should be set to a value other than STATEMENT. As of MySQL Server 5.7 and MySQL NDB Cluster 7.5, the default value for `binlog_format` is ROW. So, explicit setting of `binlog_format` is optional on MySQL NDB Cluster 7.5 or newer.

Ensure that every SQL node has a unique, specific, separate `server_id` and no combinations of SQL node have the same `server_id` within all SQL nodes on all clusters, including slaves. This is a common requirement with standard MySQL replication.

■ **Note**   Do not enable GTID, which is not yet supported for MySQL NDB Cluster.

If the SQL node is already running, you need to restart `mysqld` to enable the binary log and the other related changes. If the SQL node has not stated yet, start it at this stage. The following command is an example command to start the server on a Linux host with the old style `init` script. Start the server according to your system procedures.

```
shell$ su
shell# service mysqld start
```

Create a User for Replication on Master

Just like with standard MySQL replication, a slave connects to its master as a client. So, a user account for the slave is required on the master. Listing 6-2 shows an example command to create the user account with the appropriate privilege. The required privilege for the slave user account is REPLICATION SLAVE.

Listing 6-2. Creating a Replication User on the Master SQL Node

```
mysql> CREATE USER repl@slavehost IDENTIFIED BY 'slavepass';
mysql> GRANT REPLICATION SLAVE ON *.* TO repl@slavehost;
```

Currently, MySQL replication doesn't support authentication plugins other than the native password and sha256_password. Don't create a slave user with an unsupported plugin.

Configure Slave SQL Node for Replication

The only configuration option required for the slave is server_id. Other options can be left unchanged. Since server_id doesn't have a default value, it must be specified explicitly. Listing 6-3 is an example configuration for slave SQL node. Suppose that other required options for NDBCluster storage engine are omitted in this listing.

Listing 6-3. Example Configuration for the Slave SQL Node

```
[mysqld]
server_id = 101
skip_slave_start
```

You can find yet another option, skip_slave_start, in Listing 6-3. This option is necessary if the replication setup has more than one replication channel, which is discussed later in this chapter.

Since server_id is a dynamic variable, you can change the value using the SET GLOBAL command if you have already started the slave SQL node. If you haven't started the slave, start it to continue the replication setup.

■ **Caution**   Don't change the server_id once you have configured replication, because MySQL replication assumes that server_id is immutable throughout the replication lifecycle.

Configure Replication

Now configure the SQL node as a replication slave. Since we assume that no data is written on the cluster, it is not necessary to specify the binlog filename and position. Listing 6-4 shows an example command to set up a new slave using the CHANGE MASTER TO command.

Listing 6-4. CHANGE MASTER TO Command to Set Up a New Slave

```
mysql> CHANGE MASTER TO
    -> MASTER_HOST='masterhost',
    -> MASTER_USER='repl,
    -> MASTER_PASSWORD='PASSWORD',
    -> MASTER_PORT=3306;
```

■ **Tip**   Since the replication connection in basically a normal client connection, the MASTER_HOST, MASTER_ USER, MASTER_PASSWORD, and MASTER_PORT options are equivalent to the --host, --user, --password, and --port options for the mysql command-line client.

Secure the Connection for Replication (Optional)

If you like, it is possible to protect network communication between master and slave using a secure connection. To enable TLS connection for replication, you need to configure both master and slave properly. See Chapter 12 for details about how to set up secure connection in general. It is particularly necessary to set up certificates on the master to enable secure connection.

On the slave, you need to specify MASTER_SSL=1 on the CHANGE MASTER TO command, as shown in Listing 6-5.

Listing 6-5. Enabling TLS Connection for Replication

```
mysql> STOP SLAVE;
mysql> CHANGE MASTER TO MASTER_SSL=1;
mysql> START SLAVE;
```

A secure connection is enabled in just this much of the procedure. The connection between master and slave is ensured to be encrypted. However, there is still some room to improve security. At this stage, slaves can connect whether connections are encrypted or not. To enforce encrypted connection for all slaves, make TLS connection mandatory for the replication user. This can be achieved using the following command on the master.

```
mysql> ALTER USER repl@slavehost REQUIRE SSL;
```

This requires the user repl@slavehost to log in using an encrypted connection only. This makes replication much safer than unencrypted connection. However, some risks still remain in this setup. The problem is that the server allows connections to any accounts from any hosts only if the given credentials are valid. It sounds flawless that an authentication works properly; however, credential authentication cannot avoid the following two problems:

- If a credential for replication user is stolen or identified by *brute force attack*, an attacker may receive binary log events by using a fake slave server which pretends to be a real slave. This allows an attacker to steal important data from the replication setup.

- A slave may connect to a fake master that pretends to be a real master, because a master only accepts or rejects authentication from slaves and no authentication is required for a master itself. This allows an attacker to send fake malicious data to a slave to malfunction the victim application.

To prevent such problems, TLS has a mechanism to identify a connection peer using *certificates*. If a connection peer doesn't have a valid certificate, a connection is established. Otherwise, the connection fails. A valid certificate must be signed by a known *certification authority (CA)*, whether it is public or private. Generally, public CA is employed for public connections over the internet such as web sites. So, a private CA is suitable for private database connection which must be hidden from public.

■ **Note** The mysql_ssl_rsa_setup command creates a private CA as a part of the setup. Thus, certificates generated by mysql_ssl_rsa_setup are self-signed certificates.

To enforce the slave to specify certificates upon connection, change the user definition on the master using the following command:

```
mysql> ALTER USER repl@slavehost REQUIRE X509;
```

To verify that a slave is an authorized client, a slave must have a valid client certification. Copy *ca.pem*, *client-cert.pem*, and *client-key.pem* to the slave host. Then, specify these files in the CHANGE MASTER TO command. Assume that the files are copied into the */var/lib/mysql-cert* directory, then use the CHANGE MASTER TO command to set up a secure connection. See Listing 6-6.

Listing 6-6. Setting Up a Secure Connection on the Slave

```
mysql> CHANGE MASTER TO
    ->         MASTER_SSL_CA = 'ca.pem',
    ->         MASTER_SSL_CERT = 'client-cert.pem',
    ->         MASTER_SSL_KEY = 'client-key.pem',
    ->         MASTER_SSL_CAPATH = '/var/lib/mysql-cert';
```

On the other hand, it also makes sense for the slave to verify if the master is really an authorized server. To achieve this, a slave must specify the MASTE_SSL_VERIFY_SERVER_CERT=1 option in the CHANGE MASTER TO command. When this option is set, a slave checks if a *common name* included in the master certificate is the same as the master's hostname. The client accepts the master only if they are the same. Otherwise, the client aborts connection.

▪ **Note**   Unfortunately, a common name included in certificates generated by mysql_ssl_rsa_setup isn't a hostname and cannot be changed manually using command-line options. So, you need to generate certificates by hand if you want to use this feature. The procedure to generate certificates is a little bit complicated, and is beyond coverage of this book.

As you see, the procedure to set up replication for cluster is very close to standard MySQL replication. However, note again that the procedure in this section is applicable only when no data is stored on the cluster. When you have been running the cluster already, and the cluster stores data to be replicated, additional instructions are required, as shown in the next section.

Start Replication

Finally, start the replication using the START SLAVE command and check if the replication has really started using the SHOW SLAVE STATUS command.

```
mysql> START SLAVE;
mysql> SHOW SLAVE STATUS\G
```

Check if both Slave_IO_Running and Slave_SQL_Running are "Yes". Details about SHOW SLAVE STATUS command fields is described later in this chapter. Be aware that a special delimiter \G follows the SHOW SLAVE STATUS command. This makes the output style vertical instead of the usual table style. Since SHOW SLAVE STATUS output has many fields, the vertical style is much easier to view than the standard table style.

Setting Up NDB Cluster Replication with an Existing Database (Offline)

Even with existing data, the procedure to set up NDB Cluster Replication is close to standard MySQL replication if it is possible to secure a maintenance window. During a maintenance window, the applications must not access the cluster even if the cluster is up and running. So, you need to ensure that your applications are offline during setup. You can also achieve this goal by making the cluster single user mode and allowing access only from the SQL node, which cannot be accessed from your application. See Chapter 8 for more information about single user mode.

To add a slave cluster to an existing cluster during a maintenance window, follow the instructions in the following sections.

Install the New Cluster Used as a Slave

The first thing to do is to set up a cluster to be used as a slave. Be careful so that the slave cluster has capacity to store the same data as the master. Although it is often ideal to have slave cluster with identical configuration to the master, the configuration of the slave cluster is not necessarily identical to the master. The only prerequisite is that the slave must have sufficient capacity. If the slave cannot store the same data as the master, replication cannot be configured.

If replication filters are employed, the slave may have less data than the master. Only in such cases is it possible to employ system layout with less capacity on the slave.

Copy Master Data to Slave

Take a backup from master and restore it on the slave. Make sure that master and slave have identical data at this point. Refer to Chapter 8 for details of the backup and restore procedures.

If you use a replication filter, you can omit filtered tables from backing up and/or restoration.

Set Up Replication in the Same Way as an Empty Cluster

Continue the setup procedure from Step 2 of the previous section. If binary logging has been already enabled on the master, you can issue a RESET MASTER command before starting the replication if you like. This command clears all existing binary logs. Since there is no binary log to be applied, you don't have to specify binary log filename and position in CHANGE MASTER TO command if you issued RESET MASTER command on the master.

On the other hand, if you want to preserve binary logs on the master, note the current binary log filename and position using SHOW MASTER STATUS command. Since master and slave have identical data at this point, old binary logs must not be applied on slave. So, you have to specify the binary log filename and position in the CHANGE MASTER TO command. Find an example CHANGE MASTER TO command with the binary log filename and position in the next section.

Then, start the replication using the START SLAVE command and monitor the status using the SHOW SLAVE STATUS command.

Setting Up NDB Cluster Replication with Existing Database (Online)

In practice, it is not easy to secure a maintenance window in production systems, because applications are often used 24x7. Don't panic. MySQL NDB Cluster has a capability to add a new slave cluster to an existing cluster while the cluster is up and running and the applications are accessing or modifying data on the cluster.

To set up NDB Cluster Replication on a live system, some tricks are needed that are not seen in the offline procedures, as shown next.

Install New Cluster Used as Slave

Install a new cluster used as a slave just like offline procedure in the previous section. The prerequisites for slave cluster are the same as for the offline procedure.

Configure Master SQL Node for Replication

Enable the binary log and set the `server_id` on the master. See Listing 6-1 for more details.

Take Native Backup from Master

The only available online backup method for MySQL NDB Cluster is native backup. From the management client, execute the START BACKUP command to take a full backup of the master cluster.

Restore the Backup to Slave Cluster

To set up a new slave cluster with existing data, it is necessary to identify the binary log filename and position of the backup. The key concept used here is *epoch*, as discussed earlier in this chapter. A full backup taken from the master is a snapshot of data at a certain moment. Any native backup has an epoch that represents the moment when the backup was taken. It is possible to restore information about the epoch using the ndb_mgm command with the `--restore-epoch` (or -e, in short) option. An example command to restore the epoch along with data restoration is shown in Listing 6-7.

Listing 6-7. Restoring Metadata, Data, and Epoch to the Slave Cluster

```
shell$ ndb_restore --ndb-connectstring=mgmhost --restore_meta\
                    --restore_data --restore_epoch --nodeid=1 --backupid=1 \
                    --backup_path=/backups/cluster/BACKUP/BACKUP-1 \
                    --disable-indexes
```

As a consequence of this option, the epoch is stored in the mysql.ndb_apply_status table on the restored cluster.

■ **Note**   Upon the offline procedure in the previous section, epoch and binary log position information is not required because no data is modified during the setup and the existing binary logs are not used. On the other hand, upon online procedure, data is modified and binary logs are continuously generated every second. Therefore, replication cannot be started from the binary log position where the full backup was taken without retrieving the epoch from a backup.

On standard MySQL replication, it is possible to include the required position information within a backup. For example, the mysqldump command has the `--master-data` option for this purpose. However, this option cannot be used for MySQL NDB Cluster, because it is a distributed database and an SQL node cannot take an online backup.

Identify Binary Log Filename and Position

The first thing you must do is retrieve an epoch from the slave cluster using the following query.

```
mysql> SELECT MAX(epoch) AS latest FROM mysql.ndb_apply_status;
```

This query can be executed from any SQL node on the slave cluster, because the `mysql.ndb_apply_status` table is defined with the `ndbcluster` storage engine, which can be accessible from any SQL node.

Then, log in to an SQL node on the master cluster, which will work as a new replication master. Then issue the query in Listing 6-8 with an epoch value determined by the previous query.

Listing 6-8. Determining Binary Log Filename and Position from `mysql.ndb_binlog_index` Table

```
mysql> SET @epoch := 2101677821788177;
mysql> SELECT
    -> SUBSTRING_INDEX(File, '/', -1) AS binlog_file,
    -> Position AS binlog_position
    -> FROM mysql.ndb_binlog_index
    -> WHERE epoch > @epoch
    -> ORDER BY epoch ASC LIMIT 1;
```

Configure Replication

Go back to the slave cluster and log in to an SQL node, which will work as a new slave. Then, configure replication using the `CHANGE MASTER TO` command just like in Listing 6-9. Specify the binary log filename and position retrieved from the previous step.

Listing 6-9. Configuring Replication with Binary Log Filename and Position

```
mysql> CHANGE MASTER TO
    -> MASTER_HOST='masterhost',
    -> MASTER_USER='repl',
    -> MASTER_PASSWORD='PASSWORD',
    -> MASTER_PORT=3306,
    -> MASTER_LOG_FILE='mysql-bin.000123',
    -> MASTER_LOG_POS=1234567;
```

Substitute each parameter properly according to your system configuration and status. This `CHANGE MASTER TO` command looks the same as with the standard MySQL replication without GTID enabled. There is no difference on the `CHANGE MASTER TO` command. Only difference between the procedure to set up NDB Cluster Replication and standard MySQL replication is how to identify the binary log position, which is a preliminary step of this stage.

Optionally, you can secure a network connection between master and slave using TLS, as discussed earlier in this chapter.

Finally, you can start the replication using the `START SLAVE` command as usual. Verify if the replication setup is successful with the `SHOW SLAVE STATUS` command.

Failing Over NDB Cluster Replication Channel

It is recommended to have multiple replication channels when using NDB Cluster Replication.

As discussed earlier in this chapter, an SQL node can receive modification from the data nodes only while it's running. While offline, a certain amount of binary log events will be missed on the master SQL node. Except for a complete cluster shutdown, unavailability of master SQL node will break replication due to missing data. To avoid this problem, it is necessary to make the master SQL node redundant. To achieve this, the binary log must be enabled on more than one SQL node on the master. Then, it is possible to switch replication channel to another master SQL node and continue replication with minimal downtime when a master stops working for some reason. This scenario is shown in Figure 6-3 earlier in this chapter.

When to Failover

When a master SQL node has restarted, the binlog injector thread writes a special event called LOST_EVENTS to the binary log. This event indicates that binary log events may be missed. The event is written upon restart no matter if data is actually lost or not, because it is unknown to the SQL node whether cluster data has been modified and events has been missed while the master SQL node has been offline.

In addition to a server crash, there are several scenarios that cause a LOST_EVENTS event. If the connection between the master SQL node and the data nodes is lost, the binlog injector cannot receive events until the connection is recovered. If the progress of the binlog injector thread is too slow to catch up to the modifications made on the cluster, then events cannot be queued inside data node, the data node consider the SQL node is lagging behind and disconnects it. In these cases, the LOST_EVENT event is written to the binary log.

On the slave cluster, the slave SQL thread forcibly stops when it reads a LOST_EVENTS event from the relay log. The slave SQL thread will not recover from stop due to LOST_EVENTS event without human intervention. The error can be skipped using the sql_slave_skip_counter system variable; however, we should not do so in general, because it will leave missing data as it is and will cause data master and slave out of sync. Of course, this is the most significant symptom for time to start a failover.

Failover must be performed whenever replication stops and cannot be recovered. Of course, replication failure due to LOST_EVENTS is a green signal to begin failover. This means that failover is mandatory when the master SQL node restarts. What if the slave SQL node crashes? I recommend performing failover, because the NDB Cluster Replication slave isn't crash safe.

Still in other cases, failover must be done whenever replication slave threads are not working.

Monitor the replication status with SHOW SLAVE STATUS and see if two replication threads (Slave_IO_Running and Slave_SQL_Running fields) are working fine. If not, begin failover of the replication channel.

■ **Note** MySQL Server has an ability to avoid inconsistency between master and slave upon slave crash. This feature is called *crash-safe slave*. The implementation of crash-safe slave relies on transaction of InnoDB. With crash-safe slave, user tables and the system table called mysql.slave_relay_log_info (defined as InnoDB storage engine) are updated within the same transaction. This ensures that the binary log position and user data in InnoDB tables are synchronized even upon crashes. However, it doesn't ensure synchronization of binary log position and NDBCluster tables.

Number of SQL Nodes with Binary Logging

Although the binary log is enabled on more than one SQL node, how many SQL nodes must have binary log enabled then? The more SQL nodes have binary log, the more redundant replication will be. So, you might want to enable binary log on many SQL nodes. However, the matter is not that simple, because there exists some overhead on the data nodes, SQL node, and interconnect network to generate binary log on each SQL node.

Too many SQL nodes with binary log enabled may harm system performance and/or system stability badly, in the worst case. So, it is a good practice to enable binary log on adequate number of SQL nodes. In my opinion, two or three is sufficient in most cases. Do not enable binary log on more SQL nodes than is necessary.

Failover Procedure

To failover a replication channel, follow these steps:

1. Ensure the current slave SQL node has stopped completely.

2. Determine the current epoch on the slave cluster using the `mysql.ndb_apply_status` table.

3. Determine the binary log filename and position using the `mysql.ndb_binlog_index` table on new master SQL node.

4. Configure replication using the `CHANGE MASTER TO` command on either the current or a new slave SQL node.

5. Start replication using the `START SLAVE` command.

Actually, the procedure itself is the same as Steps 5 and 6 in the previous section (online NDB Cluster Replication setup procedure with existing database) except for the first step described previously. So, refer to the previous section for more details about the procedure.

To ensure the current slave has stopped completely, issue the `STOP SLAVE` command if the slave SQL node is running. If the slave SQL node is offline, do not start the slave SQL node unless the `skip_slave_start` option is set. Do not issue the `RESET SLAVE` command unless the current epoch is identified on the slave, because it clears the `mysql.ndb_apply_status` table. As of the MySQL NDB Cluster 7.3 series, the `ndb_clear_apply_status` option is added. When a value of this option is `OFF`, `RESET SLAVE` will not clear the `mysql.ndb_apply_status` table.

Additional Configuration for NDB Cluster Replication Channel Failover

I suggest two configuration options on the slave cluster with replication channel failover.

The first thing is to have more than one candidate slave SQL node on the slave cluster. Even though the main purpose of the channel failover is to avoid losing binary log events while master SQL node is offline, it is not possible to continue replication while the slave SQL node is offline as well. Since the MySQL Server instance can be offline somehow, you need to get prepared for the scenario that slave SQL node become offline by accident. Explicitly set `server_id` on all of the candidate slave SQL nodes in advance. Be careful that no duplicates of `server_id` occur.

The second thing is to ensure replication is running on at most one slave SQL node. It is not possible to start replication on more than one slave SQL node. It may cause problems during replication such as data inconsistency or replication stops. By default, MySQL Server including SQL node for MySQL NDB Cluster starts replication after the process has restarted if the replication is configured using the `CHANGE MASTER TO` command. Once replication is unconfigured using the `RESET SLAVE ALL` command, replication will not be started upon restart of slave SQL node. Alternatively, the `skip_slave_start` option suppresses starting replication upon restart, too. Ensure that replication doesn't start upon restart on all of slave SQL nodes. I recommend adding the `skip_slave_start` option to all the SQL nodes, because it is not possible to unconfigure replication upon crashes. Upon restart caused by crash, the only way to suppress replication is using the `skip_slave_start` option.

NDB Cluster Replication Daily Maintenance

To make NDB Cluster Replication stable, daily careful maintenance is important. Without appropriate care, no software can be executed successfully. In this section, we discuss how to maintain NDB Cluster Replication during a day-to-day business.

Monitoring NDB Cluster Replication

The most important part of maintenance is monitoring. Regularly check if the status is healthy and report issues if one is detected. The command to monitor replication status is SHOW SLAVE STATUS just like with standard MySQL replication. Listing 6-10 shows example output of the SHOW SLAVE STATUS command on MySQL NDB Cluster 7.5.

Listing 6-10. Example Output of the SHOW SLAVE STATUS Command

```
mysql> SHOW SLAVE STATUS\G
*************************** 1. row ***************************
               Slave_IO_State: Waiting for master to send event
                  Master_Host: masterhost1
                  Master_User: repl
                  Master_Port: 3306
                Connect_Retry: 60
              Master_Log_File: mysql-bin.000010
          Read_Master_Log_Pos: 154
               Relay_Log_File: relay-bin.000004
                Relay_Log_Pos: 355
        Relay_Master_Log_File: mysql-bin.000007
             Slave_IO_Running: Yes
            Slave_SQL_Running: No
              Replicate_Do_DB:
          Replicate_Ignore_DB:
           Replicate_Do_Table:
       Replicate_Ignore_Table:
      Replicate_Wild_Do_Table:
  Replicate_Wild_Ignore_Table:
                   Last_Errno: 1590
                   Last_Error: The incident LOST_EVENTS occured on the master. Message:
                               mysqld startup
                 Skip_Counter: 0
          Exec_Master_Log_Pos: 154
              Relay_Log_Space: 3296
              Until_Condition: None
               Until_Log_File:
                Until_Log_Pos: 0
            Master_SSL_Allowed: Yes
            Master_SSL_CA_File:
            Master_SSL_CA_Path:
               Master_SSL_Cert:
             Master_SSL_Cipher:
                Master_SSL_Key:
        Seconds_Behind_Master: NULL
```

```
Master_SSL_Verify_Server_Cert: No
                Last_IO_Errno: 0
                Last_IO_Error:
               Last_SQL_Errno: 1590
               Last_SQL_Error: The incident LOST_EVENTS occured on the master. Message: mysqld
                               startup
   Replicate_Ignore_Server_Ids:
             Master_Server_Id: 1
                  Master_UUID: a20a9ded-25cd-11e7-bcb2-3c970ec815c3
             Master_Info_File: /var/lib/mysql-cluster/master.info
                    SQL_Delay: 0
          SQL_Remaining_Delay: NULL
       Slave_SQL_Running_State:
            Master_Retry_Count: 86400
                  Master_Bind:
      Last_IO_Error_Timestamp:
     Last_SQL_Error_Timestamp: 170420 23:43:38
               Master_SSL_Crl:
           Master_SSL_Crlpath:
          Retrieved_Gtid_Set:
           Executed_Gtid_Set:
               Auto_Position: 0
          Replicate_Rewrite_DB:
                 Channel_Name:
           Master_TLS_Version:
1 row in set (0.00 sec)
```

The number of fields in the SHOW SLAVE STATUS command increases as the version goes up. Many fields are informative; however, it doesn't have good visibility. It is not necessary to monitor all fields. Instead, monitor the most significant fields, which are discussed next.

Slave_IO_Running

This field indicates if the slave IO thread is running. The value of this field is Yes or No. The state of slave IO thread roughly reflects state of network connection between master and slave. If the network has any problems, the value of this field should be No. In Listing 6-10, the value of this field is Yes, so the network connection must be good.

Slave_IO_State

While the value of Slave_IO_Running is Yes or No, value of this field is variety of string which indicates the state of slave IO thread. The state indicates what slave IO thread is doing, such as Waiting for master to send event, Connecting to master, or Queueing master event to the relay log.

Slave_SQL_Running

This field indicates if the slave SQL thread is running. The value of this field is Yes or No. The slave SQL thread stops running if an error occurs when applying events in the relay log.

Seconds_Behind_Master

This field shows a period of time indicating how long replication is behind. Each event in the binary log has a timestamp of event generation, which indicates roughly time when the binlog injector thread receives event from data nodes. Seconds_Behind_Master is calculated by taking a difference between the current time and the timestamp of the currently executed event on slave. If all events in the relay log have been executed, and no more events to execute are left, the value of this field is 0. Note that the value of this field is an approximation and exact delay cannot be determined, because the master and slave are separate hosts. Even if the network between the master and slave delays, it cannot be detected by this field.

Master_Log_File

The filename of the master binary log that the slave IO thread is currently reading.

Read_Master_Log_Pos

The position at the beginning of the event of master binary log where the slave IO thread is currently reading, or the position of the end of the last event of master binary log where the slave IO thread has read.

Relay_Master_Log_File

The filename of master binary log which the slave SQL thread is currently executing.

Exec_Master_Log_Pos

The position at the beginning of an event of master binary log where the slave SQL thread is currently executing, or the position of the end of the last event of master binary log where the slave SQL thread has executed.

The pair of Relay_Master_Log_File and Exec_Master_Log_Pos is more important than the pair of Master_Log_File and Read_Master_Log_Pos, because the former indicates the current position where the slave data catches up to. When a slave encounters trouble, replication can be resumed using the current data and the current values of Relay_Master_Log_File and Exec_Master_Log_Pos.

Last_*Errno*, and Last_*Error*

These fields indicate error information for the latest occurring errors. If no errors have happened since the slave threads started, these fields are empty. Table 6-2 shows a list of the fields in the SHOW SLAVE STATUS output with names starting with the Last prefix.

Table 6-2. *List of SHOW SLAVE STATUS Fields Indicating Error Information*

Field name	Description
Last_Errno	Indicates the code of the error that happened the last time either on the slave IO thread or slave SQL thread.
Last_Error	A string representation of the last error happened either on the slave IO thread or slave SQL thread. This field is more informative than Last_Errno, because additional information is added to the error string.
Last_IO_Errno	Indicates the code of the error that happened the last time on the slave IO thread.
Last_IO_Error	A string representation of the last error happened on the slave IO thread.
Last_IO_Error_Timestamp	Indicates a timestamp when the last error happened on the slave IO thread.
Last_SQL_Errno	Indicates code of the error that happened the last time on the slave SQL thread.
Last_SQL_Error	A string representation of the last error happened on the slave SQL thread.
Last_SQL_Error_Timestamp	Indicates a timestamp when the last error happened on the slave SQL thread.

Last_IO_Error_Timestamp and Last_SQL_Error_Timestamp were added on MySQL Server 5.6.3. Thus, these fields are available MySQL NDB Cluster 7.3 series or later.

Values for Last_errno/Last_Error are the same as Last_IO_Errno/Last_IO_Error or Last_SQL_Errno/Last_SQL_Error. So, these fields are essentially redundant, but handy to recognize the very latest error that happened on the slave.

As of MySQL NDB Cluster 7.5, replication related tables are added on performance schema. These performance schema tables can be used to monitor the replication status in addition to the SHOW SLAVE STATUS command. Information equivalent to SHOW SLAVE STATUS command is split into several tables. While SHOW SLAVE STATUS shows mixture of configuration and status for both slave IO thread and slave SQL thread, performance schema tables are separated by thread type by whether configuration or status. Table 6-3 shows a list of replication related performance schema tables.

Table 6-3. *List of Replication Related Performance Schema Tables on MySQL NDB Cluster 7.5*

Table Name	Description
replication_applier_configuration	Configuration for slave the SQL thread.
replication_applier_status	Status for slave the SQL thread.
replication_applier_status_by_coordinator	Status for the coordinator thread for a multi-threaded slave.
replication_applier_status_by_worker	Status for worker threads for a multi-threaded slave.
replication_connection_configuration	Configuration for the slave IO thread.
replication_connection_status	Status for the slave IO thread.
replication_group_member_stats	This table shows network and status information for replication group members.
replication_group_members	Statistical information for MySQL Group Replication members.

Since MySQL NDB Cluster doesn't support multi-thread slave and group replication, four tables out of eight in Table 6-3 are irrelevant for NDB Cluster Replication. When it comes to monitoring, configuration is unimportant. So, you need to monitor two tables—replication_applier_status and replication_connection_status. Note that information equivalent to Seconds_Behind_Master is missing from performance schema, because it is considered buggy. Since no alternative information has been added, use the SHOW SLAVE STATUS command if you want to monitor the replication lag.

■ **Note**   Design decisions for replication related performance schema tables are found in WorkLog 7374: *https://dev.mysql.com/worklog/task/?id=7374.*

Restarting Master Cluster

Care must be taken when restarting the cluster because restarting the master SQL node will lose some events while offline and will cause a LOST_EVENTS event. On the other hand, no special care is required when restarting slave cluster, because replication can be resumed safely after a restart of the slave SQL node.

There are two types of restart procedures: system restarts and rolling restarts. This section shows precaution upon restart for these two restart types.

■ **Note**   MySQL NDB Cluster has yet another restart type called initial system restart. It should not be performed upon NDB Cluster Replication setup, because it will wipe all data and break replication. Refer to Chapter 10 for further details of restart procedures.

System Restart on the Master Cluster

Upon a system restart, a LOST_EVENTS event is inevitable. Even if the SQL node is kept online, the connection between the SQL node and data nodes will be lost while the cluster is offline. However, a LOST_EVENTS event due to system restart can be ignored, because no data can be modified while the cluster is offline. When you perform a system restart on the master cluster, follow these instructions:

1. Stop the replication using the STOP SLAVE command from the slave SQL node.

2. Stop applications and ensure no data access is made.

3. Stop the master SQL nodes.

4. Shut down the cluster (SHUTDOWN command from the ndb_mgm client).

5. Perform the system restart.

6. Start the master SQL nodes.

7. Start replication using the START SLAVE command from the slave SQL node.

8. You will see that slave SQL thread stops due to LOST_EVENTS. Confirm that the error is caused by a LOST_EVENTS event. If the error is another type, stop this procedure and investigate the problem.

9. Stop replication using the STOP SLAVE command.

10. Issue SET GLOBAL sql_slave_skip_counter=1 on the slave SQL node.

11. Start replication again using the START SLAVE command from slave SQL node.

12. See if replication is running healthy using the SHOW SLAVE STATUS command.

In this scenario, no replication channel failover is required. Rather, channel failover has no meaning, because the occurrence of LOST_EVENTS event is inevitable on all SQL nodes. So, the LOST_EVENTS event due to a system restart can be ignored as long as no data can be modified while the master cluster is offline.

Rolling Restart on Master Cluster

Upon a rolling restart of the master cluster, applications will continue writing, updating, and deleting data. So, modifications will be made but not written to the binary log while the master SQL node is restarted as part of the rolling restart. Overall the procedure of rolling restart is like this on the master cluster:

1. Restart management nodes and data nodes just like usual rolling restart.

2. Restart the SQL nodes in turn except for the one that acts as the current master.

3. Failover the replication to an alternative channel.

4. Restart the SQL node that was the previous master.

5. Optionally, switch replication back to the original channel.

NDB Cluster Replication Performance Tuning

Performance is an important topic also for NDB Cluster Replication. If the performance of replication is insufficient, the slave will start lagging behind and won't catch up to the master. Such out-of-sync replica is less useful in most cases. So, you should avoid unnecessary delays on the NDB Cluster Replication.

Explicit Primary Keys

It is highly recommended to have explicit primary keys on all tables. If there is no explicit primary key, a table must be scanned to find out the target rows by slave SQL thread. A table scan is a heavy-loaded task, and should be avoided as much as possible. If a table has an explicit primary key, the row to be updated or deleted can be accessed by primary key lookup.

Hardware Considerations

It is often misunderstood that a slave cluster can have less powerful hardware than the master cluster. Of course, it's wrong. If slave cluster has hardware with poor performance, it cannot write the same amount of updates as the master cluster. So, the slave cluster must have hardware with a similar performance to master cluster; equivalent CPUs, disks, network switches.

If you plan to add slave cluster to existing cluster, consider upgrading hardware of the existing cluster to better hardware. As we discussed earlier in this chapter, more than one master SQL nodes will have binary log, while only one SQL node tends to have binary log for point-in-time recovery purpose on non-replication setup. The more SQL node have binary log, the more tasks arises on data node, SQL node, and interconnect network. Especially, high-speed network is most important.

Dedicated Master SQL Node

It is best to dedicate SQL nodes to binary logging on the master cluster. Binary logging is a somewhat heavy task. Ordinary queries may scramble resources and/or cause lock contention with binary logging.

It is ideal to dedicate SQL nodes to binary logging on separate server machines. However, it is very costly. Having dedicated SQL node instances on the same server machines as the existing SQL nodes is a reasonable alternative. It can avoid lock contention within the mysqld process at least.

Minimizing Binary Log Size on Master

Do not change two options from default; ndb_log_updated_only and ndb_log_update_as_write. If the ndb_log_updated_only option is set to ON, which is the default, only changes for updated columns are written to the binary log. If the ndb_log_update_as_write option is set to ON, which is the default, *updates* are written as *writes*. This suppresses old row values to be written to the binary log. These options must be changed when using conflict detection and resolution, otherwise, do not change them from default.

Batching Update on Slave

On the slave SQL node, enabling the slave_allow_batching option may improve performance of the slave SQL thread. This option is only effective for NDB Cluster Replication. The same option exists on standard MySQL Server, but it has no effect at all. When enabled, as the option name suggests, events are not executed one by one, but executed together in batches. It is best to set this option to ON in busy NDB Cluster Replication setups.

Maximum batch size for this option is 32KB. Batching is done per epoch. So, the batch size can be smaller than 32KB if the total size of the transactions belonging to one epoch is smaller than 32KB.

197

Reducing Synchronization of Binary Log to Disk

As the master and slave SQL nodes for NDB Cluster Replication aren't crash-safe, setting sync_binlog=1 doesn't make sense. It is recommended to set sync_binlog=1000 or similar on master SQL node. If the binary log is enabled on slave (with log_slave_updates=ON), set sync_binlog=1000 on slave SQL node, too.

As of MySQL Server 5.7 and MySQL NDB Cluster 7.5, the default value for sync_binlog option is changed to 1. This change makes sense for standard MySQL Server with InnoDB, but isn't suitable for MySQL NDB Cluster. Do not forget to set sync_binlog=1000 on MySQL NDB Cluster 7.5.

Event Buffering

On a busy cluster, it is possible that modifications are too fast and the event queue inside the data node gets full. In such cases, the data node disconnects the lagging SQL node and continues its operation. A LOST_ EVENTS event is caused by disconnection. When a lagging SQL node is disconnected, a message like this one is written in the cluster log.

```
Disconnecting node 52 because it has exceeded MaxBufferedEpochs (100 > 100), epoch 63612/1
```

Then, the following message is written on the disconnected SQL node.

```
[ERROR] cluster disconnect An incident event has been written to the binary log which will stop the slaves.
```

This is not a desired situation. In such cases, increasing MaxBufferedEpochs and MaxBufferedEpochBytes under [NDBD DEFAULT] section in *config.ini* will allow more room before disconnecting lagging SQL nodes.

Conflict Detection and Resolution

MySQL NDB Cluster has a special ability to detect conflicts happening on a multi-master replication setup, when more than one cluster acts as a master. In multi-master replication, data inconsistency can occur because replication is asynchronous. Conflict of modification is a specific issue to multi-master replication. It won't happen on standalone cluster or master-slave replication instances. So, generally speaking, maintaining multi-master replication is more difficult than master-slave replication. An ability to detect conflicts that happened during the multi-master replication can ease development and operation of multi-master NDB Cluster Replication. Since conflict detection is a little bit advanced topic and it's not necessary unless multi-master replication is used, you can skip this section for now if you like.

Multi-Master Replication

In MySQL replication, it is possible to configure a slave so it also acts as a master to other slaves. In such topology, the intermediate MySQL Server relays updates from its master. Such relaying replication topology is also known as *cascading*.

It is also possible that the head of the cascading becomes the tail slave of the cascading. In that case, the flow of replication forms a circuit. That type of replication is called *circular replication*. Figure 6-6 depicts circular replication with four sets of MySQL NDB Cluster.

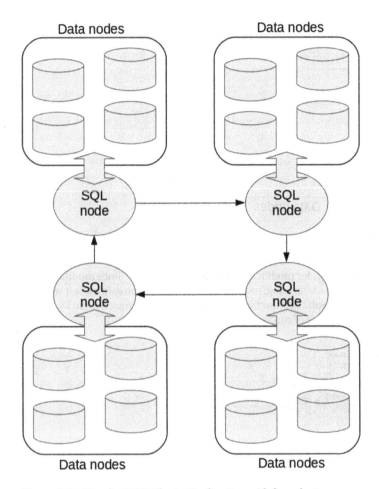

Figure 6-6. *Circular NDB Cluster Replication with four clusters*

Figure 6-7 is a special case of circular replication, whereby two clusters make up circular replication; one cluster is master and slave of another cluster. This type of replication is called *multi-master replication*.

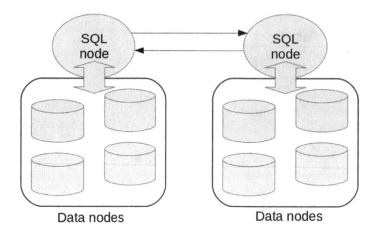

***Figure 6-7.** Multi-master NDB Cluster Replication*

By default, the slave doesn't write binary logs for modification made by replication. Since modifications are propagated only when they are written to the binary log, modifications from an upstream master won't be propagated to the downstream slaves by default. To allow binary logging for modifications done by replication, set `log_slave_updates` to `ON`. This type of configuration is depicted in Figure 6-8.

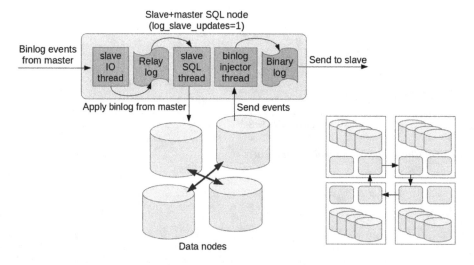

***Figure 6-8.** One SQL node acts as both master and slave*

When `log_slave_updates` is enabled in circular NDB Cluster Replication, all slave SQL nodes also act as master; one SQL node applies modifications from master, and the same SQL node also writes events produced by replication to its own binary log, which will be sent to the next slave, as depicted on the left side of Figure 6-8. The overall topology of this type of circular replication is depicted on the right side of Figure 6-8.

Alternatively, it is possible to configure circular replication on MySQL NDB Cluster without enabling `log_slave_updates`. Figure 6-9 shows circular NDB Cluster Replication without enabling `log_slave_updates`.

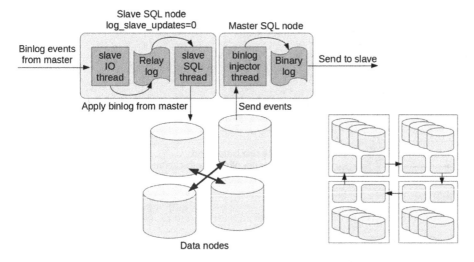

Figure 6-9. *One SQL node acts as master, the other acts as slave*

In this case, every slave doesn't store the binary log locally, but the other SQL node in the same cluster stores the binary log instead.

Currently, only two types of circular topologies are supported:

- All slaves act as master, too, as shown in Figure 6-8.

- All slaves don't store the binary log, and alternative SQL nodes become the master, as shown in Figure 6-9.

It is not okay to mix both types of setup within the same circular replication setup. The latter is not yet tested well, so I recommend configuring circular replication with `log_slave_updates=1`.

Conflicts Caused by Multi-Master Replication

The most significant problem with circular or multi-master replication is conflicts (or data inconsistencies in other words). This section describes how conflicts happen in multi-master replication. In this section, we discuss using examples with two sets of clusters.

Figure 6-10 is a simplified, abstracted, minimalized mode of the sequence of a conflict. Each cylinder indicates a table stored in MySQL NDB Cluster. A square in each cylinder indicates the same row where the value of `id` (which is a primary key of the table) is 1.

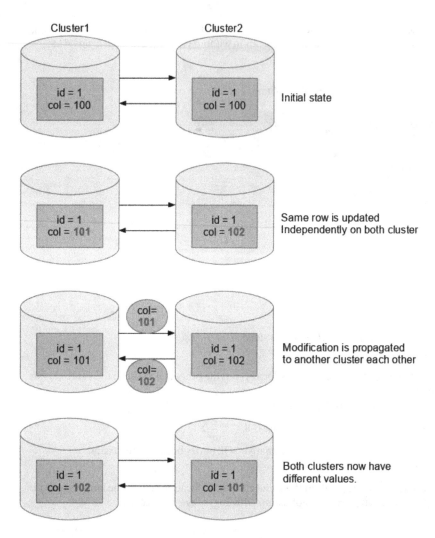

Figure 6-10. *Conflict happens due to simultaneous updates on both clusters*

At the initial state, the row with id=1 has identical values on both clusters. Then, the row is updated to different values. This is possible because they are separate clusters running independently. Then, both clusters start shipping the event in the binary log to the other cluster. Note that the values included in the events are different. This causes binary log events with different values to be applied on each cluster. Thus, the row values on both cluster become different eventually.

Of course, having different values for the same row on each cluster is a serious problem. Such a situation is a data inconsistency. While data inconsistency should be avoided, it cannot be completely avoided on standard MySQL replication, because it is asynchronous. On the other hand, MySQL NDB Cluster has a functionality to detect such conflicts and resolve them automatically. We discuss how to configure conflict detection and resolution on NDB Cluster Replication later in this section.

■ **Caution**   Conflict detection and resolution of NDB Cluster Replication certainly eases application development using multi-master replication. However, it is still much more difficult than an application that updates one cluster only, because the latter can utilize power of transactions, but the former cannot. Resolving inconsistencies after committing transactions is far more difficult than avoiding inconsistencies before committing transactions, because transactions by definition can ensure data consistency. Conflict resolution is essentially not a transactional operation, so it may break data consistency in certain scenarios. So, extra care must be taken to use conflict detection and resolution.

Conflict Detection Methods

There are several types of methods to detect conflicts on NDB Cluster Replication. Each method has pros and cons. So, you need to choose an appropriate one depending on application needs. Roughly speaking, two categories of methods exist. One is timestamp-based and the other is epoch-based.

All methods detect if modifications are in conflict by comparing data row by row. On the other hand, resolution will be done per row or per transaction depending on the method. The method can be chosen per table. So, different tables may have different conflict detection methods.

The agent to detect and resolve the conflict is the slave SQL thread. So, all conflict detection and resolution is done on the slave side only. An application can execute and commit transactions on NDBCluster tables in the same way whether conflict detection is configured or not, because conflict is not detected at commit time. Conflicts will be detected on the other cluster, which is slave of the cluster where transactions are committed, if there is a conflict.

NDB$OLD(column_name)

Conflict detection and resolution method name begin with prefix NDB$ and end with parentheses with an optional argument. In this case, NDB$OLD is a method name, and it takes one argument of column name.

NDB$OLD is a timestamp-based method. To use a timestamp-based method, a special column called *timestamp* is required on the target table. A timestamp column in context of conflict detection isn't a TIMESTAMP data type in SQL. The column is called timestamp because it indicates the oldness of the row. The actual data type for the timestamp column must be either INT UNSIGNED or BIGINT UNSIGNED. They should also be defined as NOT NULL, because the timestamp column value is required every time when detecting conflict. If the table has a suitable column already, it is not necessary to add a timestamp column explicitly. Otherwise, you should.

The NDB$OLD method detects conflict if the current timestamp value in the target table is different from what is included in the binary log event that's going to be applied.

Once a conflict is detected with the NDB$OLD method, updates for the target row are rejected even if conflicted rows are only some part of one transaction. This breaks atomicity of transaction, in other words.

■ **Caution**   As a result of the conflict resolution, the state of the database may be inconsistent in terms of transaction theory.

Figure 6-11 illustrates how conflicts are detected using the NDB$OLD method.

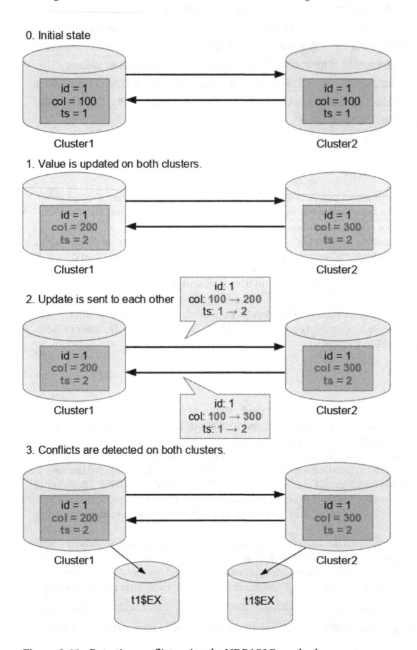

Figure 6-11. *Detecting conflicts using the NDB$OLD method*

Note that every time the target table is updated, timestamp column must be updated, too. This is typically done by incrementing the timestamp column using this statement:

```
UPDATE tbl_name SET ... ts = ts+1;
```

Every time the conflicts are detected, updates against the same data should have been made on both cluster at the same time. In other words, if the slave SQL thread on cluster2 detects a conflict, the target row must be updated on cluster2 as well. This indicates that the binary log event due to the update on cluster2 should have shipped to cluster1, which will result in a conflict on cluster1, too. Thus, conflicts must be detected and the application of the binary log event is rejected on both clusters when this method is used.

Note that the values of col column on Step 3 of Figure 6-11 have different values on both clusters. This surely is an inconsistent state. Resolving this inconsistency is up to your application; your application must determine which value is correct and will be preserved. In Figure 6-11, a table named t1$EX is depicted at the bottom. This table is called the *exceptions table*, where information about conflict and resolution is stored. Your application can use the information stored in this table when resolving inconsistencies. Details of the exception table are described later in this chapter.

NDB$MAX(column_name)

This method detects when the timestamp value has changed like NDB$OLD method, but it resolves conflicts by preserving the row value that has the higher timestamp value. So, value of the timestamp column is very important when using this method.

Although it is possible to maintain the timestamp column value by incrementing the timestamp column using statement like UPDATE tbl_name SET ... ts = ts+1 for this method, it will result in the same timestamp value on both clusters. In that case, the conflict will be detected on both clusters and the conflict won't be resolved automatically. In this case, the behavior of NDB$MAX is identical to the NDB$OLD method. So, there is no advantage to using the NDB$MAX method when the timestamp column is incremented upon each update.

To overcome this problem, an external program is required, such as a *sequence generator*. Formerly, *snowflake* developed by *Twitter* was popular for this purpose. However, the snowflake project has now been discontinued, and is not maintained anymore. There are succeeding open source projects inspired by snowflake. So, using one of them as a number generator for the timestamp column used by NDB$MAX method is a good option.

Another option is to use lightweight, high-throughput NoSQL database software for sequence generation, such as *Riak*, *Redis*, or *memcached*. Sequence generation must be extremely quick, so using SQL for this purpose is not suitable for this purpose. So, using MySQL NDB Cluster via NDB API is a good option. However, the application must access only a single instance of the cluster. Retrieving sequence number from both cluster of multi-master replication is nonsense, because such sequence numbers can conflict as well. Figure 6-12 illustrates multi-master replication using an external sequence generator.

Using wall-clock time is yet another option. It is not a perfect sequence generator in terms of the possibility of duplicate values. The following expression generates sufficiently practical timestamp values, although there is a possibility of generating values that are not arranged in chronological order within the microsecond range.

```
FLOOR(unix_timestamp(now(6)) * 10000000000) + @@server_id;
```

This expression assumes that server_id is at most 9999. It is also acceptable to use arbitrary unique identifiers instead of server_id.

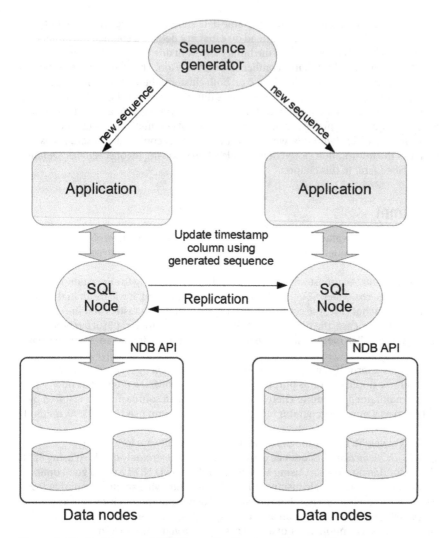

Figure 6-12. *Multi-master NDB Cluster Replication with external sequence generator*

When using an external sequence generator, the location of the generator is an issue. Since multi-master NDB Cluster Replication is often used for disaster recovery, the clusters reside in geographically distant locations. That is, a certain level of network latency must exist between them. So, if the sequence generator resides on one site, access from the other site will be slow in response. The network latency must be taken into account when using external sequence generator over the network. It is also possible that the sequence generator will go offline.

Figure 6-13 illustrates the general process flow of updates made on both clusters, which causes a conflict.

0. Initial state

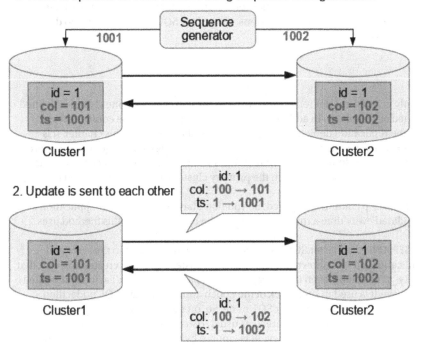

1. Value is updated on both clusters using sequence from generator..

2. Update is sent to each other

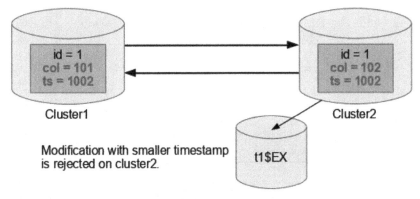

3. A conflicts is detected and resolved on cluster2.

Modification with smaller timestamp is rejected on cluster2.

Figure 6-13. *Conflict is detected and resolved with the NDB$MAX method*

On `cluster2` in Figure 6-13, updates from `cluster1` are rejected because timestamp in the table (1002) is greater than what is included in the update from `cluster1` (1001).

NDB$MAX_DELETE_WIN(column_name)

This method is identical to the `NDB$MAX` method, except for delete handling. In the `NDB$MAX` method, conflict detection and resolution for `DELETE` statements is done just like `NDB$OLD` method. This means that rows will be deleted only when the timestamp value in the binary log event is the same as the one in the table. Otherwise, a conflict is detected. This design decision is because there is no new timestamp value for the delete operation.

On the other hand, `NDB$MAX_DELETE_WIN` method has another strategy for delete handling. Delete operations always have a higher priority than other operations. If the slave SQL thread attempts to delete rows, the operation will be done even if a conflict occurs.

NDB$EPOCH()

This method is supported only in multi-master replication with exactly two clusters—one cluster is defined as *primary*, the other is defined as *secondary*. In addition, each slave SQL node must be configured as a master SQL node, just like the replication depicted in Figure 6-7 described earlier in this chapter. It is repeated to avoid having to go back several pages. With this method, conflict detection and resolution are asymmetric. This means modifications done on the primary always win when a conflict occurs. So, your application can assume that committed transactions on the primary cluster will never be changed later by conflict resolution.

With this method, no timestamp column is required. So you don't have to modify your application so that timestamp column is updated every time a row is updated. As the name suggests, this method uses epoch to detect conflicts.

The epoch used by `NDB$EPOCH` is the master SQL node's own epoch, which is sent to the slave and returns through circular replication later. As shown in Figure 6-3, the master SQL node creates an event that updates the `mysql.ndb_apply_status` table even though `mysql.ndb_apply_status` isn't actually modified on the master SQL node. This event is used to keep track of the epoch applied on slave SQL node, then identify the binary log filename and position on master SQL node. So, on the slave SQL node, the `mysql.ndb_apply_status` table is updated by the slave SQL thread as usual. Usually, updates against `mysql.ndb_apply_status` aren't recorded in the binary log, as the event is ignored by the binlog injector thread even if the binary log is enabled and `log_slave_updates` is `ON`.

Only when ndb_log_apply_status is enabled in addition to log_slave_updates, are updates against mysql.ndb_apply_status table written to the binary log in addition to virtually generated updates against the mysql.ndb_apply_status table. Thus, the master SQL node will receive a binary log event to update the mysql.ndb_apply_status generated by itself. Figure 6-14 depicts event generation and transmission when log_slave_updates and ndb_log_apply_status are ON. With this setup, the master SQL node can detect the latest epoch, which boomerangs back via replication. Thus, these two options, ndb_log_apply_status and log_slave_updates, are required for NDB$EPOCH and its variants.

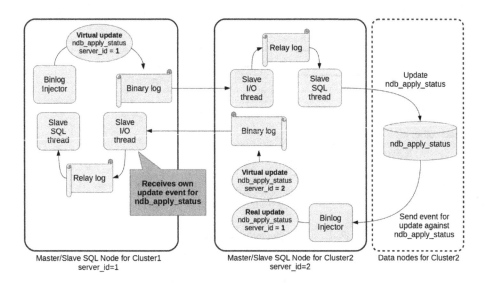

Figure 6-14. *Binary log event generation required for the NDB$EPOCH method*

Figure 6-15 depicts conflict detection and resolution using the NDB$EPOCH method.

0. Initial state

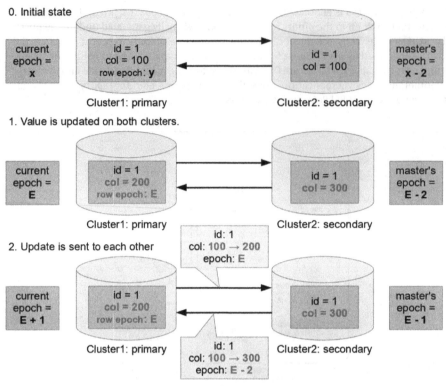

1. Value is updated on both clusters.

2. Update is sent to each other

3. A conflicts is detected and resolved on cluster1 = primary.

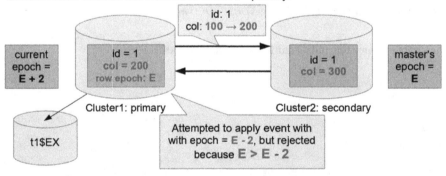

4. A conflicts is resolved on cluster2 by additional event sent from cluster1.

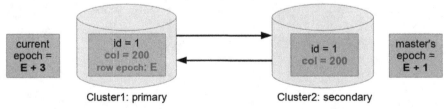

Figure 6-15. *Conflict is detected and resolved by the NDB$EPOCH method*

Note that the epoch is handled inside the data node. Epoch values are stored in the replication tables, mysql.ndb_binlog_index and mysql.ndb_apply_status, for replication purposes. In Figure 6-15, the epoch value inside of cluster1 indicates the current epoch value inside the data nodes of cluster1. For example, epoch value is x at the initial state. The epoch value inside of cluster2 indicates the epoch value of cluster1 derived via mysql.ndb_apply_status table. The epoch value is also stored in each row, described as a *row epoch* in Figure 6-14. At the initial state, the epoch values are described using constant x and y, assuming they are old. Assume too that one-way replication will take approximately 200 milliseconds.

In Step 1 of Figure 6-15, the same row is updated on both clusters. A row has epoch E on cluster1. I omitted the epoch value in the row on cluster2, because it's not relevant to conflict detection and resolution with the NDB$EPOCH method. We assume that the replication takes 200 milliseconds, so the current epoch value in mysql.ndb_apply_status on cluster2 could be $E - 2$, because the epoch is generated every TimeBetweenEpochs milliseconds, which is 100 by default. At this time, an update to mysql.ndb_apply_status with epoch value $E - 2$ has already been written to the binary log on cluster2.

In Step 2 of Figure 6-15, the binary log events are sent to each other. Focus on the epoch values included in the binary log events, which are actually values in the mysql.ndb_apply_status table. Since the epoch value E included in a row on cluster1 is bigger than the epoch value $E - 2$ returned from cluster2, an update by replication is identified as a conflict and resolved by ignoring it on the master SQL node of cluster1 in Step 3 of Figure 6-16. Then, cluster1 sends an additional binary log event to fix the conflict on the slave. So, inconsistency between the two clusters will be fixed on cluster2 after applying this event in Step 4.

NDB$EPOCH_TRANS()

This method is similar to the NDB$EPOCH method in the sense that conflict detection is done using epochs. On the other hand, the way to conflict resolution is different, as it's handled per transactions, not per row. The NDB$EPOCH_TRANS method has advantages over NDB$EPOCH because transactions executed on the secondary cluster are atomic with the NDB$EPOCH_TRANS method. With the NDB$EPOCH_TRANS method, a whole transaction may be ignored on the primary cluster, and reverted later on the secondary cluster in the event of a conflict. On the other hand, with the NDB$EPOCH method, only rows in conflict are ignored and reverted, thus the transaction on the secondary cluster will be non-atomic. In addition to the transaction in conflict, transactions dependent on the conflicted transactions also are reverted as a result of resolution.

NDB$EPOCH2() and NDB$EPOCH2_TRANS()

These methods are improved versions of NDB$EPOCH and NDB$EPOCH_TRANS, added to the MySQL NDB Cluster 7.4 series. Even though the NDB$EPOCH2 method is available, there is no practical difference between the previous method, NDB$EPOCH, even though its implementation and configuration procedure are different. Only NDB$EPOCH2_TRANS makes sense compared to the old version.

The difference between NDB$EPOCH_TRANS and NDB$EPOCH2_TRANS is delete-delete handling. There is a small chance that the primary and secondary clusters will go into inconsistent states after deleting the same row on both clusters, because no epoch is stored for deleted rows so the program cannot compare epochs for deleted rows. Listing 6-11 shows a scenario that causes this kind of inconsistency. Note that slave SQL thread cannot apply modification until the transaction locking the target row is committed. Assume that mysqlP> stands for the prompt on the primary, mysqlS> stands for the prompt on the secondary, and the sessions are not closed or reopened during this example.

Listing 6-11. An Example Scenario Where the Secondary Wins on the NDB$EPOCH_TRANS Method

```
mysqlP> INSERT INTO t VALUES (1, ... omit ...);
mysqlP> BEGIN;
mysqlP> DELETE FROM t WHERE id=1;

mysqlS> BEGIN;
mysqlS> DELETE FROM t WHERE id=1; -- delete-delete situation

mysqlP> COMMIT;
mysqlP> INSERT INTO t SET id=1 ...;
mysqlP> DELETE FROM t WHERE id=1; -- delete same row by chance

mysqlS> COMMIT; INSERT INTO t SET id=1 ...; -- the row is unlocked

mysqlP> SELECT COUNT(*) FROM t WHERE id=1;
+----------+
| COUNT(*) |
+----------+
|        1 |
+----------+
1 row in set (0.00 sec)

mysqlS> SELECT COUNT(*) FROM t WHERE id=1;
+----------+
| COUNT(*) |
+----------+
|        0 |
+----------+
1 row in set (0.00 sec)
```

According to the "primary always wins" policy, the row with id=1 must be deleted on both clusters. However, it's not deleted on the primary! Note that the INSERT following COMMIT on the secondary is executed immediately after COMMIT, as they are executed within a single line, which should be quicker than TimeBetweenEpochs. The NDB$EPOCH2_TRANS method can avoid this type of divergence, and the INSERT following COMMIT on the secondary will be marked as a conflict. The example in Listing 6-11 is not 100% reproducible, because of timing matters.

With the NDB$EPOCH2 and NDB$EPOCH2_TRANS methods, the binary log events caused by modifications done on the secondary will be executed on the primary, then sent back to the secondary. These returning events are called *reflected operations*, and will be re-executed on the secondary. Note that the binary log on SQL nodes within the primary cluster grows very fast, because reflected operations are written to the binary log.

Due to the divergence that will occur right after the delete-delete conflict, it is better to route all delete operations to one cluster unless NDB$EPOCH2_TRANS is used. It will require extra effort for the application development. On the other hand, no divergence will happen but the secondary will occasionally win due to reflected operations when using the NDB$EPOCH2_TRANS method.

Conflict Detection for Read Operations

As of the MySQL NDB Cluster 7.4 series, it is possible to detect conflicts for read operations that hold exclusive row locks. An exclusive row lock is acquired by querying rows with the SELECT ... FOR UPDATE statement.

To enable conflict detection and resolution for read operations, the ndb_log_exclusive_reads option must be set to ON on the SQL nodes. When this option is ON, reads with exclusive row locks are written to the binary log as if they are UPDATE statements without modifying the rows. This is done by setting the row values to the same values as the current ones, thus the row values are unchanged on the slave. The UPDATE events written in the binary log will trigger conflict detection and resolution as usual, whether the conflict caused by a real UPDATE or a read operation with an exclusive row lock. Thus, the conflict detection method to be used for read operations is the same as with write operations.

Note that the size of the binary log will increase when ndb_log_exclusive_reads is set to ON. Extra CPU resources will be required to handle the conflict detection and resolution. The statement must be exactly SELECT ... FOR UPDATE. A SELECT ... LOCK IN SHARE MODE isn't subject to conflict detection and resolution.

Setting Up Conflict Detection and Resolution

In this section, we discuss how to set up conflict detection and resolution. We assume that NDB Cluster Replication is already configured and running. Conflict detection and resolution must be configured per table. If you want to detect/resolve conflicts on 10 tables, you must configure it 10 times. The following is a typical procedure to set up conflict detection and resolution for a newly created table.

1. Configure the options required for conflict detection.

2. Add an entry to the mysql.ndb_replication table.

3. Create an exceptions table.

4. Create a target table.

Step 1 is common for all tables. So, it is sufficient to do it once per cluster. Repeat Steps 2-4 for each target table.

■ **Note**   It is also possible to set up conflict detection and resolution for existing tables only if method used is timestamp-based. However, this is not recommended, as all SQL nodes involving replication must be restarted after adding an entry to the mysql.ndb_replication table and creating the exceptions table.

Let's see the details of each step next.

Configure Options Required for Conflict Detection and Resolution

Some options for the SQL node are required for conflict detection and resolution in addition to what is required for usual NDB Cluster Replication. The required options vary depending on the conflict detection and resolution method described in the previous section. Table 6-4 shows a list of options required for conflict detection and resolution. Set all options required for your desired conflict detection method properly before proceeding to the next step. Some options cannot be changed online, and they require a restart of the SQL nodes. Details of each option follow.

Table 6-4. *List of Options for Conflict Detection and Resolution*

Option Name	Value To Be Set	Method
log_slave_updates	ON	Mandatory for all epoch-based methods: NDB$EPOCH, NDB$EPOCH_TRANS, NDB$EPOCH_TRANS, NDB$EPOCH2_TRANS
ndb_log_update_as_write	OFF	All
ndb_log_updated_only	OFF	All
ndb_log_apply_status	ON	Mandatory for NDB$EPOCH and its variants.
log_bin_use_v1_row_events	OFF	NDB$EPOCH_TRANS and NDB$EPOCH2_TRANS
ndb_log_transaction_id	ON	NDB$EPOCH_TRANS and NDB$EPOCH2_TRANS
ndb_slave_conflict_role	PRIMARY or SECONDARY	NDB$EPOCH2 and NDB$EPOCH2_TRANS
ndb_log_exclusive_reads	ON or OFF	All

When log_slave_updates is set to ON, the slave SQL thread writes the binary log for modifications derived from the master, which is required for a cascading replication topology. As discussed earlier in this section, there are two choices to configure multi-master NDB Cluster Replication, which is with or without log_slave_updates, as shown in Figures 6-8 and 6-9. The former is the well tested and recommended. Especially for the NDB$EPOCH method and its variants, log_slave_updates must be set to ON with exactly two clusters set up. This means that only one SQL node behaves as both master and slave on each cluster, as shown in Figure 6-14.

The default value for ndb_log_update_as_write is ON, which causes updates to be recorded as writes in the binary log. This means that old row values are not written to the binary log, thus it saves the space required for the binary log. Since a write event is treated like the REPLACE command for the NDBCluster storage engine, this saves space well. However, this behavior isn't suitable for conflict detection and resolution, because it needs the old row values to detect and/or resolve conflicts. So, this option must be set to OFF when using conflict detection and resolution.

The default value for ndb_log_updated_only is ON, which causes only the modified part of the row values and the primary key value to be stored in the binary log. This saves the extra space required for the binary log. However, this behavior is not suitable for conflict detection and resolution, because it requires the old row image. This option must be set to OFF when using conflict detection and resolution.

As discussed earlier in this section, ndb_log_apply_status must be set to ON for the NDB$EPOCH method and its variants. The default value for this option is OFF. When it's set to ON, updates for the mysql.ndb_apply_status table of the immediate master are written to the binary log on the slave SQL node. Of course, to make this option effective, log_slave_updates must be set to ON as well.

For the NDB$EPOCH_TRANS and NDB$EPOCH2_TRANS methods, two options—log_bin_use_v1_row_events and ndb_log_transaction_id—must be configured. The former must be set to OFF, and the latter must be set to ON. This is required because transaction IDs must be tracked to resolve conflicts per transaction. When these options are set to OFF and ON respectively, the transaction ID and optional flags are stored in each binary log event. The size required for this extra information is 12 bytes when flags are not set, or 14 bytes when flags are set.

When using the NDB$EPOCH2 or NDB$EPOCH2_TRANS methods, ndb_slave_conflict_role must be explicitly set on both clusters. Valid values for this option are PRIMARY, SECONDARY, NONE, and PASS. Set this option to PRIMARY or SECONDARY depending on the desired configuration. When this option is set to NONE with these methods, the slave will stop due to an error. When this option is set to PASS, conflict detection is not performed even if the tables are configured for conflict resolution using the NDB$EPOCH2 or NDB$EPOCH2_TRANS methods.

ndb_log_exclusive_reads must be set to ON when you want to detect and resolve conflicts for SELECT ... FOR UPDATE executed on both clusters. When this option is ON, SELECT ... FOR UPDATE is written as if UPDATE command, which will update row values to the same values as before. Then, exclusive reads will be subject to conflict detection and resolution.

Add Entry to mysql.ndb_replication Table

The mysql.ndb_replication system table plays a role in the configuration for conflict detection and resolution. By default, this table doesn't exist, so you must create it first when you use conflict detection and resolution. To create the mysql.ndb_replication system table, execute the statement in Listing 6-12.

Listing 6-12. Creating mysql.ndb_replication System Table

```
CREATE TABLE mysql.ndb_replication  (
    db VARBINARY(63),
    table_name VARBINARY(63),
    server_id INT UNSIGNED,
    binlog_type INT UNSIGNED,
    conflict_fn VARBINARY(128),
    PRIMARY KEY USING HASH (db, table_name, server_id)
)   ENGINE=NDB
PARTITION BY KEY(db, table_name);
```

Note that the CREATE TABLE statement for the mysql.ndb_replication table is replicated to other clusters, because circular NDB Cluster Replication is configured. So, it is sufficient to execute this command on one SQL node only.

Configuration is done by inserting rows into this table.

The db and table_name columns specify the target table for conflict detection and resolution.

The server_id column specifies the server_id of slave SQL node where conflict detection and resolution is done. If it's specified as 0, then all SQL nodes will do conflict detection and resolution. If you want to let conflict detection and resolution be done only on specific SQL nodes, insert one row per server_id. A specific server_id is required for the NDB$EPOCH and NDB$EPOCH_TRANS methods. In this case, you need to add one row to the mysql.ndb_replication table per server_id.

The binlog_type specifies the binary log image format. This column overrides the binary log generation options such as the ndb_log_update_as_write and ndb_log_updated_only options on the master SQL node. When it' set to 0 or NULL, the server options are employed. The format is specified as a number, as described in Table 6-5. Usually, you can set it to 0 or NULL to use the server default. If you have not changed ndb_log_update_as_write and ndb_log_updated_only from the default (ON) to OFF, set this column to 7.

Table 6-5. *binlog_type Column Values*

Value	Label	Description
0	NBT_DEFAULT	Use the server default.
1	NBT_NO_LOGGING	Do not log this table in the binary log.
2	NBT_UPDATED_ONLY	Only updated columns are logged.
3	NBT_FULL	All columns are logged whether they are updated or not.
4	NBT_USE_UPDATE	Updates are logged as update. (Equivalent to ndb_log_update_as_write=0.) This value isn't typically used. Specify 6 or 7 instead.
5	Not used	
6	NBT_UPDATED_ONLY_USE_UPDATE	Only updated columns are logged. Updates are logged as update (not write).
7	NBT_FULL_USE_UPDATE	All columns are logged whether they are updated or not. Updates are logged as update (not write).

The conflict_fn column specifies the conflict detection and resolution method to be used. The method takes an argument depending on the method type.

Timestamp-based methods—NDBOLD, NDBMAX, and NDB$MAX_DELETE_WIN—take the timestamp column name as an argument. If a timestamp column name is ts and a method to be used is NDB$OLD, then this column should be set to NDB$OLD(ts). You cannot omit the argument when using timestamp-based methods.

Epoch-based methods—NDB$EPOCH, NDB$EPOCH_TRANS, NDB$EPOCH2, and NDB$EPOXH2_TRANS—take a number of extra bits to be stored per row. The argument can be omitted. If it's omitted, the default value 6 is employed, which is sufficient for the default configuration. The number of required bits varies depending on the values of TimeBetweenEpochs and TimeBetweenGlobalCheckpoints.

By default, each row stores a 32-bit number, which indicates the global checkpoint ID, while the epoch consists of a 64-bit number. This is because only the upper 32-bit part of epoch is required for recovery and restart. An epoch actually consists of two 32-bit numbers. The upper is incremented upon each GCP (Global Check Point), and the lower is incremented upon each micro-GCP and reset upon GCP. So, the lower part will not grow bigger than the following value:

TimeBetweenGlobalCheckpoints / TimeBetweenEpochs - 1

Recall that the redo log is written to disk upon every GCP, not micro-GCP. So, the lower part which is incremented upon every micro-GCP and reset every GCP isn't required for recovery. However, it's required for epoch-based conflict methods. The lower part is very small usually. By default, it's at most 19, which requires 5 bits. The default value 6 is sufficient for the default GCP and micro-GCP settings. If you change TimeBetweenEpochs and TimeBetweenGlobalCheckpoints from the default, you may have to change this value from the default. Make sure sufficient bits are secured. Otherwise, false positives and negatives can happen upon conflict detection.

Due to this reason, for epoch-based methods, a target table must be created after configuring conflict detection and resolution by adding the required entries to the mysql.ndb_replication table. Otherwise, a table cannot store the lower part of the epoch, and conflict cannot be detected at all.

Create an Exceptions Table

An exceptions table is a supplemental table used by conflict detection. Various kinds of information are recorded in this table when conflicts are detected. An exceptions table can be used regardless of the method employed. Even though this table is optional, I highly recommend creating it along with conflict detection, because the information stored in this table is absolutely useful to your application. The definition of an exceptions table varies depending on the target table. The table definition looks like Listing 6-13.

Listing 6-13. Definition of an Exception Table

```
CREATE TABLE target_table$EX  (
    NDB$server_id INT UNSIGNED,
    NDB$master_server_id INT UNSIGNED,
    NDB$master_epoch BIGINT UNSIGNED,
    NDB$count INT UNSIGNED,

    [NDB$OP_TYPE ENUM('WRITE_ROW','UPDATE_ROW', 'DELETE_ROW',
                        'REFRESH_ROW', 'READ_ROW') NOT NULL,]
    [NDB$CFT_CAUSE ENUM('ROW_DOES_NOT_EXIST', 'ROW_ALREADY_EXISTS',
                        'DATA_IN_CONFLICT', 'TRANS_IN_CONFLICT') NOT NULL,]
    [NDB$ORIG_TRANSID BIGINT UNSIGNED NOT NULL,]

    target_table_pk_columns,

    target_table_non_pk_columns,

    PRIMARY KEY (NDB$server_id, NDB$master_server_id,
                        NDB$master_epoch, NDB$count)
) ENGINE = NDBCluster;
```

The name of an exceptions table is the same as the target table plus the $EX suffix, and the exceptions table should be located in the same database as the target table.

The definition of an exceptions table looks a bit complex. Columns with an NDB$ prefix and the primary key at the bottom have fixed definitions. The former four columns are always required, whereas the following three columns are optional. These columns have the meanings described in Table 6-6.

Table 6-6. *Column Definition for the Exceptions Table*

Column Name	Description
NDB$server_id	The server_id where the conflict was detected.
NDB$master_server_id	The master's server_id that sent the binary log to the slave where the conflict was detected.
NDB$master_epoch	The epoch value corresponding to the binary log that caused the conflict.
NDB$count	A counter per target table. It's reset upon restart of the slave SQL node.
NDB$OP_TYPE	An optional column. Type of operation that caused a conflict.
NDB$CFT_CAUSE	An optional column. Reason of conflict.
NDB$ORIG_TRANSID	An optional column. A transaction ID that caused a conflict. This column is useful with the NDB$EPOCH_TRANS or NDB$EPOCH2_TRANS methods, which may write multiple rows into an exception per conflict.

The optional NDB$ columns can be used as of the MySQL NDB Cluster 7.4 series. Since these columns are informative, I recommend using them.

target_table_pk_columns is a list of columns that consists of the primary key of the target table. All primary-key columns must have identical data types of the target table. Ensure that the columns have identical character set and collation to ones in the target table if the data type is a string type. Since any column included in the primary key must be NOT NULL, they must be set to NOT NULL in an exception table, too. The order of the columns is not significant. You can list the columns included in the primary key in any order. However, target_table_pk_columns must be placed before any of non-primary-key columns of the target table and after NDB$count. Actually, you can place optional NDB$ columns and target_table_pk_columns in any order. However, I recommend placing optional NDB$ columns before target_table_pk_columns to avoid confusion.

As of MySQL NDB Cluster 7.4 series, if the table has multi-column primary key, it is not necessary to include all primary-key columns of the target table into the exceptions table. You can specify only a part of primary-key columns if you like.

target_table_non_pk_columns is a list of non-primary-key columns of the target table. A new value or an old value of the column is stored upon conflict; for insert and update, a new value is stored, for delete, an old value is stored.

Beginning with the MySQL NDB Cluster 7.4 series, it is possible to let non-primary-key columns have a suffix of $OLD, $NEW, or both. As the name suggests, a non-primary-key column with an $OLD suffix will have a new value, and a non-primary-key column with a $NEW suffix will have an old value upon conflict. It is possible to have two columns with both an $OLD and a $NEW suffix per non-primary-key column. In this case, both old and new values will be stored in these columns upon conflict of update. Since it is very useful to compare a new value and an old value upon conflict of update, I recommend having both the $OLD and $NEW columns. Upon conflict of an insert or delete, one of the $OLD or $NEW columns will not have a value. So, the non-primary-key columns in an exceptions table must be nullable. Of course, it is not necessary to include all non-primary-key columns in an exceptions table. Include only the columns of interest.

If a target table t1 has a primary-key column id and non-primary-key columns col1, col2, and col3, then the exceptions table will look like Listing 6-14 for the MySQL NDB Cluster 7.4 series or newer.

Listing 6-14. Example Exceptions Table

```
CREATE TABLE t1$EX (
    NDB$server_id INT UNSIGNED,
    NDB$master_server_id INT UNSIGNED,
    NDB$master_epoch BIGINT UNSIGNED,
    NDB$count INT UNSIGNED,

    NDB$OP_TYPE ENUM('WRITE_ROW','UPDATE_ROW', 'DELETE_ROW',
                     'REFRESH_ROW', 'READ_ROW') NOT NULL,
    NDB$CFT_CAUSE ENUM('ROW_DOES_NOT_EXIST', 'ROW_ALREADY_EXISTS',
                     'DATA_IN_CONFLICT', 'TRANS_IN_CONFLICT') NOT NULL,
    NDB$ORIG_TRANSID BIGINT UNSIGNED NOT NULL,

    id INT not null,

    col1$OLD INT,
    col1$NEW INT,
    col2$OLD VARCHAR(10) CHARACTER SET utf8mb4,
    col2$NEW VARCHAR(10) CHARACTER SET utf8mb4,
    col3$OLD DATETIME,
    col3$NEW DATETIME,
```

```
    PRIMARY KEY (NDB$server_id, NDB$master_server_id,
                NDB$master_epoch, NDB$count)
) ENGINE = NDBCluster;
```

An exception table is populated only on the slave side where a conflict is detected. You can query it to find information required to fix inconsistencies. Once you have read the rows from an exceptions table, you can delete the rows using the DELETE statement. While rows are stored on one cluster, you don't have to take special care when deleting rows. Manipulation against an exceptions table will not be replicated.

■ **Caution**   Do not truncate exceptions table. Truncate table isn't a DML query on MySQL series. It's treated as DDL, and it recreates the table internally. It will break the dependency of the target table and the exceptions table, and replication will fail when a conflict is detected. If you happen to truncate an exceptions table, restart the slave SQL node to fix the problem.

Create a Target Table of Conflict Detection

Create the target table as intended. Once the table is created, conflict detection and resolution is activated.

Monitor the error log of the SQL nodes. If any problem happens, error messages will be written to the error log at this point, because entries in the mysql.ndb_replication table won't be checked and the definition of the relevant exceptions table won't be checked until the target table is created. If you find any problem, review the configuration of the mysql.ndb_replication table and the definition of the exceptions table. Then, fix the problem and start over.

Monitoring Conflict Detection

It is important to monitor if conflicts happen when using conflict detection. There are two ways to monitor the status, as described next.

Monitoring Status Variables

When a conflict is detected, the status variables in Table 6-7 is updated. All the status variables listed in Table 6-7 can be retrieved using SHOW GLOBAL STATUS LIKE 'Ndb_conflict%' on all versions, or SELECT * FROM performance_schema.global_status WHERE variable_name LIKE 'Ndb_conflict%' on MySQL NDB Cluster 7.5 or newer.

Table 6-7. *Status Variables Relevant to Conflict Detection and Resolution*

Status Variable	Description
Ndb_conflict_fn_max	Number of times that a conflict is detected using the NDB$MAX method.
Ndb_conflict_fn_old	Number of times that a conflict is detected using the NDB$OLD method.
Ndb_conflict_fn_max_del_win	Number of times that a conflict is detected using the NDB$MAX_DELETE_WIN method.
Ndb_conflict_fn_epoch	Number of times that a conflict is detected using the NDB$EPOCH method.
Ndb_conflict_fn_epoch_trans	Number of times that a conflict is detected using the NDB$EPOCH_TRANS method.
Ndb_conflict_fn_epoch2	Number of times that a conflict is detected using the NDB$EPOCH2 method.
Ndb_conflict_fn_epoch2_trans	Number of times that a conflict is detected using the NDB$EPOCH2_TRANS method.
Ndb_conflict_trans_row_conflict_count	Number of rows identified as conflicted by transaction unit methods NDB$EPOCH_TRANS and NDB$EPOCH2_TRANS.
Ndb_conflict_trans_row_reject_count	Number of rows reverted back due to conflict by transaction unit methods. The value of this status variable includes the value of Ndb_conflict_trans_row_conflict_count.
Ndb_conflict_trans_reject_count	Number of transactions reverted back due to conflict by transaction unit methods.
Ndb_conflict_trans_detect_iter_count	Number of iterations to detect dependencies of conflict by transaction unit methods.
Ndb_conflict_trans_conflict_commit_count	Number of committed transactions after resolving conflict by transaction unit methods.
Ndb_conflict_epoch_delete_delete_count	Number of times that a delete-delete conflict is detected.
Ndb_conflict_reflected_op_prepare_count	Number of rows modified on the secondary when using the NDB$EPOCH2 or NDB$EPOCH2_TRANS method.
Ndb_conflict_reflected_op_discard_count	Number of rows modified on the secondary, then sent to the primary via the binary log, applied on the primary, and sent back to the secondary but discarded when using the NDB$EPOCH2 or NDB$EPOCH2_TRANS method.
Ndb_conflict_refresh_op_count	Number of operations executed on the secondary to resolve inconsistency by overwriting data in the primary. This status variable may increase only when using the epoch-based method.
Ndb_conflict_last_conflict_epoch	Last local epoch when conflict is detected.
Ndb_conflict_last_stable_epoch	Last local epoch when modification is made but no conflict is detected.

To detect the occurrence of conflicts from your application, monitor the Ndb_conflict_fn* status variables depending on the method used.

Monitoring Exceptions Tables

Another way to monitor conflict is to query the exceptions table. One or more rows will be inserted only if conflicts occur. If the number of target tables is not huge, monitoring the exceptions table will not be an expensive, high-load operation.

This strategy has some advantages over monitoring status variables. When a conflict happens, you'll often need to take further action in your application, because some data is reverted back silently due to automatic resolution. For example, it might be necessary to notify the user that modification done by that user was canceled; the user will have to do the operation again. With this strategy, you can write additional code along with the monitoring code.

Conflict Detection Case Study

This section shows an example of the procedure to set up conflict detection and resolution using the NDB$EPOCH_TRANS and NDB$EPOCH2 methods. The name of the example table for the conflict detection and resolution is test.t_conflict with the following definition.

```
CREATE TABLE t_conflict (
  id BIGINT UNSIGNED NOT NULL PRIMARY KEY,
  col1 VARCHAR(64),
  col2 DATETIME,
  INDEX ix1 (col1, col2)
) ENGINE=NDBCluster CHARACTER SET utf8;
```

Set Up Conflict Detection Using the NDB$EPOCH_TRANS Method

This example assumes that two clusters have already been installed and have been running with multi-master replication. One SQL node per cluster acts as both master and slave. The server_ids assigned to SQL nodes for replication are 1001 for cluster1 and 2001 for cluster2. Figure 6-16 illustrates the assumed configuration.

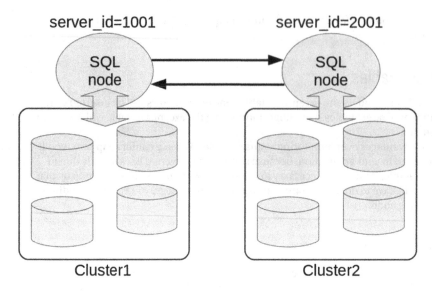

Figure 6-16. *An example multi-master NDB Cluster Replication configuration for the NDB$EPOCH_TRANS method*

Additional SQL nodes or API nodes might exist in addition to those SQL nodes depicted in Figure 6-16. They are just omitted for simplicity. With this setup, log_slave_updates should have been set already.

The first thing to do is add extra configuration to *my.cnf* on both clusters. Listing 6-15 shows an example configuration of cluster1.

Listing 6-15. Example Configuration for the NDB$EPOCH_TRANS Method

```
[mysqld]
ndbcluster
ndb_connectstring = mgmhost
log_bin = mysql-bin
log_slave_updates
server_id = 1001
... snip ...
# Additional configurations for NDB$EPOCH_TRANS method
ndb_log_update_as_write = OFF
ndb_log_updated_only = OFF
ndb_log_apply_status = ON
log_bin_use_v1_row_events = OFF
ndb_log_transaction_id = ON
```

To affect changes, SQL nodes must be restarted, because some of the options are not dynamic and cannot be changed without restarting the server. After restarting both SQL nodes, restart the replication again using the START SLAVE command. Recall that restarting the master SQL node will cause it to miss receiving events during offline. To prevent this problem, you have two choices—restart the SQL nodes while your applications are offline to ensure that no updates are made during restart, or configure SQL nodes on the alternative replication channel first, and then switch replication to the alternative channel. Note that replication will be stopped due to a LOST_EVENT event in the former case. You can safely ignore the error by SET GLOBAL sql_slave_skip_counter = 1, if no modifications are actually done during the restart.

The next step is to add entries to the `mysql.ndb_replication` table to configure conflict detection and resolution. Assume that an alternative replication channel is configured with `server_ids` 1002 and 2002, in addition to the SQL nodes with `server_ids` 1001 and 2001. In this case, conflict detection and resolution must be done only on the primary side; SQL nodes with `server_ids` 1001 and 1002. This is because the `NDB$EPOCH_TRANS` method is asymmetric, and the primary always wins. Listing 6-16 shows an example that adds entries to the `mysql.ndb_replication` table. If you have not created the table yet, create it first.

Listing 6-16. Adding Entries to `mysql.ndb_replication` Table Required for the `NDB$EPOCH_TRANS` Method

```
mysql> INSERT INTO mysql.ndb_replication VALUES ('test', 't_conflict', 1001, NULL,
'NDB$EPOCH_TRANS()');
Query OK, 1 row affected (0.00 sec)

mysql> INSERT INTO mysql.ndb_replication VALUES ('test', 't_conflict', 1002, NULL,
'NDB$EPOCH_TRANS()');
Query OK, 1 row affected (0.00 sec)
```

Since one entry is required per `server_id` for the `NDB$EPOCH` and `NDB$EPOCH_TRANS` methods, two entries are required in this case. Note that the argument against `NDB$EPOCH_TRANS()` is omitted in Listing 6-16. The default value 6 is used in this case.

Create the exceptions table prior to the target table. The table name must be `t_conflict$EX` in this case. The definition of an exceptions table varies depending on choices—whether each non-primary-column is included or not, and whether optional columns are used or not. Listing 6-17 shows an example exceptions table for the `t_conflict` target table.

Listing 6-17. Example Exceptions Table with Optional Columns and One Non-Primary-Key Column

```
CREATE TABLE t_conflict$EX (
    NDB$server_id INT UNSIGNED,
    NDB$master_server_id INT UNSIGNED,
    NDB$master_epoch BIGINT UNSIGNED,
    NDB$count INT UNSIGNED,

    NDB$OP_TYPE ENUM('WRITE_ROW','UPDATE_ROW', 'DELETE_ROW',
                        'REFRESH_ROW', 'READ_ROW') NOT NULL,
    NDB$CFT_CAUSE ENUM('ROW_DOES_NOT_EXIST', 'ROW_ALREADY_EXISTS',
                        'DATA_IN_CONFLICT', 'TRANS_IN_CONFLICT') NOT NULL,
   NDB$ORIG_TRANSID BIGINT UNSIGNED NOT NULL,

    id BIGINT UNSIGNED not null,
    col1$OLD VARCHAR(64) CHARACTER SET utf8,
    col1$NEW VARCHAR(64) CHARACTER SET utf8,

    PRIMARY KEY (NDB$server_id, NDB$master_server_id,
                    NDB$master_epoch, NDB$count)
) ENGINE = NDBCluster;
```

Finally, create the target table, as shown in Listing 6-18.

Listing 6-18. Creating the Target Table for Conflict Detection and Resolution with the NDB$EPOCH_TRANS
Method

```
mysql> CREATE TABLE t_conflict (
  id BIGINT UNSIGNED NOT NULL PRIMARY KEY,
  col1 VARCHAR(64),
  col2 DATETIME,
  INDEX ix1 (col1, col2)
) ENGINE=NDBCluster CHARACTER SET utf8;
Query OK, 0 rows affected (0.47 sec)
```

You'll find messages like Listing 6-19 in the SQL node's error log.

Listing 6-19. Example Messages Appear in the Error Log When Creating Tables

```
2017-05-06T03:28:22.329499Z 10 [Note] NDB Binlog: CREATE TABLE Event: REPLF$test/t_
conflict$EX
2017-05-06T03:28:22.778946Z 10 [Note] NDB Slave: Table test.t_conflict logging exceptions to
test.t_conflict$EX
2017-05-06T03:28:22.778965Z 10 [Note] NDB Slave: Table test.t_conflict using conflict_fn
NDB$EPOCH_TRANS.
2017-05-06T03:28:22.779511Z 10 [Note] NDB Binlog: CREATE TABLE Event: REPLF$test/t_conflict
2017-05-06T03:28:22.793209Z 10 [Note] NDB Binlog: logging ./test/t_conflict (FULL,USE_UPDATE)
```

Now you can test for conflict detection and resolution. Listing 6-20 shows an example of conflict
detection and resolution with the NDB$EPOCH_TRANS method. Assume that mysqlP> stands for the prompt
on the primary (session for the SQL node with server_id = 1001 on cluster1) and mysqlS> stands for the
prompt on the secondary (session for the SQL node with server_id = 2001 on cluster2).

Listing 6-20. Testing Conflict Detection and Resolution with the NDB$EPOCH_TRANS Method

```
##### PRIMARY #####
mysqlP> INSERT INTO t_conflict VALUES (1, 'Sun', NOW());
Query OK, 1 row affected (0.00 sec)

mysqlP> BEGIN;
Query OK, 0 rows affected (0.00 sec)

mysqlP> UPDATE t_conflict SET col1 = 'Moon';
Query OK, 1 row affected (0.00 sec)
Rows matched: 1  Changed: 1  Warnings: 0

##### SECONDARY #####
mysqlS> BEGIN;
Query OK, 0 rows affected (0.00 sec)

mysqlS> UPDATE t_conflict SET col1 = 'Jupiter';
Query OK, 1 row affected (0.00 sec)
Rows matched: 1  Changed: 1  Warnings: 0

##### PRIMARY #####
mysqlP> COMMIT;
```

```
Query OK, 0 rows affected (0.00 sec)

##### SECONDARY #####
mysqlS> COMMIT;
Query OK, 0 rows affected (0.00 sec)

##### PRIMARY #####
mysqlP> SELECT * FROM t_conflict;
+----+------+---------------------+
| id | col1 | col2                |
+----+------+---------------------+
|  1 | Moon | 2017-05-06 12:37:50 |
+----+------+---------------------+
1 row in set (0.00 sec)

mysqlP> SELECT * FROM t_conflict$EX\G
*************************** 1. row ***************************
        NDB$server_id: 1
 NDB$master_server_id: 1001
     NDB$master_epoch: 1835213755777034
           NDB$count: 3
          NDB$OP_TYPE: UPDATE_ROW
        NDB$CFT_CAUSE: TRANS_IN_CONFLICT
     NDB$ORIG_TRANSID: 1279907607296
                   id: 1
            col1$OLD: Sun
            col1$NEW: Jupiter
1 row in set (0.00 sec)

##### SECONDARY #####
mysqlS> SELECT * FROM t_conflict;
+----+------+---------------------+
| id | col1 | col2                |
+----+------+---------------------+
|  1 | Moon | 2017-05-06 12:37:50 |
+----+------+---------------------+
1 row in set (0.00 sec)

mysqlS> SELECT * FROM t_conflict$EX;
Empty set (0.01 sec)
```

Note the following facts from this test example:

- The table on both clusters have identical row values even though they are updated to different values. This means the conflict was resolved and the modification from the primary won when the row was updated from both clusters at the same time.

- Only the exceptions table on cluster1 has an entry that indicates a conflict has occurred. This means the conflict detection and resolution is done on the primary cluster only, as defined in the mysql.ndb_replication table.

If you want to test further, try the following procedures as a lesson.

- Inspect the binary logs using the `mysqlbinlog` command with the `-vv` option. See which events are written on both clusters. Note that verbosity level increases every time the option is specified. Row values are printed if the verbosity is 1 or larger. Extra information is printed if the verbosity is 2 or larger.

- Delete rows from the exceptions table.

- Truncate the exceptions table and insert new rows. See what happens.

- Test delete-delete conflict handling.

Set Up Conflict Detection Using the NDB$EPOCH2 Method

The procedure to set up the NDB$EPOCH2 method, added to the MySQL NDB Cluster 7.4 series, is similar to the NDB$EPOCH_TRANS method. The way to configure it is slightly different from the way you configure NDB$EPOCH and NDB$EPOCH_TRANS.

The first difference is the server configuration. Listing 6-21 shows an example configuration of the SQL node that acts as master and slave on cluster1.

Listing 6-21. Example Configuration of SQL Node for the NDB$EPOCH2 Method

```
[mysqld]
ndbcluster
ndb_connectstring = mgmhost
log_bin = mysql-bin
log_slave_updates
server_id = 1001
... snip ...
# Additional configurations for NDB$EPOCH_TRANS method
ndb_log_update_as_write = OFF
ndb_log_updated_only = OFF
ndb_log_apply_status = ON
ndb_slave_conflict_role = PRIMARY
```

Note that the role of this SQL node is defined using the `ndb_slave_conflict_role` option instead of entries in the `mysql.ndb_replication` table. On the other hand, don't forget to specify `ndb_slave_conflict_role` = SECONDARY for SQL nodes on the secondary cluster. The role must be explicitly set on both clusters.

The configuration does not include `log_bin_use_v1_row_events` = OFF and `ndb_log_transaction_id` = ON, which were included in the example configuration of the NDB$EPOCH_TRANS method, because the method is NDB$EPOCH2, which is not a transaction unit method.

The next step is to add an entry to the `mysql.ndb_replication` table, as shown in Listing 6-22.

Listing 6-22. Adding an Entry to the `mysql.ndb_replication` Table Required for the NDB$EPOCH2 Method

```
mysql> INSERT INTO mysql.ndb_replication VALUES ('test', 't_conflict', 0, NULL, 'NDB$EPOCH2(7)');
Query OK, 1 row affected (0.00 sec)
```

Note that the `server_id` column is set to 0. This indicates that conflict detection and resolution is done on all SQL nodes that are configured as replication slaves. The asymmetry of the NDB$EPOCH2 method is guaranteed by the `ndb_slave_confict_role` option, not the `server_id` column in the `mysql.ndb_replication` table.

Create the exceptions table and the target table just like in the NDB$EPOCH_TRANS example. Then, conflict detection and resolution is activated for the target `test.t_conflict` table.

Application Modifications Required for Conflict Detection

While the conflict detection and resolution feature of circular NDB Cluster Replication is handy when you want to update the same data from two clusters, it is not available without cost. You need to modify your application so that it fits the conflict detection and resolution. In this section, we discuss how to adopt your application so that fits with conflict detection and resolution.

Choosing the Right Conflict Detection Method

The first step to fitting your application into conflict detection and resolution is to choose the appropriate method. As discussed in this chapter, there are two categories of methods—timestamp-based methods and epoch-based methods. Table 6-8 lists the significant differences between the timestamp-based and epoch-based methods.

Table 6-8. *Major Differences Between Timestamp-Based and Epoch-Based Methods*

Characteristics	Timestamp-Based Method	Epoch-Based Method
Number of clusters supported	Any number of clusters in a circular NDB Cluster Replication.	Two
Symmetry of clusters	Symmetric; conflicts may be detected on both clusters.	Asymmetric; a cluster will have a primary or secondary role. Primary always wins.
Table change	Required; need to add a timestamp column.	Not required, but tables internally store extra bits.
Unit of conflict resolution	Row; only conflicted rows are resolved. It may break transactional consistency.	Row or transaction; transaction unit methods can ensure transactional consistency.
Is conflict resolution automatic?	Yes for NDB$MAX and NDB$MAX_DELETE_WIN. No for NDB$OLD.	Yes.

When you decide to use one of the epoch-based methods, I recommend the newer versions, NDB$EPOCH2 and NDB$EPOCH2_TRANS (over NDB$EPOCH and NDB$EPOCH_TRANS), because the newer methods are easy to configure and have delete-delete handling.

Updating Timestamp Columns

With timestamp-based conflict detection and resolution, populating the timestamp column is the application's responsibility. The application must update the timestamp column anytime it updates the table. Otherwise, conflicts cannot be detected. This requires extra effort to develop applications.

Even more, an external sequence generator is required for the NDB$MAX and NDB$MAX_DELETE_WIN methods. This requires additional development and operational cost.

Triggers are useful to populate or update timestamp values. For the NDB$OLD method, it is sufficient to implement a trigger that increments the timestamp column upon UPDATE. The INSERT trigger is not required, because it is possible to specify a default column value when the CREATE TABLE is executed. For the NDB$MAX and NDB$MAX_DELETE_WIN methods, it is a good idea to develop a user-defined function to retrieve the new timestamp value from an external sequence generator, because it can be called from the UPDATE triggers.

Monitoring Conflict Detection

Unless your application can ignore all resolved conflicts silently, you need to monitor the status of conflicts as discussed earlier in this section. Since push style notification is not available when conflicts are detected, your application must monitor conflicts periodically.

Fixing Conflicts

In some cases, automatic conflict resolution isn't sufficient for your application, and your application needs to take further actions, such as:

- Notifying users that their updates may be canceled.

- Querying another cluster to ensure modification isn't identified as a conflict.

- Verifying if the database is consistent and no constraints are violated. Readjusting the data if necessary.

Information stored in the exceptions table is useful when taking further actions against conflicts. Once you have done for conflicts, you can delete the rows in the exceptions table. If you like, you can keep the rows in the exceptions table for later review.

Cautions and Limitations of Conflict Detection

Although conflict detection is a handy functionality, there are some drawbacks and limitations. So, extra care and effort is required when using multi-master NDB Cluster Replication even if conflict detection and resolution is available.

Binary Log Size

When conflict detection and resolution is employed, more space will be needed for the binary log. It is therefore necessary to prepare more disk space and network bandwidth than what is required for NDB Cluster Replication without conflict detection.

Setting `ndb_log_update_as_write` to `OFF` increases the binary log to approximately twice for update operations. This is significant.

Since timestamp-based methods require a timestamp column in the target tables, it increases table size as well as the binary log size.

Epoch-based methods require setting the `ndb_log_apply_status` option to `ON`, which will require extra space per event in the slave's binary log. When a transaction unit method is used, make sure that `log_bin_use_v1_row_events` are set to `OFF`, and `ndb_log_transaction_id` is set to `ON`, which requires extra bytes per event.

Performance Overhead

Every time the binary log is applied on the slave SQL node, the slave SQL thread and data nodes check if a conflict occurs. This requires extra CPU resources compared to what is required for NDB Cluster Replication without conflict detection. You may have to upgrade the CPU on the SQL node that acts as a slave.

Delay Is Critical

When using conflict detection and resolution, replication delay becomes more critical than NDB Cluster Replication without conflict detection. The longer it delays, the higher chance that a conflict could arise. So it is important to apply replication as quickly as possible when using conflict detection and resolution.

Transaction Handlings

Transactions must be atomic; all modifications are applied or nothing's done at all. However, with the row unit conflict resolution methods, only rows causing conflicts will be modified after the transaction is committed. This breaks the atomicity, which is the "A" of ACID property, of the transaction. The database will enter an inconsistent state.

With epoch-based methods, a transaction will be canceled after it is committed on the secondary. This means durability, the "D" of ACID, isn't ensured on the secondary cluster.

So, it is not possible to enjoy the power of transactions on NDB Cluster Replication with conflict detection and resolution. It will make application development much more difficult than development on the usual MySQL NDB Cluster, which is fully transactional. Due to this, I don't generally recommend using multi-master NDB Cluster Replication even if conflicts can be detected and resolved. Use it only if you are prepared for the extra work caused by violations of the transaction model.

Replication to InnoDB

Standard MySQL replication supports replication from one storage engine to another with some limitations. It is also possible to configure replication from MySQL NDB Cluster to InnoDB. Even though MySQL NDB Cluster is a highly scalable system, there is a need for this type of replication to improve scalability. There are some problems that cannot be solved with standalone MySQL NDB Cluster setup, such as:

- Access to the same set of data cannot scale, because MySQL NDB Cluster employs shared-nothing architecture and data is horizontally distributed per row.

- Ordered index scans don't scale well, unless user-defined partitioning is employed, because the scans must involve all data nodes to complete.

- Analytic queries on InnoDB are often faster than on MySQL NDB Cluster.

Replication to InnoDB is a handy way to overcome these performance problems.

Requirements and Limitations

Since InnoDB and NDBCluster are different storage engines, there are requirements to replicate from a NDBCluster master to an InnoDB slave. While they are different storage engines, note that not all functions are supported upon replication.

Use mysqld Bundled with MySQL NDB Cluster

It is highly recommended that you use identical binaries for both master and slave. The InnoDB storage engine is also included in the mysqld bundled with MySQL NDB Cluster. So, you can use it not only as an SQL node but also as a slave MySQL Server. The mysqld program bundled with MySQL NDB Cluster has some additional functionality compared to the one included with the standard MySQL Server package. Since the slave must reproduce identical modifications as the master, differences in functionality may produce problems.

Binary Log Format Requirements

In NDB Cluster Replication, the master SQL node stores the binary log in a special format, which can be handled by a MySQL NDB Cluster slave only. It is necessary to let the master MySQL NDB Cluster make its binary log match InnoDB. On MySQL NDB Cluster, updates are recorded as writes in the binary log, when ndb_log_update_as_write is set to ON, which is default for MySQL NDB Cluster. On the slave side, MySQL NDB Cluster can handle such a binary log, and doesn't report errors. However, InnoDB cannot. To replicate from MySQL NDB Cluster to InnoDB, ndb_log_update_as_write = OFF must be set on the master SQL node.

On the master SQL node, duplicate entries are occasionally recorded into the binary log due to architectural reasons, which results in an ER_DUP_ENTRY error upon insert or an ER_KEY_NOT_FOUND error upon delete. To prevent issues on the slave SQL node, you must set slave_exec_mode = IDEMPOTENT. The default value for this option is STRICT, whereby these errors are handled as actual errors. When this option is set to IDEMPOTENT, the slave SQL thread simulates the behavior of NDB Cluster Replication slave. It ignores these errors, and write row events (row-based format version of "inserts") are handled as if they are REPLACE commands.

MySQL NDB Cluster System Tables

There are several system tables in mysql database. As discussed these in this chapter, the master SQL node generates events to update the mysql.ndb_apply_status table. When index statistics functionality is enabled, two system tables mysql.ndb_index_stat_head and ndb_index_stat_sample are updated with the ANALYZE TABLE command. These tables are created when the SQL node connects to the cluster. So, it will not be created automatically on an InnoDB slave. You have to create them by hand or set a replication filter to filter them out. However, I recommend not filtering the mysql.ndb_apply_status table out. The table is required when you switch to an alternative replication channel.

Circular Replication and Conflict Detection

It might be technically possible to configure circular replication involving both MySQL NDB Cluster and InnoDB. However, such a configuration is not supported. I do not recommend using inter-storage engine circular replication.

In addition, conflict detection isn't available for InnoDB. It's a unique feature of MySQL NDB Cluster. So, there's no way to detect or avoid potential conflicts caused by circular topology.

Foreign Keys

A foreign key is a useful feature when ensuring referential constraints among multiple tables. However, how foreign keys are implemented is left to the storage engine, and the implementation is different between InnoDB and NDBCluster. For example, timing is different when a foreign key constraint is checked; commit time on NDBCluster storage engine, and per statement on InnoDB. This may cause replication failure.

To prevent this problem, remove the foreign keys from the slave InnoDB tables. When foreign keys are removed from the slave, no constraint checks are performed on the slave. However, checks should have been performed on the master already. Modifications propagated to the slave must be free from constraint violation.

The only remaining problem is cascading updates and deletes done by foreign keys. Cascading updates and deletes are done inside the storage engine. So, modifications caused by cascading are not written to the binary log. This assumes that the same cascading must be executed on the slave, as was done on the master. This causes a problem when the table has a foreign key on the master, not on the slave. Do not use foreign key cascading updates and deletes if you replicate from MySQL NDB Cluster to InnoDB.

Unique Keys

NDB Cluster Replication avoids potential constraint violations against unique keys by deferring constraint checks until the transaction commits. Unique key constraints broke replication on very old versions, but it isn't a problem on recent versions. However, it is still a problem when replicating to InnoDB, because unique key constraints are checked upon every statement on InnoDB. So, remove unique key constraints on the slave side, since you can assume all modifications derived from the master do not violate unique key constraints upon every transaction commit.

Row Size Limitations

While MySQL NDB Cluster has row capacity up to 14KB, InnoDB has 8KB by default. This is may cause a problem when the table has a row larger than 8KB. In such cases, use 32KB or 64KB `innodb_page_size`.

Setting Up Replication to InnoDB

In this section, we discuss how to set up replication from MySQL NDB Cluster to InnoDB.

Configure Master SQL Node and Create a Replication User

You need to enable the binary log and set `server_id` explicitly. Do not forget to set `ndb_log_update_as_write = OFF`, which is required for replication from a `NDBCluster` master to other storage engine slaves. Listing 6-23 shows an example configuration of the master SQL node.

Listing 6-23. Example Configuration for Master SQL Node When Replicating to InnoDB

```
[mysqld]
ndbcluster
... snip ...
server_id = 1001
log_bin = mysql-bin
binlog_format = ROW
ndb_log_update_as_write = OFF
```

Create a slave user if no suitable user exists. Refer back to Listing 6-2 for an example.

Configure Slave for Replication

On the slave side, an explicit `server_id` must be set, and `slave_exec_mode` must be changed from the default. Listing 6-24 shows an example configuration of an InnoDB slave.

Listing 6-24. Example Configuration for Slave MySQL Server When Replicating from MySQL NDB Cluster Master

```
[mysqld]
server_id = 2001
slave_exec_mode = IDEMPOTENT
replicate_wild_ignore_table = mysql.ndb_index%
```

You can set additional replication filters if you like. Then, start the slave MySQL Server or restart it if it's already running.

Take a Backup from Master

Execute the START BACKUP command to take a native online backup on the master cluster. Refer to Chapter 8 for more information about native backups. The native backup is the only way to take a backup from online MySQL NDB Cluster unless it's ensured that no modifications are made while taking a backup. Listing 6-25 shows example output of a native backup.

Listing 6-25. Example Output of a Native Backup

```
ndb_mgm> START BACKUP
Connected to Management Server at: mgmhost
Waiting for completed, this may take several minutes
Node 1: Backup 1 started from node 255
ndb_mgm> Node 1: Backup 1 started from node 255 completed
 StartGCP: 527473 StopGCP: 527476
#Records: 18444 #LogRecords: 112
 Data: 575936 bytes Log: 4536 bytes
```

Note that StopGCP printed in the console when the backup completes. This value is required in the later step. StopGCP is 527476 in this example.

I recommend taking another backup for schemas using the mysqldump command, because SQL based DDL is easy to restore on the InnoDB slave. Specify the --no-data option with the mysqldump command to suppress data backup. Listing 6-26 shows an example that takes a schema backup from the master SQL node.

Listing 6-26. Taking Schema Backup from Master SQL Node

```
shell$ mysqldump -h masterhost -uroot -p db_name --no-data > dump.sql
```

Restore Schemas to Slave

Restore the schemas using the dump taken by the mysqldump command. Before restoring to the slave SQL node, change the storage engine in the dump file. This can be done using the sed command on UNIX-like systems as follows:

```
shell$ sed -i 's/ENGINE=ndbcluster/ENGINE=InnoDB/g' dump.sql
```

Then, restore the dump file as usual to the MySQL Server; for example, use the SOURCE command from the mysql CLI:

```
mysql> SOURCE dump.sql
```

Check if all tables are created on the slave.

Restore Data to Slave

This is the trickiest step of this procedure. A native NDB backup consists of two parts: the data and log. Both parts must be restored to recover a consistent snapshot at a certain point of time. There are two ways to restore the backup to the InnoDB slave.

One way is to use an intermediate temporary cluster. Restore a native backup to the temporary cluster first, ensure no modifications are done, then take a backup using the mysqldump command from the temporary cluster. The dump taken using mysqldump can be restored just like with a standard MySQL Server.

The other way is to convert the data part into tab-separated files, then restore it using the LOAD DATA INFILE command. Conversion can be done using the ndb_restore command. The required options are --print-data, --tab, and --append. The --print-data option dictates the ndb_restore command to print the data instead of restoring it to a running cluster. The --tab option specifies the target directory where the tab-separated files are created; a tab-separated file is created per table under this directory. The --append option indicates that tab-separated files are not overwritten and new data is appended when they already exist.

Listing 6-27 shows an example of converting a backup into tab-separated files.

Listing 6-27. Converting a Native Backup into Tab-Separated Files Using the ndb_restore Command

```
shell$ ndb_restore -n 1 -b 1 --print-data --tab=/backup/tab-files --append \
  /path/to/backup
```

Since a native backup is created per data node, repeat the same command for all the data nodes. The -n option in ndb_restore command specifies a node ID where the backup is generated and the -b option specifies a backup ID assigned to each backup. Refer to Chapter 8 for more information about the ndb_restore command. Then, restore the tab-separated files into the InnoDB slave using the LOAD DATA INFILE command. Make sure a data part is restored completely prior to restoration of a log part.

The next step is to restore the log file included in the native backup. As of MySQL NDB Cluster 7.5.4, the ndb_restore command can generate SQL statements that can be directly executed on MySQL Server. To generate the executable SQL log, specify the --print-sql-log option. Even when this option is specified, unnecessary header and footer lines are printed as well. To suppress these lines, execute the ndb_restore command, as shown in Listing 6-28.

Listing 6-28. Converting a Native Backup Log into SQL Format

```
shell$ ndb_restore -n 1 -b 1 --print-sql-log /path/to/backup \
  | egrep '^INSERT|^DELETE|^UPDATE' >> dump-log.sql
```

Repeat the same command for all data nodes. Then, execute the generated SQL file on the slave server. Since the ndb_restore command can be used against a backup taken from older versions, you can convert backup logs into SQL format using the ndb_restore command bundled with 7.5.4 or newer.

Create System Tables

Create the mysql.ndb_apply_status table identical to the master except for the storage engine. Create it using the InnoDB storage engine instead of NDBCluster.

Set Up Replication

Finally, set up replication using the CHANGE MASTER TO command. The first step is to retrieve binary log filename and position from the mysql.ndb_binlog_index table on the master SQL node. The required information is the StopGCP value retrieved when the backup was taken. Listing 6-29 shows an example query that retrieves the binary log filename and position.

Listing 6-29. Retrieving Binary Log Filename and Position from the mysql.ndb_binlog_index Table Using StopGCP

```
mysql> SET @stopgcp = 527476;
mysql> SELECT
    -> SUBSTRING_INDEX(File, '/', -1) AS binlog_file,
```

```
-> Position AS binlog_position
-> FROM mysql.ndb_binlog_index
-> WHERE gci > @stopgcp
-> ORDER BY epoch ASC LIMIT 1;
```

Specify the filename and position retrieved by this query in the CHANGE MASTER TO command. Then, execute the START SLAVE command to start replication, and check the replication status using the SHOW SLAVE STATUS command.

Tips When Using InnoDB as a Slave

There are several tips when using InnoDB as a slave of MySQL NDB Cluster.

Resume Replication from Alternative Channel

It is also true for the master SQL node that data can be missing from the binary log for various reasons, such as the master SQL node being offline even if the slave is InnoDB. So, redundancy is required for the master SQL node. In the event of an unrecoverable replication failure such as LOST_EVENTS event, switch to an alternative master SQL node using the epoch information stored in the mysql.ndb_apply_status table, just like for NDB Cluster to NDB Cluster replication.

Speed Up Updates by Skipping Log Synchronization

In general, the write speed of MySQL NDB Cluster is faster than InnoDB. This will cause unnecessary replication delay on the InnoDB slave. To prevent delays on the InnoDB slave, I recommend setting innodb_flush_log_at_trx_commt to 0 or 2 on the slave. This will skip synchronizing InnoDB log to disk upon transaction commit. This setting is not recommended in general, because the last committed transactions that have not synchronized to disk may be lost upon machine failures.

Since the mysql.ndb_apply_status table is updated within the same transaction to other tables, you can safely restart replication using the epoch in the table in the event of crash. Even if replication cannot be restarted for some reason, you can set up InnoDB slave again using the master data. Even more, it is also possible to clone a slave using the mysqldump command with the --dump-slave option as well as other standard method such as *MySQL Enterprise Backup*, if you have multiple slave servers.

MySQL Server Options Related to Cluster Replication

For your reference, the MySQL Server options related to NDB Cluster Replication are listed in Table 6-9.

Table 6-9. *List of NDB Cluster Replication Related Options in mysqld*

Option Name	Default	Description
log_bin	None	Enables the binary log when specified. The argument of this option is used as a base name of binary log files.
sync_binlog	0 (<= 7.4) 1 (>= 7.5)	Synchronizes the binary log to disk after handling the number of events specified by this option. Set this option to a larger value such as 1000 on MySQL NDB Cluster.
log_slave_updates	OFF	When enabled on slave, all modifications propagated from the master are recorded in the slave's binary log.
ndb_log_bin	ON	Start the binlog injector thread.
server_id	None	The server identifier assigned to the server.
server_id_bits	32	Effective bits of server_id. The range of this option is 7 ~ 32.
binlog_format	STATEMENT (<= 7.4) ROW (>= 7.5)	Format of binary log. NDB Cluster Replication only supports row format.
expire_logs_days	None	Binary logs are automatically deleted after the number of days specified with this option.
ndb_log_updated_only	ON	When enabled, only the modified part within a row is recorded in the binary log. Must be OFF when using conflict detection or InnoDB slaves.
ndb_log_update_as_write	ON	When enabled, updates against NDB tables are recorded as write in the binary log. Must be OFF when using conflict detection or InnoDB slaves.
ndb_log_apply_status	OFF	When enabled, modifications against the ndb_apply_status table from a direct master are written to the binary log. Must be OFF when using the epoch-based conflict detection method.
ndb_log_binlog_index	ON	Mapping between epoch and binary log position is written to the ndb_binlog_index table.
slave_allow_batching	OFF	When enabled, updates are applied in batches on the slave. This will improve the slave performance.
log_bin_use_v1_row_events	OFF	When disabled, version 2 of binary log format is used. Required for ndb_log_transaction_id option.
ndb_log_transaction_id	OFF	When enabled, the transaction ID of the NDBCluster storage engine is written to each binary log entry. Needed for epoch-based conflict detection method.
ndb_slave_conflict_role	None	Specifies the role of the server as PRIMARY or SECONDARY. Required for the NDB$EPOCH2 and NDB$EPOCH2_TRANS conflict detection methods.
ndb_log_exclusive_reads	OFF	When enabled, exclusive reads are written to the binary log so that they are subject to conflict detection.

Notes and Limitations of NDB Cluster Replication

There are several limitations on NDB Cluster Replication. The following features are unavailable on NDB Cluster Replication. If you want to use these features, consider using InnoDB and the standard MySQL replication instead of NDB Cluster Replication.

- GTID (Global Transaction Identifier)
- Multi-thread slave
- Multi-source replication
- Group Replication

Ensure that all tables have explicit primary keys when using replication, because an error might occur on replication in the event of node failures if there's no explicit primary key on some tables. It is also a problem when a table is scanned when applying modification if the table doesn't have explicit primary key. In general, having a primary key on all tables is highly recommended from a development point of view as well as from a replication point of view.

Summary

NDB Cluster replication is powerful feature to complement several aspects of MySQL NDB Cluster. Such as,

- Disaster recovery or standby cluster;
- Read scaling for same data set;
- Inter-storage engine replication;

This makes MySQL NDB Cluster more useful in various cases.

From the next section, we'll discuss daily tasks and maintenance related topics. To keep the database cluster healthy, it should be maintained well on a daily basis. The first topic of maintenance tasks is client and utilities for MySQL NDB Cluster.

PART III

Daily Tasks and Maintenance

■ ■ ■

The NDB Management Client and Other NDB Utilities

MySQL NDB Cluster comes with a range of utilities for managing, obtaining information from, and troubleshooting the cluster. The most commonly used utility is the NDB management client, ndb_mgm, which connects to the management nodes and can be used to get status information, create backups, etc. This chapter goes into detail about the management client and provides an overview of the other utilities.

The NDB Management Client

The NDB management client is special, as it is the only utility that exclusively communicates with the management nodes. Whereas all the data nodes, management nodes, and API/SQL nodes require a node ID in order to connect, the NDB management client does not require a node ID. This means it is always possible to connect to the cluster using the management client even if all configured API node IDs have been used. Some of the tasks that can be performed by the management client are:

- Start data nodes that are in the "no start" status. See Chapter 10 for an example.

- Stop a single management or data node, all data nodes, or all management and data nodes. See Chapter 10 for details.

- Restart management or data nodes. See Chapter 10 for examples.

- Start and abort online NDB backups. See Chapter 8 for details.

- Display information about the status of the cluster in terms of which nodes are online and from which hosts connections are accepted.

- Manage the cluster log. See Chapter 16 for details.

- Create reports.

- Create or drop node groups. See Chapter 10 for an example of creating a new node group.

- Enter and exit single user mode.

- Purge stale sessions.

- Set the text used for the prompt.

© Jesper Wisborg Krogh and Mikiya Okuno 2017
J. W. Krogh and M. Okuno, *Pro MySQL NDB Cluster*, https://doi.org/10.1007/978-1-4842-2982-8_7

The rest of this section discusses the most common uses of the ndb_mgm client, excluding cases discussed in other chapters, such as creating backups.

Invoking the NDB Management Client

There are only a few options available when starting the management client, of which the most important are the following (ordered alphabetically according to the long version of the option name):

- **--defaults-extra-file=....** Read configuration options from this file in addition to the default configuration file. See also the --defaults-file option.

- **--defaults-file=....** This works the same as for all other MySQL programs. ndb_mgm will read the [mysql_cluster] and [ndb_mgm] groups. Reading a configuration file can be useful to set the ndb-connectstring option.

- **--execute=.../-e.** A command to execute. This works the same way as for the mysql command line client. All commands that can be executed interactively through the management client can also be executed directly using the -e or --execute=... command line option. If the command consists of more than one word, the command must be quoted or the spaces escaped with a backslash (\). For example: ndb_mgm -e "START BACKUP". An advantage of executing commands this way is that the output can be redirected to another program or a file.

- **--help**. Display information about the available options and the defaults.

- **--ndb-connectstring=.../-c.** A semicolon-separated list of the hostname and port of the management nodes. The format for each management node is hostname:port. The default is localhost:1186. See Chapter 4 for details.

- **--no-defaults**. Do not read any configuration files. See also --defaults-file.

- **--prompt=.../-p.** Specify the text used for the prompt. The default is ndb_mgm>. This feature is new in MySQL NDB Cluster 7.5. The use is similar to setting the prompt of the mysql command-line client with the exception that there is no support for special sequences such as \c to add a counter.

To get additional information about the command line, including options not mentioned here, use the --help argument, as shown in Listing 7-1.

Listing 7-1. Output of ndb_mgm --help

```
shell$ ndb_mgm --help
Usage: ./mysql/bin/ndb_mgm [OPTIONS] [hostname [port]]
MySQL distrib mysql-5.7.18 ndb-7.5.6, for linux-glibc2.5 (x86_64)

Default options are read from the following files in the given order:
/etc/my.cnf /etc/mysql/my.cnf /usr/local/mysql/etc/my.cnf ~/.my.cnf
The following groups are read: mysql_cluster ndb_mgm
The following options may be given as the first argument:
--print-defaults       Print the program argument list and exit.
--no-defaults          Don't read default options from any option file,
                       except for login file.
--defaults-file=#      Only read default options from the given file #.
```

```
--defaults-extra-file=# Read this file after the global files are read.
--defaults-group-suffix=# Also read groups with concat(group, suffix)
--login-path=#          Read this path from the login file.

 -?, --usage            Display this help and exit.
 -?, --help             Display this help and exit.
 -V, --version          Output version information and exit.
 -c, --ndb-connectstring=name
                        Set connect string for connecting to ndb_mgmd. Syntax:
                        "[nodeid=<id>;][host=]<hostname>[:<port>]". Overrides
                        specifying entries in NDB_CONNECTSTRING and my.cnf
--ndb-mgmd-host=name same as --ndb-connectstring
--ndb-nodeid=#         Set node id for this node. Overrides node id specified in
                        --ndb-connectstring.
--ndb-optimized-node-selection
                        Select nodes for transactions in a more optimal way
                        (Defaults to on; use --skip-ndb-optimized-node-selection to disable.)
 -c, --connect-string=name
                        same as --ndb-connectstring
--core-file            Write core on errors.
--character-sets-dir=name
                        Directory where character sets are.
--connect-retry-delay=#
                        Set connection time out. This is the number of seconds
                        after which the tool tries reconnecting to the cluster.
--connect-retries=# Set connection retries. This is the number of times the
                        tool tries connecting to the cluster.
 -e, --execute=name    execute command and exit
 -p, --prompt=name     Set prompt to string specified
 -v, --verbose=#       Control the amount of printout
 -t, --try-reconnect=#
                        Same as --connect-retries

Variables (--variable-name=value)
and boolean options {FALSE|TRUE} Value (after reading options)
-------------------------------- ----------------------------------------
ndb-connectstring                (No default value)
ndb-mgmd-host                    (No default value)
ndb-nodeid                       0
ndb-optimized-node-selection     TRUE
connect-string                   (No default value)
core-file                        FALSE
character-sets-dir               (No default value)
connect-retry-delay              5
connect-retries                  12
execute                          (No default value)
prompt                           (No default value)
verbose                          1
try-reconnect                    12
```

Getting Help from Inside the Client

The documentation of the commands supported by the management client is in the MySQL Reference Manual at *https://dev.mysql.com/doc/refman/5.7/en/mysql-cluster-mgm-client-commands.html*. An easier way to get a quick reference is to use the HELP command inside the management client. The overview of the help is shown in Listing 7-2. This is not the same help as in the previous subsection using ndb_mgm --help, but rather provides help on the available commands.

Listing 7-2. The HELP Command in ndb_mgm

```
ndb_mgm> HELP
--------------------------------------------------------------------
 NDB Cluster -- Management Client -- Help
--------------------------------------------------------------------
HELP                                Print help text
HELP COMMAND                        Print detailed help for COMMAND(e.g. SHOW)
SHOW                                Print information about cluster
CREATE NODEGROUP <id>,<id>...       Add a Nodegroup containing nodes
DROP NODEGROUP <NG>                 Drop nodegroup with id NG
START BACKUP [NOWAIT | WAIT STARTED | WAIT COMPLETED]
START BACKUP [<backup id>] [NOWAIT | WAIT STARTED | WAIT COMPLETED]
START BACKUP [<backup id>] [SNAPSHOTSTART | SNAPSHOTEND] [NOWAIT | WAIT STARTED | WAIT
COMPLETED]
                                    Start backup (default WAIT COMPLETED,SNAPSHOTEND)
ABORT BACKUP <backup id>            Abort backup
SHUTDOWN                            Shutdown all processes in cluster
PROMPT [<prompt-string>]            Toggle the prompt between string specified
                                    or default prompt if no string specified
CLUSTERLOG ON [<severity>] ...      Enable Cluster logging
CLUSTERLOG OFF [<severity>] ...     Disable Cluster logging
CLUSTERLOG TOGGLE [<severity>] ...  Toggle severity filter on/off
CLUSTERLOG INFO                     Print cluster log information
<id> START                          Start data node (started with -n)
<id> RESTART [-n] [-i] [-a] [-f]    Restart data or management server node
<id> STOP [-a] [-f]                 Stop data or management server node
ENTER SINGLE USER MODE <id>         Enter single user mode
EXIT SINGLE USER MODE               Exit single user mode
<id> STATUS                         Print status
<id> CLUSTERLOG {<category>=<level>}+ Set log level for cluster log
PURGE STALE SESSIONS                Reset reserved nodeid's in the mgmt server
CONNECT [<connectstring>]           Connect to management server (reconnect if already
                                    connected)
<id> REPORT <report-type>           Display report for <report-type>
QUIT                                Quit management client

<severity> = ALERT | CRITICAL | ERROR | WARNING | INFO | DEBUG
<category> = STARTUP | SHUTDOWN | STATISTICS | CHECKPOINT | NODERESTART | CONNECTION | INFO
| ERROR | CONGESTION | DEBUG | BACKUP | SCHEMA
<report-type> = BACKUPSTATUS | MEMORYUSAGE | EVENTLOG
<level>    = 0 - 15
<id>       = ALL | Any database node id

For detailed help on COMMAND, use HELP COMMAND.
```

■ **Tip**   Unlike the `mysql` command-line client, there is no support for multi-line statements, so there is no need for a delimiter. This means you can execute a command in the management client without specifying a semicolon (;) at the end. Like for SQL statements, commands are case insensitive.

As the description of the HELP COMMAND command states, it is also possible to get more detailed help for a given command. For example, to learn more about the START BACKUP command, use this command:

```
ndb_mgm> HELP START BACKUP
--------------------------------------------------------------------------
 NDB Cluster -- Management Client -- Help for START BACKUP command
--------------------------------------------------------------------------
START BACKUP   Start a cluster backup

START BACKUP [<backup id>] [SNAPSHOTSTART | SNAPSHOTEND] [NOWAIT | WAIT STARTED |
WAIT COMPLETED]
                    Start a backup for the cluster.
...
```

Using the inline help is a very useful way to verify syntax and use of the commands.

Setting the Prompt

In MySQL NDB Cluster 7.5 and later, it is possible to change the prompt. The default prompt is `ndb_mgm>`. However, if you manage more than one cluster, it is useful to set the prompt to different values to reduce the risk of executing commands on the wrong cluster.

To change the prompt, use the PROMPT command followed by the string you want to use. The string should not be quoted. For example, to set the prompt to `mgm - production>`, use the following command:

```
ndb_mgm> PROMPT mgm - production>
Prompt set to mgm - production>
mgm - production>
```

There is no need for a space at the end, as that will be added automatically after all whitespace at the end of the prompt text has been trimmed.

To reset the prompt to the default, execute the PROMPT command without an argument:

```
mgm - production> PROMPT
Returning to default prompt of ndb_mgm>
ndb_mgm>
```

In MySQL NDB Cluster 7.5, the prompt can also be set on the command line and thus through the MySQL configuration file:

```
shell$ ndb_mgm --prompt="mgm - production>"
Connected to Management Server at: localhost:1186
Prompt set to mgm - production>
-- NDB Cluster -- Management Client --
mgm - production>
```

Display the Cluster Status

One of the most commonly used commands in the management client is the SHOW command. It gives an overview of the cluster's status. Additionally, the STATUS command gives a simpler output and only includes the data nodes. The SHOW command does not take any arguments, so its usage is very simple:

```
ndb_mgm> SHOW
Connected to Management Server at: 192.168.56.101:1186
Cluster Configuration
---------------------
[ndbd(NDB)]     2 node(s)
id=1    @192.168.56.103  (mysql-5.7.16 ndb-7.5.4, Nodegroup: 0, *)
id=2    @192.168.56.104  (mysql-5.7.16 ndb-7.5.4, Nodegroup: 0)

[ndb_mgmd(MGM)] 2 node(s)
id=49   @192.168.56.101  (mysql-5.7.16 ndb-7.5.4)
id=50   @192.168.56.102  (mysql-5.7.16 ndb-7.5.4)

[mysqld(API)]   6 node(s)
id=51   @192.168.56.103  (mysql-5.7.16 ndb-7.5.4)
id=52   @192.168.56.104  (mysql-5.7.16 ndb-7.5.4)
id=53 (not connected, accepting connect from 192.168.56.101)
id=54 (not connected, accepting connect from 192.168.56.102)
id=55 (not connected, accepting connect from any host)
id=56 (not connected, accepting connect from any host)
```

For the online nodes, the information includes the following data:

- The node ID allocated for the node.

- The host the node is connected from.

- The version used.

- For the data nodes, which node group the data node is part of.

- For the data nodes, there is an asterisk (*) next to the current *master (president) node*. In the example, id = 1 is the master node.

- If the data node is restarting, this will be reflected but without any details of the last completed start phase (see Chapter 10).

For currently unused slots, the information includes:

- The node ID available. If a node has been configured without an explicit *NodeId*, the management node(s) will still assign a node ID to the slot.

- Where connections are allowed from. If no *HostName* has been configured, the text will show that connections are allowed from any host.

Examples of the SHOW command are available in Chapters 10 and 11. Chapter 10 covers restart operations and Chapter 11 covers upgrades and downgrades.

The STATUS command is useful to get a quick overview of the status of one or all the data nodes. The command requires one argument—added before the STATUS keyword—and the argument must be either ALL or a node ID. As the status information includes information about the latest restart phase, it can be useful to monitor a restart of a data node. For example, to get the status of node 2:

```
ndb_mgm> 2 STATUS
Node 2: starting (Last completed phase 4) (mysql-5.7.16 ndb-7.5.4)
```

To get the status of all data nodes:

```
ndb_mgm> ALL STATUS
Node 1: started (mysql-5.7.16 ndb-7.5.4)
Node 2: starting (Last completed phase 100) (mysql-5.7.16 ndb-7.5.4)
```

Single User Mode

Single user mode is used for some maintenance situations where it is important that the application is not connected to the data nodes, or it is only connected through a single API node. In single user mode, only one API/SQL node will be allowed to connect. This also means that if an SQL node has been configured with ndb_cluster_connection_pool set to a value greater than one, it will not be able to connect as it requires all of the requested slots to be available. If the SQL nodes are configured to use a connection pool larger than one, and the single user mode maintenance window requires using an SQL node, the solution is either to use a spare SQL node available for cases like this, or restart one of the existing SQL nodes with ndb_cluster_connection_pool = 1.

The command to initialize single user mode is ENTER SINGLE USER MODE, and the command takes the node ID that will be allowed to connect to the cluster. For example, to allow node ID 54 to connect but no other API/SQL nodes, use this command:

```
ndb_mgm> ENTER SINGLE USER MODE 54;
Single user mode entered
Access is granted for API node 54 only.
```

The command may take a little while to complete while the other nodes are disconnected. While in single user mode, the SHOW and STATUS commands reflects the status, for example:

```
ndb_mgm> ALL STATUS
Node 1: single user mode (mysql-5.7.16 ndb-7.5.4)
Node 2: single user mode (mysql-5.7.16 ndb-7.5.4)
```

Once the maintenance window has completed, use the EXIT SINGLE USER MODE command to return to normal:

```
ndb_mgm> EXIT SINGLE USER MODE
Exiting single user mode in progress.
Use ALL STATUS or SHOW to see when single user mode has been exited.
```

Create Reports

The management client can be used to create a range of reports, thereby providing useful information for the cluster. A report can either be generated for one data node or for all data nodes. There are currently three report types available:

- **MemoryUsage:** The data memory and index memory usage for the data node(s).

- **BackupStatus:** The status of backups for the data node(s).

- **EventLog:** Messages from the event log on the data nodes.

The MemoryUsage report is the most commonly used report and provides information about the current memory usage both for data and (unique hash) indexes:

```
ndb_mgm> ALL REPORT MemoryUsage
Node 1: Data usage is 55%(7070 32K pages of total 12800)
Node 1: Index usage is 43%(4459 8K pages of total 10304)
Node 2: Data usage is 55%(7072 32K pages of total 12800)
Node 2: Index usage is 43%(4460 8K pages of total 10304)
```

The memory usage information is in percentage and in number of pages.

The BackupStatus report will either report that a backup is not in progress or give information of the progress of an ongoing backup. For example, when no backups are in progress and you're requesting the backup information for all data nodes:

```
ndb_mgm> ALL REPORT BackupStatus
Node 1: Backup not started
Node 2: Backup not started
```

The status for data node 1 during a backup:

```
ndb_mgm> 1 REPORT BackupStatus
Node 1: Local backup status: backup 5 started from node 49
 #Records: 556508 #LogRecords: 0
 Data: 18873520 bytes Log: 0 bytes
```

See Chapter 8 for more information about backups.

The last of the three reports is the EventLog report. This can be used to get information about the activity of the data nodes in greater detail than the out logs (see Chapter 16) and without having to log in to the data nodes. The event log is a circular buffer, so there is a limited number of events available. Listing 7-3 shows an example of the report. If events from all the data nodes are chosen, the events will be interleaved.

Listing 7-3. The EventLog Report

```
ndb_mgm> ALL REPORT EventLog
2016-12-18 16:24:13 Node 1: Node 50 Connected
2016-12-18 16:24:13 Node 1: Communication to Node 2 opened
2016-12-18 16:24:14 Node 2: Node 50 Connected
2016-12-18 16:24:14 Node 2: Communication to Node 1 opened
2016-12-18 16:24:14 Node 1: Node 2 Connected
2016-12-18 16:24:14 Node 2: Node 1 Connected
2016-12-18 16:24:17 Node 1: Node 2: API mysql-5.7.16 ndb-7.5.4
2016-12-18 16:24:17 Node 2: Node 1: API mysql-5.7.16 ndb-7.5.4
```

```
...
2016-12-18 16:38:39 Node 1: Backup 5 started from node 49
2016-12-18 16:39:28 Node 1: Backup 5 started from node 49 completed. StartGCP: 3596 StopGCP:
3600 #Records: 2423505 #LogRecords: 0 Data: 74515992 bytes Log: 0 bytes
2016-12-18 16:39:31 Node 1: LDM(1): Completed LCP, #frags = 34 #records = 1211469, #bytes =
60693392
2016-12-18 16:39:31 Node 1: LDM(2): Completed LCP, #frags = 34 #records = 1212045, #bytes =
60759696
2016-12-18 16:39:33 Node 2: LDM(1): Completed LCP, #frags = 34 #records = 1211469, #bytes =
60693392
2016-12-18 16:39:33 Node 2: LDM(2): Completed LCP, #frags = 34 #records = 1212045, #bytes =
60759696
...
2016-12-18 16:43:33 Node 2: Trans. Count = 0, Commit Count = 0, Read Count = 0, Simple Read
Count = 0, Write Count = 0, AttrInfo Count = 0, Concurrent Operations = 0, Abort Count = 0
Scans = 0 Range scans = 0, Local Read Count = 0 Local Write Count = 0
2016-12-18 16:43:33 Node 1: Operations=0
2016-12-18 16:43:33 Node 1: Global checkpoint 3718 started
2016-12-18 16:43:33 Node 1: Global checkpoint 3718 completed
2016-12-18 16:43:34 Node 1: Trans. Count = 0, Commit Count = 0, Read Count = 0, Simple Read
Count = 0, Write Count = 0, AttrInfo Count = 0, Concurrent Operations = 0, Abort Count = 0
Scans = 0 Range scans = 0, Local Read Count = 0 Local Write Count = 0
2016-12-18 16:43:35 Node 1: Global checkpoint 3719 started
2016-12-18 16:43:35 Node 1: Global checkpoint 3719 completed
2016-12-18 16:43:37 Node 1: Global checkpoint 3720 started
2016-12-18 16:43:37 Node 1: Global checkpoint 3720 completed
```

Purge Stale Sessions

This command is only very rarely needed. It can happen after a node failure that the node ID is not released, which means the node cannot rejoin the cluster. In a case like that, the PURGE STALE SESSIONS command can be used to check whether any of the node IDs can be released and, if so, release them. There are no arguments for the command. An example of using the command is:

```
ndb_mgm> PURGE STALE SESSIONS
No sessions purged
```

Other NDB Utilities

There are several utilities included in the MySQL NDB Cluster downloads. These are all installed in the *bin* directory. If you install MySQL NDB Cluster using RPM packages, the utilities are included in the client RPM for version 7.5, for example *mysql-cluster-community-client-7.5.4-1.el7.x86_64.rpm*, whereas for earlier versions the utilities are included with the server RPM. The source code for some of the utilities also serve as useful examples of using the NDB API.

Table 7-1 contains an overview of the utilities included with version 7.5.6. Throughout the book there are examples of using several of these utilities.

▪ **Tip** For more information about the utilities, see *https://dev.mysql.com/doc/refman/5.7/en/mysql-cluster-programs.html*, which includes information about all NDB Cluster programs.

Table 7-1. *Overview of Client Utilities Included with MySQL NDB Cluster 7.5.6*

Utility	Description
ndb_blob_tool	Can be used to check and repair BLOB tables. The BLOB tables were discussed in Chapter 2.
ndb_config	Get information about the current configuration and description of configuration options. Chapter 10 contains an example of using ndb_config.
ndb_delete_all	Delete all rows from a table. The equivalent of DELETE FROM <table name> without a WHERE clause in an SQL node but implemented using the NDB API. **Warning:** All data in the table will be deleted.
ndb_desc	Provide details of a table, including columns, indexes, partition info, and information about the BLOB tables. Chapter 2 includes several examples.
ndb_drop_index	Drop an index from a table. **Warning:** Never use this for a table that is used from SQL nodes—the table will become inaccessible from SQL nodes after using ndb_drop_index!
ndb_drop_table	Drop a table. It will in general be faster to use the ndb_drop_table utility than a DROP TABLE statement from an SQL node.
ndb_error_reporter	Collect the logs and trace files from the management and data nodes. This is a Perl script and requires ssh access to the nodes. See also Chapter 17.
ndb_index_stat	Enable, disable, and update index statistics. See also Chapter 9.
ndbinfo_select_all	Query information from the ndbinfo schema using the NDB API. See also Chapter 16 for information about the ndbinfo schema.
ndb_mgm	The NDB management client.
ndb_move_data	Move data between two tables using the NDB API.
ndb_print_backup_file	Print information about backup files. This utility does not connect to the management node(s).
ndb_print_file	Output information about on-disk data files. This utility does not connect to the management node(s).
ndb_print_frag_file	Output information about the fragment list files (the *S*.FragList* files in the *DBDIH* subdirectory of the *D1* and *D2* directories in the NDB file system). This utility does not connect to the management node(s).
ndb_print_schema_file	Output information about the NDB schema files (the *P0.SchemaLog* file in *DBDICT* subdirectory of the *D1* and *D2* directories in the NDB file system). This utility does not connect to the management node(s).
ndb_print_sys_file	Output information about the NDB schema files (the *P0.sysfile* file in *DBDIH* subdirectory of the *D1* and *D2* directories in the NDB file system). This utility does not connect to the management node(s).
ndb_redo_log_reader	Output the contents of the redo log files (the *S*.FragLog* files in the *D8* though *D39* directories in the NDB file system) in a human readable format. This utility does not connect to the management node(s).
ndb_restore	Restore backups. For details see Chapter 8.
ndb_select_all	Select all the data in a table using the NDB API.

(continued)

Table 7-1. (*continued*)

Utility	Description
ndb_select_count	Get the number of rows in one or more tables using the NDB API.
ndb_setup.py	Python script that starts a web daemon, thereby allowing you to set up a cluster using a web browser. See also Chapter 5.
ndb_show_tables	List the tables in the cluster. See Chapter 2 for an example and description of the output.
ndb_size.pl	Perl script that generates an estimate of the configuration options required based on an existing non-NDB Cluster database. There is an example of its usage in Chapter 18.
ndb_waiter	Wait for the cluster to reach a given status. It is commonly used in script. Chapter 10 includes an example.

Summary

In this chapter, the uses of the NDB management client have been discussed. The client can be used for a wide array of administrative tasks, ranging from getting reports of the current memory usage to restarting nodes and managing node groups. MySQL NDB Cluster also includes several other client utilities. These were briefly discussed as well. The rest of the book uses the management client and other utilities, with examples of their use and output. The next chapter on backups and restores is no exception.

Backups and Restores

For any database product, backups and restores are two very important parts of ensuring the data can be recovered in case of human errors, hardware failures, natural disasters, and the like. MySQL NDB Cluster offers two types of backups: native backups and logical backups. Both types have their uses, and in most cases, both should be used. This chapter goes through the two options, discusses when to use them, and covers how to restore the backups. First, the chapter discusses what a backup and backup procedure are.

Backups and Backup Procedures

It may sound trivial to answer the question: "What is a backup?" The definition in the Merriam-Webster dictionary (*https://www.merriam-webster.com/dictionary/backup*) is:

> *A copy of computer data (such as a file or the contents of a hard drive)*

This definition is correct and is also used in MySQL NDB Cluster—creating a backup creates a copy of the data in the cluster. However, database administrators who are used to other database systems may have something more complex in mind.

Oracle Database administrators may think of a backup of something involving Oracle Recovery Manager (RMAN; see *http://www.oracle.com/technetwork/database/features/availability/ rman-overview-096633.html*), which handles all of the details of creating a backup and integrates with Oracle Secure Backup and other solutions to write the backup to tape. MySQL Enterprise Backup (MEB) has some of the same features in the sense that it supports working with Oracle Secure Backup and third-party tape backup solutions.

In MySQL NDB Cluster, on the other hand, the native backup solution is built into the data nodes, and backups are started from a management node. This does not make the backup quality inferior to backups made with Oracle Recovery Manager or MySQL Enterprise Backup—all are professional grade backups. However, there is no support for saving the backup directory to tape or streaming it to a remote host. It is up to the database administrator to ensure that the backups are transferred to a remote location for safekeeping.

When designing backup procedures, it is important to keep in mind that a backup is worth no more than the ability to restore it. The backup procedures should not just include how to create the backup, but the whole cycle back to restoring it. This includes being able to retrieve the backup even if the whole data center is out due to a disaster (human or natural). Do not take the step of transferring the backups to a remote host or tape station lightly. The best way to confirm that the backups work is to restore them to a test system and verify that it is possible to bring back all of the data.

With the definition of a backup and backup procedures in place, it is time to look closer at how the native NDB Cluster backups work.

Native NDB Cluster Online Backups

The main method of backing up the NDBCluster tables is to use the native backup. This is to the NDBCluster tables what MySQL Enterprise Backup is to the InnoDB storage engine. The main features of the native NDB Cluster backup include:

- It is online. That is, it is possible to change data and schema while the backup is in progress.

- It is built into MySQL NDB Cluster (no additional binaries or packages are required).

- It supports creating a snapshot (the point in time where the backup is consistent) either at the start or the end of the backup; the default is to have the snapshot at the end like MySQL Enterprise Backup.

- The restore of the native backups supports parallel restores, restores to a different cluster configuration, and partial restores. Restoring backups is discussed in the section entitled "Restores".

- It uses the same underlying mechanism as the local checkpoints.

■ **Note**   Neither MySQL Enterprise Backup nor Percona XtraBackup can be used to back up MySQL NDB Cluster, as they only work at the file system level of the local host and have no means to connect to the cluster.

Overview

Backups are started from the NDB management client or from the MySQL Cluster Manager (MCM) client (see also Chapter 13). The simplest way to start a backup is:

```
shell$ ndb_mgm -e "START BACKUP"
Connected to Management Server at: localhost:1186
Waiting for completed, this may take several minutes
Node 1: Backup 1 started from node 49
Node 1: Backup 1 started from node 49 completed
 StartGCP: 91 StopGCP: 94
 #Records: 107373 #LogRecords: 2946
 Data: 20499388 bytes Log: 400956 bytes
```

The section entitled "Starting and Aborting Backups" discusses controlling backups in more detail. There are several points to note from the backup command and its output, which is discussed in the rest of this subsection.

In the example, control (the prompt) is not returned until the backup has completed. This is the default behavior. Waiting for the completion of the backup is also the only way for the invoker of the command to get the return value of the backup—whether the backup succeeded or not. Backup Monitoring discusses how to get the return code and what the meaning is.

The Backup 1 strings in the output refer to the backup ID. Each backup has an ID which is also used when restoring the backup. By default, the first backup will be number 1, the next number 2, and so forth. However, it is also possible to specify a custom backup ID. Backup IDs must be an integer with a value between 1 and 4294967294 (both inclusive). An automatically generated backup ID is always the largest previously used backup ID number, plus one.

The text Backup 1 started from node 49 means that node 49 (a management node) told node 1 (the master data node) to start the backup. Node 1 also informs when the backup has completed (the next line). However, all online data nodes will take part in the backup.

The StartGCP and StopGCP values refer to the global checkpoints that were current at the time the backup started and completed. Remember that global checkpoints is the mechanism to synchronize the flushing of the redo log to disk across the data nodes. It is possible to choose whether the backup will be consistent at the StartGCP or the StopGCP (see the next subsection, "Implementation Details").

Finally, the last two lines have statistics about the size of the backup in terms of records and rows. The "Log" part of the lines refer to collection of the transactions committed while the backup is in progress. This is discussed in the next subsection about the inner workings of the backup.

Implementation Details

The backup runs in parallel on all online data nodes, so each data node will have a part of the backup. Each node will back up the part of the data that is in its primary partitions. If a node is offline, its primary partitions are handled by another data node in the same node group. This means that the data is only backed up once—unlike local checkpoints, where each data node writes out all the data it has.

There are three parts to a backup, each using its own file. Table 8-1 shows the three parts of a backup and the filename used for each. *<backup_id>* means the backup ID chosen for the backup (see the two next subsections) and *<node_id>* means the NodeId for the node that writes the backup. The three files are written to the directory *BACKUP/BACKUP-<backup_id>*, below the path specified with the BackupDataDir option (in *config.ini*). For example, if BackupDataDir = /cluster and the backup ID is 1, the path to the three files is */cluster/BACKUP/BACKUP-1/*. The overall backup process is depicted in Figure 8-1. See the following discussion for more detail.

Table 8-1. *Filenames for Each Part of a Backup*

Part	Filename
Metadata	*BACKUP-<backup_id>.<node_id>.ctl*
Table data	*BACKUP-<backup_id>-0.<node_id>.data*
Transaction log	*BACKUP-<backup_id>.<node_id>.log*

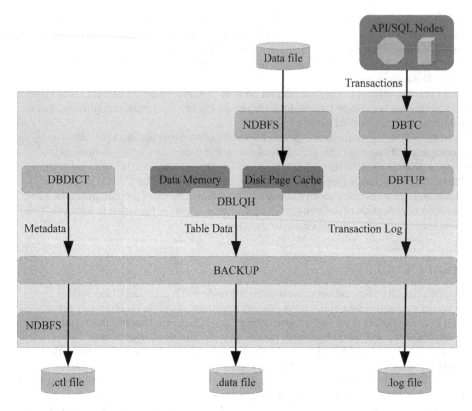

Figure 8-1. *The overall backup process*

The metadata includes the table definitions of the tables using the NDBCluster storage engine. It is important to remember that no other schema objects—including views and stored programs—are included in the backup. All data nodes back up a full copy of the metadata. It is the *DBDICT* kernel module that delivers the table metadata to the backup.

The table data is the actual data stored in the tables. Each data node only writes the data for the fragments it is the current primary node for. If a data node is offline, the other data node in the node group becomes the primary node of the fragments previously handled by the now offline node. This means that the data node handles both its own fragments and the fragments from its offline peer and will write roughly twice as much data as the rest of the data nodes. So, it is best to do backups when all the data nodes are online.

The transaction log records the changes made during the backup. This ensures that you get a consistent backup whereby all data corresponds to the same point in time. Depending on whether the backup is using a snapshot at the start or end, the log is used to roll back (an undo log) or roll forward (a redo log) the transactions committed during the backup. The transaction log is collected through internal triggers; when the *DBTUP* kernel block checks which triggers to execute, it sends the required before and/or after image of the row(s) affected to the *BACKUP* kernel block. Table 8-2 shows the transaction log type and the INSERT/UPDATE/DELETE data logged in the transaction log for a snapshot at the start and end of the backup; the primary key is denoted PK. It is clear from the table that a snapshot at the start of the backup requires storing more data in the transaction log.

Table 8-2. *The Data Stored in the Backup Transaction Log*

Event	Snapshot: Start	Snapshot: End
INSERT	PK + after image	PK + after image
UPDATE	PK + before and after image	PK + after image
DELETE	PK + before image	PK

Additionally, for snapshots at the start of the backup, the transaction log is never compressed, even if the CompressedBackup option is enabled. Compression is not supported, as the log must be read in reverse order when applying it as an undo log. For these reasons, it is generally recommended to use a snapshot at the end of the backup, which is also the default.

Starting and Aborting Backups

There are two operations available for controlling the native online backups: starting and aborting. These actions can be performed through three different means:

- **The NDB management client:** Using the START BACKUP and ABORT BACKUP commands.

- **The NDB API:** Using the ndb_mgm_start_backup() and ndb_mgm_abort_backup() functions. The NDB API is discussed in Chapter 19.

- **MySQL Cluster Manager (MCM):** Using the BACKUP CLUSTER and ABORT BACKUP commands. MCM is discussed in Chapter 13.

The NDB management client and MCM both use the NDB API functions as the underlying way of controlling backups. The rest of this section focuses on using the NDB management client for starting and aborting backups.

To start a backup, use the START BACKUP command. The command takes several optional arguments:

- **Backup ID:** The ID to use for the backup. Each backup is identified by a numeric ID between 1 and 4294967294 (inclusive). The default is to use the highest previous ID, plus one. See the subsection "Choosing the Backup ID" later in the chapter.

- **Snapshot time:** The snapshot time can take two values, which are mutually exclusive: SNAPSHOTSTART and SNAPSHOTEND: The default is SNAPSHOTEND. With the snapshot at the start of the backup, transactions committed during the backup will be rolled back when restoring the backup. On the other hand, with the snapshot at the end of the backup, the restored backup will include the transactions committed during the backup.

- **Client behavior:** This specifies how long the client should wait before returning to the user. The available values are NOWAIT, WAIT STARTED, and WAIT COMPLETED. NOWAIT will make the management client return immediately to the user; WAIT STARTED will return when the backup has started; and WAIT COMPLETED will not return until the backup has completed. The default is to wait until the backup has completed (WAIT COMPLETED).

For all three arguments, the value should be specified without an option name. However, the arguments that are specified must be included in the order they are listed. That is (line breaks added for readability purposes):

```
START BACKUP
    [backup id]
    [SNAPSHOTSTART|SNAPSHOTEND]
    [NOWAIT|WAIT STARTED|WAIT COMPLETED]
```

Note that there should not be any newlines when executing the command. For example, to create a backup with the next available backup ID with the snapshot at the start of the backup, and with the client waiting until the end of the backup before returning, use:

```
ndb_mgm> START BACKUP SNAPSHOTSTART
Waiting for completed, this may take several minutes
Node 1: Backup 5 started from node 49
Node 1: Backup 5 started from node 49 completed
 StartGCP: 49332 StopGCP: 49337
 #Records: 2398587 #LogRecords: 0
 Data: 73818288 bytes Log: 0 bytes
```

Another example is to create a backup with the ID 1612291604, with the snapshot at the end of the backup and return when the backup has started, as follows:

```
ndb_mgm> START BACKUP 1612291604 SNAPSHOTEND WAIT STARTED
Waiting for started, this may take several minutes
Node 1: Backup 1612291604 started from node 49
```

When the client returns immediately or when the backup has started, the status information will still be written as it becomes available, provided the management client is still connected. So NOWAIT and WAIT STARTED are mostly useful if the management client disconnects when the backup command has returned.

Ongoing backups can be aborted using the ABORT BACKUP command. The command takes a single argument: the backup ID to abort. For example, to abort the backup with ID 6, use:

```
ndb_mgm> ABORT BACKUP 6
Abort of backup 6 ordered
Node 1: Backup 6 started from 49 has been aborted. Error: 1321
```

Choosing the Backup ID

All backups must have a backup ID. The simplest solution is to let MySQL NDB Cluster choose the ID automatically, which uses the next higher ID in the sequence. If the previously highest used backup ID was 20, for example, then the next automatically generated ID will be 21. This is simple, but it has the disadvantage that the backup ID does not carry any meaning.

An alternative is to generate the backup IDs manually or in the backup script. One option is to make the backup reflect the time the backup is started, for example, to include the year, month, day, hour, and minute in the format %y%m%d%H%M. The meaning of each format control is as follows:

- **%y:** The year using two digits.

- **%m:** The month using two digits.

- **%d:** The day of the month using two digits.

- **%H:** The hour of the day using two digits and a 24-hour clock.

- **%M:** The minutes using two digits.

To start a backup with the backup ID generated using this format on Linux, the date command can be used:

```
shell$ ndb_mgm -e "START BACKUP $(date +'%y%m%d%H%M')"
Connected to Management Server at: localhost:1186
Waiting for completed, this may take several minutes
Node 1: Backup 1612291612 started from node 49
Node 1: Backup 1612291612 started from node 49 completed
 StartGCP: 49988 StopGCP: 49992
 #Records: 2398587 #LogRecords: 0
 Data: 73818288 bytes Log: 0 bytes
```

On Windows, the Get-Date command in PowerShell is the best option to create a backup ID. For example (keep the command on one line; it is split across two here to fit within the width of the page):

```
PS C:\> & 'C:\Program Files\MySQL\MySQL Cluster 7.5\bin\ndb_mgm.exe' -e
        "START BACKUP $(get-date -Format yyMMddHHmm)"
Connected to Management Server at: localhost:1186
Waiting for completed, this may take several minutes
Node 1: Backup 1707111936 started from node 49
Node 1: Backup 1707111936 started from node 49 completed
 StartGCP: 5469 StopGCP: 5472
 #Records: 7367 #LogRecords: 0
 Data: 497756 bytes Log: 0 bytes
```

The format string uses the following specifiers:

- **yy:** The last two digits of the year.

- **MM:** The month using two digits.

- **dd:** Day of month using two digits.

- **HH:** The hour of the day using two digits and a 24-hour clock.

- **MM:** The minutes using two digits.

An alternative is to use the %DATE% and %TIME% variables in the command prompt; however, note that the format of these variables depends on the locale set for Windows, and thus they are harder to use.

Backup Monitoring

MySQL NDB Cluster does not offer much in terms of monitoring backups. The NDB management client allows you to get a report for the status of an ongoing backup, but there is no built-in functionality to get the status of completed backups.

For completed backups, the best solution is to check the cluster log. In the cluster log, there is a log message at the start and completion of the backup:

```
2016-12-29 17:16:02 [MgmtSrvr] INFO     -- Node 1: Backup 9 started from node 49
2016-12-29 17:16:11 [MgmtSrvr] INFO     -- Node 1: Backup 9 started from node 49 completed.
StartGCP: 51829 StopGCP: 51834 #Records: 2398587 #LogRecords: 0 Data: 73818288 bytes Log:
0 bytes
```

The completion of the backup includes statistics of the backup. If the backup fails, this will also be available in the cluster log, for example:

```
2016-12-29 17:15:59 [MgmtSrvr] ALERT    -- Node 1: Backup 8 started from 49 has been
                                            aborted. Error: 1350
```

It is possible to get progress information for an ongoing backup using the BACKUPSTATUS report in the NDB management client:

```
ndb_mgm> ALL REPORT BACKUPSTATUS
Node 1: Local backup status: backup 7 started from node 49
 #Records: 1080791 #LogRecords: 0
 Data: 33553460 bytes Log: 0 bytes
Node 2: Local backup status: backup 7 started from node 49
 #Records: 354437 #LogRecords: 0
 Data: 11342376 bytes Log: 0 bytes
```

When no backup is in progress, the report states this:

```
ndb_mgm> ALL REPORT BACKUPSTATUS
Node 1: Backup not started
Node 2: Backup not started
```

Like for other similar commands in the management client, it is possible to get the report for all data nodes using the ALL keyword, or to specify a single node ID. See Chapter 7 for more information about generating reports in the NDB command-line client.

A backup shares I/O with the local checkpoints, so the I/O usage can be monitored through the ndbinfo schema. Additionally, it is possible to monitor the CPU usage. The views particularly relevant for backups are:

- **The cpustat% tables:** These views provide per thread information about the CPU usage either for the last second—the cpustat view—or the last 20 measurements at 50 milliseconds, 1 second, or 20 seconds separation—the cpustat_50ms, cpustat_1sec, and cpustat_20sec views. These views can be used to detect to what extent the CPUs are used during periods with backups executing compared to periods without ongoing backups. The views were introduced in version 7.5.2.

- **The disk_write_speed_% tables:** These views show the disk write speeds for the backup/local checkpoint data and logs. The views also include the current target write speed, so it is possible to determine whether the target can be met. There is one view (disk_write_speed_base) with the raw data, and two views (disk_write_speed_aggregate and disk_write_speed_aggregate_node) with aggregate data. The views were added in version 7.4.1.

An example of checking the disk I/O is shown in Listing 8-1.

Listing 8-1. Example Content of the ndbinfo.disk_write_speed_aggregate_node View

```
mysql> SELECT * FROM ndbinfo.disk_write_speed_aggregate_node\G
*************************** 1. row ***************************
                  node_id: 1
  backup_lcp_speed_last_sec: 7252000
       redo_speed_last_sec: 260000
backup_lcp_speed_last_10sec: 2821118
      redo_speed_last_10sec: 78243
backup_lcp_speed_last_60sec: 470000
      redo_speed_last_60sec: 64000
*************************** 2. row ***************************
                  node_id: 2
  backup_lcp_speed_last_sec: 6047000
       redo_speed_last_sec: 195000
backup_lcp_speed_last_10sec: 1493014
      redo_speed_last_10sec: 71798
backup_lcp_speed_last_60sec: 248000
      redo_speed_last_60sec: 63000
2 rows in set (0.01 sec)
```

As the same kernel block handles backups and local checkpoints, it is not possible to get details about how much of the I/O is caused by an ongoing backup and how much is from an ongoing local checkpoint. See Chapter 16 for details about the ndbinfo schema.

To get information about whether a backup succeeded, there are a few options:

- Check the return code when the backup is created using the NDB management client or the NDB API ndb_mgm_start_backup() function.

- For MySQL Cluster Manager (MCM), use the LIST BACKUPS command. This returns all the successful backups or can list a single backup based on the backup ID.

- Check the cluster log as mentioned at the beginning of this subsection.

For example, to check the return code of a backup in *bash*, use this command:

```
shell$ ndb_mgm -e "START BACKUP 8"
Connected to Management Server at: localhost:1386
Waiting for completed, this may take several minutes
Backup failed
*  3001: Could not start backup
*       Backup failed: file already exists (use 'START BACKUP <backup id>'): Temporary
        error: Temporary Resource error
shell$ echo $?
255
```

259

In Windows PowerShell, use the $LastExitCode special variable to get the exit code:

```
PS C:\> & 'C:\Program Files\MySQL\MySQL Cluster 7.5\bin\ndb_mgm.exe' -e
                                            "START BACKUP 1"
Connected to Management Server at: localhost:1186
Waiting for completed, this may take several minutes
Backup failed
*   3001: Could not start backup
*       Backup failed: file already exists (use 'START BACKUP <backup id>'): Temporary
        error: Temporary Resource error
PS C:\> echo $LastExitCode
255
```

A return code of 0 means the command was successful, a non-zero return code means the command failed. To get the overall status of the backup, it is necessary to use WAIT COMPLETED (the default), because the return code reflects the status at the time the command returns to the user.

Backup Configuration

There are a few configuration options to consider for optimal backup performance. The options are also discussed in Chapter 4. There are eight options specifically related to backups:

- **BackupDataDir:** Where to store the backups. Having the backups stored on a separate disk system from the local checkpoints can greatly improve the backup performance or reduce the cost of the storage by storing backups on less expensive disks than those used for local checkpoints. Storing the backups on a separate file system also provides redundancy, so the backup is still available even if the disk system with the local checkpoints is lost. The default for BackupDataDir is the value of FileSystemPath, which in turn defaults to DataDir.

- **BackupDiskWriteSpeedPct:** This option is new as of MySQL NDB Cluster 7.4.8 and specifies the percentage of the I/O bandwidth specified with MinDiskWriteSpeed and MaxDiskWriteSpeed to use for backups.

- **CompressedBackup:** When enabled, the backups will be compressed, trading disk I/O for increased CPU usage. When compressing backups, it may be necessary to give additional CPU resources to the I/O threads using the ThreadConfig option. The transaction log will only be compressed if the snapshot is created at the end of the backup.

- **BackupWriteSize:** The default write size for backups. The write size can be automatically increased up to the value of BackupMaxWriteSize.

- **BackupMaxWriteSize:** The maximum write size allowed.

- **BackupDataBufferSize:** The size of the in-memory buffer for buffering the writes of the data.

- **BackupLogBufferSize:** The size of the in-memory buffer for buffering the writes of the transaction log.

- **BackupReportFrequency:** How often to report backup progress to the cluster log.

■ **Note** Additionally, there is the option called BackupMemory, which is deprecated in MySQL NDB Cluster 7.4 and later. In earlier versions, it was set to the sum of BackupDataBufferSize and BackupLogBufferSize.

All the options can be changed through a *rolling restart* (or an *initial rolling restart* in case of BackupDataDir), so it is not necessary to lock into specific values at install time. There is no *one size fits all* solution for the backup options. It is important to monitor the performance (see the previous subsection as well as Chapters 14 and 16) and adjust according to the conclusions made based on the data collected. For example, if it is found that disk I/O is a bottleneck during backups, but there are spare CPU resources, a solution may be to enable compressed backups. This is also an example of why it is important to have good monitoring in place, as it is then possible to compare the monitoring data before and after the configuration change and verify the effect of the change.

Logical Backups and Binary Logs

The native (online) backup feature is great, as it provides a way to create the backups while the cluster remains available for application reads and writes. However, it has three limitations:

- The backups are mainly meant to be restored to another MySQL NDB Cluster installation.

- The backups only include the table definition and data of NDBCluster tables. Tables using other storage engines, views, stored programs, etc., are not included.

- The backups are not human readable.

While the backups can be converted to CSV files, if it is known the backup will be restored to another storage engine, it is in general better to create a logical backup. Additionally, a logical backup of the schema is good to have in case a native backup will be restored to a cluster with a different configuration than the cluster the backup is made on; this is discussed further in the next section about restores.

A logical backup is a backup that exports the data in a portable way. In MySQL, this means either as SQL statements (CREATE TABLE, INSERT, etc.) or as a CSV file. This makes it easier to restore the backup, for example, to an InnoDB replication slave. On the flip side, there is no support for online backups. In fact, as discussed next, in order to ensure a consistent backup, the cluster must be read only during the backup. It also takes longer to create the backup and even more time to restore it.

Consistency Considerations

The main advantage of logical backups is that they are portable. However, this comes at a price when it comes to ensuring a consistent backup is created. The difficulties arise from the architecture and limitations of MySQL NDB Cluster:

- MySQL NDB Cluster only supports the READ COMMITTED transaction isolation level. So, it is not possible to create a *read view* in the same way it is achieved in the InnoDB storage engine. The InnoDB read view allows for an online snapshot of the data while other connections keep updating the data.

- MySQL NDB Cluster supports several API/SQL nodes and LOCK TABLES is not global among all of those nodes.

This means that it is not possible to create a consistent backup unless the cluster is read only which is easiest to ensure by putting the cluster into single user mode. There are a couple of ways to avoid affecting the application while creating a logical backup:

- **Replication slave:** If there is a read-only replication slave, it is possible to create the backup there. The replication slave will not be able to apply replication events while the backup is made, so this must be taken into account. However, the replication slave can still save the replication events to the *relay log* to ensure it is possible to catch up to the replication master should the replication master crash while the backup is in progress.

- **Temporary cluster:** For one-off logical backups, a native backup can be restored to a temporary cluster and the logical backup can be made without impacting the production cluster.

For backups of the schema, these considerations may not be important if schema changes occur only rarely. In that case, it may be sufficient to ensure the schema backup is made while no schema changes are executed.

Creating Logical Backups

To create a logical backup, it is necessary to execute a series of SQL statements to extract the schema and/or data. That is, a logical backup that includes tables and data will essentially be created using the following queries for each of the tables:

- `SHOW CREATE TABLE ...` to get the table definition.

- `SELECT * FROM ...` to get the data.

In practice, the implementation details may be different.

MySQL NDB Cluster (and MySQL Server) ships with two client programs for creating logical backups. Additionally, there is a standalone GUI program that also supports creating backups. The three programs are as follows:

- **mysqlpump:** This is a new utility included with MySQL Server 5.7 and MySQL NDB Cluster 7.5 and later. It is meant to be a replacement of `mysqldump` and includes support for creating the backup in parallel, as well as adding the index definition after restoring the data (to avoid maintaining the indexes during the data restore).

- **mysqldump:** This is the utility traditionally used for logical MySQL backups and is included with all available versions.

- **MySQL Workbench:** *The MySQL Workbench* program adds a GUI to execute queries, manage SQL nodes, etc. It also includes an interface to control `mysqldump`.

■ **Note** The commercial version of MySQL Workbench also supports backups through MySQL Enterprise Backup. However, as mentioned in the beginning of the chapter, MySQL Enterprise Backup is not supported for MySQL NDB Cluster.

Both mysqlpump and mysqldump support creating the backup either locally or from a remote server. In MySQL NDB Cluster 7.5 and later, it is recommended to use mysqlpump unless the limitations require the use of mysqldump. The mysqlpump limitations related to MySQL NDB Cluster are:

- The backup generated is not guaranteed to be compatible with older versions of MySQL Server and MySQL NDB Cluster.

- The privilege tables are not included in the backup. However, the CREATE USER and GRANT statements required to recreate the users can be included with the *--users* option; this will be discussed in the next subsection.

- There is no feature to lock all tables during the backup.

- There is no support to include the SQL statements to recreate the logfile group and tablespace files.

- There is no support to get the replication coordinates (binary log file and position).

- There is no support for backing up to tab delimited files.

■ **Caution**   Due to the lack of an option to lock all tables during the backup, mysqlpump does not guarantee a consistent backup where all tables are current with respect to the same point in time for any other storage engine than InnoDB. It is up to the administrator creating the backup to ensure that no changes are made to the schema or data during the backup.

There are several use cases for creating a logical backup. Some of the more common cases are:

- **Schema backup:** By creating a logical backup of the schema, it is possible to include all schema objects: table definitions, stored program definitions, etc. Additionally, when a native NDB Cluster backup is restored in version 7.4 and earlier, the NDBCluster tables will be restored with the same number of partitions as the tables had when the backup was made. A logical schema backup allows the tables to be restored to a cluster with a different number of data nodes or a different configuration, and have the restored tables use the default number of partitions for the cluster the backup is restored to. It is also possible to restore the logical schema backup using a different storage engine; for example, if there is a need to have replication slave using InnoDB for complex reporting queries.

- **Full backup:** The native NDB backups only include the NDBCluster tables. InnoDB tables, stored programs (including triggers for NDBCluster tables), etc. are not included. A full backup can ensure that there is a single backup that includes everything.

- **Partial backup:** While native NDB backups support a partial restore, there is no support for partial backups. This may make the backups unnecessarily big if the aim is to copy a single table to a different system. A partial backup can also include all non-NDBCluster tables and objects. A schema backup is a special case of a partial backup.

■ **Tip** It is recommended to create a logical schema backup after each schema change. This will ensure it is possible to take advantage of the additional flexibility of logical backups and that schema objects that are not synchronized between the SQL nodes are backed up.

To create a consistent full logical backup, the cluster must first be in single user mode:

```
shell$ ndb_mgm -e "ENTER SINGLE USER MODE 51"
Connected to Management Server at: localhost:1186
Single user mode entered
Access is granted for API node 51 only.
```

In this case, the node ID allowed is 51. To avoid changes being made during the backup and to get the binary log file and position (if the SQL node has the binary logs enabled), it is necessary to lock all the tables:

```
mysql> FLUSH TABLES WITH READ LOCK;
Query OK, 0 rows affected (0.10 sec)

-- If binary logging is enabled for the SQL node:
mysql> SHOW MASTER STATUS\G
*************************** 1. row ***************************
             File: binlog.000003
         Position: 217047
     Binlog_Do_DB:
 Binlog_Ignore_DB:
Executed_Gtid_Set:
1 row in set (0.00 sec)
```

Note the File and Position values in the SHOW MASTER STATUS output and store them together with the backup. Keep the connection open while the backup itself is created. Next create the actual backup using mysqlpump:

```
shell$ mysqlpump --user=root --password --all-databases \
                 --hex-blob --triggers --routines --events > full_backup.sql
```

■ **Tip** The option --hex-blob is recommended for both mysqlpump and mysqldump. The option ensures that the binary data is always exported correctly.

Finally, unlock the tables and exit single user mode:

```
mysql> UNLOCK TABLES;
Query OK, 0 rows affected (0.00 sec)

shell$ ndb_mgm -e "EXIT SINGLE USER MODE"
Connected to Management Server at: localhost:1186
Exiting single user mode in progress.
Use ALL STATUS or SHOW to see when single user mode has been exited.
```

```
shell$ ndb_mgm -e "ALL STATUS"
Connected to Management Server at: localhost:1186
Node 1: started (mysql-5.7.16 ndb-7.5.4)
Node 2: started (mysql-5.7.16 ndb-7.5.4)
```

Creating full backups with mysqldump is similar to using mysqlpump. The main difference is that it is better to add the --lock-all-tables option, which together with the single user mode, guarantees that no changes are made to any tables during the backup. Additionally, for binary logging SQL nodes, add the --master-data option to include the binary log file and position near the top of the backup as a CHANGE MASTER TO statement. By setting the option value to 2, it will be included as a comment, so it is not automatically applied when the backup is restored:

```
--
-- Position to start replication or point-in-time recovery from
--

-- CHANGE MASTER TO MASTER_LOG_FILE='binlog.000003', MASTER_LOG_POS=217047;
```

To apply the CHANGE MASTER TO command, either comment it out before restoring the backup or execute it manually.

The mysqldump command then becomes the following command:

```
shell$ mysqldump --user=root --password --lock-all-tables --master-data=2 \
                 --all-databases --hex-blob \
                 --triggers --routines --events > full_backup.sql
```

The mysqldump backup will by default include the SQL statements to recreate the logfile group and tablespace files used for on-disk data. If these are not to be included, add the --no-tablespaces option.

When mysqldump is used, an alternative is to create the backup of the data as tab delimited files. The advantage is that there will be one SQL script with the schema definition and one tab delimited file (with the *.txt* filename extension) with the data. This makes it easier to perform partial restores and it makes it possible to restore the data in parallel. The disadvantage is that it is only possible to back one database up at a time. For example, to create a tab delimited backup of the world sample database use a command like the following example:

```
shell$ mysqldump --user=root --password \
                 --hex-blob --triggers --routines --events \
                 --tab=/backup/world world > /backup/world_programs.sql
```

The --tab option uses the SELECT ... INTO OUTFILE ... statement, which means that the following requirements apply:

- The mysqld process must be allowed to write into the directory specified in the --tab option.

- MySQL must be allowed by the --secure_file_priv option to use the directory as a destination for SELECT ... INTO OUTFILE .... The value for --secure_file_priv can be a parent directory; for example, */backup* in this case.

- The user who creates the backup must have the *FILE* privilege.

Since only one database is backed up at a time, the backup process should loop over all databases to be backed up. There is no gain by using the `--lock-all-table` option. Instead the backup process should ensure that all databases are backed up while no changes are being made to the data. For the example backup, the */backup/world* directory contains an *.sql* and a *.txt* file for each table as well as a *.sql* file for each view. The *.sql* file also includes any triggers for the table. `mysqldump` writes the backup for stored functions, stored procedures, and events to `stdout`, which in the example is redirected to the */backup/world_programs.sql* file.

■ **Note** The `--single-transaction` option for both `mysqlpump` and `mysqldump` requires the `REPEATABLE READ` transaction isolation level. Since `NDBCluster` uses the `READ COMMITTED` transaction isolation level, `--single-transaction` cannot be used to back up data with `NDBCluster` tables.

Partial backups are in most respects the same as full backups other than adding or removing options to get the desired parts of the database included in the backup. One special case that is worth considering is the *schema backup,* which is a partial backup that includes all table definitions, but no data. An example where this becomes useful is given in the "Initial System Restart" case study in Chapter 10. To create a backup that includes all table definitions, triggers, stored routines, and stored functions with `mysqlpump`, use the command:

```
shell$ mysqlpump --user=root --password --all-databases \
                 --skip-dump-rows --skip-defer-table-indexes \
                 --triggers --routines --events > schema_backup.sql
```

For `mysqldump`, the command is:

```
shell$ mysqldump --user=root --password --no-data --all-databases \
                 --triggers --routines --events > schema_backup.sql
```

The command does not lock the tables during the backup; this is not required assuming there are no schema changes made during the backup.

Logical Backups from MySQL Workbench

MySQL Workbench provides a GUI interface to create backups using `mysqldump`. There is no new functionality compared to executing `mysqldump` on the command line, but it can make it simpler to set up a backup. It is also possible to get the `mysqldump` command that MySQL Workbench uses, so it can be executed directly on the command line in the future. Figure 8-2 shows the Data Export screen for exporting the `world` sample database. To export, choose the *Data Export* option under *Management* in the *Navigator* to the left (highlighted). There are two types of backups available:

- **Export to dump project folder:** This creates one SQL script per table and one per schema with the stored programs, events, and views.

- **Export to self-contained file:** This is similar to what a single `mysqldump` command for the selected objects creates. All object definitions and data are written to the same file.

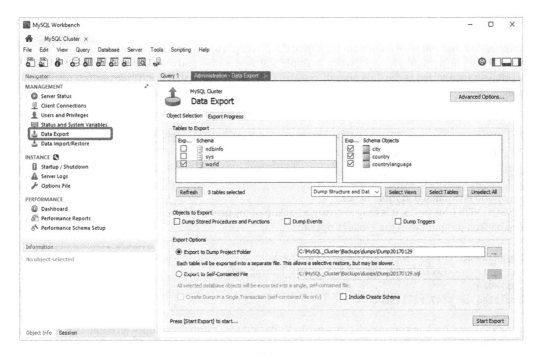

Figure 8-2. *MySQL Workbench: The Data Export screen*

It is recommended to enable the *hex-blob* option in the *Advanced Options* page; see the highlighted option in Figure 8-3. There is currently no support in MySQL Workbench for using mysqlpump for data exports.

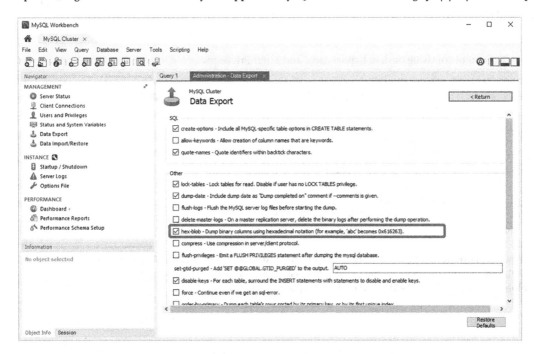

Figure 8-3. *MySQL Workbench: The Advanced Options page of the Data Export screen*

Backing Up Privileges

It is recommended that you have a separate backup of the privileges to simplify restoring users and their privileges. This can be particularly useful when multiple SQL nodes exist and *distributed privileges* (where the user privileges are stored in the data nodes—see also Chapter 12) are not in use. Three options to export the privileges are:

- mysqlpump

- Manual export using the SHOW CREATE USER and SHOW GRANTS FOR SQL statements. It is necessary to execute the commands once for each user.

- mysqldump of the privilege stables.

Each option is discussed in more detail.

In MySQL NDB Cluster 7.5, it is easy to create a backup of the users and their privileges using the mysqlpump backup program with the --users option:

```
shell$ mysqlpump --user=root --password --users \
              --exclude-databases=% > users_backup.sql
Enter password:
Dump completed in 4847 milliseconds
```

In the mysqlpump backup command, the --exclude-databases=% option excludes all databases, leaving just the CREATE USER and GRANT statements.

For older versions of MySQL NDB Cluster, there is no direct way to export the SQL statements provided with the MySQL NDB Cluster distribution. It is possible to get the required CREATE USER and GRANT statements to recreate the users using the SHOW CREATE USER and SHOW GRANTS statements. For example, using *bash*, this can be scripted as in Listing 8-2. The script first defines the SQL used to get a space separated list of all accounts in the format user@host. Then the SQL is used to set the variable USERS with this list, and finally there is a loop over the users. In the loop, SHOW CREATE USER and SHOW GRANTS FOR is executed for the current user.

Listing 8-2. Example of Using bash to Export users and Their Privileges

```
shell$ SQL="SELECT GROUP_CONCAT(
                    CONCAT('''', User, '''@''', Host, '''') SEPARATOR ' '
                ) AS Users FROM mysql.user;"
shell$ USERS=$(mysql --user=root --password --skip-column-names \
                --execute="${SQL}")
shell$ for USER in ${USERS}; do
        echo "-- CREATE USER and GRANT for: ${USER}"
        mysql --user=root --password --skip-column-names --batch \
            --execute="SHOW CREATE USER ${USER};
                      SHOW GRANTS FOR ${USER};"
    done
```

The various options to export the privileges produce similar outputs. Listing 8-3 shows an example of the SQL statements generated by the example in Listing 8-2. Note that these statements do not have a semicolon at the end to indicate the end of the statement.

Listing 8-3. Example Output of the Privileges

```
-- CREATE USER and GRANT for: 'mysql.sys'@'localhost'
Enter password:
CREATE USER 'mysql.sys'@'localhost' IDENTIFIED WITH 'mysql_native_password' AS
'*THISISNOTAVALIDPASSWORDTHATCANBEUSEDHERE' REQUIRE NONE PASSWORD EXPIRE DEFAULT ACCOUNT LOCK
GRANT USAGE ON *.* TO 'mysql.sys'@'localhost'
GRANT TRIGGER ON `sys`.* TO 'mysql.sys'@'localhost'
GRANT SELECT ON `sys`.`sys_config` TO 'mysql.sys'@'localhost'
-- CREATE USER and GRANT for: 'root'@'localhost'
Enter password:
CREATE USER 'root'@'localhost' IDENTIFIED WITH 'mysql_native_password' AS
'*13430255D7D1ODD8DCD27A6AE669F2CA263AB5EA' REQUIRE NONE PASSWORD EXPIRE DEFAULT ACCOUNT
UNLOCK
GRANT ALL PRIVILEGES ON *.* TO 'root'@'localhost' WITH GRANT OPTION
GRANT PROXY ON ''@'' TO 'root'@'localhost' WITH GRANT OPTION
```

It is also possible to use `mysqldump` to create a logical backup of the privilege tables. There are a few limitations for that method. The backup can in general only be restored to the same version of MySQL NDB Cluster (more specifically the MySQL Server version included must be the same). If the `CREATE TABLE` statements are included in the backup, it is possible to restore the privileges to the next major version, provided that `mysql_upgrade` is executed after the restore. It also requires more work if only some users need to be restored compared to a backup that returns the `CREATE USER` and `GRANT` statements. Due to these limitations, it is in general best to use one of the other options discussed.

The `mysqldump` command to back up all the privilege tables, including the `CREATE TABLE` statements, is:

```
shell$ mysqldump --user=root --password --tables mysql \
                 columns_priv db procs_priv proxies_priv tables_priv user
```

If the `CREATE TABLE` statements should not be included, add the `--no-create-info` option:

```
shell$ mysqldump --user=root --password --no-create-info --tables mysql \
                 columns_priv db procs_priv proxies_priv tables_priv user
```

In either case, after restoring the backup, you must execute `FLUSH PRIVILEGES` to make the restored privileges take effect.

Binary Logs

As discussed in Chapter 6, the binary logs are an essential component for replication between clusters. They can also be used for *point-in-time recoveries* (PITR). Essentially the binary logs are logs that record all data and schema changes. So, it is essential to back up the binary logs.

The simplest way to back up the binary logs is to copy them. An effective way to copy the binary logs is to use `rsync`, Robocopy (*https://technet.microsoft.com/en-us/library/cc733145(v=ws.11).aspx*), or a similar program. The binary logs are only appended to. After a file has reached the maximum size, it will not be modified again. So `rsync` will be able to minimize the amount of data copied.

The main disadvantage with `rsync` and Robocopy is that the binary logs are not continuously copied. Additionally, Robocopy skips open files, so only old binary logs are included. Even if the sync is made every minute, on busy systems significant amount of changes can be missing if the server goes down.

An alternative in MySQL NBD Cluster 7.3 and later is to use the `mysqlbinlog` utility to stream the binary log changes to a remote server. `mysqlbinlog` is included together with the other MySQL client programs. This minimizes the number of the binary log events that are not backed up in case of a catastrophic failure. For example, to stream the binary log starting with *binlog.000001* from the SQL node on *192.168.56.1* on port 3306, the following command can be used:

```
shell$ mysqlbinlog --read-from-remote-server --raw --stop-never \
                   --result-file=/backup/binlog/ --host=192.168.56.101 \
                   --user=backup -password binlog.000001
```

The specified options have the following functions:

- **--read-from-remote-server:** Tells `mysqlbinlog` to copy the binary logs from a remote server.

- **--raw:** By default, `mysqlbinlog` converts the binary log events to text. The `--raw` option keeps it the raw events.

- **--stop-never:** Do not stop streaming when reaching the end of the latest binary log file.

- **--result-file:** The prefix for storing the streamed binary log files. In this case a directory is given, so the binary log files will be saved into this directory with the same name as where they are copied from.

- **binlog.000001:** The first file to copy. This file must have the same name as is used on the server from which the binary logs are copied. The `SHOW BINARY LOGS` command can be used to get a list of the currently available binary logs on a given SQL node.

The remaining arguments are the standard connection options. The user who connects must have the `REPLICATION SLAVE` privilege (just like in replication) to be able to read the binary logs. If the backup user connects from *192.168.56.102* to copy the binary logs, the user can be created using this command:

```
mysql> CREATE USER backup@192.168.56.102 IDENTIFIED BY '<some password>';
Query OK, 0 rows affected (0.01 sec)

mysql> GRANT REPLICATION SLAVE ON *.* TO backup@192.168.56.102;
Query OK, 0 rows affected (0.01 sec)
```

As the binary logs contain all the data changes for the cluster, it is important that the user password with `mysqlbinlog` is kept secure. It is also best to use SSL for the connection to ensure the data is encrypted during the transfer.

An important part of backing up the binary logs is to also back up the mapping from the epochs used by the data nodes to measure the progress of time to the binary log file and position. This mapping is maintained in the `mysql.ndb_binlog_index` table. This table is local (using the `MyISAM` storage engine in MySQL NDB Cluster 7.4 and earlier and the InnoDB storage engine in version 7.5) to the SQL nodes with binary logs enabled and must be backed up separately from the native NDB Cluster backups. For example, using:

```
shell$ mysqldump --user=root --password \
                 --tables mysql ndb_binlog_index > binlog_index.sql
```

There is an example of using the `mysql.ndb_binlog_index` table later in the chapter when point-in-time recoveries are discussed.

Restores

The complement action to creating a backup is restoring it. This is often an underrated task. There are several reasons it may be necessary to restore a backup, ranging from setting up a test system or a replication slave to a disaster recovery of an important production system. In any case, knowing the right steps is critical to get the job done as quickly and painlessly as possible. The "Initial System Restart" case study in Chapter 10 gives an example of restoring a backup.

■ **Caution**   A backup is worth no more than the ability to restore it. Make sure you regularly test restoring your backups in different scenarios and that you have the restore procedures well documented. The backup must also be stored offsite—if the data center burns and the fire destroys the backup as well as the production copy, the backup is no good.

The ndb_restore Program

The main tool for restoring a native NDB Cluster backup is the ndb_restore utility, which is included with the MySQL NDB Cluster installation. If the installation is made with RPM packages, ndb_restore is included in the client RPM in version 7.5 and in the server RPM in versions 7.4 and earlier. ndb_restore is a utility that connects to the cluster in the same way as the SQL nodes or an NDB API application does. This means it can be executed from any host with network access; the only requirement is that it has to read the backup files from the file system.

■ **Tip**   Because ndb_restore is an NDB API program, it requires a mysqld or api node slot in *config.ini* in order to be able to connect to the cluster. Make sure you have enough slots available to have one ndb_restore process for each data node executing in parallel.

---

ndb_restore can read options from either the [mysql_cluster] or the [ndb_restore] group in a MySQL configuration file. There are a few common options irrespective of the action to be performed:

- **--ndb-connectstring=....** The usual connection string specifying how to connect to the management nodes.

- **--backupid=....** The ID of the backup to restore.

- **--nodeid=....** The node ID of the node the backup was created with. Each node created a part of the backup, and the node ID specified here is for the part that ndb_restore is restoring.

- **--backup_path=....** The path to where the backup is stored on the file system. The path must include the directory specific to the backup. For example, if the data nodes are configured with BackupDataDir = /backups/cluster/ and the backup with ID 1 is restored, the backup path to use is */backups/cluster/BACKUP/BACKUP-1*.

A restore where the data is restored using ndb_restore follows three high-level steps:

1. Restore the schema. This can be a restore of a logical or NDB Cluster native backup.

2. Restore the data.

3. Rebuild the indexes.

The third step of rebuilding the indexes is necessary, as the data restore will in general not work if there are any unique keys. The issue is that the restore does not replay the transaction log in the same order as the rows were originally inserted and updated (however, it still guarantees that the overall result is the same). This means that unique key violations may occur if the indexes are maintained during the restore. The unique key constraints will be checked when the indexes are recreated at the end of the backup, so at the end of the restore, the constraints are guaranteed to be valid again. The same applies for foreign keys.

Restore Schema

There are two ways to restore the schema: from the native NDB Cluster backup or from a logical backup. The main deciding factor as to whether to use one or the other is whether it is important that the table is repartitioned for version 7.4 and earlier. When the table is created from a logical backup, the number of partitions and the distribution of them is determined by the number of data nodes and the configuration of them at the time of the restore. On the other hand, creating the tables from the native NDB Cluster backup in MySQL NDB Cluster 7.4 and earlier will restore the tables using the same partitions as they had originally. This is something to be aware of if the number of data nodes or *LDM* threads has changed; in that case restoring the schema from the native NDB Cluster backup may cause a partition imbalance, with some data nodes and/or *LDM* threads not having any partition. If the number of data nodes and/or *LDM* threads decreases, it may also be required to restore the tables from a logical backup. Otherwise, the number of partitions may exceed the maximum supported for the cluster.

A change in MySQL NDB Cluster 7.5 is that ndb_restore now does partition the tables according to the cluster the restore is made to.

A logical schema backup is a series of SQL statements, so to restore it, all that is required is to source the backup through the mysql command-line client, for example:

```
mysql> warnings
Show warnings enabled.

mysql> SOURCE schema_backup.sql;
```

The warnings command tells the mysql command-line client to automatically show details of all warnings encountered. This can be very useful when executing statements from a script, as otherwise it will not be known what the reported warnings are about. It is possible to disable the automatic SHOW WARNINGS again using the nowarning command.

■ **Tip**　If the schema is restored from a logical backup and the schema includes a foreign key and a native NDB Cluster backup is used to restore the data, as described in the next subsection, make sure to drop the foreign keys before restoring the data. The last step of restoring the backup when the indexes are rebuilt will add the foreign keys. If the foreign keys already exist, this will cause an error.

To restore the schema from a native NDB Cluster backup, the `--restore_meta` option is used. The schema should only be restored from one of the backup parts (the `--nodeid` option). For example, to restore the schema from the part of the backup created by node ID 1 for backup ID 2, the `ndb_restore` command will look like this:

```
shell$ ndb_restore --ndb-connectstring=192.168.56.101,192.168.56.102 \
                   --restore_meta --nodeid=1 --backupid=2 \
                   --backup_path=/backups/cluster/BACKUP/BACKUP-2 \
                   --disable-indexes
```

The `--disable-indexes` option tells `ndb_restore` to create the tables without any indexes other than the primary key.

The `ndb_restore --restore_meta` command also recreates the log group and tablespace files by default. The files are created irrespective of whether it is a full or partial restore. If the files already exist, the restore will fail. To skip the process of restoring the disk data files, use the `--no-restore-disk-objects` option.

Full Data Restores

A full data restore is the simplest restore. In this context, a full data restore means restoring everything in the backup. If the backup itself only contains a subset of the tables and/or data, the "full restore" will only restore that subset of the tables/data.

For a logical backup, the backup is restored in the same way as described for restoring a schema. The logical backup may in fact include the schema backup together with the data backup. An example of restoring a logical backup is:

```
mysql> warnings
Show warnings enabled.

mysql> SOURCE full_backup.sql;
```

A native NDB Cluster backup is a little more complex to restore as the backup is split across all of the data nodes that were online at the time of the backup. There is no limitation on how many parts of the backup are restored in parallel other than the cluster must be able to keep up with the load. Typically, it is possible to restore all parts at the same time. A common approach is to restore each part from the same host as where the node that made the backup is installed; however, this is not required.

To restore the data backed up by node ID 1 in the backup with backup ID 2, use a command such as:

```
shell$ ndb_restore --ndb-connectstring=192.168.56.101,192.168.56.102 \
                   --restore_data --nodeid=1 --backupid=2 \
                   --backup_path=/backups/cluster/BACKUP/BACKUP-2 \
                   --disable-indexes
```

Execute `ndb_restore` like this for each part of the backup, setting the `--nodeid` option to the node ID of the data node that created that part of the backup. The `--disable-indexes` option is not required if the schema was restored using `ndb_restore` with the indexes disabled, but in that case, it is just a NOOP (no operation), so it is simpler to always include the option.

When the data has been restored from all the backup parts—that is, the ndb_restore --restore-data commands have all completed successfully, the indexes must be rebuilt. This rebuild is triggered using the --rebuild-indexes option with ndb_restore. The command to rebuild the indexes should be executed for only one of the backup parts. Continuing the example, the command to rebuild the indexes looks like this:

```
shell$ ndb_restore --ndb-connectstring=192.168.56.101,192.168.56.102 \
                   --nodeid=1 --backupid=2 \
                   --backup_path=/backups/cluster/BACKUP/BACKUP-2 \
                   --rebuild-indexes
```

Restore to a Different Number of Data Nodes

There is no restriction on the number of data nodes required in the cluster a backup is restored to (the *target cluster*) compared to the cluster where the backup was created (the *source cluster*). However, a different number of data nodes in general also means the cluster has a different default and maximum number of partitions. Because ndb_restore --restore_meta in MySQL NDB Cluster 7.4 and earlier restores the schema with the same number of partitions, as when the backup was created, it is recommended in those versions to restore the schema from a logical schema backup when the configuration of the target cluster does not match the source cluster with respect to the number of data nodes and/or the number of *LDM* threads.

The data of a native NDB Cluster backup is restored in the same way as when the two clusters are identical. If the backup parts are copied to the hosts of the data nodes, it is necessary to distribute them so some nodes get more than one backup part (if the target cluster has fewer data nodes than the source cluster) or some hosts will not have any backup parts (if the target cluster has more data nodes than the source cluster). When restoring the data, the data is automatically distributed according the partitioning of the tables on the target cluster, so there is nothing special to take into consideration.

For logical backups, there is even less to consider. Since the backup is restored by replaying an SQL script through one of the SQL nodes, the procedure is exactly the same as for restoring to a target cluster that is identical to the source cluster.

Partial Data Restores

A partial data restore is a restore in which a subset of the backup is restored. In principle, a partial backup can apply both to the tables and to the data restored. However, for the purpose of this discussion, the only case considered is when a subset of the tables is restored.

For a logical backup that has all of the backups in a single SQL script, it is necessary to edit the SQL script to remove the parts of the backup that should not be restored. This is where a backup created with mysqldump --tab=... or a dump project folder from MySQL Workbench can be an advantage, as each table is created in its own separate file, making it trivial to perform a partial restore.

■ **Caution**   The --one-database option for the mysql command-line client cannot be used to perform a partial restore of an SQL script. The option relies on the default database. As the SQL script changes the default schema for each database in the backup, the result is that --one-database will not have any effect.

---

ndb_restore on the other hand has built-in support for partial restores, and there is also support to rename the database name as part of the restore. There are five command-line arguments to ndb_restore related to partial restores:

- **--exclude-databases=....** A comma-separated list of databases to exclude from the restore.

- **--exclude-tables=....** A comma-separated list of tables to exclude from the restore. Each table must also include the database name.

- **--include-databases=....** A comma-separated list of databases to include in the backup.

- **--include-tables=....** A comma-separated list of tables to include in the backup. Like for --exclude-tables, the database name must be included for each table.

- **--rewrite-database=....** Takes two database names separated by a comma where the first value is the database name in the backup and the second is the database name to restore to. Any foreign keys in tables affected by the rename are removed as part of the rewrite. For example, to rename the world database to world_temp, you use --rewrite-database=world,world_temp. Specify multiple times to rename more than one database.

As an example, consider a backup that (among other databases) includes the world sample database, and it is required to restore the data for the City table to a database named world_temp. For example, to restore some data that was deleted by accident. In this case, the following sequence for ndb_restore commands can be used (repeat the --restore_data step for each data node that participated in the backup):

```
shell$ ndb_restore --ndb-connectstring=192.168.56.101,192.168.56.102 \
                   --restore_meta --nodeid=1 --backupid=2 \
                   --backup_path=/backups/cluster/BACKUP/BACKUP-2 \
                   --include-tables=world.City \
                   --rewrite-database=world,world_temp \
                   --disable-indexes

shell$ ndb_restore --ndb-connectstring=192.168.56.101,192.168.56.102 \
                   --restore_data --nodeid=1 --backupid=2 \
                   --backup_path=/backups/cluster/BACKUP/BACKUP-2 \
                   --include-tables=world.City \
                   --rewrite-database=world,world_temp \
                   --disable-indexes

shell$ ndb_restore --ndb-connectstring=192.168.56.101,192.168.56.102 \
                   --nodeid=1 --backupid=2 \
                   --backup_path=/backups/cluster/BACKUP/BACKUP-2 \
                   --include-tables=world.City \
                   --rewrite-database=world,world_temp \
                   --rebuild-indexes
```

It is possible to combine the include and exclude options or use the options multiple times. When multiple filters are used, the overall filter will be the combination of all of the supplied filters. In the case of using both include and exclude options, the overall filter is evaluated in the order they are supplied. Consider for example these filters:

```
shell$ ndb_restore ... --include-databases=world --exclude-tables=world.City
```

In this case, `--include-database` will include all tables in the `world` schema, and `--exclude-tables` will then remove the `world.City` table, so the overall result is that all tables in the `world` schema, except the `City` table, are restored.

Restores Using MySQL Workbench

Logical backups made with `mysqldump`, `mysqlpump`, and similar backup programs can also be restored using MySQL Workbench. There are two options for this. The first corresponds to the data export function described earlier. This supports importing a dump project folder or a self-contained file. While the dump project folder works the best using a dump project folder created by MySQL Workbench's data export feature, the self-contained file can be from any backup software that creates an SQL file. The major difference from a usability point of view is that a dump project folder offers the option of performing a full as well as a partial restore, whereas a self-contained file only supports full restores. Figure 8-4 shows the data import screen in MySQL Workbench with the options available for an import of a dump project folder.

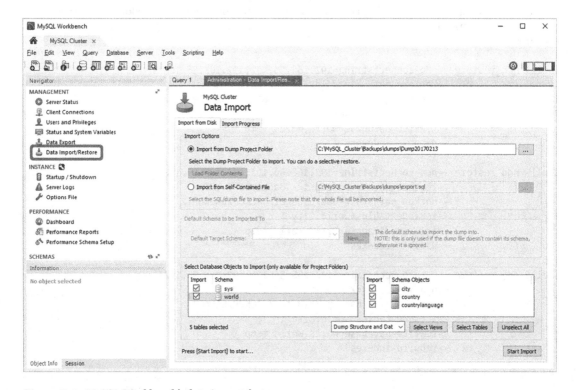

Figure 8-4. *MySQL Workbench's data import feature*

An alternative way to restore a self-contained SQL script in MySQL Workbench is to open the script in a query tab. The advantage is that it is possible to edit the contents of the script before executing it. The disadvantage is that it is difficult to handle large backups this way. A script is loaded by choosing a query tab and choosing *Open SQL Script* under *File* in the menu. This is illustrated in Figure 8-5. It is also possible to execute the script using *Run SQL Script* under *File* in the menu; this is similar to executing a self-contained SQL file from the data import screen.

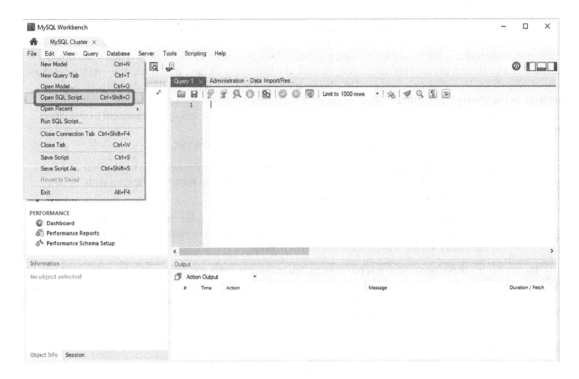

Figure 8-5. *Open SQL Script in the menu in MySQL Workbench*

Point-In-Time Recovery (PITR)

One of the more advanced restore procedures is a point-in-time recovery (PITR). As the name suggests, it consists of restoring the data to a specific point in time. There are two general cases for point-in-time recoveries:

- Restoring to just before a specific event occurred. For example, if a user has dropped a table by mistake, it is necessary to restore to just before this happened.

- Restore to the latest possible time. This can for example happen after a crash of the host where MySQL is installed.

A special case is setting up a replication slave, as that largely follows the same steps as for a point-in-time recovery.

The point-in-time recovery procedure consists of two high-level steps:

1. A regular restore of a backup, as described earlier in the chapter.

2. Replaying the binary logs from the point in time where the backup was made up to the point in time the restore should conclude. It may in some cases be necessary to skip selected events while applying the binary logs. For setting up a replication slave, replaying the binary logs will in principle never end.

At a high level, there is no difference between performing a point-in-time recovery for a logical backup and a native NDB Cluster backup as the two steps just mentioned are the same. There is however one main difference: determining the binary log file and position where the backup was created. When a backup is made with mysqldump, the backup will directly include the binary log file and position if the --master-data option was given. However, for a native NDB Cluster backup, it is not possible to have this directly in the backup, as the binary logging does not occur on the data nodes where the backup is created. Additionally, there may be several SQL nodes with binary logs enabled and the backup will not correspond to the same point in the binary logs for each SQL node.

There are two parts to determining the correct binary log file and position:

- **The mysql.ndb_apply_status table:** This table is normally only used on a replication slave. However, if the --restore_epoch option is added when restoring the data with ndb_restore, it will be populated during the restore.

- **The mysql.ndb_binlog_index table:** This is the table that was discussed as part of the backups of the binary log. It contains the mapping from the NDB Cluster epochs to the binary log file and position on that SQL node.

By combining these two tables, it is possible to determine the correct starting point to replay the binary log from. This is also required when setting up a replication slave.

Putting everything together, the steps for a point-in-time recovery are to first ensure the database has been cleanly initialized, and then restore the native NDB Cluster backup:

```
shell$ ndb_restore --ndb-connectstring=192.168.56.101,192.168.56.102 \
                   --restore_meta --nodeid=1 --backupid=2 \
                   --backup_path=/backups/cluster/BACKUP/BACKUP-2 \
                   --disable-indexes

# For each data node:
shell$ ndb_restore --ndb-connectstring=192.168.56.101,192.168.56.102 \
                   --restore_data --restore_epoch --nodeid=1 --backupid=2 \
                   --backup_path=/backups/cluster/BACKUP/BACKUP-2 \
                   --disable-indexes

shell$ ndb_restore --ndb-connectstring=192.168.56.101,192.168.56.102 \
                   --nodeid=1 --backupid=2 \
                   --backup_path=/backups/cluster/BACKUP/BACKUP-2 \
                   --rebuild-indexes
```

The next step is to restore the backup of the mysql.ndb_binlog_index table:

```
mysql> warnings
Show warnings enabled.

mysql> use mysql;
Database changed
```

```
mysql> SOURCE binlog_index.sql
Query OK, 0 rows affected (0.00 sec)
...
```

The --restore_epoch option, when used for restoring the data, populates the mysql.ndb_apply_status table similar to how it is done on a replication slave when applying the binary log. The content will be like in following output:

```
mysql> SELECT * FROM mysql.ndb_apply_status;
+-----------+--------------+----------+-----------+---------+
| server_id | epoch        | log_name | start_pos | end_pos |
+-----------+--------------+----------+-----------+---------+
|         0 | 455266533375 |          |         0 |       0 |
+-----------+--------------+----------+-----------+---------+
1 row in set (0.01 sec)
```

The data shows the latest applied epoch per server_id. Since the epoch originates from ndb_restore, the server ID is 0. In principle, there may be more than one row in which case it is the highest value of the epoch column that is of interest; in practice after a restore there is only one row. This epoch should be compared with the epochs column in the mysql.ndb_binlog_index table, which records the epoch that corresponds to binary log files and positions. The position that is of interest for a point-in-time recovery or when determining where to start replication from, is the position for the first epoch larger than the one found in mysql.ndb_apply_status. The binary log file and position can now be determined as follows:

```
mysql> SELECT i.File, i.Position
          FROM (SELECT MAX(epoch) AS MaxEpoch
                  FROM mysql.ndb_apply_status) AS e
               INNER JOIN mysql.ndb_binlog_index i ON i.epoch > e.MaxEpoch
        ORDER BY i.epoch
        LIMIT 1;
+----------------------------+----------+
| File                       | Position |
+----------------------------+----------+
| /var/lib/mysql/binlog.000003 |   216567 |
+----------------------------+----------+
1 row in set (0.00 sec)
```

The binary log can now be applied using the mysqlbinlog utility. There are four options to control which part of binary log(s) are extracted:

- **--start-position=....** The start position as found in the previous step. If multiple binary log files are specified, the position only applies to the first file.

- **--stop-position=....** The counterpart to --start-position. It specifies where to stop replaying the binary logs. If multiple binary log files are specified, the position only applies to the last file.

- **--start-datetime=....** Specifies the date and time using the format 2016-12-29 16:04:44. This option is most useful with --stop-datetime to determine the stop position for a point-in-time recovery.

- **--stop-datetime=....** Like --start-datetime, but specifies when to stop replaying the binary logs. It is not recommended to use this as part of a point-in-time recovery. The reason is that the timestamp logged with the binary log events is when the transaction started, but the events are logged in the order the transactions are committed. So, the timestamps will in general not be in order. If --stop-datetime is used, then replaying the binary log stops when the first event with a more recent timestamp than the value specified with --stop-datetime is encountered. However, the option can be useful for manually investigating the binary logs, for example, to determine the correct binary log position to use with --stop-position.

As an example, consider a point-in-time recovery where it is necessary to replay the binary log up to an event that dropped a table around 16:00 on December 29, 2016. First inspect the binary logs to determine the position of the event where the table was logged. This will look like:

```
shell$ mysqlbinlog --start-datetime='2016-12-29 15:55:00' \
                   --stop-datetime='2016-12-29 16:05:00' \
                   binlog.000005
...
# at 6432260
#161229 16:03:59 server id 57163508  end_log_pos 213382 CRC32
0x3da16db3      Query    thread_id=6    exec_time=1    error_code=0
SET TIMESTAMP=1487066639/*!*/;
/*!\C utf8 *//*!*/;
SET @@session.character_set_client=33,@@session.collation_connection=33,@@session.collation_
server=8/*!*/;
DROP TABLE `world`.`City` /* generated by server */
/*!*/;
```

■ **Tip** If you need to find an event manipulating a row, use the arguments --base64-output=decode-rows --verbose to convert the hexadecimal encoding of the row events into human readable form. Note that the binary log does not contain any character set information, so string data types such as varchar may be affected when displayed.

The DROP TABLE event starts at position 6432260, so this is the stop position to use when replaying the binary logs:

```
shell$ mysqlbinlog --start-position=216567 --stop-position=6432260 \
                   binlog.000003 binlog.000004 binlog.000005 | \
        mysql --user=root --password
```

Summary

This chapter discussed backups and restores. Backups can be made using native NDB Cluster online backups or logical backups. Often a combination of the two is used. A native NDB Cluster backup is created directly by the data nodes using the same underlying code as for local checkpoints. On the other hand, a logical backup is created using regular SQL statements to export the schema objects and data. It is also important to include backups of users, privileges, and binary logs.

Restoring backups are used for everything from setting up a test server to disaster recovery. It is important to test the restore procedures regularly to ensure familiarity with all the steps and to ensure the backups can be restored. A restore may be combined with replaying the binary logs to perform a point-in-time recovery (PITR), which for example can be useful to recover after accidentally dropping a table. Related to point-in-time recoveries is the process of setting up a replication slave.

The topic of the next chapter is the maintenance of the NDBCluster tables.

Table Maintenance

Part II covered the tasks needed to install and configure a cluster, and this part has been focusing on tools and procedures that are used on a day-to-day basis in order to maintain the cluster. An important task for the database administrator is table maintenance. This includes relatively infrequent tasks, such as adding new columns to existing tables over maintaining a good set of indexes, to more frequent tasks like defragmenting tables and updating index statistics. All of these tasks are discussed throughout this chapter.

Schema Changes

No matter how carefully a schema is planned, eventually some schema changes are required. It may be due to new requirements from the application or it may be that the schema design did not work out as well as initially planned. Schema changes in production environments are generally a painpoint for database systems; however, for NDBCluster tables, the change can in several cases be made while the table is online and the application can continue to both read and write to the table that is being changed. The rest of this section explains how to make schema changes.

Distributing Schema Changes and the Global Schema Lock

When a schema change is made for an NDBCluster table, the change must be distributed to all of the SQL nodes, and it is necessary to have a mechanism to avoid conflicting schema changes to occur concurrently. The details of the implementation of the global schema lock is beyond the scope of this book; however, some high-level information is good to know. This is the topic of this subsection.

MySQL NDB Cluster uses the hidden mysql.ndb_schema table to keep track of schema changes. It is an NDBCluster table, so all API nodes have the same view of the table. It is hidden, so it will not show up in a SHOW TABLES statement or when querying the Information Schema tables—although it is visible in the data node data dictionary using the ndb_show_tables utility or the ndbinfo.dict_obj_info view:

```
shell$ ndb_show_tables | grep ' ndb_schema$'
7      UserTable          Online  Yes    mysql      def      ndb_schema

mysql> SELECT type_name, id AS TableID, fq_name
        FROM ndbinfo.dict_obj_info
            INNER JOIN ndbinfo.dict_obj_types ON type_id = type
        WHERE fq_name = 'mysql/def/ndb_schema';
```

```
+-------------+---------+----------------------+
| type_name   | TableID | fq_name              |
+-------------+---------+----------------------+
| User table  |       7 | mysql/def/ndb_schema |
+-------------+---------+----------------------+
1 row in set (0.02 sec)
```

It is also possible to query the table directly, which can be useful when debugging. It will, for example, show the last query to modify the table and the schema version of the table. Listing 9-1 shows an example for the db1.t1 table.

Listing 9-1. The Information in mysql.ndb_schema for the db1.t1 Table

```
mysql> SELECT * FROM mysql.ndb_schema WHERE db = 'db1' AND name = 't1'\G
*************************** 1. row ***************************
     db: db1
   name: t1
  slock:
  query: ALTER TABLE t1 ADD INDEX (val)
node_id: 51
  epoch: 0
     id: 10
version: 100663299
   type: 7
1 row in set (0.08 sec)
```

Figure 9-1 shows the high-level design of the schema changes being distributed between the SQL nodes through the mysql.ndb_schema table.

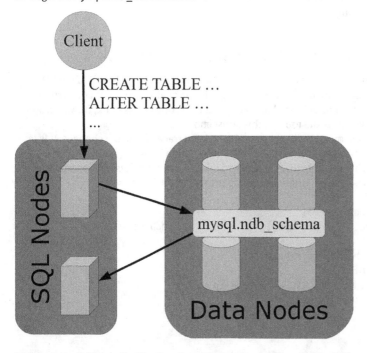

Figure 9-1. *Schema distribution through the mysql.ndb_schema table*

When two SQL nodes attempt to change the schema for the same table at the same time, the second statement to start will be blocked until the first has completed. This can for example be seen from the output of SHOW PROCESSLIST, as demonstrated in Listing 9-2, where the query is waiting for the global schema lock to be granted. A global schema lock should be treated like any other lock—the solution is to wait for the lock to be released or kill the query holding the lock. Should the lock not be released (this would be a bug), typically it will help to restart the SQL node holding the lock.

Listing 9-2. ALTER TABLE Query Waiting for the Global Schema Lock

```
mysql> SHOW PROCESSLIST\G
...
*************************** 2. row ***************************
     Id: 4
   User: root
   Host: localhost:49501
     db: db1
Command: Query
   Time: 1
  State: Waiting for ndbcluster global schema lock
   Info: ALTER TABLE t1 ADD INDEX (val)
...
```

With some of the background of how MySQL NDB Cluster handles the distribution of schema changes and how two conflicting schema changes avoid being executed at the same time, it is possible to move on to discuss the schema changes themselves.

Online Versus Offline Schema Changes

Schema changed in MySQL NDB Cluster can be divided into two categories: Those that can be performed online and those that require the table to be offline. Online schema changes have the advantage that they provide minimal interruption of the ongoing activities of the application. This is possible for several types of schema changes of NDBCluster tables. Table 9-1 summarizes the characteristics of online and offline schema changes. The next two sections go into more detail, and later in the chapter there are several examples of online and offline schema changes.

Table 9-1. *Online vs. Offline Schema Changes*

	Online	Offline
Implementation	The schema change is pushed down to the data nodes and performed in-place, i.e., without creating a new table and copying the data.	The SQL node is handling the schema change by creating a new table with the new schema and copying the data across. At the end, the old table is removed and the new table is renamed.
On the SQL node performing the change	An exclusive lock is required for the table.	An exclusive table level lock is taken. This applies even if LOCK=SHARED is specified. (Whether a shared or exclusive lock is requested affects whether the concurrent queries blocks for a metadata lock or a table lock.) Furthermore, executing concurrent queries with LOCK=SHARED will cause a deadlock when the new tale is renamed at the end of the ALTER TABLE.
On other API nodes	Both reads and writes are allowed and are safe to do.	No locking occurs for DML statements, but these are not safe to use and any data changes made during the schema change may be lost. It is thus recommended to put the cluster in single user mode, as discussed in Chapter 7.

As the comparison of the two schema change methods shows, online and offline schema changes are fundamentally different, and offline schema changes are much more intrusive than online schema changes.

Offline Schema Changes

It is worth discussing the recommendation to enable single user mode for offline schema changes in more detail. There is no transaction log keeping track of the changes to the table while the data is copied to the new table. For this reason, changes made to the part of the table that is already copied (including inserting new rows) will be lost when the old table is replaced with the new table at the end of the procedure. If it is guaranteed that only reads will occur, it is possible to keep the other nodes online during the schema change, but in practice it is better to use the single mode feature and, if necessary, redirect queries to other tables to the SQL node performing the schema change.

■ **Caution** Do not insert, update, or delete data in the table undergoing an offline schema change. The changes may be lost. It is recommended to use the single user mode feature discussed in Chapter 7 to avoid inadvertently losing data.

Performing a schema change requires resources irrespective of which algorithm is used. However, as copying schema changes requires an extra table while the change is applied, it will also require more attributes, memory, and/or disk usage during this period. As a rule of thumb, the number of attributes required for the table is three times larger than that of the original table while the schema change is ongoing.

Chapter 4 discussed how to calculate the number of attributes used for a table. To allow some spare room, MaxNoOfAttributes should be configured to allow for at least six times as many attributes. If the value of MaxNoOfAttributes is too small, an error like the one shown in Listing 9-3 is returned. In that case, it is necessary to increase the value of MaxNoOfAttributes, which requires a rolling restart of the data nodes (see Chapter 10).

Listing 9-3. Error Due to MaxNoOfAttributes Being Too Small

```
mysql> ALTER TABLE t1 ALGORITHM=COPY, ADD INDEX (val);
ERROR 1025 (HY000): Error on rename of './db1/t1' to './db1/#sql2-361e-5' (errno: 708 - Unknown
error 708)

mysql> SHOW WARNINGS\G
*************************** 1. row ***************************
  Level: Warning
   Code: 1296
Message: Got error 708 'No more attribute metadata records (increase MaxNoOfAttributes)'
from NDB
*************************** 2. row ***************************
  Level: Error
   Code: 1025
Message: Error on rename of './db1/t1' to './db1/#sql2-361e-5' (errno: 708 - Unknown error 708)
2 rows in set (0.01 sec)
```

Online Schema Changes

Online schema changes are clearly preferred: they allow the application to continue being fully online and the schema changes to happen in-place. This means the amount of work is much less and thus the schema change completes quicker. However, there is one caveat: not all schema changes can be made online. The general limitations of online schema changes are:

- The table must have an explicit primary key. When a hidden primary key is used, a copying offline schema change must always be used.

- It is only possible to do one of the following changes at a time: add an index, drop an index, or add columns. If several of these changes are required, do them in sequence.

- The schema change takes an exclusive lock on the table, which affects connections to the same SQL node. So, concurrent queries using the tables are blocked. For this reason, it can be worth having an additional SQL node reserved for administrative tasks such as table maintenance.

There are also more specific limitations for each of the operations that do support in-place changes. The supported online operations and their limitations are listed in Table 9-2.

Table 9-2. *Limitations of the Schema Changes Supporting the In-Place Algorithm*

Schema Change	Limitations and Notes
ADD INDEX	Cannot be used together with DROP INDEX or ADD COLUMN. Only one index can be created at a time. It applies to the ALTER TABLE ... ADD INDEX and ADD INDEX statements.
DROP INDEX	Cannot be used together with ADD INDEX or ADD COLUMN. Only one index can be dropped at a time. It applies to the ALTER TABLE ... DROP INDEX and DROP INDEX statements.
ADD COLUMN	The column must use the dynamic column format. If the column format is not specified explicitly, MySQL NDB Cluster will automatically choose dynamic and return a warning. TEXT and BLOB data types are not supported. The column must be DEFAULT NULL and allow null values. The column must follow all existing columns in the table definition[1].
REORGANIZE PARTITIONS	For use after adding more data nodes to the cluster or increasing the number of *LDM* threads.
OPTIMIZE TABLE	This is not an ALTER TABLE operation. Its use will be discussed in the defragmentation section.
RENAME (table)	It applies both to the ALTER TABLE ... RENAME ... and RENAME TABLE statements. Only the table name can be renamed online. Renaming an index or a column requires an offline copying ALTER TABLE.
Set the READ_BACKUP attribute	The feature is new in MySQL NDB Cluster 7.5. The read from backup replicas feature was discussed in Chapter 2.

By default, the in-place algorithm will be chosen if it is supported; otherwise, a copying schema change will be made. The next section discusses how to specify which algorithm to use with the ALTER TABLE statement.

ALTER TABLE Algorithm

The syntax to perform schema changes depends somewhat on the version of MySQL NDB Cluster. In MySQL NDB Cluster 7.2 and earlier, the ONLINE and OFFLINE keywords to ALTER TABLE were used to specify whether an online or offline schema change should be performed. In MySQL NDB Cluster 7.3 and later, the InnoDB storage engine also supports online schema changes and the syntax was changed to use the ALGORITHM attribute and the ONLINE and OFFLINE keywords were deprecated (and removed in MySQL NDB Cluster 7.5). The ALGORITHM option takes one of three values:

- **INPLACE:** This will perform the schema change within the existing copy of the table. This in general is preferred as it is faster than creating a copy of the table. For NDBCluster tables, this is a synonym for an online schema change.

- **COPY:** This makes a copy of the table with the new table definition. For NDBCluster tables, this is a synonym for an offline schema change.

- **DEFAULT:** Will choose INPLACE if possible, otherwise COPY. Specifying DEFAULT is the same as not specifying the ALGORITHM option.

---

[1]Remember, the columns are ordered in SQL databases even if they are not in relational theory

■ **Note** The terms *online* and *offline* are interchangeable with *in-place* and *copy* respectively. So, there is no change in concept between the old and new syntax.

In version 7.3 and later, it is additionally possible to set the lock type using the LOCK option to ALTER TABLE. The lock type only applies to the local SQL node executing the ALTER TABLE. It is of limited use with MySQL NDB Cluster as online schema changes always require an exclusive lock, although for offline schema changes it is, in principle, possible to choose between using a shared or an exclusive lock. (As mentioned, it is not recommended to attempt using a shared lock.)

■ **Caution** Using ALGORITHM=COPY, LOCK=SHARED to make an offline schema change will cause a deadlock if concurrent queries using the table on the same SQL node is attempted.

The following ALTER TABLE statement is an example of an online/in-place schema change:

- **MySQL NDB Cluster 7.3 and later.**

```
mysql> ALTER TABLE t1 [ALGORITHM=INPLACE, ]
                      [LOCK=EXCLUSIVE, ]
                      <schema change specification>;
```

- **MySQL NDB Cluster 7.2 and earlier.**

```
mysql> ALTER [ONLINE] TABLE <schema change specification>;
```

Here, the parts of the statement inside the square brackets ([...]) are optional, a vertical bar (|) between the two words means that one word must be chosen, and the actual schema change should go where <schema change specification> is.

An example ALTER TABLE statement for offline/copying schema change is (the same syntax is used as for online schema changes):

- **MySQL NDB Cluster 7.3 and later.**

```
mysql> ALTER TABLE t1 [ALGORITHM=COPY, ]
                      [LOCK=SHARED|EXCLUSIVE, ]
                      <schema change specification>;
```

- **MySQL NDB Cluster 7.2 and earlier.**

```
mysql> ALTER [OFFLINE] TABLE <schema change specification>;
```

Note the comma after the ALGORITHM and LOCK options. There are examples later in the chapter of various schema changes.

To maintain backward compatibility, the ONLINE and OFFLINE keywords can also be used in MySQL NDB Cluster 7.3 and 7.4; however it is recommended to start using the new syntax, and in version 7.5 and later the ALGORITHM option is the only supported syntax to specify whether the schema change should be made in-place or as a copying ALTER TABLE. Using the ONLINE and OFFLINE keywords will also cause a deprecation warning in versions 7.3 and 7.4.

This concludes the theory behind online and offline schema changes. Before moving on to partition reorganization, a series of ALTER TABLE examples are discussed.

ALTER TABLE Examples

It is worth looking at some examples, as the syntax can be difficult at first. The examples in this section use the following table as the table definition before the schema change:

```
mysql> SHOW CREATE TABLE t1\G
*************************** 1. row ***************************
       Table: t1
Create Table: CREATE TABLE `t1` (
  `id` int(10) unsigned NOT NULL,
  `val` varchar(10) DEFAULT NULL,
  PRIMARY KEY (`id`)
) ENGINE=ndbcluster DEFAULT CHARSET=latin1
1 row in set (0.02 sec)
```

Do not take the timings in the examples literally, as they are from a virtual machine on a relatively old laptop. The time it takes to perform the schema change will also depend on the amount of data. However, the relative times between in-place and copying schema changes are of relevance.

Default Behavior

By default, the INPLACE algorithm is used if this is supported, otherwise COPY is used. For example, adding a column that accepts nulls as the last column without specifying any modifiers will be made online:

```
mysql> ALTER TABLE t1 ADD COLUMN rank int unsigned;
Query OK, 0 rows affected, 1 warning (2.62 sec)
Records: 0  Duplicates: 0  Warnings: 1

mysql> SHOW WARNINGS\G
*************************** 1. row ***************************
  Level: Warning
   Code: 1478
Message: Converted FIXED field 'rank' to DYNAMIC to enable online ADD COLUMN
1 row in set (0.00 sec)
```

Notice the warning. It is presented because, by default, an integer column will use the fixed column format, but for an online schema change to occur, the dynamic column format must be used. It is possible to be more explicit about the behavior and at the same time avoid the warning. That is the next example.

Adding a Column with the Explicit Column Format

As shown in the previous example, MySQL NDB Cluster will automatically choose the dynamic column format for an in-place schema change even for data types that by default use the fixed column format, but it raises a warning. It is preferable to avoid this warning, as it may cause more important issues to be overlooked. To avoid this warning, the solution is to specify the column format explicitly:

```
mysql> ALTER TABLE t1
          ADD COLUMN rank int unsigned COLUMN_FORMAT DYNAMIC;
Query OK, 0 rows affected (2.26 sec)
Records: 0  Duplicates: 0  Warnings: 0
```

■ **Tip** It is best practice to write the queries so they do not cause any warnings. This way it is easier to identify queries that may cause problems, for example, because they are using deprecated features. Warnings can be seen with the SHOW WARNINGS statement like in the previous example or by enabling warnings automatically in the mysql command-line client using the warnings command.

What do you do, if it is not desirable to have MySQL NDB Cluster choosing the algorithm, or if it is important that the schema change is made only if it can be done using the in-place algorithm? The next two examples cover that.

Specifying Algorithm and Lock Type

It is not possible to see which algorithm will be chosen without executing the ALTER TABLE statement. This can cause surprises, if the copying algorithm is chosen where it was expected to be an in-place change. To avoid this issue, set the algorithm explicitly using the ALGORITHM option:

```
mysql> ALTER TABLE t1 ALGORITHM=INPLACE, ADD INDEX (val);
Query OK, 0 rows affected (8.29 sec)
Records: 0  Duplicates: 0  Warnings: 0
```

The same change can be made by setting the locking type for the local SQL mode explicitly. Since it is an online schema change, the lock type must be set to exclusive:

```
mysql> ALTER TABLE t1 ALGORITHM=INPLACE, LOCK=EXCLUSIVE, ADD INDEX (val);
Query OK, 0 rows affected (8.25 sec)
Records: 0  Duplicates: 0  Warnings: 0
```

The same example, but here the index is added using offline copying schema change, uses ALGORITHM=COPY:

```
mysql> ALTER TABLE t1 ALGORITHM=COPY, LOCK=EXCLUSIVE, ADD INDEX (val);
Query OK, 131072 rows affected (2 min 23.23 sec)
Records: 131072  Duplicates: 0  Warnings: 0
```

Notice how much longer it takes to add the index through a table copy.

What happens if ALGORITHM=INPLACE is chosen, but the change does not support it? That is the next thing to discuss.

Attempting Unsupported In-Place Changes

If an in-place algorithm is requested, but the schema change in question does not support it, MySQL will return an error. For example, dropping a column can only be done using the copying algorithm:

```
mysql> ALTER TABLE t1 ALGORITHM=INPLACE, DROP COLUMN rank;
ERROR 1846 (0A000): ALGORITHM=INPLACE is not supported. Reason: Detected unsupported change.
Try ALGORITHM=COPY.
```

■ **Tip**   One advantage of specifying ALGORITHM=INPLACE explicitly is that it ensures that a copying ALTER TABLE is not executed by mistake. If the INPLACE algorithm is not supported, the statement will fail with an error.

The last case to consider is schema changes in MySQL NDB Cluster 7.2 and earlier where the ALGORITHM and LOCK keywords are not supported.

Schema Changes in Version 7.2 and Earlier

In MySQL NDB Cluster 7.2 and earlier, the OFFLINE and ONLINE keywords are used instead of the ALGORITHM keyword to specify how the schema change must be executed. It is not possible to set the lock type; an exclusive lock is always taken on the SQL node where the ALTER TABLE is executed.

For example, to add an index online (in-place), use:

```
mysql> ALTER ONLINE TABLE t1 ADD INDEX (val);
```

An example of an offline (copying) schema change is to add a column using the fixed column format:

```
mysql> ALTER OFFLINE TABLE t1
        ADD COLUMN rank int unsigned COLUMN_FORMAT FIXED DEFAULT NULL;
```

This concludes the ALTER TABLE examples for making schema changes. However, ALTER TABLE is also used to reorganize the partitions; for example, after changing the number of data nodes and/or *LDM* threads. This is the topic of the next section.

Reorganize Partitions

A special case of making a schema change is reorganizing the partitions. By default, NDBCluster tables are created with the number of partitions based on the number of data nodes and the number of *LDM* threads per data node. When the configuration of the cluster changes, it is necessary to redistribute the data to take advantage of the new cluster configuration. Table 9-3 shows the various cluster configuration changes and discusses how to reorganize the partitions for each case. The overview shows that scaling up can be done with an online schema change, whereas scaling down requires an offline schema change.

Table 9-3. *Requirements to Reorganize the Partitions After a Cluster Configuration Change*

Configuration Change	Reorganize Partition Method
Increase the number of data nodes	ALTER TABLE t1 REORGANIZE PARTITION can be used. This is an online operation. See Chapter 10 for an example.
Decrease the number of data nodes	It is necessary to recreate the table. A null ALTER TABLE can be used: ALTER TABLE t1 ENGINE=NDBCluster. This is an offline operation.
Increase the number of *LDM* threads	ALTER TABLE ... REORGANIZE PARTITION can be used. This is an online operation, but it can first be performed after two rolling restarts (where the first rolling restart changes the number of *LDM* threads) or a system restart.
Decrease the number of *LDM* threads	It is necessary to recreate the table. A null ALTER TABLE can be used: ALTER TABLE t1 ENGINE=NDBCluster. This is an offline operation.

Note REORGANIZE PARTITION only supports tables using automatic partitioning. In order to repartition tables using a custom partitioning, it is necessary to rebuild the table specifying the new number of partitions, for example:

```
mysql> ALTER TABLE t1 ALGORITHM=COPY
                    PARTITION BY KEY (id) PARTITIONS 8;
```

An online reorganization of the partitions is an expensive operation even though it is performed in-place. The data must be moved around while keeping track of where it is located to be able to serve concurrent queries. Additionally, it leaves the original partitions fragmented. In general, an offline copying *null* ALTER TABLE will be faster and will defragment the table at the same time. A null ALTER TABLE rebuilds the table and (except that the new copy of the table is created with the number of partitions that is the default for the current cluster configuration), it makes no change to the table. A null ALTER TABLE is always a copying operation and must be done offline. The remainder of this section includes examples of reorganizing the partitions online versus rebuilding the table and discussion of defragmentation of tables.

An example of reorganizing the partitions online using REORGANIZE PARTITION is:

```
mysql> ALTER TABLE t1 ALGORITHM=INPLACE, REORGANIZE PARTITION;
Query OK, 0 rows affected (22 min 57.51 sec)
Records: 0  Duplicates: 0  Warnings: 0
```

To use a null ALTER TABLE instead—either after reducing the number of data nodes or *LDM* threads, or to fully defragment the table (see also the next section)—use:

```
mysql> ALTER TABLE t1 ALGORITHM=COPY, LOCK=EXCLUSIVE, ENGINE=NDBCluster;
Query OK, 131072 rows affected (3 min 41.43 sec)
Records: 131072  Duplicates: 0  Warnings: 0
```

Note that the time this table rebuild takes compared to the online REORGANIZE PARTITION statement. This is one case where the copying schema change is faster than the online approach.

Tip When it is necessary to reorganize the partitions, it is better to do it by performing a null ALTER TABLE if the downtime is acceptable. This is generally faster than the online REORGANIZE PARTITION and fully defragments the table at the same time.

Listing 9-4 shows an example of a query that can be used to find tables that are candidates to have the partitions reorganized. It requires all data nodes to be online. The MySQL NDB Cluster version must be at least 7.5. A table is included, if the current number of partitions is different from the number, a new table will be created given the current cluster configuration. It also indicates whether the table was created using automatic partitioning or manual partitioning. The query is explained after the listing.

Listing 9-4. Finding Tables That Are Candidates to Have the Partitions Reorganized

```
mysql> SELECT tds.table_id AS TableId, tbl.TableSchema, tbl.TableName,
          tds.tab_partitions AS TablePartitions,
          (
            CASE ti.partition_balance
                WHEN 'FOR_RA_BY_LDM'
                     THEN thr.NumLdmThreads/cfg.NoOfReplicas
                WHEN 'FOR_RP_BY_NODE'
                     THEN n.NumDataNodes
                WHEN 'FOR_RA_BY_NODE'
                     THEN n.NoOfNodeGroups
                ELSE thr.NumLdmThreads
            END / IF(ti.fully_replicated, n.NoOfNodeGroups, 1)
          ) AS DefaultNumPartitions,
          IF(ti.partition_balance = 'SPECIFIC',
            'YES',
            'NO'
          ) AS HasCustomPartitions
       FROM (SELECT COUNT(*) AS NumLdmThreads
            FROM ndbinfo.threads
           WHERE thread_name = 'ldm'
          ) thr
          CROSS JOIN (
             SELECT COUNT(*) AS NumDataNodes,
                    COUNT(DISTINCT group_id) AS NoOfNodeGroups
               FROM ndbinfo.membership
          ) n
          CROSS JOIN (
             SELECT config_value AS NoOfReplicas
               FROM ndbinfo.config_params p
                    INNER JOIN ndbinfo.config_values v
                            ON v.config_param = p.param_number
              WHERE p.param_name = 'NoOfReplicas'
              LIMIT 1 /* NoOfReplicas must be the same on all nodes */
          ) cfg
          INNER JOIN ndbinfo.table_distribution_status tds
          INNER JOIN ndbinfo.table_info ti ON ti.table_id = tds.table_id
          INNER JOIN (
             SELECT id AS table_id,
                    SUBSTRING_INDEX(fq_name, '/', 1) AS TableSchema,
                    SUBSTRING_INDEX(fq_name, '/', -1) AS TableName
               FROM ndbinfo.dict_obj_info doi
                    INNER JOIN ndbinfo.dict_obj_types dot
                            ON dot.type_id = doi.type
              WHERE dot.type_name = 'User table'
          ) tbl ON tbl.table_id = tds.table_id
```

```
        WHERE NOT ((tbl.TableSchema = 'mysql' AND tbl.TableName LIKE 'NDB$%')
                OR (tbl.TableSchema = 'sys'
                    AND (tbl.TableName LIKE 'NDB$%'
                        OR tbl.TableName LIKE 'SYSTAB\_%'
                        )
                    )
                )
        HAVING TablePartitions <> DefaultNumPartitions
        ORDER BY TableSchema, TableName;
```

Since the query is quite complex, it is worth taking a look at the various parts that make it up. The `CASE` statement in the `SELECT` part calculates the expected number of partitions based on the partition distribution and whether the partitions are fully replicated. If custom partitioning is used, the partition balance is set to `SPECIFIC`.

The first subquery in the `FROM` clause uses the `ndbinfo.threads` view to determine the number of *LDM* threads in the cluster. The second subquery uses the `ndbinfo.membership` view to find the number of data nodes and node groups. The third subquery checks the configuration through the `ndbinfo.config_params` and `ndbinfo.config_values` views to get the value of the `NoOfReplicas` configuration option. Each of these three subqueries returns exactly one row, so a `CROSS JOIN` can be used and overall there will still be one row.

The next join is on the `ndbinfo.table_distribution_status` view and it contains information about the number of partitions for the table. Further, the join on `ndbinfo.table_info` provides the partition balance for the table and whether the partitions are fully replicated. Finally, a subquery uses the two dictionary `ndbinfo` views—`ndbinfo.dict_obj_info` and `ndbinfo.dict_obj_types`—to get the schema and table name from the fully qualified NDB Cluster name (`fq_name`).

The `WHERE` clause filters out system tables and other internal tables that cannot be reorganized.

The `ndbinfo.table_distribution_status` table that is used in Listing 9-4 can also be used to determine whether a `REORGANIZE PARTITION` is in progress, as shown in Listing 9-5. The subquery in the `INNER JOIN` part is the same as the one used in Listing 9-4 to get the table schema and table name for each table undergoing a partition reorganization.

Listing 9-5. Finding Tables Currently Having the Partition Reorganized

```
mysql> SELECT tds.table_id AS TableId, tbl.TableSchema, tbl.TableName
        FROM ndbinfo.table_distribution_status tds
            INNER JOIN (
                SELECT id AS table_id,
                        SUBSTRING_INDEX(fq_name, '/', 1) AS TableSchema,
                        SUBSTRING_INDEX(fq_name, '/', -1) AS TableName
                    FROM ndbinfo.dict_obj_info doi
                        INNER JOIN ndbinfo.dict_obj_types dot
                                ON dot.type_id = doi.type
                    WHERE dot.type_name = 'User table'
            ) tbl ON tbl.table_id = tds.table_id
        WHERE tds.is_reorg_ongoing = 1;
+---------+-------------+-----------+
| TableId | TableSchema | TableName |
+---------+-------------+-----------+
|       4 | office      | employee  |
+---------+-------------+-----------+
1 row in set (1.98 sec)
```

The null ALTER TABLE discussed earlier in this section also has a second use to reorganizing partitions: the table rebuild also defragments the table. Defragmentation—both in-place (online) and copying (offline)—is the next topic to discuss.

Defragmentation

Over time as data is inserted, deleted, and updated, the tables will end up with gaps in the data storage and data that logically belongs together (stored in the same table) may not be in contiguous memory regions. This is known as *fragmentation*, and it causes the amount of storage used to be larger than necessary. Fragmentation can, for example, occur after the reorganization of partitions that follows adding more data nodes to a cluster.

■ **Tip** Fragmentation of the table data is not entirely different from file system fragmentation. See for example *https://en.wikipedia.org/wiki/File_system_fragmentation* for an in-depth discussion.

The free space that arises from the various changes to the data still counts toward the total data used in DataMemory or the on-disk tablespace data file. While the memory can be used for new data for the same table, it cannot be used for other tables stored in the cluster. This means that is it possible to encounter a *table is full* error while there is in principle still free memory. To reclaim any memory that is assigned to the table but otherwise free, you must defragment the table so the data is moved around to reduce or eliminate the gaps.

Figure 9-2 shows an example of how fragmentation can occur inside the data as well as the result of a defragmentation process. The example is not specific to MySQL NDB Cluster and is meant for illustrative purposes only. The light gray space between Rows 2 and 3 after updating Row 2 as well as between Rows 3 and 5 after deleting Row 4 is all empty space; that is fragmentation. The defragmentation at the end moves Rows 3 and 5 to consolidate the free space. However, note that defragmentation is an expensive and slow operation, particularly when it requires a table rebuild.

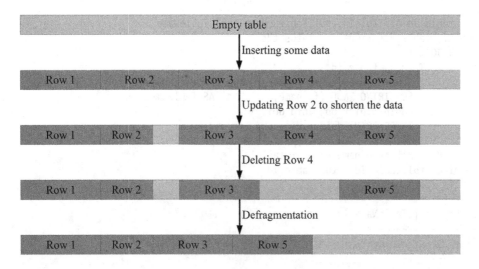

Figure 9-2. *Fragmentation and defragmentation*

For NDBCluster tables, defragmentation can be achieved in one of three ways:

- Using the OPTIMIZE TABLE statement
- Restarting the data nodes
- Rebuilding the table (a copying null ALTER TABLE)

The simplest method and the one with the least impact is the OPTIMIZE TABLE statement:

```
mysql> OPTIMIZE TABLE t1;
+--------+----------+----------+----------+
| Table  | Op       | Msg_type | Msg_text |
+--------+----------+----------+----------+
| db1.t1 | optimize | status   | OK       |
+--------+----------+----------+----------+
1 row in set (1 min 37.88 sec)
```

OPTIMIZE TABLE is an online operation in NDBCluster. However, only the variable sized memory (dynamic) will be defragmented.

A rolling restart (see Chapter 10) will also defragment the variable sized data and has the advantage that the indexes are rebuilt from scratch, so it will provide a better defragmentation than OPTIMIZE TABLE. For fixed-width memory, the only way to reclaim the fragmented memory is to rebuild the table. A table rebuild can be achieved using a null ALTER TABLE operation:

```
mysql> ALTER TABLE t1 ALGORITHM=COPY, LOCK=EXCLUSIVE, ENGINE=NDBCluster;
Query OK, 131072 rows affected (3 min 41.43 sec)
Records: 131072  Duplicates: 0  Warnings: 0
```

This is the same as was discussed earlier for repartitioning a table when an online REORGANIZE PARTITION does not work. This will rebuild the table offline, but otherwise will make no changes other than potentially repartitioning the table if the number of data nodes or *LDM* threads has changed since the last time the table was rebuild or created.

The chapter has been discussing the schema and storage of data and indexes. However, there is also another aspect related to day-to-day table maintenance: index statistics. This is the last topic of the chapter.

Index Statistics

When a query is executed through an SQL node, the statement is sent to the optimizer, which will determine the query plan to use for the actual execution. While the optimizer in general is beyond the scope of this book, one aspect related to the determination of the query plan is important to discuss: index statistics.

Index statistics provide an estimate of the number of unique values for the indexes in a table. As an example, consider the table, data, and index statistics in Listing 9-6. The table has three indexes—the primary key, an index spanning the two columns Surname and FirstName, and one on the IsManager column. The query with the COUNT() aggregate function on the table itself shows the actual number of unique values per index and part of the index for the Name index. Finally, the last query shows the same number of unique values as per the index statistics. The number of unique values is also known as the *cardinality*.

■ **Note**   The index statistics for `NDBCluster` tables also includes a *records in range* estimate—for example, how many rows have a value of x between 5 and 10. These estimates are not exposed directly and can sometimes cause non-optimal query plans. When that happens, use index hints (*https://dev.mysql.com/doc/refman/5.7/en/index-hints.html*) to get a better index. Records in range estimates will not be discussed further in this book.

Listing 9-6. Example of a Table with Its Data and Index Statistics

```
mysql> SHOW CREATE TABLE office.employee\G
*************************** 1. row ***************************
       Table: employee
Create Table: CREATE TABLE `employee` (
  `EmployeeID` int(10) unsigned NOT NULL,
  `FirstName` varchar(20) DEFAULT NULL,
  `Surname` varchar(20) DEFAULT NULL,
  `IsManager` enum('No','Yes') NOT NULL,
  PRIMARY KEY (`EmployeeID`),
  KEY `Name` (`Surname`,`FirstName`),
  KEY `IsManager` (`IsManager`)
) ENGINE=ndbcluster DEFAULT CHARSET=latin1
1 row in set (0.01 sec)

mysql> SELECT COUNT(*), COUNT(DISTINCT EmployeeID),
              COUNT(DISTINCT Surname), COUNT(DISTINCT Surname, FirstName),
              COUNT(DISTINCT IsManager)
         FROM office.employee\G
*************************** 1. row ***************************
                       COUNT(*): 10000
        COUNT(DISTINCT EmployeeID): 10000
           COUNT(DISTINCT Surname): 372
COUNT(DISTINCT Surname, FirstName): 8543
         COUNT(DISTINCT IsManager): 2
1 row in set (0.05 sec)

mysql> SELECT INDEX_NAME, NON_UNIQUE, COLUMN_NAME, CARDINALITY
         FROM information_schema.STATISTICS
         WHERE TABLE_SCHEMA = 'office' AND TABLE_NAME = 'employee';
+------------+------------+-------------+-------------+
| INDEX_NAME | NON_UNIQUE | COLUMN_NAME | CARDINALITY |
+------------+------------+-------------+-------------+
| PRIMARY    |          0 | EmployeeID  |       10000 |
| Name       |          1 | Surname     |         391 |
| Name       |          1 | FirstName   |        9204 |
| IsManager  |          1 | IsManager   |           2 |
+------------+------------+-------------+-------------+
4 rows in set (0.00 sec)
```

Looking at the cardinalities in Listing 9-6, there are a few points to note:

- The primary key has a cardinality that is equal to the number of rows. This is by definition as the primary key requires all values to be unique and null values are not allowed. The same applies to all unique indexes where the columns are defined as NOT NULL.

- The cardinality of the Name index (Surname and FirstName) does not equal the number of unique values. There is a cardinality listed both for the Surname (391) and FirstName (9204). The cardinality for the FirstName is for the combination with Surname, so the total cardinality of the index. This is due to NDBCluster not doing exact statistics when calculating the cardinalities. Instead, an estimate is found by scanning random index fragments to get a sample of the values in the index. For an index like Name that has many distinct values, the estimate will not be exact. In this case, it is roughly seven percent off, which will only rarely cause the wrong query plan to be found.

- The cardinality of the IsManager index is found to be two. That is not surprising as the column accepts exactly two values (No and Yes). In this case, the index statistics comes out exactly as the distinct count because the scanned fragments are enough to make it clear that it is unlikely the unexamined values will contain anything else other than one of these two values.

For the employee table, the Name index is very valuable for queries searching for an employee by name. It will reduce the query to only examine a few rows instead of all 10000 rows in the table. However, the IsManager index is of little use as it on average only can filter out 50% of the rows, so a table scan will anyway be the most efficient. That means the IsManager index only adds overhead: memory is used in DataMemory, and there is an overhead to maintain the index when data is inserted, updated, or deleted.

The remainder of this section discusses what options there are to affect index statistics as well as the utilities and statements used to recalculate them.

Index Statistics Internals

Before going into detail about updating index statistics and how to configure the behavior, it is worth taking a brief look at the internals of how index statistics are implemented in MySQL NDB Cluster. This is only an overview as the deeper level details are beyond the scope of this book.

The index statistics are stored internally on the data nodes in two system tables. These two tables are also exposed on the SQL nodes as the following tables in the mysql schema:

- **ndb_index_stat_head:** Meta information for the index statistics. There is one row per index where the statistics have been calculated.

- **ndb_index_stat_sample:** Actual sample data for the indexes.

These tables use the NDBCluster storage engine, so they are in sync between the SQL nodes. However, on each SQL node the statistics are loaded into a cache. This cache is updated in two ways:

- When an execution of ANALYZE TABLE completes. This occurs even if the statement was executed on a different SQL node.

- A background index statistics thread.

The background thread answers queries from the optimizer and makes sure that if the index statistics are updated directly on the data nodes (using the ndb_index_stat utility that is discussed later), the cache on the SQL node is updated. The cache update by the background thread will not happen immediately but rather as scheduled by the thread. The configuration of this is discussed later in the chapter.

The cache itself is split into several instances, which can be one of the following types:

- **Query:** This is the cache instance currently used to answer queries.

- **Build:** This is a cache currently being populated.

- **Clean:** There can be several instances of the type clean. These are old cache instances that can be deleted.

An overview of the index statistics implementation is depicted in Figure 9-3.

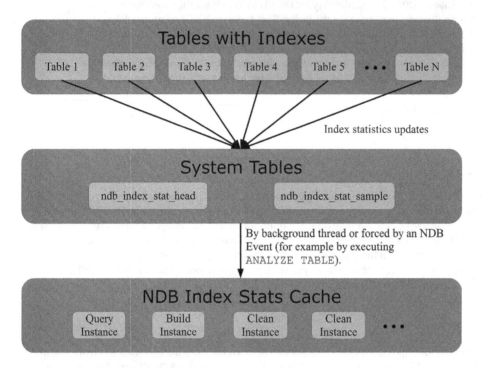

Figure 9-3. Overview of the index statistics implementation

Maintaining Index Statistics

It is important that the index statistics reflect the data distribution in the table. Otherwise the query plans will not be optimal. In complex queries with several tables joined together, the wrong query plan may in the worst case cause the query to be as much as a factor 100 slower or worse compared to the optimal query plan. There are three ways that index statistics are updated for NDBCluster tables:

- Executing ANALYZE TABLE explicitly.

- Using the ndb_index_stat utility. This can also be used for other tasks such as creating and deleting the system tables storing the index statistics.

- Automatic updates occurring in the background.

These three methods all fundamentally work the same way; however, for the user there are some differences that are worth discussing in more detail.

ANALYZE TABLE is an SQL node specific statement that calculates the index statistics for the table. It works for tables of all storage engines that support indexes. This is the most common way to update index statistics. Listing 9-7 shows examples of updating the index statistics for one and two tables. More tables can be analyzed in the same statement by adding them to the list, separating each table by a comma. If the schema name is not specified, the current schema will be used.

The first statement updates the index statistics for the employee table in the current schema, whereas the second updates the statistics for the employee and address tables in the office schema. An ANALYZE TABLE statement triggers an event at the end that ensures that the cache is updated as soon as possible; effectively it will seem like the cache is updated as part of the ANALYZE TABLE statement.

Listing 9-7. Examples of Using ANALYZE TABLE

```
mysql> ANALYZE TABLE employee;
+-----------------+---------+----------+----------+
| Table           | Op      | Msg_type | Msg_text |
+-----------------+---------+----------+----------+
| office.employee | analyze | status   | OK       |
+-----------------+---------+----------+----------+
1 row in set (0 min 56.85 sec)

mysql> ANALYZE TABLE office.employee, office.address;
+-----------------+---------+----------+----------+
| Table           | Op      | Msg_type | Msg_text |
+-----------------+---------+----------+----------+
| office.employee | analyze | status   | OK       |
| office.address  | analyze | status   | OK       |
+-----------------+---------+----------+----------+
2 rows in set (1 min 53.20 sec)
```

■ **Note**   Updating the index statistics may take a while depending on the number of rows and indexes in the tables; however, the work is performed with the table online and the gain in query performance can be significant.

The MySQL NDB Cluster distribution also includes the ndb_index_stat utility, which can perform a range of operations related to the index statistics. The utility uses the following options for performing the supported actions:

- **--delete:** Delete index statistics for the specified table. Provide the --database option and the table name to specify the table.

- **--update:** Create or update the index statistics for the specified table. Provide the --database option and the table name to specify the table.

- **--dump:** Dumps the index statistic metadata and samples for the specified table. Provide the --database option and the table name to specify the table. This is similar to querying the ndb_index_stat_head and ndb_index_stat_sample tables and is useful for debugging purposes.

- **--sys-drop:** Delete the underlying system tables (ndb_index_stat_head and ndb_index_stat_sample) that store the index statistics. This will also delete all existing index statistics. Dropping and subsequent creating the system tables can be useful should the index statistics become corrupt. When the system index statistics tables are gone, MySQL will continue to work as normal except that there will be no index statistics for the NDBCluster tables and attempts to generate the index statistics will fail with an error.

- **--sys-create:** Create the underlying system tables (ndb_index_stat_head and ndb_index_stat_sample) that store the index statistics. There are two alternate versions of the –sys-create option: --sys-create-if-not-exist and --sys-create-if-not-valid, which creates the system tables if they do not exist or after dropping any invalid objects, respectively.

■ **Tip**   The full help for ndb_index_stat can be obtained executing it with the --help option or in the MySQL Reference Manual at *https://dev.mysql.com/doc/mysql-cluster-excerpt/5.7/en/mysql-cluster-programs-ndb-index-stat.html*.

Listing 9-8 shows an example of updating the index statistics for the office.employee table. Adding the --verbose option makes the command return additional information that can be useful for debugging.

Listing 9-8. Updating the Index Statistics Using the ndb_index_stat Utility

```
shell$ ndb_index_stat --ndb_connectstring=192.168.56.101,192.168.56.102 \
                      --update --database=office employee
table:employee index:PRIMARY fragCount:4
sampleVersion:2 loadTime:1500782413 sampleCount:2513 keyBytes:10052
query cache: valid:1 sampleCount:2513 totalBytes:35182
times in ms: save: 7.435 sort: 2.228 sort per sample: 0.000
table:employee index:Name fragCount:4
sampleVersion:2 loadTime:1500782414 sampleCount:2344 keyBytes:35103
query cache: valid:1 sampleCount:2344 totalBytes:67919
times in ms: save: 9.483 sort: 2.744 sort per sample: 0.001
table:employee index:IsManager fragCount:4
sampleVersion:2 loadTime:1500782414 sampleCount:2 keyBytes:2
query cache: valid:1 sampleCount:2 totalBytes:20
times in ms: save: 1.818 sort: 0.004 sort per sample: 0.002

NDBT_ProgramExit: 0 - OK
```

An advantage of using ndb_index_stat over ANALYZE TABLE is that it is easier to script—for example, to execute it through a cron script or the Windows Task Scheduler.

Finally, MySQL NDB Cluster has support for auto updating the index statistics. Inside the *DBDICT* block, the index will be flagged for update when the number of operations exceeds a threshold. A background loop detects this later and updates the index statistics, similar to what ANALYZE TABLE and ndb_index_stat do. However, by the time the automatic update kicks in, the index statistics may be severely out of date and poor query plans may result.

There is also another more limited version of automatic updates of the index statistics working at the SQL node level. This works based on the existing statistics giving the behavior for inserts, updates, and deletes shown in Table 9-4.

Table 9-4. *The Behavior of Auto Updates of Index Statistics*

Operation	Behavior
INSERT	The cardinalities are increased with the percentage of rows added. For example, doubling the number of rows will double the cardinalities.
UPDATE	The cardinalities are not changed.
DELETE	The cardinalities are decreased with the percentage of rows deleted. For example, deleting half the rows will halve the cardinalities.

This behavior, together with the lag of the proper background update of the index statistics, means you should force an update of the index statistics whenever a table has changed significantly since the index statistics were last updated. This forced update can be triggered with ANALYZE TABLE or with the ndb_index_stat utility.

Options and Status Variables

There are two options for the SQL nodes to control the index statistics for NDBCluster tables:

- **ndb_index_stat_enable:** Enables or disabled whether index statistics are calculated and whether they are used when determining the query plan. The default is ON.

- **ndb_index_stat_option:** Specifies a range of options for updating the index statistics cache. The default values are included in Table 9-5.

It is recommended to have index statistics enabled for most systems. The only exception is systems that only query single tables with the WHERE clauses only matching one index. In that case, the index statistics are not required to determine the optimal query plan.

The ndb_index_stat_option deserves some attention as it is a relatively complex option. It consists of multiple key-value pairs, each of which is a setting on their own, but combined into one compound setting at the user facing level. Table 9-5 lists all the available settings, their default values, the allowed values, and what the settings do. The settings are listed in the order they appear in the ndb_index_stat_option option.

Table 9-5. *The Settings of the ndb_index_stat_option Variable*

Setting	Default Value	Allowed Values	Comments
loop_enable	1000ms	0ms- 4294967295ms	The amount of time to wait before checking whether the calculation of index statistics have been enabled when ndb_index_stat_enable = OFF.
loop_idle	1000ms	0ms- 4294967295ms	The amount of time to sleep before starting to update the cache again when the last batch was not fully used.
loop_busy	100ms	0ms- 4294967295ms	The amount of time to sleep before starting to update the cache again when the last batch was fully used.
update_batch	1	1- 4294967295	The batch size when updating the cache. If all loops are executed, the status is set to busy.
read_batch	4	1- 4294967295	The batch size when reading index statistics. If all loops are executed, the status is set to busy.

(continued)

Table 9-5. (*continued*)

Setting	Default Value	Allowed Values	Comments
idle_batch	32	1- 4294967295	The batch size for maintenance of the index statistics performed when the status is idle. This never sets the status to busy.
check_batch	8	1- 4294967295	The batch size when checking whether the index statistics should be updated. If all loops are executed, the status is set to busy.
check_delay	10m	0s- 4294967295s	The time between checking whether any of the index statistics should be updated.
delete_batch	8	1- 4294967295	The batch size when deleting index statistics. If all loops are executed, the status is set to busy.
clean_delay	1m	0s- 4294967295s	Used when the status is idle. The minimum time between reading index statistics from a cache instance now of the type clean and being allowed to delete the cache instance.
error_batch	4	1- 4294967295	The batch size when checking for errors in the index statistics. This never sets the status to busy.
error_delay	1m	0s- 4294967295s	The minimum time to wait before checking for errors after the previous batch found errors.
evict_batch	8	1- 4294967295	Specifies the batch size for evicting index statistics from the cache using a least recently used (LRU) list. Statistics are evicted when more than cache_lowpct percent of the cache is used. If all loops are executed, the status is set to busy.
evict_delay	1m	0s- 4294967295s	The minimum delay between evicting index statistics from the cache since the last time the statistics were read.
cache_limit	32M	0- 4294967295	The size of the index statistics cache. Increase the size if there is a large amount of index statistics. The unit is the number of bytes to allocate for the cache, and the following units can be used: K, M, G (and no unit identifier to specify bytes).
cache_lowpct	90	0-100	The percentage of the index statistics cache to be in use before starting to evict the least recently used statistics from the cache. The unit is percent.
zero_total	0	0 and1	When setting zero_total to 1, the counters in the Ndb_index_stat_status status variable are reset to 0.

For timing values for the loop_enable, loop_idle, and loop_busy settings, the value is specified in milliseconds with the ms unit optional when assigning the value. The delay timing settings take a unit of s, m, or h (seconds, minutes, or hours—the default unit is s). For the batches, the unit is the number of loops to execute; if all loops are executed, the status is set to busy.

The default values in ndb_index_stat_option work well for most deployments, and it is rarely necessary to fine-tune the settings. It is possible to set one or several of the settings in one SET statement. For example:

```
mysql> SET GLOBAL ndb_index_stat_option = 'loop_enable=1500ms,zero_total=1';
```

This sets loop_enable to 1500 milliseconds and resets the statistics in Ndb_index_stat_status. It is important that there is no whitespace in the value. Settings that are not included in the SET statement keep their current value.

The complete list of values for ndb_index_stat_option can be obtained using SHOW GLOBAL VARIABLES or by selecting the value, such as:

```
mysql> SELECT @@global.ndb_index_stat_option\G
*************************** 1. row ***************************
@@global.ndb_index_stat_option: loop_enable=1000ms,loop_idle=1000ms,loop_busy=100ms,update_
batch=1,read_batch=4,idle_batch=32,check_batch=8,check_delay=10m,delete_batch=8,clean_
delay=1m,error_batch=4,error_delay=1m,evict_batch=8,evict_delay=1m,cache_limit=32M,cache_
lowpct=90,zero_total=0
1 row in set (0.01 sec)
```

The return value in the example is also the default.

It is possible to monitor the status of the index statistics through three status variables in the SQL nodes:

- **Ndb_index_stat_status:** A range of values related to the ndb_index_stat_option setting.

- **Ndb_index_stat_cache_query:** The number of bytes currently used in the query instance of the index statistics cache. This is the same value as the query value in the cache list in Ndb_index_stat_status.

- **Ndb_index_stat_cache_clean:** The number of bytes currently used in clean instances. This is the same value as the clean value in the cache list in Ndb_index_stat_status.

The Ndb_index_stat_status status variable is similar to ndb_index_stat_option, not only that the status variable has several statistics related to the ndb_index_stat_option option, but also that it is a compound status variable with multiple statistics. The values included in Ndb_index_stat_status are listed in Table 9-6.

Table 9-6. *The Statistics Included in Ndb_index_stat_status*

Name	Description
allow	Whether queries are allowed. This will usually be the same value as ndb_index_stat_enable, but may be 0 if the index statistics have not yet been initialized.
enable	0 or 1 depending on whether ndb_index_stat_enable is off or on, respectively.
busy	Whether the statistics thread is currently busy.
loop	The current wait for the statistics thread. The unit is milliseconds.
list	Statistics about the various lists (shares). The entries in each list represent the work to be done by the index statistics thread in the loops that are limited by the corresponding batch size.
analyze	Statistics for ANALYZE TABLE for the number of tables queued and waiting to have the index statistics calculated.
stats	Special counters.
total	Total counters. For example, the value for all in analyze corresponds to the number of ANALYZE TABLE statements and the value for all in query the number of times the query statistics for an index have been looked up. The query values may both increase from regular queries requiring an index or inspecting the index statistics.
cache	Various statistics for the index statistics cache. The query value is the number of bytes currently used in the cache (the same as Ndb_index_stat_cache_query), usedpct is the same as a percentage of the available cache, and highpct is the highest usage since the statistics were last reset. These values are useful for determining whether the cache has the right size.

Listing 9-9 shows an example of the statistics in Ndb_index_stat_status as well as Ndb_index_stat_cache_query and Ndb_index_stat_cache_clean after several ANALYZE TABLE statements and queries using the indexes have been executed. An ANALYZE TABLE updating the index statistics on four tables is in progress while the output was generated. This is reflected in the values in the analyze field in Ndb_index_stat_status.

Listing 9-9. Example of the Statistics in the Index Statistics Index Variables

```
mysql> SHOW GLOBAL STATUS LIKE 'Ndb\_index\_stat\_%'\G
*************************** 1. row ***************************
Variable_name: Ndb_index_stat_status
        Value: allow:1,enable:1,busy:1,loop:100,list:(new:0,update:3,read:0,idle:5,check:0,d
elete:0,error:0,total:8),analyze:(queue:3,wait:1),stats:(nostats:0,wait:0),total:(analyze:(a
ll:43,error:0),query:(all:22,nostats:16,error:0),event:(act:0,skip:0,miss:0),cache:(refresh:
45,clean:8,pinned:0,drop:1,evict:0)),cache:(query:145667,clean:247816,drop:0,evict:0,usedpc
t:1.17,highpct:1.17)
*************************** 2. row ***************************
Variable_name: Ndb_index_stat_cache_query
        Value: 145667
*************************** 3. row ***************************
Variable_name: Ndb_index_stat_cache_clean
        Value: 247816
3 rows in set (0.00 sec)
```

Summary

It is important to keep in mind that setting up a database system is never a one-off task. Instead it's an ongoing project. In this chapter, several of the daily maintenance tasks related to NDBCluster tables were discussed. The topics discussed include:

- Online and offline schema changes

- Repartitioning a table

- Defragmentation

- Maintaining index statistics and the significance of them

Several schema changes can be made online with relatively little impact on the system. This allows the cluster to remain online in most situations. However, for some changes, an offline copying schema change is required; this also applies if a thorough defragmentation of the table is required.

The index statistics are important for the optimizer to be able to determine the optimal query plan. It was discussed how the index statistics work for NDBCluster tables and how to keep them up to date.

The next chapter covers restarting the nodes in the cluster, including several examples.

CHAPTER 10

Restarts

One of the more common routine tasks for a MySQL NDB Cluster DBA is restarting cluster nodes. As MySQL NDB Cluster is designed for high availability, most restarts can be performed with the cluster remaining online as a whole. This means that restarts play a special role in MySQL NDB Cluster and deserve special attention.

Restarts are used for several reasons in MySQL NDB Cluster, for example:

- Configuration changes
- Adding management, data, or API/SQL nodes
- Recovering from crashes
- Upgrades (discussed in Chapter 11)

For the duration of this chapter, the cluster is assumed to have the configuration shown in Listing 10-1 unless otherwise noted.

Listing 10-1. The Cluster Configuration Used in this Chapter

```
[ndb_mgmd default]
DataDir     = /cluster/

[ndbd default]
NoOfReplicas = 2
DataDir     = /cluster/

[ndbd]
NodeId      = 1
HostName    = 192.168.56.103

[ndbd]
NodeId      = 2
HostName    = 192.168.56.104

[ndb_mgmd]
NodeId      = 49
HostName    = 192.168.56.101

[ndb_mgmd]
NodeId      = 50
HostName    = 192.168.56.102
```

© Jesper Wisborg Krogh and Mikiya Okuno 2017
J. W. Krogh and M. Okuno, *Pro MySQL NDB Cluster*, https://doi.org/10.1007/978-1-4842-2982-8_10

```
[mysqld]
NodeId      = 51
HostName    = 192.168.56.103

[mysqld]
NodeId      = 52
HostName    = 192.168.56.104

[api]
NodeId      = 53
HostName    = 192.168.56.101

[api]
NodeId      = 54
HostName    = 192.168.56.102
```

Restart Types

As discussed in Chapter 2, MySQL NDB Cluster has four types of restarts:

- Node restart

- Initial node restart

- System restart

- Initial system restart

For the two node restart types (node restart and initial node restart), the cluster is online for the duration of the restart, whereas the system restart types require the cluster to be offline. The rest of this section provides more information about the four restart types.

Node Restart

A *node restart* is when one or more nodes are restarted together in such a way that the remaining online nodes at any time have all the data. That is, there is always at least one data node from each node group online. When the whole cluster is restarted in this way, it is also known as a *rolling restart* (see the next section).

The advantage of a rolling restart is that you can restart the whole cluster while it remains online. A typical use case for a rolling restart is to change the configuration of the data nodes. A node restart is only possible when you have more than one replica of the data (NoOfReplicas is greater than one), as at least one node per node group must remain online.

Initial Node Restart

An initial node restart—or an initial rolling restart if it includes the entire cluster—is a variant of the node restart. The difference is that each data node will discard all its data at the start of the restart, then recover the data from another node in the same node group during the restart. The redo log files are always recreated as part of an initial restart.

■ **Note** While all data for the data node is deleted at the start of an initial restart, the undo log and tablespace files used for on-disk data are preserved. If you want these files recreated as well, you must delete them manually before starting the data node again.

The advantage of an initial node restart is that it is possible to make some configuration changes that otherwise would not be possible. For example, the only way to change the settings for the redo log is to have the data node start from scratch. Another use of initial rolling restarts is to recover from file system corruption. The disadvantage is that the restart will take longer, because all the data must be copied from the other node(s) in the same node group.

System Restart

A system restart happens when all the data nodes have been shut down and requires at least one data node from each node group to participate in the restart. Some configuration changes—for options where the data nodes must all agree of the current value—require a system restart.

One advantage of a system restart over a rolling restart is that it is faster as all data nodes will be able to start in parallel. If it is not a problem that the cluster is offline during the restart, a system restart can be used to reduce the overall duration of the maintenance window compared to a rolling start.

Initial System Restart

Recall that an initial node restart is a specialized case of a node restart where all the data for the data node is discarded at startup. In the same way, an initial system restart is a similar special case of a system restart. First, all data nodes discard their data. This means that at the end of the restart, the state of the data nodes is like after the cluster has been started for the very first time. In fact, the very first start of the cluster is an initial system restart. The only difference between the very first start and subsequent initial system restarts is that the tablespace and undo log files for on disk tables are not deleted; the tables and the data in them are however still deleted.

Other than for the first start of the cluster, an initial system restart is only required for a few configuration changes, such as moving a data node to another node group. Additionally, it can be convenient to use, if it has been decided to restore from a backup, for example in case of rebuilding a replication slave.

Since an initial system restart deletes all the data in the cluster, it is extremely important to create a backup right before the restart.

■ **Caution** Always ensure that there is a backup and the backup can be restored before performing an initial system restart. All data will be deleted as part of the initial system restart!

Rolling Restart

A rolling restart is the act of restarting the whole cluster by never restarting more nodes concurrently than the cluster needs to remain online. It is only possible to perform a rolling restart if there is more than one replica of the data. The rolling restart can either be done using regular or initial node restarts. The steps of a rolling restart are:

1. If necessary, update the cluster configuration file (*config.ini*) with the new configuration.

2. Shut down the management nodes. If there is more than one management node, they must all be shut down.

3. Start the management nodes. To read the configuration file (*config.ini*), use the `--reload` (recommended in most cases) or `--initial` command-line options. An initial restart should only be done when it is necessary or preferred to completely clear the history of the management nodes. This includes when adding management nodes or when re-initializing the whole cluster. The use of `--reload` versus `--initial` is also discussed later in the section.

4. Restart the data nodes. Up to (`NoOfReplicas` – 1) nodes from each node group can be restarted concurrently. However, a restart adds load (both disk, CPU, and network) particularly to the hosts where the restarting nodes are installed, so be careful not to overload the system. As a rule of thumb, restart only one node on each host at a time. Restart each data node with the `--initial` option if required.

5. Restart the API/SQL nodes. Avoid restarting all at once so the application can use the remaining online nodes. If the changes do not affect the API/SQL nodes, this step is optional.

■ **Tip** The step of restarting the API/SQL nodes can be performed either before or after restarting the data nodes.

The process of a rolling restart is also summarized in Figure 10-1.

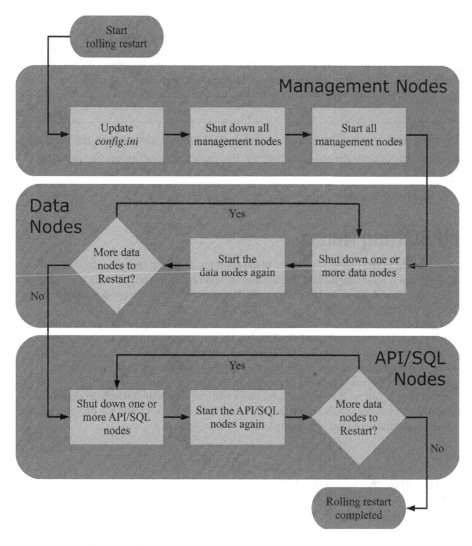

Figure 10-1. *The steps of a rolling restart*

Before moving on to the actual processes of starting and stopping the nodes, it is worth going through the steps of a rolling restart in more detail. First of all, a rolling restart is only possible when NoOfReplicas is greater than one. If there is only one replica, taking a data node offline means that some of the data will become unavailable, which will require the other data nodes to also become offline.

Between Steps 2 and 3, where the management nodes are offline, it is only the management nodes that can join the cluster. Data nodes and API/SQL nodes require the management nodes to be online to get the configuration before they can connect to the cluster.

When the data nodes are restarted in Step 4, it is necessary to ensure that at least one data node remains online for each node group at all times. The reason is the same as why NoOfReplicas must be greater than one: if there is not at least one data node online in the node group, the data in that node group is not available, and thus the whole cluster must go offline.

While the API/SQL nodes are listed as the last node type to be restarted in Step 5, they can also be restarted before the data nodes. If there are no configuration changes made as part of the rolling restart, it is not necessary to restart the management nodes. Restarts without configuration changes may for example be done to defragment the data or in some cases to work around a bug. Upgrades also in general do not require configuration changes, but will still require restarting the management nodes. In case of an upgrade without a configuration change, the API/SQL nodes can even be restarted before the management nodes.

■ **Caution**   While there is a great degree of flexibility of when the API/SQL nodes are restarted, this does not apply to the data nodes. For configuration changes and upgrades, the management nodes must be restarted before the data nodes.

Stopping and Starting Nodes

The acts of stopping and starting nodes in a cluster is one of the most fundamental tasks of a database administrator. There are several ways to do this and the methods available depend on the node type. This section goes through the options and discusses the differences. For examples of starting and stopping nodes, see the case studies later in the chapter as well.

All the binaries shipped with MySQL NDB Cluster (with the exception of the ndb_index_stat utility) support reading its arguments from a *my.cnf*/*my.ini* file. This has the advantage that options that never change between invocations can be set once and for all. The disadvantage is that the command-line arguments cannot be seen from the process list. All the binaries that need to connect to the management nodes (including mysqld) read the [mysql_cluster] group in the configuration file, so by adding the ndb_connectstring option here, it can be shared by all processes and can eliminate the need to duplicate the value within the same host. Each binary also reads its own specific section. Executing the binary with the --help option will tell which sections are read, for example:

```
shell$ ndbmtd -help
...
Default options are read from the following files in the given order:
/etc/my.cnf /etc/mysql/my.cnf /usr/local/mysql/etc/my.cnf ~/.my.cnf
The following groups are read: mysql_cluster ndbd
...
```

This shows both which files are read by default and which groups (sections) are read.

The command-line commands to start nodes in this section list all options. However, in most cases it is preferable to use a *my.cnf*/*my.ini* file with all the options used for all restarts. This will simplify starting the nodes and reduce the potential for typos.

On Microsoft Windows, all node types can be installed as a *Service*. An example of starting a node using a Microsoft Windows service is given for the management nodes. The procedure is similar for the other node types. When using a service, it is recommended you provide the startup options from a *my.cnf*/*my.ini* file, as this will allow a reconfiguration of the node without having to recreate the service.

Management Nodes

A management node is started by executing the ndb_mgmd binary. Five commonly used arguments are:

- **--config-file=…:** This option is used to specify the path to the cluster configuration file (*config.ini*). Remember that there are two types of configuration files in MySQL NDB Cluster: the *my.cnf*/*my.ini* file for the SQL nodes and the *config.ini* file that is used with management nodes. It is *config.ini* that should be used with the --config-file option. The option is required for the first start and when either the --initial or --reload option is given.

- **--config-dir=…:** This option specifies where the cached configuration is stored. The option is mandatory unless the --skip-config-cache option is given.

- **--ndb-nodeid=…:** The node ID to use for the process.

- **--initial:** Deletes all cached configurations in the directory specified with the --config-dir option and will set the new configuration as generation 1. It is mutually exclusive with the --reload option.

- **--reload:** This is the counterpart to --initial. Instead of clearing all configuration history, the management node checks if there is a difference in the current *config.ini* with the previously cached configuration. If there is a difference, the management node will increment the configuration generation, log the difference to the cluster log (see the "Configuration Change" case study later in the chapter), and store the new configuration in the configuration directory in binary format.

■ **Tip**   To see all startup options for ndb_mgmd, see *https://dev.mysql.com/doc/refman/5.7/en/mysql-cluster-programs-ndb-mgmd.html*.

Unless you must use --initial (see the "Adding Management Node" case study for a rare example), it is better to use --reload over --initial for three reasons:

- Having the difference between the old and new configuration logged to the cluster log makes it easier to follow the history of the cluster. This can be very useful when troubleshooting.

- It is less likely to mix up using --initial with a management node with --initial for a data node (which could cause total data loss).

- While only used extremely rarely, it is possible to restore an older generation configuration as long as the binary copy of it exists. --initial deletes all existing cached configurations.

An example of starting the management node using NodeId = 49 on Linux is:

```
shell$ sudo -u mysql ndb_mgmd --config-file=/etc/config.ini \
          --config-dir=/cluster/config --ndb-nodeid=49 --reload
```

The sudo in the command here is used to change to the mysql user before starting the management node. This allows the management node to execute using a non-privileged operating system account that cannot log in directly. The ndb_mgmd process will be started as a daemon by default. To start the management node as a foreground process, use the --nodaemon option.

To start the management node using Microsoft Windows services, ensure that the service has been installed as described in Chapter 5, then either use the command prompt or the Services desktop application to start the node. To start ndb_mgmd as a Microsoft Windows service from the command prompt, use this command:

```
C:\>net start "MySQL Cluster Management Server"
The MySQL Cluster Management Server service is starting.
The MySQL Cluster Management Server service was started successfully.
```

Figure 10-2 shows the Services desktop application in Windows 10. You can start the management node by clicking on *Start* the Service to the left of the list of services. Alternatively, you can start the service by right-clicking on the service name, then choosing *Start*.

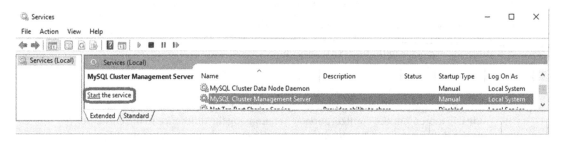

Figure 10-2. *Starting the management node through the Windows Services GUI*

The preferred way to stop a management node is to connect using the ndb_mgm management client and use the STOP command to stop the node:

```
shell$ ndb_mgm -e "49 STOP"
```

This works for all platforms. Stopping the management node in this way ensures that the shutdown is communicated to the rest of the cluster. Alternative ways to stop a management node are:

- Send a *SIGTERM* signal, for example using kill -15.

- On Microsoft Windows, if the management node is started as a service, it can be stopped though the *Services* desktop application or the command prompt similarly to how it was started.

It is not recommended to use a *SIGKILL* signal (kill -9) to shut down a management node.

■ **Caution**   Killing a management node with *SIGKILL* does not allow the node to perform a clean shutdown. This for example means that the data nodes do not know the management node has stopped until it is detected through missed heartbeats. This can cause arbitration not to work as expected and thus could cause a complete cluster outage where it could have been avoided.

Data Nodes

Starting a data node is relatively simple. All that is required is to choose whether to start a single-threaded or multi-threaded data node and to specify where the management node(s) can be found. The rest of the supported arguments are optional, although it is recommended to specify the node ID. The two binaries are:

- **ndbd:** The single-threaded binary.
- **ndbmtd:** The multi-threaded binary.

As discussed in Chapter 2, for production system it is for most systems best to use the multi-threaded binary.

Commonly used command-line arguments for the data nodes (irrespective of the binary used) include:

- **--ndb_connectstring=...:** The host and port numbers of the management nodes. As the default is localhost:1186, it is almost always necessary to specify this option for all clusters other than test setups. A management node is specified with the hostname or IP address optionally followed by a colon and the port number. Multiple management nodes are separated by commas.

- **--ndb-nodeid=...:** The node ID to use for the node. It is recommended to always include this option. If it is not set explicitly, it is assigned based on what IDs are available for that host.

- **--initial:** Perform an initial restart. Only use this option when it is required, as all data will be deleted from the node.

- **--nostart:** With this option, the data node will only go through the very early phase of the start and connect to the management node. It will then wait for the START command from the management node to continue the restart. This can be useful when restarting several nodes to ensure that all nodes restart in parallel.

- **--nowait-nodes=...:** By default, the data nodes will wait for the other offline data nodes to start up together, which saves time overall. The --nowait-nodes option tells the data node to proceed without waiting for the data node ids specified. The data nodes not to wait for are specified by their node ID in a comma-separated list. An example is given in the "Adding Data Nodes with Node Group Pre-Allocated" case study.

■ **Tip** To see all the command-line arguments for the data nodes, see *https://dev.mysql.com/doc/refman/5.7/en/mysql-cluster-programs-ndbd.html*. This also works for ndbmtd.

Here is an example of starting a data node using the multi-threaded binary:

```
shell$ sudo -u mysql ndbmtd \
         --ndb_connectstring=192.168.56.101,192.168.56.102 \
         --ndb-nodeid=1
```

When the data node is started with the --nostart option, the node will show up in the status output from the management node client as connected, but not started. For example, in the case NodeId = 2 has been started with the --nostart option:

```
shell$ ndb_mgm -e "SHOW"
Connected to Management Server at: 192.168.56.101:1186
Cluster Configuration
---------------------
[ndbd(NDB)]     2 node(s)
id=1    @192.168.56.103  (mysql-5.7.16 ndb-7.5.4, Nodegroup: 0, *)
id=2    @192.168.56.104  (mysql-5.7.16 ndb-7.5.4 , not started)
...
```

The node can be started using the <id> START command from the management client:

```
shell$ ndb_mgm -e "2 START"
Connected to Management Server at: 192.168.56.101:1186
Database node 2 is being started.
```

If multiple data nodes are connected but waiting to be started using the START command, it is also possible to use ALL instead of a node ID to start all eligible data nodes, for example:

```
shell$ ndb_mgm -e "ALL START"
Connected to Management Server at: 192.168.56.101:1186
NDB Cluster is being started.
NDB Cluster is being started.
```

To shut down a data node, it is best to stop the node using the STOP command in the management client, or if the management nodes are also to be shut down, the SHUTDOWN command. For example, to shut down NodeId= 1:

```
shell$ ndb_mgm -e "1 STOP"
Connected to Management Server at: 192.168.56.101:1186
Node 1 has shutdown.
```

The STOP command will by default refuse to shut down a node, if it is the last in a node group; i.e., it will prevent a total cluster shutdown by mistake:

```
shell$ ndb_mgm -e "2 STOP"
Connected to Management Server at: 192.168.56.101:1186
Shutdown failed.
*  2002: Stop failed
*       Node shutdown would cause system crash: Permanent error: Application error
```

If you intend to shut down all data nodes, instead either use ALL STOP or SHUTDOWN:

```
shell$ ndb_mgm -e "ALL STOP"
Connected to Management Server at: 192.168.56.101:1186
```

```
Executing STOP on all nodes.
NDB Cluster has shutdown.
```

ALL STOP only stops the data nodes. If the management nodes should be included in the shutdown, use the SHUTDOWN command instead:

```
shell$ ndb_mgm -e SHUTDOWN
Connected to Management Server at: 192.168.56.101:1186
4 NDB Cluster node(s) have shutdown.
Disconnecting to allow management server to shutdown.
```

It may be tempting to use a *SIGTERM* signal (kill -15) to stop the data nodes; however, this is not recommended. There are two major differences for a data node between stopping the node using the STOP command in the management client and a *SIGTERM* signal:

- Using the STOP command tells the data node to shut down gracefully and to cause as little interruption to the rest of the cluster as possible; for example, reducing (but not eliminating) failed transactions that will obtain a temporary error and be required to retry. On the other hand, a *SIGTERM* signal will cause a faster shutdown, but will also cause more failed transactions.

- A *SIGTERM* signal does not offer any protection against causing a cluster outage by shutting the node down.

Both the STOP command and the *SIGTERM* signal are considered "clean" shutdowns. That can, however, not be said of a *SIGKILL* signal (kill -9). Do not use a *SIGKILL* signal to shut down a data node unless the urgency is so great that corrupting the NDB file system of the node is an acceptable risk. A *SIGKILL* signal will not allow any kind of shutdown handling; the process simply stops immediately and it may for example cause partial writes of a local checkpoint.

■ **Caution** Do not stop a data node using a *SIGKILL* signal unless data loss is more acceptable than waiting. Be prepared to delete all data for the node to be able to restart (using the --initial option).

If the goal is to restart the data node immediately after the shutdown, an easy way to accomplish this is through the RESTART command in the management client, for example:

```
shell$ ndb_mgm -e "1 RESTART"
Connected to Management Server at: 192.168.56.101:1186
Node 1 is being restarted
```

The command returns once the shutdown has completed and the restart has begun. The RESTART command cannot be used for upgrades where the binary is replaced between shutdown and restart.

API/SQL Nodes

MySQL NDB Cluster does not offer any special means for starting and stopping API and SQL nodes. Whether on Linux, UNIX, or Windows, it is common to start and stop at least SQL nodes using some kind of service script, for example through *systemd* or Microsoft Windows services.

When starting an API/SQL node, it is important to remember that it cannot join the cluster until the cluster is online, and that there is at least one data node in each node group online. If an API/SQL node attempts to join the cluster before that is the case, an error similar to the following snippet will be logged in the cluster log:

```
2016-11-19 15:54:20 [MgmtSrvr] WARNING  -- Failed to allocate nodeid for API at
                                 192.168.56.103. Returned error:
                                 'No free node id found for mysqld(API).'
```

Starting an SQL node before the data nodes are ready will also cause a delay in starting the SQL node.

It is generally recommended to shut down the API/SQL nodes as the first nodes for a complete cluster shutdown. This ensures that the ongoing queries get a chance to complete. In MySQL NDB Cluster 7.4 and earlier, it was also necessary to be able to contact the management node to perform a clean shutdown. Still in MySQL NDB Cluster 7.5, messages will be reported in the *mysqld* error log if the management and data nodes are shut down before the SQL node:

```
2016-11-19 16:00:00 [NdbApi] INFO    -- Management server closed connection early. It is
                                 probably being shut down (or has problems). We will
                                 retry the connection. 1006  Illegal reply from
                                 server line: 3058
2016-11-19 16:00:05 [NdbApi] INFO    -- Management server closed connection early. It is
                                 probably being shut down (or has problems). We
                                 will retry the connection. 110 Time out talking to
                                 management server Error line: 528
```

These are just info messages and can be ignored if you know the cluster is offline.

Restart Related Configuration

Several of the configuration options available for the data nodes relate to restarts. The options fall primarily into three categories—parallelism for rebuilding ordered indexes, timeouts for waiting for other nodes, and disk write speeds for local checkpoints. Table 10-1 summarizes the most important options related to restarts.

Table 10-1. *Important Options Related to Restarts*

Option Name	Description
BuildIndexThreads	When rebuilding ordered indexes during a restart (and when using ndb_restore), BuildIndexThreads specifies how many threads to use. It can help to increase the value up to the maximum number of partitions per data node. Default is one partition per *LDM* thread, so using the default partitioning BuildIndexThreads can be set up to the number of *LDM* threads. Default is 0 (meaning single-threaded). See the TwoPassInitialNodeRestartCopy option.
MaxLCPStartDelay	During a restart, a local checkpoint is created in start phase 5 (see the next section). Sometimes some of the nodes starting together will be ready to start the local checkpoint before other nodes. Only one local checkpoint can be in progress at a time, so a data node will have to wait for ongoing local checkpoints to complete before starting its own. MaxLCPStartDelay can be used to let the nodes wait for each other and avoid serialization of the local checkpoints. Default is 0 seconds, which means no delay waiting for other nodes. It is mostly worth considering increasing MaxLCPStartDelay on clusters with a relative low write workload, so there are not constantly local checkpoints being created.
MaxDiskWriteSpeedOtherNodeRestart	The maximum disk write speed for local checkpoints and backups (combined) when another node is restarted. Default is 50 MB/s. Increasing this can help restarting data nodes complete their local checkpoints faster, but make sure not to increase the value so much the data node gets overloaded.
MaxDiskWriteSpeedOwnRestart	The maximum disk write speed for local checkpoints and backups (combined) for node being restarted. Default is 200 MB/s. This option should be set as close to the maximum throughput as the disk system for the restarting data node can sustain.
StartPartialTimeout	How long to wait for other nodes with a node group configured before proceeding. See the --nowait-nodes command-line argument for the data nodes. The default is 30000 milliseconds.
StartPartitionedTimeout	How long time to wait for other nodes if going ahead can potentially cause a partitioned cluster. See the discussion in the "Startup Process" section later in the chapter and the --nowait-nodes command-line argument for the data nodes. The default is 60000 milliseconds.

(*continued*)

Table 10-1. (*continued*)

Option Name	Description
StartNoNodegroupTimeout	How long time to wait without a node group. See the "Adding Data Nodes with Node Group Pre-Allocated" case study later in the chapter and the --nowait-nodes command-line argument for the data nodes. The default is 15000 milliseconds.
TwoPassInitialNodeRestartCopy	If BuildIndexThreads is greater than zero, enabling TwoPassInitialNodeRestartCopy allows for a multi-threaded rebuild of ordered indexes during an initial restart, which can in some cases reduce the time it takes to rebuild the ordered indexes.

■ **Tip** All the options are described in more detail in *https://dev.mysql.com/doc/refman/5.7/en/mysql-cluster-ndbd-definition.html*.

The two options—MaxDiskWriteSpeedOtherNodeRestart and MaxDiskWriteSpeedOwnRestart— should be considered together with the other disk write speed options: MinDiskWriteSpeed and MaxDiskWriteSpeed. These options define the lower (MinDiskWriteSpeed) and upper (MaxDiskWriteSpeedOtherNodeRestart, MaxDiskWriteSpeedOwnRestart, and MaxDiskWriteSpeed) bounds of the disk write speed for various stages, as indicated by the maximum settings. They go to the minimum if a delay is detected for writing the redo log or CPU usage is too high. During restarts, a higher write speed is allowed to complete the restarts faster. In MySQL NDB Cluster 7.4 and later, the disk write speed can be monitored through the disk_write_speed_aggregate, disk_write_speed_aggregate_node, and disk_write_speed_base views in the ndbinfo schema.

Startup Process

When you start a data node, it will go through several start phases numbered -1 through 9 and a start phase 101. (The missing start phases are currently not in use.) Each start phase includes specific tasks; for example start phase 5 includes creating a local checkpoint to ensure that the node can take over without data loss should the other node(s) in the node group fail immediately after the node has started. With the exception of start phase -1, the start phases can be seen from both the cluster log and the data node's out log (see the "Monitoring Restarts" section later in the chapter). This section discusses the startup process, but will not go into detail with each start phase.

■ **Tip** An overview of the start phases can be found in the MySQL Reference Manual (*https://dev.mysql.com/doc/refman/5.7/en/mysql-cluster-start-phases.html*) and more detail in the NDB Cluster Internals Manual (*https://dev.mysql.com/doc/ndb-internals/en/ndb-internals-start-phases.html*)

For further reading about the start phases, there is a lengthy comment starting at line 431 (for release 7.5.4) of the *storage/ndb/src/kernel/blocks/ndbcntr/NdbcntrMain.cpp* file in the source code. The latest source code can be downloaded from *https://dev.mysql.com/downloads/cluster/*.

At two points during the startup process, there are synchronization points where data nodes starting together may wait for each other:

- **Start phase 1:** Starting data nodes will wait for offline data nodes to join. This has two purposes: to allow multiple data nodes to start together to save time, and to avoid a partitioned restart (more on this later). This is controlled by three options: StartPartialTimeout, StartPartitionedTimeout, and StartNoNodegroupTimeout. See Table 10-1 in the previous section.

- **Start phase 5:** Data nodes starting together can wait for each other before starting the local checkpoint. As only one local checkpoint can be in progress at the same time, having the data nodes do the local checkpoint together can save time for the overall restart. The default is not to wait for each other. How long to wait is set with the MaxLCPStartDelay option. See Table 10-1.

It is worth considering the StartPartitionedTimeout a little more. Consider as an example the cluster with two data nodes and two management nodes:

```
...
[ndbd]
NodeId       = 1
HostName     = 192.168.56.103

[ndbd]
NodeId       = 2
HostName     = 192.168.56.104

[ndb_mgmd]
NodeId       = 49
HostName     = 192.168.56.101

[ndb_mgmd]
NodeId       = 50
HostName     = 192.168.56.102
...
```

Additionally, assume there is a network partition such that data node 1 can see management node 49 and data node 2 can see management node 50, but there is no connection otherwise between the two pairs, as shown in Figure 10-3.

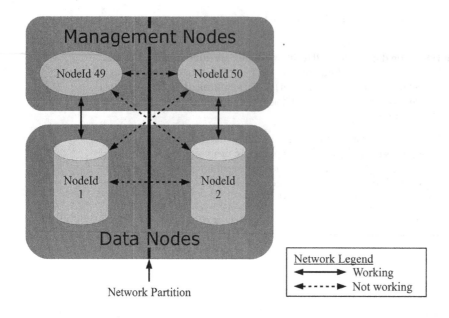

Figure 10-3. *A cluster with a network partition*

If the network fails (also called a network partition) while all nodes are online, the normal arbitration process described in Chapter 1 will handle the potential split-brain scenario. However, during a restart it is different as there is no arbitrator; the arbitrator is elected by the data nodes as a group, so it cannot be done early enough to resolve a network partition at the beginning of a startup. The arbitrator is chosen in start phase 7 during a restart. The only options in case of a network partition at startup are to deny the restart or go ahead with the risk of a partitioned cluster.

In the example shown in Figure 10-3, it will be possible to start both halves; however, it is up to the DBA to avoid starting the cluster during a network partition, or at least ensure that only one cluster group starts up. MySQL NDB Cluster handles a network partition at start up by making the starting nodes wait for the other nodes:

- First for StartPartialTimeout milliseconds to allow as many data nodes as possible to start together.

- Then another StartPartitionedTimeout milliseconds to avoid a partitioned startup in case it is possible for another group of nodes to start concurrently.

The default for StartPartitionedTimeout is 60000 milliseconds (one minute). If a partitioned startup is about to go ahead, messages like the following example are written to in the cluster log during the period added by StartPartitionedTimeout:

```
2016-11-20 11:35:52 [MgmtSrvr] INFO     -- Node 1: Waiting 60 sec for non partitioned start, nodes
                                           [ all: 1 and 2 connected: 1 missing: 2 no-wait:  ]
2016-11-20 11:35:55 [MgmtSrvr] INFO     -- Node 1: Waiting 57 sec for non partitioned start, nodes
                                           [ all: 1 and 2 connected: 1 missing: 2 no-wait:  ]
...
2016-11-20 11:36:49 [MgmtSrvr] INFO     -- Node 1: Waiting 3 sec for non partitioned start, nodes
                                           [ all: 1 and 2 connected: 1 missing: 2 no-wait:  ]
2016-11-20 11:36:52 [MgmtSrvr] INFO     -- Node 1: Start potentially partitioned with nodes 1
                                           [ missing: 2 no-wait:  ]
```

A safer solution is not to allow partitioned starts. Setting StartPartitionedTimeout to 0 is supposed to accomplish this; however, until the bug in *https://bugs.mysql.com/bug.php?id=83893* has been fixed, the best that can be done is to configure StartPartitionedTimeout to 4294962295 milliseconds (49.7 weeks). This is particularly important if the data nodes are started automatically, for example using a service script. When it is known that a partitioned restart is required, instead use the --nowait-nodes command-line argument for the data nodes to explicitly allow restarting without waiting for the nodes that are known to be offline.

Monitoring Restarts

A restart can take a while to complete and it can be useful to monitor the progress. This information can also be used to determine what can be done to improve the restart performance. There are four main places to monitor the restarts:

- The ndb_mgm management client
- The ndb_waiter utility
- The ndbinfo.restart_info table
- The logs

Examples of each of the four places are listed in the following subsections.

The Management Client

The primary way to see the progress of a restart through the management client is to use the STATUS command. The command can be used either for all data nodes or for a single data node. For example, to get the status of all data nodes during a restart:

```
shell$ ndb_mgm -e "ALL STATUS"
Connected to Management Server at: 192.168.56.101:1186
Node 1: starting (Last completed phase 3) (mysql-5.7.16 ndb-7.5.4)
Node 2: starting (Last completed phase 3) (mysql-5.7.16 ndb-7.5.4)
```

This shows that both data nodes are restarting and the last completed start phase was number 3. This indicates the current start phase is number 4. There are no details beyond that.

The ndb_waiter Utility

If the purpose of monitoring the restart is to detect when the data nodes are online, it is possible to use the ndb_waiter utility. An example of a use case is for a script to wait for the data nodes to be ready, then start the API/SQL nodes.

The ndb_waiter utility is simple as it just requires a connection string, a timeout in seconds, and the status for the data nodes to reach. The default timeout is 120 seconds and the default is to wait for all data nodes to become online. For example:

```
shell$ ndb_waiter --ndb_connectstring=192.168.56.101,192.168.56.102
Connected to Management Server at: 192.168.56.101:1186
Node 1: STARTED
Node 2: SHUTTING_DOWN
```

```
[16:43:18] Waiting for cluster enter state STARTED
Node 1: STARTED
Node 2: SHUTTING_DOWN
...
[16:43:23] Waiting for cluster enter state STARTED
Node 1: STARTED
Node 2: NO_CONTACT
...
[16:43:27] Waiting for cluster enter state STARTED
Node 1: STARTED
Node 2: STARTING
...
[16:44:32] Waiting for cluster enter state STARTED
Node 1: STARTED
Node 2: STARTED

NDBT_ProgramExit: 0 - OK
```

The status of all data nodes is printed several times per second, so the output is quite verbose. At the end the exit status can be checked. If the data nodes have not all become online by the timeout, ndb_waiter will retry 15 times before failing:

```
shell$ ndb_waiter --ndb_connectstring=192.168.56.101,192.168.56.102
Connected to Management Server at: 192.168.56.101:1186
...
waitNodeState(STARTED, -1) timeout after 15 attempts

NDBT_ProgramExit: 1 - Failed
```

▪ **Tip**   For more information about the ndb_waiter utility, see *https://dev.mysql.com/doc/refman/5.7/en/mysql-cluster-programs-ndb-waiter.html*.

The ndbinfo.restart_info Table

One of the new features in MySQL NDB Cluster 7.4 was the possibility to monitor restarts through the ndbinfo schema using the restart_info table. The advantage is that the data is readily available through the SQL nodes, so any tool that can execute SQL queries can get the information. The disadvantage is the information is not available for system restarts and it requires an SQL node to be online.

The main use of the ndbinfo.restart_info table is to monitor node restarts. The table will include data for the latest node restart, and the information will be truncated at the start of the node shutdown, and then become available when the node has completed the shutdown. An example is shown in Listing 10-2.

Listing 10-2. Example Output from `ndbinfo.restart_info`

```
mysql> SELECT * FROM ndbinfo.restart_info\G
*************************** 1. row ***************************
                                node_id: 2
                     node_restart_status: Restart completed
                 node_restart_status_int: 19
           secs_to_complete_node_failure: 0
               secs_to_allocate_node_id: 2
     secs_to_include_in_heartbeat_protocol: 1
         secs_until_wait_for_ndbcntr_master: 0
             secs_wait_for_ndbcntr_master: 0
               secs_to_get_start_permitted: 0
   secs_to_wait_for_lcp_for_copy_meta_data: 0
               secs_to_copy_meta_data: 0
                   secs_to_include_node: 2
secs_starting_node_to_request_local_recovery: 0
                 secs_for_local_recovery: 35
                 secs_restore_fragments: 13
                   secs_undo_disk_data: 0
                     secs_exec_redo_log: 0
                     secs_index_rebuild: 21
         secs_to_synchronize_starting_node: 0
               secs_wait_lcp_for_restart: 17
           secs_wait_subscription_handover: 6
                     total_restart_secs: 66
1 row in set (0.01 sec)
```

The timings are all in seconds. The `node_restart_status` column is useful to monitor the current status of the restart; some possible values are: "Node failure handling complete", "Restore fragments ongoing", "Build indexes ongoing", and "Restart completed". The `node_restart_status_int` column is an integer value corresponding to the restart status.

■ **Tip**   For more information about the `ndbinfo.restart_info` table, see *https://dev.mysql.com/doc/refman/5.7/en/mysql-cluster-ndbinfo-restart-info.html.*

A Restart Seen in the Logs

Both the cluster log and the out logs for the data nodes include detailed information about the restarts. As an example, Listing 10-3 contains part of the restart information included in the out log for a data node that has been restarted.

Listing 10-3. Data Node Out Log Excerpt

```
2016-11-19 16:58:25 [ndbd] INFO    -- Angel reconnected to '192.168.56.101:1186'
2016-11-19 16:58:28 [ndbd] INFO    -- Angel reallocated nodeid: 2
2016-11-19 16:58:28 [ndbd] INFO    -- Angel pid: 31415 started child: 32134
2016-11-19 16:58:28 [ndbd] INFO    -- Normal start of data node using checkpoint and log
                                      info if existing
2016-11-19 16:58:28 [ndbd] INFO    -- Configuration fetched from '192.168.56.101:1186',
generation: 7
2016-11-19 16:58:28 [ndbd] INFO    -- Changing directory to '/cluster'
ThreadConfig: input:  LockExecuteThreadToCPU:  => parsed: main,ldm,recv,rep
2016-11-19 16:58:28 [ndbd] INFO    -- MaxNoOfTriggers set to 1400
NDBMT: MaxNoOfExecutionThreads=4
NDBMT: workers=1 threads=1 tc=0 send=0 receive=1
2016-11-19 16:58:28 [ndbd] INFO    -- NDB Cluster -- DB node 2
2016-11-19 16:58:28 [ndbd] INFO    -- mysql-5.7.16 ndb-7.5.4 --
2016-11-19 16:58:28 [ndbd] INFO    -- Memory Allocation for global memory pools Starting
2016-11-19 16:58:28 [ndbd] INFO    -- numa_set_interleave_mask(numa_all_nodes) : OK
2016-11-19 16:58:28 [ndbd] INFO    -- Ndbd_mem_manager::init(1) min: 507Mb initial: 527Mb
2016-11-19 16:58:28 [ndbd] INFO    -- Touch Memory Starting, 2180 pages, page size = 32768
2016-11-19 16:58:28 [ndbd] INFO    -- Touch Memory Completed
...
2016-11-19 16:58:29 [ndbd] INFO    -- Start phase 0 completed
...
2016-11-19 16:59:32 [ndbd] INFO    -- Start phase 101 completed
2016-11-19 16:59:32 [ndbd] INFO    -- Phase 101 was used by SUMA to take over
responsibility for sending some of the asynchronous change events
2016-11-19 16:59:32 [ndbd] INFO    -- Node started
```

The start of the log snippet shows the angel process connecting to the management node and getting the node ID assigned. The following message mentions the restart type ("Normal start of data node using checkpoint and log info if existing" in this case), and the configuration is fetched from the management node. As part of fetching the configuration, the thread configuration is expanded, in this case MaxNoOfExecutionThreads = 4 is expanded to a ThreadConfig of main,ldm,recv,rep.

At this point the restart continues as described in the "Startup Process" section. First memory is allocated and, as can be seen, also touched. For more information about memory usage, see Chapter 2. The rest of the restart follows with a note each time a restart phase has completed.

■ **Tip**   An easy way to get to near the top of a restart logged messages is to search for "fetched".

Example Restart Scenarios

The remainder of this chapter goes through several case studies where restarts are demonstrated. The examples include:

- **Configuration Change:** Making a simple configuration change to increase the value of MaxNoOfConcurrentOperations.

- **Adding Management Node:** Increasing the number of management nodes in a cluster from one to two.

- **Adding Data Nodes:** Adding a node group to an existing cluster.

- **Adding Data Nodes with Node Group Pre-Allocated:** Adding a new node group to an existing cluster without having to restart any of the existing nodes.

- **Adding API/SQL Node:** Adding a new API/SQL node to an existing cluster.

- **Recovering from Corrupt NDB File system:** Restarting a data node after its NDB file system has become corrupt, for example after a hard crash of the host.

- **Initial System Restart:** Performing an initial system restart to increase the number of threads for the data node and redistribute the partitions to take advantage of the extra threads.

With the exception of the "Initial System Restart" case study, all of the other changes are performed online.

To make the commands less verbose, it is assumed that there exists a */etc/my.cnf* configuration file (or in a similar location depending on the platform) with the connection string defined:

```
[mysql_cluster]
ndb_connectstring = 192.168.56.101,192.168.56.102
```

All programs but ndb_mgmd require this connection string to work. As an alternative, the connection string can be given as a command-line option for each command.

As a reminder, the configuration in *config.ini* is repeated in Listing 10-4.

Listing 10-4. The Cluster Configuration Used for the Example Restart Scenarios

```
[ndb_mgmd default]
DataDir      = /cluster/

[ndbd default]
NoOfReplicas = 2
DataDir      = /cluster/

[ndbd]
NodeId       = 1
HostName     = 192.168.56.103

[ndbd]
NodeId       = 2
HostName     = 192.168.56.104

[ndb_mgmd]
NodeId       = 49
HostName     = 192.168.56.101

[ndb_mgmd]
NodeId       = 50
HostName     = 192.168.56.102

[mysqld]
NodeId       = 51
HostName     = 192.168.56.103
```

```
[mysqld]
NodeId    = 52
HostName  = 192.168.56.104

[api]
NodeId    = 53
HostName  = 192.168.56.101

[api]
NodeId    = 54
HostName  = 192.168.56.102
```

Configuration Change

A configuration change is the most common reason to perform a restart as any change to the configuration in *config.ini* requires a restart. For most changes, it will be a normal rolling restart. This example will start by using the default value for MaxNoOfConcurrentOperations (32768) and increase it to 65536. The current value can be seen from the ndbinfo.config_values and ndbinfo.config_params tables, such as:

```
mysql> SELECT param_name, param_default, node_id, config_value
        FROM ndbinfo.config_params
            INNER JOIN ndbinfo.config_values
                ON config_params.param_number = config_values.config_param
        WHERE param_name = 'MaxNoOfConcurrentOperations';
+-----------------------------+---------------+---------+--------------+
| param_name                  | param_default | node_id | config_value |
+-----------------------------+---------------+---------+--------------+
| MaxNoOfConcurrentOperations | 32768         |       1 | 32768        |
| MaxNoOfConcurrentOperations | 32768         |       2 | 32768        |
+-----------------------------+---------------+---------+--------------+
2 rows in set (0.02 sec)
```

Alternatively—and the only option in MySQL NDB Cluster 7.4 and earlier—you can use the ndb_config utility:

```
shell$ ndb_config --type=ndbd --fields=': ' --rows='\n' \
                --query=NodeId,MaxNoOfConcurrentOperations
1: 32768
2: 32768
```

The options given to ndb_config are:

- **--type:** The node type to return the result for, in this case data nodes ("ndbd" covers both single- and multi-threaded data nodes).

- **--fields:** The separator to use between the fields.

- **--rows:** The separator to use between the rows.

- **--query:** What to ask for, in this case the NodeId and the value of MaxNoOfConcurrentOperations.

The ndb_config utility has an additional trick up its sleeve: it is possible to specify a data node to get the configuration from instead of asking the management nodes. This can be useful when a configuration change is only partly applied, as you will see later in this example.

The first step of the configuration change is to update the cluster configuration file to include the new value for MaxNoOfConcurrentOperations:

```
[ndbd default]
NoOfReplicas = 2
DataDir      = /cluster/
MaxNoOfConcurrentOperations = 65536
```

Then stop both management nodes—otherwise if only one management node is restarted at a time, it will read the current configuration from the remaining online management node when restarting.

```
shell$ ndb_mgm -e "49 STOP"
Connected to Management Server at: 192.168.56.101:1186
Node 49 has shutdown.
Disconnecting to allow Management Server to shutdown

shell$ ndb_mgm -e "50 STOP"
Connected to Management Server at: 192.168.56.101:1186
Connected to Management Server at: 192.168.56.102:1186
Node 50 has shutdown.
Disconnecting to allow Management Server to shutdown
```

Note how the second execution of ndb_mgm first tried to connect to *192.168.56.101*, then changed to the other node. This happened because the management node on *192.168.56.101* (node 49) was not able to handle the request, so the next management node was used instead.

When both management nodes have completed the shutdown, they can be restarted again using the --reload option to tell the management nodes to read the new configuration file:

```
shell$ sudo -u mysql ndb_mgmd --config-file=/etc/config.ini \
          --config-dir=/cluster/config --ndb-nodeid=49 --reload
MySQL Cluster Management Server mysql-5.7.16 ndb-7.5.4

shell$ sudo -u mysql ndb_mgmd --config-file=/etc/config.ini \
          --config-dir=/cluster/config --ndb-nodeid=50 --reload
MySQL Cluster Management Server mysql-5.7.16 ndb-7.5.4
```

An interesting thing can be observed in the cluster log after the restart:

```
2016-11-17 18:02:20 [MgmtSrvr] INFO     -- Detected change of /etc/config.ini on disk, will
try to set it. This is the actual diff:
[ndbd(DB)]
NodeId=1
-MaxNoOfConcurrentOperations=32768
+MaxNoOfConcurrentOperations=65536

[ndbd(DB)]
NodeId=2
-MaxNoOfConcurrentOperations=32768
+MaxNoOfConcurrentOperations=65536
```

```
2016-11-17 18:02:20 [MgmtSrvr] INFO     -- Starting configuration change, generation: 5
2016-11-17 18:02:20 [MgmtSrvr] INFO     -- Node 1: Node 50: API mysql-5.7.16 ndb-7.5.4
2016-11-17 18:02:20 [MgmtSrvr] INFO     -- Node 2: Node 50: API mysql-5.7.16 ndb-7.5.4
2016-11-17 18:02:20 [MgmtSrvr] INFO     -- Configuration 6 commited
2016-11-17 18:02:20 [MgmtSrvr] INFO     -- Config change completed! New generation: 6
```

The cluster log includes the difference of the change (called diff in the log), and the configuration generation is incremented from 5 to 6. This is an advantage of using the --reload option over the --initial option when restarting a management node: the log will include details of the changes made to the configuration.

It can be interesting to check the effect of the configuration change as the rolling restart progresses. At this stage, the management nodes know of the new configuration, so how is that reflected using the previous methods to get the current values? First using the ndbinfo schema:

```
mysql> SELECT param_name, param_default, node_id, config_value
         FROM ndbinfo.config_params
           INNER JOIN ndbinfo.config_values
             ON config_params.param_number = config_values.config_param
         WHERE param_name = 'MaxNoOfConcurrentOperations';
+-----------------------------+---------------+---------+--------------+
| param_name                  | param_default | node_id | config_value |
+-----------------------------+---------------+---------+--------------+
| MaxNoOfConcurrentOperations | 32768         |       1 | 32768        |
| MaxNoOfConcurrentOperations | 32768         |       2 | 32768        |
+-----------------------------+---------------+---------+--------------+
2 rows in set (0.04 sec)
```

This is as expected—the data nodes are not yet aware of the configuration change. This is also reflected in the ndbinfo.nodes table:

```
mysql> SELECT * FROM ndbinfo.nodes;
+---------+--------+---------+-------------+-------------------+
| node_id | uptime | status  | start_phase | config_generation |
+---------+--------+---------+-------------+-------------------+
|       1 |    561 | STARTED |           0 |                 5 |
|       2 |    581 | STARTED |           0 |                 5 |
+---------+--------+---------+-------------+-------------------+
2 rows in set (0.02 sec)
```

The config_generation column is the same as the management node reported in the cluster log during the restart. So here the config generation is 5, the old generation. However, using ndb_config utility at first sight produces an unexpected result:

```
shell$ ndb_config --type=ndbd --fields=': ' --rows='\n' \
                 --query=NodeId,MaxNoOfConcurrentOperations
1: 65536
2: 65536
```

Why is that? The reason is that ndb_config can ask either the management nodes or any of the data nodes about the configuration. The default is to ask the management nodes, so that explains the new value for MaxNoOfConcurrentOperations. To ask data node 1 for the configuration, add the --config-from-node option:

```
shell$ ndb_config --type=ndbd --fields=': ' --rows='\n' \
                  --query=NodeId,MaxNoOfConcurrentOperations \
                  --config-from-node=1
1: 32768
2: 32768
```

This possibility to get the configuration from various nodes can be very useful to investigate issues where the configuration does not appear to be the expected. Going systematically through first the management nodes, then each data node will reveal which nodes have applied a configuration change and which have not.

All that remains now is to restart each of the remaining nodes. The data nodes can be restarted using the management client:

```
shell$ ndb_mgm -e "1 RESTART"
Connected to Management Server at: 192.168.56.101:1186
Node 1 is being restarted
```

At this point, it is necessary to wait for the restart to complete before restarting the second data node. Once the restart of the first node has completed, begin the restart of the second one:

```
shell$ ndb_mgm -e "2 RESTART"
Connected to Management Server at: 192.168.56.101:1186
Node 2 is being restarted
```

Finally restart each of the API/SQL nodes. Since this step is platform dependent, it is left as an exercise for the reader. Technically it is not necessary to restart the API/SQL nodes for a configuration change like this that does not affect the API/SQL nodes. However, by always including all nodes as part of the rolling restart, it is also ensured that none are forgotten.

Going back to check the configuration, looking at the ndbinfo schema, it can now be seen that both data nodes use the new configuration:

```
mysql> SELECT * FROM ndbinfo.nodes;
+---------+--------+---------+-------------+-------------------+
| node_id | uptime | status  | start_phase | config_generation |
+---------+--------+---------+-------------+-------------------+
|       1 |    430 | STARTED |           0 |                 6 |
|       2 |    247 | STARTED |           0 |                 6 |
+---------+--------+---------+-------------+-------------------+
2 rows in set (0.01 sec)
```

```
mysql> SELECT param_name, param_default, node_id, config_value
           FROM ndbinfo.config_params
              INNER JOIN ndbinfo.config_values
                 ON config_params.param_number = config_values.config_param
           WHERE param_name = 'MaxNoOfConcurrentOperations';
+-----------------------------+---------------+---------+--------------+
| param_name                  | param_default | node_id | config_value |
+-----------------------------+---------------+---------+--------------+
| MaxNoOfConcurrentOperations | 32768         |       1 | 65536        |
| MaxNoOfConcurrentOperations | 32768         |       2 | 65536        |
+-----------------------------+---------------+---------+--------------+
2 rows in set (0.04 sec)
```

The configuration generation has increased to 6, and the value for MaxNoOfConcurrentOperations has increased to 65536.

Adding a Management Node

This example starts with a slightly different configuration than the other case studies in this chapter. The setup is the same as in Listing 10-4 except that the management node on *192.168.0.102* is not included. The task of this example is to add the management node on *192.168.0.102*.

The steps to add a management node are:

1. Update the cluster configuration file (*config.ini*) by adding the details for the new management node.

2. Update the ndb_connectstring option for all data and API/SQL nodes (this includes utility programs such as ndb_desc).

3. Shut down the existing management node(s).

4. Restart the existing management nodes as well as the new management node with --initial.

5. Restart the data and API/SQL nodes as in a rolling restart.

The example starts with the cluster up and running:

```
shell$ ndb_mgm -e "SHOW"
Connected to Management Server at: 192.168.56.101:1186
Cluster Configuration
---------------------
[ndbd(NDB)]     2 node(s)
id=1    @192.168.56.103  (mysql-5.7.16 ndb-7.5.4, Nodegroup: 0, *)
id=2    @192.168.56.104  (mysql-5.7.16 ndb-7.5.4, Nodegroup: 0)

[ndb_mgmd(MGM)] 1 node(s)
id=49   @192.168.56.101  (mysql-5.7.16 ndb-7.5.4)

[mysqld(API)]   6 node(s)
id=51   @192.168.56.103  (mysql-5.7.16 ndb-7.5.4)
id=52   @192.168.56.104  (mysql-5.7.16 ndb-7.5.4)
id=53 (not connected, accepting connect from 192.168.56.101)
id=54 (not connected, accepting connect from 192.168.56.102)
```

The first step is to update *config.ini* to add the new management node. This requires adding an extra [ndb_mgmd] section setting the NodeId and HostName options. In the example, the new management node will be executing on *192.168.56.102* and otherwise using the option in [ndb_mgmd default] and the default configuration. The section added is as follows:

```
[ndb_mgmd]
NodeId                  = 50
HostName                = 192.168.56.102
```

The resulting *config.ini* file is the one in Listing 10-4. The configuration file also must be copied to the new node.

With the new configuration file in place, the next step is to ensure that all nodes will include the new management node when they are restarted in the future. Client programs connecting to the management nodes (such as ndb_mgm and ndb_desc) should also refer to both management nodes. To achieve this, the --ndb_connectstring option must be updated. If the option is set in the *my.cnf*/*my.ini* configuration file, it can be updated there:

```
[mysql_cluster]
ndb_connectstring = 192.168.56.101,192.168.56.102
```

It is now time for the actual restart. As with other configuration changes, the first part of the restart is to shut down the management node(s). The operation can be done from any of the nodes using the ndb_mgm management client:

```
shell$ ndb_mgm -e "49 STOP"
Connected to Management Server at: 192.168.56.101:1186
Node 49 has shutdown.
Disconnecting to allow Management Server to shutdown
```

Once the management node has shut down, the existing as well as the new management nodes must be restarted. Since a new management node necessarily will use first generation for the configuration, this is one of the rare cases where the management nodes must be started with the --initial flag to reset the management node.

▓ **Tip** It is only the management nodes that must be restarted with --initial in this case. The data nodes can perform a normal node restart.

To start the management node on *192.168.56.101*:

```
shell$ sudo -u mysql ndb_mgmd --config-file=/etc/config.ini \
          --config-dir=/cluster/config --ndb-nodeid=49 –initial
MySQL Cluster Management Server mysql-5.7.16 ndb-7.5.4
```

And on *192.168.56.102*:

```
shell$ sudo -u mysql ndb_mgmd --config-file=/etc/config.ini \
          --config-dir=/cluster/config --ndb-nodeid=50 --initial
MySQL Cluster Management Server mysql-5.7.16 ndb-7.5.4
```

The fact that there are now two management nodes can be confirmed using the SHOW command:

```
shell$ ndb_mgm -e "SHOW"
Connected to Management Server at: 192.168.56.101:1186
...
[ndb_mgmd(MGM)] 2 node(s)
id=49   @192.168.56.101  (mysql-5.7.16 ndb-7.5.4)
id=50   @192.168.56.102  (mysql-5.7.16 ndb-7.5.4)
```

All that remains now is to restart the data nodes and API/SQL nodes one by one, and they will pick up the new configuration when rejoining the cluster. To ensure that the data nodes are aware of the new connection string, stop the data nodes, then manually start them again. First node ID 1:

```
shell$ ndb_mgm -e "1 STOP"
Connected to Management Server at: 192.168.56.101:1186
Node 1 has shutdown.

shell$ sudo -u mysql ndbmtd --ndb-nodeid=1
```

Then node ID 2:

```
shell$ ndb_mgm -e "2 STOP"
Connected to Management Server at: 192.168.56.101:1186
Node 2 has shutdown.

shell$ sudo -u mysql ndbmtd --ndb-nodeid=2
```

Finally, the two API/SQL nodes can be restarted. How this restart is performed depends on the platform, whether it is SQL nodes or custom API nodes, and how they are installed. So, shut down one of the API and SQL node using the method appropriate for the installation, then start it again. Continue with the rest of the API and SQL nodes.

Adding Data Nodes

During the life time of a cluster, it may be necessary to increase the number of data nodes. Examples of why it may be required to add more data nodes are to add more storage capacity or for more parallelism for scans.

Adding extra data nodes to a cluster requires a few more steps than the previous examples:

1. Update the cluster configuration file (*config.ini*) with the details of the new data nodes. You must add a complete new node group, so for example with NoOfReplicas = 2, two new data nodes must be added.

2. Perform a rolling restart of the existing nodes in the cluster. It is important to remember to include the API/SQL nodes in this rolling restart.

3. Start the new nodes; this will be an initial restart since it is the first they are started.

4. Create a new node group for the new data nodes.

5. Reorganize the partitions for existing tables to move some of the existing data into the new data nodes.

6. Optimize the reorganized tables to reclaim variable width memory. Reorganizing the partitions is equivalent to inserting part of the data on the new nodes and deleting it on the old nodes. The deletion of data will cause fragmentation of which the memory used for variable data can be reclaimed online.

The start of this example has the configuration in Listing 10-4 and the following management and data nodes online:

```
shell$ ndb_mgm -e "SHOW"
Connected to Management Server at: 192.168.56.101:1186
Cluster Configuration
---------------------
[ndbd(NDB)]     2 node(s)
id=1    @192.168.56.103  (mysql-5.7.16 ndb-7.5.4, Nodegroup: 0, *)
id=2    @192.168.56.104  (mysql-5.7.16 ndb-7.5.4, Nodegroup: 0)

[ndb_mgmd(MGM)] 2 node(s)
id=49   @192.168.56.101  (mysql-5.7.16 ndb-7.5.4)
id=50   @192.168.56.102  (mysql-5.7.16 ndb-7.5.4)

[mysqld(API)]   6 node(s)
...
```

In this case, the new data nodes are added on the existing hosts. One point to be careful of when there are multiple data nodes on the same host is to ensure that the data nodes are not in the same node group; that could introduce a single point of failure. Since there already is one node group and the new data nodes will constitute a second node group, the new node group is automatically spread across the two hosts, so in this case the new nodes will not introduce a single point of failure.

The first step is to update the *config.ini* file on the two management nodes to add the new data nodes. This is done adding two [ndbd] sections:

```
[ndbd]
NodeId                  = 3
HostName                = 192.168.56.103

[ndbd]
NodeId                  = 4
HostName                = 192.168.56.104
```

At this point a normal rolling restart can be performed. First shut down both management nodes:

```
shell$ ndb_mgm -e "49 STOP"
Connected to Management Server at: 192.168.56.101:1186
Node 49 has shutdown.
Disconnecting to allow Management Server to shutdown

shell$ ndb_mgm -e "50 STOP"
Connected to Management Server at: 192.168.56.102:1186
Node 50 has shutdown.
Disconnecting to allow Management Server to shutdown
```

337

Then restart the management nodes using the --reload option:

```
shell$ sudo -u mysql ndb_mgmd --config-file=/etc/config.ini \
            --config-dir=/cluster/config --ndb-nodeid=49 –reload
MySQL Cluster Management Server mysql-5.7.16 ndb-7.5.4

shell$ sudo -u mysql ndb_mgmd --config-file=/etc/config.ini \
            --config-dir=/cluster/config --ndb-nodeid=50 --reload
MySQL Cluster Management Server mysql-5.7.16 ndb-7.5.4
```

The cluster log shows the new configuration:

```
...
2016-11-07 18:15:50 [MgmtSrvr] INFO     -- Detected change of /etc/config.ini on disk, will
try to set it. This is the actual diff:
[ndbd(DB)]
NodeId=3
Node removed

[ndbd(DB)]
NodeId=4
Node removed

[TCP]
NodeId1=1
NodeId2=3
Connection removed
...
```

The "diff" looks a bit odd when adding new nodes as it mentions the nodes have been removed. However, in reality all of the changes have been added. This includes the [TCP] sections. As discussed in Chapter 2, transporters are set up between all the possible node pairs whether the nodes are online or not. The cluster uses all defaults for the TCP/IP transporter settings, so that part has been hidden until now, but adding new nodes will make the management node also "discover" the new transporter settings.

At this point, restart the two existing data nodes; no special consideration has to be taken here either. First node ID 1:

```
shell$ ndb_mgm -e "1 RESTART"
Connected to Management Server at: 192.168.56.101:1186
Node 1 is being restarted
```

Wait for the restart to complete, then restart the data node with node ID 2:

```
shell$ ndb_mgm -e "2 RESTART"
Connected to Management Server at: 192.168.56.101:1186
Node 2 is being restarted
```

Once the second data node has completed its restart, restart each of the API/SQL nodes as appropriate for the platform and the API node type (SQL node or application). It is important that all nodes that were online at the start of the process have either been shut down or restarted. This is required so that they are all aware of the new nodes that are about to be added and there are transporters ready for them.

The status is now:

```
shell$ ndb_mgm -e "SHOW"
Connected to Management Server at: 192.168.56.101:1186
Cluster Configuration
---------------------
[ndbd(NDB)]     4 node(s)
id=1    @192.168.56.103  (mysql-5.7.16 ndb-7.5.4, Nodegroup: 0, *)
id=2    @192.168.56.104  (mysql-5.7.16 ndb-7.5.4, Nodegroup: 0)
id=3 (not connected, accepting connect from 192.168.56.103)
id=4 (not connected, accepting connect from 192.168.56.104)
...
```

This shows that nodes 3 and 4 are part of the cluster, but not yet started. So finally, it is time to get the new data nodes online. Since it is the first time the new data nodes are started, it must be an initial restart. The initial start of the two new nodes is done concurrently. First node ID 3:

```
shell$ sudo -u mysql ndbmtd --ndb-nodeid=3 --initial
2016-11-07 18:35:46 [ndbd] INFO     -- Angel connected to '192.168.56.101:1186'
2016-11-07 18:35:46 [ndbd] INFO     -- Angel allocated nodeid: 3
```

Next, node id 4:

```
shell$ sudo -u mysql ndbmtd --ndb-nodeid=4 --initial
2016-11-07 18:35:48 [ndbd] INFO     -- Angel connected to '192.168.56.101:1186'
2016-11-07 18:35:48 [ndbd] INFO     -- Angel allocated nodeid: 4
```

Once the restart has completed, the status is:

```
shell$ ndb_mgm -e "SHOW"
Connected to Management Server at: 192.168.56.101:1186
Cluster Configuration
---------------------
[ndbd(NDB)]     4 node(s)
id=1    @192.168.56.103  (mysql-5.7.16 ndb-7.5.4, Nodegroup: 0, *)
id=2    @192.168.56.104  (mysql-5.7.16 ndb-7.5.4, Nodegroup: 0)
id=3    @192.168.56.103  (mysql-5.7.16 ndb-7.5.4, no nodegroup)
id=4    @192.168.56.104  (mysql-5.7.16 ndb-7.5.4, no nodegroup)
...
```

One point to note here is that the new data nodes are started and part of the cluster, but there is no node group associated with them. That means tables will not have any partitions and thus not any data stored in the new data nodes. To actually store data in the new notes, it is necessary to create a new node group. This can be done using the management client:

```
shell$ ndb_mgm -e "CREATE NODEGROUP 3,4"
Connected to Management Server at: 192.168.56.101:1186
Nodegroup 1 created
```

The arguments to the CREATE NODEGROUP command are the node IDs in a comma-separated list to add to the new node group. The finale status is:

```
shell$ ndb_mgm -e "SHOW"
Connected to Management Server at: 192.168.56.101:1186
Cluster Configuration
---------------------
[ndbd(NDB)]     4 node(s)
id=1    @192.168.56.103  (mysql-5.7.16 ndb-7.5.4, Nodegroup: 0, *)
id=2    @192.168.56.104  (mysql-5.7.16 ndb-7.5.4, Nodegroup: 0)
id=3    @192.168.56.103  (mysql-5.7.16 ndb-7.5.4, Nodegroup: 1)
id=4    @192.168.56.104  (mysql-5.7.16 ndb-7.5.4, Nodegroup: 1)
...
```

The last task is to ensure that data is also added to the new nodes. This will happen automatically for all new tables, but existing tables must be redistributed first. Like the previous steps, redistributing the data is an online operation. Consider a table, such as db1.t1, that existed before the new nodes were added. Looking at the table using the ndb_desc utility shows the current distribution among the partitions (some information has been removed for clarity):

```
shell$ ndb_desc --database=db1 t1 -pn
...
-- Per partition info --
Partition   Row count   Frag fixed memory   Frag varsized memory   Nodes
0           62992       2031616             3112960                1,2
1           63392       2064384             3145728                2,1
```

Alternatively, the ndbinfo schema can be used:

```
mysql> SELECT node_id, fragment_num,
              SUM(fixed_elem_alloc_bytes) AS FixedMem,
              SUM(var_elem_alloc_bytes) AS VarMem
         FROM ndbinfo.memory_per_fragment
        WHERE fq_name = 'db1/def/t1'
        GROUP BY node_id, fragment_num;
+---------+--------------+----------+---------+
| node_id | fragment_num | FixedMem | VarMem  |
+---------+--------------+----------+---------+
|       1 |            0 |  2031616 | 3112960 |
|       1 |            1 |  2064384 | 3145728 |
|       2 |            0 |  2031616 | 3112960 |
|       2 |            1 |  2064384 | 3145728 |
+---------+--------------+----------+---------+
4 rows in set (0.05 sec)
```

To reorganize the data in existing tables, use the ALTER TABLE statement like:

```
mysql> ALTER TABLE db1.t1 ALGORITHM=INPLACE, REORGANIZE PARTITION;
Query OK, 0 rows affected (13.42 sec)
Records: 0  Duplicates: 0  Warnings: 0
```

■ **Note**   It is not possible to perform any other DDL statements while the partitions are being reorganized.

The new data distribution is:

```
mysql> SELECT node_id, fragment_num,
              SUM(fixed_elem_alloc_bytes) AS FixedMem,
              SUM(var_elem_alloc_bytes) AS VarMem
         FROM ndbinfo.memory_per_fragment
        WHERE fq_name = 'db1/def/t1'
        GROUP BY node_id, fragment_num;
+---------+--------------+----------+---------+
| node_id | fragment_num | FixedMem | VarMem  |
+---------+--------------+----------+---------+
|       1 |            0 |  2031616 | 3112960 |
|       1 |            1 |  2064384 | 3145728 |
|       2 |            0 |  2031616 | 3112960 |
|       2 |            1 |  2064384 | 3145728 |
|       3 |            2 |  1015808 | 1572864 |
|       3 |            3 |  1048576 | 1572864 |
|       4 |            2 |  1015808 | 1572864 |
|       4 |            3 |  1048576 | 1572864 |
+---------+--------------+----------+---------+
8 rows in set (0.09 sec)
```

The only thing that is missing is to free up the extra space still used in the old partitions. This can be done online using OPTIMIZE TABLE for each table. Listing 10-5 shows an example with the db1.t1 table and how this reclaims some of the variable width (dynamic) memory.

Listing 10-5. Defragmenting the Data

```
mysql> OPTIMIZE TABLE db1.t1;
+--------+----------+----------+----------+
| Table  | Op       | Msg_type | Msg_text |
+--------+----------+----------+----------+
| db1.t1 | optimize | status   | OK       |
+--------+----------+----------+----------+
1 row in set (3.35 sec)

mysql> SELECT node_id, fragment_num,
              SUM(fixed_elem_alloc_bytes) AS FixedMem,
              SUM(var_elem_alloc_bytes) AS VarMem
         FROM ndbinfo.memory_per_fragment
        WHERE fq_name = 'db1/def/t1'
        GROUP BY node_id, fragment_num;
```

```
+----------+---------------+----------+----------+
| node_id  | fragment_num  | FixedMem | VarMem   |
+----------+---------------+----------+----------+
|       1  |            0  |  2031616 | 1638400  |
|       1  |            1  |  2064384 | 1638400  |
|       2  |            0  |  2031616 | 1638400  |
|       2  |            1  |  2064384 | 1638400  |
|       3  |            2  |  1015808 | 1572864  |
|       3  |            3  |  1048576 | 1572864  |
|       4  |            2  |  1015808 | 1572864  |
|       4  |            3  |  1048576 | 1572864  |
+----------+---------------+----------+----------+
8 rows in set (0.07 sec)
```

As it can be seen, OPTIMIZE TABLE only reclaimed the memory for the variable sized memory (dynamic column format). The non-reclaimed fixed memory is still available for new rows. The only way to completely reclaim the memory is to recreate the table, for example using a null ALTER TABLE:

```
mysql> ALTER TABLE db1.t1 ENGINE=NDBCluster;
Query OK, 126384 rows affected (38.18 sec)
Records: 126384  Duplicates: 0  Warnings: 0
```

Adding Data Nodes with Node Group Pre-Allocated

An alternative way to add new data nodes, which avoids restarting any of the existing nodes, is to configure the cluster to include future data nodes ahead of time. This can be achieved by setting the node group for the future nodes to 65536 (the maximum allowed value). For example:

```
[ndbd]
NodeId                      = 3
NodeGroup                   = 65536
HostName                    = 192.168.56.103

[ndbd]
NodeId                      = 4
NodeGroup                   = 65536
HostName                    = 192.168.56.104

[ndbd]
NodeId                      = 5
NodeGroup                   = 65536
HostName                    = 192.168.56.105

[ndbd]
NodeId                      = 6
NodeGroup                   = 65536
HostName                    = 192.168.56.106
```

This configuration supports adding data nodes either to the two existing hosts or to two new hosts.

One caveat about having extra nodes configured for future use is that the current data nodes will by default wait for the future ones during a restart. This can be seen from the cluster log:

```
2016-11-12 13:07:48 [MgmtSrvr] INFO     -- Node 1: Initial start,
               waiting 13 for 3, 4, 5 and 6 to connect,
               nodes [ all: 1, 2, 3, 4, 5 and 6
                       connected: 1 and 2 missing: 3, 4, 5 and 6
                       no-wait:
                       no-nodegroup: 3, 4, 5 and 6 ]
...
2016-11-12 13:08:01 [MgmtSrvr] INFO     -- Node 1: Initial start
               with nodes 1 and 2 [ missing: 3, 4, 5 and 6 no-wait:  ]
```

The log example has been reformatted to make it easier to read. It tells that this is an initial restart, and the first note (at 13:07:48) in the second line says the cluster is waiting another 13 seconds for nodes 3, 4, 5, and 6 (i.e., the node IDs that have been reserved for future nodes) to connect. The last four lines of the first message show a summary of the nodes, a list of all known data nodes, which are connected, which the cluster will not wait for, and which do not have a node group. This shows two interesting features:

- The no-wait part refers to the possibility to tell the data node not to wait for certain nodes at startup. This can be used to skip the waiting stage.

- The no-nodegroup part shows that MySQL NDB Cluster considers NodeGroup = 65536 as not having a node group. This is what allows us to include the data nodes in the configuration even though they are not intended to be part of the cluster for the time being.

The option to avoid waiting for nodes that are known not to participate in the restart is --nowait-nodes, as discussed earlier in the chapter. To skip waiting for all of the four future nodes, start the nodes as follows:

```
shell$ sudo -u mysql ndbmtd --ndb-nodeid=1 --nowait-nodes=3,4,5,6
```

This is equivalent for node 2. An alternative is to set the StartNoNodeGroupTimeout option, which defaults to 15000 milliseconds (15 seconds). Reducing the timeout makes the nodes wait a shorter time for the nodes without a node group.

At this point, the cluster is online with two data nodes, and it is decided to add a node on each of the hosts *192.168.56.103* and *192.168.56.104*, just like in the previous example. However, as the nodes already have been added to the configuration, it is not necessary this time to perform any restarts other than getting the new nodes online. First check the status of the cluster:

```
shell$ ndb_mgm -e "SHOW"
Connected to Management Server at: 192.168.56.101:1186
Cluster Configuration
---------------------
[ndbd(NDB)]     6 node(s)
id=1    @192.168.56.103  (mysql-5.7.16 ndb-7.5.4, Nodegroup: 0, *)
id=2    @192.168.56.104  (mysql-5.7.16 ndb-7.5.4, Nodegroup: 0)
id=3 (not connected, accepting connect from 192.168.56.103)
id=4 (not connected, accepting connect from 192.168.56.104)
id=5 (not connected, accepting connect from 192.168.56.105)
id=6 (not connected, accepting connect from 192.168.56.106)
...
```

Then start the two new data nodes:

```
shell$ sudo -u mysql ndbmtd --ndb-nodeid=3 --initial
```

```
shell$ sudo -u mysql ndbmtd --ndb-nodeid=4 --initial
```

The cluster is now in the equivalent state as the previous example where the new nodes were started:

```
shell$ ndb_mgm -e "SHOW"
Connected to Management Server at: 192.168.56.101:1186
Cluster Configuration
---------------------
[ndbd(NDB)]     6 node(s)
id=1    @192.168.56.103  (mysql-5.7.16 ndb-7.5.4, Nodegroup: 0, *)
id=2    @192.168.56.104  (mysql-5.7.16 ndb-7.5.4, Nodegroup: 0)
id=3    @192.168.56.103  (mysql-5.7.16 ndb-7.5.4, no nodegroup)
id=4    @192.168.56.104  (mysql-5.7.16 ndb-7.5.4, no nodegroup)
id=5 (not connected, accepting connect from 192.168.56.105)
id=6 (not connected, accepting connect from 192.168.56.106)
...
```

Note how the new nodes (id=3 and id=4) show up without a node group after they have been started. This is exactly what NodeGroup = 65536 in the configuration file at the beginning of the example meant.

■ **Tip**　The cluster will function correctly even with the NodeGroup = 65536 setting left in the configuration for the newly added nodes. However, it makes the configuration more clear if it is removed.

With the new data nodes online, a new node group can be created:

```
shell$ ndb_mgm -e "CREATE NODEGROUP 3,4"
Connected to Management Server at: 192.168.56.101:1186
Nodegroup 1 created
```

Finally, reorganize the partitions for each table. For example, for the db1.t1 table:

```
mysql> ALTER TABLE db1.t1 ALGORITHM=INPLACE, REORGANIZE PARTITION;
Query OK, 0 rows affected (13.42 sec)
Records: 0  Duplicates: 0  Warnings: 0
```

Adding API/SQL Node

The simplest of the procedures to add extra nodes is to add new API/SQL nodes. From the point of view of the existing nodes, this is no different than making any other configuration change:

1. Update the cluster configuration file (*config.ini*) adding the new nodes.

2. Perform a rolling restart as discussed earlier.

3. Install, configure, and start the new API/SQL nodes.

The main point to consider when adding additional API/SQL nodes is that the management and data nodes will allocate send and receive buffers for the new nodes. If TotalSendBufferMemory has not been configured, the extra send buffer will cause the total memory usage to increase with the size of the send buffer (the SendBufferMemory option for the TCP sections or 2MB by default). If TotalSendBufferMemory has been configured, it is necessary to consider whether the new nodes require the total send buffer memory pool to be increased. For the receive buffer, the memory usage increases with the size of the receive buffer (the ReceiveBufferMemory option for the TCP sections or 2MB by default).

Recovering from a Corrupt NDB File System

The NDB file system of one of the data nodes can become corrupt. This is most likely to happen for one of the files created for a local checkpoint, and it typically happens after the host has crashed, the node has been killed with a *SIGKILL* signal, or due to a disk failure. However, it can also occur for other reasons. The symptom is that attempting to restart the data node fails. An example of the failed restart may be a message in the cluster log:

```
2016-11-16 16:41:40 [MgmtSrvr] ALERT    -- Node 2: Forced node shutdown completed. Occured
during startphase 5. Caused by error 2341: 'Internal program error (failed ndbrequire)
(Internal error, programming error or missing error message, please report a bug). Temporary
error, restart node'.
```

In this example, the corresponding error log message is:

```
Time: Wednesday 16 November 2016 - 16:42:11
Status: Temporary error, restart node
Message: Internal program error (failed ndbrequire) (Internal error, programming error or
missing error message, please report a bug)
Error: 2341
Error data: restore.cpp
Error object: RESTORE (Line: 507) 0x00000002 Check len < 8192 failed
Program: ndbmtd
Pid: 18633 thr: 2
Version: mysql-5.7.16 ndb-7.5.4
Trace file name: ndb_2_trace.log.3_t2
Trace file path: /cluster//ndb_2_trace.log.3 [t1..t4]
***EOM***
```

Recall that start phase 5 is where the local checkpoint is restored, which involves the *RESTORE* kernel block. In cases like this, it is necessary to recreate the NDB file system. That is, you need to perform an initial restart of the data node.

An initial restart of a data node deletes all the data nodes files in the NDB file system, with the exception of logfile group file or tablespace files. This means:

- You must make sure there is another node in the same node group online. If that is not the case, the node you are restarting will either fail to restart or restart in a partitioned mode with no data!

- If there are logfile group files or tablespace files that must be deleted, it is necessary to do it manually. If the files are missing, they will be recreated during the restart.

See the discussion of restart types at the beginning of this chapter.

Initial System Restart

An initial system restart is fortunately a rare event. The following example will change the configuration from using MaxNoOfExecutionThreads = 2 (the default) that has one *LDM* threads to MaxNoOfExecutionThreads = 8 with four *LDM* threads. As discussed in Chapter 2, the index memory is divided among the LDM threads, so increasing the number of *LDM* threads from 2 to 8 means each *LDM* thread only has a quarter the amount of index memory available. This means that if more than 23.75% of the index memory is in use for any of the *LDM* threads (the threshold for considering all the index memory used is at 95% of IndexMemory), it will not be possible to even restart the data nodes with the new configuration. So in the end, to be able to increase the *LDM* threads, it is often necessary to re-initialize the cluster and restore the data from a backup.

The steps this example uses to do this are:

1. Make the cluster read-only.

2. Create a data backup.

3. Create a schema backup.

4. Perform the restart.

5. Restore the schema.

6. Restore the data.

Because there can be multiple API/SQL nodes connected to the data nodes, it can be difficult to ensure that no one changes any data while the cluster is being backed up in Steps 2 and 3. To make this easier, MySQL NDB Cluster supports enabling a single user mode:

```
shell$ ndb_mgm -e "ENTER SINGLE USER MODE 51"
Connected to Management Server at: 192.168.56.101:1186
Single user mode entered
Access is granted for API node 51 only.
```

The command tells the cluster that the only API/SQL node that is allowed to be connected is node 51.

■ **Tip**   If the SQL nodes are using the ndb_cluster_connection_pool option to have multiple connections, either restart with ndb_cluster_connection_pool = 1 or have a spare SQL node for maintenance use with just one connection.

Combining this with enabling the super_read_only mode on SQL node 51, it is guaranteed that no changes will happen:

```
mysql> SET GLOBAL super_read_only = ON;
Query OK, 0 rows affected (0.00 sec)
```

If this is a replication slave, make sure also to stop the replication as the super_read_only flag does not apply to the SQL thread in replication.

▓ **Note**   In MySQL 7.4 and earlier, the `super_read_only` option did not exist. Instead it is necessary to use the `read_only` option, but be aware the users with the SUPER privilege (including replication) in that case are still allowed to make changes to the data.

At this point the backups can be made. In this example, it is assumed that the only user created schema with NDBCluster tables just consists of the `world` database. The data can be backed up using the native NDB backup, and the schema can be backed up using `mysqldump`:

```
shell$ ndb_mgm -e "START BACKUP"
Connected to Management Server at: 192.168.56.101:1186
Waiting for completed, this may take several minutes
Node 1: Backup 1 started from node 49
Node 1: Backup 1 started from node 49 completed
 StartGCP: 638 StopGCP: 641
 #Records: 7370 #LogRecords: 0
 Data: 498424 bytes Log: 0 bytes

shell$ mysqldump --no-data world > backup_world_schemaonly.sql
```

For production data, it is best to confirm the backup is valid by restoring it to a different cluster before proceeding. When the backup has been verified, the configuration change can be made to *config.ini* and the cluster can be shut down:

```
shell$ ndb_mgm -e "SHUTDOWN"
Connected to Management Server at: 192.168.56.101:1186
4 NDB Cluster node(s) have shutdown.
Disconnecting to allow management server to shutdown.
```

As usual, the restart begins with the management nodes. These can be started with the `--reload` flag even though the data nodes will go through an initial system restart:

```
shell$ sudo -u mysql ndb_mgmd --config-file=/etc/config.ini \
            --config-dir=/cluster/config --ndb-nodeid=49 --reload
MySQL Cluster Management Server mysql-5.7.16 ndb-7.5.4

shell$ sudo -u mysql ndb_mgmd --config-file=/etc/config.ini \
            --config-dir=/cluster/config --ndb-nodeid=50 --reload
MySQL Cluster Management Server mysql-5.7.16 ndb-7.5.4
```

When the management nodes have started, it is time to start the data nodes. This is done using the `--initial` option. If there are any logfile group files and tablespace files, it is fine to leave those as they can be reused. To start the two data nodes:

```
shell$ sudo -u mysql ndbmtd --ndb-nodeid=1 –initial

shell$ sudo -u mysql ndbmtd --ndb-nodeid=2 –initial
```

Finally, restart the API/SQL nodes.

■ **Note**   The single user and read only mode enabled before the restart does not persist after the restart. If the status must persist after the restart, enable single user mode after restarting the management nodes, and add the super read only mode to the SQL node's configuration file.

To restore the backup, use the mysqldump backup of the schema to restore the table definitions. That ensures that the tables are created using the new default number of partitions. If necessary, first create the database. This will in general not be required unless the data directory of the SQL node was also re-initialized, so the IF NOT EXISTS added to the CREATE SCHEMA statement and the sql_notes session variable is disabled to avoid false errors and warnings. (Technically, with IF NOT EXISTS, a note will be created if the schema exists, not a warning. However, the note is shown through the warnings mechanism.) Then restore the table definitions:

```
mysql> SET SESSION sql_notes = OFF;
Query OK, 0 rows affected (0.00 sec)

mysql> CREATE SCHEMA IF NOT EXISTS world;
Query OK, 1 row affected (0.05 sec)

mysql> SET SESSION sql_notes = ON;
Query OK, 0 rows affected (0.00 sec)

mysql> use world;
Database changed
mysql> SOURCE backup_world_schemaonly.sql
Query OK, 0 rows affected (0.00 sec)
```

You must remove any foreign keys; this does not affect the data integrity and the foreign keys are restored when rebuilding the indexes at the end of the restore.

Restore the data using the ndb_restore utility. This can be done in parallel for all the data nodes:

```
shell$ ndb_restore --ndb-connectstring=192.168.56.101,192.168.56.102 \
                   --backupid=1 --backup-path=/cluster/BACKUP/BACKUP-1 \
                   --restore-data --disable-indexes --nodeid=1

shell$ ndb_restore --ndb-connectstring=192.168.56.101,192.168.56.102 \
                   --backupid=1 --backup-path=/cluster/BACKUP/BACKUP-1 \
                   --restore-data --disable-indexes --nodeid=2
```

The --disable-indexes option used with ndb_restore disables the indexes, so when all data has been restored, the indexes must be rebuilt. This is done with a single command and only mentioning one node ID:

```
shell$ ndb_restore --backupid=1 --backup-path=/cluster/BACKUP/BACKUP-1 \
                   --rebuild-indexes --nodeid=1
```

For more information about restoring backups, see Chapter 8.

At this point, the cluster is back ready for use. The restored tables will have the data using the four *LDM* threads for the partitions.

Summary

This chapter covered the processes for starting, stopping, and restarting the nodes in MySQL NDB Cluster. Restarts are important, as the rolling restarts allow the database administrator to make changes to the cluster without causing downtime. These changes include, for example, configuration changes and adding more nodes. You also learned how restarts can be monitored.

The second half of the chapter was dedicated to example use cases where restarts play a central role. The examples started with a simple configuration change to one of the options for the data nodes, then went through adding management, data, and API/SQL nodes. The two final examples required an initial restart for one or all of the data nodes.

One example of using a rolling restart that has not been included in this chapter is an upgrade. Performing upgrades is a large enough topic of its own to cover a whole chapter—and this is exactly the topic of the next chapter.

■ ■ ■

Upgrades and Downgrades

In many database deployments, upgrades and downgrades are painpoints, as they require an outage. For this reason, the ability to perform online upgrades and downgrades is one of the important features of MySQL NDB Cluster. Online upgrades and downgrades are supported both for patch release changes (for example 7.5.4 to 7.5.5) as well as for major version changes (for example 7.4.13 to 7.5.4). From a technical perspective, there is little difference between an upgrade and a downgrade, so for the most part these can be treated the same.

The support for online upgrades also makes it more feasible to stay up to date with the latest releases. Having the latest release installed also means having all the latest bug fixes, which increases the stability of the cluster.

■ **Tip**   In most cases, it is recommended to use the latest patch release for a given MySQL NDB Cluster. This will ensure that all the available bug fixes—including for security bugs—have been applied.

This chapter discusses upgrades and downgrades in detail, including the considerations of when to upgrade and how to do it.

Upgrades

An upgrade is the process of replacing the current binaries of the MySQL NDB Cluster installation with new binaries of a more recent version. Upgrades can be divided into two main types: *patch release upgrades* and *major version upgrades*. These two upgrade types and upgrade considerations are discussed in the following sections. The actual steps required for an upgrade are covered later in this chapter in the section "Performing Upgrades and Downgrades".

Upgrade Types

MySQL version numbers have three components: x.y.z. For example, 7.5.4. The x-component of the MySQL NDB Cluster version numbers have not changed in several years, so for the discussion in this chapter, it is assumed only the y- and z-components change. This leaves two upgrade types:

- **Patch release upgrades:** This is an upgrade where only the z-component changes.

- **Major version upgrades:** This is an upgrade where the y-component changes.

© Jesper Wisborg Krogh and Mikiya Okuno 2017
J. W. Krogh and M. Okuno, *Pro MySQL NDB Cluster*, https://doi.org/10.1007/978-1-4842-2982-8_11

A patch release upgrade will usually only include bug fixes, although there can occasionally be new features included. This means that, in general, patch release upgrades cause only a few problems. It is of course still important to test and read the release notes before upgrading the production system.

A major release upgrade, on the other hand, includes significant new features or changes to existing features. Examples of some of the major changes introduced in the latest major versions of MySQL NDB Cluster are:

- Version 7.3: Foreign keys and the MySQL Server version (for the SQL nodes) was upgraded to version 5.6.

- Version 7.4: Rework of restarts and writing of local checkpoints and backups.

- Version 7.5: Partition balancing, read from backup replicas, and the MySQL Server version was upgraded to version 5.7.

These changes are just examples to illustrate the scope of the changes that can be expected in major release upgrades. Because there are significant changes to the data nodes and in some cases to the SQL nodes, it is important to be thorough when evaluating the upgrade and during the test phase. Another consideration that is particularly important for major release upgrades is compatibility between the old and new release.

Since the upgrades can be performed online, there will be a period where there will be nodes still using the old version while other nodes have been upgraded to the new version. This means you must be careful not to start using new features until the upgrade is complete. In some cases, it is up to the DBA and database developers to ensure that the new features are not used, before the whole cluster is available. An example of this is the introduction of foreign keys in version 7.3.

In other cases, there is a configuration option available, such as the `create_old_temporals` option for SQL nodes in 7.3.10, 7.4.7, and later (removed again in 7.5). The `create_old_temporals` option ensured that columns using temporal data types such as `TIMESTAMP` were created using the format from MySQL Server 5.5 (used in MySQL NDB Cluster 7.2). Considering backward compatibility is not restricted to the duration of the upgrade; if downgrades are also required, it is important to not make any changes that prevent a downgrade until it is known that it will not be required.

Upgrade Considerations

There are primarily two reasons for upgrading: to get bug fixes and new features. The motivation differs for each upgrade, and there is not a fixed rule that can be applied across all systems to decide when an upgrade is required. Some of the considerations to decide whether the benefits of an upgrade outweigh the cost are:

- In general, for each patch release within a major version, it becomes more stable due to the bug fixes.

- New monitoring and debugging information (typically through the `ndbinfo` schema—see Chapter 16) is added over time, both in patch releases and major release upgrades.

- The more often upgrades are performed, the fewer changes in each upgrade and thus the less chance of having to learn to adjust/configure new features.

- Each upgrade requires testing, which may favor less frequent upgrades.

- Despite extensive regression testing for each patch release, there is always a potential for regressions. This can, in some cases, favor working around a known bug rather than chasing all the latest bug fixes.

- When a new major version is released, introduction into production environments will always turn up bugs that have slipped through the testing performed during development. This can favor waiting a little before upgrading to a new major version or doing more frequent patch release upgrades in the time after the upgrade to the new major version.

- The newer the major version is, the more bug fixes it will see. That is, some bugs will not be fixed in older versions. For this reason, it is important not to lag too far behind the latest major version. For example, at the time of writing this book, versions 7.2, 7.3, 7.4, and 7.5 are under active maintenance. In that case for most users, it is recommended to be using version 7.4 or 7.5.

It is also worth noting that during the development period of a new major version, the opportunity is taken to perform refactoring, which helps fixing bugs that otherwise would be hard to fix. Bugs that have a relatively high potential to introduce regressions are also usually fixed during the development phase of a new major version to allow extra time for testing before they are introduced into production systems. This means that sometimes the only way to get a bug fix is to perform a major version upgrade.

On the downside of upgrading, is the requirement to evaluate the upgrade, including extensive testing. In the end, it is necessary for the DBA to consider each system and decide what the right balance of fixing bugs and get new features is compared to the test and preparation requirements.

Downgrades

From a basic point of view, a downgrade is the same as an upgrade except that the version number decreases rather than increases. That said, there are a few additional considerations regarding feature compatibility. As MySQL NDB Cluster supports online upgrades, it is a requirement that no feature be removed between two major versions unless an alternative was provided in the pre-upgrade version. However, new features will in general have been introduced for at least major version upgrades. Once one of the new versions has been used, it will in general not be possible to downgrade online any longer.

As an example, consider a cluster that is currently using MySQL NDB Cluster 7.5.4. Assume a new table is created using the *fully replicated tables* feature described in Chapter 2:

```
mysql> CREATE TABLE t1 (
          id int unsigned NOT NULL,
          val varchar(10) NOT NULL,
          PRIMARY KEY (id)
       ) ENGINE=ndbcluster COMMENT='NDB_TABLE=FULLY_REPLICATED=1';
```

If one attempts to downgrade to version 7.4.13 with this table, the restart will fail when trying to restore the schema:

```
2016-12-08 21:50:51 [MgmtSrvr] ALERT    -- Node 1: Forced node shutdown completed. Occurred
                                            during startphase 5. Caused by error 2355:
                                            'Failure to restore schema(Resource configuration
                                            error). Permanent error, external action needed'.
```

This is expected, and it is the responsibility of the DBA and database developers not to use any new features, until it has been confirmed that a downgrade is not required. If it is necessary to downgrade after incorporating new features, it is usually necessary to restore the data from a backup.

Another factor to consider are the other storage engines for the SQL nodes. Particularly, InnoDB does not generally allow in-place downgrades between major versions of MySQL Server. This means it may be necessary to reinitialize the SQL nodes as part of a downgrade. The "Online Downgrade" case study later in this chapter gives an example.

■ **Caution**   There are usual differences for the privilege tables between major versions of MySQL Server. For this reason, it is in general easier to restore the users and privileges using CREATE USER and GRANT statements than attempting to restore the actual content of the privilege tables.

Performing Upgrades and Downgrades

MySQL NDB Cluster supports two methods for performing an upgrade or downgrade: online or offline. The difference is whether the cluster will be available for the application during the procedure or whether the cluster will be shut down. The advantage of an online upgrade or downgrade is obviously that the impact on the application is less significant. On the other hand, the advantage of an offline upgrade or downgrade is that it will take less time and it is simpler, particularly if you have several nodes on the same host and use RPM for MySQL NDB Cluster 7.4 or earlier or Debian packages. Additionally, in a few rare cases, an online procedure may not be possible due to a bug (at the time of writing, the latest occurrence was for downgrades from version 7.2.14 or later to 7.2.13 and earlier).

■ **Note**   Online upgrades are by far the most commonly used type of upgrade and downgrade procedures. For this reason, offline upgrades and downgrades are more likely to encounter unexpected problems.

Most of the steps to perform an upgrade or downgrade are the same, whether the procedure will be online or offline:

1.   Check the MySQL Reference manual to determine if there are any special considerations for the upgrade or downgrade at *https://dev.mysql.com/doc/ refman/5.7/en/mysql-cluster-upgrade-downgrade.html*. (Use the version selector at the top-right of the page to choose a different version.) This information includes whether an online upgrade or downgrade is possible.

2.   Check the release notes. An important point to remember with MySQL NDB Cluster upgrades is that there are two upgrades taking place: both of MySQL Server (for the SQL nodes) and NDB Cluster. The release notes can be found at *https://dev.mysql.com/doc/* in the upper-right area of the page. The direct links to the MySQL Server 5.7 release notes is *https://dev.mysql.com/doc/ relnotes/mysql/5.7/en/* and for MySQL NDB Cluster 7.5 it is *https://dev.mysql. com/doc/relnotes/mysql-cluster/7.5/en/*. For major version upgrades, it is also recommended to check the "What Is New" sections of the manual—for example *https://dev.mysql.com/doc/refman/5.7/en/mysql-nutshell.html* and *https://dev. mysql.com/doc/refman/5.7/en/mysql-cluster-what-is-new.html* for MySQL NDB Cluster 7.5.

3. Test the upgrade and downgrade. This is a very important step and should be used to ensure that you have the action plan ready both for an upgrade and rolling back the upgrade (downgrading). Without good testing, the potential for problems during the actual upgrade or downgrade is much more likely. The exact testing necessary very much depends on the system, but make sure that both functionality testing and performance testing is done. The functionality testing must, for example, ensure that no warnings and errors occur—this could happen because the application uses deprecated or removed features. The performance testing must include a workload that reflects the production workload; this will ensure that, for example, optimizer changes do not cause a query plan that is worse for the application workload.

4. Perform a backup for the cluster. If the cluster also includes data for other storage engines other than NDBCluster, make sure to back those up as well.

5. Perform the actual upgrade or downgrade. This step is different whether using the online or offline procedure. The two subsections at the end of this section go into the details.

6. Verify whether everything is working as expected after the upgrade or downgrade has been completed.

Steps 1-3 should be done in advance of the time of the upgrade or downgrade, whereas Steps 4-6 constitute the upgrade or downgrade maintenance window itself. Figure 11-1 shows an overview of the procedure to upgrade a cluster for both the online and offline cases. The following two subsections discuss the specific details of the online and offline procedures.

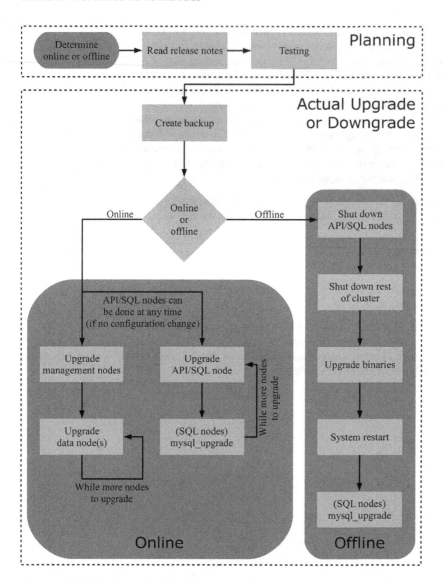

Figure 11-1. *The overview of the online and offline procedures*

■ **Caution**   While upgrading SQL nodes using *distributed privileges* (see Chapter 12) works, downgrades between major versions will not. It is important to disable the distributed privileges while the downgrade is in progress.

Online Upgrades and Downgrades

The steps to perform an online upgrade or downgrade are the same as performing a rolling restart with the addition that the binaries are replaced while the node is shut down:

1. If necessary, update the cluster configuration file (*config.ini*) with the new configuration.

2. Shut down the management nodes. If there is more than one management node, they should all be shut down.

3. Replace the binaries of the management nodes. How this is done is platform dependent and depends on whether an installer (for example, Microsoft Windows Installer .MSI file or an RPM package) or a self-contained file (.zip or .tar download) is used. The step will be similar to the installation discussed in Chapter 5.

4. Start the management nodes. To read the configuration file (*config.ini*), use either the --reload (recommended in most cases) or --initial command-line options.

5. Shut down one or more of the data nodes in such a way that there is at least one data node left online in each node group. Like for a normal rolling restart, it is recommended not to restart more than one data node on each host at a time.

6. Replace the binaries of the data node(s) that were shut down in Step 5.

7. Start the offline data node(s).

8. Repeat Steps 5-7 until all data nodes have been restarted.

9. Shut down one or more of the API/SQL nodes in such a way that at least one node is online at all times.

10. Replace the binaries of the API/SQL node(s) shut down in Step 9.

11. For SQL nodes when downgrading, reinitialize the data directory if necessary.

12. Start the offline API/SQL node(s).

13. For SQL nodes when downgrading, restore a backup of all non-NDBCluster tables if the node was reinitialized.

14. For SQL nodes when upgrading, execute the mysql_upgrade script to upgrade any tables requiring it.

15. Repeat Steps 9-12 until all of the API/SQL nodes have been restarted.

■ **Tip** The API/SQL nodes can be upgraded or downgraded at any stage through the procedure (although if configuration changes are made that affect the API/SQL nodes, the management nodes must be restarted first). This is particularly useful if the API/SQL nodes are co-hosted with other node types, as in that case the API/SQL can be upgraded or downgraded at the same time as the other node on the host.

During the rolling upgrade or downgrade, it is important not to use features that only some of the nodes can handle; particularly do not use features that only the newer version nodes know about.

The case studies section at the end of this chapter include an example of an online upgrade and downgrade.

Offline Upgrades and Downgrades

Offline upgrades and downgrades are simpler than the online procedure. It consists of shutting down the cluster, replacing the binaries, and performing a system restart. The steps are as follows:

1. Shut down all API/SQL nodes.

2. Shut down the management and SQL nodes. The best way to do this is to use the SHUTDOWN command in the management client:

   ```
   mcm> SHUTDOWN
   Connected to Management Server at: 192.168.56.101:1186
   4 NDB Cluster node(s) have shutdown.
   Disconnecting to allow management server to shutdown.
   ```

3. Replace all the binaries.

4. Perform a system restart of the management and data nodes.

5. For SQL nodes when downgrading, reinitialize the data directory if necessary.

6. Start the API/SQL nodes.

7. For SQL nodes when downgrading, restore a backup of all non-NDBCluster tables if the node was reinitialized.

8. For SQL nodes when upgrading, execute the mysql_upgrade script to upgrade any tables requiring it.

There is an example of an offline upgrade at the end of this chapter.

Case Studies

This section goes through four examples of performing upgrades and downgrades:

- Online upgrade from MySQL NDB Cluster 7.4.13 to 7.5.4 using the *generic binaries*. The generic binaries will in this discussion refer to the tarball or Zip file download that does not use any kind of installer.

- Online upgrade from MySQL NDB Cluster 7.4.13 to 7.5.4 using RPMs.

- Online downgrade from MySQL NDB Cluster 7.5.4 to 7.4.13.

- Offline upgrade from MySQL NDB Cluster 7.4.13 to 7.5.4.

All of the examples use the same configuration as in Chapter 10; see Listing 11-1.

Listing 11-1. The Cluster Configuration Used in This Chapter

```
[ndb_mgmd default]
DataDir                   = /cluster/

[ndbd default]
NoOfReplicas              = 2
DataDir                   = /cluster/

[ndbd]
NodeId                    = 1
HostName                  = 192.168.56.103

[ndbd]
NodeId                    = 2
HostName                  = 192.168.56.104

[ndb_mgmd]
NodeId                    = 49
HostName                  = 192.168.56.101

[ndb_mgmd]
NodeId                    = 50
HostName                  = 192.168.56.102

[mysqld]
NodeId                    = 51
HostName                  = 192.168.56.103

[mysqld]
NodeId                    = 52
HostName                  = 192.168.56.104

[api]
NodeId                    = 53
HostName                  = 192.168.56.101

[api]
NodeId                    = 54
HostName                  = 192.168.56.102
```

It is also assumed that all hosts have the ndb_connectstring configured in */etc/my.cnf* so it is not necessary to specify it on the command line:

```
[mysql_cluster]
ndb_connectstring         = 192.168.56.101,192.168.56.102
```

▪ **Tip**　In a real cluster installation, it is recommended to have the NodeId option configured in *my.cnf* or *my.ini* as well.

Online Upgrade Using Generic Binaries

In this example, the cluster starts out using 7.4.13 and will be upgraded online to 7.5.4. It is assumed 7.4.13 is already installed and online:

```
shell$ ndb_mgm -e "SHOW"
Connected to Management Server at: 192.168.56.101:1186
Cluster Configuration
---------------------
[ndbd(NDB)]     2 node(s)
id=1    @192.168.56.103  (mysql-5.6.34 ndb-7.4.13, Nodegroup: 0, *)
id=2    @192.168.56.104  (mysql-5.6.34 ndb-7.4.13, Nodegroup: 0)

[ndb_mgmd(MGM)] 2 node(s)
id=49   @192.168.56.101  (mysql-5.6.34 ndb-7.4.13)
id=50   @192.168.56.102  (mysql-5.6.34 ndb-7.4.13)

[mysqld(API)]   6 node(s)
id=51   @192.168.56.103  (mysql-5.6.34 ndb-7.4.13)
id=52   @192.168.56.104  (mysql-5.6.34 ndb-7.4.13)
id=53 (not connected, accepting connect from 192.168.56.101)
id=54 (not connected, accepting connect from 192.168.56.102)
```

The first step is to unpack the binaries for MySQL NDB Cluster 7.5.4:

```
shell$ cd /opt/cluster
shell$ tar -zxf mysql-cluster-gpl-7.5.4-linux-glibc2.5-x86_64.tar.gz
```

This should be done on all the hosts. To make the paths shorter, rename the directory:

```
shell$ mv mysql-cluster-gpl-7.5.4-linux-glibc2.5-x86_64 7.5.4
```

Before performing the actual upgrade, ensure you have a backup of all of your data.

At this stage, all that is required is a rolling restart where the restart is performed using the new binaries. In this example, the nodes will be upgraded in the following order:

1. Management nodes

2. Data nodes

3. SQL nodes

The first step of the rolling upgrade is to shut down both of the management nodes:

```
shell$ ndb_mgm -e "49 STOP"
Connected to Management Server at: 192.168.56.101:1186
Node 49 has shutdown.
Disconnecting to allow Management Server to shutdown
```

```
shell$ ndb_mgm -e "50 STOP"
Connected to Management Server at: 192.168.56.102:1186
Node 50 has shutdown.
Disconnecting to allow Management Server to shutdown
```

Wait for the two management nodes to shut down, then restart with the upgraded binary:

```
shell$ sudo -u mysql /opt/cluster/7.5.4/bin/ndb_mgmd \
          --config-file=/etc/config.ini --config-dir=/cluster/config \
          --ndb-nodeid=49 --reload
MySQL Cluster Management Server mysql-5.7.16 ndb-7.5.4

shell$ sudo -u mysql /opt/cluster/7.5.4/bin/ndb_mgmd \
          --config-file=/etc/config.ini --config-dir=/cluster/config \
          --ndb-nodeid=50 -reload
MySQL Cluster Management Server mysql-5.7.16 ndb-7.5.4
```

The --reload option is not required if there are no configuration changes, but it does not hurt either as it is a NOOP (no operation) if the configuration has not changed. Checking the new status shows that the management nodes are now using version 7.5.4, whereas the rest of the cluster is still using 7.4.13:

```
shell$ ndb_mgm -e "SHOW"
Connected to Management Server at: 192.168.56.101:1186
Cluster Configuration
---------------------
[ndbd(NDB)]     2 node(s)
id=1    @192.168.56.103  (mysql-5.6.34 ndb-7.4.13, Nodegroup: 0, *)
id=2    @192.168.56.104  (mysql-5.6.34 ndb-7.4.13, Nodegroup: 0)

[ndb_mgmd(MGM)] 2 node(s)
id=49   @192.168.56.101  (mysql-5.7.16 ndb-7.5.4)
id=50   @192.168.56.102  (mysql-5.7.16 ndb-7.5.4)
...
```

Now restart each data node in turn. The RESTART command in the command-line client cannot be used here as it does not replace the binary. So first stop one node:

```
shell$ ndb_mgm -e "1 STOP"
Connected to Management Server at: 192.168.56.101:1186
Node 1 has shutdown.
```

Then start it with the new binary:

```
shell$ sudo -u mysql /opt/cluster/7.5.4/bin/ndbmtd --ndb-nodeid=1
2016-11-26 19:19:10 [ndbd] INFO     -- Angel connected to '192.168.56.101:1186'
2016-11-26 19:19:10 [ndbd] INFO     -- Angel allocated nodeid: 1
```

Wait for the node to complete the restart, at which time the status is:

```
shell$ ndb_mgm -e "SHOW"
Connected to Management Server at: 192.168.56.101:1186
Cluster Configuration
---------------------
[ndbd(NDB)]     2 node(s)
id=1    @192.168.56.103  (mysql-5.7.16 ndb-7.5.4, Nodegroup: 0)
id=2    @192.168.56.104  (mysql-5.6.34 ndb-7.4.13, Nodegroup: 0, *)

[ndb_mgmd(MGM)] 2 node(s)
id=49   @192.168.56.101  (mysql-5.7.16 ndb-7.5.4)
id=50   @192.168.56.102  (mysql-5.7.16 ndb-7.5.4)
...
```

The cluster can still be used by the application despite the two data nodes using different versions, but it is very important to ensure that no new features are used at this stage. Then repeat for the other data node:

```
shell$ ndb_mgm -e "2 STOP"
Connected to Management Server at: 192.168.56.101:1186
Node 2 has shutdown.

shell$ sudo -u mysql /opt/cluster/7.5.4/bin/ndbmtd --ndb-nodeid=2
2016-11-26 19:21:37 [ndbd] INFO     -- Angel connected to '192.168.56.101:1186'
2016-11-26 19:21:37 [ndbd] INFO     -- Angel allocated nodeid: 2
```

At this point, all that remains is to upgrade the two SQL nodes in turn. First:

```
shell$ /opt/cluster/7.4.13/bin/mysqladmin --host=127.0.0.1 shutdown

shell$ /opt/cluster/7.5.4/bin/mysqld &
[1] 9227
```

Make sure to execute mysql_upgrade once the SQL node is back online. This must be done for each SQL node, and it is important to use mysql_upgrade for the new version.

```
shell$ /opt/cluster/7.5.4/bin/mysql_upgrade --host=127.0.0.1
Checking if update is needed.
Checking server version.
Running queries to upgrade MySQL server.
Checking system database.
mysql.columns_priv                           OK
mysql.db                                     OK
...
mysql.user                                   OK
Upgrading the sys schema.
Checking databases.
sys.sys_config                               OK
world.City                                   OK
world.Country                                OK
```

```
world.CountryLanguage                              OK
Upgrade process completed successfully.
Checking if update is needed.
```

As everything returns OK, there is nothing more to do. The first tables checked are the system tables in the mysql schema. These includes the privilege tables, which are the ones that most often require upgrading. The sys schema is new in MySQL Server 5.7 and thus in MySQL NDB Cluster 7.5, so it will be installed by mysql_upgrade. Chapter 15 includes examples of using the sys schema. Finally, all the user tables are checked.

The last step is to upgrade the last SQL node:

```
shell$ /opt/cluster/7.4.13/bin/mysqladmin --host=127.0.0.1 shutdown

shell$ /opt/cluster/7.5.4/bin/mysqld &
[1] 8189

shell$ /opt/cluster/7.5.4/bin/mysql_upgrade --host=127.0.0.1
Checking if update is needed.
Checking server version.
Running queries to upgrade MySQL server.
Checking system database.
mysql.columns_priv                                 OK
mysql.db                                           OK
...
mysql.user                                         OK
Found empty sys database. Installing the sys schema.
Upgrading the sys schema.
The sys schema is already up to date (version 1.5.1).
Checking databases.
sys.sys_config                                     OK
world.City                                         OK
world.Country                                      OK
world.CountryLanguage                              OK
Upgrade process completed successfully.
Checking if update is needed.
```

Note here how the sys database is reported empty. When the sys schema was installed on the first SQL node, the schema was also created on the second SQL node through the automatic schema distribution. However, as none of the sys schema objects are NDBCluster tables, the database will be empty on the subsequent SQL nodes to be upgraded. mysql_upgrade ensures that the sys schema still gets installed.

The final status after the upgrade is:

```
shell$ ndb_mgm -e "SHOW"
Connected to Management Server at: 192.168.56.101:1186
Cluster Configuration
---------------------
[ndbd(NDB)]     2 node(s)
id=1    @192.168.56.103  (mysql-5.7.16 ndb-7.5.4, Nodegroup: 0, *)
id=2    @192.168.56.104  (mysql-5.7.16 ndb-7.5.4, Nodegroup: 0)
```

```
[ndb_mgmd(MGM)] 2 node(s)
id=49   @192.168.56.101  (mysql-5.7.16 ndb-7.5.4)
id=50   @192.168.56.102  (mysql-5.7.16 ndb-7.5.4)

[mysqld(API)]   6 node(s)
id=51   @192.168.56.103  (mysql-5.7.16 ndb-7.5.4)
id=52   @192.168.56.104  (mysql-5.7.16 ndb-7.5.4)
id=53 (not connected, accepting connect from 192.168.56.101)
id=54 (not connected, accepting connect from 192.168.56.102)
```

Upgrade from 7.4 to 7.5 Using RPM

In MySQL NDB Cluster 7.4 and earlier, one difficulty of performing upgrades and downgrades on systems using RPMs to install MySQL NDB Cluster is that all of the binaries used for the cluster nodes are in the same RPM. The *server* RPM includes mysqld, ndb_mgmd, ndbd, and ndbmtd. This makes it harder to upgrade only some of the nodes in the case where one host has several nodes installed. This has changed for version 7.5, where each node type has its own RPM package. The RPMs available in the 7.4.13 RPM bundle are:

```
shell$ ls -1
MySQL-Cluster-client-gpl-7.4.13-1.el7.x86_64.rpm
MySQL-Cluster-devel-gpl-7.4.13-1.el7.x86_64.rpm
MySQL-Cluster-embedded-gpl-7.4.13-1.el7.x86_64.rpm
MySQL-Cluster-server-gpl-7.4.13-1.el7.x86_64.rpm
MySQL-Cluster-shared-compat-gpl-7.4.13-1.el7.x86_64.rpm
MySQL-Cluster-shared-gpl-7.4.13-1.el7.x86_64.rpm
MySQL-Cluster-test-gpl-7.4.13-1.el7.x86_64.rpm
```

Compare this with the RPMs available in the 7.5.4 RPM bundle:

```
shell$ ls -1
mysql-cluster-community-auto-installer-7.5.4-1.el7.x86_64.rpm
mysql-cluster-community-client-7.5.4-1.el7.x86_64.rpm
mysql-cluster-community-common-7.5.4-1.el7.x86_64.rpm
mysql-cluster-community-data-node-7.5.4-1.el7.x86_64.rpm
mysql-cluster-community-devel-7.5.4-1.el7.x86_64.rpm
mysql-cluster-community-embedded-7.5.4-1.el7.x86_64.rpm
mysql-cluster-community-embedded-compat-7.5.4-1.el7.x86_64.rpm
mysql-cluster-community-embedded-devel-7.5.4-1.el7.x86_64.rpm
mysql-cluster-community-java-7.5.4-1.el7.x86_64.rpm
mysql-cluster-community-libs-7.5.4-1.el7.x86_64.rpm
mysql-cluster-community-libs-compat-7.5.4-1.el7.x86_64.rpm
mysql-cluster-community-management-server-7.5.4-1.el7.x86_64.rpm
mysql-cluster-community-memcached-7.5.4-1.el7.x86_64.rpm
mysql-cluster-community-ndbclient-7.5.4-1.el7.x86_64.rpm
mysql-cluster-community-ndbclient-devel-7.5.4-1.el7.x86_64.rpm
mysql-cluster-community-server-7.5.4-1.el7.x86_64.rpm
mysql-cluster-community-test-7.5.4-1.el7.x86_64.rpm
```

This example starts out with the following RPMs installed:

```
shell$ rpm -qa | grep MySQL-Cluster
MySQL-Cluster-client-gpl-7.4.13-1.el7.x86_64
MySQL-Cluster-shared-compat-gpl-7.4.13-1.el7.x86_64
MySQL-Cluster-server-gpl-7.4.13-1.el7.x86_64
MySQL-Cluster-shared-gpl-7.4.13-1.el7.x86_64
MySQL-Cluster-devel-gpl-7.4.13-1.el7.x86_64
```

If a straightforward attempt to upgrade is employed, the upgrade will fail due to the changes to the RPMs:

```
shell$ yum upgrade \
          mysql-cluster-community-auto-installer-7.5.4-1.el7.x86_64.rpm \
          mysql-cluster-community-client-7.5.4-1.el7.x86_64.rpm \
          mysql-cluster-community-common-7.5.4-1.el7.x86_64.rpm \
          mysql-cluster-community-data-node-7.5.4-1.el7.x86_64.rpm \
          mysql-cluster-community-devel-7.5.4-1.el7.x86_64.rpm \
          mysql-cluster-community-java-7.5.4-1.el7.x86_64.rpm \
          mysql-cluster-community-libs-7.5.4-1.el7.x86_64.rpm \
          mysql-cluster-community-libs-compat-7.5.4-1.el7.x86_64.rpm \
          mysql-cluster-community-management-server-7.5.4-1.el7.x86_64.rpm \
          mysql-cluster-community-ndbclient-7.5.4-1.el7.x86_64.rpm \
          mysql-cluster-community-ndbclient-devel-7.5.4-1.el7.x86_64.rpm \
          mysql-cluster-community-server-7.5.4-1.el7.x86_64.rpm
Loaded plugins: langpacks, ulninfo
Examining mysql-cluster-community-auto-installer-7.5.4-1.el7.x86_64.rpm: mysql-cluster-
community-auto-installer-7.5.4-1.el7.x86_64
Package mysql-cluster-community-auto-installer not installed, cannot update it. Run yum
install to install it instead.
...
Package mysql-cluster-community-server not installed, cannot update it. Run yum install to
install it instead.
No packages marked for update
```

Since MySQL NDB Cluster 7.4.13 is already installed, it will not work either to follow the suggestion in the error message to install the RPMs instead of performing an upgrade. Instead it is necessary to first uninstall the old RPMs, which requires the --nodeps option for the rpm command:

```
shell$ rpm -e --nodeps \
          MySQL-Cluster-client-gpl-7.4.13-1.el7.x86_64 \
          MySQL-Cluster-shared-compat-gpl-7.4.13-1.el7.x86_64 \
          MySQL-Cluster-server-gpl-7.4.13-1.el7.x86_64 \
          MySQL-Cluster-shared-gpl-7.4.13-1.el7.x86_64 \
          MySQL-Cluster-devel-gpl-7.4.13-1.el7.x86_64
```

■ **Note** Uninstalling the server RPM renames the */etc/my.cnf* file to */etc/my.cnf.rpmsave*. If you reinstall the server RPM, make sure to restore the old configuration.

Then it is possible to install the new RPMs required for the host. For example, for a data node:

```
shell$ yum localinstall \
        mysql-cluster-community-data-node-7.5.4-1.el7.x86_64.rpm \
        mysql-cluster-community-ndbclient-7.5.4-1.el7.x86_64.rpm
Loaded plugins: langpacks, ulninfo
Examining mysql-cluster-community-data-node-7.5.4-1.el7.x86_64.rpm: mysql-cluster-community-
data-node-7.5.4-1.el7.x86_64
Marking mysql-cluster-community-data-node-7.5.4-1.el7.x86_64.rpm to be installed
Examining mysql-cluster-community-ndbclient-7.5.4-1.el7.x86_64.rpm: mysql-cluster-community-
ndbclient-7.5.4-1.el7.x86_64
Marking mysql-cluster-community-ndbclient-7.5.4-1.el7.x86_64.rpm to be installed
...
  Installing : mysql-cluster-community-data-node-7.5.4-1.el7.x86_64        1/2
  Installing : mysql-cluster-community-ndbclient-7.5.4-1.el7.x86_64        2/2
  Verifying  : mysql-cluster-community-ndbclient-7.5.4-1.el7.x86_64        1/2
  Verifying  : mysql-cluster-community-data-node-7.5.4-1.el7.x86_64        2/2

Installed:
  mysql-cluster-community-data-node.x86_64 0:7.5.4-1.el7
  mysql-cluster-community-ndbclient.x86_64 0:7.5.4-1.el7

Complete!
```

An alternative is to install using the rpm command directly. This has the advantage that it is possible to use the --noscripts option so the RPM scriptlets are not executed. Avoiding executing the scriptlets can particularly be an advantage with version 7.4 and earlier for SQL nodes installed on the same host as a management or data node as it avoids automatic starts of the SQL node.

The rest of the procedure for upgrading using RPMs is the same as for the generic binaries in the previous case study.

One of the issues that can occur with RPMs is that the new version of MySQL NDB Cluster depends on libraries other than the old version. In that case, attempting to install the new RPM packages might produce errors like the following:

```
shell$ yum remove mysql-cluster-community-ndbclient-7.5.4-1.el7.x86_64.rpm
Loaded plugins: langpacks, ulninfo
No Match for argument: mysql-cluster-community-ndbclient-7.5.4-1.el7.x86_64.rpm
No Packages marked for removal
[root@ol7 rpm]# yum localinstall mysql-cluster-community-server-7.5.4-1.el7.x86_64.rpm
Loaded plugins: langpacks, ulninfo
Examining mysql-cluster-community-server-7.5.4-1.el7.x86_64.rpm: mysql-cluster-community-
server-7.5.4-1.el7.x86_64
Marking mysql-cluster-community-server-7.5.4-1.el7.x86_64.rpm to be installed
Resolving Dependencies
--> Running transaction check
---> Package mysql-cluster-community-server.x86_64 0:7.5.4-1.el7 will be installed
--> Processing Dependency: mysql-cluster-community-common(x86-64) = 7.5.4-1.el7 for package:
mysql-cluster-community-server-7.5.4-1.el7.x86_64
--> Processing Dependency: mysql-cluster-community-client(x86-64) >= 5.7.9 for package:
mysql-cluster-community-server-7.5.4-1.el7.x86_64
--> Finished Dependency Resolution
```

Error: Package: mysql-cluster-community-server-7.5.4-1.el7.x86_64 (/mysql-cluster-community-server-7.5.4-1.el7.x86_64)
               Requires: mysql-cluster-community-client(x86-64) >= 5.7.9
Error: Package: mysql-cluster-community-server-7.5.4-1.el7.x86_64 (/mysql-cluster-community-server-7.5.4-1.el7.x86_64)
               Requires: mysql-cluster-community-common(x86-64) = 7.5.4-1.el7
```
You could try using --skip-broken to work around the problem
```

The same issue is reported slightly differently if the rpm command is used instead of yum:

```
shell$ rpm -ivh mysql-cluster-community-server-7.5.4-1.el7.x86_64.rpm
error: Failed dependencies:
        mysql-cluster-community-client(x86-64) >= 5.7.9 is needed by mysql-cluster-
        community-server-7.5.4-1.el7.x86_64
        mysql-cluster-community-common(x86-64) = 7.5.4-1.el7 is needed by mysql-cluster-
        community-server-7.5.4-1.el7.x86_64
```

In this case, it is because the MySQL NDB Cluster server RPM has been split into multiple RPMs to make it possible to choose to a greater degree which binaries to install. In other cases, it may be that a new library or a newer version of an existing library is required. In all cases, read the error message to see which dependency is not fulfilled. Then include the package that provides the missing dependency in the yum or rpm command.

Online Downgrade

The downgrade that will be performed in this example is the opposite of the upgrade perform in the first case study. That is, the cluster will start out using version 7.5.4 and be downgraded to version 7.4.13:

```
shell$ ndb_mgm -e "SHOW"
Connected to Management Server at: 192.168.56.101:1186
Cluster Configuration
---------------------
[ndbd(NDB)]     2 node(s)
id=1    @192.168.56.103  (mysql-5.7.16 ndb-7.5.4, Nodegroup: 0, *)
id=2    @192.168.56.104  (mysql-5.7.16 ndb-7.5.4, Nodegroup: 0)

[ndb_mgmd(MGM)] 2 node(s)
id=49   @192.168.56.101  (mysql-5.7.16 ndb-7.5.4)
id=50   @192.168.56.102  (mysql-5.7.16 ndb-7.5.4)

[mysqld(API)]   6 node(s)
id=51   @192.168.56.103  (mysql-5.7.16 ndb-7.5.4)
id=52   @192.168.56.104  (mysql-5.7.16 ndb-7.5.4)
id=53 (not connected, accepting connect from 192.168.56.101)
id=54 (not connected, accepting connect from 192.168.56.102)
id=55 (not connected, accepting connect from any host)
id=56 (not connected, accepting connect from any host)
```

It is assumed that the 7.4.13 binaries are already ready on all of the hosts.

As usual, it is best practice to start out creating a backup. As it is more likely that complications will be encountered during a downgrade than an upgrade, it is particularly important to ensure backups are available. Since the SQL nodes will be reinitialized as part of the downgrade, it is essential to have a backup of all of the non-NDBCluster data. It is also worth having a list of CREATE DATABASE statements for the schemas containing NDBCluster tables. This list can be created using the query:

```
mysql> SELECT DISTINCT
            CONCAT('CREATE SCHEMA IF NOT EXISTS `', SCHEMA_NAME, '`;')
        FROM information_schema.SCHEMATA
            INNER JOIN information_schema.TABLES ON
                    TABLES.TABLE_SCHEMA = SCHEMATA.SCHEMA_NAME
        WHERE TABLES.ENGINE = 'ndbcluster'
            AND SCHEMATA.SCHEMA_NAME <> 'mysql';
+--------------------------------------------------------------+
| CONCAT('CREATE SCHEMA IF NOT EXISTS `', SCHEMA_NAME, '`;') |
+--------------------------------------------------------------+
| CREATE SCHEMA IF NOT EXISTS `world`;                         |
+--------------------------------------------------------------+
1 row in set (0.02 sec)
```

With the backups in place, the downgrade of the management nodes and data nodes follow the same steps as for an upgrade. First shut down both management nodes, then restart them using the 7.4.13 binaries:

```
shell$ ndb_mgm -e "49 STOP"
Connected to Management Server at: 192.168.56.101:1186
Node 49 has shutdown.
Disconnecting to allow Management Server to shutdown

shell$ ndb_mgm -e "50 STOP"
Connected to Management Server at: 192.168.56.102:1186
Node 50 has shutdown.
Disconnecting to allow Management Server to shutdown
```

On the host with the management node with NodeId = 49:

```
shell$ sudo -u mysql /opt/cluster/7.4.13/bin/ndb_mgmd \
            --config-file=/etc/config.ini --config-dir=/cluster/config \
            --ndb-nodeid=49 -reload
```

And similar for NodeId = 50:

```
shell$ sudo -u mysql /opt/cluster/7.4.13/bin/ndb_mgmd \
            --config-file=/etc/config.ini --config-dir=/cluster/config \
            --ndb-nodeid=50 -reload
```

With the management nodes downgraded, move on to the data nodes. First downgrade the data node with NodeId = 1:

```
shell$ ndb_mgm -e "1 STOP"
Connected to Management Server at: 192.168.56.101:1186
Node 1 has shutdown.
```

```
shell$ sudo -u mysql /opt/cluster/7.4.13/bin/ndbmtd --ndb-nodeid=1
2016-12-17 18:21:32 [ndbd] INFO     -- Angel connected to '192.168.56.101:1186'
2016-12-17 18:21:32 [ndbd] INFO     -- Angel allocated nodeid: 1
```

And for NodeId = 2:

```
shell$ ndb_mgm -e "2 STOP"
Connected to Management Server at: 192.168.56.101:1186
Node 2 has shutdown.

shell$ sudo -u mysql /opt/cluster/7.4.13/bin/ndbmtd --ndb-nodeid=2
2016-12-17 18:55:42 [ndbd] INFO     -- Angel connected to '192.168.56.101:1186'
2016-12-17 18:55:42 [ndbd] INFO     -- Angel allocated nodeid: 2
```

The final part of the downgrade is the SQL nodes, which are also the most difficult. MySQL NDB Cluster 7.5.4 will include some InnoDB tables, as MySQL Server 5.7 (which is used for NDB Cluster 7.5) requires those. InnoDB between MySQL Server 5.7 and MySQL Server 5.6 (used for NDB Cluster 7.4) are not compatible. While MySQL knows how to handle this for an upgrade, there is no support for a downgrade of InnoDB. For this reason, the SQL nodes must be reinitialized.

To downgrade the first SQL node, first shut it down:

```
shell$ /opt/cluster/7.5.4/bin/mysqladmin --host=127.0.0.1 shutdown
```

To reinitialize the SQL node, first delete all the content in the data directory as well as any InnoDB (or files for other storage engines) located outside the data directory. For example, if datadir = /var/lib/mysql and all files are stored inside this directory, the reinitialization can be done as follows:

```
shell$ rm -rf /var/lib/mysql
shell$ mkdir /var/lib/mysql
shell$ chown mysql:mysql /var/lib/mysql
shell$ /opt/cluster/7.4.13/scripts/mysql_install_db \
        --basedir=/opt/cluster/7.4.13 --datadir=/var/lib/mysql \
        --user=mysql
Installing MySQL system tables...
...
```

It is then possible to start the node again:

```
shell$ /opt/cluster/7.4.13/bin/mysqld &
```

Restore the non-NDBCluster data for the SQL node—including setting up the privileges again. Finally repeat for the other SQL node.

Offline Upgrade

The fourth and last example will be an offline upgrade. Like the previous upgrade examples, it will be from version 7.4.13 to 7.5.4. At the start of the example, MySQL NDB Cluster 7.4.13 is installed and online:

```
shell$ ndb_mgm -e "SHOW"
Connected to Management Server at: 192.168.56.101:1186
Cluster Configuration
---------------------
[ndbd(NDB)]     2 node(s)
id=1    @192.168.56.103  (mysql-5.6.34 ndb-7.4.13, Nodegroup: 0, *)
id=2    @192.168.56.104  (mysql-5.6.34 ndb-7.4.13, Nodegroup: 0)

[ndb_mgmd(MGM)] 2 node(s)
id=49   @192.168.56.101  (mysql-5.6.34 ndb-7.4.13)
id=50   @192.168.56.102  (mysql-5.6.34 ndb-7.4.13)

[mysqld(API)]   6 node(s)
id=51   @192.168.56.103  (mysql-5.6.34 ndb-7.4.13)
id=52   @192.168.56.104  (mysql-5.6.34 ndb-7.4.13)
id=53 (not connected, accepting connect from 192.168.56.101)
id=54 (not connected, accepting connect from 192.168.56.102)
```

As usual start out creating a backup. Then as the first step of the shutdown, stop the SQL nodes. The exact method of shutting down the SQL nodes depends on the platform and which binaries are used. Once the SQL nodes are offline, shut down the management and data nodes using the SHUTDOWN command in the management client:

```
shell$ ndb_mgm -e "SHUTDOWN"
Connected to Management Server at: 192.168.56.101:1186
4 NDB Cluster node(s) have shutdown.
Disconnecting to allow management server to shutdown.
```

Wait for the shutdown to complete, then replace all the binaries and restart the cluster using the upgraded binaries. First start the management nodes:

```
shell$ sudo -u mysql ndb_mgmd --config-file=/etc/config.ini \
            --config-dir=/cluster/config --ndb-nodeid=49 –reload
MySQL Cluster Management Server mysql-5.7.16 ndb-7.5.4

shell$ sudo -u mysql ndb_mgmd --config-file=/etc/config.ini \
            --config-dir=/cluster/config --ndb-nodeid=50 --reload
MySQL Cluster Management Server mysql-5.7.16 ndb-7.5.4
```

The next step is to start the data nodes. Do this with both data nodes in parallel to reduce the time the restart takes:

```
shell$ sudo -u mysql ndbmtd --ndb-nodeid=1
2016-12-17 20:13:25 [ndbd] INFO     -- Angel connected to '192.168.56.101:1186'
2016-12-17 20:13:25 [ndbd] INFO     -- Angel allocated nodeid: 1
```

And for the other data node:

```
shell$ sudo -u mysql ndbmtd --ndb-nodeid=2
2016-12-17 20:13:35 [ndbd] INFO     -- Angel connected to '192.168.56.101:1186'
2016-12-17 20:13:35 [ndbd] INFO     -- Angel allocated nodeid: 2
```

When the data nodes have completed their restart, start the SQL nodes one by one as required by your platform. After the start of each SQL node, make sure to execute mysql_upgrade to check and upgrade the tables:

```
shell$ mysql_upgrade --host=127.0.0.1
Checking if update is needed.
Checking server version.
Running queries to upgrade MySQL server.
...
Upgrade process completed successfully.
Checking if update is needed.
```

Summary

Upgrades and downgrades are at the best of times non-trivial undertakings and if a change of major version is also included, there can be a significant amount of work involved. In some environments, an upgrade is prepared over a period of several months. MySQL NDB Cluster provides some relief as the upgrade—and a possible downgrade—can be performed online.

This chapter discussed the upgrade and downgrade steps for the online and offline procedures. Additionally, four case studies of various upgrade and downgrade scenarios were provided.

The next chapter discusses security considerations in MySQL NDB Cluster.

CHAPTER 12

Security Considerations

Back in the early days of the Internet, not a lot of thought was given to the security of the software installed around the world. Network connections were not encrypted, so the network traffic, including passwords, could be seen in plain text (remember telnet, anyone?). Even today, it is common for software or hardware devices to be delivered with standard default passwords or no password on the administration account. That level of security does not meet today's standards. This chapter discusses security from a MySQL NDB Cluster perspective. Several of the issues and solutions are by no means unique to MySQL NDB Cluster; others are very specific.

Some of the topics discussed equally belong in Chapters 3, 4, and 5 (the phases where the cluster is initially planned and set up). However, it would be wrong to think of security—including the security of the network configuration—as a one-and-done task. It should be part of the initial design and the daily tasks to evaluate and maintain the security of the cluster.

Note This chapter focuses on the software side. The physical security of the hardware is also important, as well as the risk posed by disgruntled or dishonest employees. It does very little to secure your servers and leave your server room door unlocked for anyone to walk in. Likewise, you do not want an employee who has access to your data as part of their daily work to sell the data to the highest bidder.

Network Security

The various nodes in a cluster usually communicate with each other through a TCP/IP network. As low latencies and high throughput are of great importance to NDB Cluster, some compromises have been made that require careful consideration when setting up the network, preferably using a dedicated network for communication between the cluster nodes. To add minimal overhead on network traffic, the internode communication is performed in clear text (it is non-encrypted). Additionally, there is no authentication when a node joins the cluster. In short, this means that a client that is able to connect to the data nodes will also be able to retrieve the data stored in the data nodes. Thus, it is paramount to have security in mind when configuring the network.

To illustrate how the data is visible in clear text in the network traffic, the data passing through the network was captured while inserting a row of data:

```
mysql> INSERT INTO employee (EmployeeID, FirstName, Surname, IsManager)
       VALUES (101, 'Jane', 'Doe', 'Yes');
Query OK, 1 row affected (0.00 sec)
```

The resulting file with the network capture can retrieve the data (only a single network packet displayed):

```
shell$ xxd   /tmp/insert.dump
0000000: 2420 0040 3c01 1008 f702 f704 7c08 6d00   $ .@<.......|.m.
0000010: 0400 0000 0000 0000 5ba1 9712 00c4 50a8   ........[.....P.
0000020: 0200 f500 1400 0100 0100 0000 e314 0000   ...............
0000030: 0033 8000 0000 0000 0000 0000 3300 0880   .3..........3...
0000040: 4400 0000 0816 0000 0000 0000 0000 0000   D...............
0000050: 0100 0000 0900 0000 6500 0000 0400 0000   ........e.......
0000060: 6500 0000 0500 0100 044a 616e 6500 0000   e........Jane...
0000070: 0400 0200 0344 6f65 0100 0300 0200 0000   .....Doe........
```

The last two lines are those of most interest for this example. Notice how Jane Doe can be read from the ASCII output on the right side. The other values in the row are also visible, but not quite as easy to see for a human. For example, the EmployeeId is 101, which in hexadecimal is 65, which is the first byte in the second-to-last line. So, while the packet format is efficient (and relatively easy to debug), the task from a security point of view is to prevent unauthorized users from listening in on the traffic.

The simplest and most effective way to protect the cluster from unauthorized access is to have two network levels: an internal one between the MySQL NDB Cluster nodes and an external one to access the SQL nodes or the application. This has the additional advantage that the internal network can be dedicated to the communication between the cluster nodes, which can improve the stability. Remember that MySQL NDB Cluster is a fail-early system, so network congestion can be interpreted as a network failure, making the cluster shut down one or more nodes.

Figure 12-1 illustrates how a cluster with two SQL nodes, two data nodes, and two management nodes is connected through an internal network, and the SQL nodes can be reached from the outside through the firewall. There are other options for setting up the network, but in order to ensure a secure setup, they should all use the same principle of having the insecure communication completely physically separate from the network that is external to the cluster.

■ **Caution**   If the SQL nodes are installed on the same host as management nodes or data nodes, make sure that connections are only allowed to the SQL nodes.

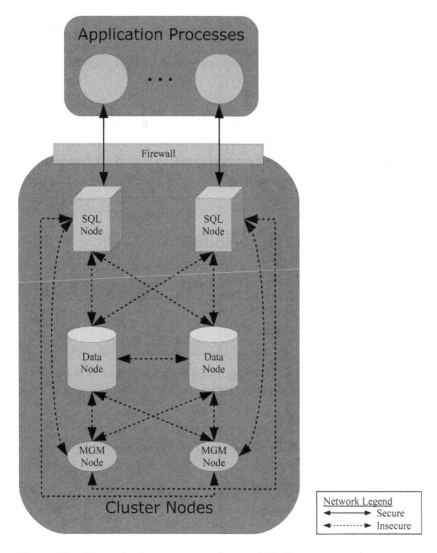

Figure 12-1. *Example of a secure network setup for a cluster*

Updates

An important part of keeping the cluster secure is to keep it updated. This does not only apply to MySQL NDB Cluster, but also to the operating system, the firmware of the network devices, etc. The whole stack should be kept up to date to ensure that not only are all of the user-level bugs fixed, but also any security bugs are fixed.

Different software vendors treat security bugs in different ways. This means you need to verify the policy of each vendor related to your cluster installation, including the infrastructure part. It is recommended that you document the policies and keep them in a central place together with all relevant references, so it is easy to look up the details. In some cases, there may also be scheduled releases of information about security bug fixes that should be incorporated into the maintenance schedule of the cluster.

375

Oracle Corporation, the vendor for MySQL NDB Cluster, has a policy of making quarterly updates for the security fixes made in Oracle products. These updates are called Critical Patch Updates (CPU), and they are released in January, April, July, and October on the Tuesday closest to the 17th of the month. The details about the release schedule and references to the individual releases can be found at *https://www.oracle.com/technetwork/topics/security/alerts-086861.html*.

■ **Caution** It can sometimes be acceptable to skip updates for normal bug fixes if the bug does not affect the application or if there is a workaround. However, be careful ignoring patches for security bugs. The information available to determine whether a system is affected by a given security bug may be minimal. So, in general, the safest approach is always to ensure all security patches are applied.

Accounts and Privileges in the SQL Nodes

The main ongoing security-related work other than keeping the system up to date with critical bug fixes is the user management. The SQL nodes come with the same built-in privilege system as MySQL Server with the addition that there is support for distributing the privileges. That is, storing them in NDBCluster tables instead of the usual MyISAM tables. Using distributed privileges means all SQL nodes have the same users and privileges defined.

■ **Note** MySQL Server 8.0 changes the privilege tables to use the InnoDB storage engine for local stored privileges. However, at the time of writing there is no MySQL NDB Cluster version available—even as a preview—that is affected by that change.

There are several aspects for the database developer and administrator to keep in mind. Some of these are:

- Ensure users are given the minimal privileges required.

- Remove privileges that are no longer needed.

- Remove users no longer in use.

- Keep the privileges in sync between the SQL nodes.

- Document and review the privileges on a regular basis.

The remainder of this section goes through these topics, except for distributed privileges, which is a large topic on its own and is discussed in its own section later in the chapter.

■ **Note** It is important that the database developer and administrator work together to ensure that the users and their privileges are set up correctly.

Accounts and Password Management

The job of managing users may seem trivial. After all, it is easy to create new users when they are required. However, there are a couple of pitfalls to be aware of with respect to keeping the system secure. Creating and maintaining users in a secure way is covered in more detail in the following discussion.

■ **Note**   There is no difference between managing users, passwords, and privileges for an SQL node in MySQL NDB Cluster and in MySQL Server. However, the topic is very important so an overview is provided. You can study this topic in more detail in the MySQL Reference Manual: *https://dev.mysql.com/doc/refman/5.7/en/privilege-system.html* and *https://dev.mysql.com/doc/refman/5.7/en/account-management-sql.html*.

MySQL supports several statements to manage users, passwords, and privileges as well as statements to view user and privilege information. The statements available as of MySQL NDB Cluster 7.5 are summarized in Table 12-1. If the statement is not supported in all versions of MySQL NDB Cluster 7.2 or later, the *Versions* column displays which versions support the statement.

Table 12-1. *Statements to Manage Users, Passwords, and Privileges*

Statement	Versions	Description
ALTER USER	7.3+	Modifies an existing user account. In versions 7.3 and 7.4, it is limited to expiring the password for the user. In version 7.5, it supports all options that can be set by CREATE USER.
CREATE USER		Creates a new user account. In version 7.4 and earlier, this is limited to creating the user and specifying the password and authentication plugin. In MySQL NDB Cluster 7.5, all account properties can be set.
DROP USER		Deletes an existing user.
GRANT		Grants privileges to a user. It can also be used to create a new user, change the password, set authentication options, and set resource options. In version 7.5 it is recommended only to use it for granting privileges. In version 7.4 and earlier, GRANT is required for most of these tasks. It is recommended never to use GRANT to create users; use CREATE USER instead.
RENAME USER		Renames a user.
REVOKE		Revokes privileges from a user.
SET PASSWORD		Changes the password for a user. In version 7.5, the new password is expected in plain text, whereas in version 7.4 and earlier a hashed password is expected.
SHOW CREATE USER	7.5+	Displays the details of a given user account, including the password hash, authentication options, etc.
SHOW GRANTS		Displays the privileges granted to a user account. In version 7.4 and earlier, it also includes the information that SHOW CREATE USER returns in version 7.5.

A new user can be created using the CREATE USER or GRANT statement. In MySQL NDB Cluster 7.5, it is preferable to use CREATE USER as it has the full functionality required to set up the user and specify not only the password, but also SSL/TLS requirements, resource limitations, passwords, and account lock options. The ALTER USER statement can be used to modify an existing user account. The features supported by CREATE USER and ALTER USER in older MySQL NDB Cluster versions are considerably more limited, and it is necessary to use the GRANT statement for anything other than creating the user, setting the initial password, or expiring a password for an existing user.

Listing 12-1 provides an example of a series of account management statements in MySQL NDB Cluster 7.5 for a user through the user's lifetime. The steps will typically not be executed all at once, but rather over a period of time. The statements are a good starting point for discussing some best practices regarding user accounts and how they are set up. The MySQL privilege system is discussed after the example.

Listing 12-1. Examples of Managing a User Account

```
mysql> CREATE USER 'appadmin'@'192.168.56.101' IDENTIFIED WITH sha256_password BY
'cxon9Fr*egAj$2P!' REQUIRE SSL PASSWORD EXPIRE;
Query OK, 0 rows affected (0.37 sec)

mysql> GRANT SELECT ON appdb.* TO 'appadmin'@'192.168.56.101';
Query OK, 0 rows affected (0.14 sec)

mysql> GRANT ALL PRIVILEGES ON 'appdb_common'.* TO 'appadmin'@'192.168.56.101';
Query OK, 0 rows affected (0.19 sec)

mysql> SHOW GRANTS FOR 'appadmin'@'192.168.56.101';
+-------------------------------------------------------------------------+
| Grants for appadmin@192.168.56.101                                      |
+-------------------------------------------------------------------------+
| GRANT USAGE ON *.* TO 'appadmin'@'192.168.56.101'                       |
| GRANT SELECT ON 'appdb'.* TO 'appadmin'@'192.168.56.101'                |
| GRANT ALL PRIVILEGES ON 'appdb_common'.* TO 'appadmin'@'192.168.56.101' |
+-------------------------------------------------------------------------+
3 rows in set (0.01 sec)

mysql> SHOW CREATE USER 'appadmin'@'192.168.56.101'\G
*************************** 1. row ***************************
CREATE USER for appadmin@192.168.56.101: CREATE USER 'appadmin'@'192.168.56.101' IDENTIFIED
WITH 'sha256_password' AS '$5$L<aLh)CU/LO:fx$ue6Lyk8tkqljAnJ..rjQrMHzWLBHjIrPxUVpgWQcGpO'
REQUIRE SSL PASSWORD EXPIRE ACCOUNT UNLOCK
1 row in set (0.01 sec)

mysql> REVOKE SELECT ON 'appdb_common'.* FROM 'appadmin'@'192.168.56.101';
Query OK, 0 rows affected (0.11 sec)

mysql> SET PASSWORD FOR 'appadmin'@'192.168.56.101' = 'rabFun[Fryn2#8D%s';
Query OK, 0 rows affected (0.26 sec)

mysql> ALTER USER 'appadmin'@'192.168.56.101' IDENTIFIED WITH sha256_password BY
'rabFun[Fryn2#8D%s' PASSWORD EXPIRE;
Query OK, 0 rows affected (0.20 sec)
```

```
mysql> ALTER USER 'appadmin'@'192.168.56.101' ACCOUNT LOCK;
Query OK, 0 rows affected (0.18 sec)

mysql> DROP USER 'appadmin'@'192.168.56.101';
Query OK, 0 rows affected (0.13 sec)
```

Note that when the user is created, there are several parts to the statement:

- **The account name:** The account name consists of a username and a hostname. User and hostnames are discussed in more detail in "The Access Control and Privilege System" section.

- **The authentication plugin:** MySQL supports several authentication plugins. The IDENTIFIED WITH clause specifies which one.

- **The password:** This is also known as the *authentication string*. Choose a strong password that cannot easily be guessed! The password is specified after the IDENTIFIED BY clause; when the authentication plugin is also specified, those two are combined as IDENTIFIED WITH <plugin name> BY <password>. The password must be quoted.

- **SSL/TLS options:** It is recommended to ensure all communication between the SQL node and clients/applications is encrypted. MySQL supports several options to specify the requirements.

- **Initial password is expired:** For new accounts that are meant to be used by interactive users—like a database administrator—it is recommended to expire the password when the account is created.

For the authentication plugin, the sha256_password plugin provides the most secure hash supported and this the recommended unless an external authentication is used. External authentication against for example LDAP servers is beyond the scope of this book. If this topic is of interest, *https://dev.mysql.com/doc/refman/5.7/en/pluggable-authentication.html* and the references therein provide a good starting point.

The simplest SSL/TLS option is REQUIRE SSL and it simply means that the connection must be encrypted, but there are no limitations on the encryption method itself or on which certificate is used by the client. There are several additional clauses that can be used to restrict the cipher, issuer, and subject of the SSL/TLS certificate used by the client for the connection.

If MySQL NDB Cluster 7.5 is compiled to use OpenSSL (this is the case for the commercial builds—MySQL Cluster Carrier Grade Edition—but not the Community Edition), MySQL is automatically set up to have self-signed certificates created when initializing the data directory of the SQL node. For extra security, a certificate signed by a trusted authority can be used. This is discussed in more detail in the next section, including an example of generating self-signed certificates using the mysql_ssl_rsa_setup utility that is included with MySQL NDB Cluster 7.5 and later.

When a user is created with an expired password, it forces the user to change the password the first time the account is used. Listing 12-2 illustrates how the user cannot perform any other action until the SET PASSWORD statement has been executed. Another observation from Listing 12-2 is that the connection is created with the option --ssl-mode=REQUIRE. This is the client-side equivalent to the REQUIRE SSL option that the account was created with. Setting the SSL mode to REQUIRE ensures that the connection will be made only if the SQL node can provide an encrypted connection.

Listing 12-2. Connecting the First Time After a User Is Created with PASSWORD EXPIRE

```
shell$ mysql --user=appadmin -password --ssl-mode=REQUIRE
Enter password:
...
mysql> SHOW SCHEMAS;
ERROR 1820 (HY000): You must reset your password using ALTER USER statement before executing
this statement.
mysql> SET PASSWORD = 'Fid.Gourt^Ob9*H3b';
Query OK, O rows affected (0.16 sec)

mysql> SHOW SCHEMAS;
+--------------------+
| Database           |
+--------------------+
| information_schema |
| appdb              |
| appdb_common       |
+--------------------+
3 rows in set (0.01 sec)
```

Continuing with the example in Listing 12-1, it is important to provide the minimal privileges required for the account. The ALL PRIVILEGES privilege can be used to provide all available privileges (except the privilege to use the GRANT statement) at the scope specified, but make sure to use it sparingly. Be aware that granting all privileges at the global (*.*) level will also allow changes to the data on the mysql schema (or any other schema).

The currently assigned privileges can be checked with the SHOW GRANTS statement or by querying the privilege tables in the mysql schema directly. If an account is found to have privileges that are no longer required, they can be revoked using the REVOKE statement. Likewise, it is possible to check the account settings using the SHOW CREATE USER statement.

It is possible for the database administrator to force a change of the password. This can be done by using the SET PASSWORD statement and adding the account to change it for. Changing the password can be combined with expiring the password by using ALTER USER like it was done when the password was first set. ALTER USER in MySQL NDB Cluster 7.5 is a very powerful statement to administrate users, as it can set or change all of the options that are also available for CREATE USER. Options not specified in an ALTER USER statement are left at their existing values.

A useful feature that is new in version 7.5 is the ability to lock an account. This can be used for several purposes, such as temporarily preventing an account from connecting or to create an account dedicated as the definer for stored programs and views. An example of the latter is the mysql.sys@localhost user, which is used for the sys schema. In the example, the ALTER USER 'appadmin'@'192.168.56.101' ACCOUNT LOCK statement is used to lock the 'appadmin'@'192.168.56.101' account while it is for example determined whether it is still needed.

Finally, but not least important, it is best practice to remove users who are no longer needed. Unused accounts still provide access to the system. If it is not possible to determine whether an account is not required or it is merely a rarely used account, one option is initially to lock it.

Regarding this last point about removing accounts that are no longer required as well as revoking privileges that are not necessary, it is also important to document and review accounts and privileges as well as other aspects of security. By regularly auditing the accounts and their privileges, you can be sure that accounts and privileges that are no longer required are removed. Documenting the outcome of the audit will help during the next audit as well.

The example of account management in Listing 12-1 uses several features that are only available in version 7.5. Over the last few MySQL Server versions, Oracle Corporation committed much work in improving the default security of MySQL and in providing better tools for managing security related features. This is particularly evident in account management when upgrading from MySQL Server 5.6 to 5.7 or MySQL NDB Cluster 7.4 to 7.5. This is another example of how keeping the system up to date can provide better security.

SSL/TLS Certificates

In order to enable encrypted connections to access the SQL nodes, it is necessary to use a protocol that handles data encryption and decryption. The technology for secure communication between connections in MySQL is called *TLS (Transport Layer Security)*, although the term *SSL (Secure Socket Layer)* is used for the MySQL options by tradition.

To enable encryption, it is required to have SSL/TLS certificates available. One option is to purchase certificates signed by a trusted third-party *certification authority* (CA). A trusted third-party CA is useful when a server must prove its identity to an unknown user; for example, an Internet bank where the customer must be sure that the web site belongs to the bank where the customer has her account.

When an application connects to an SQL node, it is often sufficient to use a self-signed certificate or a certificate signed by the company's own certification authority. The steps involved in creating a self-signed certificate can seem a little daunting at first; however, MySQL NDB Cluster 7.5 and later includes the command line utility mysql_ssl_rsa_setup, which automates the entire process. The drawback is that the certificates are generic and do not include anything that can validate that the application is connecting to the correct SQL node. Listing 12-3 shows an example of using the mysql_ssl_rsa_setup utility to generate the files required to enable SSL/TLS encryption in MySQL.

Listing 12-3. Creating the SSL/TLS Certificates for the SQL Nodes

```
shell$ mysql_ssl_rsa_setup --datadir=/var/lib/mysql --uid=mysql
Generating a 2048 bit RSA private key
...............+++
.+++
writing new private key to 'ca-key.pem'
-----
Generating a 2048 bit RSA private key
..........................+++
................................+++
writing new private key to 'server-key.pem'
-----
Generating a 2048 bit RSA private key
.............................................................+++
...............+++
writing new private key to 'client-key.pem'
-----
```

■ **Note**   The mysql_ssl_rsa_setup command first creates a private CA certificate. The server certificate generated by mysql_ssl_rsa_setup is then self-signed using that private CA certificate.

In MySQL NDB Cluster 7.5, the SSL/TLS files are automatically discovered by the mysqld process provided they are located in the data directory and the filenames are the same as when created by the mysql_ssl_rsa_setup utility. The generated certificates are not specific to MySQL NDB Cluster 7.5 and can thus also be used with older versions of MySQL; however, in that case, the SQL node must be explicitly configured using the options ssl_ca, ssl_cert, and ssl_key. An example of the configuration found in *my.cnf* is:

```
[mysqld]
ssl_ca   = /var/lib/mysql/ca-cert.pem
ssl_cert = /var/lib/mysql/server-cert.pem
ssl_key  = /var/lib/mysql/server-key.pem
```

This setup will support encryption of all communication between the client/application and the SQL node; however, two issues still exist—knowing who really connects and *man in the middle attacks*.

The first issue is that the SQL node still only relies on the user knowing the correct username and password combination in order to connect from a given host. To solve this issue, it is necessary for the client/application to use its own certificates, which are checked by the SQL node. Recall that an account can be created with restrictions on the SSL/TLS certificates that can be used with the connection.

The second issue is that the client/application does not know whether it really connected to the SQL node specified by the hostname and port when the connection was created. For example, it is possible to have a "man in the middle" situation, whereby a process intercepts the connection and decrypts all the communication before it is forwarded again.

In order to handle these two cases, it is necessary to have the certificates signed by a known certification authority. This does not have to be a third-party commercial provider, but it must be a certificate authority that is trusted by both the cluster and the client/application. For example, the IT department in the company deploying the cluster may be able to sign the certificates.

■ **Note**   If the certificates are created manually, make sure that all of the CA certificates, server certificates, and client certificates are created with a unique common name for each certificate. If any two certificates share the common name, they cannot be used to encrypt the connections.

The Access Control and Privilege System

MySQL uses a four-tiered access control and privilege system. This provides fine-grained control of who can connect, from where, and what the user is allowed to do once connected. The four tiers are as follows:

- **Username:** This is the username that is specified for example with the --user option for MySQL client programs. A user or application needs to know the appropriate username to able to connect. It is recommended to use a username that makes it easy to understand who owns the account. For example, if it is a real person, the username should reflect the name of the person. If it is an application user, choose a username that reflects the application name. That way, it is easier to determine which users can be removed after staff changes or when a new version of the application has been released.

- **Hostname:** The hostname limits from where the user can connect. It is possible to use wildcards in the hostname, but it is important to be careful not to grant access from other hosts than where the user has a need to connect. It is possible to configure the same username to be allowed to connect from different hosts, but since the combination of username and hostname defines the account, the accounts will in general have different privileges. For example, a user may have permission to change the schema when connected from the *localhost*, but is only allowed to select data when connected from a remote host.

- **Password:** The password is used to verify the user's identity. To provide additional strength to the authentication step, the password can be supplemented with requirements from the SSL/TLS certificate used.

- **Privileges:** These are the actions the account is allowed to perform. The privileges are tied to the combination of username and the hostname where the user has connected from. A privilege can be assigned to one of the following scopes: global, schema/database, table/view/procedure/function, or column. The global scope either covers all schemas or indicates a global level privilege. Examples of global level privileges are SHUTDOWN and SUPER.

There are more than 30 privileges to choose from in MySQL NDB Cluster 7.5. Determining the minimal set of privileges to grant to an account can seem like a large task. This makes it tempting to just use the ALL PRIVILEGES synonym which—as the name suggest—grants all known privileges for the specified scope to the account except the WITH GRANT OPTION privilege. Granting all privileges to accounts is a bad idea for several reasons.

When an account has all privileges to the global level or the mysql schema, this also includes access to manipulate other users, grant access (by directly manipulating the grant tables) to the data to new users, etc. Furthermore, it removes a safeguard. For example, if the application user has all privileges and a developer by mistake adds a query that deletes data from a table that the application should not be allowed to delete from, the privilege system can no longer prevent the application from proceeding. A similar issue can occur if the application is susceptible to SQL injection. Another potential threat to have in mind are disgruntled employees. Minimizing the privileges can reduce the amount of damage that can be wrought in those cases.

The SUPER privilege itself is worth a little extra attention. The privilege really covers a group of actions, ranging from being able to configure the replication settings on the slave side to killing queries run by other users.

■ **Note**   While SUPER is a very powerful privilege that should only be given to cluster-wide administration users, it is not the same as all privileges.

There are also a couple of special behaviors related to users with the SUPER privilege. First, the read_only option does not apply. A consequence of this is that the user can make changes, for example, to a replication slave that is meant to be read only. In MySQL NDB Cluster 7.5, a workaround is to use the new super_read_only option instead. Second, when all of the connections configured with max_connections are in use, there is one extra connection reserved for a user with the SUPER privilege, so the database administrator can log in to investigate and resolve the issue. Granting the SUPER privilege to the application user will defeat this functionality.

■ **Tip** MySQL Enterprise Monitor uses persistent connections, which allow it to continue monitoring an SQL node even if all connections have been used. The monitoring capability includes a report that returns the process list, similar to SHOW PROCESSLIST. Other monitoring solutions may provide similar functionalities.

Distributed Privileges

One challenge for a distributed system like MySQL NDB Cluster with several SQL nodes is keeping the accounts and privileges in sync between all of the SQL nodes. Additionally, if a password changes on one node, it is not automatically updated on the other nodes. This can cause subtle failures. The application seems to be working fine, but when the connection is routed to one specific SQL node, it fails.

The answer to this is a feature called *distributed privileges*. As the name suggests, it is a method of telling MySQL that the privileges must be the same on all nodes. In practice, this is implemented by converting the grant tables that store all of the account, password, and privilege information to use the NDBCluster storage engine. This way, the privilege data is stored inside the data nodes and, like other NDBCluster tables, all the connected SQL nodes have the same view of the data.

■ **Caution** Do not convert the grant tables manually, as that may break MySQL. Distributed privileges should only be enabled and disabled using the stored procedures, as described in this section.

To use distributed privileges, it is necessary to import the stored programs that are required to manipulate the grant tables. These stored programs are included as source code in a file named *ndb_dist_priv.sql*. The location of the *ndb_dist_priv.sql* script is in the *share* directory below the MySQL base directory. If MySQL has been installed into a global directory—such as when using the RPM management system—the *ndb_dist_priv.sql* script is in the *mysql* directory below the *share* directory. Examples of the full path to the file are shown in Table 12-2.

Table 12-2. *Examples of the Location of the ndb_dist_priv.sql Script*

Installation Type	basedir	Full Path
Linux - RPM	/usr	/usr/share/mysql/ndb_dist_priv.sql
Linux/UNIX - Tarball	/opt/mysql	/opt/mysql/share/ndb_dist_priv.sql
Windows – Install GUI	C:\Program Files\MySQL\MySQL Cluster 7.5	C:\Program Files\MySQL\MySQL Cluster 7.5\ share\ndb_dist_priv.sql

To install these stored programs, simply source the file with the mysql schema as the default schema using the SOURCE command. Verify that no errors occur and that all of the stored procedures are present at completion. Listing 12-4 shows an example of importing the script and verifying that all procedures have been installed. As stored procedures are not distributed among the SQL nodes, it is necessary to perform these steps on all SQL nodes. Notice how warnings are enabled to ensure any warnings incurred are expanded, so it is possible to inspect them. When the stored programs are created the first time, a number of warnings will occur as the *ndb_dist_priv.sql* script uses DROP PROCEDURE IF EXISTS and DROP FUNCTION IF EXISTS to remove old versions of the stored programs. These warnings can be ignored.

Listing 12-4. Importing the *ndb_dist_priv.sql* Script

```
mysql> use mysql;
Database changed

mysql> warnings
Show warnings enabled.

mysql> SOURCE /usr/share/mysql/ndb_dist_priv.sql
Query OK, 0 rows affected, 1 warning (0.13 sec)

Note (Code 1305): FUNCTION mysql.mysql_cluster_privileges_are_distributed does not exist
Query OK, 0 rows affected, 1 warning (0.15 sec)

Note (Code 1305): PROCEDURE mysql.mysql_cluster_backup_privileges does not exist
Query OK, 0 rows affected, 1 warning (0.10 sec)

Note (Code 1305): PROCEDURE mysql.mysql_cluster_move_grant_tables does not exist
Query OK, 0 rows affected, 1 warning (0.07 sec)

Note (Code 1305): PROCEDURE mysql.mysql_cluster_restore_privileges_from_local does not exist
Query OK, 0 rows affected, 1 warning (0.09 sec)

Note (Code 1305): PROCEDURE mysql.mysql_cluster_restore_privileges does not exist
Query OK, 0 rows affected, 1 warning (0.09 sec)

Note (Code 1305): PROCEDURE mysql.mysql_cluster_restore_local_privileges does not exist
Query OK, 0 rows affected, 1 warning (0.09 sec)

Note (Code 1305): PROCEDURE mysql.mysql_cluster_move_privileges does not exist
Query OK, 0 rows affected (0.14 sec)

Query OK, 0 rows affected (0.12 sec)

Query OK, 0 rows affected (0.11 sec)

Query OK, 0 rows affected (0.07 sec)

Query OK, 0 rows affected (0.07 sec)

Query OK, 0 rows affected (0.13 sec)

Query OK, 0 rows affected (0.10 sec)

mysql> SELECT ROUTINE_NAME, ROUTINE_TYPE
        FROM information_schema.ROUTINES
       WHERE ROUTINE_SCHEMA = 'mysql'
            AND ROUTINE_NAME LIKE 'mysql\_cluster\_%';
```

```
+------------------------------------------------+---------------+
| ROUTINE_NAME                                   | ROUTINE_TYPE  |
+------------------------------------------------+---------------+
| mysql_cluster_backup_privileges                | PROCEDURE     |
| mysql_cluster_move_grant_tables                | PROCEDURE     |
| mysql_cluster_move_privileges                  | PROCEDURE     |
| mysql_cluster_privileges_are_distributed       | FUNCTION      |
| mysql_cluster_restore_local_privileges         | PROCEDURE     |
| mysql_cluster_restore_privileges               | PROCEDURE     |
| mysql_cluster_restore_privileges_from_local    | PROCEDURE     |
+------------------------------------------------+---------------+
7 rows in set (0.22 sec)
```

The installation includes six stored procedures and one stored function. Table 12-3 lists each of these and discusses what they do. For briefness, the mysql_cluster_ prefix that applies to all of the seven stored programs has been removed from the name; for example, the full name of the procedure listed as backup_privileges is mysql_cluster_backup_privileges. All of the stored programs are used without any arguments.

Table 12-3. *The Seven Stored Programs for Use with Distributed Privileges*

Name	Type	Description
backup_privileges	Procedure	Creates MyISAM backup tables of the grant tables, if they do not exist. The backup table names have the _backup suffix added to their original name. Creates NDBCluster backup tables similar to the MyISAM backup tables. The tables have the ndb_ prefix and the _backup suffix. Copies the account and privilege data into the backup tables.
move_grant_tables	Procedure	Enables distributed privileges. Execute FLUSH PRIVILEGES on the SQL nodes not calling this procedure after the procedure has been executed.
move_privileges	Procedure	Combines backup_privileges and move_grant_tables. Execute FLUSH PRIVILEGES on the SQL nodes not calling this procedure after the procedure has been executed.
privileges_are_distributed	Function	Returns 0 or 1 (Boolean), depending on whether the stored procedures are enabled.
restore_local_privileges	Procedure	Deletes the distributed privileges and restores the MyISAM backup. This procedure in turn calls the restore_privileges_from_local procedure.
cluster_restore_privileges	Procedure	If distributed privileges are used, it creates the grant tables using NDBCluster if they do not exist and copies the privileges from the NDBCluster backup tables. If distributed privileges are not used, it calls restore_privileges_from_local.
restore_privileges_from_local	Procedure	Creates the grant tables using MyISAM if they do not exist. Copies the privileges from the MyISAM backup tables. FLUSH PRIVILEGES is required for the restore to take effect.

The examples that demonstrate how the distributed privileges are enabled and disabled use a view to show the backup tables. This view is defined in Listing 12-5 and can be installed in any schema; for the purpose of these examples, it is assumed to be installed in ndbutil. The view returns four columns with information about the grant tables:

- **Grant_Table:** The name of the main grant table.

- **Engine:** The storage engine currently used for the table.

- **MyISAM_Backup:** The name of the MyISAM backup table if it exists.

- **NDBCluster_Backup:** The name of the NDBCLuster backup table if it exists.

Listing 12-5. The ndbcluster_dist_priv_tables View

```
CREATE SCHEMA IF NOT EXISTS ndbutil;
CREATE OR REPLACE
  SQL SECURITY INVOKER
  VIEW ndbutil.ndbcluster_dist_priv_tables
    AS
SELECT g.TABLE_NAME AS Grant_Table, g.ENGINE AS Engine,
       IFNULL(gm.TABLE_NAME, '') AS MyISAM_Backup,
       IFNULL(gn.TABLE_NAME, '') AS NDBCluster_Backup
  FROM information_schema.TABLES g
       LEFT OUTER JOIN information_schema.TABLES gm
               ON gm.TABLE_SCHEMA = 'mysql'
               AND gm.TABLE_NAME = CONCAT(g.TABLE_NAME, '_backup')
       LEFT OUTER JOIN information_schema.TABLES gn
               ON gn.TABLE_SCHEMA = 'mysql'
               AND gn.TABLE_NAME = CONCAT('ndb_', g.TABLE_NAME, '_backup')
 WHERE g.TABLE_SCHEMA = 'mysql'
       AND g.TABLE_NAME IN ('user', 'db', 'tables_priv', 'columns_priv',
                            'procs_priv', 'proxies_priv')
 ORDER BY g.TABLE_NAME;
```

Enabling Distributed Privileges

The steps to enable distributed privileges are straightforward using the mysql_cluster_move_privileges procedure discussed in Table 12-3. Additionally, it is best to create a logical backup of the privileges before converting them. The overall procedure for enabling the distributed privileges is:

1. Create a backup of the grant tables using mysqldump or mysqlpump. This step is not strictly required, but is recommended to ensure there is a backup should it be necessary to restore the original accounts and privileges at some point.

2. On each SQL node, back up the existing grant tables using the mysql_cluster_backup_privileges procedure. It is important to only create the backup on one node at a time.

3. Convert the grant tables to store the accounts and privileges in the data nodes. This step is performed using the mysql_cluster_move_grant_tables procedure. Do only execute this step on one SQL node.

4. Execute FLUSH PRIVILEGES on all other SQL nodes than the one used in Step 3. This will ensure that any differences in the accounts and privileges are applied after the conversion.

■ **Tip** If you get this rather cryptic error:

ERROR 1534 (HY000): Writing one row to the row-based binary log failed

when converting the privileges in Step 3, it is likely due to the Timestamp columns in any of the tables_priv, columns_priv, or procs_priv tables containing a zero date (0000-00-00 00:00:00) while the NO_ZERO_DATE and NO_ZERO_IN_DATE SQL mode is enabled. The workaround is to either disable the SQL modes or update the timestamps to a non-zero value. The issue is most likely to occur if the grant tables have been manipulated directly rather than through the dedicated statements discussed earlier in the chapter.

Listing 12-6 shows an example of performing the first three steps using mysqlpump for the logical backup. The example uses the ndbutil.ndbcluster_dist_priv_tables view that was defined in Listing 12-5. It is worth noticing how the call to the mysql_cluster_move_privileges procedure causes a MyISAM backup of the grant tables to be created.

Listing 12-6. Enabling Distributed Privileges

```
# Create a logical backup
shell$ mysqlpump --user=root --password --users \
                 --exclude-databases=% > users_backup.sql
Enter password:
Dump completed in 4847 milliseconds

-- Check status of the grant tables
mysql> SELECT * FROM ndbutil.ndbcluster_dist_priv_tables;
+--------------+--------+---------------+-------------------+
| Grant_Table  | Engine | MyISAM_Backup | NDBCluster_Backup |
+--------------+--------+---------------+-------------------+
| columns_priv | MyISAM |               |                   |
| db           | MyISAM |               |                   |
| procs_priv   | MyISAM |               |                   |
| proxies_priv | MyISAM |               |                   |
| tables_priv  | MyISAM |               |                   |
| user         | MyISAM |               |                   |
+--------------+--------+---------------+-------------------+
6 rows in set (0.37 sec)

-- On each SQL node create the backup grant tables
mysql> warnings
Show warnings enabled.
mysql> CALL mysql.mysql_cluster_backup_privileges();
Query OK, 1 row affected (2.48 sec)
```

```
mysql> SELECT * FROM ndbutil.ndbcluster_dist_priv_tables;
+--------------+--------+---------------------+-------------------------+
| Grant_Table  | Engine | MyISAM_Backup       | NDBCluster_Backup       |
+--------------+--------+---------------------+-------------------------+
| columns_priv | MyISAM | columns_priv_backup | ndb_columns_priv_backup |
| db           | MyISAM | db_backup           | ndb_db_backup           |
| procs_priv   | MyISAM | procs_priv_backup   | ndb_procs_priv_backup   |
| proxies_priv | MyISAM | proxies_priv_backup | ndb_proxies_priv_backup |
| tables_priv  | MyISAM | tables_priv_backup  | ndb_tables_priv_backup  |
| user         | MyISAM | user_backup         | ndb_user_backup         |
+--------------+--------+---------------------+-------------------------+
6 rows in set (1.34 sec)

-- Convert the grant tables to NDBCluster - execute only on one SQL node
mysql> CALL mysql.mysql_cluster_move_grant_tables();
Query OK, 1 row affected (6.62 sec)

-- On the other SQL Nodes
mysql> FLUSH PRIVILEGES;
Query OK, 0 rows affected (0.21 sec)

mysql> SELECT * FROM ndbutil.ndbcluster_dist_priv_tables;
+--------------+------------+---------------------+-------------------------+
| Grant_Table  | Engine     | MyISAM_Backup       | NDBCluster_Backup       |
+--------------+------------+---------------------+-------------------------+
| columns_priv | ndbcluster | columns_priv_backup | ndb_columns_priv_backup |
| db           | ndbcluster | db_backup           | ndb_db_backup           |
| procs_priv   | ndbcluster | procs_priv_backup   | ndb_procs_priv_backup   |
| proxies_priv | ndbcluster | proxies_priv_backup | ndb_proxies_priv_backup |
| tables_priv  | ndbcluster | tables_priv_backup  | ndb_tables_priv_backup  |
| user         | ndbcluster | user_backup         | ndb_user_backup         |
+--------------+------------+---------------------+-------------------------+
6 rows in set (0.39 sec)

mysql> SELECT mysql.mysql_cluster_privileges_are_distributed();
+-------------------------------------------------+
| mysql.mysql_cluster_privileges_are_distributed() |
+-------------------------------------------------+
|                                               1 |
+-------------------------------------------------+
1 row in set (0.04 sec)
```

Disabling Distributed Privileges

If it is necessary to disable the distributed privileges, the stored procedures in Table 12-3 can be used to convert the grant tables back to the SQL nodes (MyISAM). There may be various reasons for moving back to using grant tables that are local to each SQL node. For example, you may have to convert the privileges back because you are performing a downgrade, or requirements have changed, and it is better not to have identical privileges on all SQL nodes.

The steps to disable distributed privileges are similar to enabling them:

1. Create a logical backup of the accounts and their privileges. The backup can be made with mysqldump or mysqlpump.

2. On each SQL node, update the backups of the grant tables to ensure all the changes to the privileges that have been made while they were distributed are included when restoring the local tables.

3. On one SQL node, execute the mysql_cluster_restore_local_privileges procedure. This drops the grant tables and recreates them from the MyISAM backup.

4. On all other SQL nodes than the one used in Step 3, execute the mysql_cluster_ restore_privileges_from_local procedure. This is required as the local version of the grant tables restored in Step 3 only applies to the SQL node where the step was executed.

5. On all the SQL nodes, execute FLUSH PRIVILEGES.

Listing 12-7 shows an example of disabling the distributed privileges feature.

Listing 12-7. Disabling Distributed Privileges

```
# Create a logical backup
shell$ mysqlpump --user=root --password --users \
              --exclude-databases=% > users_backup.sql
Enter password:
Dump completed in 4847 milliseconds

-- Refresh the backup grant tables - do on all SQL nodes
mysql> warnings
Show warnings enabled.
mysql> CALL mysql.mysql_cluster_backup_privileges();
Query OK, 1 row affected (2.96 sec)

-- Disable distributed privileges on first SQL node
mysql> CALL mysql_cluster_restore_local_privileges();
Query OK, 1 row affected (2.33 sec)

-- Restore local tables on remaining SQL nodes
mysql> CALL mysql_cluster_restore_privileges_from_local();
Query OK, 1 row affected (0.20 sec)

mysql> FLUSH PRIVILEGES;
Query OK, 0 rows affected (0.30 sec)
```

```
mysql> SELECT * FROM ndbutil.ndbcluster_dist_priv_tables;
+--------------+--------+---------------------+-------------------------+
| Grant_Table  | Engine | MyISAM_Backup       | NDBCluster_Backup       |
+--------------+--------+---------------------+-------------------------+
| columns_priv | MyISAM | columns_priv_backup | ndb_columns_priv_backup |
| db           | MyISAM | db_backup           | ndb_db_backup           |
| procs_priv   | MyISAM | procs_priv_backup   | ndb_procs_priv_backup   |
| proxies_priv | MyISAM | proxies_priv_backup | ndb_proxies_priv_backup |
| tables_priv  | MyISAM | tables_priv_backup  | ndb_tables_priv_backup  |
| user         | MyISAM | user_backup         | ndb_user_backup         |
+--------------+--------+---------------------+-------------------------+
6 rows in set (0.48 sec)

mysql> SELECT mysql.mysql_cluster_privileges_are_distributed();
+-------------------------------------------------+
| mysql.mysql_cluster_privileges_are_distributed() |
+-------------------------------------------------+
|                                               0 |
+-------------------------------------------------+
1 row in set (0.05 sec)
```

Special Considerations

There are a few special considerations to keep in mind when using distributed privileges. These include downgrades, restoring backups, and recovering should the password for the root@localhost account be lost.

Downgrades

The MySQL grant tables are specific to the major version of the SQL nodes. One of the main reasons you must execute the mysql_upgrade script as part of an upgrade of the SQL nodes is to ensure that the grant tables are upgraded to work with the new version. In order to support upgrades while leaving the data—and grant tables—in place, each version of the SQL nodes can also read the grant tables of the previous version.

Downgrades are different, however. The older version of the SQL node will not be able to read the newer version of the grant tables. As it was discussed in Chapter 11, even without distributed privileges, downgrading to another major version requires you to reinitialize the SQL nodes. The reinitialization step does not work with distributed privileges, as the grant tables in the data nodes will override the local tables and thus still be the new version. For this reason, it is necessary to disable distributed privileges while the downgrade is performed.

Restoring a Backup

When a full restore is performed of a native NDB Cluster backup, it is necessary to explicitly tell ndb_restore to also restore the privilege tables. Otherwise, these are left out. The option to include the privileges in the restore is --restore-privilege-tables and the option must be specified for all of the ndb_restore commands. Listing 12-8 shows an example of a full restore.

Listing 12-8. A Full Restore Including Distributed Privileges with ndb_restore

```
# Restore the schema - for one node
shell$ ndb_restore --ndb-connectstring=192.168.56.101,192.168.56.102 \
                   --restore_meta --nodeid=1 --backupid=2 \
                   --backup_path=/backups/cluster/BACKUP/BACKUP-2 \
                   --restore-privilege-tables --disable-indexes

# Restore the data - for each data node that was included in the backup
shell$ ndb_restore --ndb-connectstring=192.168.56.101,192.168.56.102 \
                   --restore_data --nodeid=1 --backupid=2 \
                   --backup_path=/backups/cluster/BACKUP/BACKUP-2 \
                   --restore-privilege-tables --disable-indexes

# Rebuild the indexes - for one node
shell$ ndb_restore --ndb-connectstring=192.168.56.101,192.168.56.102 \
                   --nodeid=1 --backupid=2 \
                   --backup_path=/backups/cluster/BACKUP/BACKUP-2 \
                   --restore-privilege-tables --rebuild-indexes
```

Recovering the root@localhost Password

The two usual methods to recover, if the database administrator is locked out of the SQL node, are to use the skip-grant-tables or init-file option. The skip-grant-tables option will disable the privilege system, so it is possible to connect without using a password, and the init-file option tells the SQL node to execute the statements in the specified file at startup. However, there is a caveat when distributed privileges are enabled—skip-grant-tables is ignored and init-file cannot be used as the statements are executed before the NDBCluster tables have become available.

This means the only option is to forcefully remove the grant tables from the data nodes. After this, it is possible to recover the root@localhost password. The steps are as follows:

1. Drop the six grant tables (columns_priv, db, procs_priv, proxies_priv, tables_priv, and user) using the ndb_drop_table utility. Listing 12-9 includes an example of dropping the columns_priv table. Add the --ndb-connectstring option if you are executing from a host without a management node and the option is not included in the MySQL configuration file.

2. Make sure the SQL node that will be used to regain access is stopped.

3. Restore the MyISAM version of the grant tables. This can be done in several ways, for example, you can copy each of the MyISAM backup tables back at the file system level, reinitialize the data directory (this will delete all non-NDBCluster tables!), or copy the grant tables from another installation. Listing 12-9 shows how to restore the columns_priv table from the MyISAM backup table created with the mysql_cluster_backup_privileges procedure. The cp commands assume the current working directory is the datadir of the SQL node.

4. Start the SQL node. Use the skip-grant-tables option if a backup copy of the grant tables was used; otherwise, start normally and use the password from the initialization.

5. Restore the privileges and set up distributed privileges again.

Listing 12-9. Dropping and Restoring the `columns_priv` Table

```
# Drop the table in the data nodes
shell$ ndb_drop_table --database=mysql columns_priv
Dropping table columns_priv...OK

NDBT_ProgramExit: 0 - OK

# Shutdown the SQL node

# Restore the backup table
shell$ cp mysql/columns_priv_backup.frm mysql/columns_priv.frm
shell$ cp mysql/columns_priv_backup.MYD mysql/columns_priv.MYD
shell$ cp mysql/columns_priv_backup.MYI mysql/columns_priv.MYI
```

The Operating System and the Rest of the Infrastructure

In the discussion about keeping the system up to date with bug fixes, it was mentioned that it is important to keep the whole stack in mind. The same applies to all aspects of securing the system. As the general infrastructure is very diverse, it is not possible to give specific advice beyond keeping all components up to date and working with the vendor to ensure that the components are configured correctly.

Security at the operating system level deserves a little more attention though. There are a few general points that should be considered when securing the operating system, for example:

- Only install services that are required.

- Ensure services—including MySQL NDB Cluster processes—are not run as the root/system administrator user.

- Disable login for users created to run services.

- Use strong passwords.

- Keep the operating system and all third-party software up to date.

- Monitor the system.

- Review the logs.

- Limit who can log in to the server and what privileges they have.

- Limit physical access to the hardware (including networking equipment) to the trusted custodians.

These items are similar to the considerations made for MySQL NDB Cluster.

All (well almost all) software has bugs, most of which do not cause big problems. The more software installed on a server, the more likely it is that some piece of software contains some bug that can be used to cause an outage, denial of service, gain privileges that the user is not supposed to have, or get access to data that is supposed to be restricted. Limiting the amount of software installed makes it is easier to ensure that all parts are up to date with the latest bug fixes. That is, in itself, a major step toward securing the data.

When a service—such as mysqld or ndbmtd—starts on a host, it will be running under a user account. The simplest approach is just to use root (on Linux/UNIX) or the System Administrator account (on Windows), as it solves all problems with privileges. It is, on the other hand, also a great way for privileges to become misused. Instead, ensure that services only have the privileges required. An example is that the mysqld process must be able to read the MySQL configuration file, but should not be able to write to it. Similarly, mysqld requires read and write access to the data directory, but it should not be allowed to read and write any random file on the system—such as the security logs. It may be that some logging must be done to files that a process is not allowed to write to directly. In that case, the writing must be done through a service that ensures that it is possible to append to the log, but deletion is prevented. These considerations are all equivalent to granting privileges to MySQL users.

■ **Note**   By convention, MySQL services uses the mysql user on Linux and UNIX. For example, when installing MySQL using RPM packages, the mysql user is automatically created as a no-login user. There is, however, no requirement for which username is actually used.

There are also steps that can be taken to detect if an attempt (successful or not) has been made to gain access to the system. These steps are beyond to scope of this discussion, but one point is worth mentioning— any kind of monitoring is only helpful if you actually pay attention to the alerts that the monitoring system generates! This applies to the monitoring discussed in Chapter 14 for MySQL NDB Cluster as well as other kinds of monitoring, such as intrusion detection software. If alerts are dismissed as not being important, sooner or later an important alert will be missed. The system administrator must ensure that alerts from the security software are categorized correctly, so that all events are handled with the appropriate urgency.

Summary

Security is an important topic in today's world and it cannot be stressed enough that it should be at the top of the list for everyone involved in software deployment. The work to secure a MySQL NDB Cluster installation starts at the planning phase, includes the initial installation, and continues with daily maintenance. It is a never-ending task.

Some of the important aspects to implement are as follows:

- Use a separate network that is shielded from the rest of the network for the communication between MySQL NDB Cluster nodes.

- Have external access to the SQL nodes and/or application protected by a firewall.

- Keep all software and firmware up to date.

- Limit the privileges given to the operating system users and to the MySQL users.

- Use encrypted connections for all external connections.

- Review logs and monitoring alerts regularly.

- At a regular basis, document and audit the accounts, privileges, and the security in general.

- Make security part of the daily routine.

Thus far, Parts II and III have been focused on how to do all installation and maintenance tasks manually. The next chapter is about MySQL Cluster Manager, which will help you automate many of these tasks.

MySQL Cluster Manager

The chapters thus far have described the internals of MySQL NDB Cluster and how to manage it by directly working with the binaries, configuration files, etc. There is another way to manage clusters though—by using *MySQL Cluster Manager*, which is also often abbreviated *MCM*. MySQL Cluster Manager is an enterprise offering that makes it considerably simpler to manage a cluster. It is only available with the *MySQL Cluster Carrier Grade Edition* subscription as well as a 30-day trial (see *https://www.mysql.com/trials/*). This chapter provides a tutorial to MySQL Cluster Manager.

Note Even if you plan to use MySQL Cluster Manager in production, it is a good idea to try managing a cluster manually on a test system first, as described in the previous chapters, in order to get experience with the processes used to manage a cluster.

Background

Before starting on the tutorial, it is worth looking a bit into the terminology and architecture of MySQL Cluster Manager to have some background understanding of the command names and how they work. This section discusses the terms used for MySQL Cluster Manager, the architecture, the available commands, and limitations.

Note There will be no difference in the application, whether the cluster is managed manually or by using MySQL Cluster Manager.

Terminology

There are a few terms that are important to know, as they are reflected in the commands and command options. S*ites*, *hosts*, *packages*, *clusters*, and *processes* are related, as described in Table 13-1.

Table 13-1. *Important Terms for MySQL Cluster Manager*

Term	Description
Site	A collection of hosts. All hosts used by a cluster must be in the same site. A host cannot be included in more than one site.
Host	A host where one or more processes is installed or is planned to be installed.
Package	The MySQL NDB Cluster files. Use the generic tarball or Zip file downloads. All processes in a cluster use the same package except while an upgrade is in progress.
Cluster	A MySQL NDB Cluster installation consisting of multiple processes.
Process	The individual processes (nodes) in a cluster. There are five supported process types: ndb_mgmd, ndbapi, ndbd, ndbmtd, and mysqld. All processes are explicitly tied to a specific host, except for the ndbapi and mysqld processes, which also support anonymous hosts. Table 13-14 includes more information about the process types.

Architecture

For MySQL Cluster Manager to be able to monitor the processes, you must have an agent installed on each host where a process is running or is about to be installed. In the same way, a package must be installed on all hosts for which there are processes defined. The agents communicate with each other using the *XCom* protocol on a dedicated port. This architecture is illustrated in Figure 13-1.

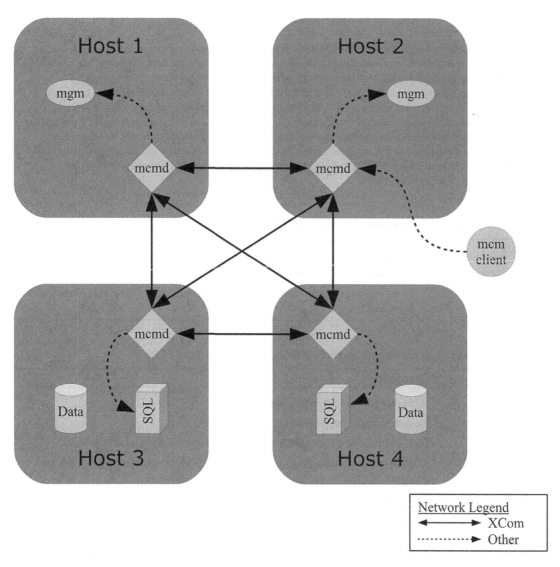

Figure 13-1. *The MySQL Cluster Manager architecture*

The communication between the MySQL NDB Cluster nodes is left out, but keep in mind that the inter-node communication will be no different whether a cluster is deployed manually or using MySQL Cluster Manager. The communication between the MySQL Cluster Manager agents is shown with solid lines and uses the XCom protocol connecting to the port specified by the xcom-port option. The agents make outbound connections to the management and SQL nodes in order to configure the cluster nodes and monitor them. The MySQL Cluster Manager client (the mcm client) can be used to connect to either of the agents in order to execute commands. The mcm client uses the standard MySQL protocol (the same used by the mysql command-line client when connecting to SQL nodes) when communicating to the agent. The connection from the mcm client connects to the port specified by the manager-port option. The mcm client may be executed from the same host as the agent or on another host.

Commands

MySQL Cluster Manager is command driven. It does not provide any new features to MySQL NDB Cluster, but rather provides an interface to manage a cluster performing tasks ranging from the initial installation through configuration, backups and restores, to upgrades. A command may cover several steps for a standalone cluster. For example, an upgrade is performed with a single command after making the new package available. Each command can be classified as *information, site and agent, package, cluster, configuration, process, backup and restore*, or *import*. Examples from each of these categories except import are explained in the tutorial. Imports greatly depend on the initial setup and platform of the cluster, so imports are beyond the scope of this chapter. Tables 13-2 through 13-9 give an overview of the commands available for each of these categories. Commands to start and stop a cluster or its processes are also discussed in more detail in Table 13-15.

Table 13-2. *Information Commands Available in MySQL Cluster Manager 1.4.2*

Command	Description
list commands	Lists the available commands.
\<command\> --help	The --help option can be used with any command for a detailed help of the command.

Table 13-3. *Site and Agent Commands Available in MySQL Cluster Manager 1.4.2*

Command	Description
add hosts	Adds one or more hosts to a site.
remove hosts	Removes one or more hosts from a site.
list hosts	Lists all hosts for a site and the status and version of the agent on the hosts.
change log-level	Changes the verbosity of agent log(s). See the "Troubleshooting MySQL Cluster Manager" section at the end of this chapter for details.
rotate log	Rotates the agent log(s).
collect logs	Collects the logs from the agents and all the cluster nodes as well as the configuration files. Useful to get all of the logs in one place, for example, to upload to MySQL Support.
create site	Creates a new site.
delete site	Deletes a site.
list sites	Lists all sites and which hosts are in each site.
show settings	Lists the agent settings or the details of the host where the agent is installed.
stop agents	Stops one or more agents.
version	Returns the agent version.
show warnings	Lists the latest warnings that occurred on the agent.

Table 13-4. *Package Commands in MySQL Cluster Manager 1.4.2*

Command	Description
add package	Adds a package to one or more hosts.
delete package	Deletes a package from one or more hosts.
list packages	Lists all packages for a site.

Table 13-5. *Cluster Commands in MySQL Cluster Manager 1.4.2*

Command	Description
create cluster	Creates a new cluster.
delete cluster	Deletes a cluster.
list clusters	Lists clusters and which package they are using for a given site.
list nextnodeids	Lists the node IDs that will be used if another data node and other nodes are added.
restart cluster	Performs a rolling restart of a cluster.
show status	Shows the status of a cluster, the operation executed for a cluster, or the processes of a cluster.
start cluster	Starts all nodes in a cluster.
stop cluster	Stops all nodes in a cluster.
autotune	Auto tunes a cluster based on the usage template and write load. Only supports MySQL NDB Cluster 7.4 and later. An example is given when configuring the cluster in the tutorial later in this chapter.
upgrade cluster	Upgrades or downgrades a cluster to use a different package.

Table 13-6. *Configuration Commands in MySQL Cluster Manager 1.4.2*

Command	Description
get	Gets the configuration of one or more nodes in a cluster based on the filters specified.
reset	Resets one or more configuration options of one or more nodes in a cluster to the option's default value.
set	Sets a value for one or more configuration options of one or more nodes in a cluster.

Table 13-7. *Process Commands in MySQL Cluster Manager 1.4.2*

Command	Description
add process	Adds one or more processes to a cluster.
change process	Changes an ndbd process to an ndbmtd process or vice versa.
list processes	Lists the processes and which host they are installed on for a cluster.
start process	Starts a process in a cluster.
stop process	Stops a process in a cluster.
update process	Updates a process in a cluster.
remove process	Removes a process from a cluster.

Table 13-8. *Backup and Restore Commands in MySQL Cluster Manager 1.4.2*

Command	Description
abort backup	Aborts an ongoing backup.
backup cluster	Backs up the data and schema for a cluster.
list backups	Lists the available backups for a cluster.
restore cluster	Restores a backup to a cluster.
backup agents	Backs up the agents' configuration data.

Table 13-9. *Import Commands in MySQL Cluster Manager 1.4.2*

Command	Description
import cluster	Imports a cluster not currently managed by MySQL Cluster Manager. Second stage of an import after the import config command.
import config	Imports the configuration of a cluster not currently managed by MySQL Cluster Manager. The first stage of an import.

Limitations

There are some limitations of MySQL Cluster Manager to be aware of. The list of supported platforms is a subset of the one for MySQL NDB Cluster. The list of supported platforms can be seen at *https://www.mysql. com/support/supportedplatforms/cluster-manager.html*. Additionally, the latest release at the time of writing of MySQL Cluster Manager (release 1.4.2) only support MySQL NDB Cluster 7.3, 7.4, and 7.5. On the user side, be aware that only one command other than checking the status should be executed at a time. This is the responsibility of the user, as MySQL Cluster Manager will not prevent conflicting commands to be executed in parallel.

■ **Caution** There is no locking between client sessions. It is the responsibility of the database administrator to ensure that no conflicting operations are executed concurrently. The recommendation is that other than checking the status, never execute more than one command at a time.

Download, Installation, and Configuration

The installation of MySQL Cluster Manager itself is straightforward. The following steps are required:

1. Download MySQL Cluster Manager if a copy of the latest release is not already downloaded.

2. Install the software.

3. Configure the software.

4. Start MySQL Cluster Manager.

The steps are discussed in the remainder of this section. The installation includes two examples: using the generic binaries on Linux and the Microsoft Windows MSI installer. Other platforms either support installing from the tarball like the Linux example or support a native packaging format such as the MSI installer or RPM.

MySQL Cluster Manager is available in two distributions:

- **Standalone:** This distribution just contains MySQL Cluster Manager itself. This is what will be used in this chapter. When downloading, the download will be labeled MySQL-Cluster-Manager, plus the patch release number and platform information. For example, *MySQL Cluster Manager 1.4.2 MSI for Windows x86 (64bit)*.

- **Bundled:** This distribution includes the most recent MySQL NDB Cluster release at the time the downloaded release of MySQL Cluster Manager was prepared. For example, MySQL Cluster Manager 1.4.2 is bundled with MySQL NDB Cluster 7.5.5. When downloading, the download will be labeled MySQL-Cluster-Manager, followed by the patch release number, the label +Cluster, and finally the platform information. For example, *MySQL Cluster Manager 1.4.2+Cluster MSI for Windows x86 (64bit)*.

■ **Note** The terms *standalone* and *bundled* are not official terms (in fact there are no official names for the two variations of how MySQL Cluster Manager is distributed). The terms are used here as they are most frequently used in MySQL Support's communication with customers and they describe the content of the downloaded files.

As MySQL Cluster Manager is released less frequently than MySQL NDB Cluster, the bundled distribution will in general not include the latest MySQL NDB Cluster release. For this reason, it is in general best to use the standalone distribution of MySQL Cluster Manager and download MySQL NDB Cluster separately. This tutorial uses the standalone MySQL Cluster Manager with MySQL NDB Cluster 7.5.5 and upgrades it to 7.5.6.

Downloading

The 30-day trial version of MySQL Cluster Manager can be downloaded from the *Oracle Software Delivery Cloud* (*https://edelivery.oracle.com/*). The trial version is identical to the download offered to paying customers. The download procedure is similar to downloading MySQL NDB Cluster, as described in Chapter 5, and requires a (free) Oracle account.

■ **Note**   Downloading software from *https://edelivery.oracle.com/* is subject to U.S. Export Administration Regulations (EAR) and other export laws. Thus, all accounts must be validated before access to the software is allowed.

The first step, once you are signed in to the Oracle Software Delivery Cloud, is to search for MySQL Cluster Manager in the search box, as shown in Figure 13-2. The available version is displayed next to MySQL Cluster Manager in the *Release* area. There is only one version available at any one time, so the version displayed will change over time.

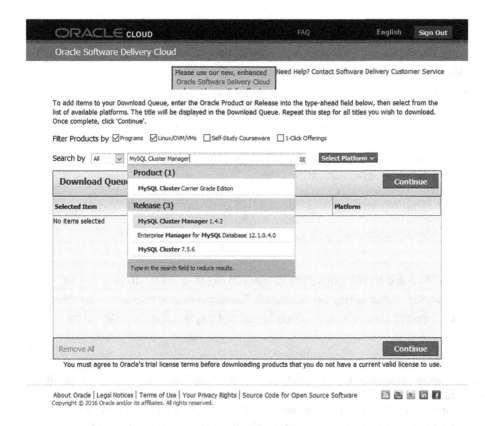

Figure 13-2. *Search by product or release name*

■ Tip   For customers who purchased MySQL Cluster Carrier Grade Edition, it is best to download MySQL Cluster Manager (and MySQL NDB Cluster) from the *Patches & Updates* tab in *My Oracle Support* (MOS), because all releases since 2011 are available there, whereas Oracle Delivery Cloud only includes one release—typically the latest.

After you choose the release, choose one or more platforms, as shown in Figure 13-3. In this example, MySQL Cluster Manager will be downloaded for the 64-bit Linux and Microsoft Windows platforms.

Figure 13-3.   *Choose the platforms*

Continue by following the screens, including the *Oracle Standard Terms and Restrictions*. Make sure to read these in full and only check the checkbox if you agree with the terms and restrictions. At the end, there is the file download screen, as displayed in Figure 13-4. The figure shows the files available. There are two files available for each supported combination of platform and installation format corresponding to the two distributions. For example, "*V860722-01.zip MySQL Cluster Manager 1.4.2 MSI for Windows x86 (64bit)*" is the standalone version, and "*V860723-01.zip MySQL Cluster Manager 1.4.2+Cluster MSI for Windows x86 (64bit)*" is the bundled distribution. The standalone version is a much smaller download than the bundled version. A typical difference for Microsoft Windows files is around 35MB compared to 1GB. Choose the standalone distribution for this tutorial: *V860730-01.zip for Linux and V860722-01.zip for Microsoft Windows (or the equivalent files available—the filenames change in each new release).*

Figure 13-4. *Choose the files to download*

As you can see in Figure 13-4, there are several options for the Linux downloads. For example, there are dedicated TAR and RPM downloads for Oracle Linux/RHEL 5+6. If there is a dedicated download for the Linux distribution in use, it is best to use that instead of the generic download.

■ **Note**　Support for Oracle Linux 5 and RHEL 5 was declared end of life as of April 30, 2017 (*https://www.mysql.com/support/eol-notice.html*). MySQL Cluster Manager 1.4.2 is the last release to support these Linux distributions.

Once the download has completed, continue with the installation. The two next subsections provide examples of installing on Linux and Windows.

Installation on Linux

The installation example on Linux for this tutorial will use the file *V860730-01.zip* that was downloaded from Oracle Software Delivery Cloud as shown in Figure 13-4. The file can be used on all recent Linux distributions.

▪ **Note** The filename changes for each new version made available from Oracle Software Delivery Cloud.

MySQL Cluster Manager must be installed on all hosts that will be used with a management, data, or SQL node. The installation can be made into any directory; for this example, the files from *V860730-01.zip* will be installed into */opt/mysql/mcm-1.4.2*.

The first step is to unzip the files included in *V860730-01.zip*:

```
shell$ mkdir -p /opt/mysql/mcm-1.4.2
shell$ cd /opt/mysql/mcm-1.4.2
# Copy V860730-01.zip into /opt/mysql/mcm-1.4.2
shell$ unzip V860730-01.zip
Archive:  V860730-01.zip
 extracting: mcm-1.4.2-linux-glibc2.5-x86-64bit.tar.gz
 extracting: mcm-1.4.2-linux-glibc2.5-x86-64bit.tar.gz.asc
 extracting: mcm-1.4.2-linux-glibc2.5-x86-64bit.tar.gz.md5
 extracting: README.txt
```

The *mcm-1.4.2-linux-glibc2.5-x86-64bit.tar.gz.asc* and *mcm-1.4.2-linux-glibc2.5-x86-64bit.tar.gz.md5* files contain a *Pretty Good Privacy (PGP)* signature and an md5 sum of the *.tar.gz* file. The *README.txt* file includes the release notes.

The MySQL Cluster Manager files themselves are included in *mcm-1.4.2-linux-glibc2.5-x86-64bit.tar.gz*:

```
shell$ tar -zxf mcm-1.4.2-linux-glibc2.5-x86-64bit.tar.gz
shell$ mv mcm-1.4.2-linux-glibc2.5-x86-64bit/mcm1.4.2 .
shell$ rmdir mcm-1.4.2-linux-glibc2.5-x86-64bit/
```

MySQL Cluster Manager has now been installed. Some of the important files included are listed in Table 13-10. The path is relative to the directory where MySQL Cluster Manager was installed (*/opt/mysql/mcm-1.4.2*).

Table 13-10. *Some of the Important MySQL Cluster Manager Files on Linux*

File	Description
bin/mcm	The MySQL Cluster Manager client.
bin/mcmd	The MySQL Cluster Manager agent (daemon). This is the long running agent process that manages the cluster.
etc/init.d/mcmd	A System V init script that can be used to automate the startup of MySQL Cluster Manager.
etc/mcmd.ini	A template for the configuration file for *bin/mcmd*.

Before moving on to the configuration and starting MySQL Cluster Manager, it is important to ensure that the mysql command-line client is also installed on all hosts, and that the mysql binary is in the program search path (explanation follows in the MySQL Cluster Manager Client subsection). To check whether the mysql binary is in the program search path, use this command:

```
shell$ which mysql
/usr/bin/mysql
```

If the which command indicates that the command is not found, be sure to install it before proceeding. An example where the mysql command-line client is not installed is:

```
shell$ which mysql
/usr/bin/which: no mysql in (/usr/lib64/qt-3.3/bin:/usr/local/bin:/usr/local/sbin:/usr/bin:/
usr/sbin:/bin:/sbin:/home/jmyuser/.local/bin:/home/myuser/bin)
```

Installation on Microsoft Windows

For Microsoft Windows, there is only one option for installing MySQL Cluster Manager. The installation is done using the Microsoft Windows *MSI* installer, as the one downloaded in the example shown in Figures 13-2 to 13-4. The installation is straightforward. The only choice during the installation is the destination directory and, in most cases, the default (*C:\Program Files (x86)\MySQL\MySQL Cluster Manager\mcm1.4.2* for version 1.4.2) is fine. See Figure 13-5.

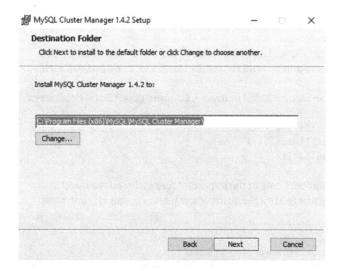

Figure 13-5. *Choose the destination directory*

When the installation is complete, the whole installation will be available in the destination folder you chose during the installation. Some of the important files in the installation are listed in Table 13-11.

Table 13-11. *Some of the Important MySQL Cluster Manager Files on Microsoft Windows*

File	Description
bin\mcm.exe	The MySQL Cluster Manager client.
bin\mcmd.exe	The MySQL Cluster Manager agent (daemon). This is the long running agent process that manages the cluster.
etc\mcmd.ini	A template for the configuration file for *bin\mcmd.exe*.

You must have the mysql command-line client installed as well and this is not included in the MySQL Cluster Manager standalone distribution. The mysql client must be in the paths searched by Windows when a command is executed without a full path. This is the Path environmental variable. Alternatively, the mysql.exe file from a Zip file download of MySQL Server or MySQL NDB Cluster can be copied into the same directory as the mcm client (*C:\Program Files (x86)\MySQL\MySQL Cluster Manager\mcm1.4.2\bin* in this example).

Assuming the mysql command-line client has been installed into *C:\MySQL_Cluster\Packages\ cluster_7.5\bin*, then Path can be configured as follows for Microsoft Windows 10; other versions will have similar procedures. Click on the Windows icon and type "settings: path", then click on *Edit Environment Variables For Your Account*, as shown in Figure 13-6. This brings up the Environment Variables dialog box, where the variables can be added.

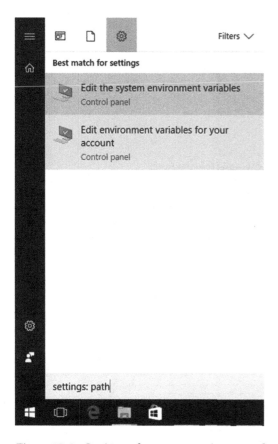

Figure 13-6. *Getting to the account environmental variables*

There are two ways to add a new path to the Path environmental variable: for the user or for the system (all users). Choose the option that best suits the system. To add the path at the user level, click on *Path* in the User variables list at the top and then click on the topmost Edit... button, as shown in Figure 13-7.

Figure 13-7. *Environmental variables*

Figure 13-8 shows you how to add a new path. First click on the *New* button, then enter the path. After adding the path to the mysql.exe binary, click *OK*.

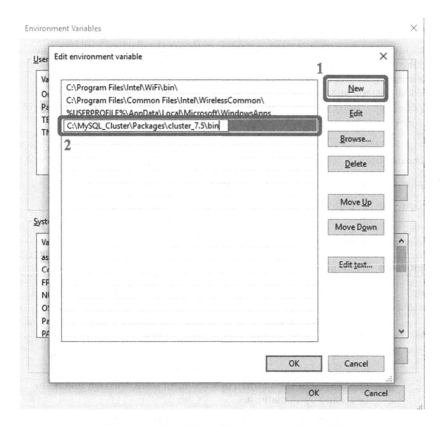

Figure 13-8. *Adding new path to the Path environmental variable*

■ **Note**   The new Path setting will only affect new command-line prompt processes, not the existing ones. You may have to restart any open command windows to use the new path.

Upgrading

An upgrade of MySQL Cluster Manager is essentially the same as an installation, just with the addition that then MySQL Cluster Manager agent is restarted using the new binary. So, download the new version, shut down all of the existing agents, install the new version, and start the agents again using the new version. Make sure that, after the upgrade, the same values for the manager-directory, manager-username, and manager-password are used as before the upgrade. For this reason, it is best to use a *mcmd.ini* file that is located outside of the MySQL Cluster Manager installation directory.

■ **Caution**   Do not have MySQL Cluster Manager agents of different versions online at the same time. Shut down all agents before starting the agents using the upgraded binaries. It is also important to ensure that the configuration is not inadvertently changed during the upgrade.

Configuration

The configuration of MySQL Cluster Manager is very similar to the configuration of other MySQL programs. It uses a configuration file in the same format as *my.cnf/my.ini* and *config.ini* discussed in Chapter 4. All settings are added under the mcmd group. Some of the most important options are described in Table 13-12. The full list of options can be found in the MySQL Cluster Manager Reference Manual at *https://dev. mysql.com/doc/mysql-cluster-manager/en/mcm-using-mcmd.html*. On Windows, there are some extra requirements for the paths; for example for the log-file and manager-directory options. These requirements are:

- The path must be absolute.

- Use forward slashes (/) instead of backslashes (\), including on Microsoft Windows.

- No spaces are allowed in the path. For example, replace spaces with underscores (_).

Table 13-12. *Some Important Options for the MySQL Cluster Manager Daemon*

Option	Default Value	Description
agent-uuid	Auto generated	An UUID identifying the agent. It is only necessary to specify this manually when there is more than one MySQL Cluster Manager agent installed on the same host. The default value is auto-generated based on information from the host.
daemon	true	Whether to execute mcmd as a foreground or daemon process. The default is to execute as a daemon process, but using a foreground process can be useful when debugging an issue. This only applies to Linux and UNIX platforms.
log-file	*mcmd.log*	The log file for mcmd. The default directory is the installation directory (*/opt/mysql/mcm-1.4.2* in this tutorial). On Microsoft Windows, an absolute path must be used. On Linux and UNIX, the path is relative to the installation directory unless an absolute path is used. It is best to use an absolute path.
log-level	message	The log level to use. Supported values are (in increased verbosity level): critical, error, warning, message, info, and debug. The default is message. See the subsection entitled "Error Messages and the Log" in the "Troubleshooting MySQL Cluster Manager" section later in the chapter.
log-use-syslog	true	When enabled, log messages are written to the syslog.
manager-directory	*../mcm_data*	The location where MySQL Cluster Manager will store its data. When a MySQL NDB Cluster node is installed without specifying the data directory explicitly, the node data directory will be in the manager directory path as well. The default is the *../mcm_data* directory relative to the installation directory. If MySQL Cluster Manager is installed in */opt/mysql/ mcm-1.4.2*, then the default manager directory is */opt/mysql/mcm_ data*. The value must be an absolute path. On Linux and UNIX, the directory must exist or the user executing mcmd must have permission to create it. On Microsoft Windows, the directory must exist.

(continued)

Table 13-12. (*continued*)

Option	Default Value	Description
manager-password	super	Dual use: Used when connecting with the mcm client to the agent, and the password used when the agent connects to the SQL nodes. You are strongly encouraged to change the password.
manager-port	1862	The port mcmd will listen to for connections from the MySQL Cluster Manager client.
manager-username	mcmd	Dual use: Used when connecting with the mcm client to the agent, and the username used when the agent connects to the SQL nodes.
xcom-port	18620	The port used for the internal communication between the agents (the XCOM communication).

■ **Tip** It is best to use the same configuration on all hosts with the exception of agent-uuid (which must have a unique value for all mcmd processes). In particular, the xcom-port setting must be the same for all hosts.

The user and password used to connect to the SQL nodes are in general configured in *mcmd.ini*, which means that MySQL Cluster Manager will refuse to start if the file system level permissions allow everyone to read the file. On Linux and UNIX, the permissions must be u=rw,g=rw,o= (0660) or stricter (fewer privileges given). If the permissions are not strict enough, mcmd will return an error like the following one when it starts:

```
2017-05-11 09:27:55.059: (critical) Failed to open given defaults-file '/etc/mcmd.ini':
permissions of /etc/mcmd.ini aren't secure (0660 or stricter required)
```

One way to ensure that only the root user can write to the configuration file, while MySQL Cluster Manager still is able to read it, is:

```
shell$ chown root.mysql /etc/mcmd.ini
shell$ chmod u=rw,g=r,o= /etc/mcmd.ini
shell$ ls -l /etc/mcmd.ini
-rw-r-----. 1 root mysql 321 May  6 17:52 /etc/mcmd.ini
```

The permission u=rw,g=r,o= is 0640 using the octal notation. This assumes that it will be the mysql user executing mcmd.

On Microsoft Windows, there are no requirements regarding the permissions of the configuration file. However, it is still best to limit access—particularly write, but also read if there are any passwords in the file—to as few users as possible. The permissions can be accessed by right-clicking on the *mcmd.ini* file in File Explorer and going to the Security tab, as shown in in Figure 13-9.

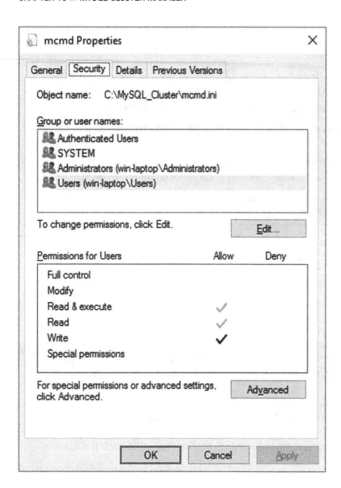

Figure 13-9. *Changing file permissions in Microsoft Windows*

For the rest of this tutorial, the configuration in Listing 13-1 is used.

Listing 13-1. The Example MySQL Cluster Manager Configuration File

```
[mcmd]
# Log file and level
log-file        = /var/log/mcmd.log
log-level       = message

# Toplevel directory for manager plugins information stored on disk
manager-directory = /var/lib/mcm_data

# Username and password connecting to the manager and for the SQL Nodes
manager-username  = mcmd
manager-password  = cjhf*jc32FH@
```

To ensure MySQL Cluster Manager can use the manager directory and the log file, create them ahead of time and set the file system permissions. Listing 13-2 shows an example of this process on Linux.

Listing 13-2. Creating the Manager Directory and Log File on Linux

```
# The manager directory
shell$ mkdir /var/lib/mcm_data
shell$ chown mysql.mysql /var/lib/mcm_data
shell$ chmod u=rwx,g=rx,o= /var/lib/mcm_data

# The log file
shell$ touch /var/log/mcmd.log
shell$ chown mysql.mysql /var/log/mcmd.log
shell$ chmod u=rw,g=r,o= /var/log/mcmd.log
```

After the agent has been started (see the next subsection), the configuration can be checked using the mcm client. You use the show settings command, as shown in Listing 13-3.

Listing 13-3. The Output of the show settings Command

```
mcm> show settings;
+-------------------+-------------------+
| Setting           | Value             |
+-------------------+-------------------+
| copy-port         | 0                 |
| log-file          | /var/log/mcmd.log |
| log-level         | message           |
| log-use-syslog    | FALSE             |
| manager-directory | /var/lib/mcm_data |
| manager-username  | mcmd              |
| manager-password  | ********          |
| manager-port      | 1862              |
| xcom-port         | 18620             |
+-------------------+-------------------+
9 rows in set (0.00 sec)

mcm> show settings --hostinfo;
+-----------------+---------------------------------+
| Property        | Value                           |
+-----------------+---------------------------------+
| Hostname        | ol7                             |
| Platform        | Linux 4.1.12-37.4.1.el7uek.x86_64 |
| Processor cores | 1                               |
| Total memory    | 992 Mb                          |
+-----------------+---------------------------------+
4 rows in set (0.00 sec)
```

With the configuration set up, it is time to start MySQL Cluster Manager.

Starting and Stopping MySQL Cluster Manager

MySQL Cluster Manager can be started and stopped either executing and stopping the process directly or by using a service management system such as System V init scripts, systemd, and Windows Services. Using a service management system to control mcmd is no different from using it for the MySQL NDB Cluster daemons and will not be discussed in more detail. Instead, the focus is on starting and stopping the mcmd process directly.

Here is an example that starts the mcmd process on Linux with the configuration file located in */etc/mcmd.ini*:

```
shell$ sudo -u mysql nohup /opt/mysql/mcm1.4.2/bin/mcmd \
                --defaults-file=/etc/mcmd.ini > /dev/null 2>&1 &
```

To start the agent on Microsoft Windows from the command prompt, the command is similar, for example:

```
C:>START /B "" "C:\Program Files (x86)\MySQL\MySQL Cluster Manager\mcm1.4.2\bin\mcmd.exe"
--defaults-file="C:\MySQL_Cluster\mcmd.ini"

MySQL Cluster Manager 1.4.2 (64bit) started
Connect to MySQL Cluster Manager by running "C:\Program Files (x86)\MySQL\MySQL Cluster
Manager\mcm1.4.2\bin\mcm" -a WIN-LAPTOP:1862
```

The recommended way to shut down an mcmd process is to use the stop agents command in the mcm client, which applies to all platforms. It is possible to shut down a single agent or multiple agents, including all the agents in a site. If the stop agents command is used without any arguments, only the agent that the mcm client is connected to is shut down:

```
mcm> stop agents;
+----------------------------+
| Command result             |
+----------------------------+
| Agents stopped successfully |
+----------------------------+
1 row in set (0.02 sec)
```

To shut down all hosts in a site, add the site name to the command:

```
mcm> stop agents test_site;
+----------------------------+
| Command result             |
+----------------------------+
| Agents stopped successfully |
+----------------------------+
1 row in set (0.18 sec)
```

If the agent is shut down using a signal on UNIX or Linux, make sure to use the SIGTERM signal or kill the process from the Microsoft Windows process list manager without a forced shutdown.

■ **Caution**   As for other MySQL NDB Cluster processes, do not use the SIGKILL signal except in critical situations, where it is not possible to get the mcmd process to stop using SIGTERM. Stopping the process with SIGKILL may cause corruption of the management directory.

The MySQL Cluster Manager Client

The MySQL Server product and SQL nodes have the mysql command-line client that can be used to manipulate the schema and data from the command line. In the same way, MySQL Cluster Manager uses the mcm command-line client to send commands to the mcmd process.

The client is started using the mcm binary in the *bin* directory of the MySQL Cluster Manager installation. With the installation directory being */opt/mysql/mcm1.4.2*, the full path is */opt/mysql/mcm1.4.2/bin/mcm*. Assuming the mcm command is in the path and the default value is used for manager-port, it is possible to connect, as shown in Listing 13-4. The username and password are the ones defined using the manager-username and manager-password options. The mcm client is the only way to interact with MySQL Cluster Manager.

Listing 13-4. Starting the mcm Command-Line Client

```
shell mcm --user=mcmd --password
MySQL Cluster Manager client started.
This wrapper will spawn the mysql client to connect to mcmd

Enter password:
Welcome to the MySQL monitor.  Commands end with ; or \g.
Your MySQL connection id is 1
Server version: 1.4.2 MySQL Cluster Manager

Copyright (c) 2000, 2016, Oracle and/or its affiliates. All rights reserved.

Oracle is a registered trademark of Oracle Corporation and/or its
affiliates. Other names may be trademarks of their respective
owners.

Type 'help;' or '\h' for help. Type '\c' to clear the current input statement.

mcm>
```

If the output seems familiar and directs the thoughts toward the mysql command-line client, it is because the mcm binary only is a wrapper for the mysql binary. This is also the reason during the installation, it was required to have the mysql command-line client installed and in the path. Because it is the mysql command-line client that is used under the hood, commands must be terminated by a semicolon (;) as for SQL statements. The commands are case insensitive, but the convention is to use all lowercase. It is also possible to execute commands using the --execute or -e option. Listing 13-5 shows an example where mcm --execute is used to get help about the create site command. The same command can be run on Microsoft Windows by invoking mcm.exe instead of mcm.

Listing 13-5. Executing a Command Directly from the Linux Shell

```
shell$ mcm --user=mcmd --password --execute="create site --help;"
MySQL Cluster Manager client started.
This wrapper will spawn the mysql client to connect to mcmd

Enter password:
+----------------------------------------------------------------+
| Help                                                           |
+----------------------------------------------------------------+
|                                                                |
| create site [options] <sitename>                               |
|                                                                |
|     Creates a site from the hosts listed in --hosts.           |
|                                                                |
|     Required options:                                          |
|     --hosts|-h              Comma separated list of hostnames.  |
|                             Format: --hosts = <host>[,<host>]*. |
|                                                                |
+----------------------------------------------------------------+
```

This also shows that the MySQL Cluster Manager commands take the argument --help, which will provide a short summary of how the command works. The next section shows you how to manage a cluster and at the same time demonstrates several of the most important commands.

Managing a Cluster

With MySQL Cluster Manager installed, it is time to use it to install and manage a cluster. This section first covers installing and configuring the cluster, then discusses starting and stopping the cluster, performing configuration changes to an online cluster, performing backups and restores, and finally upgrading the cluster.

Installing the Cluster Binaries

Before you can actually install the cluster, you must download MySQL NDB Cluster separately. If the bundled distribution of MySQL Cluster Manager is used, this is not required, but this tutorial uses the standalone distribution to allow for any supported MySQL NDB Cluster version. When it is used with MySQL Cluster Manager, you must download a tarball distribution for Linux and UNIX or the Zip file distribution for Windows. The download is done as discussed in Chapter 5.

With MySQL NDB Cluster downloaded, the file should be extracted. In this example, version 7.5.5 will be extracted into */opt/mysql/packages/7.5.5*. For example:

```
shell$ mkdir /opt/mysql/packages
shell$ cd /opt/mysql/packages/

# Copy the downloaded .tar.gz file to /opt/mysql/packages
shell$ tar -zxf mysql-cluster-gpl-7.5.5-linux-glibc2.5-x86_64.tar.gz
shell$ mv mysql-cluster-gpl-7.5.5-linux-glibc2.5-x86_64 7.5.5
```

With the MySQL NDB Cluster binaries in place, the rest of the installation is completed in the mcm client.

Preparing the Cluster Through the mcm Client

The steps to prepare the new cluster are the same irrespective of the operating system, although the paths used to link to the binaries, to the data directories for the cluster nodes, etc., of course depend on the platform and how the hardware has been set up.

It does not matter which of the MySQL Cluster Manager agents is used. You do not even have to use the same one for all of the steps, although usually it is better to keep it simple and see what has already been done.

■ **Caution** MySQL Cluster Manager does not set a password for the root@localhost user for mysqld nodes. Make sure to set a strong password for the account using the SET PASSWORD command.

The cluster that will be installed uses the same configuration as the one used to demonstrate restarts in Chapter 10 with the addition of adding two API nodes that can connect from any host. Table 13-13 summarizes the eight nodes and how they are distributed on the four hosts.

Table 13-13. *The Cluster Nodes That Will Be Installed*

Node ID	Node Type	Host
1	Data node (ndbmtd)	192.168.56.103
2	Data node (ndbmtd)	192.168.56.104
49	Management node (ndb_mgmd)	192.168.56.101
50	Management node (ndb_mgmd)	192.168.56.102
51	SQL node (mysqld)	192.168.56.103
52	SQL node (mysqld)	192.168.56.104
53	API node (not mysqld)	Any host
54	API node (not mysqld)	Any host

By convention, MySQL Cluster Manager reserves the first 48 node IDs for data nodes. This is because all data nodes must have a node ID between 1 and 48. Management, SQL, and API nodes get consecutive IDs starting at number 49.

The first step is to define the site in which to install the cluster. This is done using the create site command. The site name can be anything that is meaningful for the installation. In this case, the name test_site will be used. When creating the site, you must specify the hosts that are included on the site. Additional hosts can be added later. The complete command for this tutorial looks like this:

```
mcm> create site --hosts=192.168.56.101,192.168.56.102,192.168.56.103,192.168.56.104
test_site;
+--------------------------+
| Command result           |
+--------------------------+
| Site created successfully |
+--------------------------+
1 row in set (3.21 sec)
```

The sites that MySQL Cluster Manager is aware of can be listed using the list sites command:

```
mcm> list sites\G
*************************** 1. row ***************************
 Site: test_site
 Port: 1862
Local: Local
Hosts: 192.168.56.101,192.168.56.102,192.168.56.103,192.168.56.104
1 row in set (0.07 sec)
```

Now that the site has been created, it is possible to define the package. This is the same as assigning a name to the path where the MySQL NDB Cluster binaries were unpacked:

```
mcm> add package --basedir=/opt/mysql/packages/7.5.5 cluster_7.5.5;
+----------------------------+
| Command result             |
+----------------------------+
| Package added successfully |
+----------------------------+
1 row in set (4.19 sec)
```

By default, the same basedir is used for all of the defined hosts. It is possible to use the path for a subset of hosts by adding the --host option. However, it is best to have the same configuration for all hosts. The available packages can be listed using the list packages command:

```
mcm> list packages test_site\G
*************************** 1. row ***************************
Package: cluster_7.5.5
   Path: /opt/mysql/packages/7.5.5
  Hosts: 192.168.56.101,192.168.56.102,192.168.56.103,192.168.56.104
1 row in set (0.11 sec)
```

It is now possible to start defining the cluster, which you do using the create cluster command. There are two required arguments: the package to use and the processes to have in the cluster. Additional processes can also be added later. The format of the processes is <processname>@<host>. The supported values of <processname> are listed in Table 13-14.

Table 13-14. *Supported Process Types*

Process Name	Description
ndb_mgmd	A management node.
ndbapi	Any API node that is not an SQL node. Includes additional API node slots for use with the ndb_cluster_connection_pool option on SQL nodes.
ndbd	A single-threaded data node.
ndbmtd	A multi-threaded data node.
mysqld	An SQL node. For SQL nodes with ndb_cluster_connection_pool larger than 1, add only one mysqld node and use ndbapi for the rest of the connections in the pool.

Notice how MySQL Cluster Manager distinguishes between the single-threaded and multi-threaded data nodes when you set up the cluster by the name. This is also the case when you specify the process type when configuring the data nodes.

Except for the mysqld and ndbapi nodes, all nodes must be tied to a specific host. For the mysqld and ndbapi nodes, a host name * (asterisk) can be used to denote *any host*.

The create cluster command becomes the following command (all of the --processhosts arguments must be on one line without any spaces):

```
mcm> create cluster --package=cluster_7.5.5 --processhosts=ndbmtd@192.168.56.103,ndbmtd@192.
168.56.104,ndb_mgmd@192.168.56.101,ndb_mgmd@192.168.56.102,mysqld@192.168.56.103,mysqld@192.
168.56.104,ndbapi@*,ndbapi@* test_cluster;
+-----------------------------+
| Command result              |
+-----------------------------+
| Cluster created successfully |
+-----------------------------+
1 row in set (3.69 sec)
```

The clusters that are available in the test_site site can be listed using the list clusters command:

```
mcm> list clusters test_site;
+--------------+---------------+
| Cluster      | Package       |
+--------------+---------------+
| test_cluster | cluster_7.5.5 |
+--------------+---------------+
1 row in set (0.14 sec)
```

More interesting is the show status command. It can be used in two main ways to get the status of a cluster. Listing 13-6 returns the overall status of the test_cluster cluster as well as a detailed view that includes all processes.

Listing 13-6. Getting the Cluster Status

```
mcm> show status test_cluster;
+--------------+---------+---------+
| Cluster      | Status  | Comment |
+--------------+---------+---------+
| test_cluster | created |         |
+--------------+---------+---------+
1 row in set (0.09 sec)

mcm> show status --process test_cluster;
+--------+----------+----------------+--------+-----------+---------------+
| NodeId | Process  | Host           | Status | Nodegroup | Package       |
+--------+----------+----------------+--------+-----------+---------------+
| 49     | ndb_mgmd | 192.168.56.101 | added  |           | cluster_7.5.5 |
| 50     | ndb_mgmd | 192.168.56.102 | added  |           | cluster_7.5.5 |
| 1      | ndbmtd   | 192.168.56.103 | added  | n/a       | cluster_7.5.5 |
| 2      | ndbmtd   | 192.168.56.104 | added  | n/a       | cluster_7.5.5 |
```

```
| 51     | mysqld    | 192.168.56.103 | added  |           | cluster_7.5.5 |
| 52     | mysqld    | 192.168.56.104 | added  |           | cluster_7.5.5 |
| 53     | ndbapi    | *              | added  |           |               |
| 54     | ndbapi    | *              | added  |           |               |
+--------+-----------+----------------+--------+-----------+---------------+
8 rows in set (0.09 sec)
```

There are several other modes for show status. Listing 13-7 shows the complete output of the help text for the command. The output has been reformatted to reduce the width of the text.

Listing 13-7. The Help for the show status Command

```
mcm> show status --help;
+---------------------------------------------------------------------------+
| Help                                                                      |
+---------------------------------------------------------------------------+
|                                                                           |
| show status [options] <clustername>                                       |
|                                                                           |
|     Shows cluster, process, operation, progress or backup status for the  |
|     specified cluster.                                                     |
|     Defaults to --cluster if no option specified.                         |
|                                                                           |
|     Valid options:                                                        |
|     --backup|-k          Show backup details.                             |
|     --cluster|-c         Show cluster details.                            |
|     --operation|-o       Show operation details.                          |
|     --process|-r         Show process details.                            |
|     --progress|-g        Show progress details.                           |
|     --progressbar|-b     Show progress bar.                               |
|                                                                           |
+---------------------------------------------------------------------------+
14 rows in set (0.02 sec)
```

If all nodes should have all options set to their default values, this is all there is to it. However, in practice that will not be the case, so the next topic covers how to make configuration changes.

Cluster Configuration: Auto Tuning

A feature unique to MySQL Cluster Manager is the autotune command. This can be a very useful way to get a good base configuration which then can be fine-tuned as required. The autotune command requires a template and optionally a write workload. The template defines the general workload, and there are three available templates:

- **web:** For web-based production workloads. MySQL Cluster Manager will attempt to maximize the performance given the available hardware.

- **realtime:** As for the web-based workload, it is aimed at maximizing the performance given the available workload. Additionally, the time to detect failures will be reduced.

- **test:** For test setups. The resource usage will be reduced compared to the web and realtime workloads.

The `--writeload` option can be used to set the write load to `low`, `medium`, or `high`. The definition of each write load is as follows:

- **low:** Fewer than 100 write transactions per second.

- **medium:** Between 100 and 1000 write transactions per second. This is the default if the `--writeload` option is omitted.

- **high:** More than 1000 write transactions per second.

The auto tuning feature issues several `set` commands. As will be discussed shortly, the `set` command changes the configuration of the cluster. If the `--dryrun` option is specified, MySQL Cluster Manager will generate the `set` commands and output them to a file rather than applying them. This is an excellent way to inspect the suggested changes before applying them. Optionally, the `set` commands can be applied manually with the possibility of making changes to them to fine-tune the configuration.

Since this is a test cluster, the `test` template will be used. Only a small number of write transactions are expected, so the low `writeload` value is appropriate. A dry run of the `autotune` command gives the following result:

```
mcm> autotune --dryrun --writeload=low test test_cluster\G
*************************** 1. row ***************************
Command result: Autotuning calculation complete. Please check /var/lib/mcm_data/clusters/
test_cluster/tmp/autotune.31b68d15_85_1.mcm on host 192.168.56.102 for settings that will be
applied.
1 row in set (4.35 sec)
```

Listing 13-8 contains the content of */var/lib/mcm_data/clusters/test_cluster/tmp/autotune. 31b68d15_85_1.mcm*, showing the suggested `set` commands to tune the cluster.

Listing 13-8. The Configuration Changes Suggested by the `autotune` Command

```
# The following will be applied to the current cluster config:
set HeartbeatIntervalDbDb:ndbmtd=15000 test_cluster;
set HeartbeatIntervalDbApi:ndbmtd=15000 test_cluster;
set RedoBuffer:ndbmtd=32M test_cluster;
set SendBufferMemory:ndbmtd+ndbmtd=2M test_cluster;
set ReceiveBufferMemory:ndbmtd+ndbmtd=2M test_cluster;
set SendBufferMemory:ndb_mgmd+ndbmtd=2M test_cluster;
set ReceiveBufferMemory:ndb_mgmd+ndbmtd=2M test_cluster;
set SendBufferMemory:mysqld+ndbmtd=2M test_cluster;
set ReceiveBufferMemory:mysqld+ndbmtd=2M test_cluster;
set SendBufferMemory:ndbapi+ndbmtd=2M test_cluster;
set ReceiveBufferMemory:ndbapi+ndbmtd=2M test_cluster;
set SharedGlobalMemory:ndbmtd=20M test_cluster;
set FragmentLogFileSize:ndbmtd=64M test_cluster;
set NoOfFragmentLogFiles:ndbmtd=16 test_cluster;
```

As the content of *autotune.31b68d15_85_1.mcm* shows, configuration changes are made using the set command. The syntax in its symbolic form is as follows:

```
mcm> set <option name>:<process(es)>[:NodeId]=<value> <cluster name>;
```

The `<option name>` is the name of the option, for example `HeartbeatIntervalDbDb`. Then you indicate what to apply the option to. For most options, this is a single process (as opposed to a pair of processes); for example, `HeartbeatIntervalDbDb` applies to the `ndbtmd` process. If an option should be applied to a single process only, the node ID can be added. Finally, you specify the value and which cluster to apply the change to. It is possible to set more than one option in one command; in that case, the options are combined as a comma-separated list. Some options, noticeably TCP-related options, require two processes. For example, the SendBufferMemory option specifies the size of the send buffer when sending from one node to another; this buffer is specific to each pair of nodes. The *autotune.31b68d15_85_1.mcm* file includes examples of single-process and dual-process options.

The settings look fine for this cluster, so they can be applied with the autotune command without the --dryrun option:

```
mcm> autotune --writeload=low test test_cluster;
+---------------------------------------------------+
| Command result                                    |
+---------------------------------------------------+
| Cluster successfully autotuned to template test   |
+---------------------------------------------------+
1 row in set (4.44 sec)
```

Cluster Configuration: The set Command

The test cluster has the SQL nodes located on the same hosts as the data nodes. It was also determined that the write load will be low. That is a good use case for enabling ndb_read_backup, which reduces the latency for read operations by always reading from the data node on the same host as the SQL node. Additionally, enable the binary log on NodeId = 51, but not on NodeId = 52. These two changes can be combined into one set command, like so:

```
mcm> set ndb_read_backup:mysqld=ON,log_bin:mysqld:51=binlog test_cluster;
+----------------------------------+
| Command result                   |
+----------------------------------+
| Cluster reconfigured successfully |
+----------------------------------+
1 row in set (3.79 sec)
```

Another change that will be made for the test cluster (overwriting one of the settings of the auto tuning) is to increase the send buffers for communication between the two data nodes:

```
mcm> set SendBufferMemory:ndbmtd+ndbmtd=4M test_cluster;
+----------------------------------+
| Command result                   |
+----------------------------------+
| Cluster reconfigured successfully |
+----------------------------------+
1 row in set (4.88 sec)
```

To ensure that the backups for the cluster are not deleted if the data administrator deletes the data directory before an initial system restart, configure the backup directory to be outside the */var/lib/mcm_data* path. First create the directory and set the ownership on each host that will have a data node:

```
shell$ mkdir /backups
shell$ mkdir /backups/ndbmtd /backups/mysqld
shell$ chown -R mysql:mysql /backups
```

Then execute the configuration change:

```
mcm> set BackupDataDir:ndbmtd=/backups/ndbmtd test_cluster;
+-----------------------------------+
| Command result                    |
+-----------------------------------+
| Cluster reconfigured successfully |
+-----------------------------------+
1 row in set (5.03 sec)

mcm> set backupdatadir:mysqld=/backups/mysqld test_cluster;
+-----------------------------------+
| Command result                    |
+-----------------------------------+
| Cluster reconfigured successfully |
+-----------------------------------+
1 row in set (3.25 sec)
```

The backupdatadir option for the SQL nodes is a MySQL Cluster Manager specific option that defines where the schema backup made during backup will be stored.

MySQL Cluster Manager verifies the option name and the value. If the validation fails, an error will be returned:

```
mcm> set ndb_batch_sizes:mysqld=64K test_cluster;
ERROR 6003 (00MGR): No such configuration parameter ndb_batch_sizes for process mysqld

mcm> set ndb_batch_size:mysqld=64M test_cluster;
ERROR 6002 (00MGR): Value 64M is outside legal range [0 - 31536000] for configuration
parameter ndb_batch_size
```

One side effect of this validation is that new options introduced for the cluster processes cannot be used until MySQL Cluster Manager also has been upgraded. This is particularly required for a major version upgrade of MySQL NDB Cluster, which usually includes several new options and/or new ranges of valid values.

Cluster Configuration: The get Command

The counterpart to the set command is the get command. It retrieves the value(s) of one or more options. It is possible to filter the options and processes in the same way as for the set command. Listing 13-9 shows how to get the value of the log_bin option for all mysqld processes, and the value of SendBufferMemory for sending from the data node with NodeId = 1 to the data node with NodeId = 2.

Listing 13-9. Getting the Values of Two Configuration Options

```
cm> get log_bin:mysqld test_cluster\G
*************************** 1. row ***************************
     Name: log_bin
    Value: binlog
 Process1: mysqld
  NodeId1: 51
 Process2:
```

```
NodeId2:
  Level:
Comment:
1 row in set (0.15 sec)

mcm> get SendBufferMemory:ndbmtd:1+ndbmtd:2 test_cluster\G
*************************** 1. row ***************************
    Name: SendBufferMemory
   Value: 4M
Process1: ndbmtd
 NodeId1: 1
Process2: ndbmtd
 NodeId2: 2
   Level: Process
 Comment:
1 row in set (0.21 sec)
```

In the output of the log_bin option, notice how there is only a row for NodeId = 51 despite the command asking for all mysqld processes. Why is that? By default, the get command only returns the options that are set to non-default values. To include options using the default value, add the --include-defaults or -d option (removing the Process2 and NodeId2 columns to reduce the width of the output):

```
mcm> get --include-defaults log_bin:mysqld test_cluster;
+---------+--------+----------+---------+...+---------+---------+
| Name    | Value  | Process1 | NodeId1 |...| Level   | Comment |
+---------+--------+----------+---------+...+---------+---------+
| log_bin | binlog | mysqld   | 51      |...|         |         |
| log_bin | OFF    | mysqld   | 52      |...| Default |         |
+---------+--------+----------+---------+...+---------+---------+
2 rows in set (0.19 sec)
```

A special use of the get command is to not add any filter other than the cluster name. This will return all options. Be aware that if the --include-defaults option is added, even this small test cluster returns 1896 rows.

Cluster Configuration: The reset Command

If it turns out that you made a mistake and you need to reset an option to its default value, you can use the reset command. Listing 13-10 disables binary logging from NodeId = 51 and checks the settings after running the reset command.

Listing 13-10. Resetting the log_bin Option

```
mcm> reset log_bin:mysqld:51 test_cluster;
+-----------------------------------+
| Command result                    |
+-----------------------------------+
| Cluster reconfigured successfully |
+-----------------------------------+
1 row in set (5.21 sec)
```

```
mcm> get --include-defaults log_bin:mysqld test_cluster;
+---------+-------+----------+---------+...+---------+---------+
| Name    | Value | Process1 | NodeId1 |...| Level   | Comment |
+---------+-------+----------+---------+...+---------+---------+
| log_bin | OFF   | mysqld   | 51      |...| Default |         |
| log_bin | OFF   | mysqld   | 52      |...| Default |         |
+---------+-------+----------+---------+...+---------+---------+
2 rows in set (0.27 sec)
```

With the cluster configuration set, it is time to start the cluster.

Starting and Stopping Processes

The test cluster is ready to be started. MySQL Cluster Manager has four commands to control whether a cluster and its processes are started or stopped, as well as a restart cluster command. The five commands are summarized in Table 13-15. The cluster name is mandatory for all four commands. The Options column shows the options for performing an initial restart and the options required to specify the nodes to start. Additional options exist for the commands; see the help text or documentation for details.

Table 13-15. *The Commands to Start and Stop a Cluster or Its Processes*

Command	Options	Description
restart cluster		Perform a rolling restart. Initial rolling restarts are not supported.
start cluster	[--initial]	Starts all processes in the cluster.
stop cluster		Shuts down the entire cluster. Equivalent to stopping the SQL nodes followed by the SHUTDOWN command in the ndb_mgm client.
start process	[--initial] Node ID or --added	Starts a single process or all nodes added (but not yet started) with the add process command (not discussed in this book).
stop process	Node ID	Stops a single process.

Since the test cluster is completely shut down, start it using the start cluster command:

```
mcm> start cluster test_cluster;
+-----------------------------+
| Command result              |
+-----------------------------+
| Cluster started successfully |
+-----------------------------+
1 row in set (2 min 25.02 sec
```

The command takes a while to complete. The progress can be followed using the show status command in another mcm client. Listing 13-11 shows the status using various options at the time when the two data nodes are starting. The --progressbar output can be particularly useful in a command that refreshes automatically; an example is the watch command on Linux.

Listing 13-11. The Status While Starting the Cluster

```
mcm> show status --cluster test_cluster;
+--------------+-----------------+---------+
| Cluster      | Status          | Comment |
+--------------+-----------------+---------+
| test_cluster | non-operational |         |
+--------------+-----------------+---------+
1 row in set (0.06 sec)

mcm> show status --process test_cluster;
+--------+----------+----------------+----------+-----------+--------------+
| NodeId | Process  | Host           | Status   | Nodegroup | Package      |
+--------+----------+----------------+----------+-----------+--------------+
| 49     | ndb_mgmd | 192.168.56.101 | running  |           | cluster_7.5.5 |
| 50     | ndb_mgmd | 192.168.56.102 | running  |           | cluster_7.5.5 |
| 1      | ndbmtd   | 192.168.56.103 | starting | n/a       | cluster_7.5.5 |
| 2      | ndbmtd   | 192.168.56.104 | starting | n/a       | cluster_7.5.5 |
| 51     | mysqld   | 192.168.56.103 | added    |           | cluster_7.5.5 |
| 52     | mysqld   | 192.168.56.104 | added    |           | cluster_7.5.5 |
| 53     | ndbapi   | *              | added    |           |              |
| 54     | ndbapi   | *              | added    |           |              |
+--------+----------+----------------+----------+-----------+--------------+
8 rows in set (1.81 sec)

mcm> show status --operation test_cluster;
+---------------+-----------+--------------+
| Command       | Status    | Description  |
+---------------+-----------+--------------+
| start cluster | executing | <no message> |
+---------------+-----------+--------------+
1 row in set (0.06 sec)

mcm> show status --progress test_cluster;
+---------------+-----------+----------+
| Command       | Status    | Progress |
+---------------+-----------+----------+
| start cluster | executing | 62%      |
+---------------+-----------+----------+
1 row in set (0.10 sec)

mcm> show status --progressbar test_cluster;
+---------------+-----------+----------------------------+
| Command       | Status    | Progress                   |
+---------------+-----------+----------------------------+
| start cluster | executing | 62% [############        ] |
+---------------+-----------+----------------------------+
1 row in set (0.12 sec)
```

When the start cluster command returns, the status of the cluster is fully operational:

```
mcm> show status --cluster test_cluster;
+--------------+--------------------+---------+
| Cluster      | Status             | Comment |
+--------------+--------------------+---------+
| test_cluster | fully operational  |         |
+--------------+--------------------+---------+
1 row in set (0.07 sec)
```

Starting and stopping individual nodes is performed similarly. For example, to stop the SQL node with NodeId = 51:

```
mcm> stop process 51 test_cluster;
+-----------------------------+
| Command result              |
+-----------------------------+
| Process stopped successfully |
+-----------------------------+
1 row in set (10.51 sec)
```

To start the node again:

```
mcm> start process 51 test_cluster;
+-----------------------------+
| Command result              |
+-----------------------------+
| Process started successfully |
+-----------------------------+
1 row in set (14.48 sec)
```

There are essentially three ways to trigger a rolling restart of a cluster—use the restart cluster command, perform a configuration change that requires a restart, or upgrade the cluster. Performing a configuration change is the next topic discussed, whereas upgrading the cluster is the last topic in this section.

Configuration of an Online Cluster

When the configuration of an online cluster changes, a restart is sometimes required. For changes to mysqld options where it is possible to make the change dynamic with a SET GLOBAL statement, this method will be used. The configuration file is also updated to persist the change when the node is restarted the next time. An example is to change the value of sort_buffer_size:

```
mcm> set sort_buffer_size:mysqld=32768 test_cluster;
+----------------------------------+
| Command result                   |
+----------------------------------+
| Cluster reconfigured successfully |
+----------------------------------+
1 row in set (0.87 sec)
```

If a restart is required, MySQL Cluster Manager will automatically perform it. This means it is preferable to combine all of the changes into one single set command when the cluster is online. The automatic restart is made as a rolling restart, where up to half the data nodes (one data node from each node group) restart in parallel to minimize the time it takes to perform the restart. However, to avoid overloading a host, no two data nodes on the same host will be restarted at the same time.

■ **Tip**　If multiple configuration changes are required of an online cluster, combine the changes into a single set command to avoid multiple rolling restarts.

As an example, consider changing the value of DataMemory for the data nodes:

```
mcm> set DataMemory:ndbmtd=100M test_cluster;
+-----------------------------------+
| Command result                    |
+-----------------------------------+
| Cluster reconfigured successfully |
+-----------------------------------+
1 row in set (2 min 22.02 sec)
```

If the progress of the set command is monitored using the show status --process command, it is possible to see how the nodes are restarted as part of the rolling restart:

```
mcm> show status --process test_cluster;
+--------+----------+----------------+----------+-----------+---------------+
| NodeId | Process  | Host           | Status   | Nodegroup | Package       |
+--------+----------+----------------+----------+-----------+---------------+
| 49     | ndb_mgmd | 192.168.56.101 | running  |           | cluster_7.5.5 |
| 50     | ndb_mgmd | 192.168.56.102 | running  |           | cluster_7.5.5 |
| 1      | ndbmtd   | 192.168.56.103 | starting | 0         | cluster_7.5.5 |
| 2      | ndbmtd   | 192.168.56.104 | running  | 0         | cluster_7.5.5 |
| 51     | mysqld   | 192.168.56.103 | running  |           | cluster_7.5.5 |
| 52     | mysqld   | 192.168.56.104 | running  |           | cluster_7.5.5 |
| 53     | ndbapi   | *              | added    |           |               |
| 54     | ndbapi   | *              | added    |           |               |
+--------+----------+----------------+----------+-----------+---------------+
8 rows in set (0.08 sec)
```

The temporary configuration difference during the restart can also be seen in the ndbinfo.memoryusage view (the timing of the following query must be just right to see both data nodes online with different DataMemory sizes) on the SQL node using the mysql command-line client:

```
mysql> SELECT node_id, total
         FROM ndbinfo.memoryusage
        WHERE memory_type = 'Data memory';
+---------+-----------+
| node_id | total     |
+---------+-----------+
|       1 | 104857600 |
|       2 |  83886080 |
+---------+-----------+
2 rows in set (0.02 sec)
```

The ndbinfo schema is discussed in more detail in Chapter 16.

Backups

MySQL Cluster Manager creates two backups—a full backup using the native NDB Cluster backup and a schema backup using mysqldump. Backups are created using the backup cluster command and both backups are always created. It is not possible to ensure that the native NDB Cluster backup and the schema backup are consistent with each other unless no schema changes are made during the period the backup is executing.

■ **Note** MySQL Cluster Manager does not provide any service to back up the binary logs. Use the techniques described in Chapter 8 instead.

The backup cluster command supports the same backup options as the START BACKUP command in the ndb_mgm client, but specified in the same way as other optional parameters in MySQL Cluster Manager. Table 13-16 lists the options available with the backup cluster command. The options are available both with a long name and a single letter, with the former displayed in the first column and the latter in the second. Additionally, the cluster name must be specified.

Table 13-16. *The Backup Cluster Options*

Long Option	Shortcut	Description
--background	-B	Execute the backup in the background. The mcm client will return control immediately.
--backupid	-I	The backup ID for the backup. This behaves the same way as when the backup is started through the ndb_mgm client, i.e., it must be an integer between 1 and 4294967294 (both inclusive). By default, the next in sequence from the previous highest used backup ID will be used.
--snapshotend	-E	Create the backup with a snapshot at the end of the backup. This is the default.
--snapshotstart	-S	Create the backup with a snapshot at the start of the backup.
--waitcompleted	-W	MySQL Cluster Manager will keep the connection to the management node open until the backup has completed. This is the default.
--waitstarted	-w	MySQL Cluster Manager will only keep the connection to the management node open until the backup has started.

As an example of creating a backup with the backup ID set to 170511211, the following command can be used:

```
mcm> backup cluster --backupid=1705112111 test_cluster;
+-------------------------------+
| Command result                |
+-------------------------------+
| Backup completed successfully |
+-------------------------------+
1 row in set (55.27 sec)
```

While the backup is in progress, the show status command with the --backup option will show the following status:

```
mcm> show status --backup test_cluster;
+----------------------------------------------------------+
| Command result                                           |
+----------------------------------------------------------+
| BackupId 1705112111 currently active in test_cluster     |
+----------------------------------------------------------+
1 row in set (0.13 sec)
```

The completed backups can be listed with the list backups command. By default, only the native NDB Cluster backups will be listed. This can be changed by adding the --all option. If only one backup is of interest, the --backupid option can be used to filter the list. Listing 13-12 shows examples of using the list backups command. The timestamps are around the time the backup completed.

Listing 13-12. Listing the Completed Backups

```
mcm> list backups test_cluster;
+------------+--------+----------------+----------------------+---------+
| BackupId   | NodeId | Host           | Timestamp            | Comment |
+------------+--------+----------------+----------------------+---------+
| 1705112054 | 1      | 192.168.56.103 | 2017-05-11 10:55:56Z |         |
| 1705112054 | 2      | 192.168.56.104 | 2017-05-11 10:55:56Z |         |
| 1705112103 | 1      | 192.168.56.103 | 2017-05-11 11:04:03Z |         |
| 1705112103 | 2      | 192.168.56.104 | 2017-05-11 11:04:03Z |         |
| 1705112111 | 1      | 192.168.56.103 | 2017-05-11 11:12:00Z |         |
| 1705112111 | 2      | 192.168.56.104 | 2017-05-11 11:12:00Z |         |
+------------+--------+----------------+----------------------+---------+
6 rows in set (0.28 sec)

mcm> list backups --backupid=1705112111 --all test_cluster;
+------------+--------+----------------+----------------------+---------+
| BackupId   | NodeId | Host           | Timestamp            | Comment |
+------------+--------+----------------+----------------------+---------+
| 1705112111 | 1      | 192.168.56.103 | 2017-05-11 11:12:00Z |         |
| 1705112111 | 2      | 192.168.56.104 | 2017-05-11 11:12:00Z |         |
| 1705112111 | 51     | 192.168.56.103 | 2017-05-11 11:12:11Z | Schema  |
| 1705112111 | 52     | 192.168.56.104 | 2017-05-11 11:12:18Z | Schema  |
+------------+--------+----------------+----------------------+---------+
4 rows in set (0.32 sec)
```

The backup files can be found in the backup data directories that were configured when the test cluster was first set up. The directory structure is the same as for native NDB Cluster backups created through the ndb_mgm client. For example, on NodeId = 1 and NodeId = 51:

```
shell$ ls /backups/ndbmtd/BACKUP/BACKUP-1705112111/
BACKUP-1705112111-0.1.Data   BACKUP-1705112111.1.ctl   BACKUP-1705112111.1.log

shell$ ls /backups/mysqld/BACKUP/BACKUP-1705112111/
BACKUP-1705112111.51.schema.sql
```

■ **Tip** As always, make sure the backups are copied off the hosts and that there is a copy of the backups outside the data center as well.

With the backups in place, it is possible to simulate a disaster where it is necessary to restore the backup.

Restoring a Backup

In order to simulate a situation where it is necessary to restore the backup made in the previous step, perform an initial system restart of the test cluster. This will delete all the data from the cluster, so the only way to recover is to restore the data from a backup. MySQL Cluster Manager uses the ndb_restore program to restore a backup. As it is possible for the agent to communicate with the agents on the other hosts, it is possible to perform the restore with a single command from any of the MySQL Cluster Manager agents.

■ **Caution** Do not perform an initial system restart of a production cluster unless it is absolutely necessary and then only after verifying that a backup exists and it is possible to restore the backup!

The first step of the initial system restart is to stop the cluster:

```
mcm> stop cluster test_cluster;
+----------------------------+
| Command result             |
+----------------------------+
| Cluster stopped successfully |
+----------------------------+
1 row in set (34.13 sec)
```

Then perform the initial system restart:

```
mcm> start cluster --initial test_cluster;
+----------------------------+
| Command result             |
+----------------------------+
| Cluster started successfully |
+----------------------------+
1 row in set (1 min 19.63 sec)
```

For the restore in this example, the backup with the 170511211 ID will be used. The MySQL Cluster Manager command to execute the restore is restore backup. As with ndb_restore, there are a number of options to affect the restore, such as to specify which tables to restore. One important difference to executing ndb_restore directly is that MySQL Cluster Manager will by default restore the metadata (the schema definition) from the native NDB Cluster backup. So, the simplest way to perform a restore that restores both the schema and data is as follows:

```
mcm> restore cluster --backupid=1705112111 test_cluster;
+------------------------------+
| Command result               |
+------------------------------+
| Restore completed successfully |
+------------------------------+
1 row in set (2 min 31.16 sec)
```

Upgrades

Remember the steps used when the upgrade was performed manually? MySQL Cluster Manager completes the upgrade in four simple steps. This makes upgrades much simpler to execute, and simpler procedures lead to fewer errors.

The four steps are:

1. Download the new version to upgrade to.

2. Unpack the downloaded file on each host.

3. Add a package for the new version in MySQL Cluster Manager.

4. Tell MySQL Cluster Manager to execute the upgrade.

Under the hood, the same steps are required compared to the manual upgrade. It is just that in this case, MySQL Cluster Manager will keep track of what has to be done and when.

For this example, the upgrade is to version 7.5.6 with the downloaded file unpacked into */opt/mysql/packages/7.5.6* in the same way as it was done for version 7.5.5 used for the initial installation:

```
shell$ cd /opt/mysql/packages/
shell$ tar -zxf mysql-cluster-gpl-7.5.6-linux-glibc2.5-x86_64.tar.gz
shell$ mv mysql-cluster-gpl-7.5.6-linux-glibc2.5-x86_64 7.5.6
```

This must be done on all hosts.

The new version can then be added as a package in MySQL Cluster Manager:

```
mcm> add package --basedir=/opt/mysql/packages/7.5.6 cluster_7.5.6;
+----------------------------+
| Command result             |
+----------------------------+
| Package added successfully |
+----------------------------+
1 row in set (7.80 sec)
```

All that remains now is to execute the upgrade using the upgrade cluster command:

```
mcm> upgrade cluster --package=cluster_7.5.6 test_cluster;
+------------------------------+
| Command result               |
+------------------------------+
| Cluster upgraded successfully |
+------------------------------+
1 row in set (9 min 7.22 sec)
```

As usual, the show status command can provide information about the progress, for example:

```
mcm> show status --process test_cluster;
+--------+----------+----------------+----------+-----------+--------------+
| NodeId | Process  | Host           | Status   | Nodegroup | Package      |
+--------+----------+----------------+----------+-----------+--------------+
| 49     | ndb_mgmd | 192.168.56.101 | running  |           | cluster_7.5.6 |
| 50     | ndb_mgmd | 192.168.56.102 | running  |           | cluster_7.5.6 |
| 1      | ndbmtd   | 192.168.56.103 | running  | 0         | cluster_7.5.6 |
| 2      | ndbmtd   | 192.168.56.104 | starting | 0         | cluster_7.5.6 |
| 51     | mysqld   | 192.168.56.103 | running  |           | cluster_7.5.5 |
| 52     | mysqld   | 192.168.56.104 | running  |           | cluster_7.5.5 |
| 53     | ndbapi   | *              | added    |           |              |
| 54     | ndbapi   | *              | added    |           |              |
+--------+----------+----------------+----------+-----------+--------------+
8 rows in set (0.08 sec)
```

Notice how the management nodes as well as the data node with NodeId = 1 have already been upgraded and restarted, while the data node with NodeId = 2 is in the process of restarting with the upgraded version. The SQL nodes are still waiting for their turn and are still using version 7.5.5.

This concludes the MySQL Cluster Manager tutorial. The remainder of the chapter is an introduction to troubleshooting MySQL Cluster Manager problems.

Troubleshooting MySQL Cluster Manager

The main sources of information to perform troubleshooting in MySQL Cluster Manager are the error messages and the log file specified with the log-file option. It is also worth keeping in mind that MySQL Cluster Manager is self-healing, so in most cases a restart of an agent that crashed will recover on its own; in a worst-case scenario, whereby it is impossible to start an agent, the agent can be recovered by deleting the agent repository. The error messages, the log, and the self-healing process are all discussed in this section.

Error Messages and the Log

Often the error message will be enough for you to diagnose the issue. Consider for example the following error:

```
mcm> set log_bin:mysqld:51=binlog test_cluster;
ERROR 1002 (00MGR): Agent on host 192.168.56.101:18620 is unavailable
```

The error indicates that there is a communication problem between the agent where the command is executed and the agent on *192.168.56.101*. In that case, investigate whether the agent is online on *192.168.56.101*, whether the firewall permits the agents to communicate, etc.

If more information is required, it is necessary to look in the log file. It is possible to control the verbosity of the log by setting the log-level option. Table 13-17 lists the log levels in order of increased verbosity. The info and debug levels can generate a fair bit of log messages, the message somewhat less but still enough to be able to start investigating most cases. The message level for example includes all commands executed through the mcm client. The warning, error, and critical levels will, in general, not produce enough information to be used for an investigation. It is best to use the message level during normal operations and increase to the debug level when troubleshooting.

Table 13-17. *The MySQL Cluster Manager Log Levels*

Log Level	Description
critical	The most severe errors. This could include a corrupted repository for the agent.
error	Still a severe level for the agent. This could include configuration errors.
warning	For conditions that may require a corrective action. A warning level message while executing a command will cause the command to fail.
message	Messages about the operation of the agent. This includes the commands executed through the mcm client. This is the default and recommended log level.
info	Informational messages. These generally do not require any action.
debug	Additional information that can be required to debug errors.

The log level can be changed dynamically at runtime using the change log-level command. The change can be applied to the agent on which the command is executed, to a list of hosts, or to a site. For example, to change the log level to debug for the test_site site:

```
mcm> change log-level debug test_site;
+-------------------------------+
| Command result                |
+-------------------------------+
| Log-level changed successfully |
+-------------------------------+
1 row in set (0.02 sec)
```

In the previous example, where the set command failed because the agent could not communicate with the agent on host *192.168.56.101*, it will not work to set the log level for the whole site. That will require telling the agents on all the other hosts about the change. In a case like that, it is useful to change the log level on the agent where the error is returned:

```
mcm> change log-level debug;
+-------------------------------+
| Command result                |
+-------------------------------+
| Log-level changed successfully |
+-------------------------------+
1 row in set (0.00 sec)
```

When the log level is set to debug, the log file will contain messages like those shown in Listing 13-13. Notice how each message includes the log level in parentheses after the timestamp. From the log snippet, it can be seen that message level messages include the executed commands (the first message in the sample output) and that an error was returned to the client (the last message). The highest severity message in this example is a warning that it was not possible to deliver a message to the agent on host *192.168.56.101* port 18620 (the Xcom port). The debug messages include a confirmation that the cluster test_cluster exists and the parsed components of the command.

Listing 13-13. Example of the MySQL Cluster Manager Log

```
2017-05-16 21:07:50.520: (message) [T0x14eb320 chass] Received command: set log_
bin:mysqld:51=binlog test_cluster
2017-05-16 21:07:50.520: (debug) [T0x14eb320 chass@commands.c:1474] Verifying that cluster
exists
2017-05-16 21:07:50.520: (debug) [T0x14eb320 chass@commands.c:3993] Getting existing config
for test_cluster
2017-05-16 21:07:50.520: (debug) [T0x14eb320 chass@commands.c:3757] Sec='', key='log_bin',
proc1='mysqld', pid1='51', proc2='', pid2='', val='binlog'
2017-05-16 21:07:50.520: (info) [T0x14eb320 chass@manager-api-util.c:391] Appended: sec=''
key='log_bin' proct1='mysqld' pid1='51' proct2='' pid2='' val='binlog' pri=1 readonly=0
...
2017-05-16 21:07:50.612: (info) [T0x1572450 CMGR @cluster-manager.c:10199] First unavailable
host in view is 192.168.56.101:1
8620
2017-05-16 21:07:50.612: (warning) [T0x1572450 CMGR ] Message delivery failed: err->
message='Agent on host 192.168.56.101:186
20 is unavailable' mgr_set_configvalues
2017-05-16 21:07:50.612: (info) [T0x1572450 CMGR @reply.c:161] Error reply to client
127.0.0.1:50173 req_id 6 { 1002, 'Agent
on host 192.168.56.101:18620 is unavailable' }
2017-05-16 21:07:50.613: (debug) [T0x14eb320 chass@message_broker.c:418] Updating last
replied req_id 5 -> 6
2017-05-16 21:07:50.613: (message) [T0x14eb320 chass] Returning error to client : 1002 Agent
on host 192.168.56.101:18620 is unavailable
```

Self-Healing Agents

One of the features of MySQL Cluster Manager is that it is self-healing. So, when a MySQL Cluster Manager agent has been down, it will try to recover itself by getting the information it is missing from one of the other agents. In rare cases—such as after a host crash—the state of the agent repository may become so bad that a recovery is not possible. In those cases, one solution is to delete the agent repository and then start the agent. First ensure the agent is not running by checking the process list on the host for the mcmd process. For example:

```
shell$ ps auxf | grep mcmd | grep -v grep
```

This command should not return anything. In Microsoft Windows, check the Task Manager for the existence of the mcmd process, as shown in Figure 13-10. In the figure, the mcmd process is there, so you must first stop it.

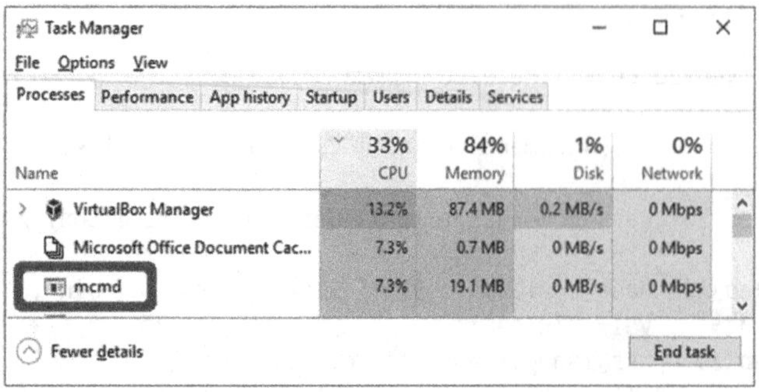

Figure 13-10. *The mcmd process in the Microsoft Windows Task Manager*

With the agent down, remove everything in the repository directory together with the repository checksum file. The repository is the *rep* directory under the path specified with the manager-directory option, and the checksum file is the repchksum file in manager-directory. Using the configuration used for the tutorial in the previous sections, the full paths on Linux are */var/lib/mcm_data/rep* and */var/lib/mcm_data/repchksum*:

```
shell$ rm -f /var/lib/mcm_data/rep/* /var/lib/mcm_data/repchksum
```

For Microsoft Windows, the default paths are *C:\Program Files (x86)\MySQL\MySQL Cluster Manager\mcm_data\rep* and *C:\Program Files (x86)\MySQL\MySQL Cluster Manager\mcm_data\repchksum*. Assuming the default paths are used (otherwise substitute with the actual paths), delete them either through File Explorer or from the command prompt:

```
C:\Users\wisborg>del /s "C:\Program Files (x86)\MySQL\MySQL Cluster Manager\mcm_data\rep"
"C:\Program Files (x86)\MySQL\MySQL Cluster Manager\mcm_data\repchksum"
C:\Program Files (x86)\MySQL\MySQL Cluster Manager\mcm_data\rep\*, Are you sure (Y/N)? y
Deleted file - C:\Program Files (x86)\MySQL\MySQL Cluster Manager\mcm_data\rep\clustat.
test_cluster.8005fafe_10_0
Deleted file - C:\Program Files (x86)\MySQL\MySQL Cluster Manager\mcm_data\rep\config.test_
cluster.8005fafe_10_0
Deleted file - C:\Program Files (x86)\MySQL\MySQL Cluster Manager\mcm_data\rep\opstat.test_
cluster.8005fafe_10_0
Deleted file - C:\Program Files (x86)\MySQL\MySQL Cluster Manager\mcm_data\rep\site.test_
site.8005fafe_1_0
Deleted file - C:\Program Files (x86)\MySQL\MySQL Cluster Manager\mcm_data\rep\sitepackage.
cluster_7.5.5.8005fafe_8_0
Deleted file - C:\Program Files (x86)\MySQL\MySQL Cluster Manager\mcm_data\repchksum
```

Finally, start the agent again.

Summary

This chapter provided a tour of MySQL Cluster Manager, which is a product included in the commercial offering of MySQL NDB Cluster. After downloading, installing, and configuring MySQL Cluster Manager itself, a test cluster was set up and several of the same tasks discussed earlier in the book were performed:

- Installing the cluster.

- Configuring the cluster.

- Starting and stopping the cluster and single processes.

- Making subsequent configuration changes.

- Backing up and restoring the data and schema.

- Updating the cluster.

The chapter also discussed how to troubleshoot issues that pop up while using MySQL Cluster Manager.

This completes the daily tasks and maintenance for MySQL NDB Cluster, and it is time to move on to monitoring and troubleshooting. The next chapter looks at monitoring solutions and monitoring the operating system.

PART IV

■ ■ ■

Monitoring and Troubleshooting

CHAPTER 14

■ ■ ■

Monitoring Solutions and the Operating System

An often-forgotten part of maintaining a database is that it must be monitored. There are two sources of data to monitor—data collected by an external monitoring solution or the database administrator and logs written by the processes running on the operating system. Irrespective of the source of the data, monitoring has a threefold purpose. This chapter, together with the next three chapters, will go through the various parts of monitoring from the high-level monitoring solutions to the actual troubleshooting using the collected data and logs.

The journey through the world of monitoring and troubleshooting will start in this chapter with a discussion about monitoring at the high level and going through monitoring solutions and the reasons that you need to monitor. The chapter concludes with considerations of how to monitor the operating system. The next two chapters go through MySQL data sources and MySQL specific logs, with an emphasis in Chapter 15 on the sources and logs that are also available for MySQL Server installations. Chapter 16 is devoted to the data sources and logs exclusive to MySQL NDB Cluster. Chapter 17 discusses troubleshooting, including examples of using the logs.

Why Monitor?

Monitoring might seem like a boring task that does not provide any direct improvement to a MySQL NDB Cluster installation. However, the importance of having a good monitoring in place cannot be stressed enough. It is the best line of defense to avoid issues in the first place and is invaluable to investigate issues.

This section covers the three main reasons to monitor a cluster:

- **Establish a baseline:** Makes it possible to see the effect of making changes. This is primarily useful for performance issues and to help predict when maintenance is required.

- **Perform a root cause analysis:** Something went wrong, but what and why?

- **Perform preventive maintenance:** Prevent issues from happening.

Since MySQL NDB Cluster is often used for high-availability systems, the importance of monitoring is even more important than in some other cases.

© Jesper Wisborg Krogh and Mikiya Okuno 2017
J. W. Krogh and M. Okuno, *Pro MySQL NDB Cluster*, https://doi.org/10.1007/978-1-4842-2982-8_14

Establish a Baseline

When monitoring data is recorded over time, the historical data can be used as a baseline. That is, for comparison with newly collected data to see the differences. This is particularly useful for determining whether a change made to the system was successful, such as whether the performance or availability has been improved.

Consider the following use case: One of the users of the application complains about the time it takes to perform some action, for example, the time to load a web page. The investigation concludes that the solution will be to add an index to a table to reduce the number of rows examined. How can monitoring be used to determine whether the issue has been resolved after adding the index? This is where the baseline comes into play.

■ **Note** Sometimes a solution may be found, but it turns out that the change does not improve the situation or even makes it worse. A good baseline combined with data comparisons ensure that the investigation does not end before the issue is really resolved.

Figure 14-1 shows metrics of the query in question for the period before and after the index was added to improve the query. The index was added around 12:57, which is obvious from the change to the data. The execution time improves by almost an order of magnitude and the number of executions increases by around the same factor. So, from the perspective of the query, it is mission accomplished. There is a little more to the story, though.

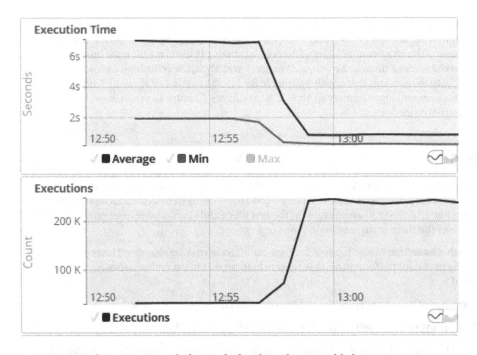

Figure 14-1. *The query metrics before and after the index was added*

Figure 14-2 shows some more metrics for the same index addition, but at the cluster level. The increase of the number of statements per second reflects the increase in the number of executions of the query. Is that expected? Or does that show that the query is executed more often than it should be? It might also be that the change simply allowed the cluster to handle all of the queries expected now that the index was added.

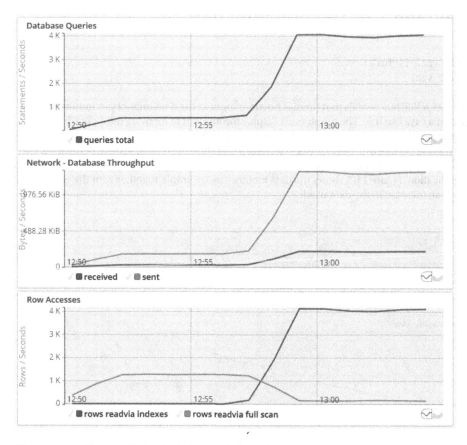

Figure 14-2. *The overall metrics before and after adding an index*

It is also worth noting the network throughput on the cluster. The *Row Accesses* graph shows that the work went from being table scans to index scans and lookups. This was the aim of the schema change, so that is good. However, despite each query now accessing fewer rows, the increase in number of queries has caused the overall network usage to increase. Does that warrant an upgrade of the network infrastructure? The send throughput peaks at around 10 mbit (1.25 MB/s), so if that is the maximum supported throughput of the network, an upgrade is required. The network utilization is also useful to investigate through preventive maintenance, as described later.

Perform a Root Cause Analysis

Another common use case of monitoring is to determine the root cause of an issue. As an example, users complain that they are getting a "table is full" error. The following shows the query and the error returned:

```
mysql> INSERT INTO t1 (val) VALUES (UUID());
ERROR 1114 (HY000): The table 't1' is full

mysql> SHOW WARNINGS\G
*************************** 1. row ***************************
  Level: Warning
   Code: 1296
Message: Got error 827 'Out of memory in Ndb Kernel, table data (increase DataMemory)' from NDB
```

```
*************************** 2. row ***************************
   Level: Error
    Code: 1114
Message: The table 't1' is full
2 rows in set (0.00 sec)
```

The output of SHOW WARNINGS reveals that there is no more room in the data memory. A monitoring graph is very helpful in a case like this. The graph must display the amount of memory used out of DataMemory over time. This makes it possible to determine how quickly the memory has been used. For example, if it was a gradual change over several years, it is likely just showing regular growth of the data. On the other hand, if the growth happened over a few minutes, it suggests a change to the use of the cluster or even a bug in the application. Figure 14-3 shows the data memory usage graph, together with the queries that may have caused an increase in the data used.

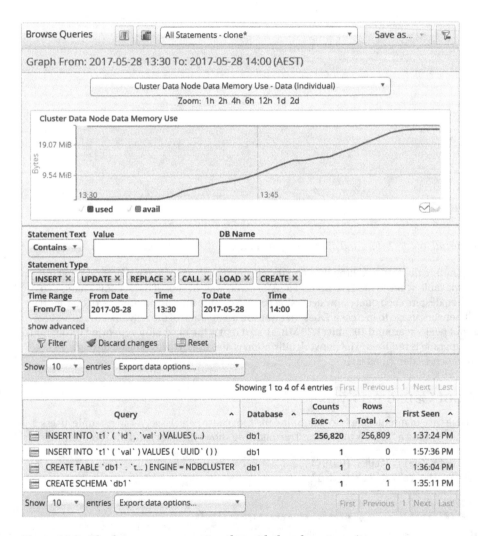

Figure 14-3. The data memory usage together with the relevant queries

Figure 14-3 is from the Query Analyzer in MySQL Enterprise Monitor. The graph displays the total amount of DataMemory (the horizontal line at the top) and the increasing line shows the memory used out of DataMemory. This makes the amount of free memory the difference between the two lines. The graph shows that the amount of free memory gradually decreased over 25 minutes until 95% of the memory was used (with the last 5% reserved for restarts).

The lower part of the screenshot shows that there can only be one source of the increased data memory usage: the INSERT INTO 't1' ('id', 'val') VALUES (...) query. This query was executed more than 250,000 times in the half hour that was selected. There is also a CREATE TABLE statement for the table, so this suggests that some kind of batch job storing data in the table or a data import job or similar was executed. With this information, it is time to determine whether the issue should be resolved by avoiding the data in the t1 table or whether it is necessary to increase the value of DataMemory. The section entitled "MySQL Enterprise Monitor" later in the chapter covers the Query Analyzer in more detail.

It would have been even better if the issue had been discovered before all of the data memory had been exhausted and the database started to return errors. How to use monitoring to avoid these potential issues is the next topic.

Perform Preventive Maintenance

The best kind of issues are the ones that are resolved before they become a problem. Monitoring is the best place to look for potential issues. The two examples in this section show how preventive maintenance can be used to avoid a problem.

The baseline example saw the network usage of the cluster increase after a new index made it possible to increase the number of queries per second on the cluster. This may cause the network to become a bottleneck, so the usage should be monitored. If it is determined that the current network configuration will not be able to sustain the workload, corrective actions in the form of changes to the workload or improving the capacity of the network must be taken.

The root cause analysis example had the data memory usage increase over a period of time. Typically for these kind of issues, it is a slow change that occurs over several months. With a monitoring system such as MySQL Enterprise Monitor that alerts of potential issues before they become critical, it is possible to make the required changes ahead of time. In this case, either add data memory or stop the job that loaded all of the data into the table.

Analyzing the monitoring data is among the database administrators' and system administrators' most important tasks. Having a good monitoring system installed with alert events configured appropriately is an important step to simplify this work.

Monitoring Solutions

It will become apparent in this and the two next chapters that there is a vast amount of data that can be collected for monitoring purposes. Any attempt to manually keep on top of the raw data and detect potential issues is bound to fail, and investigations of ongoing issues and root cause analysis will take longer than they should. This is where monitoring solutions show their strength.

A monitoring solution is software dedicated to collect and display monitoring data. Additionally, the most useful solutions either send notifications of problems on their own or can be combined with notification software. The exact way monitoring solutions are implemented varies and there are different opinions as to which solution is the best. In that respect, the important thing is to find a product that provides the necessary monitoring and become familiar with it.

■ **Tip**   Treat the monitoring solution as a production system. With the requirements that applications are available 24 hours a day, monitoring becomes increasingly important. So make sure the monitoring system is itself monitored, the required availability has been defined, etc.

MySQL Monitoring Solutions

MySQL provides two monitoring solutions. Both solutions are part of the *MySQL Enterprise Edition* and *MySQL Cluster Carrier Grade Edition* subscriptions, but like MySQL Cluster Manager, they are available in a 30-day trial version (*https://www.mysql.com/trials/*). The solutions are as follows:

- **MySQL Enterprise Monitor:** A standalone monitoring solution written by the MySQL team. Often abbreviated *MEM*.

- **Oracle Enterprise Manager for MySQL:** A plugin for monitoring MySQL Server instances from within *Oracle Enterprise Manager (OEM)*.

The same development team works on both solutions. However, since Oracle Enterprise Manager for MySQL is part of a larger monitoring solution from Oracle Corporation, it does not have all of the features included in MySQL Enterprise Monitor. Specifically, there are no MySQL NDB Cluster specific metrics included in Oracle Enterprise Manager for MySQL. For this reason, it is better to use MySQL Enterprise Monitor, and this is the only one of the two solutions discussed in more detail in this book. The next section provides a brief overview of MySQL Enterprise Monitor.

■ **Tip**   To monitor MySQL NDB Cluster, MySQL Enterprise Monitor is preferred over Oracle Enterprise Manager for MySQL.

MySQL Enterprise Monitor (MEM)

MySQL Enterprise Manager was first released more than 10 years ago. At the time of writing, the latest version is version 3.4, but version 4.0 has later been released. It is written by the MySQL developer team specifically to monitor MySQL and the hosts MySQL is installed on. This section goes through the components of MySQL Enterprise Monitor, how to install and upgrade it and its most important features.

■ **Tip**   New versions of MySQL Enterprise Monitor are released frequently. Each new version includes new features. For example, version 3.2 included a new replication dashboard, version 3.3 included a dashboard for monitoring backups, version 3.4 included support for Group Replication, and version 4.0 includes improved monitoring of MySQL NDB Cluster and a new user interface as some of the new features. Make sure to use the latest version to have all the monitoring features available. The manual at *https://dev.mysql.com/doc/mysql-monitor/en/* includes a description of the latest features and has a link to the release notes.

Components

MySQL Enterprise Monitor consists of several components. The database administrator can choose to install the components required for the system that should be monitored. Table 14-1 lists the four types of components that are available.

Table 14-1. *Types of MySQL Enterprise Monitor Components*

Component	Description
MySQL Enterprise Service Manager	This is the main component where the collected data is stored and can be viewed. There are three subcomponents to the MySQL Enterprise Service Manager: Apache Tomcat, Java Runtime Environment (JRE), and MySQL Server (optional). The user interface is accessed through a web browser.
MySQL Enterprise Monitor Agent	The MySQL Enterprise Monitor Agent collects the data and sends it to the MySQL Enterprise Service Manager.
MySQL Enterprise Monitor Proxy and Aggregator	The MySQL Enterprise Monitor Proxy and Aggregator can be used to collect query information for the *Query Analyzer*. In MySQL NDB Cluster 7.3 and later the source of this data will usually be the Performance Schema. The MySQL Enterprise Monitor Proxy and Aggregator are not required when the data is colelcted from the Performance Schema.
MySQL Enterprise Plugin for Connector/PHP *MySQL Enterprise Plugin for Connector/J* *MySQL Enterprise Plugin for Connector/Net*	There are plugins available for PHP, .Net, and Java. The plugins can send query data directly to the MySQL Enterprise Service Manager (.Net and Java) or via the MySQL Enterprise Monitor Aggregator (PHP).

In most setups, only the MySQL Enterprise Service Manager and the MySQL Enterprise Monitor Agent are used, so these are the only components that are discussed in more detail.

A MySQL Enterprise Monitor Agent is responsible for collecting data and sending it to the MySQL Enterprise Service Manager for storage and analysis. An agent can collect data by executing queries against an SQL node either on the same host or a remote host. Additionally, the agent can collect host level data such as CPU statistics, memory usage metrics, disk utilization, and network throughput from the host it is installed on. So, in order to collect all data, you must install an agent on all hosts in a cluster.

The MySQL Enterprise Monitor Service Manager stores the data in a MySQL Server instance called the repository. It is possible to use either a bundled repository or an existing MySQL Server instance. It is in most cases best to use the bundled repository as it ensures that all requirements are met and the repository is upgraded when the MySQL Enterprise Service Manager is upgraded.

■ **Caution** Never choose the repository to be one of the MySQL instances that MySQL Enterprise Monitor is set up to monitor. Doing so will prevent the detection of problems with the cluster, for example, if the SQL node becomes unavailable.

The MySQL Enterprise Service Manager includes an agent. This allows MySQL Enterprise Monitor to automatically set up monitoring of its own repository and the host on which the MySQL Enterprise Service Manager is installed. Since the agent can monitor remote MySQL instances, in principle the MySQL Enterprise Service Manager is all that is required if host-level monitoring of remote hosts is not required.

Installation and Upgrades

The installation and upgrade of the MySQL Enterprise Service Manager and the MySQL Enterprise Monitor Agent are straightforward. The downloads include two binaries, one of which is for new installations and the other that is for upgrades. Each installer includes everything required to install the component. Table 14-2 includes examples of the filenames from version 3.4.0 for the installers on Linux and Microsoft Windows.

Table 14-2. *Installer Binaries*

Action	Installer Filename
New install	*mysqlmonitor-3.4.0.4144-linux-x86_64-installer.bin*
	mysqlmonitor-3.4.0.4144-windows64-installer.exe
Upgrade	*mysqlmonitor-3.4.0.4144-linux-x86_64-update-installer.bin*
	mysqlmonitor-3.4.0.4144-windows64-update-installer.exe

Notice how the binaries for new installations end with *installer* (plus the file extension) and for upgrades, they end in *update-installer* (plus the file extension). The exact filenames will depend on the release installed, as the version numbers and build numbers (4144 in this case) are included in the filename.

An installation or upgrade can be performed in one of three modes:

- **GUI:** A GUI-based installation with dialogs to set up MySQL Enterprise Monitor.

- **Text:** The text mode provides the same functionality as the GUI mode, but all the dialogs are in text mode. This is useful when no graphical user interface is installed on the target server.

- **Unattended:** All options are provided on the command line. This is great for scripting installs.

It is best the first time to use either the GUI or text mode to get familiar with the configuration options. Later installations, particularly of the agents, can be automated using the unattended installation. When the installer is executed with root or administrator rights, it will attempt to add the component as a service (for example as System V init script on Linux or as a Microsoft Windows Service), so MySQL Enterprise Monitor is automatically started and stopped together with the operating system. Figure 14-4 shows one of the screens in GUI mode for the MySQL Enterprise Service Manager, where the settings for the bundled repository are configured.

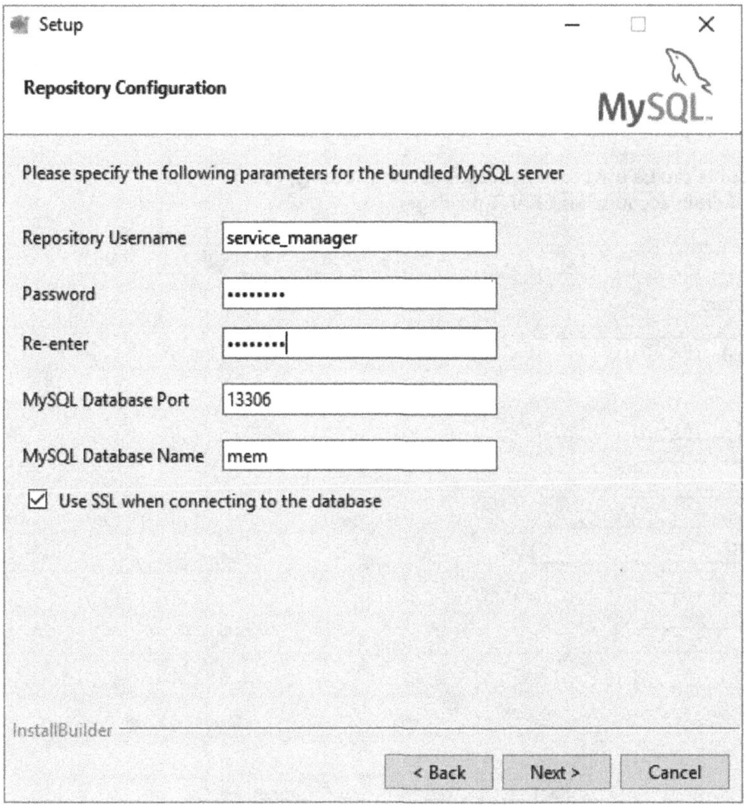

Figure 14-4. *Configuring the repository during the installation*

Remember the discussion in Chapter 12 about giving the minimum required privileges to the users? This also applies to the users involved in monitoring. The MySQL Enterprise Monitor Agent supports using three different users: an administrator account, a general account, and a limited account. When all accounts are present, MySQL Enterprise Monitor will choose the account with the fewest privileges that can perform the task. This also ensures that the extra login that is reserved in addition to max_connections for a user with the SUPER privilege is not used by the monitoring system.

The installer for the agent supports creating the general and limited accounts automatically, provided the administrator account has been configured with the WITH GRANT privilege. Figure 14-5 shows the setup screen in the GUI installer for MySQL Enterprise Monitor Agent that enables you to set up the less privileged accounts.

Figure 14-5. *Adding less privileged users while installing the agent*

■ **Tip** The MySQL Enterprise Monitor Agent installer supports adding two users with fewer privileges than the administrator account used for the installation. It is strongly recommended that you choose this option by checking the *Auto-Create Less Privileges Users* checkbox.

Features

MySQL Enterprise Monitor has a range of features, most of which are similar to those offered by other monitoring solutions. Additionally, there are some features that are unique. These features fit into four groups, as shown in Table 14-3. Some of the features are discussed in more detail.

Table 14-3. *MySQL Enterprise Monitor Feature Groups*

Feature Group	Description
Dashboards	The dashboards provide an overview of instances, replication, etc.
Events	Events are triggered when some condition is met. The rules that decide which metrics are outside the normal range are called *advisors*.
Query Analyzer	The Query Analyzer shows statistics of the queries executed in MySQL. It is possible to display a time series graph together with the query statistics.
Reports & Graphs	There is a range of reports and time series graphs; for example, a snapshot of the process list, the number of queries per second, etc.

The events are the mechanism for MySQL Enterprise Monitor to alert the database administrator and system administrator that some metric is outside the expected operational range. It may range from a catastrophic event indicating that a MySQL instance can no longer be reached (for example, because the host has crashed) to informational messages that the disk will be out of space a month from now if no action is taken. The rules used to decide whether an event should be triggered are called advisors. As of version 3.4.0, there are over 230 preconfigured advisors in 14 categories. Figure 14-6 shows a subset of the advisors (the MySQL NDB Cluster specific advisors).

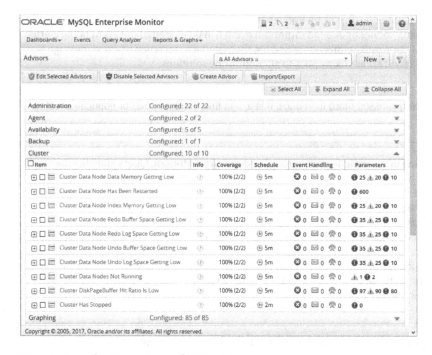

Figure 14-6. *The MySQL NDB Cluster advisors*

There are four severity levels for events:

- **Notice:** This is a heads up that the metrics are getting outside the expected range. The issue is not expect to be severe enough to impact the performance or availability, so no immediate action is required. For example, it could be that the amount of data memory used has reached a level where it is time to start considering whether archiving should be implemented or additional memory should be added to the hosts.

- **Warning:** The situation is not yet impacting performance or availability, but an investigation should not be held off for long.

- **Critical:** Performance or availability is assumed to be affected or will very soon be affected. Investigate and take action immediately.

- **Emergency:** The service is unavailable or so slow that it is essentially an outage. Immediate action is required.

The threshold for each advisor can be set per severity level. When an event triggers, it is possible to have emails sent or *Simple Network Management Protocol (SNMP)* traps triggered to alert the relevant people in the organization. The alerts can be sent based on the affected system, the advisor, and the severity. For example, an alert may be sent to the system administrator if the disk is running out of space, but a warning that replication has stopped will be sent to the database administrator.

Make sure to configure the notification of events and the thresholds for triggering the events, so the urgency is correctly reflected. For example, if an alert arrives as a text message and wakes the database administrator up at 2:00 am, it better be important enough to get out of bed. Once notifications are dismissed with, "oh, it can wait," sooner or later an important event will be missed. If the event being alerted by 2:00 am by text message is not worth getting out of bed for, then send it as an email or a text message at the start of the next business day. This advice applies to all monitoring solutions.

▪ **Tip**   If notifications can be dismissed more than once, it is a sign that the thresholds or notification setup should be changed.

The Query Analyzer is one of the main features in MySQL Enterprise Monitor. Query statistics are collected and the Query Analyzer allows the user to compare the queries executed in a given time frame with the other data collected. An example of this was shown in the root cause analysis example in the "Why Monitor?" section. Additionally, the Query Analyzer can be used to find badly tuned queries, the most frequently executed queries, etc. The data for the Query Analyzer is by default collected from the Performance Schema (covered in the next chapter), but it is also possible to use one of the connector plugins or the proxy plugin.

The reports and graphs feature includes various ways to display collected data. This ranges from traditional time series graphs, as those shown in the graphs earlier in the chapter, to ad hoc reports that show a snapshot of the current process list.

▪ **Note**   The monitoring graphs included in this chapter originate from MySQL Enterprise Monitor.

▪ **Note**   Third-party monitoring and alerting solutions commonly used with MySQL include Cacti, Nagios, and Zabbix. Each solution works in different ways and has its strengths and weaknesses, so it is important to become familiar with your specific monitoring solution.

The Operating System

Database management systems are resource hungry processes, and MySQL NDB Cluster is no exception. This means that it is important to monitor the usage and availability of resources at the operating system level. As will be seen in the two next chapters, the SQL nodes have some data about CPU, network, and disk usage; however, it is no way a substitute for monitoring the hosts directly through the operating system.

The details of monitoring operating system metrics depend entirely on the operating system and version. Even different flavors of Linux and UNIX have different ways of obtaining the same metrics. For this reason, it is beyond the scope of this book to provide information on how to collect the data. Instead, the focus is on what kind of data to collect.

■ **Note** If MySQL is deployed in virtual machines, make sure to monitor the host system and the hypervisor (virtual machine platform) as well as the virtual machine. The performance of the host system may impact the processes inside the virtual machine.

The fail early strategy of the data nodes also means that overloads of any part of the operating system—down to contention on a single CPU thread—can cause problems. This makes monitoring the operating system on the hosts with data nodes particularly important. Do also ensure that hardware related to the cluster but not necessarily with nodes installed is monitored; this for example includes network components between the nodes.

The data nodes start warning about stalls after 100 milliseconds and the watchdog shuts down a data node after 18 seconds if a thread is unresponsive. A typical sampling interval for a monitoring solution may be one minute. It is likely with one minute between measurements that the contention leading to a watchdog shutdown will not be detected. In fact, the one-minute average may be lower than normal, as the data node stops using resources once it is shut down. In general, the data collection must be done more frequently on hosts with data nodes than for other hosts, while still taking care to avoid the overhead of monitoring becoming a problem.

This section continues going through the most important metrics to monitor at the operating system level. The discussion focuses on the data node requirements, but also in general applies to other hosts.

CPU Usage

The data nodes primarily have an in-memory workload. This means the data nodes are typically CPU bound (as opposed to I/O bounds from reading data from disk). The ndbinfo schema (see Chapter 16) has excellent CPU metrics for the data node threads, but it does not include information about the CPU usage of other processes on the machine, including SQL nodes. So, the monitoring should fill in this gap.

Each data node thread may have very different CPU usages, so if possible collect CPU usage data for each virtual CPU. The ndbinfo.threadstat view includes the operating system thread ID for each data node thread. Combining the monitoring data for each virtual CPU with the data collected from ndbinfo. threadstat will allow the database and system administrators to correlate the data to determine whether data node performance issues are related to the CPU usage.

Network Usage

Given that MySQL NDB Cluster is a distributed system relying on the network for the inter-node communication, it comes as no surprise that network monitoring is important. Even a 10Gbit dedicated network between the data nodes can get saturated for high performance clusters.

As for the CPU usage, the ndbinfo schema can provide details for the network usage for the data nodes through the ndbinfo.transporters view. The SQL nodes similarly have status variables providing the amount of data sent and received. So, the operating system monitoring must collect data for the overall usage and if possible the network usage of other processes.

An example that could cause cluster problems is a process that copies large amounts of data through the same network interfaces that the data node uses. One scenario is the backups being copied off the host. It may even be a host that is not related to the cluster that causes problems, if it is using the same network infrastructure as the cluster nodes.

Disk Usage

It is easy to forget about the disks when it comes to monitoring MySQL NDB Cluster. After all, it is primarily an in-memory database. However, all in-memory data is persisted through local checkpoints, the redo logs, and backups. There is also support for on-disk data tablespaces, which also demands a high performing disk system.

In the example with the ndbinfo log space report in Chapter 16, you learn that the longer it takes to write out the data to the local checkpoints, the more data must be stored in the redo logs. That means bottlenecks in the disk performance can directly affect how much disk space is required for the redo logs. Changing the size of the redo logs requires an initial rolling restart, so this is a relatively major change.

The disk_write_speed_% views in ndbinfo provide inside information about the disk write speeds that the data nodes achieves. The operating system monitoring needs to collect information that can be used to investigate if the data nodes cannot achieve the expected throughput—or prevent the disk system from being saturated by making changes to the storage ahead of time. If possible, also collect data that shows the disk usage per process. For a disk system with a battery backed write cache (*https://en.wikipedia.org/wiki/Disk_buffer#Write_acceleration*), the battery status can also greatly affect the performance. If a battery becomes faulty or goes through a relearning procedure, the disk system will enter a degraded mode. The same issue can occur if a disk in a raid-array becomes faulty or is being rebuilt.

Aside from the disk throughput used for the processes, the amount of disk space used is also important to monitor. As the amount of data in the data nodes increases, the local checkpoints and backups become larger, so they take up more disk space. It may also be that more tablespace and/or undo log files are added for on-disk data.

A surprising culprit of running out of disk may also be the redo logs. The size of the redo logs will in principle not change, except if the fragment log file options are changed through an initial (rolling) restart. However, by default, the files are created sparse, so they do not consume much disk space at first. No part of the redo log can be reused until all the files have been used, so it may take a while before all of the disk space reserved for the redo logs will actually be used. If the monitoring does not watch the free disk space, this can cause the data nodes to run out of disk (failing to write the redo log may cause data loss).

Memory Usage

Memory usage is typically not a problem for the data nodes. When a data node starts, it not only requests all the memory it has been configured to use, it also writes to (touches) all of the memory to ensure the operating system really allocates it. So, it is rare for a data node to run out of memory unless another process is the culprit. That said, monitoring should still collect memory usage statistics.

Do not rely on the memory instrumentation in the Performance Schema (see Chapter 15) to monitor the overall memory usage of the SQL nodes. While the memory instrumentation is very useful, it does not have 100% coverage. So even if the performance overhead of permanently enabling the memory instruments is acceptable, supplement the monitoring by collecting data at the operating system level.

Logs

It is important to keep an eye on the logs. The operating system logs include a wide range of message types, from recording execution of jobs through the task scheduler over general operating system messages to audit logs. It may not be possible to automate the monitoring of the logs, in which case a manual inspection of the logs must be part of the routine. Even if fully automated monitoring is not possible, it may be possible to monitor for certain events and strings in the logs and notify the system administrator when the test is positive.

Log monitoring should focus on detecting hardware problems, out of memory issues, intrusions, etc. The system logs can also be very valuable for root cause analysis, so be sure that there is a retention policy in place that ensures the logs are kept for a period and possibly backed up to another host.

Summary

This chapter covered monitoring at a high level as well as what to be aware of when monitoring at the operating system level. The topics discussed in this chapter are:

- Why monitoring is important, with three examples of using monitoring for baseline monitoring, root cause analysis, and preventive maintenance.

- Monitoring solutions, including MySQL's enterprise solution, MySQL Enterprise Monitor.

- At the operating system level, the most important things to monitor are the network, CPU, disk, and memory.

- Watch the logs. This includes the operating system level logs.

The next chapter dives into the data sources and logs available in general for both MySQL Server and MySQL NDB Cluster.

CHAPTER 15

■ ■ ■

Sources for Monitoring Data

Monitoring data can be collected from a variety of sources. No matter how good a monitoring solution is, it is important not only to know where the data comes from, but also how it is collected, the units of measure, the limitations of the data source, and how it can be used for analysis. That helps you understand what can be read out of the data. Additionally, it may be necessary to collect some data manually while performing a test or investigating an issue, whereas other data is more geared toward manual use. An example of the latter is the process list.

There are numerous ways to collect data. The five main areas that are available on both MySQL Server and MySQL NDB Cluster are:

- The Information Schema

- The Performance Schema

- The sys schema

- SHOW statements

- The MySQL error log

This chapter goes through all of these areas and provides several examples of how to use the sources.

The Information Schema

The Information Schema was introduced to MySQL in version 5.0. It is a common feature across several relational database management systems (though not all). MySQL aims to follow the SQL:2003 standard for *F021 Basic information schema* with some changes to reflect the specific nature of MySQL (for example, the standard does not take into account that there are several storage engines).

The Information Schema was the first metadata schema in MySQL, so it has also ended up being the home for many tables that do not really belong there. Recently work has been started to make the Information Schema focused on relatively static data such as schema information, which plugins are available, etc. The first step was to move the tables with configuration variables and status counters to the Performance Schema; this was done in MySQL Server 5.7.6 (a development milestone release) and MySQL NDB Cluster 7.5 (all releases). The work is continuing, and some deprecation warnings may be encountered in MySQL NDB Cluster 7.5 and later.

This section introduces the Information Schema tables and explains how to use them. At the end, the tables that have data that is specific to NDB Cluster will be discussed, with examples.

© Jesper Wisborg Krogh and Mikiya Okuno 2017

J. W. Krogh and M. Okuno, *Pro MySQL NDB Cluster*, https://doi.org/10.1007/978-1-4842-2982-8_15

Information Schema Tables

The list of available Information Schema tables varies with the version and the features that have been enabled. Tables 15-1 through 15-4 show all the Information Schema tables in a default MySQL NDB Cluster 7.5 SQL node, except for the tables specific to InnoDB. The tables are split into four groups:

- System information such as available character sets, storage engines, etc.
- Schema information such as the schemata, tables, etc.
- Privilege information
- Configuration and performance monitoring metrics

InnoDB is required for the SQL nodes to work in MySQL NDB Cluster 7.5 and adds another 30 tables, but for brevity these are not included here.

Except for OPTIMIZER_TRACE (introduced in version 7.3), all tables are available in at least MySQL NDB Cluster version 7.2 and later. The convention is that Information Schema table names are in all uppercase (an exception is ndb_transid_mysql_connection_map, which is lowercase).

Table 15-1 lists the Information Schema tables with information about the system such as character sets, plugins, etc. These can be useful for verifying which features are available.

Table 15-1. *The Information Schema: MySQL System Information Tables*

Table	Description
CHARACTER_SETS	The available character sets. All char, varchar, and text columns have a character set associated with them.
COLLATIONS	The available collations. Each collation belongs to a character set and defines the comparison and sorting rules.
COLLATION_CHARACTER_SET_APPLICABILITY	The mapping of each collation to a character set. This is the same as the first two columns of the COLLATIONS table.
ENGINES	Information about the storage engines.
PLUGINS	Available plugins, including status. Plugins are for example storage engines and authentication plugins.

Table 15-2 goes through the tables that provide information about the schemas, tables, columns, stored routines, etc. These are often used to answer questions such as which tables have a foreign key to a specific table and what are the index statistics for an index.

Table 15-2. *The Information Schema: Schema Information*

Table	Description
COLUMNS	The column definitions for the tables.
EVENTS	Information about events defined on the SQL node (remember that events are not automatically distributed among the SQL nodes).
FILES	Information about tablespace and log group files created by MySQL. Before MySQL Server 5.7/MySQL NDB Cluster 7.5, this was an NDB Cluster specific table. It, for example, includes information about the amount of free space in the files.
KEY_COLUMN_USAGE	Information about the columns used in referential constraints (primary keys, unique keys, and foreign keys).
PARAMETERS	Information about the parameters in stored programs.
PARTITIONS	Information about each partition in the tables.
REFERENTIAL_CONSTRAINTS	Information about foreign keys.
ROUTINES	Details including the full definition of stored procedures and stored functions.
SCHEMATA	Schema (database) information.
STATISTICS	The equivalent of SHOW INDEXES.
TABLES	Information of all tables. The equivalent of SHOW TABLE STATUS.
TABLESPACES	Tablespace information.
TABLE_CONSTRAINTS	Summary of the primary, unique, and foreign keys.
TRIGGERS	Details for all user-level table triggers (not the internal NDB Cluster triggers).
VIEWS	Details of the views.

The privilege information tables are listed in Table 15-3. The privileges are stored in tables in the mysql schema, and the four Information Schema privilege tables are views into the cached privileges (i.e., if the mysql privilege tables are updated directly using INSERT, UPDATE, DELETE, etc., then the Information Schema privilege tables will not show the change until after the execution of FLUSH PRIVILEGES). The table definitions of the Information Schema tables are not the same as for the mysql tables. The tables are, for example, useful for finding users with a specific privilege or access to a given schema, table, or column.

Table 15-3. *The Information Schema: Privilege Information*

Table	Description
COLUMN_PRIVILEGES	Contains the column-level privileges given to users.
SCHEMA_PRIVILEGES	Contains the schema-level privileges given to users.
TABLE_PRIVILEGES	Contains the table-level privileges given to users.
USER_PRIVILEGES	Contains the global-level privileges granted to users.

There are several tables related to monitoring in the Information Schema. These are included in Table 15-4. Some of these tables already have new implementations in the Performance Schema. The ndb_transid_mysql_connection_map table is of particular interest to MySQL NDB Cluster and will be used in examples later in this chapter and in the next chapter.

459

Table 15-4. *The Information Schema: Monitoring Related Data*

Table	Description
GLOBAL_STATUS	The same as the output of SHOW GLOBAL STATUS. This table is disabled by default in MySQL NDB Cluster 7.5 and later and has been removed in version MySQL Server 8.0. Use the performance_schema.global_status table instead.
GLOBAL_VARIABLES	The same as the output of SHOW GLOBAL VARIABLES. This table is disabled by default in MySQL NDB Cluster 7.5 and later and has been removed in version MySQL Server 8.0. Use the performance_schema.global_variables table instead.
ndb_transid_mysql_connection_map	Provides a mapping between an NDB transaction ID and the SQL node ID and connection ID that uses the transaction. Examples are provided later.
OPTIMIZER_TRACE	Can be used to get detailed information about the decision process made by the optimizer when a query is executed.
PROCESSLIST	The same as SHOW FULL PROCESSLIST. In MySQL NDB Cluster 7.3 and later it is better to use the performance_schema.threads table instead.
PROFILING	The same information as in using SHOW PROFILE after profiling a query. The table has been deprecated in favor of the Performance Schema in MySQL NDB Cluster 7.5 and later.
SESSION_STATUS	The same as the output of SHOW SESSION STATUS. This table is disabled by default in MySQL NDB Cluster 7.5 and later and has been removed in MySQL Server 8.0. Use the performance_schema.session_status table instead.
SESSION_VARIABLES	The same as the output of SHOW SESSION VARIABLES. This table is disabled by default in MySQL NDB Cluster 7.5 and has been removed in MySQL Server 8.0. Use the performance_schema.session_variables table instead.

Using the Information Schema

The Information Schema tables can be used and joined as user-defined tables. They can also be combined in queries with tables from other schemata, such as the Performance Schema and ndbinfo. For example, you can get the number of columns per table in the world sample database, as shown in the following output:

```
mysql> SELECT TABLE_SCHEMA, TABLE_NAME, COUNT(*) AS NumColumns
          FROM information_schema.TABLES
            INNER JOIN information_schema.COLUMNS
              USING (TABLE_SCHEMA, TABLE_NAME)
        WHERE TABLE_SCHEMA = 'world'
        GROUP BY TABLE_SCHEMA, TABLE_NAME;
+--------------+-----------------+------------+
| TABLE_SCHEMA | TABLE_NAME      | NumColumns |
+--------------+-----------------+------------+
| world        | City            |          5 |
| world        | Country         |         15 |
| world        | CountryLanguage |          4 |
+--------------+-----------------+------------+
3 rows in set (0.07 sec)
```

Queries involving schema information will in general be relatively slow, particularly if the tables are not in the table cache. The reason is that the information is stored in the *.frm* files in the file system in MySQL Server 5.7 and earlier, and reading data from one file at a time to get the schema information is slow. So, be careful with queries against tables, columns, indexes, etc. that are not limited by a WHERE clause and the schema and/or table name. There is no support for indexes in the Information Schema until MySQL Server 8.0 where a new data dictionary is available. However, for tables like TABLES there is limited support for pushing down the restrictions on the schema and table name.

Another performance issue to consider when using the Information Schema is the mutex required by the PROCESSLIST table (and SHOW [FULL] PROCESSLIST). In extreme cases, this can impact the performance of MySQL and it has in the past effectively caused outages. For this reason, it is recommended to use the performance_schema.threads table or one of the sys schema views derived from it. Additionally, the threads table provides more information and flexibility. The Performance Schema threads table is available in MySQL NDB Cluster 7.3 and later.

The Information Schema and NDB Cluster

Two of the tables are of particular interest for MySQL NDB Cluster are the FILES and the ndb_transid_mysql_connection_map tables. The FILES table was exclusively used for NDB Cluster until version 7.5 (where InnoDB also started to use it with the introduction of the general tablespaces). Both tables are MySQL extensions to the SQL standard for the Information Schema.

The Information Schema FILES Table

The FILES table provides detailed information about the logfile group and tablespace files, such as the size and amount of free space. Listing 15-1 shows an example where a log group is added with one undo log file and a tablespace with one data file. The output from the FILES table has two parts—three rows for the tablespace files and three rows for the logfile group. There is one row for each file on each node as well as a row for the logfile group and tablespace themselves.

Listing 15-1. Using the information_schema.FILES Table

```
mysql> CREATE LOGFILE GROUP lg_1
            ADD UNDOFILE 'undo_1.log'
            INITIAL_SIZE 16M
            UNDO_BUFFER_SIZE 2M
            ENGINE NDBCLUSTER;
Query OK, 0 rows affected (1.48 sec)

mysql> CREATE TABLESPACE ts_1
            ADD DATAFILE 'data_1.dat'
            USE LOGFILE GROUP lg_1
            INITIAL_SIZE 32M
            ENGINE NDBCLUSTER;
Query OK, 0 rows affected (9.51 sec)

mysql> CREATE TABLE db1.t1 (
          id int unsigned NOT NULL auto_increment,
          val varchar(36) NOT NULL,
          PRIMARY KEY (id)
       ) ENGINE=NDBCluster
```

```
            TABLESPACE ts_1
            STORAGE DISK;
Query OK, 0 rows affected (0.22 sec)

mysql> INSERT INTO db1.t1 (val)
        VALUES (UUID()), (UUID()), (UUID()), (UUID()), (UUID());
Query OK, 5 rows affected (0.00 sec)
Records: 5  Duplicates: 0  Warnings: 0

mysql> INSERT INTO db1.t1 (val)
        SELECT UUID()
          FROM db1.t1 a
               CROSS JOIN db1.t1 b;
Query OK, 25 rows affected (0.01 sec)
Records: 25  Duplicates: 0  Warnings: 0

mysql> INSERT INTO db1.t1 (val)
        SELECT UUID()
          FROM db1.t1 a
               CROSS JOIN db1.t1 b;
Query OK, 900 rows affected (0.06 sec)
Records: 900  Duplicates: 0  Warnings: 0

mysql> SELECT FILE_NAME, FILE_TYPE, LOGFILE_GROUP_NAME, ENGINE, FREE_EXTENTS,
              TOTAL_EXTENTS, EXTENT_SIZE, INITIAL_SIZE, MAXIMUM_SIZE, EXTRA
         FROM information_schema.FILES
              WHERE ENGINE='NDBCluster'\G
*************************** 1. row ***************************
          FILE_NAME: data_1.dat
          FILE_TYPE: DATAFILE
LOGFILE_GROUP_NAME: lg_1
             ENGINE: ndbcluster
       FREE_EXTENTS: 30
      TOTAL_EXTENTS: 32
        EXTENT_SIZE: 1048576
       INITIAL_SIZE: 33554432
       MAXIMUM_SIZE: 33554432
              EXTRA: CLUSTER_NODE=1
*************************** 2. row ***************************
          FILE_NAME: data_1.dat
          FILE_TYPE: DATAFILE
LOGFILE_GROUP_NAME: lg_1
             ENGINE: ndbcluster
       FREE_EXTENTS: 30
      TOTAL_EXTENTS: 32
        EXTENT_SIZE: 1048576
       INITIAL_SIZE: 33554432
       MAXIMUM_SIZE: 33554432
              EXTRA: CLUSTER_NODE=2
*************************** 3. row ***************************
```

```
          FILE_NAME: NULL
          FILE_TYPE: TABLESPACE
LOGFILE_GROUP_NAME: lg_1
             ENGINE: ndbcluster
       FREE_EXTENTS: NULL
      TOTAL_EXTENTS: NULL
        EXTENT_SIZE: 1048576
       INITIAL_SIZE: NULL
       MAXIMUM_SIZE: NULL
              EXTRA: NULL
*************************** 4. row ***************************
          FILE_NAME: undo_1.log
          FILE_TYPE: UNDO LOG
LOGFILE_GROUP_NAME: lg_1
             ENGINE: ndbcluster
       FREE_EXTENTS: NULL
      TOTAL_EXTENTS: 4194304
        EXTENT_SIZE: 4
       INITIAL_SIZE: 16777216
       MAXIMUM_SIZE: 16777216
              EXTRA: CLUSTER_NODE=1;UNDO_BUFFER_SIZE=2097152
*************************** 5. row ***************************
          FILE_NAME: undo_1.log
          FILE_TYPE: UNDO LOG
LOGFILE_GROUP_NAME: lg_1
             ENGINE: ndbcluster
       FREE_EXTENTS: NULL
      TOTAL_EXTENTS: 4194304
        EXTENT_SIZE: 4
       INITIAL_SIZE: 16777216
       MAXIMUM_SIZE: 16777216
              EXTRA: CLUSTER_NODE=2;UNDO_BUFFER_SIZE=2097152
*************************** 6. row ***************************
          FILE_NAME: NULL
          FILE_TYPE: UNDO LOG
LOGFILE_GROUP_NAME: lg_1
             ENGINE: ndbcluster
       FREE_EXTENTS: 4121268
      TOTAL_EXTENTS: NULL
        EXTENT_SIZE: 4
       INITIAL_SIZE: NULL
       MAXIMUM_SIZE: NULL
              EXTRA: UNDO_BUFFER_SIZE=2097152
6 rows in set (0.01 sec)
```

From a monitoring perspective, the number of free extents are of particular interest. These show how much space is left. Multiplying by the extent size gives the amount of free space in bytes. When using on-disk data, it is important to monitor the free space, so in case space is running out, either more space can be allocated or the existing data can be purged. Listing 15-2 shows an example of checking the data files and the undo log for free space.

Listing 15-2. Determining the Amount of Free Space for the On-Disk Data Files and Undo Log

```
mysql> SELECT FILE_NAME, FILE_TYPE,
              (FREE_EXTENTS*EXTENT_SIZE) AS FreeBytes,
              ROUND(100*FREE_EXTENTS/TOTAL_EXTENTS, 2) AS FreePct,
              EXTRA
         FROM information_schema.FILES
        WHERE ENGINE='NDBCluster' AND FREE_EXTENTS IS NOT NULL;
+------------+----------+-----------+---------+-------------------------+
| FILE_NAME  | FILE_TYPE | FreeBytes | FreePct | EXTRA                   |
+------------+----------+-----------+---------+-------------------------+
| data_1.dat | DATAFILE | 31457280  |   93.75 | CLUSTER_NODE=1          |
| data_1.dat | DATAFILE | 31457280  |   93.75 | CLUSTER_NODE=2          |
| NULL       | UNDO LOG | 16485072  |    NULL | UNDO_BUFFER_SIZE=2097152 |
+------------+----------+-----------+---------+-------------------------+
3 rows in set (0.01 sec)
```

The Information Schema ndb_transid_mysql_connection_map Table

The ndb_transid_mysql_connection_map table provides a mapping of connections in SQL nodes and the NDB transaction IDs. This is used to filter the cluster locks, transactions, and operations in the ndbinfo tables cluster_locks, cluster_operations, and cluster_transactions to create the corresponding tables at the server level. Listing 15-3 shows the SELECT statement used in the definition of the ndbinfo.server_transactions view (reformatted and slightly rewritten), where the ndb_transid_mysql_connection_map table is used to get the transactions for the SQL node. The ndb_transid_mysql_connection_map table is in general not required for manual use, but an example will be provided when investigating locks in the next chapter.

Listing 15-3. The Definition of the ndbinfo.server_transactions View

```
SELECT map.mysql_connection_id, t.node_id, t.block_instance,
       t.transid, t.state, t.count_operations, t.outstanding_operations,
       t.inactive_seconds, t.client_node_id, t.client_block_ref
  FROM information_schema.ndb_transid_mysql_connection_map map
       INNER JOIN ndbinfo.cluster_transactions t
                ON map.ndb_transid >> 32 = t.transid >> 32;
```

The ndbinfo schema used in the previous example is a schema specific to MySQL NDB Cluster and will be discussed in the next chapter.

Whereas the future aim for the Information Schema is to provide relatively static data, the opposite is true for the Performance Schema, which is the next data source to discuss.

The Performance Schema

Since 2010 there has been an ongoing effort to improve the possibility to monitor MySQL and investigate performance issues through the Performance Schema. This is a collection of tables using the Performance_Schema storage engine which stores all data in-memory. The data is not persistent, so the overhead with the default settings is in general low. The downside from a MySQL NDB Cluster perspective is that only the mysqld process is instrumented, so there is no information in the Performance Schema related to the data nodes. This section provides an introduction to the Performance Schema.

MySQL Server 5.6 and thus MySQL NDB Cluster 7.3 and later have seen some major changes for the Performance Schema compared to MySQL Server 5.5 and MySQL NDB Cluster 7.2. Only the current implementation is discussed.

As mentioned, the data in the Performance Schema is not persistent, so it will be lost when restarting the SQL nodes. Additionally, the table size is limited to cap the memory usage and once the tables become full, old data will either be purged to make room for new, or additionally data will be grouped in an "overfill bin".

Performance Schema Threads

Before discussing the details of using the Performance Schema, it is necessary to first discuss threads: The Performance Schema refers to threads and uses a thread ID to uniquely identify each thread. A thread can either be a foreground thread, which is the same as the connections showing in SHOW PROCESSLIST or a background thread. This can be the main thread listening for new connections or internal InnoDB threads.

Listing 15-4 shows a typical example of the threads available using the performance_schema.threads table compared with the process list output from the Information Schema (same as SHOW PROCESSLIST but here only including select columns). The ID column of the performance_schema.threads query corresponds to the ID column of the information_schema.PROCESSLIST query. The two threads with the name thread/sql/one_connection are normal connections (thread IDs 29 and 31).

Listing 15-4. Example of Performance Schema Threads

```
mysql> SELECT THREAD_ID, NAME, TYPE, PROCESSLIST_ID AS ID
       FROM performance_schema.threads;
+-----------+------------------------------------------+------------+------+
| THREAD_ID | NAME                                     | TYPE       | ID   |
+-----------+------------------------------------------+------------+------+
|         1 | thread/sql/main                          | BACKGROUND | NULL |
|         2 | thread/sql/thread_timer_notifier         | BACKGROUND | NULL |
|         3 | thread/innodb/io_ibuf_thread             | BACKGROUND | NULL |
|         4 | thread/innodb/io_log_thread              | BACKGROUND | NULL |
|         5 | thread/innodb/io_read_thread             | BACKGROUND | NULL |
|         6 | thread/innodb/io_read_thread             | BACKGROUND | NULL |
|         7 | thread/innodb/io_read_thread             | BACKGROUND | NULL |
|         8 | thread/innodb/io_read_thread             | BACKGROUND | NULL |
|         9 | thread/innodb/io_write_thread            | BACKGROUND | NULL |
|        10 | thread/innodb/io_write_thread            | BACKGROUND | NULL |
|        11 | thread/innodb/io_write_thread            | BACKGROUND | NULL |
|        12 | thread/innodb/io_write_thread            | BACKGROUND | NULL |
|        13 | thread/innodb/page_cleaner_thread        | BACKGROUND | NULL |
|        15 | thread/innodb/srv_lock_timeout_thread    | BACKGROUND | NULL |
|        16 | thread/innodb/srv_error_monitor_thread   | BACKGROUND | NULL |
|        17 | thread/innodb/srv_monitor_thread         | BACKGROUND | NULL |
|        18 | thread/innodb/srv_master_thread          | BACKGROUND | NULL |
|        19 | thread/innodb/srv_purge_thread           | BACKGROUND | NULL |
|        20 | thread/innodb/srv_worker_thread          | BACKGROUND | NULL |
|        21 | thread/innodb/srv_worker_thread          | BACKGROUND | NULL |
|        22 | thread/innodb/buf_dump_thread            | BACKGROUND | NULL |
|        23 | thread/innodb/srv_worker_thread          | BACKGROUND | NULL |
|        24 | thread/innodb/dict_stats_thread          | BACKGROUND | NULL |
|        25 | thread/sql/signal_handler                | BACKGROUND | NULL |
|        26 | thread/sql/compress_gtid_table           | FOREGROUND |    3 |
|        29 | thread/sql/one_connection                | FOREGROUND |    7 |
|        31 | thread/sql/one_connection                | FOREGROUND |    8 |
+-----------+------------------------------------------+------------+------+
27 rows in set (0.00 sec)
```

```
mysql> SELECT ID, USER, COMMAND, STATE
         FROM information_schema.PROCESSLIST
         ORDER BY ID;
+----+-------------+---------+-----------------------------------+
| ID | USER        | COMMAND | STATE                             |
+----+-------------+---------+-----------------------------------+
|  1 | system user | Daemon  | Waiting for event from ndbcluster |
|  7 | root        | Sleep   |                                   |
|  8 | root        | Query   | executing                         |
+----+-------------+---------+-----------------------------------+
3 rows in set (0.00 sec)
```

Notice that thread ID 26 is a foreground thread, but this particular one does not show up in the process list output and is thus an example of a kind of in-between thread that is not fully a background neither a foreground thread. On the other hand, the process list row with ID = 1 does not show up in the performance_schema.threads output. This is the NDB binlog thread waiting for events from the data nodes.

As the example shows, it is possible to convert between the process list ID and the Performance Schema thread ID using the performance_schema.threads table. An alternate way is to use the sys.ps_thread_id() function if the sys schema is installed. sys.ps_thread_id() only supports converting from the process list ID to the Performance Schema thread ID. These two ways of converting the ID are illustrated in Listing 15-5. The CONNECTION_ID() function gets the process list ID for the current connection. The sys.ps_thread_id() function can also take NULL as an argument, in which case it returns the Performance Schema thread ID for the current connection.

Listing 15-5. Converting the Process List ID to the Performance Schema Thread ID

```
mysql> SELECT CONNECTION_ID();
+-----------------+
| CONNECTION_ID() |
+-----------------+
|               7 |
+-----------------+
1 row in set (0.00 sec)

mysql> SELECT THREAD_ID
         FROM performance_schema.threads
         WHERE PROCESSLIST_ID = 7;
+-----------+
| THREAD_ID |
+-----------+
|        29 |
+-----------+
1 row in set (0.00 sec)

mysql> SELECT sys.ps_thread_id(7);
+---------------------+
| sys.ps_thread_id(7) |
+---------------------+
|                  29 |
+---------------------+
1 row in set (0.00 sec)
```

```
mysql> SELECT sys.ps_thread_id(NULL);
+------------------------+
| sys.ps_thread_id(NULL) |
+------------------------+
|                     29 |
+------------------------+
1 row in set (0.00 sec)
```

> ■ **Note** Unfortunately, the term *thread* is overloaded in MySQL and is in some places used as a synonym for connection. In this chapter, a *connection* refers to a user connection and a *thread* refers to a Performance Schema thread, i.e., it can either be a background or foreground (including connections) thread.

Performance Schema Tables Overview

As of MySQL NDB Cluster 7.5.6, there is a total of 87 tables in the Performance Schema. Most table names are self-descriptive. For example, the tables used to configure the Performance Schema have the prefix setup_ and the summary table names include _summary_ and what data they group and how. All of the Performance Schema tables are listed in tables throughout this section and are grouped according to the following groups:

- **Setup tables:** Tables that are used for configuring the Performance Schema and get information related to the Performance Schema configuration.

- **Event tables:** Tables with details for the events that have been recorded.

- **Summary tables:** Report tables with the data from the events tables grouped according to the purpose of the table.

- **Connection and thread tables:** Data related to foreground and background threads.

- **Variable and status tables:** The system variables and status variables at the global or session/thread level.

- **Replication tables:** Tables showing information related to replication.

- **Instance tables:** Tables with data about instances that range from mutexes to prepared statements.

- **Lock tables:** Tables about table level and metadata locks.

The remainder of this section goes through these tables and provides examples of using the most important of them.

Setup Tables and Configuration

The setup tables in Table 15-5 allow the database administrator to change the settings of the Performance Schema dynamically. There are five setups tables. The most commonly used of these are the setup_ consumers and setup_instruments tables. Additionally, there is performance_timers, which is a reference table.

Table 15-5. *Performance Schema Setup Tables*

Table Name	Description
performance_timers	Overview of the timers available for the setup_timers table.
setup_actors	Configure which accounts should be instrumented and timed by default.
setup_consumers	Configure which consumers are enabled to consume the data generated by the instruments.
setup_instruments	Configure which instrumentation points should be enabled.
setup_objects	Configure which tables, triggers, stored procedures, stored functions, and stored events should be instrumented.
setup_timers	Configure which timers should be used for the different event types.

The rest of this section discusses the setup tables as well as provides an introduction to the terms.

Instruments

Instruments are the code points where the measurements are done. It is possible to count and time an instrument. For memory related instruments, counting means summing the memory allocation and deallocation size. The instrument names are self-descriptive and follow the convention that forward slashes (/) separate group levels. An example of an instrument name is statement/sql/select. As the name suggests, it instruments a SELECT SQL statement. By enabling it, each SELECT statement will be counted and optionally timed. All instruments for SQL statements have the prefix statement/sql/ followed by the statement type.

The data generated by the instruments must be consumed in order for the data to be available in the Performance Schema tables. This is done by consumers.

Consumers

The setup_consumers table defines what can consume the instruments. The consumers form a hierarchy, as shown in Figure 15-1. For the events consumers in the two lowest levels, the % can be stages, statements, transactions (version 7.5 and later only), or waits.

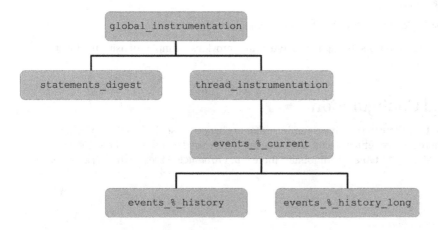

Figure 15-1. *The Performance Schema consumers*

For a consumer to be effectively enabled, not only must the consumer itself be enabled, but also all of the ancestor consumers in the hierarchy must be enabled. For example, for events_statements_history to be consuming instruments, the events_statements_current, thread_instrumentation, and global_instrumentation consumers must also be enabled. When the sys schema is installed, the sys.ps_is_consumer_enabled() function can be used to take the hierarchy into consideration. Listing 15-6 lists all of the consumers in version 7.5 and the default values for whether they are enabled in setup_consumers and whether they also have all of the ancestor consumers enabled. In versions 7.3 and 7.4, the events_statements_history consumer was not enabled by default.

Listing 15-6. The Consumers in MySQL NDB Cluster 7.5.

```
mysql> SELECT NAME, ENABLED, sys.ps_is_consumer_enabled(NAME) AS Collects
          FROM performance_schema.setup_consumers;
+----------------------------------+---------+----------+
| NAME                             | ENABLED | Collects |
+----------------------------------+---------+----------+
| events_stages_current            | NO      | NO       |
| events_stages_history            | NO      | NO       |
| events_stages_history_long       | NO      | NO       |
| events_statements_current        | YES     | YES      |
| events_statements_history        | YES     | YES      |
| events_statements_history_long   | NO      | NO       |
| events_transactions_current      | NO      | NO       |
| events_transactions_history      | NO      | NO       |
| events_transactions_history_long | NO      | NO       |
| events_waits_current             | NO      | NO       |
| events_waits_history             | NO      | NO       |
| events_waits_history_long        | NO      | NO       |
| global_instrumentation           | YES     | YES      |
| thread_instrumentation           | YES     | YES      |
| statements_digest                | YES     | YES      |
+----------------------------------+---------+----------+
15 rows in set (0.00 sec)
```

The statement_digest consumer is responsible for collecting statistics about normalized queries. The digest name comes from the digest that is calculated for each of the normalized queries. The data can be found in the events_statements_summary_by_digest table—an example of the data collected will be shown later.

There is an events table for each of the events consumers. The name of the table is the same as for the consumer. The details of the events consumers and tables as well as the relationship between the event types is discussed in the next section about the event tables.

Actors, Objects, and Timers

The setup_actors and setup_objects tables define which accounts (user@hostname) and which schema objects (tables, stored programs, etc.) are instrumented. By default, everything is instrumented except for schema objects in the information_schema, mysql, and performance_schema schemas. The setup_timers table define the timers are used for different event types. The timers are set up automatically based on how expensive they are to use and how accurate they are. The default timers chosen are system dependent, and usually there is no need to change them. Details of the available timers and the overhead for them can be found in the performance_timers table.

Configuration Recommendations and How to Change Settings

The default settings are a good starting point and usually only minor changes are required if at all any except when investigating specific issues. An example of a change that may be worth considering is to enable the events_transactions_current consumer and the transaction instrument. This will allow additional details of transactions, such as finding all statements executed in a transaction, to be available. An example is shown later when discussing the events tables. To enable the consumer and instrument dynamically, use the statements in Listing 15-7. Optionally the last 10 transactions for each current connection can be kept by also enabling the events_transactions_history consumer.

■ **Note**   None of the examples in this chapter requires enabling anything beyond the defaults unless explicitly noted.

Listing 15-7. Enabling Transaction Monitoring

```
mysql> UPDATE performance_schema.setup_consumers
          SET ENABLED = 'YES'
        WHERE NAME = 'events_transactions_current';
Query OK, 1 row affected (0.00 sec)
Rows matched: 1  Changed: 1  Warnings: 0

mysql> UPDATE performance_schema.setup_instruments
          SET ENABLED = 'YES', TIMED = 'YES'
        WHERE NAME = 'transaction';
Query OK, 1 row affected (0.00 sec)
Rows matched: 1  Changed: 1  Warnings: 0
```

It is also possible to enable instruments and consumers in the MySQL Server configuration file (*my.cnf*/*my.ini*). To enable the transaction consumer and instrument like it was done dynamically in Listing 15-7, add the settings:

```
[mysqld]
performance_schema_consumer_events_transactions_current = ON
performance_schema_instrument                           = transaction=ON
```

The performance_schema_instrument option supports the % wildcard and the option can be specified multiple times.

■ **Caution**   Do not be tempted to enable all consumers and instruments in production. Monitoring does have overhead, and enabling everything will have a major impact on the performance! Particularly the wait/synch/% instruments and events_waits_% consumers add overhead. As a rule of thumb, the more fine grained the monitoring is, the more overhead it adds.

There are several other configuration options for the Performance Schema. The complete list of the variables available in MySQL NDB Cluster 7.5.6 can be seen in Listing 15-8 together with their default values. A value of -1 means the option is auto-sized. For more details, see *https://dev.mysql.com/doc/refman/5.7/ en/performance-schema-options.html*.

Listing 15-8. The Performance Schema Variables

```
mysql> SHOW GLOBAL VARIABLES LIKE 'performance\_schema%';
+-------------------------------------------------------------+-------+
| Variable_name                                               | Value |
+-------------------------------------------------------------+-------+
| performance_schema                                          | ON    |
| performance_schema_accounts_size                            | -1    |
| performance_schema_digests_size                             | 10000 |
| performance_schema_events_stages_history_long_size          | 10000 |
| performance_schema_events_stages_history_size               | 10    |
| performance_schema_events_statements_history_long_size      | 10000 |
| performance_schema_events_statements_history_size           | 10    |
| performance_schema_events_transactions_history_long_size    | 10000 |
| performance_schema_events_transactions_history_size         | 10    |
| performance_schema_events_waits_history_long_size           | 10000 |
| performance_schema_events_waits_history_size                | 10    |
| performance_schema_hosts_size                               | -1    |
| performance_schema_max_cond_classes                         | 80    |
| performance_schema_max_cond_instances                       | -1    |
| performance_schema_max_digest_length                        | 1024  |
| performance_schema_max_file_classes                         | 80    |
| performance_schema_max_file_handles                         | 32768 |
| performance_schema_max_file_instances                       | -1    |
| performance_schema_max_index_stat                           | -1    |
| performance_schema_max_memory_classes                       | 320   |
| performance_schema_max_metadata_locks                       | -1    |
| performance_schema_max_mutex_classes                        | 210   |
| performance_schema_max_mutex_instances                      | -1    |
| performance_schema_max_prepared_statements_instances        | -1    |
| performance_schema_max_program_instances                    | -1    |
| performance_schema_max_rwlock_classes                       | 40    |
| performance_schema_max_rwlock_instances                     | -1    |
| performance_schema_max_socket_classes                       | 10    |
| performance_schema_max_socket_instances                     | -1    |
| performance_schema_max_sql_text_length                      | 1024  |
| performance_schema_max_stage_classes                        | 150   |
| performance_schema_max_statement_classes                    | 193   |
| performance_schema_max_statement_stack                      | 10    |
| performance_schema_max_table_handles                        | -1    |
| performance_schema_max_table_instances                      | -1    |
| performance_schema_max_table_lock_stat                      | -1    |
| performance_schema_max_thread_classes                       | 50    |
| performance_schema_max_thread_instances                     | -1    |
| performance_schema_session_connect_attrs_size               | 512   |
| performance_schema_setup_actors_size                        | -1    |
| performance_schema_setup_objects_size                       | -1    |
| performance_schema_users_size                               | -1    |
+-------------------------------------------------------------+-------+
42 rows in set (0.00 sec)
```

The events consumers discussed before are closely related to the event tables, which is the next group of Performance Schema tables to look at.

Event Tables

The event tables are directly related to the event consumers with one event table per event consumer. There are four event types and for each there are three scopes. This and the relationship between the event types is discussed in this section.

Table 15-6 shows the 12 event tables available in MySQL NDB Cluster 7.5. The table names follow the scheme events_{type}_{scope}. The type is one of stages, statements, transactions, and waits, and the scope is current, history, or history_long.

Table 15-6. *Performance Schema Event Tables*

Table Name	Description
events_stages_current	Current or latest stage event for each existing thread.
events_stages_history	Up to the last 10 stage events for each existing thread.
events_stages_history_long	Up to the last 10000 stage events for the SQL node.
events_statements_current	Current or latest statement for each existing thread.
events_statements_history	Up to the last 10 statements for each existing thread.
events_statements_history_long	Up to the last 10000 statements for the SQL node.
events_transactions_current	Current or latest transaction for each existing thread.
events_transactions_history	Up to the last 10 transactions for each existing thread.
events_transactions_history_long	Up to the last 10000 transactions for the SQL node.
events_waits_current	Current or latest wait event for each existing thread.
events_waits_history	Up to the last 10 wait events for each existing thread.
events_waits_history_long	Up to the last 10000 wait events for the SQL node.

For the events consumers, the current consumers monitor the current or last event. The history consumers keep the last 10 (by default) events for each connection, but the data is purged when the connection disconnects. On the other hand, the history_long consumers by default keep the last 10000 events irrespective of the connection and the events persist when the connection disconnects; when all events are used, the oldest are purged.

The event types are summarized in Table 15-7 with the relationship between them depicted in Figure 15-2. The transactions are the highest level including one or more statements. A statement goes through stages while being executed. At the bottom are the wait events that are low-level interactions such as I/O or mutex waits. Other than I/O waits for example for the binary logs, the wait events are not very interesting for an SQL node in a cluster given the bulk of the work query is performed on the data nodes. The columns available in the event table only depend on the event type, for example events_statements_current, events_statements_history, and events_statements_history_long all have the same columns.

Table 15-7. *Performance Schema Event Types in Order of Increased Details*

Event Type	Description
Transactions	The highest level (fewest details). Includes details such as the transaction isolation level requested (but not necessarily the transaction isolation level used as NDBCluster tables always use READ-COMMITTED), transaction status, etc. This event type was added in MySQL NDB Cluster 7.5. None of the event scopes for transaction events are enabled by default.
Statements	This is the most commonly used event type. It records data for each statement. There are a lot of useful information such as the duration; how many rows were examined, returned, and affected; whether internal temporary tables were used; whether indexes where used; and more. The current scope is enabled by default in version 7.3 and later and the history scope is also enabled in 7.5
Stages	This roughly corresponds to the states reported by SHOW PROCESSLIST. These are not enabled by default.
Waits	The lowest level (most details). The wait events for example includes I/O and waiting for mutexes. These are very specific and very useful for low level performance tuning, but they are also the most expensive. None of the wait events consumers are enabled by default.

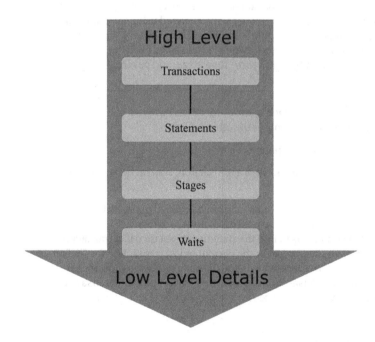

Figure 15-2. *The relationship between the event types*

The event scopes specify how many and which records are kept. A prerequisite for the history scopes to collect data is that the current scope is also collected. The history can either be collected per connection (history) or per SQL node (history long). The current event is always per connection though it is in some cases possible to have more than one event per connection. The current and history events are purged as soon as the connection is closed. The three scopes are summarized in Table 15-8.

Table 15-8. *Performance Schema Event Scopes*

Event Scopt	Description
Current	Currently ongoing events. If a connection does not have a currently ongoing event, the last event is returned. For statement events, the current scope is similar to SHOW PROCESSLIST but including the last executed statement for currently idle connections. The sys schema uses this to provide a much more detailed process list as it is shown in the next section. The current scope only includes threads that exist at the time the events are queried.
History	Keeps the last 10 (by default) events for each connection and background thread. This is most useful for the higher-level event types as lower level events often have so short duration that 10 events only represent the last few fractions of a second. The history scope only includes threads that exist at the time the events are queried. The number of events stored per thread can be changed with the following options in the MySQL configuration file: performance_schema_events_transactions_history_size, performance_schema_events_statements_history_size, performance_schema_events_stages_history_size, and performance_schema_events_waits_history_size.
History long	Keeps the last 10000 (by default) events irrespective of the thread triggering the event. Events in the history long scope are kept even if the thread is closed. This makes the events_%_history_long tables useful for examining the most recent history across all connections. The number of events to store can be changed using the following options in the MySQL configuration file: performance_schema_events_transactions_history_long_size, performance_schema_events_statements_history_long_size, performance_schema_events_stages_history_long_size, and performance_schema_events_waits_history_long_size.

One event can be the parent of another event. So, each of the event tables have two columns to essentially define a (virtual) foreign key to one of the events in the other tables:

- **NESTING_EVENT_ID:** The event ID for the parent event.

- **NESTING_EVENT_TYPE:** Whether the parent ID is a transaction, statement, stage or wait event.

Since in general not all events are captured and the events may not be purged in the order they are captured, this relationship is not complete. However, it is in most cases not a problem.

A simple example of using the nesting columns is to find the statements executed in a transaction. Listing 15-9 shows how to find up to the last 10 statements for the current or last transaction for THREAD_ID = 35 and return the queries in the order they were executed with the oldest first and the most recent at the bottom. This example requires the events_transactions_current consumer and the transaction instrument to be enabled. The details of the events_statements_% tables are discussed later as well as timing values in the Performance Schema.

Listing 15-9. Find the Latest Statements in a Transaction

```
mysql> SELECT s.EVENT_ID, s.SQL_TEXT,
              sys.format_time(s.TIMER_WAIT) AS QueryTime
         FROM performance_schema.events_transactions_current t
              INNER JOIN performance_schema.events_statements_history s
                  ON s.NESTING_EVENT_ID = t.EVENT_ID
```

```
        WHERE t.THREAD_ID = 35
              AND s.NESTING_EVENT_TYPE = 'transaction'
        ORDER BY s.EVENT_ID\G
*************************** 1. row ***************************
 EVENT_ID: 202
 SQL_TEXT: UPDATE queue SET status = 1, locked_by = 23 WHERE status = 0 AND locked_by IS
NULL LIMIT 1
QueryTime: 3.30 ms
*************************** 2. row ***************************
 EVENT_ID: 203
 SQL_TEXT: SELECT id, val FROM queue WHERE locked_by = 23
QueryTime: 1.08 ms
*************************** 3. row ***************************
 EVENT_ID: 204
 SQL_TEXT: UPDATE queue SET status = 2, locked_by = NULL WHERE locked_by = 23
QueryTime: 2.60 ms
*************************** 4. row ***************************
 EVENT_ID: 205
 SQL_TEXT: COMMIT
QueryTime: 966.89 us
4 rows in set (0.00 sec)
```

In general, the nesting level may be deeper. The following sets up a test, then executes a transaction that calls a stored procedure to add an employee and finally commits the transaction. At the same time as the transaction is executing, another connection monitors the event tables (actually the history long event tables) using the sys schema stored procedure sys.ps_trace_thread(). The procedure saves its output in a DOT graph description language file (see *https://en.wikipedia.org/wiki/DOT_(graph_description_language)*) with the filename given as one of the arguments (*/mysql/out/trace.dot* in this case). The arguments to sys.ps_trace_thread() are:

- The thread is to monitor (28).

- The file to save the output to ('/mysql/out/trace.dot').

- How many seconds to monitor for (10 seconds).

- How frequently to poll the events tables—in seconds (0.1 second).

- Whether to truncate the Performance Schema tables before starting to monitor (TRUE). Enabling this avoids including old events in the trace, but also discards all existing data in the tables. So enabling the option is mostly useful on test systems.

- Whether to automatic enable Performance Schema settings (FALSE). When enabled, the settings are restored at the end of the procedure. Setting up the Performance Schema manually allows a more fine-grained control of what is included in the trace.

- Whether to add the file and line number of the events in the trace (FALSE).

The events_transactions_current, events_transactions_history_long, and events_statements_history_long consumers as well as the transaction instrument must be enabled in addition to the default settings for this example to work.

■ **Tip**   In recent versions of MySQL Server and MySQL NDB Cluster, it is only possible to save data to a file from inside MySQL if the target directory is below the directory specified by the secure_file_priv option.

The test execution is shown in Listing 15-10.

Listing 15-10. A Test Used to Trace a Transaction

```
-- Setup the test
mysql> CREATE TABLE employee (
          id char(36) PRIMARY KEY,
          Name varchar(40) NOT NULL
       ) ENGINE=NDBCluster;
Query OK, 0 rows affected (2.46 sec)

mysql> DELIMITER $$
mysql> CREATE PROCEDURE AddEmp(IN in_name varchar(40), OUT out_uuid char(36))
       BEGIN
           SET out_uuid = UUID();
           SELECT
                   out_uuid AS id;
           INSERT
             INTO employee
           VALUES (out_uuid, in_name);
       END$$
Query OK, 0 rows affected (0.01 sec)

mysql> DELIMITER ;

-- Enable consumers and instrument
mysql> UPDATE performance_schema.setup_consumers
          SET ENABLED = 'YES'
        WHERE NAME IN ('events_transactions_current',
                       'events_transactions_history_long',
                       'events_statements_history_long');
Query OK, 3 rows affected (0.00 sec)
Rows matched: 3  Changed: 3  Warnings: 0

mysql> UPDATE performance_schema.setup_instruments
          SET ENABLED = 'YES',
              TIMED = 'YES'
        WHERE NAME = 'transaction';
Query OK, 1 row affected (0.00 sec)
Rows matched: 1  Changed: 1  Warnings: 0

-- Determine the Performance Schema thread ID
mysql> SELECT sys.ps_thread_id(NULL);
+------------------------+
| sys.ps_thread_id(NULL) |
+------------------------+
|                     28 |
+------------------------+
1 row in set (0.01 sec)
```

```
-- Start the data collection in another connection using the thread id
-- from the previous statement.
Other Connection> CALL sys.ps_trace_thread(28, '/mysql/out/trace.dot',
                                    10, 0.1, TRUE, FALSE, FALSE);

-- Execute the test in the connection with Performance Schema thread id = 28
mysql> BEGIN;
Query OK, 0 rows affected (0.00 sec)

mysql> CALL AddEmp
            ('John Doe', @id);
+--------------------------------------+
| id                                   |
+--------------------------------------+
| 17ecdc78-5265-11e7-a0a3-080027fa42a9 |
+--------------------------------------+
1 row in set (0.00 sec)

Query OK, 1 row affected (0.00 sec)

mysql> COMMIT;
Query OK, 0 rows affected (0.00 sec)

-- Optionally reset the Performance Schema settings to the defaults.
mysql> CALL sys.ps_setup_reset_to_default(FALSE);
Query OK, 0 rows affected (0.07 sec)
```

The DOT formatted file can be converted into a graphical representation using software such as the dot program included in the *Graphviz* toolset (*http://www.graphviz.org/*). Graphviz is available from several Linux package repositories and for download from Graphviz's homepage for Linux, Oracle Solaris, Microsoft Windows, and macOS. An example of converting the DOT file to a PNG file is:

```
shell$ dot -Tpng -o trace.png /mysql/out/trace.dot
```

Figure 15-3 shows the resulting graph. Two modifications have been made to make the data easier to read: The graph has been cropped so only the edge of the box with the BEGIN statement is visible to the far left of the figure, and the color scheme has been changed to work better in a black and white book.

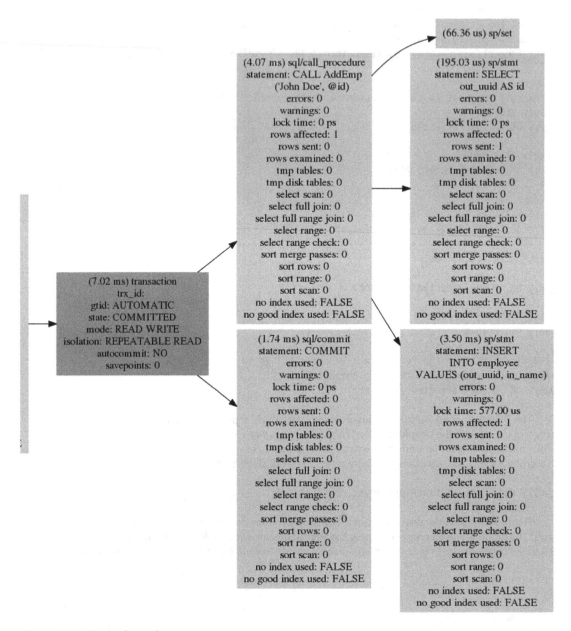

Figure 15-3. *Trace of nested events*

There are some interesting observations to make from the image in Figure 15-3:

- The details of each event are included in a box with one box per event. For the BEGIN statement, all metrics are either 0 or FALSE.

- The trace includes one transaction (the second column, darker grey) and six statements in four levels.

- The transaction event includes information such as whether GTIDs are used (not supported for NDB Cluster), the state (COMMITTED), the transaction isolation mode, etc. Notice that the transaction isolation level is listed as REPEATABLE READ, which is what was requested (as it is the default). However, MySQL NDB Cluster only supports READ COMMITTED. So, for MySQL NDB Cluster, the listed and actual transaction isolation level may not be the same.

- The overall time it took to execute the transaction was 7.02 milliseconds.

- The parent of the transaction is the BEGIN statement. The transaction itself is parent of two statements of which the CALL statement again is parent of another three statements.

- For each statement except the SET statement inside the stored procedure, there is a long list of details. These include the execution time (also included for the SET statement), whether errors or warnings occurred, the number of rows affected/sent/examined, index use, etc.

- The events for the statements (see the string next to the time the event took, for example sql/call_procedure for the CALL statement) differ whether the statement is executed directly or through the stored procedure. Events for statements executed directly starts with sql/, whereas events for statements executed through the procedure starts with sp/.

The only source of all of the details in Figure 15-3 is the events tables, which show how useful they can be for collecting information.

While the number of tables and amount data can seem overwhelming at first, there is a high degree of similarity between data showing similar data, and the names used for tables and columns are quite consistent. For example, the events tables all have similar columns describing the event at a high level, then specific columns based on whether it is a wait, stage, statement, or transaction event. The current, history, and history long tables for the same event type, all have the same columns. Summary tables for an event type will have columns that are easy to relate to the per event tables. The next example will use the events_statements_current table to illustrate how to read the raw data.

Listing 15-11 shows the example of the raw output for the most recent query for thread ID 31 from the events_statements_current table. The details are similar to what was seen in the trace graph, but a couple of things warrant a bit more consideration.

Listing 15-11. Example Output from performance_schema.events_statements_current

```
mysql> SELECT *
         FROM performance_schema.events_statements_current
        WHERE THREAD_ID = 31\G
*************************** 1. row ***************************
            THREAD_ID: 31
             EVENT_ID: 35
         END_EVENT_ID: 36
           EVENT_NAME: statement/sql/select
               SOURCE: socket_connection.cc:101
          TIMER_START: 7030638806624000
            TIMER_END: 7030640657767000
           TIMER_WAIT: 1851143000
            LOCK_TIME: 224000000
             SQL_TEXT: SELECT * FROM world.City WHERE CountryCode = 'AUS' ORDER BY
Population DESC
               DIGEST: d21ff2e30ed268303522831878e8e1d6
```

```
        DIGEST_TEXT: SELECT * FROM `world` . `City` WHERE `CountryCode` = ? ORDER BY
`Population` DESC
     CURRENT_SCHEMA: db1
        OBJECT_TYPE: NULL
      OBJECT_SCHEMA: NULL
        OBJECT_NAME: NULL
OBJECT_INSTANCE_BEGIN: NULL
         MYSQL_ERRNO: 0
    RETURNED_SQLSTATE: NULL
        MESSAGE_TEXT: NULL
             ERRORS: 0
           WARNINGS: 0
       ROWS_AFFECTED: 0
           ROWS_SENT: 14
       ROWS_EXAMINED: 28
CREATED_TMP_DISK_TABLES: 0
    CREATED_TMP_TABLES: 0
     SELECT_FULL_JOIN: 0
SELECT_FULL_RANGE_JOIN: 0
        SELECT_RANGE: 0
   SELECT_RANGE_CHECK: 0
         SELECT_SCAN: 0
    SORT_MERGE_PASSES: 0
          SORT_RANGE: 1
           SORT_ROWS: 14
           SORT_SCAN: 0
       NO_INDEX_USED: 0
   NO_GOOD_INDEX_USED: 0
     NESTING_EVENT_ID: NULL
   NESTING_EVENT_TYPE: NULL
  NESTING_EVENT_LEVEL: 0
1 row in set (0.00 sec)
```

TIMER_START, TIMER_END, TIMER_WAIT, and LOCK_TIME all have huge values. All timings in the Performance Schema are in picoseconds (10^{-12} second). The reason for choosing this unit is performance (it ensures no division is required, and divisions are computational more expensive than multiplication). When software consumes the timing values, this choice of unit is not a problem, but it makes it hard for humans to read the values. The sys schema includes several formatting functions, one of which is format_time(). This function can be used to convert the picoseconds into human readable units:

```
mysql> SELECT EVENT_ID, sys.format_time(TIMER_START) AS TimeStart,
              sys.format_time(TIMER_END) AS TimeEnd,
              sys.format_time(TIMER_WAIT) AS TimeWait,
              sys.format_time(LOCK_TIME) AS LockTime
         FROM performance_schema.events_statements_current
        WHERE THREAD_ID = 31;
+----------+-----------+---------+----------+-----------+
| EVENT_ID | TimeStart | TimeEnd | TimeWait | LockTime  |
+----------+-----------+---------+----------+-----------+
|       35 | 1.95 h    | 1.95 h  | 1.85 ms  | 224.00 us |
+----------+-----------+---------+----------+-----------+
1 row in set (0.00 sec)
```

The meaning of the four timing values are:

- **TimeStart:** The amount of time in hours since the timer was last reset until the start of the event. The reset happens when MySQL is restarted or the timer overflows (which happens after 2^{64} picoseconds or approximately 30.5 weeks).

- **TimeEnd:** The amount of time in hours since the timer was last reset until the end of the event.

- **TimeWait:** The total duration of the event in milliseconds. This is the same as the difference between TIMER_END and TIMER_START.

- **LockTime:** The time spent waiting for table locks in microseconds. This value is not very useful for NDBCluster tables as they use row-level locks.

Since different events use different timers as noted in the description of the setup_timers table, the TIMER_START and TIMER_END values of different events cannot in general be compared. Instead always use the EVENT_ID columns to compare the order of events.

Another interesting detail are the DIGEST and DIGEST_TEXT columns:

```
       SQL_TEXT: SELECT * FROM world.City WHERE CountryCode = 'AUS' ORDER BY
Population DESC
         DIGEST: d21ff2e30ed268303522831878e8e1d6
    DIGEST_TEXT: SELECT * FROM `world` . `City` WHERE `CountryCode` = ? ORDER BY
`Population` DESC
```

The DIGEST_TEXT column is the normalized version of the query. The Performance Schema normalization of a query is similar to what the mysqldumpslow script can do for the slow query log to allow grouping queries that are the same except for the parameters used. In the example, the value for CountryCode is replaced with a question mark (?), so if the query is repeated for a different country, the digest text will be the same:

```
       SQL_TEXT: SELECT * FROM world.City WHERE CountryCode = 'USA' ORDER BY
Population DESC
         DIGEST: d21ff2e30ed268303522831878e8e1d6
    DIGEST_TEXT: SELECT * FROM `world` . `City` WHERE `CountryCode` = ? ORDER BY
`Population` DESC
```

The DIGEST is an MD5 hash based on the normalized query (although not as simple as MD5(DIGEST_TEXT)). Having the digest hash makes it simpler to query for similar queries. For example:

```
mysql> SELECT sys.format_time(TIMER_WAIT) AS TimeWait,
           CONCAT(LEFT(SQL_TEXT, 56), ' ...') AS 'SQL'
      FROM performance_schema.events_statements_history
     WHERE DIGEST = 'd21ff2e30ed268303522831878e8e1d6';
+----------+-------------------------------------------------------------+
| TimeWait | SQL                                                         |
+----------+-------------------------------------------------------------+
| 1.85 ms  | SELECT * FROM world.City WHERE CountryCode = 'AUS' ORDER ... |
| 1.61 ms  | SELECT * FROM world.City WHERE CountryCode = 'USA' ORDER ... |
+----------+-------------------------------------------------------------+
2 rows in set (0.00 sec)
```

However, the digests are even more useful than this. They are also used internally in the Performance Schema to generate a summary of the queries on the SQL node. Summary tables is the next group of tables to look at.

Summary Tables

The events tables that were the topic of the previous section contains the raw data. This is very useful for inspecting specific events like one query that is slow. However, particularly on SQL nodes with a high number of queries per second, the events tables are not always useful as the events are evicted too quickly. This is where the summary tables enter the picture.

MySQL NDB Cluster 7.5 has 36 summary tables as listed in Table 15-9 through Table 15-14. The naming convention is {what}_summary_by_{group by}, where {what} is which data is summarized and {group by} is what the data is grouped by. For some summary tables the "by_{group by}" pattern is repeated to signify that the data is grouped by more than one thing. A "global_" is also added after "summary_" for some summary tables to make it explicit that there is only one grouping level.

Table 15-9 shows the summary tables for stage events. As most stage events are disabled by default, most of the summary values in these tables are 0.

Table 15-9. *The Stage Events Summary Tables*

Table Name	Description
events_stages_summary_by_account_by_event_name	Stages grouped by account and event name.
events_stages_summary_by_host_by_event_name	Stages grouped by host and event name.
events_stages_summary_by_thread_by_event_name	Stages grouped by thread and event name.
events_stages_summary_by_user_by_event_name	Stages grouped by use and event name.
events_stages_summary_global_by_event_name	Stages grouped only by event name.

The statement event summary tables listed in Table 15-10 are the summary tables used most often. An example using the events_statements_summary_by_digest table is discussed after Table 15-14.

Table 15-10. *The Statement Events Summary Tables*

Table Name	Description
events_statements_summary_by_account_by_event_name	Statements grouped by account and event name.
events_statements_summary_by_digest	Statements grouped by digest.
events_statements_summary_by_host_by_event_name	Statements grouped by host and event name.
events_statements_summary_by_program	Statements grouped by stored procedure, stored function, stored event, or trigger.
events_statements_summary_by_thread_by_event_name	Statements grouped by thread and event name.
events_statements_summary_by_user_by_event_name	Statements grouped by user and event name.
events_statements_summary_global_by_event_name	Statements grouped only by event name.

Table 15-11 lists the transaction events summary tables. Transactions are not instrumented by default, so the summary data will be all zeros.

Table 15-11. *The Transaction Events Summary Tables*

Table Name	Description
events_transactions_summary_by_account_by_event_name	Transactions grouped by account and event name.
events_transactions_summary_by_host_by_event_name	Transactions grouped by host and event name.
events_transactions_summary_by_thread_by_event_name	Transactions grouped by thread and event name.
events_transactions_summary_by_user_by_event_name	Transactions grouped by user and event name.
events_transactions_summary_global_by_event_name	Transactions grouped only by event name.

The final category of events summary tables is for wait events. These are summarized in Table 15-12.

Table 15-12. *The Wait Events Summary Tables*

Table Name	Description
events_waits_summary_by_account_by_event_name	Wait events grouped by account and event name.
events_waits_summary_by_host_by_event_name	Wait events grouped by host and event name.
events_waits_summary_by_instance	Wait events grouped by instance. See the instance tables later.
events_waits_summary_by_thread_by_event_name	Wait events grouped by thread and event name.
events_waits_summary_by_user_by_event_name	Wait events grouped by user and event name.
events_waits_summary_global_by_event_name	Wait events grouped only by event name.

Table 15-13 shows the memory summary tables. Memory instrumentation is only enabled by default for the Performance Schema memory events, so by default the summary tables only have non-zero data for these events. If instrumentation has been enabled for all memory events, these summary tables are very useful to determine where the SQL nodes uses its memory.

Table 15-13. *The Memory Summary Tables*

Table Name	Description
memory_summary_by_account_by_event_name	Memory usage grouped by account and event name.
memory_summary_by_host_by_event_name	Memory usage grouped by host and event name.
memory_summary_by_thread_by_event_name	Memory usage grouped by thread and event name.
memory_summary_by_user_by_event_name	Memory usage grouped by user and event name.
memory_summary_global_by_event_name	Memory usage grouped only by event name.

The last set of summary tables are for files, objects, sockets, and tables. These are summarized in Table 15-14.

Table 15-14. *Summary Tables for Files, Objects, Sockets, and Tables*

Table Name	Description
file_summary_by_event_name	Files grouped by event name. This includes I/O latencies and amount of data read and written.
file_summary_by_instance	Files grouped by file instance and event name. This includes I/O latencies and amount of data read and written.
objects_summary_global_by_type	The number of times tables, stored procedures, stored functions, stored events, and triggers have been used and the amount of time spent in them.
socket_summary_by_event_name	Statistics based on connection type (TCP/IP, UNIX socket, etc.)
socket_summary_by_instance	Statistics grouped by the socket instances.
table_io_waits_summary_by_index_usage	Table I/O wait events grouped by index.
table_io_waits_summary_by_table	Table I/O wait events grouped by table.
table_lock_waits_summary_by_table	Table lock wait events grouped by table.

The summary tables are essentially reports on their own, making them very useful for investigating issues. One summary table that is particularly worth considering in more detail is the events_statements_summary_by_digest table. This table uses the digests discussed in the previous section to group the statement events. The statistics are aggregated for the combination of the default schema and the digest (to allow distinguishing the same query executed for two different schemas). The result is similar to the report generated by the mysqldumpslow script on the slow query log, but being automatically kept up to date for all instrumented queries and available using the SELECT statement which makes it very easy to filter and order the data as required.

The events_statements_summary_by_digest table can, by default, hold 10000 combinations of the default schema and the digest. The size can be changed using the performance_schema_digests_size option (requires a restart of the SQL node). When the last available row in the table is taken into use, the default schema and digest will both be set to NULL and all queries not matching an existing row will be combined in this NULL row.

■ **Note** The events_statements_summary_by_digest table is also the default source for the MySQL Enterprise Monitor Query Analyzer.

As an example, consider a request to find the most often executed queries. Listing 15-12 gives an example of this using a requirement that the queries must have been executed at least 500 times.

Listing 15-12. Summary of Queries Executed at Least 500 Times

```
mysql> SELECT SCHEMA_NAME, DIGEST, DIGEST_TEXT, COUNT_STAR,
              sys.format_time(SUM_TIMER_WAIT) AS TotalTime,
              sys.format_time(AVG_TIMER_WAIT) AS AvgTime,
              SUM_ROWS_AFFECTED, SUM_ROWS_SENT, SUM_ROWS_EXAMINED
         FROM performance_schema.events_statements_summary_by_digest
        WHERE COUNT_STAR >= 500
        ORDER BY COUNT_STAR DESC\G
*************************** 1. row ***************************
      SCHEMA_NAME: world
           DIGEST: 127979ff01aa4392cc363ae5c71177d5
      DIGEST_TEXT: SELECT * FROM `City` WHERE `ID` = ?
       COUNT_STAR: 1000
        TotalTime: 552.40 ms
          AvgTime: 552.40 us
SUM_ROWS_AFFECTED: 0
    SUM_ROWS_SENT: 1000
SUM_ROWS_EXAMINED: 1000
*************************** 2. row ***************************
      SCHEMA_NAME: world
           DIGEST: 22a2a36f23374320e7a9739086957192
      DIGEST_TEXT: UPDATE `City` SET `Population` = `Population` + ? WHERE `ID` = ?
       COUNT_STAR: 1000
        TotalTime: 1.62 s
          AvgTime: 1.62 ms
SUM_ROWS_AFFECTED: 1000
    SUM_ROWS_SENT: 0
SUM_ROWS_EXAMINED: 1000
2 rows in set (0.00 sec)
```

The output shows that SUM_ROWS_EXAMINED is the same as COUNT_STAR (the total number of executions) for the two statements, so on average each execution only needs to examine one row. That is a good as it gets (and comes from using the primary key to locate the rows).

Another very useful summary table is the table_io_waits_summary_by_index_usage table. This makes it possible to check whether indexes are used or not. Unused indexes cause an overhead both storage and performance wise. So, it is useful to monitor whether indexes are used, and if not investigate whether it is possible to remove it. For an example of checking for unused indexes, see the example with the sys.schema_index_statistics view in the next section about the sys schema.

The table_io_waits_summary_by_index_usage table can also be used to find tables with many rows found using table scans. This is done by filtering with the INDEX_NAME set to NULL. An example of this will also be provided in the discussion of the sys schema—see the example with the sys.schema_tables_with_full_table_scans view in the next section.

The next group of tables to consider are the connection and thread tables.

Connection and Thread Tables

The connection and threat tables give access to statistics and metadata for the connections made to the SQL node and which threads exist. There are a total of seven tables, all listed in Table 15-15.

485

Table 15-15. *Performance Schema Connection Tables*

Table Name	Description
accounts	Number of current and total threads grouped by username and hostname.
host_cache	Details for TCP/IP connections from non-loopback interfaces.
hosts	Number of current and total threads grouped by hostname.
session_account_connect_attrs	Session attributes for the same account querying the table.
session_connect_attrs	Session attributes for all connections.
threads	Details for all threads, including similar information as the process list.
users	Number of current and total threads grouped by username.

The threads table is the most interesting for general usage. This was the table that was used earlier to link connection IDs with the Performance Schema thread IDs and to show that both foreground and background threads are instrumented. It includes various metadata for each thread as well as the same information as the process list for user connections. Listing 15-13 shows an example for a user connection.

Listing 15-13. The performance_schema.threads Table

```
mysql> SELECT * FROM performance_schema.threads WHERE THREAD_ID = 12595\G
*************************** 1. row ***************************
          THREAD_ID: 12595
               NAME: thread/sql/one_connection
               TYPE: FOREGROUND
     PROCESSLIST_ID: 12572
   PROCESSLIST_USER: app_user
   PROCESSLIST_HOST: ol7
     PROCESSLIST_DB: db1
PROCESSLIST_COMMAND: Query
   PROCESSLIST_TIME: 12
  PROCESSLIST_STATE: Sending data
   PROCESSLIST_INFO: SELECT * FROM t1 INNER JOIN t2 USING (val)
   PARENT_THREAD_ID: NULL
               ROLE: NULL
       INSTRUMENTED: YES
            HISTORY: YES
    CONNECTION_TYPE: TCP/IP
       THREAD_OS_ID: 14131
1 row in set (0.00 sec)
```

It is preferred to use the threads table over the SHOW PROCESSLIST statement or the information_schema.PROCESSLIST table as those requires a mutex on the executing queries to generate the process list. The mutex is required as SHOW PROCESSLIST and an query on information_schema.PROCESSLIST requires fetching the status from each thread. The Performance Schema works the other way around that the threads update the Performance Schema when the status changes, so a table lock on the threads table is enough to give a consistent result. Additionally, the threads table offer more details and can be joined with the events_statements_current table to provide even more information including sub second precision on the execution time. The sys schema views processlist and session, which are discussed in the next section, will give an example of this.

The accounts, hosts, and users tables all show the number of current threads and total threads but grouped by the account, host, and user, respectively. Listing 15-14 shows examples of this. The NULL users and hosts are for the background threads and system users. Notice that the column names uses the word "connection", however it is really threads.

Listing 15-14. Getting the Number of Threads

```
mysql> SELECT * FROM performance_schema.accounts;
+----------+-----------+---------------------+-------------------+
| USER     | HOST      | CURRENT_CONNECTIONS | TOTAL_CONNECTIONS |
+----------+-----------+---------------------+-------------------+
| NULL     | NULL      |                  25 |             12952 |
| root     | localhost |                   2 |                21 |
| app_user | ol7       |                   1 |               254 |
+----------+-----------+---------------------+-------------------+
3 rows in set (0.00 sec)

mysql> SELECT * FROM performance_schema.hosts;
+-----------+---------------------+-------------------+
| HOST      | CURRENT_CONNECTIONS | TOTAL_CONNECTIONS |
+-----------+---------------------+-------------------+
| NULL      |                  25 |             12956 |
| localhost |                   2 |                21 |
| ol7       |                   1 |               254 |
+-----------+---------------------+-------------------+
3 rows in set (0.00 sec)

mysql> SELECT * FROM performance_schema.users;
+----------+---------------------+-------------------+
| USER     | CURRENT_CONNECTIONS | TOTAL_CONNECTIONS |
+----------+---------------------+-------------------+
| NULL     |                  25 |             12962 |
| root     |                   2 |                21 |
| app_user |                   1 |               254 |
+----------+---------------------+-------------------+
3 rows in set (0.00 sec)
```

The host_cache table can be used to get details of the TCP connections from non-loopback interfaces (but not UNIX socket connections and for example *127.0.0.1*). Listing 15-15 provides an example. This can be used to find out where connection errors are originating from and whether any hosts are close to being blocked due to too many protocol handshake errors. A host is blocked if SUM_CONNECT_ERRORS for a host reached the value of the max_connect_errors configuration option.

Listing 15-15. Details of the Host Cache

```
mysql> SELECT * FROM host_cache\G
*************************** 1. row ***************************
                       IP: 192.168.56.101
                     HOST: ol7
           HOST_VALIDATED: YES
       SUM_CONNECT_ERRORS: 3
COUNT_HOST_BLOCKED_ERRORS: 0
```

```
                 COUNT_NAMEINFO_TRANSIENT_ERRORS: 0
                 COUNT_NAMEINFO_PERMANENT_ERRORS: 0
                             COUNT_FORMAT_ERRORS: 0
                 COUNT_ADDRINFO_TRANSIENT_ERRORS: 0
                 COUNT_ADDRINFO_PERMANENT_ERRORS: 0
                             COUNT_FCRDNS_ERRORS: 0
                           COUNT_HOST_ACL_ERRORS: 0
                     COUNT_NO_AUTH_PLUGIN_ERRORS: 0
                        COUNT_AUTH_PLUGIN_ERRORS: 0
                         COUNT_HANDSHAKE_ERRORS: 3
                       COUNT_PROXY_USER_ERRORS: 0
                   COUNT_PROXY_USER_ACL_ERRORS: 0
                     COUNT_AUTHENTICATION_ERRORS: 8
                               COUNT_SSL_ERRORS: 0
              COUNT_MAX_USER_CONNECTIONS_ERRORS: 0
     COUNT_MAX_USER_CONNECTIONS_PER_HOUR_ERRORS: 0
                  COUNT_DEFAULT_DATABASE_ERRORS: 0
                      COUNT_INIT_CONNECT_ERRORS: 0
                             COUNT_LOCAL_ERRORS: 0
                           COUNT_UNKNOWN_ERRORS: 0
                                     FIRST_SEEN: 2017-06-17 18:58:38
                                      LAST_SEEN: 2017-06-17 19:03:16
                               FIRST_ERROR_SEEN: 2017-06-17 18:58:38
                                LAST_ERROR_SEEN: 2017-06-17 19:03:17
1 row in set (0.00 sec)
```

The last two tables—session_account_connect_attrs and session_connect_attrs—both show attributes for the user connections. The attributes are provided by the client and thus which attributes are available depends on how the connection was made. The difference between the two tables is that session_account_connect_attrs only includes attributes for connections for the same account as the account of the connection executing the query, whereas session_connect_attrs includes the attributes for all accounts. By having this separation, it is possible to grant the SELECT privilege on the session_account_connect_attrs to users who should be allowed to check the attributes for its own connections without showing information for other accounts. Listing 15-16 shows an example of the attributes for two connections.

Listing 15-16. Session Attributes

```
mysql> SELECT PROCESSLIST_ID AS ID, ATTR_NAME, ATTR_VALUE, ORDINAL_POSITION
          FROM session_connect_attrs;
+-------+-----------------+----------------------+------------------+
| ID    | ATTR_NAME       | ATTR_VALUE           | ORDINAL_POSITION |
+-------+-----------------+----------------------+------------------+
|     9 | _os             | linux-glibc2.5       |                0 |
|     9 | _client_name    | libmysql             |                1 |
|     9 | _pid            | 1959                 |                2 |
|     9 | _client_version | 5.7.18-ndb-7.5.6     |                3 |
|     9 | _platform       | x86_64               |                4 |
|     9 | program_name    | mysql                |                5 |
| 26106 | _runtime_version| 1.8.0_111            |                0 |
| 26106 | _client_version | 5.1.42               |                1 |
| 26106 | _client_name    | MySQL Connector Java |                2 |
| 26106 | _client_license | GPL                  |                3 |
```

```
| 26106 | _runtime_vendor   | Oracle Corporation   |                4 |
+-------+-------------------+----------------------+------------------+
11 rows in set (0.00 sec)
```

The connection with connection ID 9 is using the mysql command-line client from version 5.7.18-ndb-7.5.6 connecting from a Linux system. Connection ID 26106 is, on the other hand, a Java application using Connector/J version 5.1.42. One of the advantages of these attributes is that it is easy to check the version of the client and connectors used; this can be used to verify that all instances of the application are using the appropriate version.

The attributes tables expose variables for the client side of the connection. Next are the variable and status tables that provide information from the server side.

Variable and Status Tables

The Performance Schema provides a range of tables to get the values of variables (options) and status variables. There are both global and session level tables as well as status variables grouped by account, host, thread, and user. The tables are listed in Table 15-16. The global_status, global_variables, session_status, and session_variables have replaced the corresponding tables from the Information Schema in MySQL NDB Cluster 7.5 as part of the effort to move tables that are more about performance and are more dynamic into the Performance Schema.

Table 15-16. *Performance Schema Variable and Status Tables*

Table Name	Description
global_status	The global status variables. The same as SHOW GLOBAL STATUS except for variables starting with Com_.
global_variables	The global configuration variables. The same as SHOW GLOBAL VARIABLES.
session_status	The session status variables. The same as SHOW SESSION STATUS except for variables starting with Com_.
session_variables	The session configuration variables. The same as SHOW SESSION VARIABLES.
status_by_account	The status variables grouped by username and hostname.
status_by_host	The status variables grouped by hostname.
status_by_thread	The status variables grouped by thread.
status_by_user	The status variables grouped by username.
user_variables_by_thread	The user variables (for example @id) for each current connection.
variables_by_thread	The session-level configuration variables for each current connection.

The variables_by_thread table is a more general version of session_variables. Whereas session_variables includes the variables for the connection querying the table, the variables_by_thread table has data for all of the connections. However, there is one additional difference: variables_by_thread strictly only includes session level variables, whereas session_variables adds the global variables that do not have a session counterpart. For example, tls_version is included in session_variables but not in variables_by_thread.

Listing 15-17 shows an example of how variables_by_thread can be used together with global_variables to detect when a client connection has changed any of the configuration options.

Listing 15-17. Determining Connections Using Non-Global Variable Values

```
mysql> SELECT t.THREAD_ID, VARIABLE_NAME,
              t.VARIABLE_VALUE AS SessionValue,
              g.VARIABLE_VALUE AS GlobalValue
         FROM performance_schema.variables_by_thread t
              INNER JOIN performance_schema.global_variables g
                    USING (VARIABLE_NAME)
        WHERE t.VARIABLE_VALUE <> g.VARIABLE_VALUE
          AND VARIABLE_NAME NOT IN ('character_set_database',
                                    'collation_database');
+-----------+------------------+--------------+-------------+
| THREAD_ID | VARIABLE_NAME    | SessionValue | GlobalValue |
+-----------+------------------+--------------+-------------+
|     32412 | sort_buffer_size | 2097152      | 262144      |
+-----------+------------------+--------------+-------------+
1 row in set (0.02 sec)
```

The database character set and collation is filtered out as they depend on how the current schema for the connection was created rather than what the connection have set. Similarly, it may be necessary to filter out other options that are known to be changed. In this case, the sort buffer has been increased to 2MB by one of the connections. Large buffers can cause performance issues and too high memory usage, so if this value is not expected for the connection, it may warrant further investigation.

The next group of tables to look at are the replication tables.

Replication Tables

Until MySQL Server 5.7 and MySQL NDB Cluster 7.5, the only way to get information about the replication status and configuration was to use the SHOW SLAVE STATUS statement. In MySQL NDB Cluster 7.5, the eight tables in Table 15-17 has been added to make some of the information available through the Performance Schema. The tables were also discussed in Chapter 6, and will not be discussed further here.

Table 15-17. *Performance Schema Replication Tables*

Table Name	Description
replication_applier_configuration	Configuration for slave the SQL thread.
replication_applier_status	Status for slave the SQL thread.
replication_applier_status_by_coordinator	Status for the coordinator thread for a multi-threaded slave.
replication_applier_status_by_worker	Status for worker threads for a multi-threaded slave.
replication_connection_configuration	Configuration for the slave IO thread.
replication_connection_status	Status for the slave IO thread.
replication_group_member_stats	This table shows network and status information for replication group members. Group Replication is not supported for MySQL NDB Cluster.
replication_group_members	Statistical information for MySQL Group Replication members. Group Replication is not supported for MySQL NDB Cluster.

Instance Tables

There are a number of instances that are tracked. These range from mutexes to prepared statements. Table 15-18 lists the six tables available for these instances. Most of the tables are not often required, but can be useful in some debugging situations.

Table 15-18. *Performance Schema Instance Tables*

Table Name	Description
cond_instances	The condition synchronization instances. Includes just the instance name and memory address.
file_instances	File instances. Includes filename, event name, and the number of open file descriptors to the file.
mutex_instances	Mutex instances. Includes the memory address and which thread (if any) holds a lock on the mutex.
prepared_statements_instances	Prepared statement statistics similar to events_statements_current.
rwlock_instances	Read and write lock instances. Includes the memory address, which thread (if any) holds a write lock, and how many read locks that exits for the instance.
socket_instances	Each of the TCP/IP socket, UNIX socket, etc. Includes the memory address, thread ID using the socket, socket ID, IP address, port number, and state.

One table stands out as being somewhat different that the others: the prepared_statements_instances table. This is very similar to the events_statements_current table, except it is for prepared statements. There are no tables equivalent of the events history or history long tables, so only current existing prepared statements (i.e. existing in the prepared statement cache) can be viewed.

Listing 15-18 shows an example where there are two prepared statements in the cache. Notice how the statement name and SQL text are the same for the two prepared statements—this is not an error. The scope of the prepared statement is the connection, so two connections are free to create prepared statements with the same name.

Listing 15-18. The Prepared Statement Instances

```
mysql> SELECT * FROM prepared_statements_instances\G
*************************** 1. row ***************************
    OBJECT_INSTANCE_BEGIN: 140468851714864
             STATEMENT_ID: 1
           STATEMENT_NAME: stmt_city
                 SQL_TEXT: SELECT * FROM world.City WHERE ID = ?
          OWNER_THREAD_ID: 32412
           OWNER_EVENT_ID: 10
        OWNER_OBJECT_TYPE: NULL
      OWNER_OBJECT_SCHEMA: NULL
        OWNER_OBJECT_NAME: NULL
            TIMER_PREPARE: 230446000
          COUNT_REPREPARE: 0
            COUNT_EXECUTE: 4
        SUM_TIMER_EXECUTE: 3560169000
```

```
           MIN_TIMER_EXECUTE: 671388000
           AVG_TIMER_EXECUTE: 890042000
           MAX_TIMER_EXECUTE: 1107494000
              SUM_LOCK_TIME: 504000000
                  SUM_ERRORS: 0
                SUM_WARNINGS: 0
           SUM_ROWS_AFFECTED: 0
               SUM_ROWS_SENT: 4
           SUM_ROWS_EXAMINED: 4
  SUM_CREATED_TMP_DISK_TABLES: 0
       SUM_CREATED_TMP_TABLES: 0
         SUM_SELECT_FULL_JOIN: 0
   SUM_SELECT_FULL_RANGE_JOIN: 0
            SUM_SELECT_RANGE: 0
       SUM_SELECT_RANGE_CHECK: 0
             SUM_SELECT_SCAN: 0
        SUM_SORT_MERGE_PASSES: 0
              SUM_SORT_RANGE: 0
               SUM_SORT_ROWS: 0
               SUM_SORT_SCAN: 0
            SUM_NO_INDEX_USED: 0
       SUM_NO_GOOD_INDEX_USED: 0
*************************** 2. row ***************************
        OBJECT_INSTANCE_BEGIN: 140469259951328
                STATEMENT_ID: 1
              STATEMENT_NAME: stmt_city
                    SQL_TEXT: SELECT * FROM world.City WHERE ID = ?
              OWNER_THREAD_ID: 35411
               OWNER_EVENT_ID: 3
            OWNER_OBJECT_TYPE: NULL
          OWNER_OBJECT_SCHEMA: NULL
            OWNER_OBJECT_NAME: NULL
               TIMER_PREPARE: 313392000
             COUNT_REPREPARE: 0
               COUNT_EXECUTE: 1
           SUM_TIMER_EXECUTE: 1281026000
           MIN_TIMER_EXECUTE: 1281026000
           AVG_TIMER_EXECUTE: 1281026000
           MAX_TIMER_EXECUTE: 1281026000
              SUM_LOCK_TIME: 165000000
                  SUM_ERRORS: 0
                SUM_WARNINGS: 0
           SUM_ROWS_AFFECTED: 0
               SUM_ROWS_SENT: 1
           SUM_ROWS_EXAMINED: 1
  SUM_CREATED_TMP_DISK_TABLES: 0
       SUM_CREATED_TMP_TABLES: 0
         SUM_SELECT_FULL_JOIN: 0
   SUM_SELECT_FULL_RANGE_JOIN: 0
            SUM_SELECT_RANGE: 0
       SUM_SELECT_RANGE_CHECK: 0
             SUM_SELECT_SCAN: 0
```

```
     SUM_SORT_MERGE_PASSES: 0
            SUM_SORT_RANGE: 0
             SUM_SORT_ROWS: 0
             SUM_SORT_SCAN: 0
          SUM_NO_INDEX_USED: 0
     SUM_NO_GOOD_INDEX_USED: 0
2 rows in set (0.00 sec)
```

Lock Tables

Lock wait issues are typical issues that database administrators will have to investigate. Locks can occur at several levels from the global level in the SQL node over metadata and table level locks to row level locks. The Performance Schema includes two tables listed in Table 15-19 that can be used to investigate metadata locks and table locks.

Table 15-19. Performance Schema Lock Tables

Table Name	Description
metadata_locks	Metadata lock information. One row per metadata lock currently in use or being waited for.
table_handles	Information about table locks. Rows may be returned even if no lock currently exists or is being requested.

Given that these will only be an issue for NDBCluster tables while schema changes are being made, and the NDBCluster storage engine does not support concurrent queries for the table on the same SQL node, the Performance Schema lock tables will not be discussed in more detail here. In the next chapter, it will be shown how to investigate lock contention at the row level for NDBCluster tables.

This concludes the tour of the Performance Schema. As it can be seen, there is a lot of data available, and each new version of MySQL Server adds more tables and instruments. It is easy to become overwhelmed and it can be hard to remember all of the queries in the heat of the battle. This is where the sys schema comes into play.

■ **Tip** There is much more to know about the Performance Schema. The full documentation can be found in the MySQL Reference Manual at *https://dev.mysql.com/doc/refman/en/performance-schema.html*.

The sys Schema

The sys schema is the brainchild of Mark Leith, one of the managers for MySQL Enterprise Monitor. He started the ps_helper project to experiment with monitoring ideas and to showcase what the Performance Schema was able to do while making it simpler at the same time. The project was later renamed to the sys schema and moved into MySQL. There have since been contributions from several other people, including one of the authors of this book.

This section looks at the installation process for the sys schema as well as demonstrates some use cases including the Performance Reports in MySQL Workbench.

Installation

The `sys` schema is available for MySQL Server 5.6 and later, which means MySQL NDB Cluster 7.3 and later. Starting with MySQL Server 5.7/MySQL NDB Cluster 7.5, it is installed by default in the same way as the other system schemas such as the `mysql` schema. For users of MySQL NDB Cluster 7.3 and 7.4, it is necessary to install it manually from the GitHub repository, MySQL Workbench, or MySQL Enterprise Monitor. Should the `sys` schema become corrupted or there is an upgrade available, it is possible for all MySQL NDB Cluster versions to reinstall using the GitHub downloads.

The `sys` schema GitHub repository is available at *https://github.com/mysql/mysql-sys*. The repository is administrated by the MySQL development team in the same way as the server (which includes MySQL NDB Cluster) GitHub repository. From the front page of the repository, choose the branch to download. In most cases, it is recommended to choose the master branch, which is the same as is installed with MySQL. Then click on the green *Clone or Download* button followed by *Download ZIP* to download the installation files. This is also shown in Figure 15-4.

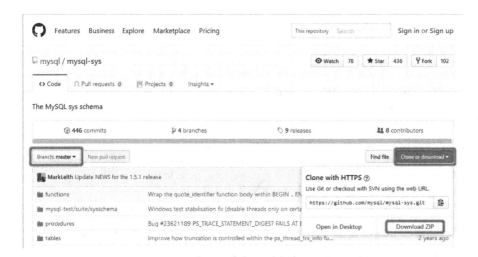

Figure 15-4. *Downloading the sys schema from GitHub*

After the downloaded Zip file has been extracted, go into the *mysql-sys-master* directory (if another branch than master was downloaded, the directory name will be different) where the installation files are located. There is one SQL script per supported version:

- **sys_56.sql:** For MySQL Server 5.6 and MySQL NDB Cluster 7.3 and 7.4.

- **sys_57.sql:** For MySQL Server 5.7 and MySQL NDB Cluster 7.5 and 7.6.

Connect to an SQL node using the `mysql` command-line client with the current directory being *mysql-sys-master* and execute (using the appropriate installation file for the MySQL NDB Cluster version):

```
mysql> SOURCE sys_56.sql
Query OK, 0 rows affected (0.00 sec)

Query OK, 0 rows affected (0.00 sec)

Query OK, 0 rows affected (0.00 sec)
```

```
Query OK, 1 row affected (0.45 sec)

Database changed
Query OK, 0 rows affected (0.04 sec)
...
```

It is also possible to install the sys schema using a GUI using either MySQL Enterprise Monitor or MySQL Workbench. Figure 15-5 shows the install screen in the Performance Reports in MySQL Workbench. Do note that MySQL Workbench only supports installing the sys schema if it is not already there; there is no support for upgrades.

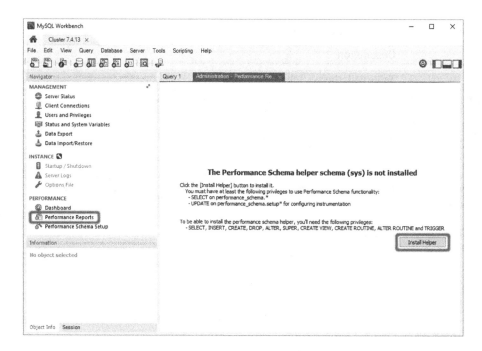

Figure 15-5. *Installing the sys schema from the MySQL Workbench Performance Reports*

With the sys schema installed, it is time to look close at what it provides.

sys Schema Objects

At its core, the sys schema is a collection of views, stored functions, and stored procedures. Additionally, there is one table with two triggers for the configuration. While originally it was aimed at providing an interface to the Performance Schema, it has evolved to include the Information Schema and provide some general utilities.

One of the main goals of the sys schema is ease of use. For this reason, the views in most cases include an ORDER BY clause. Additionally, the columns including Performance Schema timings, paths, byte values, or statements are formatted to make it easier for humans to read and to make it more likely for the output to fit inside a screen width. The formatting may not always be wanted, for example if a custom ordering is required or software needs to analyze the data. To accommodate that, each view that uses formatting functions also exist in a version with x$ prefixed to the view name. These views return the unformatted data.

The remainder of this section lists all of the sys schema objects and provides a brief description.

■ **Note**   For the full documentation of the sys schema objects, see the Reference Manual at *https://dev. mysql.com/doc/refman/5.7/en/sys-schema-reference.html* or the GitHub README file at *https://github.com/ mysql/mysql-sys/blob/master/README.md*.

The sys schema only includes one table for the configuration. The table has two triggers to set who updates the configuration. The table and triggers are listed in Table 15-20. The sys schema configuration in discussed in the next section.

Table 15-20. *sys Schema Configuration Table and Triggers*

Table/Trigger Name	Description
sys_config	Table with the sys schema configuration.
sys_config_insert_set_user	Trigger that sets the username of the user inserting new configuration options.
sys_config_update_set_user	Set the username of the user updating configuration options.

Table 15-21 lists the views providing summaries grouped by hostname. The hostname is where the users are connecting from, so the views can, for example, be used to determine whether the workload from multiple application hosts is even.

Table 15-21. *sys Schema Host Summary Views*

View Name	Description
host_summary x$host_summary	Overall host summary grouped by the hostname.
host_summary_by_file_io x$host_summary_by_file_io	File I/O latencies grouped by the hostname.
host_summary_by_file_io_type x$host_summary_by_file_io_type	File I/O latencies grouped by the hostname and event name.
host_summary_by_stages x$host_summary_by_stages	Latencies grouped by the hostname and stage event name.
host_summary_by_statement_latency x$host_summary_by_statement_latency	Statement statistics grouped by the hostname.
host_summary_by_statement_type x$host_summary_by_statement_type	Statement statistics grouped by the hostname and statement type.

There are a few views specific for the InnoDB storage engine. These are listed in Table 15-22. In MySQL NDB Cluster, these are most often useful when replicating to an InnoDB instance.

Table 15-22. *sys Schema InnoDB Views*

View Name	Description
innodb_buffer_stats_by_schema x$innodb_buffer_stats_by_schema	InnoDB buffer pool allocations grouped by schema.
innodb_buffer_stats_by_table x$innodb_buffer_stats_by_table	InnoDB buffer pool allocations grouped by table.
innodb_lock_waits x$innodb_lock_waits	Information about ongoing InnoDB lock contention.

Investigating issues related to disk I/O can be difficult to track down. However, the sys schema includes several views that can tell what is causing I/O from within the SQL node. These views are summarized in Table 15-23.

Table 15-23. *sys Schema I/O Views*

View Name	Description
io_by_thread_by_latency x$io_by_thread_by_latency	I/O latencies grouped by thread.
io_global_by_file_by_bytes x$io_global_by_file_by_bytes	I/O amounts grouped by file.
io_global_by_file_by_latency x$io_global_by_file_by_latency	I/O latencies grouped by file.
io_global_by_wait_by_bytes x$io_global_by_wait_by_bytes	I/O amounts grouped by event name.
io_global_by_wait_by_latency x$io_global_by_wait_by_latency	I/O latencies grouped by event name.
latest_file_io x$latest_file_io	The latest file I/O events.

In MySQL NDB Cluster 7.5 and later, it is possible to enable instrumentation of when memory is allocated and deallocated. This can be used to investigate what is contributing to the overall memory usage of the SQL node. The views available for this are listed in Table 15-24.

Table 15-24. *sys Schema Memory Usage Views*

View Name	Description
memory_by_host_by_current_bytes x$memory_by_host_by_current_bytes	Current memory usage grouped by host.
memory_by_thread_by_current_bytes x$memory_by_thread_by_current_bytes	Current memory usage grouped by thread.
memory_by_user_by_current_bytes x$memory_by_user_by_current_bytes	Current memory usage grouped by user.
memory_global_by_current_bytes x$memory_global_by_current_bytes	Current memory usage grouped by event name.
memory_global_total x$memory_global_total	The total current memory usage.

For the memory views, note that memory usage is only instrumented from the time the corresponding memory instruments are enabled. This means that memory usages are in general only accurate if memory instrumentation is enabled in the MySQL configuration file, so the instruments are enabled from the time MySQL starts. By default, only memory instrumentation of the Performance Schema is enabled.

There are several views to investigate the schema. The groupings are at the table and index levels. These views are useful for investigating whether the indexes are optimal, whether a table is running out of auto-increment values, etc. The section entitled "Command-Line Usage and Examples" includes examples of using some of these views. The views are summarized in Table 15-25.

Table 15-25. *sys Schema Schema Views*

View Name	Description
schema_auto_increment_columns	Information about auto-increment columns, including data type and used values.
schema_index_statistics x$schema_index_statistics	Information about the usage of the indexes.
schema_object_overview	Overview of the number of tables, indexes, etc. grouped by schema.
schema_redundant_indexes	Finds indexes where there are two indexes covering the same uses and provides suggestions as to which to drop.
schema_table_lock_waits x$schema_table_lock_waits	Lists current table metadata lock contentions.
schema_table_statistics x$schema_table_statistics	Table usage statistics, including latencies and amount of data read.
schema_table_statistics_with_buffer x$schema_table_statistics_with_buffer	The same as the schema_table_statistics view, but also including the InnoDB buffer pool allocation statistics.
schema_tables_with_full_table_scans x$schema_tables_with_full_table_scans	Shows information about table scans.
schema_unused_indexes	Lists unused indexes.
x$schema_flattened_keys	Helper view for schema_redundant_indexes.

One of the strengths of the Performance Schema is the ability to look for queries that fulfills certain criteria such as it uses sorting, internal temporary tables, no use of index, etc. To make it easier to look for such queries, the sys schema has the views in Table 15-26. All the statement views are grouped by the default schema and digest.

Table 15-26. *sys Schema Statement Views*

View Name	Description
statement_analysis x$statement_analysis	General statement statistics.
statements_with_errors_or_warnings x$statements_with_errors_or_warnings	Statements returning error and/or warnings.
statements_with_full_table_scans x$statements_with_full_table_scans	Information about statements using full table scans.
statements_with_runtimes_in_95th_percentile x$statements_with_runtimes_in_95th_percentile	Statements with their average runtime in the 95th percentile.
statements_with_sorting x$statements_with_sorting	Statements that sort the result set.
statements_with_temp_tables x$statements_with_temp_tables	Statements using internal temporary tables.
x$ps_digest_95th_percentile_by_avg_us	Helper view for statements_with_runtimes_in_95th_percentile.
x$ps_digest_avg_latency_distribution	Helper view for x$ps_digest_95th_percentile_by_avg_us.

Similar to the views grouping by hostname, there are summaries grouped by the username. These are particularly useful for systems with several users, for example, multiple applications using the same cluster for storage. The user views are listed in Table 15-27.

Table 15-27. *sys Schema User Views*

View Name	Description
user_summary x$user_summary	Overall user summary grouped by the username.
user_summary_by_file_io x$user_summary_by_file_io	File I/O latencies grouped by the username.
user_summary_by_file_io_type x$user_summary_by_file_io_type	File I/O latencies grouped by the username and event name.
user_summary_by_stages x$user_summary_by_stages	Latencies grouped by the username and stage event name.
user_summary_by_statement_latency x$user_summary_by_statement_latency	Statement statistics grouped by the username.
user_summary_by_statement_type x$user_summary_by_statement_type	Statement statistics grouped by the username and statement type.

The views grouped by the wait events can be used if low level events are investigated. These are not used very often, particularly for MySQL NDB Cluster. The wait event views are summarized in Table 15-28.

Table 15-28. *sys Schema Wait Views*

View Name	Description
wait_classes_global_by_avg_latency x$wait_classes_global_by_avg_latency	Latency statistics grouped by the wait classes (the first three components separated by / of the event name) order by average latency.
wait_classes_global_by_latency x$wait_classes_global_by_latency	Latency statistics grouped by the wait classes (the first three components separated by / of the event name) ordered by total latency.
waits_by_host_by_latency x$waits_by_host_by_latency	Wait latencies grouped by the event name and hostname.
waits_by_user_by_latency x$waits_by_user_by_latency	Wait latencies grouped by the event name and username.
waits_global_by_latency x$waits_global_by_latency	Wait latencies grouped by the event name.

The last group of views are for the general status. These range from the version of the sys schema and the SQL node over metrics including the global status variables to a modern implementation of the process list. Table 15-29 lists the views.

Table 15-29. *sys Schema General Status Views*

View Name	Description
metrics	The global status variables, the InnoDB metrics (the INNODB_METRICS table in the Information Schema), overall memory usage, and the time of the query.
processlist x$processlist	An advanced process list view based on several Performance Schema tables such as threads and events_statements_current. Both foreground and background threads are included.
ps_check_lost_instrumentation	Checks whether any instrumentation has been lost due to the Performance Schema sizing being too small.
session x$session	The same as the processlist view, but filtered so only connections are included.
session_ssl_status	SSL information for connections.
version	The sys schema and MySQL version.

There are several functions in the sys schema. Most of these are helper functions of one sort or another. The first group can be used to format the bytes, paths, statements, and timings found in the Performance Schema. These are listed in Table 15-30.

Table 15-30. sys Schema Formatting Functions

Function Name	Description
format_bytes	Formats bytes to include units.
format_path	Formats a path to replace parts of the path with configuration options, for example datadir.
format_statement	Truncates a statement to statement_truncate_len (see the "sys Schema Configuration" section) characters while preserving both the start and end of the statement.
format_time	Converts picoseconds into a human-readable format including units.

The second group of functions can be used to manipulate information, for example, to extract the schema or table name from a filename, or manipulating lists. Table 15-31 lists these utility functions.

Table 15-31. sys Schema Utility Functions

Function Name	Description
extract_schema_from_file_name	Extracts the schema name from a filename.
extract_table_from_file_name	Extracts the table name from a filename.
list_add	Adds an element to a comma separated list if the element is not already in the list.
list_drop	Removes an element from a comma separated list.
quote_identifier	Quotes a MySQL identifier using backticks (`).
sys_get_config	Retrieve a sys schema configuration option. See the "sys Schema Configuration" section.
version_major	Returns the major version for MySQL Server (for example returns 5 for 5.7.18).
version_minor	Returns the minor version for MySQL Server (for example returns 7 for 5.7.18).
version_patch	Returns the patch release version for MySQL Server (for example returns 18 for 5.7.18).

The third and last group of functions directly uses the Performance Schema tables. These can for example be used to determine what is enabled, convert a connection ID to a Performance Schema thread ID, etc. The functions are listed in Table 15-32.

Table 15-32. *sys Schema Performance Schema Functions*

Function Name	Description
ps_is_account_enabled	Returns whether an account has instrumentation enabled.
ps_is_consumer_enabled	Returns whether a consumer will collect data (based on the hierarchy).
ps_is_instrument_default_enabled	Returns whether an instrument is enabled by default based on the MySQL version.
ps_is_instrument_default_timed	Returns whether an instrument is timed by default based on the MySQL version.
ps_is_thread_instrumented	Returns whether a given thread is instrumented.
ps_thread_account	Returns username@hostname for a thread ID.
ps_thread_id	Returns the Performance Schema thread ID for a connection ID.
ps_thread_stack	Generates a JSON-formatted stack for a given thread.
ps_thread_trx_info	Generates a JSON object with details of the current transaction for a thread.

The stored procedures in the sys schema can also be divided into three groups. The first group contains the procedures aimed at making it easier to make configuration changes to the Performance Schema. Table 15-33 lists all of these.

Table 15-33. *sys Schema Performance Schema Setup Procedures*

Procedure Name	Description
ps_setup_disable_background_threads	Disables instrumentation of all background threads.
ps_setup_disable_consumer	Disables all consumers that have the provided string as part of the name.
ps_setup_disable_instrument	Disables all instruments that have the provided string as part of the name.
ps_setup_disable_thread	Disables instrumentation for the connection with the provided connection ID.
ps_setup_enable_background_threads	Enables instrumentation for all background threads.
ps_setup_enable_consumer	Enables all consumers that have the provided string as part of the name.
ps_setup_enable_instrument	Enables all instruments that have the provided string as part of the name.
ps_setup_enable_thread	Enables instrumentation for the connection with the provided connection ID.
ps_setup_reload_saved	Restores the Performance Schema setup that was previously saved with the ps_setup_save() procedure in the same session.
ps_setup_reset_to_default	Resets the Performance Schema settings to the default. This was the one used for the trace example earlier in the chapter.
ps_setup_save	Saves the current Performance Schema settings.
ps_setup_show_disabled	Shows all disabled Performance Schema related settings.
ps_setup_show_disabled_consumers	Shows all disabled consumers.
ps_setup_show_disabled_instruments	Shows all disabled instruments.
ps_setup_show_enabled	Shows all enabled Performance Schema settings.
ps_setup_show_enabled_consumers	Shows all enabled consumers.
ps_setup_show_enabled_instruments	Shows all enabled instruments.

The second group of stored procedures is useful for investigating statements or group of statements. The ps_trace_thread procedure used in the discussion of the Performance Schema to trace a transaction is among them. The statement and trace procedures are listed in Table 15-34.

Table 15-34. *sys Schema Statement and Trace Procedures*

Procedure Name	Description
ps_statement_avg_latency_histogram	Generates a histogram based on the average digest latencies.
ps_trace_statement_digest	Tracks the occurrence of statements with a given digest for a period of time.
ps_trace_thread	Generates a DOT formatted trace file. Used earlier in the Performance Schema section.
ps_truncate_all_tables	Truncates all Performance Schema tables (resets the statistics to the same as after a restart of the SQL node).

The third group of sys schema objects includes a few utility procedures that make it easy to collect diagnostics data, execute one-off dynamically created statements, etc. These are described in Table 15-35.

Table 15-35. *sys Schema Utility Procedures*

Procedure Name	Description
create_synonym_db	Creates a schema with the specified name containing views to the original schema. Can be used to for example have ps as a synonym for performance_schema.
diagnostics	Collects diagnostics data for a given period of time. This includes data from the ndbinfo views.
execute_prepared_stmt	Executes an SQL query passed in the argument by using a prepared statement and deallocate the prepared statement after use. Useful for dynamically generated queries.
table_exists	Returns whether a table exists and if so whether it is a base table, temporary table, or a view.

sys Schema Configuration

The sys schema comes with its own configuration management since it must also work as an add-on to older versions of MySQL, where it is not included as part of the normal installation. The configuration consists of two parts—the persisted part which is stored in the sys_config table and a temporary part using user variables. The default configuration can be seen from Listing 15-19.

Listing 15-19. The Default sys Schema Configuration

```
mysql> SELECT * FROM sys.sys_config;
+-----------------------------------+-------+---------------------+--------+
| variable                          | value | set_time            | set_by |
+-----------------------------------+-------+---------------------+--------+
| diagnostics.allow_i_s_tables      | OFF   | 2017-06-11 12:30:17 | NULL   |
| diagnostics.include_raw           | OFF   | 2017-06-11 12:30:17 | NULL   |
| ps_thread_trx_info.max_length     | 65535 | 2017-06-11 12:30:17 | NULL   |
```

```
| statement_performance_analyzer.limit | 100  | 2017-06-11 12:30:17 | NULL   |
| statement_performance_analyzer.view  | NULL | 2017-06-11 12:30:17 | NULL   |
| statement_truncate_len               | 64   | 2017-06-11 12:30:17 | NULL   |
+--------------------------------------+------+---------------------+--------+
6 rows in set (0.00 sec)
```

The set_time column is updated automatically unless set explicitly as the column is defined as DEFAULT
CURRENT_TIMESTAMP ON UPDATE CURRENT_TIMESTAMP and the set_by user is updated by a trigger to reflect
the username executing the INSERT or UPDATE. A set_by that is set to NULL means the configuration was
inserted as part of the sys schema installation.

For each of the variables in the sys_config table, it is possible to override the value at the session
level using a user variable with the name @sys. as a prefix concatenated on the option name. Listing 15-20
shows an example where the format_statement() function is used to format a query. The function uses the
statement_truncate_len option to decide where to truncate the query.

Listing 15-20. Example of Using sys Schema Session Level Settings

```
mysql> SELECT sys.format_statement('SELECT * FROM world.City INNER JOIN world.Country on
Country.Code = City.CountryCode') AS FormattedQuery\G
*************************** 1. row ***************************
FormattedQuery: SELECT * FROM world.City INNER ... ountry.Code = City.CountryCode
1 row in set (0.00 sec)

mysql> SET @sys.statement_truncate_len = 128;
Query OK, 0 rows affected (0.01 sec)

mysql> SELECT sys.format_statement('SELECT * FROM world.City INNER JOIN world.Country on
Country.Code = City.CountryCode') AS FormattedQuery\G
*************************** 1. row ***************************
FormattedQuery: SELECT * FROM world.City INNER JOIN world.Country on Country.Code = City.
CountryCode
1 row in set (0.00 sec)

mysql> SET @sys.statement_truncate_len = NULL;
Query OK, 0 rows affected (0.00 sec)

mysql> SELECT sys.format_statement('SELECT * FROM world.City INNER JOIN world.Country on
Country.Code = City.CountryCode') AS FormattedQuery\G
*************************** 1. row ***************************
FormattedQuery: SELECT * FROM world.City INNER ... ountry.Code = City.CountryCode
1 row in set (0.00 sec)
```

By setting @sys.statement_truncate_len the truncation point can be change. Setting the value of the
user variable to NULL resets the option, so the sys schema will use the value from sys_config again.

Some features, such as the diagnostics() procedure, support additional custom settings. The
Reference Manual contains the details of these custom settings.

With the sys schema installed and configured, it is time to look at some examples of using it.

Command-Line Usage and Examples

One of the main goals of the sys schema is ease of use. For this reason, the views are in general created so no joins, or ORDER BY clauses are required to use them. A plain SELECT * FROM <view name> possibly with a WHERE and/or LIMIT clause is the typical use case. The Performance Schema sections have already shown several examples of using the sys schema, and more examples will follow in the next chapter when using the ndbinfo schema. So, this section will be limited to a couple of complementary use cases.

A view that already has been mentioned is the session view. It will also be used to find details for the connections in the ndbinfo locks report in the next chapter. The session view is an advanced version of the SHOW PROCESSLIST statement. Listing 15-21 shows an example where there are two connections.

Listing 15-21. Using the sys.session View

```
mysql> SELECT * FROM sys.session\G
*************************** 1. row ***************************
                thd_id: 32
                conn_id: 9
                   user: root@localhost
                     db: NULL
                command: Sleep
                  state: NULL
                   time: 3
      current_statement: NULL
      statement_latency: NULL
               progress: NULL
           lock_latency: 3.19 ms
          rows_examined: 1
              rows_sent: 1
          rows_affected: 0
             tmp_tables: 0
        tmp_disk_tables: 0
              full_scan: NO
         last_statement: SELECT * FROM world.City WHERE ID = 130
 last_statement_latency: 3.88 ms
         current_memory: 0 bytes
              last_wait: NULL
      last_wait_latency: NULL
                 source: NULL
            trx_latency: 641.43 us
              trx_state: COMMITTED
          trx_autocommit: YES
                    pid: 29378
           program_name: mysql
*************************** 2. row ***************************
                thd_id: 28
                conn_id: 5
                   user: root@localhost
                     db: db1
                command: Query
                  state: Sending data
                   time: 0
      current_statement: SELECT * FROM sys.session
```

```
      statement_latency: 1.37 ms
               progress: NULL
           lock_latency: 852.00 us
          rows_examined: 0
              rows_sent: 0
          rows_affected: 0
             tmp_tables: 4
        tmp_disk_tables: 1
              full_scan: YES
         last_statement: NULL
 last_statement_latency: NULL
         current_memory: 0 bytes
              last_wait: NULL
      last_wait_latency: NULL
                 source: NULL
            trx_latency: 564.17 us
              trx_state: ACTIVE
         trx_autocommit: YES
                    pid: 4246
           program_name: mysql
2 rows in set (0.05 sec)
```

The first row (thd_id: 32) shows an idle connection. Because the session view join on the performance_ schema.events_statements_current table, the previous statement can be included. The second row (thd_id: 28) is an example of a connection executing the query. In both cases, detailed information is available.

There is a sibling view to the session view: the processlist view. The difference is that the processlist view not only includes the connections, but also the background threads.

A common consideration for database administrators is which indexes are required. Table scans are a killer for performance and may also affect other queries. Too many indexes will also hurt performance as they must be maintained when data is changed, and the optimizer has to consider more options when deciding on the query plan. To review whether the correct indexes are in place, the sys schema includes three views that can be used.

Listing 15-22 uses the schema_redundant_indexes view to look for redundant indexes.

Listing 15-22. Finding Redundant Indexes

```
mysql> SELECT * FROM sys.schema_redundant_indexes\G
*************************** 1. row ***************************
            table_schema: world
              table_name: City
     redundant_index_name: Name
  redundant_index_columns: Name
redundant_index_non_unique: 1
      dominant_index_name: Name_2
   dominant_index_columns: Name,District
 dominant_index_non_unique: 1
           subpart_exists: 0
           sql_drop_index: ALTER TABLE `world`.`City` DROP INDEX `Name`
*************************** 2. row ***************************
            table_schema: world
              table_name: CountryLanguage
     redundant_index_name: CountryCode
  redundant_index_columns: CountryCode
```

```
redundant_index_non_unique: 1
        dominant_index_name: PRIMARY
     dominant_index_columns: CountryCode,Language
 dominant_index_non_unique: 0
              subpart_exists: 0
              sql_drop_index: ALTER TABLE `world`.`CountryLanguage` DROP INDEX `CountryCode`
2 rows in set (0.03 sec)

mysql> SHOW CREATE TABLE world.CountryLanguage\G
*************************** 1. row ***************************
       Table: CountryLanguage
Create Table: CREATE TABLE `CountryLanguage` (
  `CountryCode` char(3) NOT NULL DEFAULT '',
  `Language` char(30) NOT NULL DEFAULT '',
  `IsOfficial` enum('T','F') NOT NULL DEFAULT 'F',
  `Percentage` float(4,1) NOT NULL DEFAULT '0.0',
  PRIMARY KEY (`CountryCode`,`Language`),
  KEY `CountryCode` (`CountryCode`),
  CONSTRAINT `countryLanguage_ibfk_1` FOREIGN KEY (`CountryCode`) REFERENCES `Country`
(`Code`) ON DELETE NO ACTION ON UPDATE NO ACTION
) ENGINE=ndbcluster DEFAULT CHARSET=latin1
1 row in set (0.00 sec)

mysql> ALTER TABLE world.CountryLanguage DROP INDEX CountryCode;
ERROR 1553 (HY000): Cannot drop index 'CountryCode': needed in a foreign key constraint
```

The result shows that the world.City table both has an index covering the Name and District columns as well as one just covering the Name column. The index just on the Name column is redundant as the Name column is a left prefix of the Name_2 index on (Name, District). So, the Name_2 index can be used for queries just requiring an index on the Name column. There is a catch, as can be seen for the redundant index on the world.CountryLanguage table. When trying to drop the redundant index, the statement fails because the foreign key requires the index.

After checking for redundant indexes, it is time to check for unused indexes. The schema_unused_ indexes view is included for this purpose. An example of using the view is:

```
mysql> SELECT * FROM sys.schema_unused_indexes;
+---------------+-----------------+-------------+
| object_schema | object_name     | index_name  |
+---------------+-----------------+-------------+
| world         | City            | CountryCode |
| world         | City            | Name        |
| world         | CountryLanguage | CountryCode |
+---------------+-----------------+-------------+
3 rows in set (0.00 sec)
```

The view automatically excludes indexes that are primary keys or on a table in the mysql schema (as those tables should not be changed). As with the redundant index check, indexes that exist for a foreign key cannot be dropped. Another thing to remember is that since the statistics come from the Performance Schema, they only cover the period since the statistics were last reset (no longer back than the last restart of the SQL node). This means that while the index at the time of the query shows up as unused, it may just not have been used yet. It may, for example, be that the index is essential for a weekly or monthly batch job. So, make sure that the statistics covers a long enough time to include all uses.

Finally, it is time to look for tables where indexes are required. The schema_tables_with_full_table_scans view can be used to find tables where table scans are performed. The result includes the number of rows scanned and how long time it has taken to scan these rows. Before going ahead and adding an index, remember that some queries cannot possible use an index, and a table scan may be more efficient in some cases even if an index can be used—Chapter 18 will include some discussions of this. For example:

```
mysql> SELECT * FROM sys.schema_tables_with_full_table_scans;
+---------------+-------------+--------------------+---------+
| object_schema | object_name | rows_full_scanned  | latency |
+---------------+-------------+--------------------+---------+
| world         | City        |            2370382 | 32.35 s |
+---------------+-------------+--------------------+---------+
1 row in set (0.00 sec)
```

While it is now known that the world.City table are subject to table scans, it is not known which queries are causing them, and which columns may benefit from an index. Listing 15-23 shows how to use the statements_with_full_table_scans view to find queries using full table scans. For clarity, a filter on the db column has been added, but in general be careful as that filters on the default schema for the connection executing the query.

Listing 15-23. Finding queries in the world Schema by Doing Full Table Scans

```
mysql> SELECT *
          FROM sys.statements_with_full_table_scans
         WHERE db = 'world'\G
*************************** 1. row ***************************
                    query: SELECT * FROM `world` . `City` WHERE `Population` > ?
                       db: world
               exec_count: 10000
            total_latency: 33.85 s
      no_index_used_count: 10000
 no_good_index_used_count: 0
        no_index_used_pct: 100
                rows_sent: 2370000
            rows_examined: 2370000
            rows_sent_avg: 237
        rows_examined_avg: 237
               first_seen: 2017-06-18 17:35:50
                last_seen: 2017-06-18 17:36:26
                   digest: e2842f4964f77841445bae18495f9dfe
1 row in set (0.00 sec)
```

The output shows that the query causing the table scans has a filter on the Population column. If the query is commonly executed, it may be worth adding the index.

The observant reader may note that the statistics in Listing 15-23 shows the number of rows sent to be the same as rows examined. This would normally indicate that a table scan is required as all rows are required from the table. However, there is a catch here. The EXPLAIN plan for the query shows that despite the fact there is not any index on the Population column, the condition is still pushed down to the storage engine:

```
mysql> EXPLAIN SELECT * FROM world.City WHERE Population > 1000000\G
*************************** 1. row ***************************
           id: 1
  select_type: SIMPLE
```

```
           table: City
      partitions: p0,p1
            type: ALL
   possible_keys: NULL
             key: NULL
         key_len: NULL
             ref: NULL
            rows: 4079
        filtered: 33.33
           Extra: Using where with pushed condition (`world`.`City`.`Population` > 1000000)
1 row in set, 1 warning (0.00 sec)
```

This means the filtering is done on the data node, so for the SQL node it looks like all rows in the table are required which makes the statistics in performance_schema.events_statements_summary_by_digest (that is the source for sys.statements_with_full_table_scans) somewhat deceiving.

To conclude the discussion about the sys schema, the performance reports in MySQL Workbench will be demonstrated.

MySQL Workbench Performance Reports

MySQL Workbench is the desktop client GUI tool from MySQL. In addition to allowing the user to execute queries and manage the schema, MySQL Workbench includes various reports for monitoring the MySQL instance it is connected to. One group of these reports are known as the Performance Reports.

The source for the Performance Reports is the sys schema views with one report per view. Figure 15-6 shows an example of using one of the reports. The Performance Reports use the views with the unformatted data (those with the x$ prefix), so it is possible to change the sorting order and the unit used. In Figure 15-6, the unit for the Total Time column has been changed to milliseconds.

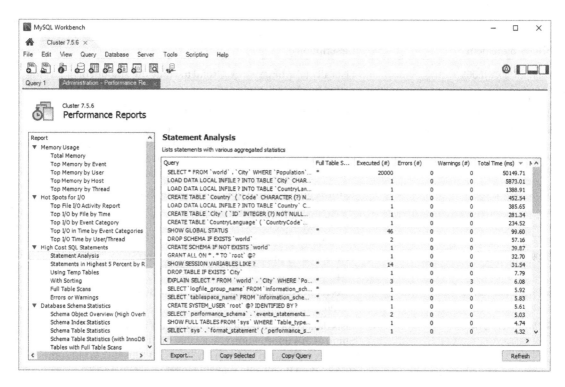

Figure 15-6. *The MySQL Workbench Performance Reports*

At the bottom of the report there are four buttons. The *Export ...* button makes it possible to save the result in a CSV file. The *Copy Selected* button performs a similar export, but copies the selected rows as well as the heading line to the clipboard—also using the CSV format. The *Copy Query* button copies the query used for the report to the clipboard. In this example, the query is:

```
select * from sys.`x$statement_analysis`
```

Finally, the *Refresh* button refreshes the report.

This concludes the tour of the sys schema. The final data source to consider from inside MySQL is the SHOW statements.

SHOW Statements

Traditionally—going back to the days before MySQL 5.0—the only way to get to get performance and status data was to use SHOW statements. While increasingly more of the data provided by the SHOW statements is now available from other sources such as the Information Schema, ndbinfo, the Performance Schema, and the sys schema, it is still not all information that can be obtained from the new sources. Additionally, the SHOW statements can be handy at the command line as they are typically shorter to type than querying the other sources.

There is a total of 40 SHOW statements in MySQL NDB Cluster 7.5 ranging from queries like SHOW TABLES to SHOW SLAVE STATUS and SHOW BINLOG EVENTS. Table 15-36 summarizes the most important SHOW statements from a MySQL NDB Cluster monitoring perspective. A keyword in square brackets indicates an optional keyword.

Table 15-36. *Common SHOW Statements for NDB Cluster Monitoring*

SHOW Statement	Description
SHOW BINARY LOGS	Lists all of the binary logs. Useful to verify the amount of binary log stored for the SQL node.
SHOW ENGINE NDBCluster STATUS	Shows statistics for the NDBCluster storage engine.
SHOW [FULL] PROCESSLIST;	Returns one row per connection to the SQL node with details of the user, query being executed, etc. It is recommended to use performance_schema.threads, sys.processlist, or sys.session instead for MySQL NDB Cluster 7.3 and later.
SHOW PROFILE	Returns profiling for a query with details for each thread state used. Requires profiling to be enabled before executing the query. This feature has been deprecated and will be removed in a later version. Use the Performance Schema instead.
SHOW PROFILES	Lists all query profiles that can be used with SHOW PROFILE. Deprecated together with SHOW PROFILE.
SHOW SLAVE HOSTS	Lists replication slaves connected to the SQL node that is acting as a replication master.
SHOW SLAVE STATUS	Lists details for the replication status on a replication slave. Some of this information is available from the Performance Schema replication tables in MySQL NDB Cluster 7.5, but some information is still only available in SHOW SLAVE STATUS.
SHOW [GLOBAL|SESSION] STATUS	Shows session or global status variables. The same as querying the Information Schema status tables in MySQL NDB Cluster 7.4 and earlier and the Performance Schema status tables in version 7.5. If neither GLOBAL nor SESSION is specified, the session status is returned.
SHOW TABLE STATUS	The same as querying the information_schema.TABLES table.
SHOW [GLOBAL|SESSION] VARIABLES	Shows session or global configuration variables. The same as querying the Information Schema variables tables in MySQL NDB Cluster 7.4 and earlier and the Performance Schema variables tables in version 7.5. If neither GLOBAL nor SESSION is specified, the session variables is returned.
SHOW WARNINGS	Not directly monitoring. Returns the warnings and errors generated by the previous statement. It is important to watch for warnings and errors both when executing queries directly in the mysql command-line client and through the application.

As an NDB Cluster specific statement, consider the SHOW ENGINE statement for NDBCluster. An example output is shown in Listing 15-24.

Listing 15-24. SHOW ENGINE NDBCluster STATUS

```
mysql> SHOW ENGINE NDBCluster STATUS\G
*************************** 1. row ***************************
  Type: ndbcluster
  Name: connection
Status: cluster_node_id=52, connected_host= 192.168.56.101, connected_port=1186, number_of_
data_nodes=2, number_of_ready_data_nodes=2, connect_count=0
*************************** 2. row ***************************
  Type: ndbcluster
  Name: NdbTransaction
Status: created=2, free=0, sizeof=368
*************************** 3. row ***************************
  Type: ndbcluster
  Name: NdbOperation
Status: created=4, free=4, sizeof=944
*************************** 4. row ***************************
  Type: ndbcluster
  Name: NdbIndexScanOperation
Status: created=1, free=1, sizeof=1152
*************************** 5. row ***************************
  Type: ndbcluster
  Name: NdbIndexOperation
Status: created=0, free=0, sizeof=952
*************************** 6. row ***************************
  Type: ndbcluster
  Name: NdbRecAttr
Status: created=8, free=8, sizeof=88
*************************** 7. row ***************************
  Type: ndbcluster
  Name: NdbApiSignal
Status: created=16, free=16, sizeof=144
*************************** 8. row ***************************
  Type: ndbcluster
  Name: NdbLabel
Status: created=0, free=0, sizeof=200
*************************** 9. row ***************************
  Type: ndbcluster
  Name: NdbBranch
Status: created=0, free=0, sizeof=32
*************************** 10. row ***************************
  Type: ndbcluster
  Name: NdbSubroutine
Status: created=0, free=0, sizeof=72
*************************** 11. row ***************************
  Type: ndbcluster
  Name: NdbCall
Status: created=0, free=0, sizeof=24
```

```
*************************** 12. row ***************************
  Type: ndbcluster
  Name: NdbBlob
Status: created=0, free=0, sizeof=496
*************************** 13. row ***************************
  Type: ndbcluster
  Name: NdbReceiver
Status: created=2, free=0, sizeof=128
*************************** 14. row ***************************
  Type: ndbcluster
  Name: NdbLockHandle
Status: created=0, free=0, sizeof=48
*************************** 15. row ***************************
  Type: ndbcluster
  Name: binlog
Status: latest_epoch=1319821975224330, latest_trans_epoch=1309823291359243, latest_received_
binlog_epoch=1319821975224330, latest_handled_binlog_epoch=1319821975224330, latest_applied_
binlog_epoch=1307057332420613
15 rows in set (0.03 sec)
```

The information returned includes details of the connection to the rest of the cluster, the number of various objects created and the size of each object as well as details of the epochs related the binary log. These metrics are not easily accessible from other sources.

This concludes the tour of the general data sources for monitoring inside the SQL nodes. One important source of information has not been discussed yet: the MySQL log files.

MySQL Logs

The final piece of the monitoring puzzle to be considered in this chapter is the MySQL logs. MySQL provides a number of logs ranging from logs meant for auditing to the general-purpose error log on the SQL nodes. It is important to review the error logs at regular bases to spot potential issue before they occur, and all logs are in play when investigating incidents. Depending on the application and certification requirements, it may also be required to analyze the audit logs. This section goes through the logs available on the SQL nodes.

SQL Node Error Logs

The error log on the SQL nodes—also often referred to as the MySQL error log—should be familiar to any database administrator who is used to working with MySQL Server. If it is not, now is a good time to make it part of your daily routine.

The MySQL error log is a simple style log with messages appended to the end of it. There are a number of options that can be used to control the logging. These are summarized in Table 15-37.

Table 15-37. *Options for the SQL Node Error Log*

Option	Versions	Default	Description
log_error	All	(stderr)	The path/filename of the error log.
log_error_verbosity	7.5+	3	The log verbosity level. Has replaced log_warnings in MySQL NDB Cluster 7.5. Level 1 is errors only, level 2 adds warnings, and level 3 adds notes. As startup and shutdown messages are notes, it is recommended to use level 3.
log_syslog	7.5+	OFF	Whether to log to a syslog facility.
log_syslog_facility	7.5+	daemon	The syslog facility to use if log_syslog is set to ON.
log_syslog_include_pid	7.5+	ON	Whether to include the process ID of the SQL node when logging to a syslog facility.
log_syslog_tag	7.5+		An optional tag to add to the SQL node identifier when writing to the syslog.
log_timestamps	7.5+	UTC	Whether to use UTC or the SYSTEM time zone for the timestamps used in the log messages.
log_warnings	7.4 and earlier	1	Takes a value of 0 or higher, but effectively only 0, 1, and 2 have distinct logging verbosities. A value of 2 primarily adds connections related messages. Due to the lack of clear distinction what the levels do, the option has been deprecated in version 7.5 and replaced with log_error_verbosity.

Of the available options, the only one that is recommended to always set explicitly is log_error unless logging is only done to a syslog facility. Setting the path and filename of the error log ensures it is well known where the error log is and that it is not written to *stderr*. In case of an emergency, it is important to be able to locate the error log quickly.

As mentioned in the start of the discussion about the MySQL error log, checking the log should be part of the daily routine. This will allow the database administrator to get early warnings of issues. An example is that during restarts, all deprecated options in use will be listed with a warning.

Three examples of warnings from the MySQL NDB Cluster 7.5 error log are:

```
2017-06-20T06:45:42.986780Z 0 [Warning] The syntax '--log_warnings/-W' is deprecated and
will be removed in a future release. Please use '--log_error_verbosity' instead.
2017-06-20T06:45:42.986844Z 0 [Warning] TIMESTAMP with implicit DEFAULT value is deprecated.
Please use --explicit_defaults_for_timestamp server option (see documentation for more
details).
2017-06-20T06:45:42.988522Z 0 [Warning] Insecure configuration for --secure-file-priv:
Location is accessible to all OS users. Consider choosing a different directory.
```

These are three of the first messages during the restart. The first message is caused by having the log_warnings option in the configuration and tells to use the log_error_verbosity option instead. The second is another deprecation warning. This one is interesting as it says to use the explicit_defaults_for_timestamp option to avoid using the deprecated behavior. However, explicit_defaults_for_timestamp is itself deprecated, as it is meant as for a transitional period where there are two defaults behavior supported for columns using the timestamp data type. In both cases, it is a heads up to the database administrator that changes are on the way. Paying attention to these deprecation warnings can greatly improve future upgrade experiences.

The third message warns that the secure-file-priv option points to a path that can be accessed by all operating system users. It is not very safe, if other than the administrators can access the host. This is an example of how the warning provides instructions on how to improve the security of the SQL node.

Audit Logs

The final logs to discuss are logs that in some way can be used for auditing. These logs ranges from the traditional slow query log and general query log to the enterprise level audit log. Table 15-38 lists the four audit logs available in MySQL. All of the logs are per SQL node.

Table 15-38. *Logs with Auditing Capabilities*

Log	Description
Audit log plugin	The audit log plugin is part of the Enterprise Edition and MySQL Cluster Carrier Grade Edition subscriptions as MySQL Enterprise Audit. It can log all or a subset of the executed queries as well as events such as connections and server startup and shutdown. There are options to control performance, filtering, auto-rotation, etc. Details of MySQL Enterprise Audit can be found at *https://dev.mysql.com/doc/refman/en/audit-log.html*.
Query Analyzer	While not a traditional log, the MySQL Enterprise Monitor Query Analyzer discussed in the previous chapter does log the queries in intervals which can be used to audit what type of queries are executed. It can also possible to aggregate queries from all of the SQL nodes in the cluster.
Slow query log	Logs queries based on the execution time and optionally if no indexes are used. The mysqldumpslow script that is included with the SQL nodes can be used to aggregate statistics for the queries in the slow query log.
General query log	Logs all queries and connections. This makes it very useful to determine the statements and connections, but it comes at a high-performance overhead, big disk space consumption, and there are no filtering options.
Binary log	The primary purposes of the binary log are replication and point-in-time recoveries. However, as it records all data and schema changes, it is also an excellent audit log for changes. Additionally, as the only one of the logs, it records events from all nodes. The mysqlbinlog program can be used to read the events from the binary logs.

To what extent audit logs are required depends on the system. However, in all cases being able to go back and inspect what activity there has been on the node is an invaluable resource for a postmortem analysis. An example of this was shown in the previous chapter where the Query Analyzer in MySQL Enterprise Monitor was used to determine the reason the data memory was exhausted.

Auditing logs can also be used proactively. If the Query Analyzer shows increasing response times or the rate queries are added to the slow query log increases, it may be a sign that changes are required. Optimally this is picked up before the increased response times become a problem. It may be that the amount of data has increased, so queries using a table scan are starting to suffer and it is necessary to look at improved indexing—for example using the techniques described in the sys schema section. It may also be that the query rate is increasing and starting to put a strain on the SQL node or cluster, so it is necessary to add more SQL nodes or scale out with a read-replica to be able to spread the load.

The Performance Schema digest summary table may seem to obsolete the slow query log. Particularly with the Query Analyzer built on top. However, the slow query log has some advantages: it logs query at the time they complete, and unlike the Performance Schema the data is persisted to disk. The slow query log also records the actual queries executed whereas the Performance Schema stores the normalized queries.

■ **Caution** Auditing logs are great, but there are two caveats. They have an overhead. They not only provide the administrator with auditing capabilities, but they can also be used by intruders to get access to data. Be sure to test the performance before deploying auditing solutions and protect the logs.

Summary

MySQL Server includes several sources of monitoring data as well as several logs. This chapter has gone through and discussed how the available tables, views, statements, and logs can be useful in MySQL NDB Cluster.

The Information Schema is the grand old lady of monitoring schemas in MySQL. It has been around for over a decade and is still the central place to get schema information and information about plugins, character set, privileges, etc. The newer Performance Schema provides a way to get information of transactions to mutexes and almost anything in between. The number of tables and amount of data available in the Performance Schema can seem overwhelming, so the sys schema has been developed to provide views that can work as reports, and stored programs to manipulate the data. Finally, there are still the SHOW statements that is a classic MySQL tool to get monitoring information. The logs can easily be forgotten among all of the other information, but those are also very important to review regularly.

This concludes the whirlwind tour of the resources generally available in MySQL. However, for MySQL NDB Cluster there are additional data sources and logs to be aware of. These are discussed in the next chapter.

CHAPTER 16

■ ■ ■

Monitoring MySQL NDB Cluster

Thus far the discussion about monitoring and logs has, with a couple of exceptions, included information that is not specific to MySQL NDB Cluster, but rather also for standalone MySQL Server installations. Just like there are information schema tables that are specific to InnoDB, there are tables and views with monitoring data that is specific to the data nodes and NDBCluster tables.

The data that the data nodes make available through the SQL nodes can be found in the NDB Cluster Information Database—better known as the ndbinfo schema, which is the main topic of this chapter. The discussion first goes through the configuration of the ndbinfo schema and the available views, then provides several examples of generating reports using the ndbinfo views. The third part of the chapter goes through the log and trace files available on the management and data nodes.

The NDB Cluster Information Database (ndbinfo)

Originally the only data that could be extracted from the data nodes had to be found in the cluster log and the data node out logs. In MySQL NDB Cluster 7.1.1, the NDB Cluster Information Database was introduced. This is also commonly called the ndbinfo schema after the default schema name. It has since been expanded several times with more data. As of MySQL NDB Cluster 7.5.6, there are 41 views plus 43 hidden tables. The tables use the NDBInfo storage engine.

The advantage of the ndbinfo schema over the logs is that it consists of tables and views that can be queried using the SELECT statement. In many ways, it resembles the Information Schema and the Performance Schema, but with information specific to MySQL NDB Cluster.

This section discusses the configuration of the ndbinfo schema and its available views. The next section goes through a series of examples using the views.

Configuration

There are seven configuration options and variables that are related to the ndbinfo schema. These are listed in Table 16-1. In practice, it is uncommon to change any of these values, although the ndbinfo_offline and ndbinfo_show_hidden views have some good use cases, as discussed later.

Table 16-1. *ndbinfo Configuration Options*

Option	Default Value	Description
ndbinfo_database	ndbinfo	The name of the schema used for the NDB Cluster Information Database. While a different value can be set at restart (for example, in the MySQL configuration file), the actual value can only be changed at compile time.
ndbinfo_max_bytes	0	For debugging purposes only.
ndbinfo_max_rows	10	For debugging purposes only.
ndbinfo_offline	OFF	Put the ndbinfo schema into offline mode. This will avoid errors if the underlying tables and views do not actually exist (such as if the data nodes are offline). Instead, the tables will always appear empty. Listing 16-2 shows an example.
ndbinfo_show_hidden	OFF	Whether to show the hidden tables that contain the actual data from the data nodes. Listing 16-3 shows an example.
ndbinfo_table_prefix	ndb$	The table name prefix used for the hidden tables. This can be changed at start up, but the actual value used can only be changed at compile time.
ndbinfo_version	N/A	The ndbinfo version. This is a read-only variable and for information only.

The current settings can be found using SHOW GLOBAL VARIABLES on the SQL node, as demonstrated in Listing 16-1.

Listing 16-1. Retrieving the ndbinfo Related Variables

```
mysql> SHOW GLOBAL VARIABLES LIKE 'ndbinfo%';
+----------------------+---------+
| Variable_name        | Value   |
+----------------------+---------+
| ndbinfo_database     | ndbinfo |
| ndbinfo_max_bytes    | 0       |
| ndbinfo_max_rows     | 10      |
| ndbinfo_offline      | OFF     |
| ndbinfo_show_hidden  | OFF     |
| ndbinfo_table_prefix | ndb$    |
| ndbinfo_version      | 460038  |
+----------------------+---------+
7 rows in set (0.00 sec)
```

ndbinfo_offline

The ndbinfo_offline option can be useful for avoiding errors while the data nodes are offline. As Listing 16-2 shows, if ndbinfo is used while the data nodes are offline, it will result in an error that says the connection to the data nodes to failed. However, with ndbinfo_offline = ON, a warning and an empty result set are returned instead.

Listing 16-2. Using the ndbinfo_offline Mode

```
mysql> SELECT * FROM ndbinfo.table_info;
ERROR 1296 (HY000): Got error 157 'Connection to NDB failed' from NDBINFO

mysql> SET GLOBAL ndbinfo_offline = ON;
Query OK, 0 rows affected (0.00 sec)

mysql> SELECT * FROM ndbinfo.table_info;
Empty set, 1 warning (0.00 sec)

mysql> SHOW WARNINGS\G
*************************** 1. row ***************************
  Level: Note
   Code: 1
Message: 'NDBINFO' has been started in offline mode since the 'NDBCLUSTER' engine is
disabled or @@global.ndbinfo_offline is turned on - no rows can be returned
1 row in set (0.00 sec)
```

ndbinfo_show_hidden

By default, all of the tables using the NDBInfo storage engine are hidden and the data is exposed through
views. In a few cases, such as when debugging, it can be useful to see the underlying tables; for example, the
table definitions of the underlying NDBInfo tables have comments explaining what the data means. Only the
references to the table names are hidden—it is still possible to query the underlying tables even if they are
hidden.

Listing 16-3 shows an example of the nodes view that uses the ndb$info table as the source of the data.
Both the view and table can be used even with ndbinfo_show_hidden set to OFF, but SHOW TABLES (and
the information_schema.TABLES table) only includes the ndb$info table when ndbinfo_show_hidden is
set to ON. The output of SHOW CREATE TABLE ndbinfo.ndb$nodes have been reformatted to improve the
readability.

Listing 16-3. The ndbinfo.nodes View and Its Underlying Table

```
mysql> SELECT @@session.ndbinfo_show_hidden;
+-------------------------------+
| @@session.ndbinfo_show_hidden |
+-------------------------------+
|                             0 |
+-------------------------------+
1 row in set (0.00 sec)

mysql> SHOW TABLES FROM ndbinfo LIKE '%nodes%';
+----------------------------+
| Tables_in_ndbinfo (%nodes%) |
+----------------------------+
| nodes                      |
+----------------------------+
1 row in set (0.00 sec)
```

```
mysql> SHOW CREATE VIEW ndbinfo.nodes\G
*************************** 1. row ***************************
                View: nodes
         Create View: CREATE ALGORITHM=UNDEFINED DEFINER='root'@'localhost' SQL SECURITY
                      INVOKER VIEW 'nodes' AS select 'ndb$nodes'.'node_id' AS 'node_id',
                      'ndb$nodes'.'uptime' AS 'uptime',(case 'ndb$nodes'.'status' when 0
                      then 'NOTHING' when 1 then 'CMVMI' when 2 then 'STARTING' when 3 then
                      'STARTED' when 4 then 'SINGLEUSER' when 5 then 'STOPPING_1' when 6
                      then 'STOPPING_2' when 7 then 'STOPPING_3' when 8 then 'STOPPING_4'
                      else '<unknown>' end) AS 'status','ndb$nodes'.'start_phase' AS
                      'start_phase','ndb$nodes'.'config_generation' AS 'config_generation'
                      from 'ndb$nodes'
character_set_client: latin1
collation_connection: latin1_swedish_ci
1 row in set (0.01 sec)

mysql> SHOW CREATE TABLE ndbinfo.ndb$nodes\G
*************************** 1. row ***************************
       Table: ndb$nodes
Create Table: CREATE TABLE `ndb$nodes` (
  `node_id` int(10) unsigned DEFAULT NULL,
  `uptime` bigint(20) unsigned DEFAULT NULL
           COMMENT 'time in seconds that node has been running',
  `status` int(10) unsigned DEFAULT NULL
           COMMENT 'starting/started/stopped etc.',
  `start_phase` int(10) unsigned DEFAULT NULL
               COMMENT 'start phase if node is starting',
  `config_generation` int(10) unsigned DEFAULT NULL
                      COMMENT 'configuration generation number'
) ENGINE=NDBINFO DEFAULT CHARSET=latin1 COMMENT='node status'
1 row in set (0.00 sec)

mysql> SELECT * FROM ndbinfo.nodes;
+---------+--------+---------+-------------+-------------------+
| node_id | uptime | status  | start_phase | config_generation |
+---------+--------+---------+-------------+-------------------+
|       1 |   2000 | STARTED |           0 |                 1 |
|       2 |   2000 | STARTED |           0 |                 1 |
+---------+--------+---------+-------------+-------------------+
2 rows in set (0.02 sec)

mysql> SELECT * FROM ndbinfo.ndb$nodes;
+---------+--------+---------+-------------+-------------------+
| node_id | uptime | status  | start_phase | config_generation |
+---------+--------+---------+-------------+-------------------+
|       1 |   2005 |       3 |           0 |                 1 |
|       2 |   2005 |       3 |           0 |                 1 |
+---------+--------+---------+-------------+-------------------+
2 rows in set (0.01 sec)
```

```
mysql> SET SESSION ndbinfo_show_hidden = ON;
Query OK, 0 rows affected (0.00 sec)

mysql> SHOW TABLES FROM ndbinfo LIKE '%nodes%';
+-----------------------------+
| Tables_in_ndbinfo (%nodes%) |
+-----------------------------+
| ndb$nodes                   |
| nodes                       |
+-----------------------------+
2 rows in set (0.01 sec)
```

Notice how the SHOW CREATE TABLE ndbinfo.ndb$nodes output includes a comment for most of the columns documenting the column. This can be a useful way to get information about the contents of the views without looking up the view in the MySQL Reference Manual.

The ndbinfo Views

The 41 views are listed in Tables 16-2 through 16-5, with one table for each of these four categories:

- **Cluster configuration and overall status:** These views provide information about the configuration of the cluster and the status.

- **Ongoing locks, operations, and transactions:** These views give insight into where the operational and transactional resources are used and where the locks are held.

- **Performance metrics:** Various performance metrics such as the disk write speed, CPU usage, etc.

- **Objects and memory usage:** Information about the overall memory usage, per fragment memory usage, log buffers and spaces, etc.

The four tables include the table name as well as the version or versions where the table was first included and a description of the table. The first version is only specified when the view has been introduced after version 7.1.1. As you can see, new views are often added; additionally, new columns are sometimes added to existing views. In some cases, views have been added to existing general available (GA) versions and not just to the latest development release. In those cases, there will be more than one first version listed. Since the ndbinfo views are a great source of monitoring information, it is a reason in itself to consider upgrading to the latest version.

■ **Tip** A detailed description of each table can be found in the MySQL Reference Manual at *https://dev.mysql. com/doc/refman/5.7/en/mysql-cluster-ndbinfo.html*.

The first group of views is for the cluster configuration and overall status. These views are listed in Table 16-2. The views are useful for extracting general information such as the value of a configuration option or for monitoring the status of the cluster.

Table 16-2. *The ndbinfo Views: Cluster Configuration and Overall Status*

Table	First Version	Description
arbitrator_validity_detail	7.0.37 7.1.26 7.2.10	Details of the arbitration status as seen by each of the data nodes.
arbitrator_validity_summary	7.0.37 7.1.26 7.2.10	Summary of the arbitration status. This should only contain one line indicating which node is the active arbitrator. If there is more than one line, it suggests that the data nodes do not agree.
blocks		Mapping between kernel block numbers and names. This is a reference table that can be used to resolve block numbers in other views.
config_nodes	7.5.7 7.6.2	The nodes that are in the cluster. The output is similar to information provided by the SHOW command in the NDB management client.
config_params		Includes the configuration options available for the data nodes (those that can be specified in *config.ini*). Before version 7.5.0, this only included the parameter number and name, but since 7.5.0 several other columns have been added with the default value, minimum and maximum values, etc.
config_values	7.5.0	The configuration value for each option in the config_params table.
membership	7.0.37 7.1.26 7.2.10	Detailed information about the data node memberships, including which nodes are considered the left and right nodes and arbitrator information.
nodes		Summary of the data nodes status.
processes	7.5.7 7.6.2	Information about the nodes connected to the cluster, including the process ID.
threadblocks	7.1.17 7.2.2	Mapping of kernel blocks to threads and block instances.
threads	7.5.2	Overview of the threads configured.

Table 16-3 includes the views that provide information about ongoing locks, operations, and transactions. These views can for example be great for investigating issues about where the cluster is running out of concurrent operations (the MaxNoOfConcurrentOperations option) and lock contention.

Table 16-3. *The ndbinfo Views: Ongoing Locks, Operations, and Transactions*

Table	First Version	Description
cluster_locks	7.5.3	Details of all locks held or waited for in the cluster.
cluster_operations	7.1.17 7.2.2	Details of all operations (see also the MaxNoOfConcurrentOperations and MaxNoOfLocalOperations configuration options) in the cluster as seen from the DBLQH kernel block.
cluster_transactions	7.1.17 7.2.2	Details of all transactions in the cluster.
locks_per_fragment	7.5.3	Details of locks and which fragments they are in.
operations_per_fragment	7.4.3	Details of the operations grouped by the fragments.
server_locks	7.5.3	The equivalent to the cluster_locks table but filtered to only show locks originating from the SQL node issueing the query.
server_operations	7.1.17 7.2.2	The equivalent to the cluster_operations table but filtered to only show operations originating from the SQL node issueing the query.
server_transactions	7.1.17 7.2.2	The equivalent to the cluster_transactions table but filtered to only show transactions originating from the SQL node issueing the query.

There are both cluster-level and server-level views showing the current locks, operations, and transactions. The server-level views show just the locks, operations, or transactions from that SQL node, whereas the cluster-level views include all nodes. The server-level views are derived from the cluster-level views using the information_schema.ndb_transid_mysql_connection_map table, as shown in Listing 15-3 in the previous chapter. For reference, here is a listing again with the definition of the ndbinfo.server_transactions view (reformatted and slightly rewritten):

```
SELECT map.mysql_connection_id, t.node_id, t.block_instance,
       t.transid, t.state, t.count_operations, t.outstanding_operations,
       t.inactive_seconds, t.client_node_id, t.client_block_ref
  FROM information_schema.ndb_transid_mysql_connection_map map
       INNER JOIN ndbinfo.cluster_transactions t
                ON map.ndb_transid >> 32 = t.transid >> 32;
```

Table 16-4 lists the views that are related to performance monitoring. The views range from the simple counters view to detailed views for disk, CPU, and network usage. These views are among the most useful for investigating performance issues. Chapter 20 gives examples of using the cpustat and threadstat views.

Table 16-4. *The ndbinfo Views: Performance Metrics*

Table(s)	First Version	Description
counters		Includes metrics for events in the kernel blocks such as the number of scan slowdowns, number of reads, etc.
cpustat cpustat_1sec cpustat_20sec cpustat_50ms	7.5.2	CPU usage information for each thread in the data nodes. The cpustat view contains data for the previous second. The other views contain 20 measurements per the time interval indicated by the table name. For example, cputstat_1sec includes a total of 20 seconds of data sampled every second. Chapter 20 has an example of using the cpustat table.
disk_write_speed_aggregate disk_write_speed_aggregate_node disk_write_speed_base	7.4.1	Information about the I/O performance of local checkpoints, backups, and redo (fragment) logs, including the current write speed and whether it has been necessary to slow down. disk_write_speed_base includes the raw data, disk_write_speed_aggregate groups by thread and disk_write_speed_aggregate_node groups by data node.
resources		Various metrics such as query memory.
restart_info	7.4.2	Detailed timing information for the last node restart (system restarts are not included).
tc_time_track_stats	7.4.9	Time-tracking statistics from the DBTC kernel block. This includes scan, primary, and unique key operations.
threadstat	7.1.17 7.2.2	Information for each threat about number of signals sent, CPU time, context switches, etc. Chapter 20 includes an example of using the table.
transporters		Information about the transporters such as number of bytes sent and received, slowdowns, overloads, etc.

Views that give information about the objects and memory use are listed in Table 16-5. Objects include user tables, system tables, indexes, the internal NDB triggers, etc. The memory tables (including logbuffers and logspaces) are important to monitor over time to be able to identify trends and peak uses.

Table 16-5. *The* ndbinfo *Views: Objects and Memory Use*

Table	First Version	Description
dict_obj_info	7.5.4	Information for various kinds of objects such as tables, indexes, foreign keys, internal data node triggers, etc. The type for each object can be found in the dict_obj_types table. The information includes the ID, parent object, and the fully qualified name.
dict_obj_types	7.4.1	The object types available. For example, used with the dict_obj_info view.
diskpagebuffer		Metrics about the disk page buffer (the cache for on-disk data).
logbuffers		Information about the use of the redo and disk data undo log buffer.
logspaces		Information about the use of the redo and disk data undo log files.
memory_per_fragment	7.4.1	Details of the memory usage grouped per fragment.
memoryusage		Information about the use of DataMemory, IndexMemory, and LongMessageBuffer (included in 7.1.31, 7.2.16, 7.3.5, and later).
table_distribution_status	7.5.4	Various information about tables such as number of partitions and fragments, the status of local checkpoints, whether a partition reorganization is ongoing, etc.
table_fragments	7.5.4	Detailed status of the fragments for each table, for example on which data node the primary replicate and the backups are located.
table_info	7.5.4	Information about tables such as whether the read_backup flag is set, the default storage, etc.
table_replicas	7.5.4	Information about the distribution of tables such as latest global and local checkpoints.

The ndbinfo views are important to monitor for all of the three reasons discussed in the "Why Monitor?" section of Chapter 14—to establish a baseline, to perform a root cause analysis, and to perform preventive maintenance. The next section includes examples of using the views. Additional examples have been presented throughout the book.

NDB Cluster Reports

Just like for the Performance Schema discussed in the previous chapter, the ndbinfo schema can seem overwhelming at first. However, with a little practice, it becomes easier to retrieve information. This section will show several examples of how to generate reports using the ndbinfo schema. These reports are useful on their own, but also serve as an introduction on writing queries against the views, so additional reports can be created.

Memory Usage Report

The memoryusage view can be used to monitor how much DataMemory, IndexMemory, and LongMessageBuffer memory has been allocated and how much is currently used. There is one row per data node and memory type. Listing 16-4 shows the plain output from the view.

Listing 16-4. The ndbinfo.memoryusage View

```
mysql> SELECT * FROM ndbinfo.memoryusage;
+---------+----------------------+---------+------------+----------+-------------+
| node_id | memory_type          | used    | used_pages | total    | total_pages |
+---------+----------------------+---------+------------+----------+-------------+
|       1 | Data memory          | 3309568 |        101 | 41943040 |        1280 |
|       1 | Index memory         |  638976 |         78 | 15990784 |        1952 |
|       1 | Long message buffer  |  524288 |       2048 | 67108864 |      262144 |
|       2 | Data memory          | 3309568 |        101 | 41943040 |        1280 |
|       2 | Index memory         |  638976 |         78 | 15990784 |        1952 |
|       2 | Long message buffer  |  393216 |       1536 | 67108864 |      262144 |
+---------+----------------------+---------+------------+----------+-------------+
6 rows in set (0.02 sec)
```

This output is great for machine usage—such as in monitoring systems—but for human reading, the query in Listing 16-5 may be better suited. The query uses the sys.format_bytes() function from the sys schema to add units to the number of bytes.

Listing 16-5. Formatted Output from the ndbinfo.memoryusage View

```
mysql> SELECT node_id, memory_type, sys.format_bytes(used) AS UsedBytes,
              sys.format_bytes(total) as TotalBytes,
              sys.format_bytes(total-used) AS FreeBytes,
              ROUND(100*used/total, 2) AS UsedPct
         FROM ndbinfo.memoryusage;
+---------+----------------------+------------+------------+-----------+---------+
| node_id | memory_type          | UsedBytes  | TotalBytes | FreeBytes | UsedPct |
+---------+----------------------+------------+------------+-----------+---------+
|       1 | Data memory          | 3.16 MiB   | 40.00 MiB  | 36.84 MiB |    7.89 |
|       1 | Index memory         | 624.00 KiB | 15.25 MiB  | 14.64 MiB |    4.00 |
|       1 | Long message buffer  | 512.00 KiB | 64.00 MiB  | 63.50 MiB |    0.78 |
|       2 | Data memory          | 3.16 MiB   | 40.00 MiB  | 36.84 MiB |    7.89 |
|       2 | Index memory         | 624.00 KiB | 15.25 MiB  | 14.64 MiB |    4.00 |
|       2 | Long message buffer  | 384.00 KiB | 64.00 MiB  | 63.62 MiB |    0.59 |
+---------+----------------------+------------+------------+-----------+---------+
6 rows in set (0.02 sec)
```

Now the three bytes columns have the values in KiB and MiB units. The units will depend on the actual values and can be up to GiB as of MySQL NDB Cluster 7.5. Additionally, a UsedPct column was added to make it easier to see how close the cluster is to exhausting the memory.

Disk Page Buffer Report

The disk page buffer is used to cache the disk data in memory. Like the InnoDB buffer pool, the disk page buffer improves performance by keeping disk data in memory, so subsequent queries using the same data can retrieve the data from memory instead of requiring expensive disk operations. This is explained in more detail in Chapter 18. The effectiveness of the disk page buffer is important to the performance of on-disk data. Two columns in the `ndbinfo.diskpagebuffer` view are of particular interest when determining the effectiveness:

- **page_requests_direct_return:** Pages returned from the cache. These contribute to improving the hit rate.

- **page_requests_wait_io:** Pages returned from disk. These contribute to lowering the hit rate.

The sum of the two is the total number of page requests. So, using these two columns, the cache hit rate for the disk page buffer can be calculated, as shown in Listing 16-6. Some of the columns have been renamed in the output to reduce the width of the result. The `IF(...)` clause is there to avoid dividing by zero if there have been no page requests yet.

Listing 16-6. Querying the Disk Page Buffer Hit Rate

```
mysql> SELECT node_id, block_instance,
              page_requests_direct_return AS PageDirectReturn,
              page_requests_wait_io AS PageWaitIo,
              IF(page_requests_direct_return+page_requests_wait_io = 0,
                 NULL,
                 ROUND(100*page_requests_direct_return/
                       (page_requests_direct_return+page_requests_wait_io),
                       2)
              ) AS CacheHitPct
         FROM ndbinfo.diskpagebuffer;
+---------+----------------+------------------+------------+-------------+
| node_id | block_instance | PageDirectReturn | PageWaitIo | CacheHitPct |
+---------+----------------+------------------+------------+-------------+
|       1 |              1 |            10488 |         17 |       99.84 |
|       1 |              2 |                1 |          1 |       50.00 |
|       2 |              1 |            10408 |         17 |       99.84 |
|       2 |              2 |                1 |          1 |       50.00 |
+---------+----------------+------------------+------------+-------------+
4 rows in set (0.02 sec)
```

The `block_instance` column is the instance of the *PGMAN* kernel block used. Listing 16-7 shows how to find the threads where the block instances exist.

■ **Note**   The number of *PGMAN* block instances depends on the configuration of `MaxNoOfExecutionThreads` and `ThreadConfig`.

Listing 16-7. Getting Information About the *PGMAN* Kernel Block Instances

```
mysql> SELECT node_id, thr_no, tb.block_instance, t.thread_name
          FROM ndbinfo.threadblocks tb
             INNER JOIN ndbinfo.threads t USING (node_id, thr_no)
          WHERE tb.block_name = 'PGMAN'
          ORDER BY node_id, block_instance;
+---------+--------+----------------+-------------+
| node_id | thr_no | block_instance | thread_name |
+---------+--------+----------------+-------------+
|       1 |      1 |              0 | rep         |
|       1 |      2 |              1 | ldm         |
|       1 |      1 |              2 | rep         |
|       2 |      1 |              0 | rep         |
|       2 |      2 |              1 | ldm         |
|       2 |      1 |              2 | rep         |
+---------+--------+----------------+-------------+
6 rows in set (0.03 sec)
```

So, in this case the *LDM* threads used for queries have a cache hit rate of 99.84%, which is good. The low hit rate of the replication thread is not a concern, given the low number of pages returned. The two queries in Listings 16-6 and 16-7 can be combined, as shown in Listing 16-8.

Listing 16-8. Combined Query to Determine the Disk Page Buffer Hit Rate per Thread

```
mysql> SELECT node_id, block_instance, t.thread_name,
            dpb.page_requests_direct_return AS PageDirect,
            dpb.page_requests_wait_io AS PageWait,
            IF(dpb.page_requests_direct_return+page_requests_wait_io = 0,
              NULL,
              ROUND(100*dpb.page_requests_direct_return/
                 (dpb.page_requests_direct_return+
                  dpb.page_requests_wait_io),
                2)
            ) AS HitPct
       FROM ndbinfo.diskpagebuffer dpb
           INNER JOIN ndbinfo.threadblocks tb
                   USING (node_id, block_instance)
           INNER JOIN ndbinfo.threads t USING (node_id, thr_no)
       WHERE tb.block_name = 'PGMAN'
       ORDER BY node_id, block_instance;
+---------+----------------+-------------+------------+----------+--------+
| node_id | block_instance | thread_name | PageDirect | PageWait | HitPct |
+---------+----------------+-------------+------------+----------+--------+
|       1 |              1 | ldm         |      10488 |       17 |  99.84 |
|       1 |              2 | rep         |          1 |        1 |  50.00 |
|       2 |              1 | ldm         |      10408 |       17 |  99.84 |
|       2 |              2 | rep         |          1 |        1 |  50.00 |
+---------+----------------+-------------+------------+----------+--------+
4 rows in set (0.05 sec)
```

Transporters Report

The network is one of the parts of the cluster infrastructure that most easily can become a bottleneck. The ndbinfo.transporters view provides an easy way to monitor for overloaded transporters and identify which node-to-node connections contribute most to overall data use.

■ **Note**   The transporter metrics reset every time the status of the transporter changes to connected. However, the metrics will be retained after a disconnect until the connection is re-established.

There are two thresholds that are considered when determining the status of a transporter:

- **Overloaded:** This occurs when the send buffer use is more than OverloadLimit bytes. By default, OverloadLimit is 80% of SendBufferMemory for the transporter.

- **Slowdown:** This occurs at 60% of the overload limit.

If a transporter tends to become overloaded, it is necessary to look into improving the network or increasing the size of the send buffer. The ndbinfo.transporters view has four columns related to overload and slowdown situations:

- **overloaded:** Whether the transporter is currently overloaded.

- **overload_count:** The number of times the transporter has been overloaded.

- **slowdown:** Whether the transporter is currently in the slowdown state.

- **slowdown_count:** The number of times the transporter has been in the slowdown state.

The overload and slowdown states often only last for a short period of time, so the counts are in general more useful from a monitoring point of view.

Listing 16-9 shows an example of querying the ndbinfo.transporters view to get the status of the transporter between two data nodes with NodeId = 1 and NodeId = 2. The data is shown in both directions.

Listing 16-9. The Transporters Data and Metrics Between Two Data Nodes

```
mysql> SELECT * FROM transporters WHERE (node_id = 1 AND remote_node_id = 2) OR (node_id = 2
AND remote_node_id = 1)\G
*************************** 1. row ***************************
         node_id: 1
  remote_node_id: 2
          status: CONNECTED
  remote_address: 192.168.56.104
      bytes_sent: 139508260
  bytes_received: 117712512
   connect_count: 1
      overloaded: 0
  overload_count: 0
        slowdown: 0
  slowdown_count: 0
```

```
*************************** 2. row ***************************
         node_id: 2
  remote_node_id: 1
          status: CONNECTED
  remote_address: 192.168.56.103
      bytes_sent: 117712512
  bytes_received: 139508260
   connect_count: 1
      overloaded: 0
  overload_count: 0
        slowdown: 0
  slowdown_count: 0
2 rows in set (0.02 sec)
```

In this case, the data is symmetric, but for the four overload and slowdown columns, this is not always the case. The bytes_sent and bytes_received columns can optionally be formatted using the sys.format_bytes() function, like it was done for the memory usage report. If the overload or slowdown counters increase, it is an indication of problems. Similarly, if the connect_count increases without a deliberate restart of one of the nodes, it may mean there are network problems.

Disk Write Speed Report

In MySQL NDB Cluster 7.4 and later, it is possible to monitor the disk write speed of local checkpoints (LCPs), backups, and redo logs. Since local checkpoints and backups are handled by the same code, their disk write metrics are combined.

The ndbinfo.disk_write_speed_base view has the raw metrics recorded. An example of one of the rows in the view is as follows:

```
mysql> SELECT * FROM disk_write_speed_base LIMIT 1\G
*************************** 1. row ***************************
                 node_id: 1
                  thr_no: 0
              millis_ago: 0
           millis_passed: 1001
 backup_lcp_bytes_written: 0
      redo_bytes_written: 131072
 target_disk_write_speed: 20971520
1 row in set (0.01 sec)
```

The data is for the reporting period that ended millis_ago milliseconds ago, and data collection lasted millis_passed milliseconds. The target_disk_write_speed value is the number of bytes per second that the *LDM* thread aims to be writing per second. This target will vary according to the MaxDiskWriteSpeed, MaxDiskWriteSpeedOtherNodeRestart, MaxDiskWriteSpeedOwnRestart, and MinDiskWriteSpeed options for the data node.

The base table has 61 rows per *LDM* thread and each period is close to a second. As one record for each *LDM* thread is always completed 0 milliseconds ago, the oldest period finished around a minute ago. The one-second intervals are also what the *LDM* threads uses for the internal monitoring of the disk write speed, and the target disk write speed may be adjusted after each of these periods.

The raw data is great for a monitoring system, as it allows one to calculate any statistics it may support. However, for a manual inspection, one of the ndbinfo.disk_write_speed_aggregate and ndbinfo.disk_write_speed_aggregate_node views is usually preferred. The two views aggregate the data for the last second, last 10 seconds, and last minute. Additionally, the ndbinfo.disk_write_speed_aggregate view calculates the standard deviations[1] and whether any of the following conditions applied (with the corresponding column name):

- **slowdowns_due_to_io_lag:** The I/O was slowed down due the I/O subsystem being the bottleneck.

- **slowdowns_due_to_high_cpu:** The I/O was slowed down due to high CPU.

- **disk_write_speed_set_to_min:** The disk write speed was set to MinDiskWriteSpeed.

- **current_target_disk_write_speed:** The target write speed that the *LDM* thread is currently attempting to achieve.

These columns are great to troubleshoot performance issues, and the slowdown columns cannot be derived from the base data without also considering other metrics.

The ndbinfo.disk_write_speed_aggregate view groups the aggregate data per *LDM* thread, whereas the ndbinfo.disk_write_speed_aggregate_node view groups the data per data node. Listing 16-10 shows an example output of the ndbinfo.disk_write_speed_aggregate view.

Listing 16-10. The ndbinfo.disk_write_speed_aggregate View

```
mysql> SELECT * FROM ndbinfo.disk_write_speed_aggregate\G
*************************** 1. row ***************************
                          node_id: 1
                           thr_no: 0
           backup_lcp_speed_last_sec: 134000
                redo_speed_last_sec: 0
         backup_lcp_speed_last_10sec: 13479
              redo_speed_last_10sec: 65261
std_dev_backup_lcp_speed_last_10sec: 40000
       std_dev_redo_speed_last_10sec: 65000
         backup_lcp_speed_last_60sec: 26000
              redo_speed_last_60sec: 65000
std_dev_backup_lcp_speed_last_60sec: 179000
       std_dev_redo_speed_last_60sec: 65000
           slowdowns_due_to_io_lag: 5
         slowdowns_due_to_high_cpu: 0
        disk_write_speed_set_to_min: 0
    current_target_disk_write_speed: 20971520
*************************** 2. row ***************************
                          node_id: 2
                           thr_no: 0
           backup_lcp_speed_last_sec: 1061000
                redo_speed_last_sec: 0
         backup_lcp_speed_last_10sec: 106169
              redo_speed_last_10sec: 65209
std_dev_backup_lcp_speed_last_10sec: 318000
       std_dev_redo_speed_last_10sec: 65000
         backup_lcp_speed_last_60sec: 42000
              redo_speed_last_60sec: 65000
```

---

[1]*https://en.wikipedia.org/wiki/Standard_deviation*

```
std_dev_backup_lcp_speed_last_60sec: 198000
       std_dev_redo_speed_last_60sec: 64000
             slowdowns_due_to_io_lag: 6
          slowdowns_due_to_high_cpu: 0
          disk_write_speed_set_to_min: 0
    current_target_disk_write_speed: 20971520
2 rows in set (0.01 sec)
```

The view has the data per thread. The write speeds are available for the last one, 10, and 60 seconds for backup/LCP writes, redo writes, and their standard deviation. (There is no standard deviation for the one second data as it is a single measurement.) The 10 and 60 seconds values are per second.

There are also statistics for slowdowns, such as how many seconds the write speed has been set to MinDiskWriteSpeed since the last node restart, and the current target speed. In the example, notice that there were six occasions where a slowdown was detected due to I/O lag.

Listing 16-11 shows an example of the ndbinfo.disk_write_speed_aggregate_node view.

Listing 16-11. The ndbinfo.disk_write_speed_aggregate_node View

```
mysql> SELECT * FROM disk_write_speed_aggregate_node\G
*************************** 1. row ***************************
                   node_id: 1
  backup_lcp_speed_last_sec: 75000
         redo_speed_last_sec: 130000
backup_lcp_speed_last_10sec: 7540
       redo_speed_last_10sec: 65235
backup_lcp_speed_last_60sec: 1000
       redo_speed_last_60sec: 65000
*************************** 2. row ***************************
                   node_id: 2
  backup_lcp_speed_last_sec: 74000
         redo_speed_last_sec: 129000
backup_lcp_speed_last_10sec: 7537
       redo_speed_last_10sec: 65209
backup_lcp_speed_last_60sec: 1000
       redo_speed_last_60sec: 65000
2 rows in set (0.01 sec)
```

In this case the aggregation is per node, and it only includes the 1, 10, and 60 second values with no standard deviation. It may at first seem that this view is not very useful, but consider a cluster with multiple *LDM* threads (there can be up to 32). In that case, the ndbinfo.disk_write_speed_aggregate view will have one row per *LDM* thread per data node, so the one row per node in ndbinfo.disk_write_speed_aggregate_ node can be useful to get an overview of how the nodes work.

Locks Report

A common issue in transactional systems is that two transactions fight for the same locks. In a worst-case scenario, the two transactions may hold locks that the other transaction require. This is called a *deadlock*. Lock waits and deadlocks are handled the same way in MySQL NDB Cluster: after TransactionDeadlockDetectionTimeout milliseconds, a transaction gives up waiting and fails with a lock wait timeout error.

■ **Note** The locks discussed here are at the NDBCluster level (that is, inside the storage engine in the data nodes). The locks discussed with the Performance Schema in the previous chapter were for tables and metadata (but only within the one SQL node).

The challenge is to determine which transactions wait for which locks, and what the transactions that holds the blocking lock is doing. The three ndbinfo views—cluster_locks, locks_per_fragment, and cluster_transactions—can be used to get this information. Listing 16-12 shows an example of determining the blocking and waiting locks as well as finding information about the two conflicting connections.

Listing 16-12. Investigating Locks

```
-- Find information about conflicting locks
mysql> SELECT lb.tableid, lb.fragmentid, lpf.fq_name,
              lpf.parent_fq_name, lpf.type,
              '-----------------' AS '------------------------',
              lb.transid AS BlockingTransId, lb.op AS BlockingOp,
              lb.duration_millis AS BlockingMilliSeconds,
              tb.state AS BlockingState,
              tb.count_operations AS BlockingOperations,
              tb.inactive_seconds AS BlockingInactiveSeconds,
              tb.client_node_id AS BlockingNodeId,
              '-----------------' AS '------------------------',
              lw.transid AS WaitingTransId, lw.op AS WaitingOp,
              lw.duration_millis AS WaitingMilliSeconds,
              tw.state AS WaitingState,
              tw.count_operations AS WaitingOperations,
              tw.inactive_seconds AS WaitingInactiveSeconds,
              tw.client_node_id as WaitingNodeId
         FROM ndbinfo.cluster_locks lw
         INNER JOIN ndbinfo.cluster_locks lb
                   ON lb.lock_num = lw.waiting_for
         INNER JOIN ndbinfo.cluster_transactions tb
                   ON tb.transid = lb.transid
         INNER JOIN ndbinfo.cluster_transactions tw
                   ON tw.transid = lw.transid
         INNER JOIN ndbinfo.locks_per_fragment lpf
                   ON lpf.table_id = lb.tableid
                      AND lpf.fragment_num = lb.fragmentid
                      AND lpf.node_id = lb.node_id\G
*************************** 1. row ***************************
          tableid: 12
       fragmentid: 1
          fq_name: world/def/City
   parent_fq_name: NULL
             type: User table
-----------------: -----------------
```

```
          BlockingTransId: 36084872111980557
              BlockingOp: READ
    BlockingMilliSeconds: 2028919
           BlockingState: Started
      BlockingOperations: 2
BlockingInactiveSeconds: 2009
          BlockingNodeId: 51
-----------------------: -----------------
           WaitingTransId: 40588471739351055
               WaitingOp: READ
     WaitingMilliSeconds: 3323
            WaitingState: Started
       WaitingOperations: 1
 WaitingInactiveSeconds: 3
           WaitingNodeId: 51
1 row in set (0.28 sec)

-- Blocking connection information
mysql> SELECT session.*
          FROM information_schema.ndb_transid_mysql_connection_map map
              INNER JOIN sys.session
                      ON session.conn_id = map.mysql_connection_id
          WHERE (map.ndb_transid >> 32) = (36084872111980557 >> 32)\G
*************************** 1. row ***************************
                thd_id: 134
                conn_id: 111
                  user: root@localhost
                    db: world
               command: Sleep
                 state: NULL
                  time: 2038
     current_statement: NULL
     statement_latency: NULL
              progress: NULL
          lock_latency: 159.54 ms
         rows_examined: 1
             rows_sent: 0
         rows_affected: 1
            tmp_tables: 0
       tmp_disk_tables: 0
             full_scan: NO
        last_statement: UPDATE world.City SET Population = Population + 1 WHERE ID = 130
last_statement_latency: 163.07 ms
        current_memory: 0 bytes
             last_wait: NULL
      last_wait_latency: NULL
                source: NULL
           trx_latency: NULL
             trx_state: NULL
```

```
          trx_autocommit: NULL
                     pid: 26941
            program_name: mysql
1 row in set (0.05 sec)


-- Waiting connection information
mysql> SELECT session.*
          FROM information_schema.ndb_transid_mysql_connection_map map
               INNER JOIN sys.session
                         ON session.conn_id = map.mysql_connection_id
         WHERE (map.ndb_transid >> 32) = (40588471739351055 >> 32)\G
*************************** 1. row ***************************
                  thd_id: 141
                 conn_id: 118
                    user: root@localhost
                      db: world
                 command: Query
                   state: updating
                    time: 21
       current_statement: UPDATE world.City SET Population = Population + 1 WHERE ID = 130
       statement_latency: 20.38 s
                progress: NULL
            lock_latency: 146.00 us
           rows_examined: 0
               rows_sent: 0
           rows_affected: 0
              tmp_tables: 0
         tmp_disk_tables: 0
               full_scan: NO
          last_statement: NULL
  last_statement_latency: NULL
          current_memory: 0 bytes
               last_wait: NULL
       last_wait_latency: NULL
                  source: NULL
             trx_latency: NULL
               trx_state: NULL
          trx_autocommit: NULL
                     pid: 26986
            program_name: mysql
1 row in set (0.05 sec)
```

The query to find the blocking and waiting transactions looks large, but is a straightforward joining of tables. For the blocking and waiting transactions, there is a pair of cluster_locks and cluster_transactions views, and the locks_per_fragment view is used to retrieve additional information about the table and/or index where the lock is registered. The dashed columns are there to make it easier to see the three groups of data—the table, blocking, and waiting information.

The two queries to find additional information must be executed on the SQL node where the connection originates. The node ID can be found from the ndbinfo query. The connection information is found using the sys.session view.

The locks views can also be used to determine which tables and fragments constitute hot spots. The ndbinfo.locks_per_fragment view is excellent for this purpose. Listing 16-13 shows an example row of this view. The numbers are somewhat exaggerated compared to the expected values of a production system, as they were obtained using an artificially large value of TransactionDeadlockDetectionTimeout to make testing easier.

Listing 16-13. The ndbinfo.locks_per_fragment View

```
mysql> SELECT *
       FROM ndbinfo.locks_per_fragment
       WHERE node_id = 2 AND table_id = 12 AND fragment_num = 1\G
*************************** 1. row ***************************
         fq_name: world/def/City
  parent_fq_name: NULL
            type: User table
        table_id: 12
         node_id: 2
  block_instance: 1
    fragment_num: 1
          ex_req: 2008
       ex_imm_ok: 1998
      ex_wait_ok: 1
    ex_wait_fail: 9
          sh_req: 0
       sh_imm_ok: 0
      sh_wait_ok: 0
    sh_wait_fail: 0
  wait_ok_millis: 2360
wait_fail_millis: 550811
1 row in set (0.04 sec)
```

The columns prefixed with ex_ are for exclusive locks, whereas the sh_ prefix is for shared locks. In this example, there has been 2008 requests for exclusive locks (ex_req), of which 1998 have been granted immediately (ex_imm_ok), one was granted after waiting for it (ex_wait_ok), and nine were waiting but did not get granted (ex_wait_fail). If a fragment or table (by aggregating the data) has many lock requests waiting or failing, it suggests that there is contention in that area. Better indexing or different query patterns may help to resolve this issue, or possibly increasing TransactionDeadlockDetectionTimeout can be used to resolve or mitigate the issues.

Log Buffers and Spaces Report

Chapter 2 discussed how the changes made by transactions are written into the redo buffer on commit, then flushed to the redo log during a global checkpoint. The redo log is used to persist committed transactions until the changes are included in a local checkpoint. Figure 16-1 shows an overview of this mechanism. There is a similar mechanism for on-disk data where there is an undo log and undo log buffer for transactions that need to be rolled back (see also Chapter 18).

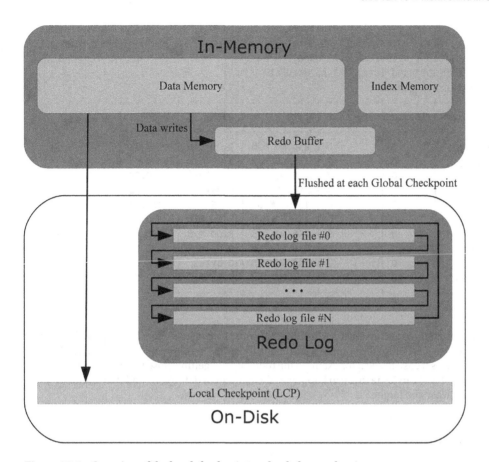

Figure 16-1. *Overview of the local checkpoint and redo log mechanism*

Monitoring the redo and undo buffers as well as the redo and undo logs is very important to avoid aborted transactions and the cluster becoming read-only. The ndbinfo schema has two views for this purpose: logbuffers to monitor the buffers, and logspaces to monitor the logs. Listing 16-14 shows an example of querying the usage of both the buffers and logs.

Listing 16-14. Querying the ndbinfo.logbuffers and ndbinfo.logspaces Views

```
mysql> SELECT node_id, log_type, log_id, log_part,
              sys.format_bytes(total) AS total,
              sys.format_bytes(used) AS used,
              ROUND(100*used/total, 2) AS UsedPct
         FROM ndbinfo.logbuffers;
+---------+----------+--------+----------+----------+-----------+---------+
| node_id | log_type | log_id | log_part | total    | used      | UsedPct |
+---------+----------+--------+----------+----------+-----------+---------+
|       1 | REDO     |      0 |        1 | 16.00 MiB | 320.00 KiB |    1.95 |
|       1 | DD-UNDO  |     20 |        0 | 2.00 MiB  | 5.08 KiB   |    0.25 |
|       2 | REDO     |      0 |        1 | 16.00 MiB | 320.00 KiB |    1.95 |
|       2 | DD-UNDO  |     20 |        0 | 2.00 MiB  | 31.48 KiB  |    1.54 |
+---------+----------+--------+----------+----------+-----------+---------+
4 rows in set (0.01 sec)
```

539

```
mysql> SELECT node_id, log_type, log_id, log_part,
              sys.format_bytes(total) AS total,
              sys.format_bytes(used) AS used,
              ROUND(100*used/total, 2) AS UsedPct
         FROM ndbinfo.logspaces;
+---------+----------+--------+----------+------------+----------+---------+
| node_id | log_type | log_id | log_part | total      | used     | UsedPct |
+---------+----------+--------+----------+------------+----------+---------+
|       1 | REDO     |      0 |        0 | 256.00 MiB | 2.00 MiB |    0.78 |
|       1 | REDO     |      0 |        1 | 256.00 MiB | 2.00 MiB |    0.78 |
|       1 | REDO     |      0 |        2 | 256.00 MiB | 0 bytes  |    0.00 |
|       1 | REDO     |      0 |        3 | 256.00 MiB | 0 bytes  |    0.00 |
|       1 | DD-UNDO  |     20 |        0 | 16.00 MiB  | 2.05 MiB |   12.80 |
|       2 | REDO     |      0 |        0 | 256.00 MiB | 2.00 MiB |    0.78 |
|       2 | REDO     |      0 |        1 | 256.00 MiB | 2.00 MiB |    0.78 |
|       2 | REDO     |      0 |        2 | 256.00 MiB | 0 bytes  |    0.00 |
|       2 | REDO     |      0 |        3 | 256.00 MiB | 0 bytes  |    0.00 |
|       2 | DD-UNDO  |     20 |        0 | 16.00 MiB  | 1.95 MiB |   12.17 |
+---------+----------+--------+----------+------------+----------+---------+
10 rows in set (0.02 sec)
```

In this example, the redo log is less than 1% full, but that could be because a local checkpoint has just completed. What is usage just before the completion? Having the usage logged regularly in a monitoring system with graphs makes it easy to see if for example the redo logs are getting close to full before the local checkpoints complete. This is an issue that can happen as the amount of data grows and thus the local checkpoints become larger and larger.

Configuration Report

In MySQL NDB Cluster 7.4 and earlier, the only way to query the configuration of the data nodes was to use the ndb_config utility. This was a cumbersome way to get the configuration values—for example it was necessary to know the exact spelling of the option name. To recap the ndb_config usage from Chapter 10, to use ndb_config to get the value of DataMemory from each of two data nodes, it is necessary to use two requests. For example:

```
shell$ ndb_config --type=ndbd --fields=': ' --rows='\n' \
                  --query=NodeId,DataMemory \
                  --config-from-node=1 --nodeid=1
1: 41943040

shell$ ndb_config --type=ndbd --fields=': ' --rows='\n' \
                  --query=NodeId,DataMemory \
                  --config-from-node=2 --nodeid=2
2: 41943040
```

It is even more difficult to get information about the option using ndb_config. To do this, use the --config-info option. However, there are no filtering options, so information for all options is always returned:

```
shell$ ndb_config -configinfo
...
IndexMemory (Non-negative Integer)
Number bytes on each ndbd(DB) node allocated for storing indexes
Default: 18874368 (Min: 1048576, Max: 1099511627776)

DataMemory (Non-negative Integer)
Number bytes on each ndbd(DB) node allocated for storing data
Default: 83886080 (Min: 1048576, Max: 1099511627776)

UndoIndexBuffer (Non-negative Integer)
Number bytes on each ndbd(DB) node allocated for writing UNDO logs for index part
Default: 2097152 (Min: 1048576, Max: 4294967039)
...
```

As of MySQL NDB Cluster 7.5, you can use the ndbinfo schema with the config_params and config_values views.

The config_params view has information about the configuration options and includes a description, the data type, the default value, minimum and maximum values, and whether the option is mandatory. For example, for the DataMemory parameter:

```
mysql> SELECT *
         FROM ndbinfo.config_params
        WHERE param_name = 'DataMemory'\G
*************************** 1. row ***************************
     param_number: 112
       param_name: DataMemory
param_description: Number bytes on each ndbd(DB) node allocated for storing data
       param_type: unsigned
    param_default: 83886080
        param_min: 1048576
        param_max: 1099511627776
  param_mandatory: 0
     param_status:
1 row in set (0.01 sec)
```

The config_params view also exists in older versions of MySQL NDB Cluster, but it only includes the param_number and param_name columns.

Being able to query information about the configuration options is nice, but joining the param_values view is what makes it really interesting. Listing 16-15 shows how to get the value of a single configuration option—DataMemory.

Listing 16-15. Configuration Information for the DataMemory Option

```
mysql> SELECT v.node_id, p.param_name, v.config_value, p.param_default,
              IF(v.config_value = p.param_default, 'YES', 'NO') AS IsDefault
         FROM ndbinfo.config_params p
              INNER JOIN ndbinfo.config_values v
                       ON v.config_param = p.param_number
        WHERE p.param_name = 'DataMemory';
+---------+------------+--------------+---------------+-----------+
| node_id | param_name | config_value | param_default | IsDefault |
+---------+------------+--------------+---------------+-----------+
|       1 | DataMemory | 41943040     | 83886080      | NO        |
|       2 | DataMemory | 41943040     | 83886080      | NO        |
+---------+------------+--------------+---------------+-----------+
2 rows in set (0.02 sec)
```

By comparing the actual value (the `config_value` column) to the default value (the `param_default` column), it is possible to determine whether the option is using the default value. Listing 16-16 uses this to return a report containing all configuration options that are set to non-default values.

Listing 16-16. Finding All Options with Non-Default Values

```
mysql> SELECT v.node_id, p.param_name, v.config_value
         FROM ndbinfo.config_params p
              INNER JOIN ndbinfo.config_values v
                       ON v.config_param = p.param_number
        WHERE v.config_value <> p.param_default;
+---------+-------------------------------+-------------------------+
| node_id | param_name                    | config_value            |
+---------+-------------------------------+-------------------------+
|       1 | NodeId                        | 1                       |
|       1 | DataDir                       | /cluster/node_1         |
|       1 | MaxNoOfTables                 | 130                     |
|       1 | MaxNoOfAttributes             | 1009                    |
|       1 | MaxNoOfTriggers               | 1400                    |
|       1 | MaxNoOfConcurrentTransactions | 1024                    |
|       1 | MaxNoOfConcurrentOperations   | 5120                    |
|       1 | DataMemory                    | 41943040                |
|       1 | IndexMemory                   | 15728640                |
|       1 | FileSystemPath                | /cluster/node_1         |
|       1 | BackupDataBufferSize          | 4194304                 |
|       1 | BackupLogBufferSize           | 4194304                 |
|       1 | Arbitration                   | 1                       |
|       1 | RedoBuffer                    | 16777216                |
|       1 | BackupDataDir                 | /backups/cluster/node_1 |
|       1 | DiskPageBufferMemory          | 16777216                |
|       1 | Nodegroup                     | 0                       |
|       1 | SharedGlobalMemory            | 20971520                |
|       2 | NodeId                        | 2                       |
|       2 | DataDir                       | /cluster/node_2         |
|       2 | MaxNoOfTables                 | 130                     |
|       2 | MaxNoOfAttributes             | 1009                    |
```

```
|       2 | MaxNoOfTriggers                |  1400                    |
|       2 | MaxNoOfConcurrentTransactions  |  1024                    |
|       2 | MaxNoOfConcurrentOperations    |  4096                    |
|       2 | DataMemory                     |  41943040                |
|       2 | IndexMemory                    |  15728640                |
|       2 | FileSystemPath                 |  /cluster/node_2         |
|       2 | BackupDataBufferSize           |  4194304                 |
|       2 | BackupLogBufferSize            |  4194304                 |
|       2 | Arbitration                    |  1                       |
|       2 | RedoBuffer                     |  16777216                |
|       2 | BackupDataDir                  |  /backups/cluster/node_2 |
|       2 | DiskPageBufferMemory           |  16777216                |
|       2 | Nodegroup                      |  0                       |
|       2 | SharedGlobalMemory             |  20971520                |
+---------+--------------------------------+--------------------------+
36 rows in set (0.03 sec)
```

> **Note** Not all options have a default value defined. An example is `FileSystemPath`. These options will always end up being included in the report to find all options with a non-default value.

Finally, the configuration views can be used to detect when the data nodes do not have the same configuration. This is an issue that, for example, can occur if a node was missed during a rolling restart where a configuration change was made. When the data nodes have diverting configurations, it can cause subtle issues that appear to happen at random, and thus are hard to debug. Listing 16-17 shows an example of detecting parameters where the data nodes do not have the same settings.

Listing 16-17. Finding Options with Different Values on the Data Nodes

```
mysql> SELECT p.param_name, v.node_id, v.config_value
        FROM (SELECT config_param
               FROM ndbinfo.config_values
             GROUP BY config_param
             HAVING COUNT(DISTINCT config_value) > 1
            ) t
            INNER JOIN ndbinfo.config_params p
                    ON p.param_number = t.config_param
            INNER JOIN ndbinfo.config_values v
                    ON v.config_param = t.config_param
        WHERE param_name NOT IN ('BackupDataDir', 'DataDir',
                                 'FileSystemPath', 'NodeId', 'Nodegroup')
        ORDER BY p.param_name, v.node_id;
+------------------------------+---------+--------------+
| param_name                   | node_id | config_value |
+------------------------------+---------+--------------+
| MaxNoOfConcurrentOperations  |       1 | 5120         |
| MaxNoOfConcurrentOperations  |       2 | 4096         |
+------------------------------+---------+--------------+
2 rows in set (0.04 sec)
```

A few options that are expected to be different. To avoid having data returned that may hide real issues, these options are explicitly removed using the WHERE clause. The list of excluded options will vary from cluster to cluster depending on the expected configuration.

This concludes the example reports for the NDB Cluster Information Database. While these reports are great for accessing data, they cannot replace the logs. The logs have additional information and the messages remain even after an event has completed. The logs in MySQL NDB Cluster are the next monitoring source to discuss.

NDB Cluster Logs

Like SQL nodes, the management and data nodes have their own log files. The management nodes maintain the cluster log, which is an overall log for cluster. On the data nodes, there are three log types: a general log, an error log, and trace logs (files). This section provides an overview of the logs, as well as discuses how to configure them.

Cluster Logs

The cluster logs are the best place to get an overview of what is going on in the cluster as a whole. The logs are maintained by the management nodes, with one set of logs per management node, but it records messages related to all nodes in the cluster—thus the name.

Since the management nodes control the cluster logs, messages will only be written to them while at least one of the management nodes is online. Given that each management node writes to its own log, there may be gaps while a node is offline, so it is in general necessary to check the cluster log for each management node.

■ **Tip** The cluster log messages are documented in *https://dev.mysql.com/doc/refman/5.7/en/mysql-cluster-logs-cluster-log.html*.

The default is that the cluster logs are written to files, with each cluster log consisting of a set of files (more on the configuration shortly, including how to change the destination, filenames, maximum file size, and maximum number of files). The file currently written to will not have a suffix, whereas the old files have a suffix, including a number. For the sake of illustration, assume that the currently active cluster log file is *ndb_49_cluster.log* (the default for a management node with NodeId = 49). This filename is the base filename for the cluster log.

When the cluster is installed, the cluster log will just consist of *ndb_49_cluster.log*. Log messages are then written to the file and at the time it reaches its maximum size, it is renamed to *ndb_49_cluster.log.1* and a new file called *ndb_49_cluster.log* will be created. When the new file also has reached its maximum size, it is renamed *ndb_49_cluster.log.2* and so forth. At some point, there are as many old cluster log files as the configuration allows. At that time, *ndb_49_cluster.log.1* is reused. So, the cluster log is a circular log, but always with *ndb_49_cluster.log* as the most recent file, and either of the archived log files being the next oldest, then the rest following in order.

This is illustrated in Figure 16-2 for a configuration with at most four files. For brevity, the base name of the files in the figure is *cluster.log*, but for production systems, it is strongly recommended to include the node ID of the management node in the base filename—for example, the ndb_error_reporter script that is discussed in Chapter 17 requires unique cluster log base names to collect all cluster log file sets.

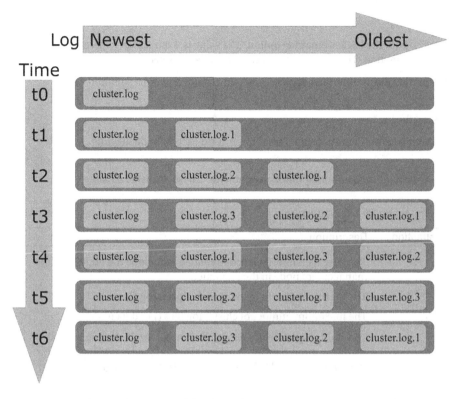

Figure 16-2. *The circular nature of the cluster log*

■ **Tip** Always have unique base filenames for the cluster logs across all management nodes.

Table 16-6 contains the configuration options related to the cluster log. It is best to keep the settings the same on all nodes except for the cluster log base filename. More details about the options as well as how to control what is logged is discussed in the rest of this section.

Table 16-6. *The Cluster Log Configuration Options*

Option	Nodes	Default	Description
LogDestination	Management	See text	Where the cluster log is written, the maximum number of files, and file size.
MemReportFrequency	Data	0	How many seconds between reporting the DataMemory and IndexMemory usage.
StartupStatusReportFrequency	Data	0	How frequently progress of creating the fragment log files during initial node restarts.

Log Destination

The cluster log is configured with the LogDestination option. The value is a semicolon-separated list where each part configures a log destination. There is support for three log destinations:

- **FILE:** Write to a log file as described earlier. This is the default and most common log destination.

- **SYSLOG:** Send the log to a syslog facility.

- **CONSOLE:** Write the log to the console. This is rarely used except for debugging purposes.

The FILE and SYSLOG destinations support additional arguments. These are listed in Table 16-7.

Table 16-7. *Additional Arguments for Log Destinations*

Option	Log Destination	Description
filename	FILE	The base filename. It is recommended to include the node ID of the management node in the filename.
maxsize	FILE	The maximum size in bytes of each cluster log files.
maxfiles	FILE	The maximum number of cluster log files (per data node).
facility	SYSLOG	The syslog facility to use. Supported values for the facility are auth, authpriv, cron, daemon, ftp, kern, lpr, mail, news, syslog, user, uucp, local0, local1, local2, local3, local4, local5, local6, and local7.

For FILE where several options can be specified, the options are separated with a comma. The default value for LogDestination is FILE:filename=ndb_<NodeId>_cluster.log,maxsize=1000000,maxfiles=6 where <NodeId> is the node ID of the management node. The default size is good for test systems, but it is in most cases recommended to increase the size for production systems.

When deciding on the size and number of files for the FILE destination, make the file size as large as it is practical – for example it must still be possible to review the log file and search it. Exactly what this means in terms of file size depends on the tools used to read log files. For example, the less command on Linux can large files of several gigabytes. Dealing with a large file is mainly an issue of how long it takes to search and read it. Other tools such as Notepad++ may have maximum file sizes. In practice, a size of at most 10-20 megabytes works well.

Then increase maxfiles so the total size (maxsize * maxfiles) is large enough to include at least a week of log data. Be aware that restarts include data for each table and index, so a single rolling restart for clusters with a large number of tables, indexes, and/or data nodes can use a couple of megabytes of log space.

Memory Report Frequency

Setting the MemReportFrequency to a value greater than 0 will cause the data nodes to generate a report for its DataMemory and IndexMemory usage every MemReportFrequency seconds. The report looks like the following report excerpt.

```
2017-06-19 20:26:02 [MgmtSrvr] INFO     -- Node 1: Data usage is 13%(174 32K pages of total 1280)
2017-06-19 20:26:02 [MgmtSrvr] INFO     -- Node 1: Index usage is 5%(113 8K pages of total 1952)
2017-06-19 20:26:03 [MgmtSrvr] INFO     -- Node 2: Data usage is 13%(174 32K pages of total 1280)
2017-06-19 20:26:03 [MgmtSrvr] INFO     -- Node 2: Index usage is 5%(113 8K pages of total 1952)
```

The same data can be obtained from ndbinfo.memoryusage, which is better for monitoring purposes, although having occasional memory usage reports in the log can be useful to correlate with other log messages.

Memory usage reporting is not entirely turned off even when MemReportFrequency = 0. There will still be messages if the memory threshold crosses the thresholds of 80% and 90% in either direction for the data or index memory. Listing 16-18 shows an example of the memory increasing through 80% and 90%, and then reducing back below 80% again.

Listing 16-18. Messages About Increasing and Decreasing Memory Usage

```
2017-06-19 21:12:39 [MgmtSrvr] INFO     -- Node 1: Data usage increased to 81%(1044 32K pages
                                           of total 1280)
2017-06-19 21:12:40 [MgmtSrvr] INFO     -- Node 2: Data usage increased to 81%(1045 32K pages
                                           of total 1280)
2017-06-19 21:12:51 [MgmtSrvr] INFO     -- Node 2: Data usage increased to 90%(1153 32K pages
                                           of total 1280)
2017-06-19 21:12:52 [MgmtSrvr] INFO     -- Node 1: Data usage increased to 90%(1160 32K pages
                                           of total 1280)
2017-06-19 21:18:36 [MgmtSrvr] INFO     -- Node 2: Data usage decreased to 88%(1132 32K pages
                                           of total 1280)
2017-06-19 21:18:37 [MgmtSrvr] INFO     -- Node 1: Data usage decreased to 88%(1132 32K pages
                                           of total 1280)
2017-06-19 21:22:08 [MgmtSrvr] INFO     -- Node 2: Data usage decreased to 79%(1013 32K pages
                                           of total 1280)
2017-06-19 21:22:09 [MgmtSrvr] INFO     -- Node 1: Data usage decreased to 79%(1013 32K pages
                                           of total 1280)
```

Startup Status Report Frequency

The final cluster log configuration option is StartupStatusReportFrequency. This option is only used during initial data node restarts when the redo logs are recreated. Particularly, if the logs are created in full (as opposed to sparse) this can take a long time, so it can be useful to have progress reports logged.

The default (StartupStatusReportFrequency = 0) only logs information of the redo log file generation at the start and completion. When the value is set to a non-zero value, a progress report will be logged every StartupStatusReportFrequency seconds.

Controlling What Is Logged

It is possible to some degree to control what is logged to the cluster log through the CLUSTERLOG command in the ndb_mgm command-line client. There are eight log categories and each is set to a log threshold. The categories are:

- **CHECKPOINT:** For messages created during execution of local and global checkpoints.

- **CONNECTION:** For messages created when connections are made between cluster nodes.

- **ERROR:** Messages related to errors that do not cause node failures. This includes missed heartbeats.

- **INFO:** For informational messages such as when sending a heartbeat.

- **NODERESTART:** Similar to STARTUP and SHUTDOWN but for data node restarts.

- **STARTUP:** For messages created during the startup of data nodes.

- **STATISTICS:** Various statistics such as number of transaction, current operations, etc.

- **SHUTDOWN:** For messages created during the shutdown of data nodes.

The default threshold is 7 for all categories except ERROR, which has a default threshold of 15. The allowed range for the threshold is 0 through 15 where 0 only includes the most important messages and 15 includes all messages.

Each log message has a priority which is compared to the threshold. If the priority is less than or equal to the threshold, then the message is logged. For example, a message with priority 12 will be logged if the threshold is 12 or higher. In other words, the higher the configured threshold, the more log messages there are.

The threshold is set by specifying which data node to apply it to followed by the CLUSTERLOG command and the category with the threshold. For example, to set the STATISTICS category to 15 for the data node with NodeId = 1, use this command:

```
ndb_mgm> 1 CLUSTERLOG STATISTICS=15
Executing CLUSTERLOG STATISTICS=15 on node 1 OK!
```

To make the same change to all data nodes, use this command:

```
ndb_mgm> ALL CLUSTERLOG STATISTICS=15
Executing CLUSTERLOG STATISTICS=15 on node 1 OK!
Executing CLUSTERLOG STATISTICS=15 on node 2 OK!
```

■ **Note**   The threshold is set for a given management and data node pair (or one management node to all data nodes). If there are several management nodes and the threshold should apply to all cluster logs, the CLUSTERLOG command must be executed while connected to each management node.

In older versions of MySQL NDB Cluster, it was more common to use increased thresholds to get information. For example, for the statistics, it is in general better to get the data from ndbinfo.

In addition to the priority, each log message has a severity. It is possible to filter messages by their severity using the CLUSTERLOG command with slightly different arguments. For example, you can toggle the logging of INFO level messages by using:

```
ndb_mgm> CLUSTERLOG FILTER INFO;
INFO disabled
```

Execute again to re-enable:

```
ndb_mgm> CLUSTERLOG FILTER INFO;
INFO enabled
```

There are six severity levels which, in order of decreasing severity, are:

- **ALERT:** The most severe issues that must be corrected immediately. This includes information about network partitioning, node failures, failed backups, etc.

- **CRITICAL:** This level is currently not used.

- **ERROR:** Still very important events that must be handled urgently. An example is a transporter error.

- **WARNING:** Important messages such as missed heartbeats (but where the node has not yet been declared dead). These messages generally require attention.

- **INFO:** Informational messages that in general do not require any action. An example is a backup that has started or completed.

- **DEBUG:** Very detailed messages, for example, that a transporter has received an end-of-file message. These messages are mostly useful when working with the source code.

By default, all but the DEBUG severity level is enabled.

■ **Tip** Details of the cluster log events, how to control what is logged, and classification of the events including their priorities and severities are documented in *https://dev.mysql.com/doc/refman/5.7/en/mysql-cluster-event-reports.html* and in the subpages listed near the top of the page.

Data Node Logs

While the cluster log provides a good overview of the cluster activity, it is at times necessary to get more information. Each data node has three log types that cover general messages, unscheduled shutdown details, and trace logs. All data node log files are located in the path specified with DataDir. Table 16-8 summarizes the three logs.

Table 16-8. *Data Node Log Files*

Log	Filename	Description
Out log	*ndb_<NodeId>_out.log*	General log messages. Similar to the MySQL Server error log but for data nodes.
Error log	*ndb_<NodeId>_error.log*	One message block per unscheduled shutdown with details of why the node was shut down.
Trace log	*ndb_<NodeId>_trace.log.<count>*	One set of log files for each unscheduled shutdown. Each set has one file per data node thread.

<NodeId> is a placeholder for the NodeId for the data node and *<count>* is a placeholder for a counter that increments for each unscheduled shutdown. The MaxNoOfSavedMessages option sets the limit to the number of message blocks in the error log and the sets of trace files. It defaults to 25.

Chapter 17 is dedicated to troubleshooting and includes more information about the data node logs.

Summary

This chapter covered the ndbinfo schema, including several examples of creating reports that can be used for monitoring purposes. Additionally, the logs and trace files available on the management and data nodes were discussed. It also concludes the tour of monitoring, the sources of monitoring, and the logs available in MySQL NDB Cluster setups. As you can see in this and the previous two chapters, monitoring is a very large topic for which an entire book can be written on its own. Implementing good monitoring on MySQL NDB Cluster is not something that is done in a single day—instead it is an ongoing process.

There is one topic related to monitoring and logs that still needs to be discussed: troubleshooting. This is the topic of the next chapter.

CHAPTER 17

Typical Troubles and Solutions

This chapter discusses problems that may occur on MySQL NDB Cluster. Since nothing is perfect, your MySQL NDB Cluster installation may face some troubles. It is important for your service quality to minimize downtime due to these troubles. You need to be prepared for troubles and fix them as quickly as possible. In this chapter, learn how to cope with troubles using typical examples of problems.

Typical Problems on Data Nodes

Since the data node is a heart of MySQL NDB Cluster, troubles on data nodes can affect the entire database cluster system. Even though data nodes are usually redundant, and the absence of a single data node doesn't lead to an entire system outage, it can happen because of multiple node failures. So, it is important to minimize the probability of multiple node failures. To achieve this goal, it is necessary to identify problems and resolve them quickly.

■ **Tip** When you face a problem, be sure to search the bug database, as the same problem might have been reported. If you cannot find the identical problem, file a new bug at *https://bugs.mysql.com/*. Contact Oracle Corporation for support if you have a support license. Commercial support is a good way to save time and cost required for investigation.

General Information about Node Failures

A data node can crash for various reasons. Since MySQL NDB Cluster has a fail-early strategy, a data node will shut down by itself when something goes wrong. The strategy expects data nodes to have redundancy, which can prevent an entire system outage when you have single node failures. A single node failure is not a fatal problem for MySQL NDB Cluster. Take the appropriate actions against node failures. It is rather likely that you will face node failures at some point if you run the cluster with many data nodes for a long time.

This section discusses how to collect the information required to investigate node failures.

Cluster Log

The first thing you must check upon node failure is the *cluster log*, which is a centralized consolidated log of the entire cluster. It's stored on each management node. The content of the cluster log varies depending on its filtering configuration. See Chapter 16 for more details of the cluster log, and see Chapter 4 for more details of configuration of the cluster log. The cluster log has a filename such as *ndb_NODEID_cluster.log* by default, where NODEID is the NodeId for the management node that writes the cluster log.

Upon a node failure, the data node reports why it's going to be abnormally shut down, before it shuts down completely. There could be some sign in the cluster log before the node failure, which leads a node to crash. Carefully examine the cluster log and see what happened prior to crash. Listing 17-1 shows an example cluster log when a node failed due to a heartbeat failure. In this example, Node 1 was forced to shut down because Node 2, the "left" node of Node 1, detected that heartbeat signal didn't arrive for a certain period. See Chapter 1 for more information about heartbeats and the "left" node.

Listing 17-1. Cluster Log When a Data Node Failed Due to Missed Heartbeat

```
2017-05-13 17:27:09 [MgmtSrvr] WARNING  -- Node 2: Node 1 missed heartbeat 2
2017-05-13 17:27:14 [MgmtSrvr] WARNING  -- Node 2: Node 1 missed heartbeat 3
2017-05-13 17:27:19 [MgmtSrvr] WARNING  -- Node 2: Node 1 missed heartbeat 4
2017-05-13 17:27:19 [MgmtSrvr] ALERT    -- Node 2: Node 1 declared dead due to missed
                                            heartbeat
... snip ...
2017-05-13 17:27:22 [MgmtSrvr] ALERT    -- Node 1: Forced node shutdown completed. Caused by
                                            error 2315: 'Node declared dead. See error log
                                            for details(Arbitration error). Temporary error,
                                            restart node'.
```

Node Log

As the name suggests, the node log is a node specific log stored locally on each node. It may have more detailed messages compared to the cluster log, and may be useful for debugging purposes. The node log has a filename such as *ndb_NODEID_out.log*, where NODEID is the NodeId for the data node. Listing 17-2 shows an example node log when the data node was shut down due to a missed heartbeat.

Listing 17-2. Example Node Log When a Data Node Was Marked as Dead Due to Missed Heartbeats

```
2017-05-13 17:27:22 [ndbd] WARNING  -- thr: 1: Overslept 23577 ms, expected ~10ms
2017-05-13 17:27:22 [ndbd] WARNING  -- thr: 2: Overslept 23572 ms, expected ~10ms
2017-05-13 17:27:22 [ndbd] WARNING  -- thr: 0: Overslept 23572 ms, expected ~10ms
2017-05-13 17:27:22 [ndbd] WARNING  -- timerHandlingLab, expected 10ms sleep, not scheduled
                                        for: 23572 (ms)
2017-05-13 17:27:22 [ndbd] WARNING  -- thr: 3: Overslept 23571 ms, expected ~10ms
2017-05-13 17:27:22 [ndbd] INFO     -- Watchdog: User time: 93  System time: 681
2017-05-13 17:27:22 [ndbd] WARNING  -- Watchdog: Warning overslept 23669 ms, expected 100 ms.
2017-05-13 17:27:22 [ndbd] INFO     -- We(1) have been declared dead by 2 (via 2) reason:
                                        Heartbeat failure(4)
2017-05-13 17:27:22 [ndbd] INFO     -- QMGR (Line: 4213) 0x00000002
2017-05-13 17:27:22 [ndbd] INFO     -- Error handler shutting down system
2017-05-13 17:27:22 [ndbd] INFO     -- Error handler shutdown completed - exiting
2017-05-13 17:27:22 [ndbd] ALERT    -- Node 1: Forced node shutdown completed. Caused by
                                        error 2315: 'Node declared dead. See error log for
                                        details(Arbitration error). Temporary error, restart
                                        node'.
```

You can see that the threads in the data node overslept a long time, so watchdog warnings were reported. A thread in data node intentionally sleeps for a certain period when there are no more signals to process.

However, a thread may oversleep (fail to wake up) longer than planned for various reasons; for example, the OS failed to allocate CPU time to the thread due to a high load. In this example, the threads overslept because I paused the ndbmtd process using a debugger (GDB) for a while. It prevented data node 1 from sending the heartbeat signal to data node 2, thus data node 2 marked data node 1 as dead due to these missed heartbeats. While this is an artificial failure, similar log content can happen by chance on your production system, too.

Error Log

The data node writes an event in its error log when it encounters an unplanned shutdown. The information written to the error log includes when the error happened, the error code, where the error happened, and so forth. The error log has a filename such as *ndb_NODEID_error.log*, where NODEID indicates the NodeId for the data node. Listing 17-3 shows an example of the error log when a data node was marked as dead due to missed heartbeats.

Listing 17-3. Example Error Log When a Data Node Was Marked as Dead Due to Missed Heartbeats

```
Time: Saturday 13 May 2017 - 17:27:22
Status: Temporary error, restart node
Message: Node declared dead. See error log for details (Arbitration error)
Error: 2315
Error data: We(1) have been declared dead by 2 (via 2) reason: Heartbeat failure(4)
Error object: QMGR (Line: 4213) 0x00000002
Program: ndbmtd
Pid: 29262 thr: 0
Version: mysql-5.7.18 ndb-7.5.6
Trace file name: ndb_1_trace.log.1
Trace file path: /var/lib/mysql-cluster/ndb_1_trace.log.1 [t1..t4]
***EOM***
```

In this error log, you can see that the error number was 2315; data node 2 marked this node as dead due to four contiguous heartbeat failures. Then, the QMGR block forcibly shut down this node. You can also see that the version of MySQL NDB Cluster is 7.5.6. For this case, the error log is informative enough and no more investigation is required. However, further information is often required in various cases. The source of information required for further investigation is the trace file, which is described in next section.

Trace Files

Upon a node failure, a special log file called a *trace file* is generated under the DataDir of the failed data node. Don't confuse the trace file in this section with the one retrieved from the debug version of mysqld. The trace file in this section is a facility of the NDB kernel, which is enabled by default on non-debug binaries of ndbd and ndbmtd. The trace file has a filename such as *ndb_NODEID_trace.log.N*, where NODEID indicates the NodeId for the data node and N indicates the ID of the trace file. The ID is increased up to MaxNoOfSavedMessages and reset to 1 if it has reached MaxNoOfSavedMessages.

■ **Note** Increase MaxNoOfSavedMessages if the data node crashes frequently, so that the new trace files do not overwrite the existing ones. The size of each trace file is trivial, so you don't have to worry about the file system consumption due to the trace file. The default value for this option is 25.

The trace file is the most significant data source when investigating crashes. One or more trace files are created per each crash. Listings 17-4 and 17-5 show examples of the trace file content. Listing 17-4 shows the beginning of an example trace file. Listing 17-5 shows the middle of an example trace file.

Listing 17-4. Example Content of Trace File at its Beginning

```
$ head -20 ndb_1_trace.log.1
JAM CONTENTS up->down left->right
SOURCE FILE          LINE  LINE  LINE  LINE  LINE  LINE  LINE  LINE  LINE

QmgrMain.cpp         02804 02821 02989 02828 02926 00050 00051 00052 00053
                     00255
---> signal
DbdihMain.cpp        00359 00530 27209 16403 16492 16492 16492 16492
---> signal
DbdihMain.cpp        16857
---> signal
DbdihMain.cpp        16497 16510
---> signal
DbdihMain.cpp        17581 17527 17527 17527 17527 17527 17527 17527 17527
                     17527 17527 17527 17527 17527 17527 17527 17527 17527
                     17527 17527 17527 17527 17527 17527 17527 17527 17527
                     17527 17527 17527 17527 17527 17527 17527 17527 17527
                     17527 17527 17527 17527 17527 17527 17527 17527 17527
                     17527 17527 17527 17527 17562
DbtcMain.cpp         05571
Ndbfs.cpp            01593 01426
```

Listing 17-5. Example Content in the Middle of the Trace File

```
$ head -461 ndb_1_trace.log.1 | tail -12
---> signal
QmgrMain.cpp          00220 04130
SimulatedBlock.cpp    02018

-------------- Signal ----------------
r.bn: 252 "QMGR", r.proc: 1, r.sigId: 146516 gsn: 254 "FAIL_REP" prio: 0
s.bn: 252 "QMGR", s.proc: 2, s.sigId: 96525 length: 3 trace: 0 #sec: 0 fragInf: 0
 FailedNode: 1, FailCause: 4
-------------- Signal ----------------
r.bn: 246 "DBDIH", r.proc: 1, r.sigId: 146515 gsn: 164 "CONTINUEB" prio: 0
s.bn: 246 "DBDIH", s.proc: 1, s.sigId: 146502 length: 1 trace: 0 #sec: 0 fragInf: 0
 Check GCP Stop
```

If you have not seen it before, this can look like garbage, despite its importance. The content of the trace file consists of two parts. One is a program trace like Listing 17-4; the other is a dump of recently executed signals, like the latter half of Listing 17-5.

The program trace is required to investigate problems on a data node, because the unit of the job in the data node is a signal. Usual lock based multi-threaded programs implement a complex algorithm by calling functions in a nested manner, which solve race conditions using locks. So, it is possible to figure out what the thread was doing when it crashed by examining the stack trace; it's a history indicating which function is called by which function. Since `mysqld` is a lock based multi-threaded program, the stack trace is a good starting point to investigate the cause of crashes.

However, this is not true for `ndbmtd` and `ndbd`. In these processes, complex algorithms are broken into signals, where a signal is a unit of tasks in these processes. An algorithm that handles each signal is designed to be very small and simple. If a signal needs further processing, it is done by one or more additional signals, which is sent to the kernel blocks, either its own or others, instead of the calling functions. The stack trace of `ndbmtd` and `ndbd` is fairly small and it doesn't include sufficient data to figure out the history of program execution. Thus, when it comes to crash analysis, you need the trace file instead of the stack trace.

The first part of the trace file indicates on which line of which source file the thread in question executed. For example, Listing 17-4 indicates that `ndbmtd` executed line 2804 of *QmgrMain.cpp*, then lines 2821, 2989, 2828, and so forth of same file. The signal processing ended at line 255, then it switched to the next signal, which started from line 359 of *DbdihMain.cpp*.

The second half of the trace file is a list of signals in the order from newest to oldest. As discussed in Chapter 2, signals are stored in two *job buffers* depending on the priority of the signals. Since the job buffers are fixed-sized arrays used in a circular fashion, old signals already executed remain in the job buffer for a while. When each signal is executed, a monotonically increasing identifier is assigned to the signal. So, signals in job buffers can be sorted in the order they were executed, using this identifier even though two buffers exist.

Review Listing 17-5, which shows the boundary of jam buffer content and job buffer content. Since the jam buffer content is sorted from oldest to newest, and job buffer content is sorted from newest to oldest, newest data is located around the boundary. So, it is possible to figure out what was going on at the very moment when the data node crashed by examining the data around the boundary. The first thing to do when analyzing a trace file is to scroll down to the boundary. Then, grab the source code around the latest job buffer along with the signal data.

Note that the multi-threaded version of data node, `ndbmtd`, has multiple sets of job buffers and jam buffers; one set per thread. So, one trace file is created per instance, and each trace file has the suffix _*tN* where *N* indicates thread number. To write trace files, all execution threads must be stopped in advance. A thread that's not the cause of the crash is stopped by the `STOP_FOR_CRASH` signal. So, investigate a trace file that doesn't include the `STOP_FOR_CRASH` signal first. Note that the error log entry also tells you which thread it believes is the culprit.

Core Files

Even though the data node is designed using a signal processing architecture, it is sometimes required to analyze the core file to access values in memory. Information that can be retrieved from the trace file is mainly line numbers and signal data. If you need to examine more data that's not seen in the trace file, such as the global variables, a core file is required just like for usual programs.

You can retrieve a core file upon a crash on UNIX-like systems by using the following instructions:

- Make sure your program binary includes debugging symbols. Binaries officially shipped from Oracle Corporation include debugging symbols. Be careful when you're using binaries compiled from source.

- Ensure sufficient free space is available on your file system. Since the data node process consumes a large amount of memory, the same amount of free disk space is required to store a core file.

- Use the `ulimit` command to allow the process to generate sufficiently large core files before starting `ndbmtd` and `ndbd`. Specify `unlimited` to generate the whole process memory image.

- Specify the `--core-file` option when starting `ndbmtd` and `ndbd`.

To analyze a core file, a debugger such as GDB, LLDB, dbx, or mdb is required.

■ **Note** Currently, data nodes don't generate core files on Windows. Refer to the bug report for details of the problem on Windows: *https://bugs.mysql.com/bug.php?id=86358*.

NDB Error Reporter Utility

When a data node crashes, we need to examine the various kinds of files including the configuration file and logs. The NDB Error Reporter Utility, the ndb_error_reporter command, collects various files required for investigation. It logs in to remote host using SSH and copies files to the local host. The following files are collected from data nodes and management nodes:

- *config.ini*
- PID file
- Cluster log
- Error log
- Node log
- Trace file
- Data files under FileSystemPath (optional)

The command takes the configuration file as its argument. A typical command is:

```
$ ndb_error_reporter ./config.ini
```

Then, it generates a compressed archive file under the current working directory named *ndb_error_report_DATETIME.tar.bz2*, where DATETIME indicates the current timestamp in numeric format (YYYYMMDDhhmmss). The command may take additional arguments to specify a username for a remote login. See ndb_error_reporter --help for more details.

I recommend running this command for testing purposes once you have set up the cluster. If you face any problems, solve them in advance before you need to use this utility for collecting information about a crash.

Since the command is written in the Perl script, you need to install the Perl interpreter on your system in advance.

■ **Tip** MySQL Cluster Manager can also collect configuration files and logs. See Chapter 13 for more details of MySQL Cluster Manager.

Watchdog Timeout

On a data node, all threads that handle signals are monitored by the *watchdog thread*. The watchdog thread wakes up every TimeBetweenWatchDogCheck milliseconds and checks if the watchdog counter has been changed by the monitored thread to a non-zero value, then resets the counter to zero. If the watchdog counter remains zero, then the watchdog thread thinks that the monitored thread is stuck and not proceeding.

Since MySQL NDB Cluster is designed to be a real-time database system, which responds within a guaranteed period, being stuck on one signal is a critical problem. Recall that MySQL NDB Cluster takes a fail-early strategy. The stuck data node is forcibly shut down when the watchdog timeout is detected. Listing 17-6 shows an error log whereby the data node died due to a watchdog timeout.

Listing 17-6. An Error Log Caused by a Data Node That Died Due to a Watchdog Timeout

```
Time: Thursday 18 May 2017 - 15:53:34
Status: Temporary error, restart node
Message: WatchDog terminate, internal error or massive overload on the machine running this
node (Internal error, programming error or missing error message, please report a bug)
Error: 6050
Error data: Job Handling
Error object: /srctopdir/storage/ndb/src/kernel/vm/WatchDog.cpp
Program: ndbmtd
Pid: 2082
Version: mysql-5.7.18 ndb-7.5.6
Trace file name: ndb_2_trace.log.1
Trace file path: /var/lib/mysql-cluster/ndb_2_trace.log.1 [t1..t4]
***EOM***
```

You can see that the Error Data in Listing 17-6 is "Job Handling", which indicates the state when the thread got stuck. This status indicates that the data node was stuck when processing signals. Table 17-1 shows a list of possible thread status.

Table 17-1. *List of Possible Thread Status on Data Node*

Status	Description
Job Handling	Execution thread is handling signals.
Scanning Timers	Execution thread is detecting if the clock has ticked backward.
External I/O	A send thread is releasing local memory.
Print Job Buffers at crash	A thread is dumping the jam buffer and signal memory upon crash.
Checking connections	A receiver thread is checking the connection status.
Performing Send	A send thread is performing a send operation.
Polling for Receive	A receiver thread is polling the socket.
Performing Receive	A receiver thread is performing a receive operation.
Allocating memory	A thread is allocating memory. This status can be shown only at startup.
Packing Send Buffers	A thread is packing send buffers to make memory available to other threads.

A watchdog timeout is likely to be caused for the following reasons:

- A data node is overloaded.

- A data node process is swapped out due to memory shortage.

- Unnecessary delay is caused when using a virtual machine.

- The network interface is faulty.

- Something slow is happening inside the kernel, such as memory compaction.

- A bug in the data node, such as an infinite loop.

LCP Watchdog Timeout

When a data node encounters a disk problem, it might fail to write the *Local Checkpoint (LCP)* to disk for a long time. If there is no progress on an LCP for more than LcpScanProgressTimeout seconds, which is 60 seconds by default, a data node shuts down itself due to the fail-early strategy. A stuck LCP is a problem, because it exhausts the redo log space. Note that all redo log entries written after the last LCP must be kept until the next LCP completes. Listing 17-7 shows an example error log in which a data node died due to an LCP watchdog timeout.

Listing 17-7. An Error Log Caused by a Data Node That Died Due to an LCP Watchdog Timeout

```
Time: Thursday 18 May 2017 - 18:32:57
Status: Temporary error, restart node
Message: LCP fragment scan watchdog detected a problem.  Please report a bug. (Internal
error, programming error or missing error message, please report a bug)
Error: 7200
Error data: Please report this as a bug. Provide as much info as possible, especially
all the ndb_*_out.log files, Thanks. Shutting down node due to lack of LCP fragment scan
progress
Error object: DBLQH (Line: 25454) 0x00000002
Program: ndbmtd
Pid: 30777 thr: 2
Version: mysql-5.7.18 ndb-7.5.6
Trace file name: ndb_3_trace.log.1_t2
Trace file path: /var/lib/mysql-cluster/ndb_3_trace.log.1 [t1..t4]
***EOM***
```

This problem was most likely caused by faulty and/or overloaded disks. You would need to monitor the I/O activity of the disks and replace any faulty ones.

Swap Insanity

As discussed in Chapters 3 and 4, recent CPUs often have built-in memory controllers for faster memory access. RAM is connected directly to each CPU. Because of this, memory access speed varies depending on which CPU has the target memory to be accessed. This type of system architecture is called *Non-Uniform Memory Access (NUMA)*. Figure 17-1 shows a conceptual view of NUMA system with two CPUs. Each CPU and its local memory is called a *NUMA node*. If CPU0 accesses the RAM under CPU1, which is in a different NUMA node, data must be transferred via the bus between the two CPUs, which is a much slower process than when accessing the local RAM.

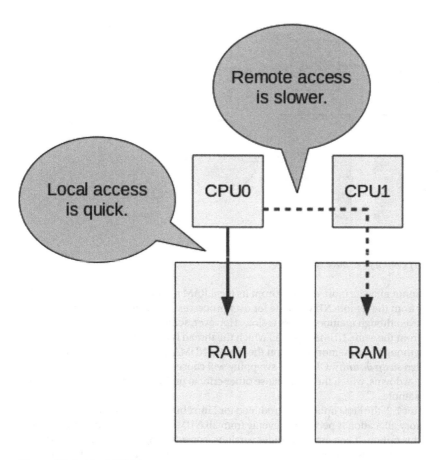

Figure 17-1. *The NUMA concept*

Recent Linux kernels attempt to allocate memory from the same NUMA node that's running the thread allocating the memory. If free space is running out on the current NUMA node, the memory is allocated from the other NUMA node. This strategy works well with programs that allocate small amounts of memory, because memory access within the same NUMA node is fast. However, it doesn't work well for programs that require memory larger than the RAM size of one NUMA node. Figure 17-2 depicts a situation in which memory runs out on one NUMA node.

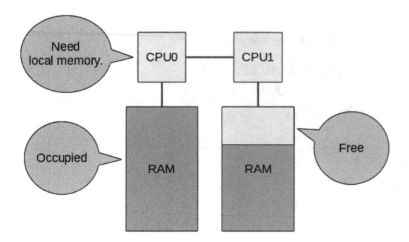

Figure 17-2. *Memory is short even if free space exists*

In Figure 17-2, CPU0 cannot allocate more memory from its local RAM module. In such a case, the OS kernel will allocate memory from the remote NUMA node for user processes. This is not a problem from a functionality point of view, even though memory access is slow. However, some kernel modules occasionally require allocating memory from the same NUMA node on which the thread is currently running. In such cases, memory is short even though free memory exists on the remote NUMA node. Then, some processes are swapped out. This is called *swap insanity*. Of course, swapping will cause various negative effects on the running program, such as slowdowns, which then may cause other critical problems for the data nodes, such as watchdog timeouts, for example.

As of MySQL NDB Cluster 7.2, the Numa option is introduced for Linux binaries. When the option is set to 1, which is the default, memory allocation is performed evenly from all NUMA nodes using the functionality of *libnuma*. Do not disable this option. If you are using older versions, consider upgrading to MySQL NDB Cluster 7.2 or newer. If you don't want to upgrade, run the data node via the numactrl command as shown:

```
$ numactrl --interleave all ndbmtd -c mgmhost
```

GCP Stop

On versions prior to the 7.2 series, the *Global Checkpoint (GCP)* stop was a major problem. Due to the fail-early strategy, a data node was designed to separate a lagging node to keep the entire system stable. As part of the strategy, a data node that caused GCP lag was forcibly shut down, and this was called a *GCP stop*. GCP may take time for various reasons, and excessive lag will result in GCP stop.

A GCP stop is detected when the micro-GCP doesn't finish within TimeBetweenEpochsTimeout milliseconds. A micro-GCP usually finishes quickly, because it's an operation on memory. However, it may take a long time on (non-micro) GCP because the data node writes the redo log to disk, which is done every TimeBetweenGlobalCheckpoints milliseconds. A GCP stop is most likely to happen due to the slowness of disks. Disk gets slow for various reasons:

- Faulty disks.

- Disk I/O is overloaded due to read/write against disk data tables.

- Other processes using the disks including copying a backup off the server.

- Too many writes to the redo log.

As of MySQL NDB Cluster 7.2, the default value for `TimeBetweenEpochsTimeout` has changed to 0, which disables the timeout for micro-GCP completely. In very old versions (older than 7.0.21 and 7.1.10), the timeout cannot be disabled and the default value of this option was four seconds. As of MySQL NDB Cluster 7.0.21 and 7.1.10, the maximum value was increased from 32 seconds to 256 seconds, and it was made possible to disable the micro-GCP timeout. (Actually, a setting of 32 seconds wasn't enough in some cases.) This change improved the availability of the data node by avoiding data node failure due to the fail-early strategy. However, there is a trade-off that the response of transaction processing may become slow when disks become slow due to reasons like those discussed previously. Any active transactions cannot be committed until the on-going micro-GCP finishes. So, it will take a very long time to complete these transactions when GCP stop is disabled.

To overcome this problem, yet another feature was added to the MySQL NDB Cluster 7.2 series— the *redo overcommit*. As the name suggests, writes to the redo log are tentatively assumed to progress even if they actually do not. This can prevent slowness of transaction processing upon sudden slowness of disks. There is no problem if writing to the redo log catches up later. If disk is too slow so that redo log flush operation takes longer than `RedoOverCommitLimit` seconds `RedoOverCommitCounter` times, then pending transactions will be aborted. This is better than shutting down data nodes from a stability point of view. Then, NDB API clients, including SQL node, will take further actions defined by the `DefaultOperationRedoProblemAction` option. One drawback of a redo overcommit is that it will increase the chances of losing data upon complete system outage, because it may enlarge the period in which redo logging has not actually completed.

Thus, GCP stop isn't a major problem on recent versions. However, it still makes sense to configure the data node with a non-zero `TimeBetweenEpochsTimeout` value, so that it intentionally causes GCP stop upon disk slowness if you prefer the fail-early strategy to aborting transactions. It will maximize performance instead of sacrificing stability.

Network Partitioning (Split Brain)

As discussed elsewhere in this book, such as in Chapters 1 and 3, a problem called *network partitioning* (also known as *split brain*) can happen with MySQL NDB Cluster data nodes. Network partitioning is when the network the between data nodes is disconnected evenly so that one data node within each node group can run and connect. In such case, more than one cluster can continue operating. Since they are disconnected, writes to one cluster can cause data inconsistency in another, which is a fatal situation for a database system, since consistency of data is crucial.

To prevent network partitioning, MySQL NDB Cluster performs *arbitration* to determine which cluster will survive. When arbitration is performed and one cluster wins, the other cluster is forcibly shut down. This process is so called *STONITH (Shoot The Other Node In The Head)*. Network partitioning will not happen if arbitration works properly. Network partitioning will not happen even if arbitration is not working, because all data nodes will be shut down due to arbitration failure. The entire cluster shutdown is also a bad problem that should be avoided.

Make sure that the arbitrator is reachable from all data nodes even when the network connection between the data nodes is lost. Use separate network switches for connections between data nodes and make the network connection redundant using a network layer such as a bonding driver, as discussed in Chapter 3.

The only way that network partitioning can become an actual problem is at startup, because no arbitration is performed upon startup even if network partitioning happens. Make sure that network partitioning will never happen during startup. I strongly recommend setting `StartPartitionedTimeout` to a very large value to prevent network partitioning at startup.

If you find network partitioning is happening by chance, resolve the problem using the following instructions:

1. Stop your application as soon as possible.

2. Decide which partition should survive. If you are uncertain, choosing arbitrarily is okay.

3. Shut down one partition.

4. Solve the network problems.

5. Reconnect the stopped data nodes using the --initial option, one by one.

6. Solve the data inconsistency if possible. Otherwise, consider restoring the latest successful backup. In the former case, you will partially lose the latest modifications. In the latter case, you will lose whole recent modifications.

7. Restart your application.

Unplanned Shutdown of Entire System

The entire system could go offline even if the system is fault tolerant; it can happen for the following reasons:

- Upon data node failure, a surviving data node within the same node group may also go down before the failed node comes back online. If no data nodes within one node group are available, the entire database cluster system goes down.

- Power outage of the whole data center where the cluster is running. To prevent a catastrophic situation, a *UPS (Uninterruptible power supply)* is often employed.

- A serious bug that causes a failure on multiple data nodes.

When you face a complete system failure, you must restart the cluster. Consider these tips when you restart the cluster:

- Make a complete copy of the NDB file system for a backup. This is typically a file system under the FileSystemPath subdirectory.

- It is not necessary to perform further operations upon restart, because the data will be automatically recovered.

- Some of the most recent committed transactions may be lost when there is an unplanned entire system shutdown, because the redo log is not written to disk upon transaction commit. The redo log is written to disk upon every GCP.

- Determine if the hardware machines are okay. See if all the CPUs are running, if the RAM size is identical to before, and if all the file systems are mounted.

- Check the network connectivity to prevent unnecessary network partitioning. The ping command is sufficient for this purpose.

- If some machines cannot be recovered anyway, consider starting the cluster without them. The MySQL NDB Cluster can start with missing data nodes if at least one data node is available per node group. Such a start type is also known as a *partial start*. If you perform a partial start, specify the --nowait-nodes option when starting ndbmtd or ndbd. See Chapter 10 for more information about restart operations.

Typical Problems on SQL Nodes

The SQL node is yet another important component of the MySQL NDB Cluster, because applications often access data via an SQL node, and it is required for daily operations such as monitoring, table maintenance, replication, and so forth. It is important to quickly solve problems raised on an SQL node. Note that the examples in this section show typical problems. Not all the problems are shown, and you may encounter further problems in your production system.

Errors While Executing Queries

The SQL node is the primary source of error while executing queries, because it reports to its client if an error happens in the course of a query execution. It is important for the application to retrieve the error information to handle an error properly. We discuss how to handle errors (exceptions) in the next chapter. It is necessary to implement an error-handling mechanism in your application to prepare for errors. An application will retry transactions or execute other error-handling algorithms, depending on the content of errors, as discussed in the following subsections.

Resource Temporary Errors

The error ER_GET_TEMPORARY_ERRMSG (Errno = 1297) raised from mysqld during query execution indicates a resource temporary error, which means some resource is temporarily short. When an application receives this error, follow these steps to handle the error:

1. Explicitly roll back the current transaction. (Reconnect to mysqld if you like.)

2. Let the program wait for a while. (A few seconds are sufficient in most cases.)

3. Retry the same transaction.

Don't forget to close the session upon error handling, because abandoned connections cause problems such as connection shortages and unplanned disconnection of sessions.

As the name suggests, temporary resource errors happen due to a resource shortage. Increase resources sufficiently so that temporary resource errors are less likely to happen. The parameter to be increased is written in the error message like so:

```
Out of operation records in transaction coordinator (increase MaxNoOfConcurrentOperations)
```

In this case, MaxNoOfConcurrentOperations should be increased if the same error happens frequently.

Non-Temporary Errors

The SQL node may report non-temporary errors as ER_GET_ERRMSG (Errno = 1296). In this case, the cluster is not working properly. The problem on the SQL node might be non-recoverable. An example error message for ER_GET_ERRMSG is:

```
ERROR 1296 (HY000): Got error 157 'Unknown error code' from NDBCLUSTER
```

In this case, human intervention is required to recover from the problem. You may need to recover data nodes first, for example.

Connection to Data Node Is Lost

One of most serious problems the SQL node can encounter is a lost connection to the data nodes. Since all data is stored in the data nodes, the SQL node can do nothing when it loses the connection to the data nodes. While the SQL node is disconnected from the data nodes, an ER_GET_ERRMSG will happen, as discussed in the previous subsection.

Disconnection happens due to:

- The entire cluster being shut down.

- Network device failures.

- Slow networks (due to overload etc.).

Disconnection caused by a slow network may be an automatically recoverable error. It might be caused by a heartbeat error or a lagging event transmission. The former is easy to understand, but the latter requires some explanation.

In a data node, epochs used for event generation for binary logging are buffered for a while, because network communication does not complete immediately. So, data transmission for event generation should be done in the background. To make it in the background, a sufficient buffer is required to store data for a while. If the data transmission of such events lags behind, this buffer may get full. In such cases, it is not possible to keep more data in the buffer, so some events will be lost. It will make it difficult for queries to be executed on the SQL node. So, lagging SQL nodes are disconnected.

The buffer size is determined by two options: MaxBufferedEpochs and MaxBufferedEpochBytes. MaxBufferedEpochs specifies the buffer size in number of epochs. The default is 100. So, 100 unsent epochs can be stored in the buffer at most. Since epochs are generated every 100 milliseconds by default, the buffer can store epochs for 10 seconds in total. However, 10 seconds of delay in network communication is too strict. The default value might be set to a smaller value because MySQL NDB Cluster is a real-time database system and takes a fail-early strategy. MaxBufferedEpochBytes specifies the buffer size in bytes.

When the buffer is running out, the data node disconnects the SQL node with a message in the cluster log:

```
2017-05-21 13:28:05 [MgmtSrvr] INFO     -- Node 3: Disconnecting lagging nodes
'0000000000000000000000000000000000000000000000010000000000000',
```

If the SQL node is disconnected frequently due to this problem, consider increasing MaxBufferedEpochs and/or MaxBufferedEpochBytes twice. If the problem still happens, increase them twice again until it's resolved.

As discussed in Chapter 6, LOST_EVENTS are written to the binary log upon disconnection. The event indicates possible data loss from the binary log, and it will cause replication failure.

After the SQL node is disconnected from the data nodes, all tables become read-only for a while even if the connection is resumed. This is because there might be possible schema changes while the SQL node was disconnected. Once the connection resumes, the NDB binary log injector thread restarts and all schemas are checked. Then the tables are writable with the following message in the error log of the SQL node.

```
2017-05-21 13:42:09 9047 [Note] NDB Binlog: ndb tables writable
```

Errors Related to Transaction Handling

An SQL node may raise various errors to its client when something goes wrong. Some errors are specific to the NDBCluster storage engine, but others are not. For example, the duplicate key error is not specific to the NDBCluster storage engine. It happens on any storage engine that supports unique constraints. We discuss the details of such error handling in the next chapter.

Crashes

The mysqld process faces crashes for various reasons just like other programs. When the process faces a crash, it is important to identify the cause of the crash to prevent further crashes. In this section, we discuss how to cope with mysqld crashes.

Error Log

When mysqld crashes, it prints relevant information to the error log. It also prints a stack trace when it crashes. Stack traces may not be printed for various reasons; for example, due to corrupted stack memory, hardware failure, and so forth. The stack trace for mysqld is much more informative than the one for ndbd or ndbmtd, because mysqld is a multi-threaded (lock based) program. So, the stack trace for mysqld indicates the history of function calls.

The error log might also include information that can help you investigate the cause of the crash. The mysqld might report some symptoms before it crashes, which can help you determine the cause.

Core File

Even though the stack trace is useful for mysqld, further information is often required, such as a core file. The stack trace included in the error log lacks the following information:

- The stack trace in error log is one for the thread that caused the crash. The stack trace for other threads is not available in the error log.

- Local variables are not printed in the stack trace even though they are stored in a stack.

- Global variables and heap memory aren't stored in a stack.

■ **Note** The core file is not generated by default. You need to specify the --core-file option to retrieve a core file.

If you need such information, retrieve a core file and open it using a debugger. To retrieve a core file on Linux, follow these instructions:

1. Allow the operating system to dump the core. Set the --core-file-size option to unlimited for myqld_safe. If mysqld is started using systemd, set the LimitCORE option to infinity in the mysqld.service configuration file.

2. Enable the --core-file option for mysqld.

3. Set the fs.suid_dumpable kernel parameter to 1.

4. Restart MySQL Server and wait until it crashes.

The fs.suid_dumpable kernel parameter is required when retrieving a core file from a process that changes the effective user by calling the setuid(2) system call by itself. Also change the kernel.core_pattern kernel parameter if you like. You can change the kernel parameters online using the sysctl -w command, as shown:

```
# sysctl -w fs.suid_dumpable = 1
```

However, settings changed with the sysctl -w command will be lost after an OS reboot. To make the changes persistent, edit */etc/sysctl.conf* or create a new file with a two-digit prefix and *.conf* suffix under the */etc/sysctl.d* directory.

The core file of mysqld can be retrieved on Windows, too. You simply specify the --core-file option for mysqld.

The process for examining the data in the core file is dependent on the debugger. Consult with the manual of the debugger for more information about how to use it.

■ **Tip**   You will often see the <optimized out> string when you examine a core file. This indicates that the variable in question is stored only in the register, and not stored in memory. In such cases, you cannot retrieve the value of the variable from the core file directly.

OOM Killer

If you find the mysqld disappears without printing anything to the error log, the mysqld process was likely killed by someone else. The most common thing that kills mysqld on Linux machines is the *OOM killer*, where OOM stands for out-of-memory.

Since the Linux kernel allows *overcommits* for memory allocation, it may cause memory shortages after the process has acquired a pointer to heap memory returned by the allocator. At this stage, the kernel may allocate only virtual memory space, and mapping to physical memory may not have been done yet. Physical memory is allocated when the process accesses the memory area. This behavior is known as *deferred page allocation* or *optimistic memory allocation*. This process saves memory in certain cases, because not all memory is necessarily used and a process may end up accessing only part of the allocated memory. This saves CPU time, too, because physical memory allocation is a heavy task. This also improves availability of processes because the out-of-memory error isn't detected until the process accesses the allocated memory area, even if the size of the allocated memory is bigger than the actual free memory. On the other hand, the kernel returns an out-of-memory error if the kernel expects that memory will short. Thus, deferred page allocation works fine in most cases.

The main drawback of deferred page allocation is that memory shortage might become obvious afterward, even if the kernel returns an okay for memory allocation, because it's optimistic. In such cases, the system may not be able to continue its execution due to the memory shortage. The OOM killer is a program that solves such problematic situations by killing one of the running processes. The mysqld process, as well as ndbmtd and ndbd, are likely to be victims of the OOM killer, because these processes consume large amounts of memory.

To prevent the OOM killer from killing them, adjust the score of likelihood to be killed by the OOM killer. Write -17 to the */proc/[pid]/oom_adj* file, where *[pid]* is the actual PID of the target process. Then the OOM killer will not kill the processes. The following example helps adjust the score for the mysqld process:

```
$ su
# cd /proc/`pidof mysqld`
# echo -17 > oom_adj
```

Do this every time you start the process that must not be killed by OOM killer. It is also important to monitor memory usage so that memory will not be running out.

■ **Tip** Windows doesn't have OOM killer, because OOM situations will never happen on Windows. Since Windows doesn't overcommit memory allocation, an error for memory shortage is detected at the memory allocation stage.

■ **Note** Various types of problems may happen on an SQL node, which will also happen on standard MySQL Server. See the following page for more details about example problems and solutions for MySQL Server:

https://dev.mysql.com/doc/refman/en/problems.html

Typical Problems on Management Nodes

The management node is less important from an availability point of view, because the data nodes and SQL nodes can run without the management node if no management tasks are required (such as rejoining a failed data node to the cluster). So, we will not dive into the details of management troubles in this book. Whatever the type of the problem is, there are common actions that must be taken when facing a problem:

- Stop all management nodes, one at a time. Then restart them one by one.

- Clear the configuration cache and restart.

- Start the management server with the --verbose option.

Summary

In this chapter, we discussed general data collection methods for dealing with troubles and the typical problems that data nodes and SQL nodes encounter. Since data nodes and SQL nodes have different architectures, different types of data are required to investigate their problems.

It is important to quickly collect the necessary information about the issues, because you must identify the cause of problems as quickly as possible to keep the database up and running. Prompt data collection is required even when you have a support license. Be prepared for troubles and take the necessary actions promptly once an issue occurs.

Development and Performance Tuning

■ ■ ■

Developing Applications Using SQL with MySQL NDB Cluster

This chapter discusses various topics regarding application development using SQL with MySQL NDB Cluster. While MySQL NDB Cluster can be used as relational database system via SQL nodes, it can be used as NoSQL storage via the native NDB API. This chapter covers the former topic, accessing MySQL NDB Cluster via an SQL node. Even though it is possible to access MySQL NDB Cluster just like other relational databases, it is important to understand the techniques specific to MySQL NDB Cluster.

Designing Tables

The first step when developing a database application is to design its tables. Although it is possible to use the NDBCluster storage engine just like others, important aspects such as access performance and space efficiency will vary depending on their designs. The maximum load the cluster can handle is dependent on the table design.

We discuss the basic concepts of table objects using the NDBCluster storage engine. We do not discuss application specific matters such as what data should be included in each table. For example, we do not discuss about what kinds of tables are required and what types of columns must be included in each table when developing financial application.

Creating NDB Cluster Tables

You create a new table the same way you do using the standard MySQL Server. The only difference is the storage engine name. The storage engine name should be NDBCluster or NDB like in following listing. The storage engine name is case insensitive, and NDBCluster and NDB are synonyms. You can specify either of them as you like.

```
mysql> CREATE TABLE tbl (id SERIAL, col VARCHAR(100)) ENGINE NDBCluster;
```

CREATE TABLE can be executed from an arbitrary SQL node. Tables using the NDBCluster storage engine is automatically propagated through the hidden mysql.ndb_schema system table to all SQL nodes. Figure 18-1 shows a conceptual view of schema propagation. So, you don't have to take care of which SQL node should be used to create a table. It is possible to issue other DDL statements from any SQL node; however, you should keep in mind that a table lock is acquired on a local SQL node for an online ALTER TABLE statement. So, you need to take care of which SQL node is used for the online ALTER TABLE. Further care must be taken for the offline ALTER TABLE. See Chapter 9 for more information about schema changes.

© Jesper Wisborg Krogh and Mikiya Okuno 2017
J. W. Krogh and M. Okuno, *Pro MySQL NDB Cluster*, https://doi.org/10.1007/978-1-4842-2982-8_18

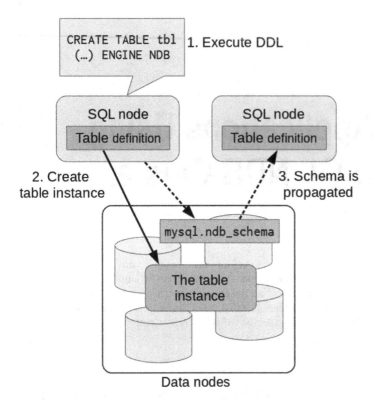

Figure 18-1. *Schema definition is propagated via mysql.ndb_schema table*

Supported Data Types

Any data type supported by standard MySQL Server is supported in MySQL NDB Cluster. So, you can design a table using the NDBCluster storage engine just like when using the standard MySQL Server.

As a limitation of MySQL NDB Cluster, the space required for each column is a multiple of four bytes. If the space required to store some variable length data is 13 bytes, 16 bytes is allocated anyway. BLOB and its variants including TEXT are implemented using hidden support tables. The first 256 bytes of a BLOB column is stored in the main table. If the column value is larger than 256 bytes, the rest of the value is stored in the hidden table. Each row in the hidden table is 2000 bytes. A single BLOB value may consume multiple rows in the hidden table.

■ **Caution**   Since this space requirement is not efficient, the use of BLOB columns must be avoided as much as possible.

Although the standard MySQL Server has efficient data types for small numeric data types, such as TINYINT, SMALLINT, and MEDIUMINT, they consume four bytes per row in the NDBCluster storage engine. So, using such small numeric data types on NDBCluster storage engine is not as efficient as with the standard MySQL Server.

Similarly, the space for BIT column is allocated four bytes at a time. So, a BIT(1) column consumes four bytes. However, unlike other data types, multiple BIT columns are stored in one place per row. So, no extra four bytes are required unless the total size exceeds 32 bits. Thus, 32 BIT(1) columns and a single BIT(32) column require same space. Note that a nullable column also requires a bit to indicate if the column is NULL or not, and it's stored in the same space as the BIT columns.

As of the MySQL NDB Cluster 7.5 series, JSON columns and generated columns are supported. If you want to use these features, install MySQL NDB Cluster 7.5 or later. Spatial columns are supported, but spatial indexes are not supported in MySQL NDB Cluster.

Three Types of Indexes

When designing tables on relational database systems, the index is one of the most important factors. It is very important to understand its characteristics and uses. You need to understand what type of index is available on MySQL NDB Cluster, and the architecture of each type of index. That is the first step of table design. The structure of an index in MySQL NDB Cluster is a little bit different from the other storage engines such as InnoDB.

In MySQL NDB Cluster, you can use three types of indexes:

- **Unique hash index:** This type of index is used for the primary key only. The only capable search operation is equality comparison.

- **Ordered index:** This type of index is used for non-unique secondary index. This index can be used for general purposes, just like B-Tree index in InnoDB.

- **Secondary unique hash index:** This type of index is used for a secondary unique index. This type of index is essentially the same as the primary index, but implemented using hidden support tables.

The following sections go into detail about each index type.

Unique Hash Index for Primary Key

A *unique hash index* is an index type for the primary key. As the name suggests, it ensures uniqueness of individual key value. It's also called a *hash index* in short. We call it the hash index throughout this chapter.

Just like a general hash index, hash indexes in MySQL NDB Cluster can be used for equality comparison only. It is not possible to use it for range or inequality comparisons. A query like the one in Listing 18-1 can use the hash index.

Listing 18-1. Querying a Table Using Equality Comparison

```
mysql> EXPLAIN SELECT Name, CountryCode FROM City WHERE Id = 100\G
*************************** 1. row ***************************
           id: 1
  select_type: SIMPLE
        table: City
   partitions: p0,p1,p2,p3
         type: eq_ref
possible_keys: PRIMARY
          key: PRIMARY
      key_len: 4
          ref: const
         rows: 1
     filtered: 100.00
        Extra: NULL
1 row in set, 1 warning (0.00 sec)
```

Note that type is eq_ref, so the table is accessed through an equality comparison using PRIMARY KEY. A hash index is also used for joins even if the key is not compared to a constant value directly in the WHERE clause. Listing 18-2 shows an example query execution plan where two tables are joined using the primary key of the inner table. Note that the City table (inner table) is accessed with the eq_ref access type.

Listing 18-2. Example Execution Plan for a Join of Two Tables

```
mysql> EXPLAIN SELECT Country.Name, City.Name FROM Country INNER JOIN City ON Country.
Capital = City.Id WHERE Country.Code LIKE 'J%'\G
*************************** 1. row ***************************
           id: 1
  select_type: SIMPLE
        table: Country
   partitions: p0,p1,p2,p3
         type: range
possible_keys: PRIMARY
          key: PRIMARY
      key_len: 3
          ref: NULL
         rows: 11
     filtered: 100.00
        Extra: Parent of 2 pushed join@1; Using where with pushed condition
((`world`.`Country`.`Code` like 'J%') and (`world`.`Country`.`Capital` is not null));
Using MRR
*************************** 2. row ***************************
           id: 1
  select_type: SIMPLE
        table: City
   partitions: p0,p1,p2,p3
         type: eq_ref
possible_keys: PRIMARY
          key: PRIMARY
      key_len: 4
          ref: world.Country.Capital
         rows: 1
     filtered: 100.00
        Extra: Child of 'Country' in pushed join@1
2 rows in set, 1 warning (0.01 sec)
```

At most one hash index can be created for each table internally. If a table doesn't have an explicit primary key, the NDBCluster storage engine automatically creates a hidden primary key defined as BIGINT UNSIGNED NOT NULL AUTO_INCREMENT PRIMARY KEY USING HASH. So, every table has a primary key whether it's explicit or not. So, the cluster as a whole can at most have MaxNoOfTables hash indexes.

It is highly recommended to have an explicit primary key, because the hidden one is created if it's not explicitly defined. Hidden primary keys cannot be accessed using SQL. If a primary key is not defined explicitly, a table is scanned on the slave SQL node in an NDB Cluster Replication setup.

Hash indexes are stored in IndexMemory, and they are the only objects stored in IndexMemory. They consume 21 to 25 bytes per row for hash value and pointer to the row. Consumption of IndexMemory is quite small.

Ordered Index

As the name suggests, an ordered index is an index that has all the index rows sorted in the order of key values. An ordered index can be used just like usual B+tree index. It can be used for:

- **Equality comparison (=):** Comparing a value to a key using equals sign.

- **Inequality comparison (!=, <>):** Not equal.

- **Range scan (<, <=, >, >=, and combination of these):** Less than, less than or equal, greater than, greater than or equal, or between.

- **Full index scan:** This execution plan is chosen when there is no condition to filter rows using this index, but the query can be solved by accessing only columns included in the index.

- **Sorting:** Sort can be solved by reading rows in index order.

Note that an ordered index is local to the partition. This means that an ordered index cannot search rows in other partitions, thus it cannot search rows in other node groups. Recall that rows on NDBCluster tables are partitioned horizontally. See Chapter 2 for more information about partition balancing. This makes equality comparison using ordered index more expensive than a primary key lookup in default partition balancing.

Figure 18-2 shows a conceptual flow of an ordered index scan. *TC* in Figure 18-2 stands for *transaction coordinator*, which is selected at the beginning of each transaction. Note that all data nodes must be accessed to find rows that match the specified key value or value range when using default partition balancing, because all partitions may have rows that match the given key value or value range.

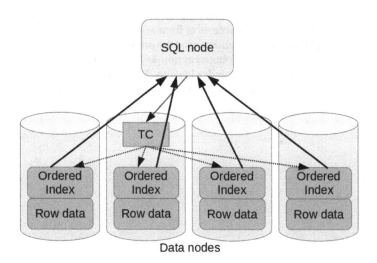

Figure 18-2. Ordered index scan process flow

There are two exceptions to this scenario:

- **User-defined partitioning:** The table is partitioned by user-defined partitioning and equality comparison against partition key is included in the search criteria. In this case, only partitions that have the given partition key value are searched.

- **Fully-replicated table:** The table is a fully-replicated table, whereby all data nodes have an identical whole copy of the table. In this case, ordered index lookup can be solved by accessing an arbitrary data node.

A lookup using an ordered index has more overhead than a primary key lookup in general. So it will not be as quick as a primary key lookup in average. The overhead of a lookup increases in proportion to the number of data nodes, and the overhead may have more impact if size of query result is small. On the other hand, if the query result is big, many rows are matched against the given range. In other words, an ordered index scan is very efficient because all data nodes are searched in parallel. In such cases, a range scan using ordered index will be faster if there are more data nodes in the cluster.

Note that ordered index is stored on `DataMemory`, *not* `IndexMemory`, even though it's an index. This is a mistake many people make. Only hash indexes are stored in `IndexMemory` on MySQL NDB Cluster. Each index row in an ordered index consumes 10 bytes. It is possible to create up to `MaxNoOfOrderedIndexes` ordered indexes.

Unique Hash Index for Secondary Index

Hash indexes have similar but different structures when they are used for secondary indexes. The only object that can ensure uniqueness of key values in MySQL NDB Cluster is a hash index. However, a hash index can essentially be an implementation of the primary key itself. How does MySQL NDB Cluster ensures uniqueness of key values on secondary indexes?

■ **Note** If a table doesn't have an explicit primary key, but has unique keys, the first defined non-nullable unique key is chosen as a primary key of the table.

The answer is that MySQL NDB Cluster creates an internal hidden *support table* to ensure uniqueness of secondary unique key values. The support table is not directly accessible from SQL nodes. The support table is defined so that columns in the unique index of the main table consist the primary key of the support table, and columns of the primary key values of the main table are stored as non-key column in the support table. Figure 18-3 depicts the conceptual flow of secondary unique index lookups. The support table is accessed first and the primary key value is retrieved. Then, the actual row data is retrieved by looking up the retrieved primary key value.

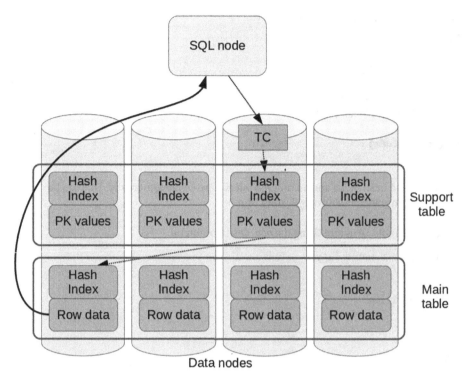

Figure 18-3. *A unique key lookup using the secondary hash index*

A unique index lookup is more efficient than an ordered index lookup, because the ordered index on all data nodes must be accessed unless the partition distribution is changed from the default. Of course, a secondary unique index lookup is slower than a primary key lookup, because it requires accessing two tables to solve the query. In addition, the secondary unique index lookup may require an extra network hop.

In general, secondary indexes and primary keys have irrelevant values even if the secondary index is defined as a unique index. So, the target row might be stored on a different data node than the data node where the unique index row is stored, because they should have different hash values. Of course, the query will be quick if the secondary unique index row and the target row are stored on a same data node. Otherwise, unique index lookup requires one extra network hop to complete, which is slower than the former case. The probability that they are stored in the same data node decreases in inverse proportion to the number of data nodes.

Note that updating rows on support table consumes operation records. So, MaxNoOfConcurrentOperations may have to be increased when using a secondary hash index.

A secondary hash index consumes both IndexMemory and DataMemory, because the support table has its own hash index and non-key columns representing primary key column values of the main table. It is possible to create up to MaxNoOfUniqueHashIndexes secondary hash indexes.

Defining Indexes

It is important to understand how to use the three types of indexes properly. The most significant point is that two indexes are created internally for the PRIMARY KEY and the UNIQUE secondary by default. This is because the hash index cannot be used for any operations except for the equality comparison. In general, indexes are also used for other purposes such as range scans and sorting. Listing 18-3 shows an example CREATE TABLE statement that defines a table with an explicit primary key.

Listing 18-3. Defining a Table with an Explicit Primary Key

```
CREATE TABLE City (
  ID int(11) NOT NULL AUTO_INCREMENT,
  Name char(35) NOT NULL DEFAULT '',
  CountryCode char(3) NOT NULL DEFAULT '',
  District char(20) NOT NULL DEFAULT '',
  Population int(11) NOT NULL DEFAULT '0',
  PRIMARY KEY (ID),
  KEY CountryCode (CountryCode)
) ENGINE=NDBCluster;
```

In this case, two indexes—a hash index and an ordered index—are created internally. This can be confirmed by the ndb_desc command, as shown in Listing 18-4.

Listing 18-4. Showing Actual Table Structure Using the ndb_desc Command

```
shell$ ndb_desc -c mgmhost -d world City
-- City --
Version: 16777217
Fragment type: HashMapPartition
K Value: 6
Min load factor: 78
Max load factor: 80
Temporary table: no
Number of attributes: 5
Number of primary keys: 1
Length of frm data: 338
Max Rows: 0
Row Checksum: 1
Row GCI: 1
SingleUserMode: 0
ForceVarPart: 1
PartitionCount: 4
FragmentCount: 4
PartitionBalance: FOR_RP_BY_LDM
ExtraRowGciBits: 0
ExtraRowAuthorBits: 0
TableStatus: Retrieved
Table options:
HashMap: DEFAULT-HASHMAP-3840-4
-- Attributes --
ID Int PRIMARY KEY DISTRIBUTION KEY AT=FIXED ST=MEMORY AUTO_INCR
Name Char(35;latin1_swedish_ci) NOT NULL AT=FIXED ST=MEMORY DEFAULT ""
CountryCode Char(3;latin1_swedish_ci) NOT NULL AT=FIXED ST=MEMORY DEFAULT ""
District Char(20;latin1_swedish_ci) NOT NULL AT=FIXED ST=MEMORY DEFAULT ""
Population Int NOT NULL AT=FIXED ST=MEMORY DEFAULT 0
-- Indexes --
PRIMARY KEY(ID) - UniqueHashIndex
PRIMARY(ID) - OrderedIndex
CountryCode(CountryCode) - OrderedIndex

NDBT_ProgramExit: 0 - OK
```

Find that there are two indexes—PRIMARY KEY and PRIMARY—in the output of the ndb_desc command in Listing 18-4. The former is the hash index, the latter is the ordered index. Note that the hash index is printed as UniqueHashIndex. If the query is an equality comparison, the hash index is used. Otherwise, the ordered index is used. If the application requires equality comparisons only on the given table, you can prevent the ordered index from being created by specifying the USING HASH keyword in the DDL, as shown in Listing 18-5.

Listing 18-5. Creating a Table Without an Ordered Index in the Primary Key

```
CREATE TABLE City (
  ID int(11) NOT NULL AUTO_INCREMENT,
  Name char(35) NOT NULL DEFAULT '',
  CountryCode char(3) NOT NULL DEFAULT '',
  District char(20) NOT NULL DEFAULT '',
  Population int(11) NOT NULL DEFAULT '0',
  PRIMARY KEY (ID) USING HASH,
  KEY CountryCode (CountryCode)
) ENGINE=NDBCluster;
```

Note that the USING HASH keyword is included in the primary key definition. When the table is created by this statement, the index part of the ndb_desc command looks like following listing.

```
-- Indexes --
PRIMARY KEY(ID) - UniqueHashIndex
CountryCode(CountryCode) - OrderedIndex
```

I recommend initially creating tables with the USING HASH keyword for the primary key, because the equality comparison is the most used operation for the primary key. It is worth saving memory for the ordered index, because memory is not free. If you later find your application actually requiring an ordered index, you can add the ordered index as a secondary index online at any time. Functionality of ordered indexes doesn't change whether they are a part of primary key or an independent secondary index.

Just like the primary key, both hash index and ordered index are created for the secondary UNIQUE index underneath. If you don't need an ordered index, you can skip it with USING HASH keyword in the same way as with the primary key. Hash index is a support table, but it's printed as UniqueHashIndex just like the primary key. You need to identify if it's a primary key or not by checking the index name. Listing 18-6 shows an example of the ndb_desc command output for a table that has a primary key and one unique secondary index. Note that the table in Listing 18-6, Country, isn't what is shown in previous examples in this chapter, because the City table didn't have a suitable set of columns for a secondary unique index.

Listing 18-6. Index Structure of a Table with one Secondary Unique Index

```
shell$ ndb_desc -c mgmhost -d world Country
-- Country -
... snip ...
-- Indexes --
PRIMARY KEY(Code) - UniqueHashIndex
PRIMARY(Code) - OrderedIndex
Name(Name) - OrderedIndex
Name$unique(Name) - UniqueHashIndex

NDBT_ProgramExit: 0 - OK
```

If you want to create a non-unique secondary index, just create it as usual.

```
ALTER TABLE City ADD INDEX (Name);
```

Adding indexes is an in-place (online) operation for MySQL NDB Cluster. Refer to Chapter 9 for more details about online schema changes.

Table 18-1 lists the combinations of index types for the NDBCluster storage engine. Keep in mind that you need to pick one index type. To pick an appropriate index type, you must understand the characteristics of each index type and your application needs.

Table 18-1. *Possible Combinations of Index Types*

Index Type	Operation	Storage	Data Size Per Row
PRIMARY KEY	Various	IndexMemory + DataMemory	21 to 25 bytes in IndexMemory 10 bytes in DataMemory
PRIMARY KEY with USING HASH	Equality comparisons	IndexMemory	21 to 25 bytes in IndexMemory
UNIQUE	Various	IndexMemory + DataMemory	21 to 25 bytes in IndexMemory size of primary key value of main table + 10 bytes in DataMemory
UNIQUE with USING HASH	Equality comparisons	IndexMemory + DataMemory	21 to 25 bytes in IndexMemory size of primary key value of main table in DataMemory
Non-unique secondary index	Various	DataMemory	10 bytes in DataMemory

The T-Tree Index

The structure of an ordered index in MySQL NDB Cluster is not a B+tree index, which is widely used on relational database systems (and in MySQL in particular). MySQL NDB Cluster employs T-tree index instead. T-tree can be used just like B+tree index, however, its structure is different from a B+tree index. Figure 18-4 depicts the conceptual view of several nodes in a T-tree index. The term "node" here indicates a unit of data consisting the tree, not nodes in the cluster. Be aware that the shape of each node in the figure looks like the letter T. The name of T-tree index is named after the shape of a node. Of course, you could draw the same thing differently. The shape of a node in the original paper of T-tree index looks like the letter T.

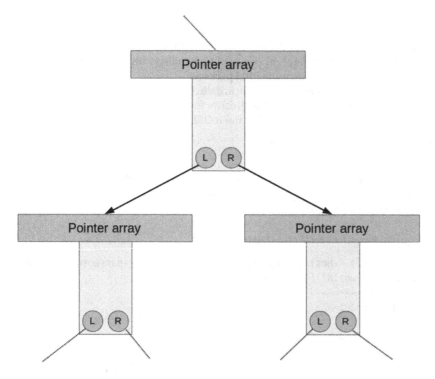

Figure 18-4. *Overview of the T-tree structure*

The T-tree index is optimized for in-memory database systems. Unlike the B+tree index, the T-tree index itself doesn't have index data. It has pointers to the data instead. Storing pointers is sufficient for the T-tree index used for in-memory database system, because key values always exist on memory. T-tree can also save CPU resources because it requires less comparison when searching, inserting, or deleting rows on the index.

Each node has an array of pointers to the row data in a sorted state. L is a pointer to a subtree where all values are smaller than all values in this node. R value is a pointer to a subtree where all values are larger than all values in this node.

Search starts from the root node of the tree. When searching a node, firstly it checks if the key value is included in the range of the array in the current node. If the given key value is included in the range of the current node, the node is called a bounding node. If the row is found in the bounding node, the row is returned. Otherwise, the search fails. If the given key value is smaller than all values in the current node, the left subtree is searched in the same manner. Likewise, if the given key value is larger, the right subtree is searched.

Estimating Table Size

When you design a table on MySQL NDB Cluster, you may want to know how much memory or disk is consumed per row, because capacity is an important topic for database systems. There are two options available; one is ndb_size.pl, which is bundled in the official package, the other is sizer, which is developed by a third party.

The ndb_size.pl Command

If you don't care about details too much, ndb_size.pl command is a good choice, because data size for each data type has not changed drastically and the ndb_size.pl command is bundled with MySQL NDB Cluster package. It is included in the client package if you are using RPM packages.

To use the ndb_size.pl command, Perl interpreter must be installed onto your system, because it is written in Perl. In addition, *MethodMaker*, *Perl DBI*, and MySQL driver for Perl (*DBD::mysql*) are required to use this command. Refer to the following page for information about *DBD::mysql*.

http://search.cpan.org/dist/DBD-mysql/lib/DBD/mysql.pm

The ndb_size.pl command calculates the required resources for existing non-NDB tables when the storage engine for the given tables is NDBCluster. The storage engine for the existing tables is arbitrary. To calculate the required resources, create the tables using another storage engines such as InnoDB, then run the ndb_size.pl command, as shown in Listing 18-7.

Listing 18-7. Calculating Required Resources for World Database

```
shell$ ndb_size.pl --database=world --hostname=sqlnode1 --user=msandbox --password=msandbox
ndb_size.pl report for database: 'world' (3 tables)
-----------------------------------------------------
Connected to: DBI:mysql:host=sqlnode1

Including information for versions: 4.1, 5.0, 5.1

world.Country
-------------

DataMemory for Columns (* means varsized DataMemory):
... snip ...
Parameter Minimum Requirements
------------------------------
* indicates greater than default
```

Parameter	Default	4.1	5.0	5.1
NoOfOrderedIndexes	128	6	6	6
IndexMemory (KB)	18432	368	176	176
NoOfTriggers	768	39	39	39
NoOfUniqueHashIndexes	64	3	3	3
DataMemory (KB)	81920	672	672	736
NoOfTables	128	6	6	6
NoOfAttributes	1000	32	32	32

The ndb_size.pl command prints the resource consumption for each table. (Output for each table is omitted in Listing 18-10.) Then, it prints a summary of required resources at the end. As you can see, the version numbers printed there (such as 4.1, 5.0, and 5.1) are outdated. However, you can still use this command as an estimation for resource consumption because there's not a huge difference in the latest version.

The sizer Command

If you want to estimate the data size based on the version you are using, sizer is a good option. It is an NDB API application developed by severalnines. The sizer command is shipped with a simple *Makefile* as a source code. You can get the source code from GitHub. To build a sizer command, you need the libraries (*libmysqlclient_r.so* and *libndbclient.so*) and the relevant header files. Set the MYSQL_BASEDIR variable for the *Makefile* to point to the directory where the libraries and header files are installed. The default value for the MYSQL_BASEDIR variable is /usr, which is suitable for OS native package installation such as RPM. If you installed the package to another directory such as */usr/local/mysql-cluster*, then run the make command as described in the following command example. The binary is created under the source top directory. Move it to any directory if you like.

```
shell$ git clone https://github.com/severalnines/sizer.git
shell$ cd sizer
shell$ make MYSQL_BASEDIR=/usr/local/mysql-cluster
```

The use of sizer is similar to ndb_size.pl, but it connects to the management node and data nodes as in Listing 18-8; it doesn't connect to an SQL node like ndb_size.pl. You need to install MySQL NDB Cluster and populate the tables with sample data before executing the sizer command.

Listing 18-8. The sizer Command Example

```
shell$ export LD_LIBRARY_PATH=/usr/local/mysql-cluster
shell$ sizer -c mgmhost -d world
... snip ...
Record size (incl OH):
        #Rows found=239 records
        #OrderedIndexes=2
        #UniqueHashIndexes=2
        #blob/text=0
        #attributes=15
        DataMemory=440 bytes
        IndexMemory=40 bytes
        Diskspace=0 bytes

Appending the following to world.csv
world,Country,239,1,2,2,0,15,40,440,0,0,0
```

The sizer command generates a CSV file with a filename like *database_name.csv*. Each column indicates following data (data in parentheses indicates the example value for world.Country table in the example of Listing 18-8.):

- Database name (world)
- Table name (Country)
- Number of rows in the table (239)
- Number of table objects (always 1)
- Number of ordered indexes in the table (2)
- Number of unique hash index, including primary and secondary (2)
- Number of BLOB/TEXT columns (0)
- Number of attributes (15)
- Size of consumed IndexMemory per row (40)
- Size of consumed DataMemmory per row (440)

- Size of consumed disk space for disk tables (0)
- If variable length column is used in this table (0)
- If variable length column is used in the support table of secondary unique hash index (0)

Refer to the following page for more information about `sizer`: *https://github.com/severalnines/sizer*.

Estimating Required Objects per Table

It is also important to estimate the number of required objects for every table, because the number of objects is manually defined by user in the configuration file (*config.ini*). If you have the table definitions, the `ndb_size.pl` command does the job for you. Review Listing 18-7 in the previous section for example outputs of these commands. Note that the `sizer` command just displays the number of columns instead of consumed attributes.

If you have not completed designing your table yet, you can estimate the number of required attributes using the table in the following list:

- **Non-BLOB column:** 1
- **BLOB (TEXT) column:** 5
- **Hash index in the primary key:** 0
- **Secondary unique hash index:** 1 + number of columns consisting the index
- **Ordered index:** 1 + number of columns consisting the index

For example, the number of attributes for the `world.Country` table is calculated as:

- **Non-BLOB column:** 1 * 15 = 15
- **BLOB (TEXT) column:** 5 * 0 = 0
- **Hash index in the primary key:** 0 * 1 = 0
- **Secondary unique hash index:** (1 + 0) * 0 = 0
- **Ordered index:** 1 + 1 (for primary key if not specifying USING HASH) = 2
- **Total:** 17

Defining Foreign Key Constraints

As of MySQL NDB Cluster 7.3, foreign keys are supported. You can use foreign keys to keep tje integrity of reference relationship between two tables by specifying a set of referencing columns on a child table and a set of referenced columns on a parent table. Any inserts or updates to the child table are rejected if there are no matching rows on the parent table. It is also possible to define actions when rows are updated or deleted on the parent table.

The following list shows a typical definition of a foreign key with actions upon update and delete:

```
mysql> ALTER TABLE Country ADD CONSTRAINT fk_capital FOREIGN KEY (Capital) REFERENCES
City(ID) ON UPDATE SET NULL ON DELETE SET NULL;
Query OK, 0 rows affected (2.74 sec)
Records: 0  Duplicates: 0  Warnings: 0
```

A foreign key constraint is checked on the data node every time a row is inserted, updated, or deleted on the child or parent table. To define a foreign key on a child table, the referenced column or set of columns on a parent table must be a set of columns that constitutes a primary key or secondary unique index. Every referenced column must have identical data type to referencing column. For example, you cannot define a foreign key that references the BIGINT column from an INT column. Referencing columns must be listed in the same order of definition as the referenced primary key or secondary unique index. These requirements are a little bit stricter than InnoDB. Referenced columns must be indexed, but not necessarily be unique on InnoDB. Referenced columns and referencing columns must have similar data types, but not necessarily be identical.

Table 18-2 lists actions for the ON UPDATE and ON DELETE clauses supported by the SQL standard and its status in MySQL NDB Cluster.

Table 18-2. Actions for Modifications on Parent Table of Foreign Key Constraint

Action	Supported on NDBCluster	Description
RESTRICT	Yes	Rejects update or delete on a parent table if matching rows exist on a child table. If this action is specified, you must modify the child table first so that no rows reference the rows to be updated or deleted on the parent table.
CASCADE	Limited	Updates or deletes on the parent table are propagated to matching rows on the child table. MySQL NDB Cluster doesn't support the CASCADE action for ON UPDATE if the referenced set of columns is a primary key of a parent table.
SET NULL	Yes	Referencing columns for matching rows on the child table are set to NULL upon update or delete of rows on the parent table.
NO ACTION	Same as RESTRICT	On MySQL Server and MySQL NDB Cluster, it is defined the same as RESTRICT. Some database systems implement NO ACTION as a deferred check, but MySQL doesn't support it.
SET DEFAULT	No	Setting a default value upon update or delete of rows on the parent table. MySQL doesn't support this action.

Reviewing Table Definition

You can review the definition of a table in various ways. Specifically, the SHOW CREATE TABLE statement, just like usual tables on MySQL Server, the ndb_desc command, and ndbinfo tables are all useful to review the table definition precisely. Listing 18-9 shows an example of the SHOW CREATE TABLE command output.

Listing 18-9. Example of the SHOW CREATE TABLE Command Output

```
mysql> SHOW CREATE TABLE City\G
*************************** 1. row ***************************
       Table: City
Create Table: CREATE TABLE `City` (
  `ID` int(11) NOT NULL AUTO_INCREMENT,
  `Name` char(35) NOT NULL DEFAULT '',
  `CountryCode` char(3) NOT NULL DEFAULT '',
  `District` char(20) NOT NULL DEFAULT '',
```

```
  `Population` int(11) NOT NULL DEFAULT '0',
  PRIMARY KEY (`ID`),
  KEY `CountryCode` (`CountryCode`),
  CONSTRAINT `fk_countrycode` FOREIGN KEY (`CountryCode`) REFERENCES `Country` (`Code`) ON
DELETE SET NULL ON UPDATE SET NULL
) ENGINE=ndbcluster AUTO_INCREMENT=4080 DEFAULT CHARSET=latin1
1 row in set (0.00 sec)
```

The SHOW CREATE TABLE command is useful in the sense that the value of the Create Table field can be reused as an executable SQL command. You can modify the SQL command printed by SHOW CREATE TABLE and create a similar table.

The ndb_desc command is a dedicated tool for MySQL NDB Cluster. It prints a table definition with some extra information specific to MySQL NDB Cluster. Listing 18-10 shows an example of ndb_desc command output for the same table as Listing 18-9.

Listing 18-10. Example of ndb_desc Command Output

```
shell$ ndb_desc -c mgmhost -d world City
-- City --
Version: 67108865
Fragment type: HashMapPartition
K Value: 6
Min load factor: 78
Max load factor: 80
Temporary table: no
Number of attributes: 5
Number of primary keys: 1
Length of frm data: 338
Max Rows: 0
Row Checksum: 1
Row GCI: 1
SingleUserMode: 0
ForceVarPart: 1
PartitionCount: 4
FragmentCount: 4
PartitionBalance: FOR_RP_BY_LDM
ExtraRowGciBits: 0
ExtraRowAuthorBits: 0
TableStatus: Retrieved
Table options:
HashMap: DEFAULT-HASHMAP-3840-4
-- Attributes --
ID Int PRIMARY KEY DISTRIBUTION KEY AT=FIXED ST=MEMORY AUTO_INCR
Name Char(35;latin1_swedish_ci) NOT NULL AT=FIXED ST=MEMORY DEFAULT ""
CountryCode Char(3;latin1_swedish_ci) NOT NULL AT=FIXED ST=MEMORY DEFAULT ""
District Char(20;latin1_swedish_ci) NOT NULL AT=FIXED ST=MEMORY DEFAULT ""
Population Int NOT NULL AT=FIXED ST=MEMORY DEFAULT 0
```

```
-- Indexes --
PRIMARY KEY(ID) - UniqueHashIndex
PRIMARY(ID) - OrderedIndex
CountryCode(CountryCode) - OrderedIndex
-- ForeignKeys --
27/24/fk_countrycode CountryCode (CountryCode) REFERENCES world.Country/PRIMARY KEY () on
update set null on delete set null

NDBT_ProgramExit: 0 - OK
```

The ndb_desc command is useful when you want to review the internal structure of a table such as partitioning definitions and number of extra bits, which is not printed in SHOW CREATE TABLE.

As of the MySQL NDB Cluster 7.5 series, various useful tables to retrieve metadata and status of tables are added on ndbinfo database. Especially, table_fragments, table_info, and table_replicas are useful for the table metadata and status. These table don't have any columns to directly identify table names. You need to refer to the dict_obj_info table to identify table identifiers from table names. Listing 18-11 shows an example query to retrieve table metadata from the ndbinfo.table_info table.

Listing 18-11. Retrieving Table Metadata from the ndbinfo.table_info Table

```
mysql> SELECT * FROM dict_obj_info d JOIN table_info t ON d.id = t.table_id  WHERE fq_name
LIKE 'world/def/City'\G
*************************** 1. row ***************************
                  type: 2
                    id: 24
               version: 67108865
                 state: 4
       parent_obj_type: 0
         parent_obj_id: 0
               fq_name: world/def/City
              table_id: 24
          logged_table: 1
     row_contains_gci: 1
row_contains_checksum: 1
           read_backup: 0
      fully_replicated: 0
          storage_type: MEMORY
            hashmap_id: 1
     partition_balance: FOR_RP_BY_LDM
            create_gci: 0
1 row in set (0.02 sec)
```

See Chapter 16 for more details about the ndbinfo database.

You can also use other tools to review the table definitions just like you do on standard MySQL Server, such as DESC, EXPLAIN, SHOW FULL FIELDS, and the Information Schema. Listing 18-12 shows an example output of the DESC command for the world.City table.

Listing 18-12. DESC Command Output for `world.City` Table

```
mysql> DESC City;
+-------------+----------+------+-----+---------+----------------+
| Field       | Type     | Null | Key | Default | Extra          |
+-------------+----------+------+-----+---------+----------------+
| ID          | int(11)  | NO   | PRI | NULL    | auto_increment |
| Name        | char(35) | NO   |     |         |                |
| CountryCode | char(3)  | NO   | MUL |         |                |
| District    | char(20) | NO   |     |         |                |
| Population  | int(11)  | NO   |     | 0       |                |
+-------------+----------+------+-----+---------+----------------+
5 rows in set (0.00 sec)
```

Disk Data Tables

MySQL NDB Cluster supports disk data tables (or disk based tables) as an option to use less expensive storage medium for big storage size with a reasonable performance penalty. It has been supported as of MySQL NDB Cluster 6.2 series.

I strongly recommend using SSD when you employ disk data tables. In the past when SSD was not available, disk data tables were very slow because the storage medium was a *hard disk drive* (HDD). It takes a very long time to move the header and seek the target sector on HDD, because it's mechanically controlled. So, disk data tables can be used only for very specific purposes such as archiving. In these days, we can choose *solid state drive* (SSD) with reasonable costs in the sense that it is cheaper than RAM. It doesn't have mechanical components, thus has much better read/write performance in both response and throughput. In addition, SSD products with very fast interface such as *PCIe* and *NVMe* are available on the market recently. With such fast SSDs, disk data tables are a realistic choice for general use with little performance penalty.

Disk Data Tables Architecture

Since disk data tables are stored differently, the way tables are updated is different from in-memory tables. Figure 18-5 depicts the conceptual flow when writing to disk data tables.

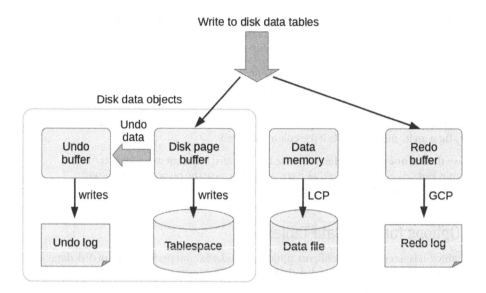

Figure 18-5. *Overview of disk data table architecture: write transactions*

When writing to disk data tables, all modification is done on a *disk page buffer* just like all modifications on InnoDB tables are done in the InnoDB buffer pool. Old row values are copied to the undo log in order to be used for rollback; old rows values are restored from *undo log* upon rollback and crash recovery. Redo logging is still required for disk data tables, because the redo log is used for crash recovery and micro-GCP is required for replication even if the modified tables are disk data tables.

When crash recovery is performed on the disk data tables, the state of the tablespace is reverted to the time when the latest LCP was performed so that tablespace for the disk data tables and the data memory for in-memory tables are synchronized. Then, you apply the redo logs together with in-memory tables. This means that sufficient redo log space is still needed for disk data tables. To synchronize tablespace and LCP, all changes done before the LCP must be flushed to disk before the next LCP.

Known Limitations for Disk Data Tables

When using disk data tables, you must keep in mind the following limitations to prevent problems. Major limitations for disk data tables are:

- **It is not possible to store indexes and indexed columns on disk:** The complete disk data table is not supported in MySQL NDB Cluster yet. The primary key columns are stored in memory even for disk data tables.

- **Disk data tables don't improve data durability:** Durability is assured by checkpointing in MySQL NDB Cluster. To recover the latest data, the redo log is required anyway.

- **A large buffer is required to improve performance of disk data tables:** The larger the disk page buffer that is allocated, the faster table access is. To allocate large memory to a disk page buffer, it is necessary to reduce the data memory instead. A disk data table is slower than an in-memory table even if ample disk page buffer is allocated and fast SSD is employed.

- **Space efficiency is not optimal:** More space is required when using disk data tables than when using in-memory tables. Since the required storage medium is disk, not memory, it may be possible to store much larger data if the system has a lot of disk space.

- **Space reusability is not optimal:** It is not possible to reclaim disk area using OPTIMIZE TABLE. Once the disk space is allocated to a table, the space will not be deallocated until the table is dropped.

- **Each column in a disk data table requires an 8-byte pointer:** It consumes more memory than an in-memory table if the column is small.

- **Response time is not predictable:** Response time against an in-memory table is predictable. But this is not true for disk data tables, because the response time largely differs whether the target data is cached on memory or not.

Configuration Options for Disk Data Tables

As in other types of tables, it is necessary to configure options to make exhibit performance of disk data tables. In this section, we discuss the options for disk data tables to be adjusted. Refer to Chapter 4 for more information about configuration options.

- **DiskPageBufferMemory:** This option determines how much memory is allocated to the disk page buffer. The larger the buffer is, the more it can save disk I/O. Allocate as much memory as possible when you need better performance on disk data tables. The default is 64MB.

- **SharedGlobalMemory:** This option is not dedicated to disk data tables, but the undo log buffer is allocated from this memory. The maximum size of the undo log buffer is 600MB per data node. The default is 128MB.

- **DiskIOThreadPool:** This option specifies the number of IO threads for disk data tables. If fast SSDs are employed, or multiple disks are used to spread IO among them, you should consider increasing threads. The default is 2.

- **FileSystemPathDD, FileSystemPathDataFiles, FileSystemPathUndoFiles:** These options specify directories where disk data objects are stored. FileSystemPathDD is the default value for the two others, when they are not specified. FileSystemPathDataFiles specifies a directory for tablespace data files. FileSystemPathUndoFiles specifies a directory for undo logs. These options are required when multiple disks per data node host are employed to spread the IO load. The default value for FileSystemPathDD is FileSystemPath.

- **InitialLogFileGroup, InitialTablespace:** When these options are specified upon initial system restart, undo logs and tablespace are created. Otherwise, these disk data objects must be created manually, as described in the next section. These options do not have default values.

Preparing the Logfile Group

To use disk data tables, you must create the disk data objects in advance. The required objects are logfile group (undo log) and tablespace (data file).

The logfile group is created using the CREATE LOGFILE GROUP command from an arbitrary SQL node. The following listing shows an example command to create the logfile group. Currently, it is possible to create only one logfile group per cluster.

```
mysql> CREATE LOGFILE GROUP lg1 ADD UNDOFILE 'undo1.log' INITIAL_SIZE = 10G UNDO_BUFFER
_SIZE = 600M ENGINE NDB;
Query OK, 0 rows affected (35 min 17.13 sec)
```

This command takes quite a long time to complete, because the undo logfile must be initialized. Each clause in the CREATE LOGFILE GROUP command has the following meanings:

- **ADD UNDOFILE 'filename':** This clause adds an undo logfile to the logfile group. With the CREATE LOGFILE GROUP command, only one undo log file can be specified and an undo log file is mandatory.

- **INITIAL_SIZE = size:** This clause specifies the size of the undo log file. As the name implies, it's not only an initial size, but also the size throughout the lifecycle of the undo log file. It cannot be changed later. If you find that the undo log is too small, you can add more undo log files later using the ALTER LOGFILE GROUP command. This clause can be omitted. The default size for the undo file is 128MB.

- **UNDO_BUFFER_SIZE = size:** This clause specifies the size of the undo buffer, a buffer to store undo data temporarily before writing it to the undo log files. Larger undo buffers may improve writing performance. Be careful because the buffer size cannot be changed later. The maximum size for the undo log buffer is 600MB. This clause can be omitted. The default value for the undo buffer is 8MB.

Note that the default sizes for the undo log file and undo buffer are too small in most cases. If you use disk data tables under a high volume of load, the sizes must be increased properly. Since the undo buffer size cannot be changed later, be very careful when determining the size. It is highly recommended to do benchmarks on test systems before creating the logfile group in the production systems.

The undo log file size can be estimated just like the redo log. The undo log is used to revert data in a tablespace back to the time when the latest LCP completed. To revert back to the latest LCP, undo log entries must be kept until the next LCP completes. Thus, you can calculate the theoretical maximum size of the undo log entries using this formula:

```
time_taken_to_complete_lcp * io_speed_of_undo_logging
```

This formula is identical to what is used to calculate the redo log size. See Chapter 4 for more information about redo log size estimation.

Preparing Tablespace

Once you have created a logfile group, it's time to create the tablespace to store disk data tables using the CREATE TABLESPACE command. The following command output shows an example command that creates a tablespace. Note that the logfile group must be created before the tablespace, because each tablespace is linked to a certain logfile group. Unlike the logfile group, it is possible to create multiple tablespaces in one cluster.

```
mysql> CREATE TABLESPACE ts1 ADD DATAFILE 'ts1-1.dat' USE LOGFILE GROUP lg1 EXTENT_SIZE =
256K INITIAL_SIZE = 8G ENGINE NDB;
Query OK, 0 rows affected (33 min 6.03 sec)
```

Each clause in the CREATE TABLESPACE command has the following meanings:

- **ADD DATAFILE 'filename':** This clause adds a data file to the tablespace to be created. This clause cannot be omitted, and only one data file can be added in the CREATE TABLESPACE command.

- **USE LOGFILE GROUP lg_name:** This clause specifies the associated logfile group for this tablespace.

- **EXTENT_SIZE = size:** This clause specifies the size of an extent, the allocation unit for each disk data table partition. The minimum size is 32KB, the maximum size is 2G. This clause can be omitted. The default value is 1MB. Be cautious because an extent that's too big will reduce the number of extents within a data file, because extent is an allocation unit that cannot be shared among multiple tables. An extent that's too big results in inefficient disk space utilization. The default is fine in most cases. Do not set it to too small or too large.

- **INITIAL_SIZE = size:** This clause specifies the size of data file. Just like with the undo log file, it is not possible to change file size. If you find that the tablespace is too small, you need to add a data file using the ALTER TABLESPACE command.

You need to be careful about the extent size and data file size. Each data file can have up to 64K extents. The recommended maximum extents per data file is 32K. So, you can create up to a 32GB data file with the default extent size. In Listing 18-18, the extent size is set to 256KB, which is four times smaller than the default, and the size of the data file is set to 8GB, which is four times smaller than the maximum size with 32KB extents.

If you need a larger tablespace, add more data files or enlarge the extent. Alternatively, you can create more than one tablespace.

Creating Disk Data Tables

To create disk data tables, you must specify the STORAGE DISK clause and the TABLESPACE clause in the CREATE TABLE statement. Listing 18-13 shows an example command that creates a disk data table.

Listing 18-13. Creating a Disk Data Table

```
mysql> CREATE TABLE ddCity (
    ->   ID int(11) NOT NULL AUTO_INCREMENT,
    ->   Name char(35) NOT NULL DEFAULT '',
    ->   CountryCode char(3) NOT NULL DEFAULT '',
    ->   District char(20) NOT NULL DEFAULT '',
    ->   Population int(11) NOT NULL DEFAULT '0',
    ->   PRIMARY KEY (ID),
    ->   KEY CountryCode (CountryCode)
    -> ) ENGINE=NDB STORAGE DISK TABLESPACE ts1;
Query OK, 0 rows affected (5.79 sec)
```

In this example, the whole table is defined as disk data. It is also possible to store only certain columns to be stored on disk. Since it's not possible to store indexes and indexed columns on disk, they are automatically defined as in-memory data. You can review which storage is actually used for each column with the ndb_desc command. The following command output is an excerpt from the ndb_desc command output for the ddCity table in Listing 18-13.

```
-- Attributes --
ID Int PRIMARY KEY DISTRIBUTION KEY AT=FIXED ST=MEMORY AUTO_INCR
Name Char(35;latin1_swedish_ci) NOT NULL AT=FIXED ST=DISK DEFAULT ""
CountryCode Char(3;latin1_swedish_ci) NOT NULL AT=FIXED ST=MEMORY DEFAULT ""
District Char(20;latin1_swedish_ci) NOT NULL AT=FIXED ST=DISK DEFAULT ""
Population Int NOT NULL AT=FIXED ST=DISK DEFAULT 0
```

You can see that the ID and CountryCode columns are stored in memory as ST=MEMORY is displayed. The other columns are stored on disk as ST=DISK is displayed.

It is possible to specify the storage per column. Although Population column is stored on disk, it is inefficient because it requires an 8-byte pointer on memory for four bytes of column data. Listing 18-14 shows an example CREATE TABLE statement that defines the same table as in Listing 18-13, but with storage preferences.

Listing 18-14. Defining a Table with Disk Data for Specific Columns

```
mysql> CREATE TABLE ddCity (
    ->    ID int(11) NOT NULL AUTO_INCREMENT,
    ->    Name char(35) NOT NULL DEFAULT '' STORAGE DISK,
    ->    CountryCode char(3) NOT NULL DEFAULT '',
    ->    District char(20) NOT NULL DEFAULT '' STORAGE DISK,
    ->    Population int(11) NOT NULL DEFAULT '0',
    ->    PRIMARY KEY (ID),
    ->    KEY CountryCode (CountryCode)
    -> ) ENGINE=NDB TABLESPACE ts1;
Query OK, 0 rows affected (1.35 sec)
```

As you can see, STORAGE DISK is not specified on the last line of the table definition. Instead, STORAGE DISK is specified in the column definitions. This causes only the specified columns to be stored on disk. You can confirm this point by using the ndb_desc command like in the following command output, which is an excerpt from the ndb_desc output.

```
-- Attributes --
ID Int PRIMARY KEY DISTRIBUTION KEY AT=FIXED ST=MEMORY AUTO_INCR
Name Char(35;latin1_swedish_ci) NOT NULL AT=FIXED ST=DISK DEFAULT ""
CountryCode Char(3;latin1_swedish_ci) NOT NULL AT=FIXED ST=MEMORY DEFAULT ""
District Char(20;latin1_swedish_ci) NOT NULL AT=FIXED ST=DISK DEFAULT ""
Population Int NOT NULL AT=FIXED ST=MEMORY DEFAULT 0
```

You can see that the ID, CountryCode, and Population columns are stored in memory. The Name and District columns are stored on disk, as specified in CREATE TABLE statement.

Monitoring Disk Data Tables

When you are using disk data tables, monitor the metadata and status for the disk data tables using the following schema and ndbinfo database information. See Chapter 16 for more information about these ndbinfo tables.

Consideration for Normalization

As a database practitioner, I insist that normalization still makes sense for MySQL NDB Cluster, because it is a relational database management system. When a table is not normalized, the tables may include duplicates. If only some part of the duplicated rows is updated by chance, it results in an anomaly, because updated rows and rows not updated will be different, even though logically they must be same.

A table that's not normalized is a result of a join of more than one table. The process of normalization is decomposing such a table into multiple tables without losing data. This eliminates potential duplicate data within a table. The original table can be reconstructed by joining those tables.

A major drawback of normalization is that more joins are needed. It was a big problem for MySQL NDB Cluster in older versions, because joins were very slow. However, recent versions of MySQL NDB Cluster have good join algorithms, pushdown joins, and batched-key-access joins, even though InnoDB still usually beats NDB. Since joins are reasonably fast in recent versions of MySQL NDB Cluster, you do not have to worry so much about joining tables.

Major Limits Regarding Table Design

Table 18-3 describes the major limits when you design tables in MySQL NDB Cluster.

Table 18-3. *Major Limits Regarding Table Design*

Item	Description of limits
Total number of database objects	You can create up to a total of 20320 database objects. This hard limit includes databases, tables, and indexes.
Total number of tables	Capped by the MaxNoOfTables setting.
Total number of indexes	Capped by the MaxNoOfOrderedIndexes and MaxNoOfUniqueHashIndexes settings.
Data size per index	3072 bytes
Number of attributes per table	512. Attribute is an element that belongs to a table, such as a column or index. See Chapter 4 for more information about attributes.
Number of columns per index	32
Supported index types	Hash index and ordered index. (Spatial index and full-text index are not supported.) Index prefix is not supported.
Indexable column types	All but for BLOB including TEXT and BIT.
Maximum row size	14000 bytes. Note that each BLOB column contributes 264 bytes to this total.
Supported partitioning type	KEY or HASH
Maximum number of partitions	Eight per node group
Total number of tablespaces for disk data tables	2^{32}
Data file per tablespace for disk data tables	2^{16}
Extents per data file for disk data tables	2^{15}
Maximum recommended data file size for disk data tables	32GB
Auto-increment column values	Values are non-monotonical between SQL nodes, because each SQL node reserves some range of values in advance.
Use as temporary table	Not supported

Accessing Data via SQL

Once the tables are ready, it's time to manipulate the data in them. Since MySQL NDB Cluster is a relational database management system, SQL is the primary method for the job, even though it has *NoSQL* style methods. In this section, we discuss how to access the database in MySQL NDB Cluster using SQL from applications.

Connecting to SQL Node

An application can connect to an SQL node just like for standard MySQL Server, although the storage engine is different. The only question for the application is which SQL node to connect to. As discussed in elsewhere in this book, MySQL NDB Cluster can have multiple SQL nodes. An application can access identical data from any SQL node. There are three typical choices to solve this problem:

- An application has multiple instances, each application instance always connects to the same SQL node. In this case, an application instance and SQL node typically reside on the same host.

- Use the load balancing facility of Connector/J for Java applications.

- Spread the load using an external load balancers.

Each method has pros and cons. Carefully choose a method suitable for your application.

One SQL Node per Application Instance

This is the most promising method. If the number of application servers is not too big, deploying one SQL node per application server instance is a good choice, because there is no extra program required for this topology. Figure 18-6 is a conceptual view of the topology where each application server connects to the SQL node within the same host. Since they reside in the same host, an application server can connect via a UNIX domain socket. A connection through a UNIX domain socket has very little overhead compared to a remote network connection, so this topology has an advantage in terms of performance as well as simplicity.

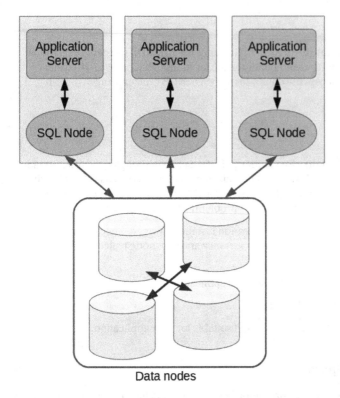

Data nodes

Figure 18-6. *Each application server connects to the SQL node that resides in the same host*

Load Balancing with Connector/J

If you are developing an application using Java, it is possible to solve this problem by just using Connector/J. Connector/J has a load balancing facility against MySQL NDB Cluster and 1:N MySQL replication setup. To enable load balancing, you simply adjust the connection parameters. There are two parameters to be adjusted, the connection URL and loadBalanceStrategy. The connection URL for load balancing has the following format:

```
jdbc:mysql:loadbalance://{comma separated list of servers}/{database name}
```

Listing 18-15 shows an example configuration of Connector/J to enable load balancing.

Listing 18-15. Setting URL and Properties for Load Balancing with Connector/J

```
Class.forName("com.mysql.jdbc.Driver");
String url = "jdbc:mysql:loadbalance://host1,host2,host3/db";
Properties props = new Properties();
props.setProperty("user", "username");
props.setProperty("password", "my password");
props.setProperty("loadBalanceStrategy", "random");
Connection conn = DriverManager.getConnection(url, props);
```

With this setup, the connections to SQL node are spread across multiple servers, as depicted in Figure 18-7.

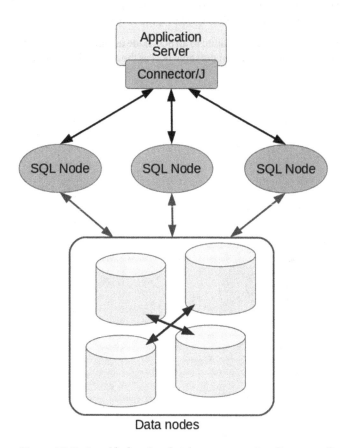

Figure 18-7. *Load balancing database access using Connector/J*

An acceptable value for `loadBalanceStrategy` is `random` or `bestResponseTime`. When `random` is set, the connection is retrieved randomly from the server list. When `bestResponseTime` is set, the driver picks the server that had the best response time in the previous transaction. The default value is `random`.

Using Load Balancers

There are many load balancers on the market. The type of load balancer is roughly categorized into following three types:

- Hardware load balancer: Load balancing is done by dedicated hardware. It looks like a network switch.

- TCP/IP level load balancer: Load balancing is done by software that can be generally used for TCP/IP connection, such as *LVS* and *HAProxy*.

- MySQL protocol load balancer: Load balancing is done by software at the MySQL protocol level. This type of load balancer can only be used by MySQL or other databases that support the MySQL protocol. (See the following descriptions for specific product names.) In this book, only this one is discussed in more detail.

Figure 18-8 depicts an overview of the connection from an application to an SQL node using a load balancer. If the load balancer is software based, it is highly possible that it runs on the same host as the application server.

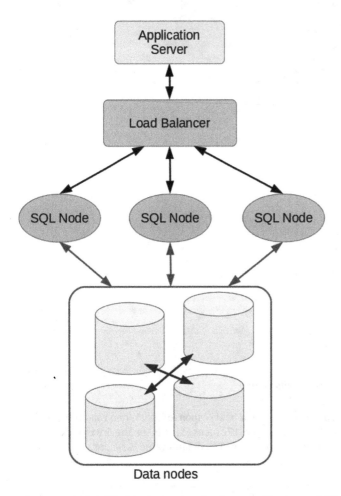

Figure 18-8. *Load balancing connection from application to SQL nodes using a load balancer*

Unfortunately, there is no suitable load balancer released from Oracle Corporation that can be used with MySQL NDB Cluster for the time being. *MySQL Router* was a potential candidate in its development stage. However, it has become a dedicated software for *InnoDB Cluster*, which is a HA solution based on standard MySQL replication. So, it cannot be used for MySQL NDB Cluster.

There are several third-party software programs that can be used for load balancing with MySQL NDB Cluster. I personally recommend *ProxySQL*, because it is practical to use and has a free software licensed under *GPLv3*. The source code of ProxySQL is released on GitHub:

https://github.com/sysown/proxysql

ProxySQL is not just a load balancer, it also has rich features such as query rewriting, query routing, query caching, a firewall, and so forth. In this book, only the load balancing feature is discussed.

Currently, there is no detailed manual page for ProxySQL, so refer to the *wiki* page of the GitHub repository, and the *doc* directory included in the source code. Since the configuration of ProxySQL is a bit confusing, we will discuss typical usage of ProxySQL.

Firstly, install ProxySQL onto your host. You can download the source code or binary (*RPM* and *DEB*) packages from GitHub. Unlike general open source projects, it doesn't have an automatic configuration facility such as a `configure` script or a `cmake` configuration file. Just run `make` from the source top directory. Listing 18-16 shows a typical command that builds it from source.

Listing 18-16. Building ProxySQL from Source Code

```
shell$ git clone https://github.com/sysown/proxysql.git
shell$ cd proxysql
shell$ make
shell$ sudo make install
```

This will install the systemd service, *proxysql.service*, and the default configuration file, */etc/proxysql. conf*, together with the `proxysql` command. You can either start it from `systemd` or from the command line.

The configuration system for ProxySQL is puzzling. There are four layers within the configuration system of ProxySQL; `RUNTIME`, `MEMORY`, `DISK`, and `CONFIG FILE`. Figure 18-9 shows a screenshot of the wiki page of ProxySQL GitHub repository. `RUNTIME` is the only effective configuration to control the behavior of ProxySQL. `MEMORY` is an in-memory SQLite database, and `DISK` is an on-disk SQLite database. Any configuration is first loaded to `MEMORY`, then applied to `RUNTIME`. It is not possible to load the configuration from `DISK` or `CONFIG FILE` into `RUNTIME` directly. As the name suggests, configurations in `MEMORY` are not persistent and will be lost upon restart. You must save changes to `DISK` to be persistent. `CONFIG FILE` is a supplemental source of configuration. Use it only if you prefer a file-based configuration style.

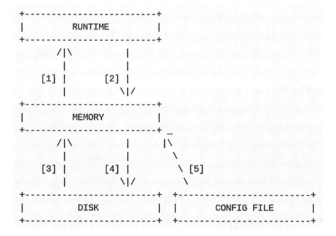

Figure 18-9. *Four configuration layers for ProxySQL*

The initial configuration is empty except for some basic configuration and comments. If you prefer to configure it using the configuration file, comment out, copy, and edit some configurations in it before starting the `proxysql` daemon. This step can be skipped when you configure using the administrative interface.

The admin interface for ProxySQL is built on top of the MySQL protocol. So, the runtime configuration is done by connecting to ProxySQL using the `mysql` command and issuing SQL statements over it. The default port for the admin interface is 6032, and the default username and password are both `admin`. You must change the credentials in your production system. Listing 18-17 shows an example command output when connecting to the admin interface.

Listing 18-17. Connecting ProxySQL Admin Interface Using the `mysql` Command

```
shell $ mysql -h 127.0.0.1 -P 6032 -uadmin -p
Enter password:
Welcome to the MySQL monitor.  Commands end with ; or \g.
Your MySQL connection id is 6
Server version: 5.5.30 (ProxySQL Admin Module)

Copyright (c) 2000, 2017, Oracle and/or its affiliates. All rights reserved.

Oracle is a registered trademark of Oracle Corporation and/or its
affiliates. Other names may be trademarks of their respective
owners.

Type 'help;' or '\h' for help. Type '\c' to clear the current input statement.

mysql>
```

Be aware that the server version is printed as "Proxy Admin Module". There are several databases and tables to configure in ProxySQL, as shown in Listing 18-18.

Listing 18-18. Listing Administrative Databases and Tables in the Main Database

```
mysql> SHOW DATABASES;
+-----+---------+-------------------------------+
| seq | name    | file                          |
+-----+---------+-------------------------------+
| 0   | main    |                               |
| 2   | disk    | /var/lib/proxysql/proxysql.db |
| 3   | stats   |                               |
| 4   | monitor |                               |
+-----+---------+-------------------------------+
4 rows in set (0.00 sec)

mysql> SHOW TABLES;
+--------------------------------------+
| tables                               |
+--------------------------------------+
| global_variables                     |
| mysql_collations                     |
| mysql_query_rules                    |
| mysql_replication_hostgroups         |
| mysql_servers                        |
| mysql_users                          |
| runtime_global_variables             |
| runtime_mysql_query_rules            |
```

```
| runtime_mysql_replication_hostgroups |
| runtime_mysql_servers                |
| runtime_mysql_users                  |
| runtime_scheduler                    |
| scheduler                            |
+--------------------------------------+
13 rows in set (0.00 sec)
```

The output looks like MySQL, but a little bit different. (The SHOW DATABASES command in the actual MySQL Server has only one field in its result set.) We don't discuss the details of each table in this book. Refer to the documentation and the wiki for more details about these tables.

To set up load balancing in ProxySQL, you simply set up monitoring and add the MySQL servers (the SQL nodes) to connect to.

ProxySQL monitors the target MySQL servers. ProxySQL must log in to the monitored servers, and you must create a monitoring user on each monitored MySQL Server. The monitoring user requires the USAGE privilege only. The following command output shows an example command that creates a monitoring user. Run these commands using the root user on each monitored MySQL Server.

```
mysql> CREATE USER proxysqlmon@proxyhost IDENTIFIED BY 'proxypassword';
Query OK, 0 rows affected (0.26 sec)

mysql> GRANT USAGE ON *.* TO proxysqlmon@proxyhost;
Query OK, 0 rows affected (0.00 sec)
```

Be sure to substitute the password in this example with a stronger one in the production system. Then, configure ProxySQL so that it logs in using this credential. Listing 18-19 shows an example command that sets up the monitoring user and password in the ProxySQL admin interface.

Listing 18-19. Configuring Monitoring User on the ProxySQL Admin Interface

```
mysql> UPDATE global_variables SET variable_value='proxysqlmon' WHERE variable_name =
'mysql-monitor_username';
Query OK, 1 row affected (0.00 sec)

mysql> UPDATE global_variables SET variable_value='proxypassword' WHERE variable_name =
'mysql-monitor_password';
Query OK, 1 row affected (0.00 sec)

mysql> LOAD MYSQL VARIABLES TO RUNTIME;
Query OK, 0 rows affected (0.00 sec)

mysql> SAVE MYSQL VARIABLES TO DISK;
Query OK, 74 rows affected (0.02 sec)
```

Note that the UPDATE statements in Listing 18-19 only modify the configuration in the MEMORY layer. It must be applied to the running ProxySQL instance using the LOAD command, then must be saved to DISK using the SAVE command for persistence.

Add the servers to be connected for load balancing, as shown in Listing 18-20. The LOAD and SAVE commands are required, just like in the previous step.

Listing 18-20. Configuring MySQL Servers to Be Connected

```
mysql> INSERT INTO mysql_servers (hostgroup_id, hostname, port) VALUES(0, 'sqlnode1', 3306);
Query OK, 1 row affected (0.00 sec)

mysql> INSERT INTO mysql_servers (hostgroup_id, hostname, port) VALUES(0, 'sqlnode2', 3306);
Query OK, 1 row affected (0.00 sec)

mysql> LOAD MYSQL SERVERS TO RUNTIME;
Query OK, 0 rows affected (0.00 sec)

mysql> SAVE MYSQL SERVERS TO DISK;
Query OK, 0 rows affected (0.01 sec)
```

Now you can connect to the backend SQL nodes through ProxySQL. The default port number is 6033, with the digits in a reverse sequence from the default MySQL port number 3306. Listing 18-21 shows an example command that connects SQL node via ProxySQL. Be aware that the server version string is printed as "ProxySQL". The connected MySQL Server is chosen randomly per query or per an explicitly started transaction from the list of servers configured in Listing 18-20. This means that the connected backend server may change even without reconnecting to ProxySQL.

Listing 18-21. Connecting to SQL Node via ProxySQL

```
shell$ mysql -h proxyhost -P 6033 -p
Enter password:
Welcome to the MySQL monitor.  Commands end with ; or \g.
Your MySQL connection id is 9
Server version: 5.5.30 (ProxySQL)

Copyright (c) 2000, 2017, Oracle and/or its affiliates. All rights reserved.

Oracle is a registered trademark of Oracle Corporation and/or its
affiliates. Other names may be trademarks of their respective
owners.

Type 'help;' or '\h' for help. Type '\c' to clear the current input statement.

mysql> SELECT VERSION();
+------------------+
| VERSION()        |
+------------------+
| 5.7.18-ndb-7.5.6 |
+------------------+
1 row in set (0.00 sec)
```

Transaction Handling for NDBCluster Tables

In most aspects, NDBCluster tables can be accessed in the same manner as InnoDB. You can write transactions just like InnoDB. However, there are some big differences between the transaction handling of NDBCluster and InnoDB. You must keep in mind some characteristics of the transaction handling in MySQL NDB Cluster when you develop transactional applications.

- **Only the READ-COMMITTED isolation level is supported:** The NDBCluster storage engine supports only the READ-COMMITTED isolation level. REPEATABLE-READ or SERIALIZABLE are not supported. If these isolation levels are required for your application, NDBCluster may not be a good choice.

- **No deadlock detection is available:** MySQL NDB Cluster doesn't have the ability to detect deadlocks caused by conflicting row-level locks like InnoDB does. So, any lock problems are detected as lock-wait-timeout, instead of deadlock.

- **Commit is not durable on disk:** While all data is replicated among the node group, committed transactions are not durable until the redo log entries are written by a GCP. This means transactions are not durable upon entire cluster failures.

- **Savepoints are not supported:** MySQL NDB Cluster does not support savepoints. You must always roll back the whole transaction when you want to revert uncommitted changes.

- **The LOCK TABLES command doesn't block access from other SQL nodes:** The LOCK TABLES statement is effective for the same SQL node only where the statement is issued. So, it is not possible to block transactions executed on other SQL nodes using the LOCK TABLES statement.

- **It's not possible to disable binary logging temporarily:** If binary logging is enabled in an SQL node, it is not possible to disable binary logging for individual statements by setting the sql_log_bin system variable to OFF.

Error-Handling Techniques

It is important to prepare for errors when you develop transactional database applications, because transaction theory does not ensure that transactions can complete successfully. It only ensures that the state of all transactions become either COMMIT or ABORT. This simplifies application development, because it is not necessary to consider the possibility of an unfinished, halfway state.

This property is so called *atomicity*; one of four important properties of transactions called *ACID*. Thus, all changes done by a transaction are rolled back when the transaction fails. The state of the database reverts as if the failed transaction wasn't executed at all. So, the only error-handling needed for a transactional application is to retry a failed transaction from the beginning. However, in other words, error handling is mandatory for transactional applications even though its algorithm is simple.

The error-handling flow varies depending on the type of programming language. When using a *procedural programming language*, it judges if an error happens or not by examining the return code from functions. When using an *object oriented programming language*, an error is often detected by exceptions. Listing 18-22 shows conceptual code of a transaction, including a retry algorithm using C API. Note that the code is just a concept, so many things are omitted and represented in an abbreviated form. You cannot compile it. Read the comments in Listing 18-22 to understand what this program is doing. When retrying a transaction, be sure that all the read values within a failed transaction are obsolete. Don't reuse a read value even if it still exists in memory.

Listing 18-22. Conceptual Transaction Handling Code with Retry Algorithm in C

```
int do_transaction1(...) {
  /* Variable declaration */
  MYSQL      *mysql;
  MYSQL_RES  *res;
  MYSQL_ROW  row;
```

```
  int       status;
  int       exit_code;
  int       retry_count = 5;
  useconds_t retry_delay = 100000;

loop:
  /* Get connection */
  mysql = mysql_init(NULL);
  if (!mysql_real_connect(mysql, ...)) {
    goto err;
  }

  /* Execute transaction */
  if(mysql_autocommit(mysql, 0))
    goto err;
  ...
  status = mysql_real_query(mysql, ...);
  if(status) {
    if(transaction is retriable) {
      goto retry;
    } else {
      goto err;
    }
  }
  ...

  goto end;

retry:
  /* Retry transaction for recoverable error */
  status = mysql_rollback();
  if(retry_count++ > 0) {
    usleep(retry_delay);
    goto loop;
  }

err:
  /* Critical error */
  exit_code = THE_ERROR_CODE;

end:
  /* Closing connection */
  mysql_close(mysql);

  return exit_code;
}
```

A program to do same thing can be written differently in an object oriented programming language such as Java. Listing 18-23 shows example source code for a Java program to execute a transaction. This Java program is shorter than the C program in Listing 18-22, as Java is more compact than C.

Listing 18-23. Conceptual Transaction Handling Code with Retry Algorithm in Java

```java
public void doTransaction1() throws SQLException {
  Connection    conn = null;
  Statement     stmt = null;
  ResultSet     rs = null;
  int           retryCount = 5;
  int           sleepDelay = 100;

  do {
    try {
      // Get connection
      conn = getConnection();
      conn.setAutoCommit(false);

      // Execute transaction
      stmt = conn.createStatement();

      String query = "SELECT ... FROM tbl WHERE ...";
      rs = stmt.executeQuery(query);
      ...

      retryCount = 0;
    } catch (SQLException sqlEx) {
      String sqlState = sqlEx.getSQLState();

      // Determine if transaction is retryable
      if (transaction is retryable) {
        Thread.sleep(sleepDelay);
        retryCount--;
      } else {
        retryCount = 0;
      }
    } finally {
      try {
        if (rs != null) rs.close();
        if (stmt != null) stmt.close();
        if (conn != null) conn.close();
      } catch (SQLException sqlEx) {
        // Write log etc
        ...
      }
    }
  } while (retryCount > 0);
}
```

The key point when writing a program to execute a transaction is how to determine if a transaction is retriable. It is determined by what error is reported from the server via the driver. So, an application must retrieve the error information from the driver first. MySQL drivers provide the following type of error information:

- **Errno:** MySQL specific error code assigned to each error type. You can find the list of error codes at *https://dev.mysql.com/doc/refman/5.7/en/error-messages-server.html* and *https://dev.mysql.com/doc/refman/5.7/en/error-messages-client.html*.

- **Error message:** A description of the error in text format. You may find additional information in the error message such as location of syntax error, a table name causing duplicate rows, etc.

- **SQLSTATE:** The five-character code that represents an error type, which is defined in the SQL standard.

Errno (or error code) and SQLSTATE are used to judge if the transaction is retriable, and what further action is required. Note that errno also has a text label that represents the type of error. You can find the label in the reference manual. The error message is a human readable error information. The error message is mainly used for logging to be reviewed later by the DBA.

The way to retrieve error information varies depending on the programming language and the driver implementation. Table 18-4 lists how to retrieve error information when an error occurs.

Table 18-4. *Retrieving Error Information for Each Programming Language*

Language/Driver	Error Detected By	Methods to Retrieve Error Information
Connector/J	SQLException	SQLException#getSQLState() SQLException#getErrorCode() SQLException#getMessage()
Connector/Python	mysql.connector.Error	mysql.connector.Error#sqlstate mysql.connector.Error#errno mysql.connector.Error#msg
C API	Return code	mysql_sqlstate() mysql_errno() mysql_error()
PHP, mysqli	Return code	mysqli_sqlstate()/mysqli->sqlstate() mysqli_errno()/mysqli->errno() mysqli_error()/mysqli->error()
PHP, PDO	PDOException	PDOException::$errInfo[0] ... SQLSTATE PDOException::$errInfo[1] ... Errno PDOException::$errInfo[2] ... Error
Perl, DBD::mysql	Exception or return code depends on RaiseError setting	$dbh->state $dbh->err $dbh->errstr
Ruby/MySQL	Mysql::Error	Mysql::Error#sqlstate Mysql::Error#errno Mysql::Error#error

The simplest way to implement a retry routine is to retry blindly against all types of errors. This works fine in most cases, because the retry itself is harmless unless the transaction is committed. Do not forget to roll back the transaction before retrying. Otherwise, the retry will not succeed.

If you prefer a cleverer choice, consider implementing a routine that judges if the transaction is retriable according to the SQLSATE and error code before retrying it. There are not many kinds of retriable errors, because most errors are fatal for the application. For example, errno 1146 has a label ER_NO_SUCH_TABLE, it means "the table referenced by statement does not exist". A table that does not exist is highly unlikely to appear upon retry. So, it's not a retriable error. In such cases, human intervention is required anyway. A DBA may need to fix the schema problem or fix a bug in the application code. Anyway, retrying transaction is effective only when an error is temporary.

The information that must be checked first is SQLSTATE. While SQLSTATE consists of five characters, the first two characters stand for the error class, and the following three characters stand for the error subclass. Table 18-5 lists the major error classes of SQLSTATE.

Table 18-5. *Major Error Classes Defined in SQLSTATE*

Class	Class Text	Retriable?	Description
00	Successful completion	No (No need to retry)	No error.
01	Warning	No (No need to retry)	The statement was executed successfully, but some warnings were raised.
02	No data	No (Used in Procedures)	No more data exists.
08	Connection exception	**Yes**	Connection related error.
22	Data exception	No (Used in Procedures)	Data is invalid for data type.
23	Integrity constraint violation	No (Used in Procedures)	Constraint is violated.
25	Invalid transaction state	No	Tried to transit invalid state of transaction.
28	Invalid authorization specification	No	Authorization failed.
40	Transaction rollback	Yes	Transaction was rolled back for some reason. Currently, not available for MySQL NDB Cluster. (Happens with InnoDB.)
42	Syntax error or access rule violation	No	Parser detected syntax error.
HY	General error	**Depends**	Vendor specific.
XA	XA transaction error	Depends	XA transactions are not supported in MySQL NDB Cluster.

As you see in Table 18-5, the only SQLSTATE classes to be retried are 08 and in some cases HY. An application needs to reconnect to SQL node when the SQLSTATE class is 08. Temporary errors discussed in Chapter 15 are included in the HY class. Note that 40 or XA can be raised from InnoDB, but it will not happen with the NDBCluster storage engine.

> ■ **Caution** If you get a syntax error (SQLSTATE class = 42), it might be a symptom of an SQL injection attack. Syntax errors could be the result of an attacker altering the SQL syntax. Even if they are not due to an attack, syntax errors indicate a potential risk of SQL injection attack, so they should be fixed as soon as possible.

When the SQLSTATE class is HY, an application must examine the error code retrieved from the driver. In MySQL NDB Cluster, the error codes listed in Table 18-6 are worth a retry.

Table 18-6. *List of Error Codes to Retry for MySQL NDB Cluster*

Error Code	Label	Description
1028	ER_FILSORT_ABORT	Sort is aborted for various reasons. This is not specific to the NDBCluster storage engine.
1036	ER_OPEN_AS_READONLY	An accessed table is opened in read-only mode. This can happen before the binlog injector is ready.
1038	ER_OUT_OF_SORTMEMORY	Memory is short when sorting rows. This is not specific to the NDBCluster storage engine.
1041	ER_OUT_OF_RESOURCES	Memory is short in the SQL node. This is not specific to the NDBCluster storage engine.
1180	ER_ERROR_DURING_COMMIT	An error happened during commit.
1181	ER_ERROR_DURING_ROLLBACK	An error happened during rollback.
1135	ER_CANT_CREATE_THREAD	Thread creation failed for some reason such as memory shortage. This is not specific to the NDBCluster storage engine.
1205	ER_LOCK_WAIT_TIMEOUT	A transaction cannot acquire lock due to lock-wait-timeout.
1297	ER_GET_TEMPORARY_ERRMSG	Resource temporary error.

There is one corner case that cannot be retried without inspecting further. That is, the connection failure (SQLSTATE class = 08) when executing commit, because an application itself cannot determine if the COMMIT was successful or not by only inspecting the error information retrieved from the driver. An application knows only the fact that it issued COMMIT to SQL node, but its result is unknown due to a network problem. Such a problem can be handled properly by an XA transaction; however, it has not been implemented on MySQL NDB Cluster yet. An application must inspect the table data to judge if changes made by the transaction are available or not, or raise an error for human intervention.

Summary

This chapter discussed how to develop applications in MySQL NDB Cluster as a usual relational database using SQL. It covered the following topics:

- Creating tables and indexes, and the various types of database objects.

- Understanding what types of indexes are available in MySQL NDB Cluster.

- Estimating table sizes and their required objects.

- Using disk data tables.

- Connecting to the SQL node from an application

- Employing transaction and error-handling techniques.

SQL is a good old, but actively used, data manipulation language. SQL is easy to use and is commonly used in real world database application development. Since MySQL NDB Cluster can be accessed via SQL, you can enjoy the power of SQL when developing applications on it.

The next chapter discusses how to develop applications on MySQL NDB Cluster using NoSQL APIs. While SQL is very powerful programming language, there are still some problem areas that SQL cannot address. In such cases, NoSQL APIs may come in handy.

CHAPTER 19

■ ■ ■

MySQL NDB Cluster as a NoSQL Database

This chapter discusses various ways to develop applications using MySQL NDB Cluster as a NoSQL database. MySQL NDB Cluster has several types of NoSQL protocols, and they can access the same data as SQL but without the overhead of using an SQL query interface. Being able to access the same data via different protocols is one of the best things about MySQL NDB Cluster when developing practical applications.

Why NoSQL?

SQL is a perfect, self-contained language in the sense that it can do everything that a relational database provides. However, it's sometimes imperfect from a performance point of view. In some cases, a simpler and faster access method is preferred. MySQL NDB Cluster has a native *NDB API* that accesses data nodes. It also supports several NoSQL APIs built on top of the NDB API.

This chapter discusses the following major NoSQL APIs supported by MySQL NDB Cluster.

- **memcached API:** A well-known, simple, fast, and easy to use API over well-defined network protocol. MySQL NDB Cluster package bundles memcached server, which can access data nodes. While memcached protocol is very simple, it provides far less functionality compared to SQL. You can find details of the protocol at *https://github. com/memcached/memcached/blob/master/doc/protocol.txt*

- **NDB API:** An application can access the data node directly using the NDB API protocol. Since the NDB API is a C++ API, an application must be written using C++. This makes implementing an algorithm to access data using the NDB API more difficult than with SQL. For example, joins, subqueries, stored routines, GROUP BY, and ORDER BY, etc. are all very powerful and easy to use operations in SQL. However, it is very cumbersome task to implement these same operations using the NDB API.

- **ClusterJ:** Java wrapper of the NDB API. The application can invoke NDB API functions via the *Java Native Interface (JNI)*. Developing Java applications is less difficult than with C++, but they have more performance overhead.

Each protocol can access the same data as SQL with less performance overhead than SQL. However, SQL is the most powerful API available for MySQL NDB Cluster, so every NoSQL protocol has its own drawbacks in exchange for performance advantages. So, it is not practical to develop a whole application using NoSQL protocols only. The best strategy is to combine SQL and NoSQL. Complex algorithms are implemented using SQL, and simple but fast algorithms are implemented using NoSQL.

© Jesper Wisborg Krogh and Mikiya Okuno 2017
J. W. Krogh and M. Okuno, *Pro MySQL NDB Cluster*, https://doi.org/10.1007/978-1-4842-2982-8_19

Accessing Data via memcached

memcached is the name of the software that stores (caches) data in memory. Data is stored in the form of key-value pairs. This kind of data storage software is called a *key-value store (KVS)*.

As of the MySQL NDB Cluster 7.2 series, the memcached server is bundled as part of the package. The bundled memcached has a special version that can use MySQL NDB Cluster as its underlying storage engine.

Why Use NDB-memcached

The memcached protocol is well-known, simple, easy to use, and fast. Many readers may have worked with memcached before. Although there are more advanced KVS products in the market, memcached is still a good choice for caching purposes.

Figure 19-1 shows an overview architecture of memcached working with MySQL NDB Cluster. The memcached server directly connects to data nodes using the NDB API. So, it acts as a kind of API node just like an SQL node. An application accesses data via the memcached protocol via memcached server, then memcached server accesses actual data on the data nodes using the NDB API. We call functionality of the memcached server that can use MySQL NDB Cluster as its storage engine *NDB-memcached* for convenience throughout this chapter. Note that the process name is still memcached, even though we call it NDB-memcached as a product name. NDB-memcached and memcached without the prefix indicate the same thing, and we use these terms interchangeably in this chapter.

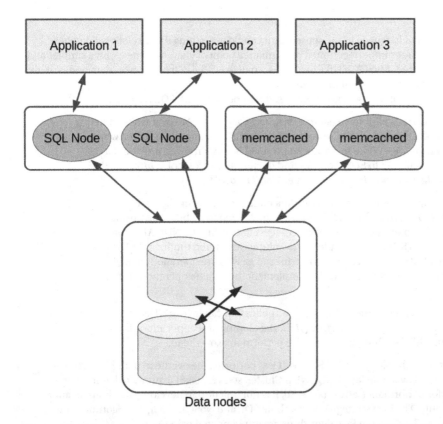

Data nodes

Figure 19-1. Overview architecture of memcached working with MySQL NDB Cluster

When the data is modified in NDB-memcached, row data inside data nodes is directly modified. On the other hand, NDB-memcached can see the latest row data modified from the SQL node. So, there is no need to synchronize data between memcached and the relational database. This makes application development easier than if memcached is used only as a cache and the standard MySQL Server is used as persistent storage. In addition, data on data nodes will survive even if memcached crashes. Unlike sharding, where the overall data is split into smaller shards, every memcached server in NDB-memcached can access all data in the data nodes. Thus, NDB-memcached has clear advantages compared to the standard memcached.

The most important aspect of memcached is its performance in terms of both response time and throughput. Since the memcached protocol is much simpler than SQL, it is more efficient than SQL. When processing SQL, it is necessary to parse the SQL, check privileges, optimize the query execution plans, and so forth. SQL processing has much more overhead than accessing data via memcached. However, memcached cannot handle complex queries such as joins. So, it is possible to take on different access method based on these requirements:

- Use NDB-memcached for simple and fast data access.

- Use SQL for complex queries.

This strategy brings both flexibility and performance to your application.

Setting Up NDB-memcached

In this section, we discuss how to set up NDB-memcached.

Installing NDB-memcached

Install the package that includes the memcached binary and related files.

When you are using the RPM or DEB package manager on Linux, memcached is included in a separate dedicated package in the MySQL NDB Cluster 7.5 series or newer. The package name is *mysql-cluster-community-memcached-7.5.6-1.el7.x86_64.rpm* or *mysql-cluster-community-memcached_7.5.6-1ubuntu16.04_amd64.deb,* for example. In MySQL NDB Cluster 7.4 or older, memcached is included in the server RPM package or in one DEB package. For other package formats, the package is all-in-one and it's not separated by functionality regardless of the operating system type. Refer to Chapter 5 for more information about installation.

■ **Note**   NDB-memcached is not currently available for Windows packages, because memcached doesn't officially support the Windows platform. Consider using UNIX-like operating systems.

Preparing the ndbmemcache Schema

Then, set up the system schema required for NDB-memcached; the schema name is ndbmemcache. To create the ndbmemcache schema and the tables in it, execute the SQL statements included in *ndb_memcache_metadata.sql*. It's located in the */usr/share/mysql/memcached-api/* directory for MySQL NDB Cluster 7.5 or newer RPM and the DEB package. It's located in the *share/mysql/memcached-api/* subdirectory of the installation directory for other package types. Load the SQL file as shown in Listing 19-1. You can see 11 tables under the ndbmemcache database.

Listing 19-1. Creating the ndbmemcache Schema and Tables

```
mysql> source /usr/share/mysql/memcached-api/ ndb_memcache_metadata.sql
Query OK, 1 row affected (1.87 sec)

Database changed
Query OK, 0 rows affected (0.81 sec)
...
mysql> use ndbmemcache
Database changed
mysql> SHOW TABLES;
+-----------------------+
| Tables_in_ndbmemcache |
+-----------------------+
| cache_policies        |
| containers            |
| demo_table            |
| demo_table_large      |
| demo_table_tabs       |
| external_values       |
| key_prefixes          |
| last_memcached_signon |
| memcache_server_roles |
| meta                  |
| ndb_clusters          |
+-----------------------+
11 rows in set (0.00 sec)
```

Starting the memcached Server

Make sure that there is a free [API] or [MYSQLD] slot in your *config.ini* file, because memcached connects to the cluster as an API node. One memcached process will consume up to four slots. If there is no free slot available, add at least one API node before you start the memcached server. Refer to Chapter 10 for the procedure to add API nodes.

To start the memcached server, run the memcached command, as shown in Listing 19-2.

Listing 19-2. Starting the memcached Server

```
shell$ memcached -E /usr/lib64/mysql/ndb_engine.so \
    -e "connectstring=mgmhost;role=db-only"
```

As you can see, two options are explicitly specified in Listing 19-2. These options are specific to NDB-memcached. Each option has the meaning listed here.

- **-E:** Specifies a shared library that implements the storage engine to be used.

- **-e:** Specifies options passed to the storage engine. Options are specified in text separated by semicolons..

The engine-specific options passed via -e option are listed in Table 19-1.

Table 19-1. *Engine Specific Options Passed to ndb_engine.so*

Option	Description
connectstring=*string*	The connection string. Specify in the same format as for common NDB programs. The default value is localhost:1186.
role=*string*	The role assigned to this memcached server. The default value is default_role. See the next section.
scheduler=*string*	Specify the scheduler properties in the format name:configuration. The default is "S:c0,f0,t1", which indicates that the scheduler name is S, and options for *S-scheduler* are c0,f0,t1.
reconf={true|false}	Specify if online reconfiguration is allowed. The default value is true.
debug={true|false}	Set to true if you want to debug NDB-memcached. The default value is false.

The configuration for the scheduler is a little bit complex. There are schedulers other than the S-scheduler (scheduler names are 73, stockholm, trondheim), but S-scheduler is the most tested and sufficient in most cases. The parameters to the S-scheduler are represented in a comma-separated string without spaces, each string begins with one letter followed by one digit. Each parameter has the following meanings.

- **c:** Specify the number of connections to the cluster just like --ndb-cluster-connection-pool in mysqld. Possible range is 0 – 4. The default is 0, which means automatic.

- **f:** Specify if force send is used. The default is 0 (false). This option has the same effect of --force-send option in mysqld.

- **t:** Set send thread timer in milliseconds. The possible range is 1 – 10. The default is 1.

Other options for memcached are also available, just like for the standard memcached. See the output of memcached -h for a complete list of available options. By default, memcached is listening on port 11211. You can test NDB-memcached using the telnet command, as shown in Listing 19-3. If you don't have the telnet command on your operating system, as it's an outdated command, try the memclient command shipped with memcached in the package.

Listing 19-3. Connecting to NDB-memcached and Running Some Tests

```
shell$ telnet localhost 11211
Trying ::1...
Connected to localhost.
Escape character is '^]'.
set love 0 0 5
peace
STORED
set b:big 0 0 5
small
STORED
^]
telnet> quit
Connection closed.
```

```
shell$ memclient -a
Memclient 1.0 using Term::ReadLine::Stub
Attempting ASCII connection to localhost:11211 ...
Connected.
memcache > get love
        KEY        | FLAGS |Value
love               | 0     |peace
```

You can see that the values are stored in NDBCluster tables, as shown in Listing 19-4.

Listing 19-4. Accessing the Same Data from the SQL Node as NDB-memcached

```
mysql> SELECT * FROM ndbmemcache.demo_table;
+------+------------+-------+-------------+--------------+
| mkey | math_value | flags | cas_value   | string_value |
+------+------------+-------+-------------+--------------+
| love |       NULL |     0 | 83214991362 | peace        |
+------+------------+-------+-------------+--------------+
1 row in set (0.00 sec)

mysql> SELECT * FROM ndbmemcache.demo_table_large;
+------+-------+-------------+--------------+--------+----------+
| mkey | flags | cas_value   | string_value | ext_id | ext_size |
+------+-------+-------------+--------------+--------+----------+
| big  |     0 | 83214991365 | small        |   NULL |     NULL |
+------+-------+-------------+--------------+--------+----------+
1 row in set (0.00 sec)
```

As you see in Listing 19-4, values are stored in demo_table and demo_table_large. Why are they stored in these tables? Is it possible to access arbitrary tables via NDB-memcached? That is a next topic.

Defining Mapping to NDB Cluster Tables

You see that two keys, love and b:big, are stored in separate tables in Listing 19-4. This is because the latter key has a prefix b:. NDB-memcached can access different tables depending on the prefix values. A prefix b: is predefined by default. This functionality is very important, because it is useless if it is just accessing the demo table.

To understand mappings to tables, the following concepts are the key points:

- **Role:** A role assigned to each memcached server. Defined in the memcache_server_ roles table and specified in the -e option upon startup of the memcached process.

- **Prefix:** A prefix of each key.

- **Policy:** Caching policy mapped to each value.

- **Container:** Defines which table or tables are used to store key-value pairs in the NDBCluster storage engine.

In short, the pair of role and prefix determines which pair of policy and container is used.

Defining Containers

Container defines table and columns to be accessed from NDB-memcached. Of course, the target table must be an NDB Cluster table. The key part mapped to the table can consist of up to four columns. The set of key columns must consist either of a primary key or secondary unique index on the target table. The value part mapped to the table can consist of up to 16 columns. If the key part or value part consists of more than one column, it must be specified in tab-delimited format in the memcached client.

Once the target table is ready, insert an entry into the containers table under the ndbmemcache database. The containers table has the columns listed in Table 19-2.

Table 19-2. *Columns in the containers Table*

Column	Nullable	Description
name	No	Name of the container.
db_schema	No	Database name of the target table.
db_table	No	The target table name.
key_columns	No	Comma-delimited list of columns used as the key of memcached operation. Can be specified with up to four columns. If multiple columns are specified in this table, values must be specified in tab-separated format in memcached API.
value_columns	Yes	Comma-delimited list of columns used as the value stored/read by memcached. Can be specified with up to 16 columns. If multiple columns are specified in this table, values must be specified or retrieved in tab-separated format in memcached API.
flags	No	Currently not used.
increment_column	Yes	Column to store the numeric value used in memcached INCR and DECR operations. If set, the column must be defined as BIGINT UNSIGNED in the target table.
cas_column	Yes	Column used for *Compare and Swap* (*CAS*) operations on memcached. If set, the column must be defined as BIGINT UNSIGNED on the target table.
expire_time_column	Yes	Column used to determine if the row is expired or not. If set, the column must be defined as TIMESTAMP in the target table. A row is deleted from the target table when accessed from memcached if the column value is older than the current time.
large_values_table	Yes	Table used to store large data like BLOB data.

The following SQL command inserts an entry to access the world.City table via NDB-memcached. The container is named world_city in this example. Two of the non-primary-key columns in the world.City table are listed in the value_columns value.

```
mysql> INSERT INTO containers VALUES('world_city', 'world', 'City', 'ID',
'Name,CountryCode', 0, NULL, NULL, NULL, NULL);
Query OK, 1 row affected (0.00 sec)
```

If `large_values_table` is not empty, the table to store large values must have a definition, as shown in Listing 19-5.

Listing 19-5. Definition of a Table to Store Large Values

```
CREATE TABLE IF NOT EXISTS `external_values` (
  `id` INT UNSIGNED AUTO_INCREMENT NOT NULL,
  `part` SMALLINT NOT NULL,
  `content` VARBINARY(13950) NOT NULL,
  PRIMARY KEY (id,part)
) ENGINE = NDBCluster;
```

Review Policies

NDB-memcached can store data inside memcached as well as in the `NDBCluster` tables. The preference of whether to store the data in memcached or an `NDBCluster` table is defined in the `cache_policies` table under the ndbmemcache database. There are six predefined policies in the `cache_policies` table, as shown in Listing 19-6.

Listing 19-6. Displaying Predefined Cache Policies

```
mysql> SELECT * FROM cache_policies\G
*************************** 1. row ***************************
  policy_name: memcache-only
   get_policy: cache_only
   set_policy: cache_only
delete_policy: cache_only
flush_from_db: false
*************************** 2. row ***************************
  policy_name: caching-with-local-deletes
   get_policy: caching
   set_policy: caching
delete_policy: cache_only
flush_from_db: false
*************************** 3. row ***************************
  policy_name: ndb-read-only
   get_policy: ndb_only
   set_policy: disabled
delete_policy: disabled
flush_from_db: false
*************************** 4. row ***************************
  policy_name: ndb-test
   get_policy: ndb_only
   set_policy: ndb_only
delete_policy: ndb_only
flush_from_db: true
*************************** 5. row ***************************
  policy_name: ndb-only
   get_policy: ndb_only
   set_policy: ndb_only
delete_policy: ndb_only
flush_from_db: false
```

```
*************************** 6. row ***************************
  policy_name: caching
   get_policy: caching
   set_policy: caching
delete_policy: caching
flush_from_db: false
6 rows in set (0.00 sec)
```

Each column in cache_policies has the meaning listed in Table 19-3.

Table 19-3. *Description of Columns in the cache_policies Table*

Column	Description
policy_name	Name of the policy. The name is used for mapping with role and prefixes.
get_policy	Policy applied to the get operation of memcached.
set_policy	Policy applied to the set operation of memcached.
delete_policy	Policy applied to the delete operation of memcached.
flush_from_db	Specifies if all rows in the table are deleted upon the flush_all operation of memcached.

Acceptable values for the three policy columns in cache_policies table are described in the following list:

- **cache_only:** Data is get, set, and deleted in the in-memory storage of memcached itself only.

- **ndb_only:** Data is get, set, and deleted in the associated container table only.

- **caching:** Data is stored in both the in-memory storage of memcached and the associated container table. Storage of memcached is used as a cache for the container table. The cache is searched first upon a get operation, any further search is skipped if data is found in in-memory data storage of memcached. Upon the set and delete operation, data in both the in-memory storage of memcached and the associated container table is updated or deleted.

- **disabled:** The operation is not allowed.

Review the predefined policies and pick the one that's suitable for your application. If you simply want to access the same data as a NDB Cluster table via memcached protocol, ndb-only is the choice. Or choose ndb-read-only if you want to allow read only access to a NDB Cluster table from memcached. The ndb-test policy is very much like the ndb-only policy, except for the flush_from_db setting. Since deleting all rows upon flush_all operation is a somewhat dangerous operation, I recommend not using this policy.

With caching policies, caching and caching-with-local-deletes, of course it is possible that data in the in-memory storage of memcached and the container table will be out of sync if only one of them is updated. Be careful when you use caching policies. The memcache-only policy doesn't access the container tables. Data is not durable nor synchronized to other memcached instances.

If there is no policy that exactly matches your needs, you can add your own policy to the cache_policies table.

Define Server Roles

Each memcached server has a role assigned to it. The role itself is just a label defined in the memcache_
server_roles table under the ndbmemcache database. Listing 19-7 shows an example memcached_server_
roles table that includes the predefined roles.

Listing 19-7. Example Content of the memcached_server_roles Table

```
mysql> SELECT * FROM memcache_server_roles;
+--------------+---------+---------+---------------------+
| role_name    | role_id | max_tps | update_timestamp    |
+--------------+---------+---------+---------------------+
| large        |       4 |  100000 | 2017-06-11 17:13:35 |
| default_role |       0 |  100000 | 2017-06-11 17:13:35 |
| db-only      |       1 |  100000 | 2017-06-11 17:13:35 |
| ndb-caching  |       3 |  100000 | 2017-06-11 17:13:35 |
| mc-only      |       2 |  100000 | 2017-06-11 17:13:35 |
+--------------+---------+---------+---------------------+
5 rows in set (0.00 sec)
```

As you can see, each role has a numeric identifier, as shown in the role_id column. This value is used
to define the mappings between the prefix and the pair of caching policy and container.

You can use predefined roles if you like or you can add your own. Since each memcached server
instance will behave differently depending on the assigned role, define as many roles as if you want to run
memcached servers with different behaviors.

Define Mappings

Now, you can define mappings between role and prefix pairs and caching policy and container pairs. The
definition is done by adding entries to the key_prefixes table under the ndbmemcache database. Table 19-4
lists the columns in the key_prefixes table.

Table 19-4. Columns in the key_prefixes Table

Column	Description
server_role_id	Specify the role using a value from the role_id column in the memcached_server_roles table.
key_prefix	Prefix of the key specified for memcached operations.
cluster_id	Specify the identifier for cluster to be accessed. Set 0 when accessing to the default cluster. Use of multiple clusters with NDB-memcached isn't dealt with this book, because it is not a common usage.
policy	The policy name to be applied. The value of this column must be defined in the policy_name column of the cache_policies table.
container	The container name to be stored. The value of this column must be defined in the name column of the containers table. This column can be NULL if the policy doesn't require table access like memcache-only.

The following SQL command is an command that adds an entry to the key_prefixes table. With this example, rows in the world.City table via the world_city container are accessed without caching using the prefix wc: on the memcached servers with the db-only (role_id is 1) role.

```
mysql> INSERT INTO key_prefixes VALUES(1, 'wc:', 0, 'ndb-only', 'world_city');
```

Apply Settings to a Running memcached Instance

Prefix mappings are read when the memcached server starts. So, you can apply settings to the memcached server by restarting it. This is the simplest and safest way to apply settings.

If you want to apply changes without stopping the memcached server, update the update_timestamp column of the memcache_server_roles table to the current timestamp, as in the following example.

```
mysql> UPDATE memcache_server_roles SET update_timestamp = NOW() WHERE role_name = 'db-
only';
Query OK, 1 row affected (0.00 sec)
Rows matched: 1  Changed: 1  Warnings: 0
```

The memcached process will then reconfigure the mappings by reading the configuration from tables under the ndbmemcache database. Now, you can access world.City table with the prefix wc:, as in Listing 19-8. Notice that the retrieved value includes many spaces. It's a trailing space caused by the CHAR data type plus the tab character to separate two column values.

Listing 19-8. Accessing the world.City Table from memcached

```
memclient -a
Memclient 1.0 using Term::ReadLine::Stub
Attempting ASCII connection to localhost:11211 ...
Connected.
memcache > get wc:1532
      KEY          | FLAGS |Value
wc:1532            | 0     |Tokyo                             JPN
```

When you use NDB-memcached in a production system, I recommend truncating the key_prefixes table before defining mappings. The predefined mappings are useless in most cases other than for demonstration purposes. You can also drop demo tables in the ndbmemcache database.

Accessing NDBCluster Tables via the memcached Protocol in Your Application

To access NDBCluster tables via the memcached protocol in your application, you must install the memcached client library suitable for your programming language. Client libraries to access memcached aren't bundled in the MySQL NDB Cluster packages, so you must get them by yourself. Since memcached is well-known, commonly-used software, there are many choices for client libraries in the market.

For example, the following client libraries are available:

- **Java:** *https://github.com/gwhalin/Memcached-Java-Client*

- **.NET:** *https://github.com/enyim/EnyimMemcached*

- **PHP:** memcached (*libmemcached* binding) and memcached (original implementation) available on PECL

- **Python:** *https://github.com/linsomniac/python-memcached, https://github.com/pinterest/pymemcache*

- **Ruby:** *https://github.com/arthurnn/memcached*

- **Perl:** Cache::Memcached CPAN module

Performance Tuning

There are several parameters to be tuned for NDB-memcached.

- **Scheduler:** Scheduler settings can be adjusted via the scheduler part of the -e option, as described earlier in this section. Consider increasing the number of connections to data nodes (c parameter) and send thread timer (t parameter) if you prefer to have better throughput. Turn on force send (set 1 to f parameter) if you prefer to have better response time.

- **Number of NDB objects used in memcached:** Adjust the max_tps column value in the memcache_server_roles table and the microsec_rtt column value in the ndb_clusters table. The more max_tps or microsec_rtt, the more NDB objects are used in memcached. More NDB objects are required to handle more access to the cluster in parallel to the expense of increased memory usage.

Accessing Data via the NDB API

While NDB-memcached is a powerful choice to get better performance using the handy memcached API, it still lacks some capabilities and has some performance overhead. To meet the stringent requirements, a native NoSQL access method, the NDB API, is the last resort.

Why Use the NDB API?

While the NDB API is a great method to access tables in MySQL NDB Cluster, it's not a panacea for application development. Of course, there are pros and cons to using the NDB API just like with any other software.
Pros of the NDB API are:

- An application linked with the NDB API client library connects directly to the data nodes. There is no relay point between them, which causes overhead. So, the NDB API is the best choice for performance in terms of response time and throughput.

- It is a transactional API like SQL. While memcached is handy, its operations are non-transactional.

- It can do everything that the data node provides. While the memcached is handy, its functionality is very limited; it can do look-up based operations against predefined tables only. The NDB API can do not only lookups, but also scans, conditional searches, and parameterized queries against any tables in the cluster.

Cons of the NDB API are:

- It is a very low-level API so it requires more work to implement. While it can do everything on the cluster theoretically, many lines of codes are required to implement the same functionality as with SQL. For example, JOIN is a common operation in SQL, and theoretically it can be implemented using NDB API; however, it requires a lot of code.

- It targets C++ applications. While there are bindings for other programming languages, there is some overhead when using such bindings. Developing a C++ application is more difficult than writing an application using popular web programming languages such as Java, PHP, Python, and Ruby.

Consider carefully if the NDB API is suitable for your application needs. SQL is sufficient for common application development in terms of functionality. NDB-memcached is available when better performance is required. Although it is slower than the NDB API and doesn't provide transactions, using NDB-memcached is much easier.

Installing Header Files and Libraries for the NDB API

To develop applications using the NDB API, header files and libraries must be installed on your development machine. In MySQL NDB Cluster 7.5 series or newer, the required files are included in the following packages:

- **RPM:** The *ndbclient-devel* package includes the header files and static library. The *ndbclient* package includes the shared library.

- **DEB:** The *ndbclient-dev* package includes the header files and static library. The *ndbclient* package includes the shared library.

- **All-in-one package:** Required files are bundled in the package.

In MySQL NDB Cluster 7.4 series or older, the required files are included in the following packages:

- **RPM:** The *devel* package includes the header files and static library. The *server* package includes the shared library.

- **DEB:** Only the deb package is not separated per functionality. The only available package type is an all-in-one DEB package.

- **All in one package:** Required files are bundled in the package.

Since only all-in-one packages are available for Windows and macOS, the required library is bundled in the package. However, it appears that the Windows MSI package doesn't have a dynamic link version of ndbclient library (*ndbclient.dll*). Use the Zip archive package for now.

Building an Application with the NDB API

To build an application with the NDB API, you need a C++ compiler. So, install a compiler on your development machine beforehand. To compile your program and link it to the *libndbclient* library, the appropriate options must be passed to the compiler and linker.

The compiler option can be retrieved using the mysql_config command. The mysql_config command shows the required compiler options according to the installation layout of your package. The general compiler options can be retrieved with the --cflags option, as shown in the following command. Note that the second line of this example is the result displayed by this command.

```
shell$ mysql_config --cflags
-I/usr/include/mysql -g -fno-strict-aliasing    -DNDEBUG
```

The options to specify the location of the include files are also required. The options can be retrieved using the mysql_config command with the --include option. The include files are placed in the *storage/ndb*, *storage/ndb/ndbapi*, and *storage/ndb/mgmapi* subdirectories under the include path retrieved by the mysql_config --include command. So, you can set the CXXFLAGS compiler option as shown in the following command.

```
shell$ CXXFLAGS="`mysql_config --cflags` \
  `mysql_config --include`/storage/ndb \
  `mysql_config --include`/storage/ndb/ndbapi \
  `mysql_config --include`/storage/ndb/mgmapi"
shell$ export CXXFLAGS
```

If you want to pass these options to the compiler via an environment variable, you can export them, like this example. If you also use the standard MySQL C API as well, add the output of mysql_config --include command without any subdirectories to the compiler option.

The linker option must be set in addition to the compiler option. To retrieve the linker options, run the mysqld_config command with the --libs_r option. The linker also requires a list of libraries to be linked. The required library for NDB API applications is *libndbclient*. Add -lndbclient to the linker option according to the convention of the library name specification. The following command sets the linker option. If you also use the standard MySQL C API as well, add -lmysqlclient to the option too.

```
shell$ LDFLAGS="`mysql_config --libs_r` -lndbclient"
```

Then, you can compile your application using a compiler, as shown in the following command example. In this example, g++, a C++ compiler from the *GNU Compiler Collection* is used to compile the program source file example.cc.

```
shell$ g++ $CXXFLAGS $LDFLAGS example.cc -o example
```

References and Examples

This section discusses how to write NDB API applications. We will discuss only a simplified flow of the NDB API programs to let you understand the overview. Refer to the MySQL NDB Cluster API Developer Guide at *https://dev.mysql.com/doc/ndbapi/en/* for a complete reference to NDB API programming.

In this book, we discuss the native NDB API and Java binding of it, *ClusterJ*. We'll discuss ClusterJ in the next section. There is a yet another binding of the NDB API for JavaScript. You can find the details of JavaScript binding in the MySQL NDB Cluster API Developer Guide.

The source code of MySQL NDB Cluster also includes good examples. You can browse the source code online at GitHub at *https://github.com/mysql/mysql-server/tree/cluster-7.5/storage/ndb/ndbapi-examples*.

Of course, these examples are included in the downloaded or cloned source code, too. These examples are useful for understanding how to write NDB API programs. I recommend reviewing all of these example programs before you write any NDB API programs.

Typical Program Flow

You need include *NdbApi.hpp* at the beginning of the program. Call ndb_init() to initialize the NDB API right after the program begins. Call ndb_end(0) to clean up before the program exits.

Even when developing NDB API programs, the MySQL C API (or MySQL C++ driver if you like) is often used alongside. These two API libraries are used depending on the situation:

- An application accesses SQL node using MySQL C API to create, drop, or examine database objects. It is worth it to execute complex queries such as joins via SQL node.

- An application accesses data nodes directly using the NDB API for data access.

If you want to use the MySQL C API, you need to include *mysql.h* as well as NdbApi.hpp, as shown in Listing 19-9. Don't forget to adjust the compiler option so that the path to mysql.h is added in addition to the NDB API header files. Make sure ndb_exit(0) is called when the program exits in error. A program is likely to end without calling ndb_exit(0) if terminating using the exit() function. I recommend writing a function to perform the necessary cleanup and exit that's called when the program exits upon error.

Listing 19-9. Typical Structure of a Program That Uses the NDB API and the MySQL C API

```
#include <NdbApi.hpp>
#include <mysql.h>
... snip ...
int main(int argc, char *argv[])
{
    ndb_init();
    ... snip ...
    ndb_end(0);
    return 0;
}
```

Since the NDB API is written in C++, a typical object-oriented programming language, functionalities are implemented as various classes. Table 19-5 lists the major classes used in NDB API programs.

Table 19-5. Classes Often Used in NDB API Programs

Class	Description
Ndb_cluster_connection	This class manages the connection to the cluster. The connect string is passed to its constructor.
Ndb	A handle to access the data node. There is an upper limit to the number of Ndb objects within a single program. A program can create up to 4711 Ndb objects.
NdbDictionary	A class to work with the metadata required to specify the target objects. This class has various child classes to handle dedicated objects, such as Dictionary, Table, Column, Index, and Event.
NdbTransaction	A class to execute transactions and record-based operations.
NdbOperation	A class to specify the operation to be executed. There are several subclasses to handle specific operations: NdbIndexOperation class for secondary unique index lookups, NdbScanOperation class for table scans, and NdbIndexScanOperation class for index scans. The NdbOperation class itself is used for operations based on primary-key lookups.
NdbScanFilter	A class to define filters applied to scans on data node.
NdbRecAttr	A class to manipulate data per each attribute.
NdbRecord	A class to manipulate data per each row record.
NdbBlob	A class to manipulate blob data.
NdbInterpretedCode	A class represents interpreted code, which is directly executed on data nodes. This class is used with NdbRecord.
NdbEventOperation	A class to work with events that are notified upon modification of each table through micro-GCP.
NdbError	A class to retrieve error information.

Figure 19-2 depicts the typical workflow of an NDB API program. In this workflow, the program utilizes the classes listed in Table 19-6.

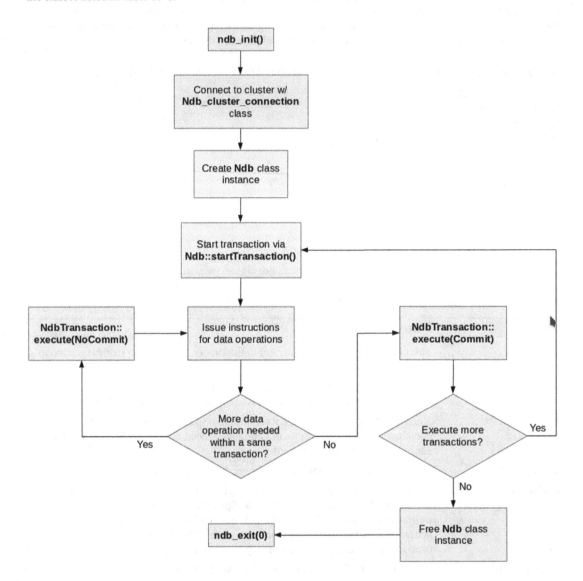

Figure 19-2. *Semantic diagram for the typical flow of an NDB API program*

Simple Read Example

As they say, "seeing is believing". So, this section shows you a working example in Listing 19-11. Review the comments in the code of the example. To run the example program in this section, you need to set up the *world example database* in your cluster. Then drop foreign keys and change storage engine to NDBCluster. To set up the world example database, refer to the manual at *https://dev.mysql.com/doc/world-setup/en/world-setup-installation.html* Listing 19-10 shows an example command that sets up the world database using the NDB Cluster storage engine.

Listing 19-10. Setting Up the world Database Using the NDB Cluster Storage Engine

```
mysql> source /path/to/world.sql
... snip ...

mysql> use world
Database changed
mysql> ALTER TABLE City DROP FOREIGN KEY city_ibfk_1;
Query OK, 0 rows affected (0.11 sec)
Records: 0  Duplicates: 0  Warnings: 0

mysql> ALTER TABLE CountryLanguage DROP FOREIGN KEY countryLanguage_ibfk_1;
Query OK, 0 rows affected (0.09 sec)
Records: 0  Duplicates: 0  Warnings: 0

mysql> ALTER TABLE Country ENGINE NDBCluster;
Query OK, 239 rows affected (1.61 sec)
Records: 239  Duplicates: 0  Warnings: 0

mysql> ALTER TABLE City ENGINE NDBCluster;
Query OK, 4079 rows affected (2.42 sec)
Records: 4079  Duplicates: 0  Warnings: 0

mysql> ALTER TABLE CountryLanguage ENGINE NDBCluster;
Query OK, 984 rows affected (1.87 sec)
Records: 984  Duplicates: 0  Warnings: 0
```

Listing 19-11. Sample NDB API Program That Reads a Row from a Table

```cpp
#include <NdbApi.hpp>
#include <iostream>
#include <string>

const char *connectstring = "mgmhost";
const char *db = "world";

class NdbApiExample1 {
public:
  NdbApiExample1() : cluster_connection(NULL), myNdb(NULL),
              myDict(NULL), myTable(NULL) {};
  ~NdbApiExample1();
  int doTest();

private:
  void print_error(const NdbError &e, const char *msg)
  {
    std::cerr << msg << ": Error code (" << e.code << "): "
              << e.message << "." << std::endl;
  }
```

```
  Ndb_cluster_connection *cluster_connection;
  Ndb *myNdb;
  const NdbDictionary::Dictionary* myDict;
  const NdbDictionary::Table *myTable;
  NdbTransaction *myTransaction;
  NdbOperation *myOperation;
};

int NdbApiExample1::doTest()
{
  // Step 1. Initialize NDB API
  ndb_init();

  // Step 2. Connecting to the cluster
  cluster_connection = new Ndb_cluster_connection(connectstring);
  if (cluster_connection->connect(4 /* retries              */,
                                  5 /* delay between retries */,
                                  1 /* verbose              */)) {
    std::cerr << "Could not connect to MGMD." << std::endl;
    return 1;
  }

  if (cluster_connection->wait_until_ready(30,0) < 0) {
    std::cerr << "Could not connect to NDBD." << std::endl;
    return 2;
  }

  // Step 3. Connect to 'world' database
  myNdb = new Ndb(cluster_connection, db);
  if (myNdb->init()) {
    print_error(myNdb->getNdbError(),
                "Could not connect to the database object.");
    return 3;
  }

  // Step 4. Get table handle
  myDict= myNdb->getDictionary();
  myTable= myDict->getTable("Country");

  if (myTable == NULL) {
    print_error(myDict->getNdbError(), "Could not retrieve a table.");
    return 4;
  }

  // Step 5. Start transaction
  myTransaction= myNdb->startTransaction();
  if (myTransaction == NULL) {
    print_error(myNdb->getNdbError(), "Could not start transaction.");
    return 5;
  }
```

```cpp
// Step 6. Get operation handle
myOperation= myTransaction->getNdbOperation(myTable);
if (myOperation == NULL) {
  print_error(myTransaction->getNdbError(),
              "Could not retrieve an operation.");
  return 6;
}


// Step 7. Specify type of operation and search condition
myOperation->readTuple(NdbOperation::LM_Read);
myOperation->equal("Code", "JPN");


// Step 8. Get buffers for results
NdbRecAttr *Name = myOperation->getValue("Name", NULL);
NdbRecAttr *Capital = myOperation->getValue("Capital", NULL);
if (Name == NULL || Capital == NULL) {
  print_error(myTransaction->getNdbError(),
              "Could not allocate attribute records.");
  return 7;
}


// Step 9. Send a request to data nodes
if (myTransaction->execute( NdbTransaction::Commit ) == -1) {
  print_error(myTransaction->getNdbError(), "Transaction failed.");
  return 8;
}


// Step 10. Retrieve values
std::cout << " Name:           "
          << std::string(Name->aRef(),
                         Name->get_size_in_bytes())
          << std::endl;
std::cout << " Capital Code: "
          << Capital->u_32_value()
          << std::endl;

  return 0;
}

NdbApiExample1::~NdbApiExample1()
{
  // Step 11. Cleanup
  if (myTransaction) myNdb->closeTransaction(myTransaction);
  if (myNdb) delete myNdb;
  if (cluster_connection) delete cluster_connection;
  ndb_end(0);
}
```

```
int main(int argc, char *argv[])
{
  NdbApiExample1 ex;
  return ex.doTest();
}
```

This code is straightforward and simple. All jobs are done in the doTest() function of the NdbApiExample1 class. Let's examine each step in this program.

Step 1. Initialize the NDB API

ndb_init() must be called at the beginning of the program.

Step 2. Connect to the Cluster

The connect string is passed to the constructor of the Ndb_cluster_connection class. After an instance of the class is created successfully, the code calls the connect() member function to connect to the cluster.

Step 3. Connect to the world Database

Connect to the world database using an Ndb class instance. Since the Ndb class is not thread-safe, you must create an Ndb class instances dedicated to each thread. Don't share Ndb class instances among threads. There can be up to 4177 Ndb class instances per process.

Step 4. Get the Table Handle

A handle is retrieved to access the Country table. When accessing objects, you retrieve an instance of the NdbDictionary::Dictionary class. Then ask the retrieved dictionary to get more objects.
You can reuse objects retrieved from the dictionary.

Step 5. Start the Transaction

Transactions must be started explicitly.

Step 6. Get the Operation Handle

Retrieve the operation handle objects from an instance of the NdbTransaction class, which is retrieved when a transaction starts. Since this example is for a primary-key lookup, an instance of NdbOperation class is retrieved using the NdbTransaction::getNdbOperation() function. Call the appropriate function from the following functions to get a suitable operation handle:

- NdbTransaction::getNdbOperation()
- NdbTransaction::getNdbIndexOperation()
- NdbTransaction::getNdbScanOperation()
- NdbTransaction::getNdbIndexScanOperation()

Step 7. Specify the Type of Operation and Search Condition

In this step, declare the type of operation that's going to be executed. In this case, read is specified as the operation by calling the NdbOperation::readTuple() function. The name of this function is confusing in the sense that the name of the function gives an impression that the read operation is performed when this function is called. However, the function just declares the type of the upcoming operation. The operation will be executed a little bit later.

In the NdbOperation class, the following five operations are defined:

- **readTuple:** A row is read based on the primary key value.

- **insertTuple:** A row is inserted.

- **updateTuple:** A row is updated where the primary key value is matched.

- **writeTuple:** A row is updated if a matching row already exists, or inserted if there is no matching row.

- **deleteTuple:** A row is deleted where the primary key value is matched.

Note that NdbOperation::readTuple() takes one argument, NdbOperation::LM_Read. The argument specifies a lock mode, and it's a shared lock in this case. You can specify the lock mode using the following four modes:

- **LM_Read:** Shared lock is held on the row throughout the transaction lifecycle.

- **LM_Exclusive:** Exclusive lock is held on the row throughout the transaction lifecycle.

- **LM_CommittedRead:** No lock is acquired and read committed rows.

- **LM_SimpleRead:** Shared lock is acquired, but released right after the operation.

In the second line of this step, NdbOperation::equal() is called. This specifies a primary key name and value to be searched. In this case, a row that has the value of the Code column matching JPN is searched. If the primary key consists of multiple key parts (columns), call the NdbOperation::equal() function multiple times, so that values are given for all key parts.

Step 8. Get Buffers for Results

In this step, buffers to store fetched values are allocated by calling NdbOperation::getValue().
This function just prepares the buffer, and the actual operation is executed a little bit later, just like NdbOperation::readTuple(). In this example, the column name of the fetch value is specified as the first argument of NdbOperation::getValue(). The first argument of NdbOperation::getValue() would be:

- An attribute (column) name in a null terminated string (char*)

- Attribute identifier in Uint32

- Instance of NdbDictionary::Column class retrieved from a dictionary

Note that the column name in the NDB API is case-sensitive. Specify exactly what can be seen in the table definition. The second argument is a pointer to the memory area where data will be stored. If NULL just like in this example, memory is allocated automatically and freed later when the instance of NdbRecAttr is deleted. So, you must copy the retrieved data before closing the transaction if you want to reuse it later.

I recommend specifying the second argument of the NdbOperation::getValue() function to avoid unnecessary data copy for better performance. In such cases, the memory area where the fetched value is stored will not be freed even when the NdbRecAttr instance is deleted. However, the NDB API doesn't know whether the buffer has sufficient space to store the data, because the argument is just a pointer. Ensure that sufficient space is allocated. You can calculate the required size to store the column value from the table definition.

Step 9. Send a Request to the Data Nodes

A request is sent to the data node by calling NdbTransaction::execute(). Then, the data node will process the request and send the reply to the NDB API program. The NDB API sets the values according to specification of the NdbRecAttr instances.

Note that the argument of the NdbTransaction::execute() function in this example is NdbTransaction::Commit. This indicates that the ongoing transaction is committed as the name implies. This function will take one of the following values as an argument:

- **NdbTransaction::NoCommit:** When this value is specified, a request is sent to data nodes, but transaction continues. Specify this value when there are more operations to be done within the same transaction.

- **NdbTransaction::Commit:** The ongoing transaction will be committed.

- **NdbTransaction::Rollback:** The ongoing transaction will be rolled back.

Step 10. Retrieve the Values

Values are retrieved from the NdbRecAttr instances. You can retrieve the string value by calling the NdbRecAttr::aRef()function. However, the string value is not null terminated. You must determine the size of the string value using NdbRecAttr::get_size_in_bytes(). Since the Capital is an UNSIGNED INT column, you can access the value by calling NdbRecAttr::u_32_value().

Step 11. Clean Up

In this step, the necessary cleanup is performed. Note that the cleanup is done in the destructor of the NdbApiExample1 class. It's called when a program exits the scope where the instance of NdbApiExample1 is declared as a local variable. Performing the necessary cleanup upon scope exit is a handy technique for a C++ program.

Accessing Data Using NdbRecord

When working with the NdbRecAttr class, it is necessary to create instances of the class so many times, because the NdbRecAttr class instances are retrieved from the NdbOperation class instance. It causes a certain overhead within NDB API programs. To reduce the overhead caused by this, the NdbRecord class was added in MySQL NDB Cluster 6.2.15.

What NdbRecord does is to define the relative memory layout to the pointer where the data is stored or loaded from the NDB API to interact with the data nodes. When using the NdbRecord interface, data is exchanged using a contiguous memory area per row, while NdbRecAttr binds the memory area to exchange data per column. Other than the difference upon specifying memory layout, the flow of program is same for the NdbRecAttr and NdbRecord programming interfaces.

Listing 19-12 shows an example program that uses the NdbRecord class to exchange data. Only the different part is excerpted. Steps 1 to 4 and 11 are the same as in Listing 19-11. Some extra header files for standard libraries must be included in addition to what's included in Listing 19-11.

Listing 19-12. Sample NDB API Program That Reads a Row from a Table Using `NdbRecord`

```
...
#include <stddef.h>
#include <cstdint>
#include <cstring>
...
  // Step 5. Define NdbRecord memory area for rows of City table
  struct CountryRow {
    char    nullBits;
    char    Code[3];
    char    Name[52];
    Uint32  Capital;
  };

  NdbDictionary::RecordSpecification recordSpec[3];

  // Code
  recordSpec[0].column = myTable->getColumn("Code");
  recordSpec[0].offset = offsetof(struct CountryRow, Code);
  recordSpec[0].nullbit_byte_offset = 0;    // Not nullable
  recordSpec[0].nullbit_bit_in_byte = 0;

  // Name
  recordSpec[1].column = myTable->getColumn("Name");
  recordSpec[1].offset = offsetof(struct CountryRow, Name);
  recordSpec[1].nullbit_byte_offset = 0;    // Not nullable
  recordSpec[1].nullbit_bit_in_byte = 0;

  // Capital
  recordSpec[2].column = myTable->getColumn("Capital");
  recordSpec[2].offset = offsetof(struct CountryRow, Capital);
  recordSpec[2].nullbit_byte_offset =
    offsetof(struct CountryRow, nullBits);;   // Nullable
  recordSpec[2].nullbit_bit_in_byte = 0;

  const NdbRecord *pkRecord =
    myDict->createRecord(myTable, recordSpec, 1, sizeof(recordSpec[0]));
  const NdbRecord *valsRecord =
    myDict->createRecord(myTable, recordSpec, 3, sizeof(recordSpec[0]));
  if (pkRecord == NULL || valsRecord == NULL) {
    print_error(myNdb->getNdbError(), "Could not create NdbRecord.");
    return 5;
  }

  // Step 6. Start transaction
  myTransaction= myNdb->startTransaction();
  if (myTransaction == NULL) {
    print_error(myNdb->getNdbError(), "Could not start transaction.");
    return 6;
  }
```

```
// Step 7. Specify type of operation and search condition
CountryRow rowData;
std::memset(&rowData, 0, sizeof rowData);
std::memcpy(&rowData.Code, "JPN", 3);
const NdbOperation *pop=
  myTransaction->readTuple(pkRecord,
                           (char*) &rowData,
                           valsRecord,
                           (char*) &rowData);
if (pop==NULL) {
  print_error(myTransaction->getNdbError(),
              "Could not execute record based read operation");
  return 7;
}
```

```
// Step 8. Send a request to data nodes
if (myTransaction->execute( NdbTransaction::Commit ) == -1) {
  print_error(myTransaction->getNdbError(), "Transaction failed.");
  return 8;
}
```

```
// Step 9. Retrieve values
std::string nameStr = std::string(rowData.Name, sizeof(rowData.Name));
std::cout << " Name:         "
          << nameStr.substr(0, nameStr.find_last_not_of(' ') + 1)
          << std::endl;
std::cout << " Capital Code: "
          << (rowData.nullBits & 0x01 ? std::string("NULL") :
                                        std::to_string(rowData.Capital))
          << std::endl;

  return 0;
}
```

Let's examine each new step of this program.

Step 5. Define the NdbRecords

NdbRecord is a descriptor of the memory layout for a given set of columns per row mapped to a contiguous memory area. The CountryRow struct represents a memory area to be accessed via the NdbRecord interface. Typically, a struct like in this example is used as a container of data. So, the application can access the column data in a row via the struct members. Of course, it can be a class instead of a struct.

Then, the program declares an array of NdbDictionary::RecordSpecification with three elements. This class specifies the memory location and property of each column accessed via the NdbRecord interface. Since this program accesses three columns, three instances of the NdbDictionary::RecordSpecification struct are used. The column member specifies the target column. The offset member specifies the relative offset from the beginning of the contiguous memory area to exchange row data. The nullbit_byte_offset and nullbit_bit_in_byte members specify the location of null-bit set when a column is NULL. The former is a relative offset of bytes where the null-bit is stored. The latter is which bit within a byte is used to indicate if the column is NULL or not. Thus, acceptable values for the nullbit_bit_in_byte member are 0 to 7.

Next, two NdbRecord class instances are created, one for the primary key value to be passed as a search condition, and one for the column values to be fetched from the data nodes. The third argument of the Nd bDictionary::Dictionary::createRecord() function is the number of columns mapped by the created NdbRecord instance.

Step 6. Start the Transaction

Start a new transaction just like when you're using the NdbRecAttr interface.

Step 7. Specify the Type of Operation and Search Condition

A variable of the CountryRow struct, rowData, is declared and initialized by 0. Then, the Code member of rowData is set to JPN to be used as a search condition.

A pointer to the NdbOperation class is retrieved by calling the NdbTransaction::readTuple() function. This instructs the NDB API that the type of upcoming operation is readTule, and which NdbRecord and relevant memory area are used as containers for the search condition and result.

Recall that the same thing is done in the NdbRecAttr interface by acquiring the NdbOperation class instance from NdbTransaction first, then specifying the operation type by calling readTuple(), specifying the search condition by calling NdbOperation::equal(), and specifying the memory containers for each column by calling NdbOperation::getValue().

Thus, the number of calls of NDB API functions is much fewer in the NdbRecord interface. Be aware that number of steps in this example program is one less than the number of steps in the NdbRecAttr example program.

Step 8. Send a Request to the Data Nodes

Execute a transaction just like when using the NdbRecAttr interface.

Step 9. Retrieve the Values

Value retrieval is very simple in NdbRecord. It can be achieved by just accessing the struct members.

Remarks About Using the NdbRecord Interface

While the code to create the NdbRecord instances is somewhat messy, it is possible to reuse the created NdbRecord instances once they are defined. So, this code has a clear advantage in terms of performance when implementing repeating program routines. The table access in the NDBCluster storage engine is implemented using the NDBRecord interface.

Scan Example

A scan is much more complex operation than primary-key based lookup operations. All other operations are scans. There are two types of scans:

- Table scan
- Ordered index scan

Due to the nature of scan operations, it is not possible to scan a unique hash index.

The most powerful feature of a scan via the NDB API is that it can filter data inside the data nodes. This will dramatically reduce size of data transferred to the NDB API client. This functionality is also known as *engine condition pushdown* optimization for the NDB Cluster storage engine. Scan filtering can be used together with ordered indexes, too. Figure 19-3 shows a typical architectural overview of scan filtering. A scan is typically performed on all data nodes in parallel unless the table uses a non-standard distribution strategy.

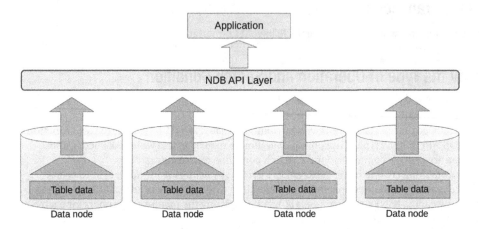

Figure 19-3. *Concept of search filtering on a data node*

A scan is very similar to a cursor operation in SQL; a cursor is defined first, then handle the row data in a loop, update, or delete the row if needed. Figure 19-4 shows a typical program flow for scan operations. Be aware that the bottom-right part consists of a loop.

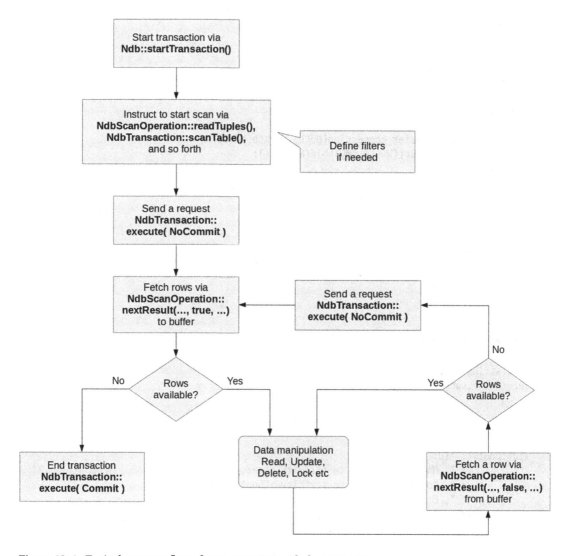

Figure 19-4. *Typical program flow of scan operation with the NDB API*

Just like with a non-scan operation, a scan can be performed using the NdbRecAttr or NdbRecord interface. Since there are good examples in the manual for the NdbRecAttr interface, you'll see an example of a scan using the NdbRecord interface. Listing 19-13 shows an example scan operation. The program includes three scan examples—table scan, index scan, and update with table scan. Since the program is long, it's split into three parts for explanation. Listings 19-13 to 19-15 consist of one sample program as a whole. This example program needs an index on the Population column of the world.City table.

Listing 19-13. Simple Example of the Scan Operation: First Part of Three

```
#include <NdbApi.hpp>
#include <iostream>
#include <string>
#include <stddef.h>
```

```cpp
#include <cstdint>
#include <cstring>

const char *connectstring = "mgmhost";
const char *db = "world";

class NdbApiExample3 {
public:
  NdbApiExample3() : cluster_connection(NULL), myNdb(NULL),
                     myDict(NULL), myTable(NULL) {};
  ~NdbApiExample3();
  int doTest();

private:
  struct CityRow {
    Int32 ID;
    char   Name[35];
    char   CountryCode[3];
    char   District[20];
    Int32 Population;
  };

  std::string char_to_str(char *s, int max_len)
  {
    std::string str(s, max_len);
    return str.substr(0, str.find_last_not_of(" ") + 1);
  }

  void print_city(CityRow *city)
  {
    std::cout << "Id: " << city->ID
              << ", Name: " << char_to_str(city->Name, 35)
              << ", Code: " << char_to_str(city->CountryCode, 3)
              << ", District: " << char_to_str(city->District, 20)
              << ", Population: " << city->Population
              << std::endl;
  }

  int do_scan_read();
  int do_index_scan_read();
  int do_scan_update();

  void print_error(const NdbError &e, const char *msg)
  {
    std::cerr << msg << ": Error code (" << e.code << "): "
              << e.message << "." << std::endl;
  }

  Ndb_cluster_connection *cluster_connection;
  Ndb *myNdb;
  NdbDictionary::Dictionary* myDict;
  const NdbDictionary::Table *myTable;
```

```
  const NdbDictionary::Index *myIndex;
  const NdbDictionary::Column *myColumn;
  const NdbRecord *pkRecord, *valsRecord, *indexRecord;
};

int NdbApiExample3::doTest()
{
  // Step 1. Initialize NDB API
  ndb_init();

  // Step 2. Connect to the cluster
  cluster_connection = new Ndb_cluster_connection(connectstring);
  if (cluster_connection->connect(4 /* retries               */,
                                  5 /* delay between retries */,
                                  1 /* verbose               */)) {
    std::cerr << "Could not connect to MGMD." << std::endl;
    return 1;
  }

  if (cluster_connection->wait_until_ready(30, 0) < 0) {
    std::cerr << "Could not connect to NDBD." << std::endl;
    return 2;
  }

  // Step 3. Connect to 'world' database
  myNdb = new Ndb(cluster_connection, db);
  if (myNdb->init()) {
    print_error(myNdb->getNdbError(),
                "Could not connect to the database object.");
    return 3;
  }

  // Step 4. Get table metadata
  myDict = myNdb->getDictionary();
  myTable = myDict->getTable("City");
  myIndex = myDict->getIndex("Population", "City");
  myColumn = myTable->getColumn("CountryCode");
  if (myTable == NULL || myIndex == NULL || myColumn == NULL) {
    print_error(myDict->getNdbError(),
                "Could not retrieve database object.");
    return 4;
  }

  // Step 5. Define NdbRecord's
  NdbDictionary::RecordSpecification recordSpec[5];
  std::memset(recordSpec, 0, sizeof recordSpec);
  // Id
  recordSpec[0].column = myTable->getColumn("ID");
  recordSpec[0].offset = offsetof(struct CityRow, ID);

  // Name
  recordSpec[1].column = myTable->getColumn("Name");
  recordSpec[1].offset = offsetof(struct CityRow, Name);
```

```
// CountryCode
recordSpec[2].column = myTable->getColumn("CountryCode");
recordSpec[2].offset = offsetof(struct CityRow, CountryCode);

// District
recordSpec[3].column = myTable->getColumn("District");
recordSpec[3].offset = offsetof(struct CityRow, District);

// Population
recordSpec[4].column = myTable->getColumn("Population");
recordSpec[4].offset = offsetof(struct CityRow, Population);

int rssz = sizeof(recordSpec[0]);
pkRecord = myDict->createRecord(myTable, recordSpec, 1, rssz);
valsRecord = myDict->createRecord(myTable, recordSpec, 5, rssz);
indexRecord = myDict->createRecord(myIndex, &recordSpec[4], 1, rssz);

if (pkRecord == NULL || valsRecord == NULL || indexRecord == NULL) {
  print_error(myDict->getNdbError(), "Failed to initialize rssz.");
  return 5;
}

// Run tests. See lines of routines for details.
int err = 0;
if ((err = do_scan_read()) ||
    (err = do_index_scan_read()) ||
    (err = do_scan_update())) {
  std::cout << "Transaction failed due to error ("
            << err << ")." << std::endl;
}
  return err;
}

int NdbApiExample3::do_scan_read()
{
  // Step 6. Start a new transaction
  NdbTransaction *myTransaction = myNdb->startTransaction();
  if (myTransaction == NULL) {
    print_error(myNdb->getNdbError(), "Could not start transaction.");
    return 6;
  }

  // Step 7. Prepare filter to be applied
  NdbInterpretedCode code(myTable);
  NdbScanFilter filter(&code);
  if (filter.begin(NdbScanFilter::AND) < 0 ||
      filter.cmp(NdbScanFilter::COND_LIKE,
                 myColumn->getColumnNo(), "JPN", 3) < 0 ||
      filter.end() < 0) {
    print_error(myTransaction->getNdbError(), "Failed to get a filter.");
    myNdb->closeTransaction(myTransaction);
    return 7;
  }
```

```
Uint32 scanFlags = NdbScanOperation::SF_TupScan;
NdbScanOperation::ScanOptions options;
options.optionsPresent =
  NdbScanOperation::ScanOptions::SO_SCANFLAGS |
  NdbScanOperation::ScanOptions::SO_INTERPRETED;
options.scan_flags = scanFlags;
options.interpretedCode= &code;

// Step 8. Instruct NDB API to scan table
NdbScanOperation *sop =
  myTransaction->scanTable(valsRecord,
                           NdbOperation::LM_CommittedRead,
                           NULL,
                           &options,
                           sizeof(NdbScanOperation::ScanOptions));
if (sop == NULL) {
  print_error(myTransaction->getNdbError(),
              "Could not retrieve an operation.");
  myNdb->closeTransaction(myTransaction);
  return 8;
}

// Step 9. Send a request to data nodes
if (myTransaction->execute( NdbTransaction::NoCommit ) == -1) {
  print_error(myTransaction->getNdbError(), "Failed to prepare a scan.");
  myNdb->closeTransaction(myTransaction);
  return 5;
}

// Step 10. Fetch rows in a loop
int check = 0;
bool needToFetch = true;
CityRow *row;
while((check = sop->nextResult((const char**) &row,
                              needToFetch, false)) >= 0) {
  if (check == 0) {
    // Row available
    needToFetch = false;
    print_city(row);
  } else if (check == 2) {
    // Need to fetch
    myTransaction->execute(NdbTransaction::NoCommit);
    needToFetch = true;
  } else if (check == 1) {
    // No more rows
    break;
  }
}
```

```
// Step 11. End transaction and free it
if (check == -1) {
  print_error(myTransaction->getNdbError(), "Error during scan.");
  myNdb->closeTransaction(myTransaction);
  return 11;
} else {
  myTransaction->execute(NdbTransaction::Commit);
}
myNdb->closeTransaction(myTransaction);
return 0;
}
```

We skip the discussion for steps that do the same things as in the previous examples. Only parts specific to a scan operation are explained in the following discussion.

Step 5. Define NdbRecords

The indexRecord variable is created using myIndex as the first argument of the NdbDictionary::Dictionary ::createRecord() function. This is because indexRecord is used for an index scan operation.

Step 7. Prepare the Filter To Be Applied

A variable of type NdbInterpretedCode is created from the NdbDictionary::Table instance. Then, a variable of type NdbScanFilter is created from the NdbInterpretedCode instance. NdbScanFilter is the class to define a filter.

The argument of the NdbScanFilter::begin() function is NdbScanFilter::AND, NdbScanFilter::OR, NdbScanFilter::NAND, or NdbScanFilter::NOR.

This specifies the logical operator applied when there is more than one search condition defined in the filter.

The call of the NdbScanFilter::cmp() function defines the filter to be applied. In this example, the defined filter is used to fetch rows where the CountryCode column is JPN. The first argument of the NdbScanFilter::cmp() function specifies the type of operation. While NdbScanFilter::COND_LIKE is specified in this case, it is a condition type for strings. Table 19-6 lists the available condition types.

Table 19-6. *Condition Types Defined in NdbScanFilter*

Condition Type	Data Type	Description
COND_LE	Numeric	Less than or equal (<=)
COND_LT	Numeric	Less than (<)
COND_GE	Numeric	Greater than or equal (>=)
COND_GT	Numeric	Greater than (>)
COND_EQ	Numeric	Equal (=)
COND_NE	Numeric	Not equal (!=)
COND_LIKE	String	Like search for strings
COND_NOT_LIKE	String	Not like search for strings

(continued)

Table 19-6. (*continued*)

Condition Type	Data Type	Description
COND_AND_EQ_MASK	BIT	A column value equals the result of the bit operation
COND_AND_NE_MASK	BIT	A column value does not equal the result of the bit operation
COND_AND_EQ_ZERO	BIT	Result of bit operation is zero
COND_AND_NE_ZERO	BIT	Result of bit operation is a non-zero value

When the like search is employed, you can search data in string columns using the '%' or '_' character as wildcards just like in SQL. The NdbScanFilter class has other comparison functions—eq(), ne(), le(), lt(), ge(), and gt()—as a human readable shorthand of cmp() with the specific condition type. To test if the column is NULL or not, the NdbScanFilter class has the isnull() and isnotnull() functions, too.

NdbScanOperation::ScanOptions is a struct to options of scan. The interpreted code created by the filter we just discussed and scan flags are passed to this struct in the example program. Scan flags specify some additional properties of the scan, as described in Table 19-7. Although scan flags are defined in the NdbScanOperation class, the class name is omitted in Table 19-7.

Table 19-7. *Scan Flags*

Flag Name	Description
SF_TupScan	Scan in the order of rows in the DBTUP kernel block.
SF_DiskScan	Scan in the order of rows on disk.
SF_OrderBy	Scan in the order of rows in the index. This is applicable to ordered index scan operations only.
SF_OrderByFull	Same as SF_OrderBy except that all key columns are added automatically to the read bitmask.
SF_Descending	Ordered index scan is done in descending order.
SF_ReadRangeNo	Upon a multi-range scan, identifier of range is returned.
SF_MultiRange	Multi-range scan is performed.
SF_KeyInfo	Requests KeyInfo to be sent back to the caller, which is required for further operation.

Step 8. Instruct the NDB API to Scan the Table

In this step, NdbTransaction::scanTable() is called to declare that the program is going to perform a table scan using the NdbRecord interface. This is followed by NdbTransaction::execute() in Step 9. Be aware that the argument is NoCommit, because scans need further operations.

Step 10. Fetch Rows in a Loop

NdbScanOperation::nextResult() fetches a row from the data nodes. A fetch from the data node is done in a batch, then stored temporarily in a buffer in the NDB API library. When the second argument is true, the fetch is done from the data node. Otherwise, a row is just retrieved from a buffer.

When a row is fetched, NdbScanOperation::nextResult() returns 0. If fetch is done, but no more matching rows are found, it returns 1. If it attempted to retrieve a row from the local buffer, but no rows are available locally, it returns 2. When an error happens, it returns -1.

While it is possible to write a scan program by always specifying true for the second argument of NdbSc anOperation::nextResult(), I do not recommend doing so. Batching is a very efficient method, and it can improve the application performance dramatically.

This is a basic program flow of a scan operation. The scan operation is done in a similar way no matter how complex it is. The example ordered index scan program is shown in Listing 19-14, which is continued from Listing 19-13.

Listing 19-14. Simple Example of the Scan Operation: Second Part of Three

```
int NdbApiExample3::do_index_scan_read()
{
// Step 1. Start a new transaction
 NdbTransaction *myTransaction = myNdb->startTransaction();
 if (myTransaction == NULL) {
   print_error(myNdb->getNdbError(), "Could not start transaction.");
   return 1;
 }


// Step 2. Prepare filter to be applied
 NdbInterpretedCode code(myTable);
 NdbScanFilter filter(&code);
 if (filter.begin(NdbScanFilter::AND) < 0 ||
     filter.cmp(NdbScanFilter::COND_LIKE,
               myColumn->getColumnNo(), "JPN", 3) < 0 ||
     filter.end() < 0) {
   print_error(myTransaction->getNdbError(), "Failed to set a filter.");
   myNdb->closeTransaction(myTransaction);
   return 2;
 }


 Uint32 scanFlags =
     NdbScanOperation::SF_OrderBy | NdbScanOperation::SF_Descending;
 NdbScanOperation::ScanOptions options;
 options.optionsPresent =
     NdbScanOperation::ScanOptions::SO_SCANFLAGS |
     NdbScanOperation::ScanOptions::SO_INTERPRETED;
 options.scan_flags = scanFlags;
 options.interpretedCode= &code;


// Step 3. Define index boundary
 CityRow low, high;
 low.Population = 1000000;
 high.Population = 2000000;
 NdbIndexScanOperation::IndexBound bound;
 bound.low_key= (char*)&low;
 bound.low_key_count = 1;
 bound.low_inclusive = true;
 bound.high_key = (char*)&high;
 bound.high_key_count =1 ;
```

```
bound.high_inclusive = false;
bound.range_no = 0;
```

// Step 4. Instruct NDB API to scan index
```
NdbIndexScanOperation *isop =
  myTransaction->scanIndex(indexRecord,
                           valsRecord,
                           NdbOperation::LM_Read,
                           NULL,
                           &bound,
                           &options,        -
                           sizeof(NdbScanOperation::ScanOptions));
if (isop == NULL) {
  print_error(myTransaction->getNdbError(),
              "Could not retrieve an operation.");
  myNdb->closeTransaction(myTransaction);
  return 4;
}
```

// Step 5. Send a request to data nodes
```
if (myTransaction->execute( NdbTransaction::NoCommit ) == -1) {
  print_error(myTransaction->getNdbError(), "Failed to prepare a scan.");
  myNdb->closeTransaction(myTransaction);
  return 5;
}
```

// Step 6. Fetch rows in a loop
```
int check = 0;
bool needToFetch = true;
CityRow *row;
while((check = isop->nextResult((const char**) &row,
                                needToFetch, false)) >= 0) {
  if (check == 0) {
    // Row available
    needToFetch = false;
    print_city(row);
  } else if (check == 2) {
    // Need to fetch rows
    myTransaction->execute(NdbTransaction::NoCommit);
    needToFetch = true;
  } else if (check == 1) {
    // No more rows
    break;
  }
}
```

// Step 7. End transaction and free it
```
if (check == -1) {
  print_error(myTransaction->getNdbError(), "Error during index scan.");
  myNdb->closeTransaction(myTransaction);
  return 7;
```

```
  } else {
    myTransaction->execute(NdbTransaction::Commit);
  }
  myNdb->closeTransaction(myTransaction);
  return 0;
}
```

As you can see, the program in Listing 19-14 is very close to the scan program in Listing 19-13. The only different part is the boundary definition in Step 3 and the operation type in Step 4.

Step 3. Define the Index Boundary

The NdbIndexScanOperation::IndexBound class is used to define a boundary of the index for the NdbRecord interface. Two variables of the CityRow struct are used to specify the lower and upper bounds of the scanned range of the index. The boundary is passed to an argument of the NdbTransaction::scanIndex() function, as described in the next step. It is possible to apply the boundary after calling the NdbTransaction::scanIn dex()the boundary argument as NULL. In this case, NdbIndexScanOperation::setBound() must be called to set the boundary before calling NdbTransaction::execute().

Step 4. Instruct the NDB API to Scan the Index

In this example, NdbTransaction::scanIndex() is called to perform the ordered index scan, instead of NdbTransaction::scanTable() in the previous example.

The last example of a scan operation involves updating rows during the scan. Listing 19-15 shows an example program that updates rows along with the scan operation.

Listing 19-15. Simple Example of the Scan Operation: Third Part of Three

```
int NdbApiExample3::do_scan_update()
{
  // Step 1. Start a new transaction
  NdbTransaction *myTransaction = myNdb->startTransaction();
  if (myTransaction == NULL) {
    print_error(myNdb->getNdbError(), "Could not start transaction.");
    return 1;
  }

  // Step 2. Prepare filter to be applied
  NdbInterpretedCode code(myTable);
  NdbScanFilter filter(&code);
  if (filter.begin(NdbScanFilter::AND) < 0 ||
      filter.cmp(NdbScanFilter::COND_LIKE,
                 myColumn->getColumnNo(), "JPN", 3) < 0 ||
      filter.end() < 0) {
    print_error(myTransaction->getNdbError(), "Failed to set a filter.");
    myNdb->closeTransaction(myTransaction);
    return 2;
  }
```

```
Uint32 scanFlags = NdbScanOperation::SF_KeyInfo;
NdbScanOperation::ScanOptions options;
options.optionsPresent =
  NdbScanOperation::ScanOptions::SO_SCANFLAGS |
  NdbScanOperation::ScanOptions::SO_INTERPRETED;
options.scan_flags = scanFlags;
options.interpretedCode= &code;

// Step 3. Instruct NDB API to scan table
NdbScanOperation *sop =
  myTransaction->scanTable(valsRecord,
                           NdbOperation::LM_Exclusive,
                           NULL,
                           &options,
                           sizeof(NdbScanOperation::ScanOptions));
if (sop == NULL) {
  print_error(myTransaction->getNdbError(),
              "Could not retrieve an operation.");
  myNdb->closeTransaction(myTransaction);
  return 3;
}

// Step 4. Send a request to data nodes
if (myTransaction->execute( NdbTransaction::NoCommit ) == -1) {
  print_error(myTransaction->getNdbError(), "Failed to prepare a scan.");
  myNdb->closeTransaction(myTransaction);
  return 4;
}

// Step 5. Update rows in a loop
int check = 0;
bool needToFetch = true;
CityRow *row;
while((check = sop->nextResult((const char**) &row,
                              needToFetch, false)) >= 0) {
  if (check == 0) {
    // Row available
    needToFetch = false;
    CityRow newCity = *row;
    std::memcpy(&newCity.CountryCode, "ZPG", 3);
    const NdbOperation *uop =
        sop->updateCurrentTuple(myTransaction,
                                valsRecord,
                                (char*) &newCity);
    if (uop == NULL) {
      print_error(myTransaction->getNdbError(), "Failed update row.");
      myNdb->closeTransaction(myTransaction);
      return 5;
    }
  } else if (check == 2) {
    // Need to fetch rows
```

```
      myTransaction->execute(NdbTransaction::NoCommit);
      needToFetch = true;
    } else if (check == 1) {
      // No more rows
      break;
    }
  }

  // Step 6. End transaction and free it
  if (check == -1) {
    print_error(myTransaction->getNdbError(), "Error during scan update.");
    myNdb->closeTransaction(myTransaction);
    return 6;
  } else {
    myTransaction->execute(NdbTransaction::Commit);
  }
  myNdb->closeTransaction(myTransaction);
  return 0;
}

NdbApiExample3::~NdbApiExample3()
{
  // Step 7. Cleanup
  if (myNdb) delete myNdb;
  if (cluster_connection) delete cluster_connection;
  ndb_end(0);
}

int main(int argc, char *argv[])
{
  NdbApiExample3 ex;
  return ex.doTest();
}
```

The program in Listing 19-15 is mostly same as the one in Listing 19-13, except that rows are updated inside the loop of fetching rows at Step 5. The way to update a row is very simple; you just call the NdbScanO peration::updateCurrentTuple() function. As the name implies, it updates the latest fetched row by the NdbScanOperation::nextResult() function by replacing the value of the row with new value. You can also delete the current row using NdbScanOperation::deleteCurrentTuple() and lock the current row using Ndb ScanOperation::lockCurrentTuple().

Error-Handling Considerations

The example programs in this section don't have sufficient error-handling facilities. They are just examples; the primary goal of these programs is ease of understanding. While the NDB API is a transactional database manipulation API, transactions may fail for various reasons. The transaction theory guarantees that every transaction ends in two states—COMMIT or ABORT. The former is a successful state, and the latter is a state where the transaction is rolled back due to some error. The theory doesn't guarantee that transaction will succeed every time.

Thus, error handling, including a retry of the transaction, is required for NDB API applications just like with SQL applications. To implement error-handling routines on an NDB API application, note the following points.

Acquiring Error Information

As you have seen in this section, error information can be referred using the NdbError struct instance, which can be retrieved by calling the Ndb::getNdbError() function. Since it's retrieved from the Ndb object, it is not available before the Ndb object is retrieved to connect to the database. So you need separate error-handling implementatiosn in the early stages of your application. While the getNdbError() function is implemented on other classes than Ndb, all of them are created using the existing Ndb class object.

To implement a routine to retry transactions, it is necessary to judge if the unsuccessful transaction is retriable. This can be done by examining the status member of the NdbError struct. If it is equal to NdbError::TemporaryError, the transaction can be retried.

Transaction Is Automatically Rolled Back

In MySQL NDB Cluster, when a transaction failed for some reason, it is automatically rolled back and no further operations are acceptable through the failed transaction. You need to close the transaction right away and then retry the transaction using a new instance of NdbTransaction.

Insert Reasonable Wait Before Retry

Temporary errors won't go away immediately, because the resources will not be available until other transactions release their own. So, it is a good idea to insert some reasonable wait time before retrying a transaction. Otherwise, the attempt to retry a transaction will likely to fail due to the same temporary error.

Together with the story so far in this section, you can write code to retry the transaction, as shown in Listing 19-16. Note that this code is just conceptual. You need to write your own code to do the actual work.

Listing 19-16. Overview Concept Code to Retry Transactions on the NDB API

```
int exitCode = incomplete;
int retryCount = 10;
int retryDelay = 50;
while (retryCount-- > 0) {
  // Obtain a new transaction handle
  NdbTransaction myTransaction = myNdb->startTransaction();
  ... Write code to execute some operation here ...
  if (found_error) {
    const NdbError err = myNdb->getNdbError();
    // Judge if error is retriable
    if (err.status == NdbError::TemporaryError) {
      // Close transaction
      myNdb->closeTransaction(myTransaction);
      // Sleep before retry
      millisleep(retryDelay);
      continue;
    } else {
      exitCode = failure;
      break;
    }
  } else {
    exitCode = successful;
  }
}
```

In this section, you learned how to develop applications using the NDB API. You can modify data using transactions on the NDB API. Transactions make development easier.

Operations described in this section, such as lookup and scan, are low-level functionalities. While they are low-level, it is technically possible to implement high-level functionalities just like with SQL, by combining low-level functionalities as building blocks. Even when possible, it will take more time than if you're developing an application using high-level APIs such as SQL. However, the effort will pay off if the application requires superb performance.

In the next section, we discuss how to use ClusterJ, an API for the Java programming language. It is not common to develop entire database applications in C++; it is sometimes used partially where performance is important. Java is more widely used than C++ for database application development.

Accessing Data via ClusterJ

An official Java binding of the NDB API library, *ClusterJ*, has been available since the MySQL NDB Cluster 7.1 series. Although ClusterJ is a binding of the *libndbclient* library that calls the NDB API C++ functions through the *Java Native Interface* (or *JNI* in short), use of ClusterJ is much different from the NDB API itself. ClusterJ has an O/R mapper like interface. It uses ClusterJ much easier than the direct use of the NDB API.

Since Connector/J is available for Java applications to work with the SQL node, ClusterJ and Connector/J can be used depending on the situation, just like C++ application can use the MySQL C API and the NDB API.

A plugin for *OpenJPA*, a Java persistence project at *The Apache Software Foundation*, also exists, and it's called *ClusterJPA*. It automatically switches between the use of ClusterJ and Connector/J for the best possible performance. We will not discuss ClusterJPA in this book, because it's no longer supported as of following versions of MySQL NDB Cluster: 7.2.30, 7.3.18, 7.4.16, and 7.5.7.

Installing ClusterJ

A separate package is available for the *RPM* and *DEB* package managers in the MySQL NDB Cluster 7.5 series. The package name includes the string "java", like *mysql-cluster-community-java-7.5.6-1.el7.x86_64. rpm*. In older versions, ClusterJ is included in the *server* RPM package, and all-in-one type package for other package formats.

Since ClusterJ is a wrapper of the NDB API, the `libndbclient` library must also be installed on the same host. Refer to the installation section of the NDB API earlier in this chapter.

To run ClusterJ programs, *clusterj.jar* must be added to the classpath. The *clusterj.jar* is typically installed under */usr/share/mysql/java* on RHEL or Debian-based operating systems, and it has a string indicating the version number in its filename, like *clusterj-7.5.6.jar*. The path to the `libndbclient` library is also required to be passed to JVM via the `-Djava.library.path` option. It is typically installed under */usr/lib/mysql*. So, the command to run a ClusterJ application looks like this:

```
shell$ java -classpath /usr/share/mysql/java/clusterj-7.5.6.jar:. \
>           -Djava.library.path=/usr/lib/mysql ClusterJAppName
```

When compiling a ClusterJ application, *clusterj-api.jar* must be passed to the `javac` via the classpath. The command to compile ClusterJ application looks like this:

```
shell$ javac -classpath /usr/share/mysql/java/clusterj-api-7.5.6.jar \
>            ClusterJAppName.java
```

Writing a ClusterJ Application

To access the cluster, the first thing to do is acquire an instance of the com.mysql.clusterj.Session class. This is the counterpart to the Ndb class of the NDB API. An instance of the Session class is retrieved from com.mysql.clusterj.SessionFactory, which is retrieved from com.mysql.clusterj.ClusterJHelper.

You get data access via an interface with annotations. Mapping between the class member and column is accomplished by annotations. The interface must have a getter and setter for each column. Once the getter and setter are declared, ClusterJ identifies that the column should exist in the table. ClusterJ assumes that column names are lowercase. If the column name includes uppercase characters, annotation must be added just before the getter and setter declaration. It is necessary to write one interface for every table accessed by the application.

ClusterJ Example

Listings 19-17 to 19-19 show a ClusterJ example program. While they consist of three files, the main routine is shown in Listing 19-18 and called *ClusterJSimple.java*. We don't discuss the details of what is done in this example program. The purpose of the example program is to let you see the overall use of ClusterJ. Read the comments in the program to understand what is done at each stage of the program.

Listing 19-17. City.java: Interface Definition for the City Table

```
import com.mysql.clusterj.annotation.Column;
import com.mysql.clusterj.annotation.Index;
import com.mysql.clusterj.annotation.PersistenceCapable;
import com.mysql.clusterj.annotation.PrimaryKey;

// Step 1. Define an interface
@PersistenceCapable(table="City")
public interface City {
    @PrimaryKey
    @Column(name="ID")
    int getId();
    void setId(int id);

    @Column(name="Name")
    String getName();
    void setName(String name);

    @Column(name="District")
    String getDistrict();
    void setDistrict(String district);

    @Column(name="CountryCode")
    @Index(name="CountryCode")
    String getCountryCode();
    void setCountryCode(String countryCode);

    @Column(name="Population")
    int getPopulation();
    void setPopulation(int population);
}
```

Listing 19-18. ClusterJSimple.java: Example ClusterJ Program

```java
import com.mysql.clusterj.ClusterJHelper;
import com.mysql.clusterj.SessionFactory;
import com.mysql.clusterj.Session;
import com.mysql.clusterj.Query;
import com.mysql.clusterj.query.QueryBuilder;
import com.mysql.clusterj.query.QueryDomainType;

import java.io.*;
import java.util.Properties;
import java.util.List;
import java.util.ArrayList;
import java.util.Map;

public class ClusterJSimple {

    public static void main (String[] args)
        throws java.io.FileNotFoundException,
                java.io.IOException,
                com.mysql.clusterj.ClusterJException {

        // Step 2. Load properties from file
        File propsFile = new File("clusterj.properties");
        InputStream inStream = new FileInputStream(propsFile);
        Properties props = new Properties();
        props.load(inStream);

        // Step 3. Get a session instance
        SessionFactory factory = ClusterJHelper.getSessionFactory(props);
        Session session = factory.getSession();

        // Step 4. Create a new City instance and add one row
        City newCity = session.newInstance(City.class);
        newCity.setId(4080);
        newCity.setName("Tochigi");
        newCity.setDistrict("Tochigi");
        newCity.setCountryCode("JPN");
        newCity.setPopulation(140000);
        session.persist(newCity);
        System.out.println("Saved Tochigi-shi.");

        // Step 5. Find a row with ID = 1532
        City whatsThis = session.find(City.class, 1532);
        System.out.println("Name of city where ID = 1532 is "
                            + whatsThis.getName().trim() + ".");

        // Step 6. Find all rows with CountryCode = "JPN". Watch Step 9
        List<City> cities = findByCountryCode(session, "JPN");
        System.out.println("Cities in Japan.");
        int n = 1;
```

```
    for (City c: cities) {
        System.out.println((n++) + ":" + c.getName().trim());
    }

    // Step 7. Updating a row: increment population of Tokyo by 1000000
    City tokyo = whatsThis;
    tokyo.setPopulation(tokyo.getPopulation() + 1000000);
    session.updatePersistent(tokyo);

    // Step 8. Delete a row
    City tochigi = session.newInstance(City.class);
    tochigi.setId(4080);
    session.deletePersistent(tochigi);
    System.out.println("Deleted Tochigi-shi");
}

// Step 9. Scan example using a query builder
static List<City> findByCountryCode(Session session, String cc)
    throws com.mysql.clusterj.ClusterJException {
    QueryBuilder builder = session.getQueryBuilder();
    QueryDomainType<City> domain =
        builder.createQueryDefinition(City.class);
    domain.where(domain.get("countryCode")
                .equal(domain.param("cc")));
    Query<City> query = session.createQuery(domain);
    query.setParameter("cc", cc);
    printExplain(query);
    return query.getResultList();
}

// 10. Print execution plan
static <T> void printExplain(Query<T> q) {
    Map<String, Object> explain = q.explain();
    for (String k: explain.keySet()) {
        System.err.println(k + ":" + explain.get(k).toString());
    }
}
}
```

Listing 19-19. clusterj.properties: Example Connection Properties

```
com.mysql.clusterj.connectstring=mgmhost
com.mysql.clusterj.database=world
```

Since ClusterJ uses the NDB API internally, the programming style of ClusterJ is close to the NDB API. If you are familiar with the NDB API, you can use ClusterJ without struggling. Read the manual when you develop an application using ClusterJ: *https://dev.mysql.com/doc/ndbapi/en/mccj.html.*

Summary

The chapter discussed the NoSQL interface available for MySQL NDB Cluster. The major APIs covered in this chapter were memcached, the NDB API, and ClusterJ.

As you see, development in MySQL NDB Cluster is very flexible. Such flexibility is one of the strongest advantages of MySQL NDB Cluster. In general, a single application has various parts—one part may need complex queries, the other part may need very fast data access. It is possible to satisfy the performance and functionality needs using a variety of MySQL NDB Cluster APIs.

The only remaining topic to consider is performance, which is discussed in the next chapter.

CHAPTER 20

■ ■ ■

MySQL NDB Cluster and Application Performance Tuning

Performance is a very important topic for database management systems. A database management system without sufficient performance is useless. It is also true for MySQL NDB Cluster. This chapter discusses how to improve the performance of MySQL NDB Cluster.

MySQL NDB Cluster Tuning

To leverage computer resources, it is very important to set up the system properly, so that MySQL NDB Cluster utilizes the underlying processor, disk, network, and so forth. This section discusses how to configure the system so it's optimized for MySQL NDB Cluster.

Disabling Powersave and CPU Frequency Scaling

While *powersave* and *CPU frequency scaling* are good for power consumption, they are not good in terms of performance on MySQL NDB Cluster. They are even bad for the predictability of response time. When powersave and/or CPU frequency scaling are enabled, the CPU clock speed is adjusted according to the current system load. A CPU core may go into the idle state if there are not tasks to do on the CPU core.

For example, Intel CPUs have several power modes, called *C-states*, to save power. The name of each state defined in the C-state is labeled with the letter C followed by one digit and an extra letter if applicable. For example, C0, C1, C1E, C2 ... and so forth. The bigger the number, the deeper the CPU core sleeps and the more circuits are powered off. C0 indicates the core is operating and isn't sleeping. When the system is idle for a while, the operating system lets the CPU core go into idle C-state mode, such as C1.

The most significant problem when using the powersave mode with MySQL NDB Cluster is that it takes a long time to wake up sleeping CPU cores. It also takes time to increase the CPU clock speed when it's operating in a low clock speed and determines that the CPU core is busy. These time lags greatly impact the performance and response times of MySQL NDB Cluster.

To prevent such negative impacts due to idle states and CPU frequency scaling on Linux, use the performance CPU governor. The way to configure CPU governor depends on the distribution. Refer to the distribution's manual for details of CPU governor configurations. The following command is an example of how to set the governor to perform well on systems where the *cpupower* utility is installed. The command is common among distributions in which the cpupower utility is installed.

```
shell$ sudo cpupower frequency-set --governor performance
```

© Jesper Wisborg Krogh and Mikiya Okuno 2017
J. W. Krogh and M. Okuno, *Pro MySQL NDB Cluster*, https://doi.org/10.1007/978-1-4842-2982-8_20

Typically, the configuration file for the cpupower command is located at */etc/default/cpupower*. Edit the file and set governor='performance' on your hosts. The default value is ondemand in most cases, which causes an idle CPU core to go into idle C-state.

Optionally, if you are using Intel CPUs, it is possible to disable the idle state completely by setting the kernel parameter intel_idle.max_cstate=0. It is typically set in the line that starts with GRUB_CMDLINE_LINUX_DEFAULT= of */etc/default/grub* on systems using grub as the boot loader. (You need to create the actual grub configuration file from using the grub-mkconfig command after editing */etc/default/grub*.)

On Windows, you can choose the *High Performance* power plan from the Power Options screen of the Windows Control Panel, as shown in Figure 20-1. Note that the High Performance setting is hidden initially. You can expand the plan by clicking *Show Additional Plans*.

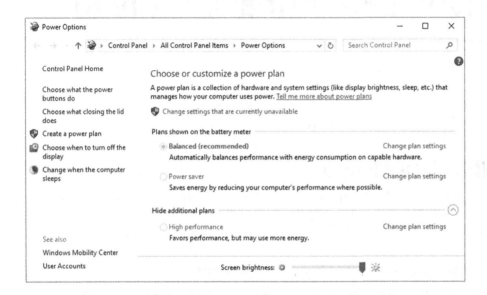

***Figure 20-1.** Setting the high performance power plan on Windows*

On Windows 10, you can open the *Power Options* screen by opening *Windows Settings*, then clicking on the *Systems* menu. Choose *Power & Sleep* and then *Additional Power Settings*, as shown in Figure 20-2.

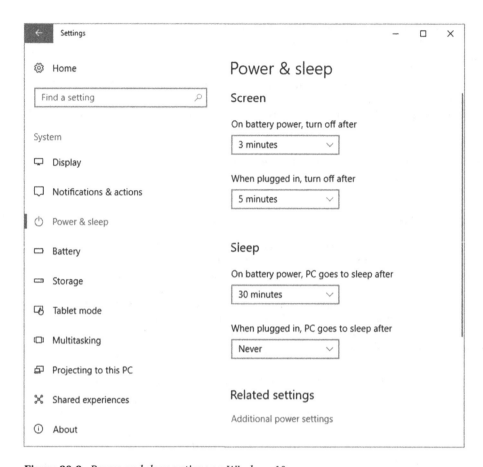

Figure 20-2. *Power and sleep options on Windows 10*

Note that power consumption will increase when you're using high performance mode. However, it is a worthy cost to pay, because the performance gain by disabling powersave and CPU frequency scaling is significant. We need more server machines to achieve the same level of performance if powersave is enabled. Running more server machines is much more expensive than disabling powersave with fewer server machines in terms of both money and electric power. Even when you're running more server machines with powersave mode enabled, the response time is usually worse than running fewer server machines with powersave mode disabled.

CPU Binding Strategy

CPU binding, or *processor affinity*, is the most significant factor for impacting the performance of the data node. However, configuring CPU binding is not an easy task. Performance degrades when you improperly bind threads to the CPUs. This section discusses how to maximize performance using CPU binding.

Hyper-Threading and CPU Binding

Hyper-threading (HT) is a commonly implemented in recent CPUs, such as Core series and Xeon series. With HT, multiple virtual CPU cores are identified on every physical CPU core from an operating system. A virtual CPU core behaves as if it were a physical CPU core. Since each virtual core can run a thread on it, more than one thread runs concurrently on the one physical CPU core.

657

HT may improve throughput of an application that runs many threads in parallel by sharing CPU hardware resources efficiently among threads. On the other hand, application response may be sacrificed by HT as a side-effect.

Sharing one physical core between threads brings poorly affects the MySQL NDB Cluster data node, because the number of signals that can be processed by one thread decreases when threads share one physical core. Such slow threading can be a bottleneck of the entire cluster. Don't bind more than one busy thread to virtual cores sharing the same physical core. The two threads will disturb the execution of each other.

■ **Caution**　Never bind more than one busy thread to a virtual code that shares the same physical core.

CPU Usage and Binding

It is important to balance the load of the CPU cores to maximize the performance of MySQL NDB Cluster. To achieve this goal, it is necessary to monitor the CPU utilization and adjust the configuration accordingly.

While typical busy thread types are ldm and tc, other type of threads may also be busy by chance. See Chapter 4 for further information about thread types. To identify which thread is busy, the ndbinfo.cpustat table comes in handy. It displays CPU utilization for each thread. The table shows CPU resource utilization bound for each thread. In other words, the table is useful only when the thread is bound to specific the CPU, because it is nonsense to see CPU utilization for a thread that runs on an arbitrary CPU core.

Listing 20-1 shows example output from the ndbinfo.cpustat table.

Listing 20-1. Inspecting CPU Utilization Using the cpustat Table

```
mysql> SELECT node_id, thr_no, thread_name, OS_user, OS_system, OS_idle FROM cpustat JOIN
threads USING (node_id, thr_no) WHERE node_id=1;
+---------+--------+-------------+---------+-----------+---------+
| node_id | thr_no | thread_name | OS_user | OS_system | OS_idle |
+---------+--------+-------------+---------+-----------+---------+
|       1 |      0 | main        |       0 |         1 |      99 |
|       1 |      8 | send        |       1 |         3 |      99 |
|       1 |      1 | rep         |       0 |         0 |     100 |
|       1 |      2 | ldm         |      65 |         2 |      33 |
|       1 |      3 | ldm         |       0 |        12 |      88 |
|       1 |      4 | tc          |       0 |        10 |      90 |
|       1 |      5 | tc          |       0 |        10 |      90 |
|       1 |      6 | recv        |       0 |         7 |      93 |
|       1 |      7 | recv        |       1 |         5 |      95 |
+---------+--------+-------------+---------+-----------+---------+
9 rows in set (0.08 sec)
```

According to this output, the data node has two ldm threads, two tc threads, two recv threads, one rep thread, one main thread, and one send thread. Only the one ldm thread with id=2 appears to be busy; the tc and recv threads consume CPU time. It is worth it to increase the number of ldm threads on this cluster. CPU usage of two ldm threads differ significantly because one handles the primary fragment of one table, and the other handles the backup fragment. Load will be balanced when the table has the READ_BACKUP=1 table comment and workload type is read.

While ndbinfo.cpustat displays the CPU utilization reported by the operating system, it may sometimes be unreliable, because it will include the CPU utilization caused by other programs, including interrupts handled inside the kernel. It will cause imbalanced CPU utilization among threads even if they are the same types of threads. In such case, you need to verify if the CPU utilization is really caused by an imbalanced workload within a data node.

To analyze the workload of each thread, the ndbinfo.threadstat table is useful. The table shows statistics per thread such as a count of signals handled by each thread. Listing 20-2 is an example of a stored procedure to see if workloads are balanced. If specific threads handle more signals than other, same types of threads, the workload is imbalanced.

Listing 20-2. Stored Procedure to Examine Load Balance Among Threads

```
delimiter //
CREATE PROCEDURE sigcount(t INT)
  BEGIN
    DROP TEMPORARY TABLE IF EXISTS tmpstat;
    CREATE TEMPORARY TABLE tmpstat ENGINE MEMORY
        SELECT * FROM ndbinfo.threadstat;
    SELECT SLEEP(t) FROM DUAL;

    SELECT STRAIGHT_JOIN
        s2.node_id,
        s2.thr_no,
        s2.thr_nm,
        (s2.os_now - s1.os_now) AS time_ms,
        (s2.c_loop - s1.c_loop) AS loops,
        (s2.c_exec - s1.c_exec) AS execs,
        (s2.c_wait - s1.c_wait) AS waits,
        (s2.c_exec - s1.c_exec) / (s2.c_loop - s1.c_loop) AS spl --signals_per_loop
      FROM
        tmpstat s1 INNER JOIN
        ndbinfo.threadstat s2 USING (node_id, thr_no)
      ORDER BY
        s1.node_id, s1.thr_no;

    DROP TEMPORARY TABLE tmpstat;
END;//
delimiter ;
mysql> CALL sigcount(5);
+-----------+
| SLEEP(t)  |
+-----------+
|         0 |
+-----------+
1 row in set (5.03 sec)
```

node_id	thr_no	thr_nm	time_ms	loops	execs	waits	spl
1	0	main	5046	3412	3531	1299	1.0349
1	1	rep	5046	1780	804	951	0.4517
1	2	ldm	5046	35380	608922	1628	17.2109
1	3	ldm	5046	46202	56861	12600	1.2307
1	4	tc	5046	35006	133170	11096	3.8042
1	5	tc	5046	35935	133070	11817	3.7031
1	6	recv	5047	27803	108	0	0.0039
1	7	recv	5045	20830	108	0	0.0052
2	0	main	5026	3219	2631	1257	0.8173
2	1	rep	5026	1741	803	948	0.4612
2	2	ldm	5027	48346	56283	13616	1.1642
2	3	ldm	5027	38280	634545	1727	16.5764
2	4	tc	5027	35159	132148	11385	3.7586
2	5	tc	5026	37624	134823	12528	3.5834
2	6	recv	5026	27683	107	0	0.0039
2	7	recv	5026	20722	107	0	0.0052

16 rows in set (5.07 sec)

Query OK, 0 rows affected (5.07 sec)

The spl (signals per loop) column indicates the approximate business of each thread. In Listing 20-2, the busiest thread type is ldm. Only the ldm thread with id=2 is loaded heavily; the other ldm thread is loaded only a little. The tc threads seem somewhat busy, but not as busy as the ldm threads.

Interrupts and CPU Binding

Yet another consideration when binding threads to CPUs is whether you should avoid binding to CPUs that are busy due to interrupts. An interrupt is a way for hardware or software to notify the CPU when immediate action is required. Each single interrupt finishes quickly and requires very few CPU resources. However, interrupts can add up and tons of interrupts may use lots of CPU resources. High-speed devices may cause lots of interrupts; for example, a high-IOPS NVMe connected SSDs and high-speed 10 gigabyte network interface card will cause a high volume of interrupts.

Linux systems are often configured so that specific CPUs handle interrupts by default. Such configuration may cause problems like these:

- Execution of the user program may be impeded by busy interrupts.

- CPU resources are insufficient to handle all the interrupts from busy devices.

To prevent such problems, *irqbalance* is useful. It can spread the load caused by interrupts into all or specific CPUs. The mechanism to bind interrupts to CPUs is called the *interrupt affinity*. It is important not to bind interrupts to too few CPUs. Otherwise, the speed of interrupt handling becomes a bottleneck. Note that not all devices support interrupt affinity being bound to multiple CPUs. The irqbalance just sets up interrupt affinity if the device supports it. A network interface card often supports *Receive Side Scaling* (*RSS*), also known as *multi-queue receive*. When RSS is enabled, interrupts caused by received packets on the network interface card can be redirected to multiple CPUs. Otherwise, it is not possible to spread workload among multiple CPUs.

To secure good performance of MySQL NDB Cluster, it is important not to bind interrupts and busy data node threads such as ldm and tc to the same CPU. The easiest way to avoid congestion between interrupts and busy threads is to spread interrupts to all the CPUs. In this case, all the CPUs will share the workload for interrupts, and the required resources needed per CPU will be small. The CPU resources required to handle interrupts will never be short, because all CPUs are involved in handling interrupts. This configuration is easy; however, it cannot achieve optimal performance.

Optimal performance can be achieved only when interrupts and busy threads are bound to separate CPUs explicitly. In this case, busy threads in a data node can monopolize the whole resource of the given CPU core. So, a bound thread can process the most signals on the given system.

When binding interrupts and threads to CPUs explicitly, you need to ensure that CPU resources bound to interrupts is sufficient. To see CPU utilization caused by interrupts on Linux, show the content of the */proc/stat* file. The sixth column of each CPU line indicates the time taken to handle interrupts. To analyze interrupts, the CONFIG_IRQ_TIME_ACCOUNTING configuration flag must be enabled in your kernel. To determine if the flag is enabled, execute the following command:

```
shell$ gunzip -c /proc/config.gz | grep CONFIG_IRQ_TIME_ACCOUNTING
```

If the CONFIG_IRQ_TIME_ACCOUNTING flag is disabled, you must compile the kernel from the source to enable it. While the way to build the Linux kernel is beyond scope of this book, it is not very difficult. Refer your Linux distribution manuals for kernel compilation details. You might even face a problem when executing this command if */proc/config.gz* doesn't exist. It should be because the CONFIG_IKCONFIG and CONFIG_IKCONFIG_PROC configuration flags are disabled in your kernel. If the */proc/config.gz* file doesn't exist, you need to recompile the kernel first.

On a macOS, users are not allowed to change interrupt settings. CPUs that handle interrupts are automatically selected. Even worse, you cannot retrieve separate CPU usage consumed by interrupts. It is included in the total CPU usage. To monitor system CPU time on a macOS, choose *Activity Monitor* and open *Window* ➤ *CPU History* from menu. Figure 20-3 shows a screenshot of CPU History window of Activity Monitor on two CPU core Mac machines.

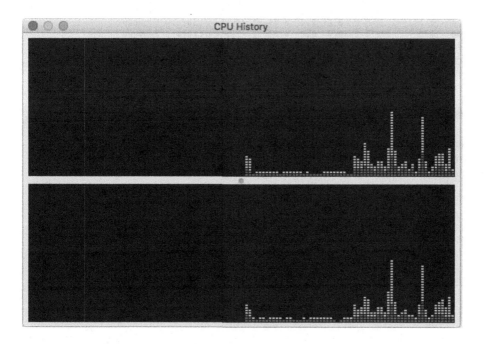

Figure 20-3. *CPU History screen of Activity Monitor on two CPU core Mac machines*

If you don't mind installing free software, *htop* works very nicely. If you have *homebrew*, a popular third-party package manager for macOS, installed on your system, you can install the htop command as follows:

```
shell$ brew install htop
```

See the following web site for more information about homebrew.

https://brew.sh/

Figure 20-4 shows example output of the htop command.

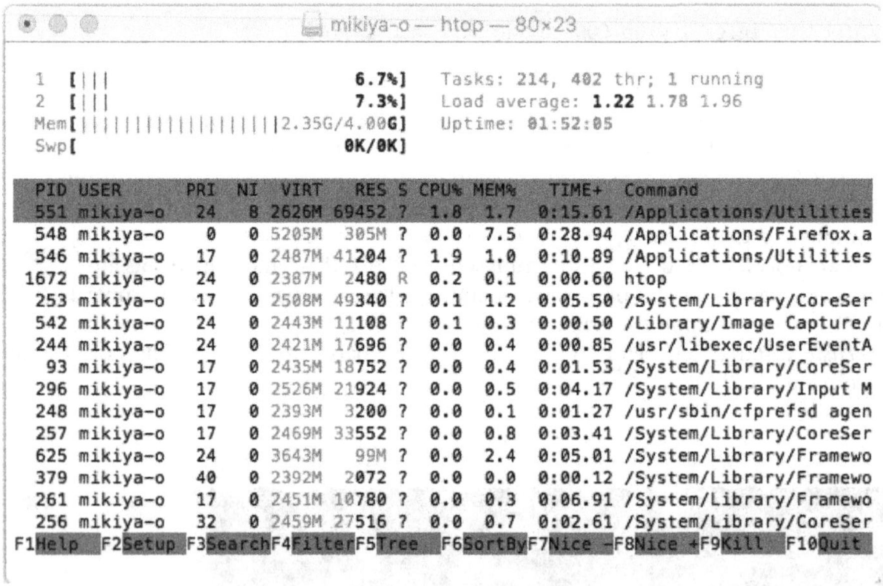

Figure 20-4. *htop command output example*

At the top-left side of the htop command output in Figure 20-4, CPU usage is displayed per CPU core. On Windows, you can see CPU usage for interrupts per CPU core using the *Performance Monitor*. Figure 20-5 shows the Performance Monitor when recording performance statistics data.

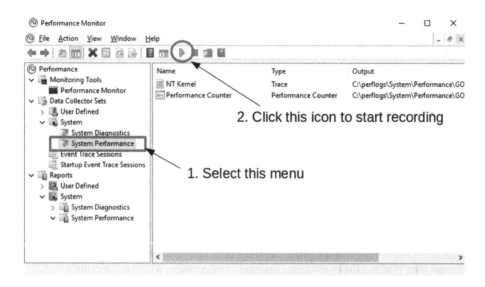

Figure 20-5. *Recording system performance statistics data using Performance Monitor*

To see system performance, you must record the statistics data first. To record the data, select System Performance from the side menu under Data Collector Sets ➤ System, and then click triangular icon at the toolbar. Wait for a while and click the square icon at the right of the triangular icon. Then, you can see a report by choosing Reports ➤ System ➤ System Performance. Figure 20-6 shows a screenshot of Performance Monitor displaying a report.

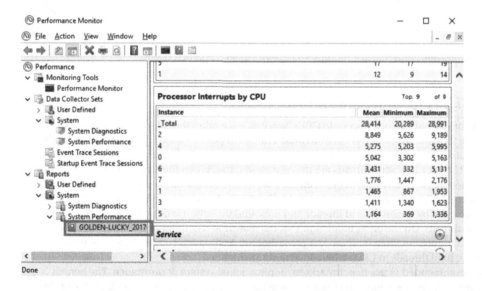

Figure 20-6. *Displaying a system performance report on Performance Monitor*

Performance indicators are grouped into categories. You can find Processor Interrupts by CPU under the CPU ➤ Process category. According to the numbers in Figure 20-6, the number of interrupts are somewhat imbalanced. CPU 2 handles approximately eight times more interrupts than CPU 5.

It is possible to specify interrupt affinity for network interface cards on Windows if the device supports Receive Side Scaling (RSS). In general, interrupt affinity is especially important for network interface devices. So, enabling RSS is often sufficient for interrupt affinity purposes on Windows systems. The following command enables RSS from a Windows shell.

```
PS C:\> netsh int tcp set global rss=enabledUsing Real-Time Scheduler
```

When using CPU binding, it is a good idea to employ the real-time scheduler and assign high priority to the bound threads. When using the real-time scheduler, threads run uninterrupted until a thread with a higher priority is ready to run, or until the given thread reaches sleep or wait events. This allows the real-time thread to utilize CPU resources at a maximum.

To run a thread as a real-time thread on Linux and POSIX systems using an unprivileged user, you must configure the resource limit. You need to edit */etc/security/limits.conf* and add a line like the following:

```
mysql    -    rtprio    99
```

This assumes that ndbd or ndbmtd is executed using the mysql user. Substitute the username if you run a data node using a different user. Without the appropriate resource configuration, a data node cannot start.

Alternatively, it is possible to assign a higher priority to a given thread via the thread_prio parameter in ThreadConfig. The thread_prio parameter adjusts the niceness (the priority of process scheduling in the UNIX world) of the given thread on Linux and UNIX systems, which needs a different resource limit than the real-time scheduler. In the ThreadConfig option, the realtime and thread_prio parameters are mutually exclusive. If you can use the real-time scheduler, it's a better choice than specifying thread_prio. See Chapter 4 for more information about the TheadConfig option.

The real-time scheduler for the ThreadConfig option is also available for Windows. Setting thread priority is a different process from UNIX systems. It is done by calling the SetThreadPriority() Windows API function. When a real-time scheduler is selected, the THREAD_PRIORITY_TIME_CRITICAL priority is set for the given thread. See the following page for further details about the SetThreadPriority() Windows API function.

https://msdn.microsoft.com/en-us/library/windows/desktop/ms686277(v=vs.85).aspx

Mix Bound Thread and Unbound Thread

Even if you want to bind some threads to certain CPUs, you can leave other threads unbound. It is not necessary to bind all threads. Whether it is better to bind a thread depends on the type of thread. ldm and tc are the primary candidates to be bound, because they must respond quickly and must handle as many signals as possible. The recv and send threads are the next candidates. When they are bound to CPUs and have a real-time scheduler, communication between the nodes will be more responsive.

In my opinion, other threads are not necessary to bind to CPUs. Optimal performance using given hardware can be achieved by mixing bound threads and unbound threads. It is desirable to set the real-time scheduler to bound threads. On the other hand, don't set the real-time scheduler to unbound threads. Just configure a sufficient number of threads when they are unbound. As discussed earlier in this section, it is also important not to bind threads to CPUs where interrupts are handled.

It is strongly recommended to use benchmarks to monitor actual system performance. The benefit of benchmarking is that it reveals actual data from real systems. Determine the best makeup of threads by examining benchmark results. Observed real data is always more reliable than hypotheses formulated on from the "armchair".

Disk Type and File System Block Size

Using a fast disk is very important for MySQL NDB Cluster, even when only in-memory tables are used, because logs and checkpoints are written to disk to ensure persistence of data. Writing speed to the NDBCluster tables is limited by the redo logging speed. Local checkpoint (LCP) also limits writing speed, because new redo log entries cannot be written to the redo log if the redo log space runs out. In such cases, it is necessary to free space occupied by old redo log entries, but it's not possible to free old redo log entries until the on-going LCP completes.

Disk speed is more important when using disk data tables, because they not only write to disk but also read data from disk. For disk data tables, it is necessary to write undo logs in addition to the data file and redo log. Thus, you need better disk bandwidth in this case than with in-memory tables. It is very important to employ fast disks when using disk data tables.

There are several considerations when optimizing disk I/O performance:

- Adjust the block size (or cluster size on NTFS) of the file system to 32KB when formatting it. This is because the page size of data memory and disk data table is 32KB in MySQL NDB Cluster.

- Use the deadline or noop I/O scheduler on Linux. They perform better for database systems than the cfq I/O scheduler, which is the default for the Linux kernel. Note that some Linux distribution sets use deadline as the default I/O scheduler.

- Append the noatime mount option on Linux and UNIX systems. It will improve file read performance, as the last access time is not recorded. This is important when you're restarting a data node and using disk data tables.

- You should leave some free space on the disk. In general, the closer the disk is filled to capacity, the slower its performance becomes. It is recommended to leave at least 20% free space unallocated to any disk partitions.

- Enable the *Trim* command on SSDs, which is a command to mark unused area as discarded. Trim may improve disk performance because it can omit unnecessary disk writes.

  - On Windows, Trim is supported since Windows 7. Trim is enabled by default. To check if Trim is enabled, run fsutil behavior query DisableDeleteNotify from the command prompt or a Windows shell with administrator privilege. If the value is 1, Trim is disabled. In such cases, enable it with the fsutil behavior set DisableDeleteNotify 0 command. If the value is not set, Trim is enabled. For more information, see *https://www.tenforums.com/tutorials/40028-enable-disable-trim-support-solid-state-drives-windows-10-a.html*.

  - On macOS, Trim is supported only for Apple branded SSDs from mac OS X 10.6.8 (Snow Leopard). As of macOS X 10.10.4 (Yosemite), Trim is supported on all brand SSDs. To enable Trim on third-party SSDs, execute sudo trimforce enable.

- On Linux, Trim is supported as of Linux Kernel version 2.6.33. On Linux systems, whether Trim is enabled by default or not depends on the distribution. For example, Trim is enabled by default on Ubuntu as of 14.04. Before enabling it, run hdparm -I /dev/sdX to verify if your device supports the Trim command. To enable it on Linux systems, add discard to the mount option. If you are using LVM, set issue_discard = 1 in the */etc/lvm/lvm.conf* file. You also need to configure the trim option for the file system in addition to LVM. If you prefer to use periodic batched trim, use the fstrim command from cron. Otherwise, add the discard option in the mount options. For more information, see *https:// access.redhat.com/documentation/en-US/Red_Hat_Enterprise_Linux/7/html/ Performance_Tuning_Guide/chap-Red_Hat_Enterprise_Linux-Performance_ Tuning_Guide-Storage_and_File_Systems.html.*

■ **Note** Don't enable Trim on dm-crypt, because it increases security risks. It leaks minimal data from freed blocks. At least it may allow attackers to extrapolate file system type in use when Trim is enabled. See the following page for more information: *http://asalor.blogspot.jp/2011/08/trim-dm-crypt-problems.html.*

SQL Tuning

This section discusses how to maximize performance by tuning SQL. The previous section was all about performance tuning on the MySQL NDB Cluster side. This section discusses performance tuning from the application point of view. In general, writing efficient SQL statements is very important, because performance can be many times faster if you understand the characteristics of the database management system and write the SQL accordingly.

Commit Sizing

The most significant characteristic to be aware of is that MySQL NDB Cluster is optimized for many small transactions. When modifying a given number of rows, it is much faster to modify them in lots of smaller transactions in parallel, rather than modifying all the rows with one big transaction. So, if you want to update tons of rows, separate the modifications into multiple transactions, and keep every transaction as small as possible. Execute the small transactions in parallel, if possible. MySQL NDB Cluster will complete the modifications much faster and will make the data nodes less busy.

Of course, separating one big modification into multiple smaller pieces may break atomicity. If atomicity is a must, don't break a transaction into smaller ones no matter how large. Be aware that a transaction may fail due to the upper limit of MaxNoOfConcurrentOperations or RedoBufferSize if you execute a large enough transaction. Even if atomicity is must, but it is not possible to raise the upper limits of these options, you will have to separate the transaction into smaller pieces.

What is the optimal size of a transaction, then? It depends on the configuration or the table definitions. If a transaction is for a *online transaction processing* (*OLTP*) type workload, limit the number of rows modified in the transaction to 1,000 approximately. If it's a batch or *online analytical processing* (*OLAP*) type workload, limit the number of rows to 100,000.

Non-Transactional Batch Processing

If you need to modify many rows at a time, but it is not necessary to be transactional, you can use the ndb_use_transaction option on the SQL node. By default, this option is ON, and transactions are enabled. If you set it to OFF, transaction support is disabled and modifications will be much faster. This option can be set at the session level. So, you can disable this option on a command basis like in the following example:

```
mysql> SET ndb_use_transaction = OFF;
mysql> DELETE FROM world.City;
mysql> SET ndb_use_transaction = ON;
```

Disabling transactions will break transaction properties such as atomicity. So, you cannot roll back an SQL command that is only partially executed due to problems. If you disable ndb_use_transaction, the modification must be recoverable or retrievable, like in the following situation:

- In a batch process, it creates a table and loads huge amounts of data into the table from file.

- Deletes unused rows matching some criteria, such as certain date ranges.

In these cases, you can repeat the same query if it fails.

Engine Condition Pushdown Optimization

One of the most powerful features of MySQL NDB Cluster is the capability to filter rows at the data nodes. It will minimize the network bandwidth usage between the data node and SQL node, and maximize the performance because filtering is done in parallel on data nodes. Filtering can be done whether there are suitable indexes or not. This feature is called *engine condition pushdown* optimization on the SQL node. Engine condition pushdown is enabled by default.

When engine condition pushdown is used, it is indicated in the Extra field of the EXPLAIN command, as shown in Listing 20-3. Note that pushed condition is displayed on the Extra field in parentheses. The condition isn't displayed in MySQL NDB Cluster 7.4 or older.

Listing 20-3. Query Execution Plan with Engine Condition Pushdown Enabled

```
mysql> EXPLAIN SELECT * FROM City WHERE District = 'Tochigi'\G
*************************** 1. row ***************************
           id: 1
  select_type: SIMPLE
        table: City
   partitions: p0,p1,p2,p3
         type: ALL
possible_keys: NULL
          key: NULL
      key_len: NULL
          ref: NULL
         rows: 4079
     filtered: 10.00
        Extra: Using where with pushed condition (`world`.`City`.`District` = 'Tochigi')
1 row in set, 1 warning (0.00 sec)
```

To disable engine condition pushdown, adjust the `optimizer_switch` option, as shown in Listing 20-4. In general, there is no advantage to disabling it.

Listing 20-4. Disabling Engine Condition Pushdown Optimization

```
mysql> set optimizer_switch='engine_condition_pushdown=off';
Query OK, 0 rows affected (0.00 sec)

mysql> EXPLAIN SELECT * FROM City WHERE District = 'Tochigi'\G
*************************** 1. row ***************************
           id: 1
  select_type: SIMPLE
        table: City
   partitions: p0,p1,p2,p3
         type: ALL
possible_keys: NULL
          key: NULL
      key_len: NULL
          ref: NULL
         rows: 4079
     filtered: 10.00
        Extra: Using where
1 row in set, 1 warning (0.00 sec)
```

Even though engine condition pushdown is fast and useful, you must be aware that all rows are scanned on the data nodes. This skews the query statistics. For example, `Rows_examined` in the slow query log indicates only rows returned to the SQL node. Rows scanned but filtered on the data nodes are excluded from the statistics. So, when you look for candidate queries to be optimized, engine condition pushdown may make your job more difficult.

Note that engine condition pushdown can be used together with indexes. If engine condition pushdown is used with indexes, unmatched rows are filtered at data nodes. This is pretty much like the *index condition pushdown* optimization, and more efficient than engine condition pushdown with a table scan. So, having a good index is still very important even when engine condition pushdown takes effect.

Optimizing Joins

In very old versions of MySQL NDB Cluster, join was a glass jaw for MySQL NDB Cluster, because the SQL node only had the *nested-loop-join* (*NLJ*) algorithm and its variant *block-nested-loop join* (*BNLJ*) algorithm. These algorithms required many traversals between the SQL node and data nodes. So, joins were very slow and caused tons of workload on the data nodes. In recent versions of MySQL NDB Cluster, more powerful join algorithms became available.

Pushdown Join Optimization

A join is a reasonably fast operation for MySQL NDB Cluster, because joins can be pushed down to the data nodes just like search criteria can be pushed down to the data nodes. With the pushdown join optimization, a join is performed inside the data nodes, and the SQL node just receive the joined rows from the data nodes.

A pushdown join is added as of the MySQL NDB Cluster 7.2 series. It was initially called *adaptive query localization* (*AQL*) or *select-project join* (*SPJ*). The latter name remains in the kernel block name that handles pushdown joins. To use pushdown joins, the `ndb_join_pushdown` option must be enabled; it is enabled by default.

Pushdown joins have some limitations. To enable pushdown joins, you need to satisfy these conditions:

- Key columns on joined tables must have identical data types.

- Queries must not reference BLOB or TEXT columns.

- Queries must not include explicit locking clauses—FOR UPDATE and LOCK IN SHARE MODE.

- The access method for the child (inner) table must be ref, eq_ref, or const for inner joins, and only eq_ref for outer joins. This means join key columns must be indexed for inner joins, and must have unique hash indexes for outer joins.

- There is limited support for pushdown joins and GROUP BY queries.

- Experimental user-defined partitioning types (other than [LINER] KEY) are not supported.

As you see, table design is very important when using pushdown joins. Use identical data types for identical data across tables and define the appropriate indexes on the join key columns.

When a pushdown join is employed, the Extra field of the EXPLAIN command will display the pushdown join, as shown in Listing 20-5. If engine condition pushdown optimization is not employed, execute SHOW WARNINGS, which will show the reason.

Listing 20-5. Query Execution Plan with a Pushdown Join

```
mysql> EXPLAIN SELECT * FROM City JOIN Country ON Country.Capital = City.Id\G
*************************** 1. row ***************************
           id: 1
  select_type: SIMPLE
        table: Country
   partitions: p0,p1,p2,p3
         type: ALL
possible_keys: NULL
          key: NULL
      key_len: NULL
          ref: NULL
         rows: 239
     filtered: 100.00
        Extra: Parent of 2 pushed join@1; Using where with pushed condition
(`world`.`Country`.`Capital` is not null)
*************************** 2. row ***************************
           id: 1
  select_type: SIMPLE
        table: City
   partitions: p0,p1,p2,p3
         type: eq_ref
possible_keys: PRIMARY
          key: PRIMARY
      key_len: 4
          ref: world.Country.Capital
         rows: 1
     filtered: 100.00
        Extra: Child of 'Country' in pushed join@1
2 rows in set, 1 warning (0.00 sec)
```

In example of Listing 20-5, the Extra field for the Country table includes information about the engine condition pushdown in addition to the pushdown join, even though no WHERE clause exists in this query. This is because the optimizer finds that the Country.Capital column is defined as nullable but cannot be NULL in this query as it's joined with a non-nullable column. In such cases, the optimizer thinks it can efficiently filter out rows from the parent table using an additional search condition.

Batched-Key-Access Join Optimization

Batched-key access join (*BKAJ*) is yet another fast join algorithm available with MySQL NDB Cluster. It is a variant of *Block Nested Loop Join* (*BNLJ*). BNLJ is an improved version of *Nested Loop Join* (NLJ), which reduces the number of scans for an inner table if the table has no suitable indexes. The algorithm for BKAJ is identical to BNLJ, except that access to the inner table is batched using the *multi-range read* (*MRR*) optimization.

To describe the BKAJ algorithm, we will discuss the NLJ and BNLJ algorithms first. NLJ is a very simple algorithm that performs joins like a loop. The following code is a conceptual algorithm of a join of two tables.

```
for each row in t1 matching where condition {
  for each row in t2 matching join key and where condition {
    send joined row to client
  }
}
```

If the inner table has an appropriate index to fetch rows, NLJ is very fast even if lots of rows are returned from the outer table and the inner table must be accessed many times. Otherwise, it will be very inefficient. Suppose that the inner table doesn't have suitable indexes, and the query fetches 1 million rows from the outer table, then inner table is scanned 1 million times. If the inner table is large, the query is unlikely to end in a practical amount of time.

To overcome this performance problem, BNLJ was introduced. With BNLJ, rows fetched from an outer table are first stored into a buffer, called the *join buffer*. Rows from an outer table will be fetched until the buffer becomes full. Then, it fetches rows one by one from an inner table using the search criteria, and tests if a fetched row can be joined to rows in the join buffer. This dramatically reduces the number of scans of the inner table.

Figure 20-7 is a conceptual view of the BNLJ algorithm. As you see in Figure 20-7, BNLJ is only useful when no suitable keys are available on the inner table.

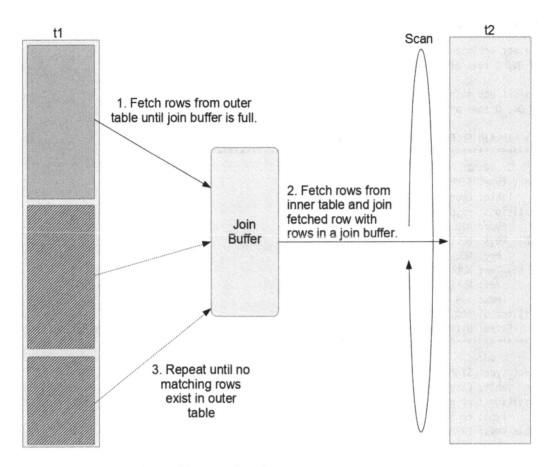

Figure 20-7. *Conceptual view of the BNLJ algorithm*

BNLJ is a very strong algorithm when the inner table doesn't have suitable indexes and a scan is needed. However, there are some more problems to be solved. Even if the inner table has suitable indexes for the join, accessing the inner table is not necessarily optimal. BKAJ solves the performance issue in such cases; access to the inner table is not scanned, but not efficient enough.

In theory, the order of rows in separate tables is irrelevant. So, access to the inner table will be done in random order with NLJ, which is often inefficient. In MySQL NDB Cluster, accessing the inner table row by row is not efficient even if the inner table has a suitable index for the join, because row access operations involve network traversal. To overcome this problem, BKAJ is useful.

With BKAJ, the rows are first fetched from the outer table and stored into the join buffer. Then, BKAJ retrieves the key values from the buffered rows. Next, the rows are fetched from the inner table using the MRR optimization. With MRR, rows are fetched using multiple key values sorted in key order. Finally, rows fetched from the inner table are joined with the buffered rows. Since access to the inner table is batched using multiple key values, this type of join is called a *batched-key-access join*.

BKAJ is disabled by default. To use BKAJ, modify the optimizer switch so that the optimizer can choose BKAJ, as shown in Listing 20-6. Note that the pushdown join is disabled in Listing 20-6, because it's more efficient than BKAJ. If a pushdown join is available, the optimizer tends to choose it over BKAJ. The example query in Listing 20-6 is identical to Listing 20-5. The only difference is the query execution plan. You can see `Using join buffer (Batched Key Access)` in the `Extra` field of the `City` table in Listing 20-6.

Listing 20-6. Enabling BKAJ and Examining the Query Execution Plan

```
mysql> set optimizer_switch='batched_key_access=on';
Query OK, 0 rows affected (0.00 sec)

mysql> SET ndb_join_pushdown = 0;
Query OK, 0 rows affected (0.00 sec)

mysql> EXPLAIN SELECT * FROM City JOIN Country ON Country.Capital = City.Id\G
*************************** 1. row ***************************
           id: 1
  select_type: SIMPLE
        table: Country
   partitions: p0,p1,p2,p3
         type: ALL
possible_keys: NULL
          key: NULL
      key_len: NULL
          ref: NULL
         rows: 239
     filtered: 100.00
        Extra: Using where with pushed condition (`world`.`Country`.`Capital` is not null)
*************************** 2. row ***************************
           id: 1
  select_type: SIMPLE
        table: City
   partitions: p0,p1,p2,p3
         type: eq_ref
possible_keys: PRIMARY
          key: PRIMARY
      key_len: 4
          ref: world.Country.Capital
         rows: 1
     filtered: 100.00
        Extra: Using join buffer (Batched Key Access)
2 rows in set, 1 warning (0.00 sec)
```

Offloading Joins

If it is not possible to employ efficient join algorithms, consider to setup replication from MySQL NDB Cluster to InnoDB. InnoDB generally has good join performance, and it is possible to spread read load among multiple slaves using a 1:N topology. See Chapter 6 for more information about the procedure to set up replication from MySQL NDB Cluster to InnoDB.

Optimizing Partitioning

Understanding and adjusting partitioning on MySQL NDB Cluster is very important. In MySQL NDB Cluster, data is spread into data nodes row by row. Each table is split into partitions, and each partition belongs to only one node group unless the table is fully replicated. So, it is possible to identify which data node stores the target row. Thus, the partition key also works as a distribution key among the data nodes.

Characteristics of Partitioning on MySQL NDB Cluster

For the time being, the only supported partitioning method by MySQL NDB Cluster is KEY partitioning, including its variant LINER KEY partitioning. KEY partitioning is similar to HASH partitioning, except for the expression to calculate the key value. For HASH partitioning, a user specifies a partition expression. On the other hand, for KEY partitioning, MySQL Server provides a partition expression; MySQL NDB Cluster uses MD5() for this purpose.

There are several differences as to how partition pruning works in the NDBCluster storage engine from InnoDB:

- All partitions are scanned in parallel in the NDBCluster storage engine. The scan speed is fast even if partition pruning isn't employed.

- The partitioning expression cannot be changed manually, and the number of partitions is limited by the system configuration. See Chapter 2 for more information about partition balancing.

User-Defined Partitioning

By default, the primary key works as a partition key. It is not a bad choice in most cases. However, in certain cases, choosing a different column as a partition key can be a better choice. For example, the world.City table in the world example database may have to be partitioned using CountryCode, instead of its primary key ID, because the world.City table is often queried for a specific country.

MySQL NDB Cluster can partition a table differently than the default. This functionality is called *user-defined partitioning*. User-defined partitioning is useful in the following scenario:

- A value for the partition key is often specified as an equality comparison for a range scan using additional search criteria.

- A table is joined as the inner table using a partition key.

In these cases, partition pruning can be applied when querying user-defined partitioned tables. It makes the query more efficient, thus it improves the scalability of your application.

For example, the query in Listing 20-7 must scan all partitions according to its execution plan. You can see that all partitions are listed in the partitions field of the EXPLAIN output. All the data nodes will be accessed by this query.

Listing 20-7. A Query That Scans All Partitions

```
mysql> EXPLAIN SELECT * FROM City
    ->   WHERE CountryCode='JPN' AND Name LIKE 'T%'\G
*************************** 1. row ***************************
           id: 1
  select_type: SIMPLE
        table: City
   partitions: p0,p1,p2,p3
         type: ref
possible_keys: CountryCode
          key: CountryCode
      key_len: 3
          ref: const
         rows: 3
     filtered: 11.11
        Extra: Using where with pushed condition (`world`.`City`.`Name` like 'T%')
1 row in set, 1 warning (0.00 sec)
```

Now consider changing the table definition, as shown in Listing 20-8. In this example, the primary key and partition definition change. The partition key for the City table has changed from the ID column to the CountryCode column.

Listing 20-8. Changing Table Definition of the City Table

```
mysql> ALTER TABLE City MODIFY ID INT NOT NULL, DROP PRIMARY KEY;
Query OK, 4079 rows affected (2.27 sec)
Records: 4079  Duplicates: 0  Warnings: 0

mysql> ALTER TABLE City ADD PRIMARY KEY (ID, CountryCode)
    ->                     PARTITION BY KEY (CountryCode);
Query OK, 4079 rows affected (0.88 sec)
Records: 4079  Duplicates: 0  Warnings: 0
```

With the table definition in Listing 20-8, the same query as in Listing 20-7 will have a different execution plan, as shown in Listing 20-9.

Listing 20-9. An Example Execution Plan for a User-Defined Partitioned Table

```
mysql> EXPLAIN SELECT * FROM City
    ->    WHERE CountryCode='JPN' AND Name LIKE 'T%'\G
*************************** 1. row ***************************
           id: 1
  select_type: SIMPLE
        table: City
   partitions: p2
         type: ref
possible_keys: CountryCode
          key: CountryCode
      key_len: 3
          ref: const
         rows: 3
     filtered: 11.11
        Extra: Using where with pushed condition (`world`.`City`.`Name` like 'T%')
1 row in set, 1 warning (0.00 sec)
```

You can see that only p2 is scanned by the query in Listing 20-9, because it has an explicit value for the partition key CountryCode. This query can be parallelized with the execution plan in Listing 20-9 more than the execution plan in Listing 20-7, because less workload will be caused by the scan.

User-defined partitioning also works with joins. Listing 20-10 shows an example execution plan for a join when the City table isn't user-defined partitioned. You can see that all partitions must be scanned to look for rows matching the given condition CountryCode = 'JPN'.

Listing 20-10. Execution Plan for a Join Without User-Defined Partitioning

```
mysql> EXPLAIN SELECT * FROM City JOIN Country ON
    -> Country.Code = City.CountryCode WHERE Country.Code = 'JPN'\G
*************************** 1. row ***************************
           id: 1
  select_type: SIMPLE
        table: Country
```

```
    partitions: p2
          type: eq_ref
 possible_keys: PRIMARY
           key: PRIMARY
       key_len: 3
           ref: const
          rows: 1
      filtered: 100.00
         Extra: NULL
*************************** 2. row ***************************
            id: 1
   select_type: SIMPLE
         table: City
    partitions: p0,p1,p2,p3
          type: ref
 possible_keys: CountryCode
           key: CountryCode
       key_len: 3
           ref: const
          rows: 3
      filtered: 100.00
         Extra: NULL
2 rows in set, 2 warnings (0.00 sec)
```

When the City table is user-defined partitioned, the query execution plan looks like Listing 20-11.

Listing 20-11. Execution Plan for a Join with User-Defined Partitioning

```
mysql> EXPLAIN SELECT * FROM City JOIN Country ON
    -> Country.Code = City.CountryCode WHERE Country.Code = 'JPN'\G
*************************** 1. row ***************************
            id: 1
   select_type: SIMPLE
         table: Country
    partitions: p2
          type: eq_ref
 possible_keys: PRIMARY
           key: PRIMARY
       key_len: 3
           ref: const
          rows: 1
      filtered: 100.00
         Extra: NULL
*************************** 2. row ***************************
            id: 1
   select_type: SIMPLE
         table: City
    partitions: p2
          type: ref
```

```
possible_keys: CountryCode
          key: CountryCode
      key_len: 3
          ref: const
         rows: 3
     filtered: 100.00
        Extra: NULL
2 rows in set, 2 warnings (0.00 sec)
```

Now, you can see that only p2 is accessed on both tables in Listing 20-11. This is very efficient in terms of network traversal. When *optimized node selection* is enabled, the query can be solved by accessing only one data node. We discuss optimized node selection later in this section.

Figure 20-8 depicts which partitions are accessed by this query. The left one is the case without user-defined partitioning. The right one is the case with user-defined partitioning. The effect of user-defined partitioning becomes more significant when the cluster has more data nodes.

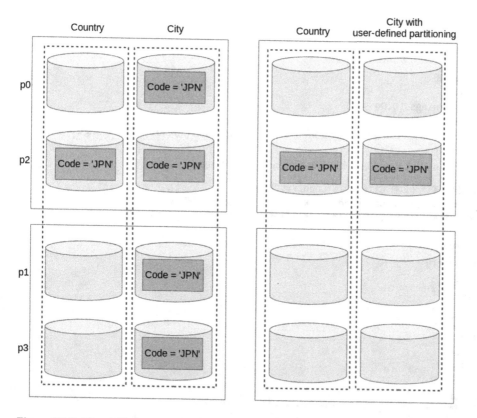

Figure 20-8. *How tables are accessed by a join with user-defined partitioning and without it*

The drawback to user-defined partitioning is that primary key definition must be changed in most cases. This is due to a limitation of MySQL Server; all unique indexes must include all the columns that are part of the partition key. This limitation is required because MySQL Server doesn't support global indexes for partitioned tables. Changing the primary key (or secondary unique index) may be unacceptable in most cases, because it would loosen the unique constraints. If the unique constraint for the original unique index is a must, user-defined partitioning cannot be used.

Read from Backup Replica and Fully Replicated Tales

As of the MySQL NDB Cluster 7.5 series, it is possible to adjust the partition balancing. See Chapter 2 for more information about partition balancing.

When a partition balance is employed and you're reading from a backup replica, a read workload may be spread more efficiently among data nodes than the default balance. Even though it is an interesting feature added to MySQL NDB Cluster 7.5, I think the effect of reading from a backup replica is not significant, except when the number of replicas is two, with the two data nodes set up and it works like fully replicated tables.

On the other hand, the effect of fully replicated tables, also added to MySQL NDB Cluster 7.5, is significant. When a table is fully replicated, every data node has all data of that table. So, any read query can be solved by accessing only one data node. As a trade-off, write performance against fully-replicated tables will be much worse than non-fully replicated tables, because modifications must be synchronized to all data nodes. The write overhead is larger when the cluster has more data nodes.

Fully replicated tables are suitable for tables that have the following characteristics:

- Data that rarely changes.

- Tables that are read very frequently from an application.

- Tables that are often joined with other tables.

- The data is small.

Optimizing Access from SQL Node to Data Node

It is also important to optimize the access from the SQL node to data nodes to maximize the performance. The SQL node must send requests to the data nodes and receive responses from the data nodes every time it is executing queries.

Connection Pooling

When an SQL node is running on a machine with many CPU cores, it is worth to consider increasing the number of connections between the SQL node and the data nodes, because a single instance of the NDB API will cause lock contention among the threads.

To increase the number of connections between the SQL node and data nodes, configure the ndb_cluster_connection_pool option in *my.cnf*. This option cannot be changed online. You need to restart the SQL node after changing it.

The default value for this option is 1. Increasing this option may increase the throughput of SQL handling for the given SQL node. While the maximum allowed value is 63 for this option, 4 is sufficient for most cases. Don't set it too big. Benchmark your application with a different ndb_cluster_connection_pool value and find the best setting for the application and the current cluster installation.

To increase this option, sufficient free slots for SQL nodes must be secured in *config.ini*. In other words, for the management and data nodes, each connection from ndb_cluster_connection_pool looks like a different SQL node. Refer to Chapter 10 for the procedure to add SQL nodes.

Optimized Node Selection

An arbitrary data node can be used as the *transaction coordinator* (*TC*) when executing transactions on data nodes. It is important to choose an appropriate TC to maximize performance of transactions in terms of response and throughput.

To minimize the overhead required for the communication between the SQL node and data nodes, MySQL NDB Cluster has a functionality called *distribution awareness*. It's a functionality to choose the TC based on the distribution of rows for the very first query within a transaction. If the query is looked up based on its distribution key, choosing the TC as the same host where the target row resides is the best choice, because no extra network communication is required to solve the query.

Figure 20-9 is a non-optimal node selection for a lookup query based on the distribution key; the TC and the data node where the target row exists don't match. In this case, the TC must send a signal to another data node to request to send the row data.

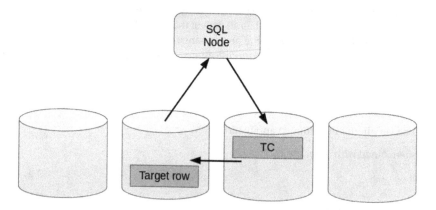

Figure 20-9. Non-optimal, distribution-unaware node selection

---

■ **Tip** The distribution key can be the primary key for an implicitly partitioned table or the partition key for a user-defined partitioned table.

Figure 20-10 shows an optimal node selection; the TC and the data node where the target row exists match. In this case, the lookup query based on the distribution key can be solved by just accessing one data node.

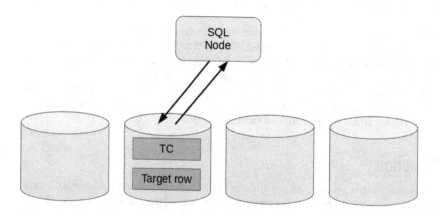

Figure 20-10. Optimal distribution-aware node selection

To let the SQL node select the TC based on the distribution, the `ndb_optimized_node_selection` option must be set to 2 or 3. 3 is the default. This option may take a value from 0 to 3, defined as follows:

- **0:** Distribution-aware node selection is not done. TC is selected in a round-robin fashion.

- **1:** Distribution-aware node selection is not done. TC is selected based on the network hops between the SQL node and the data node. If the SQL node and the data node reside in a same host, the data node is the closest to this SQL node, so it is always chosen as the TC.

- **2:** The SQL node first attempts to choose the TC based on distribution awareness. If the given query cannot prune the target partition, such as a scan without a user-defined partition, it falls back to the same behavior as 0.

- **3:** Same as 2, except that it falls back to 1 instead of 0.

In most cases, you don't have to change this option from the default. On the other hand, you need to consider the following points when you write transactions:

- Execute a query that accesses only one partition at the very beginning of each transaction. Look up or scan the partition key over a user-defined partitioned table.

- Apply user-defined partitioning if possible. It will increase the chances of executing the whole transaction within only one data node.

- Distribution-aware node selection is done by examining the first statement of each transaction. If a transaction includes many statements, the distribution-aware node selection will have little effect.

- Distribution-aware node selection may even cause bad performance in certain cases. For example, suppose that the first query in a given transaction accesses a table with only one row. In such case, the same node is selected as the TC for the given transaction. This causes imbalanced workload among data nodes if `ndb_optimized_node_selection=3`. It is worth to changing it to 0 or 1.

Adding Nodes

When the hardware resources are not sufficient for the ongoing workload, it might be time to add new nodes to the cluster. You can add any type of node online to the existing cluster. Refer to Chapter 10 for more details about adding nodes. There are two choices—adding data nodes and/or SQL nodes. Data nodes must be added when facing the following problems:

- The application needs more capacity.

- Accessing the table data is the major bottleneck.

Whether performance will be improved by adding data nodes or not depends on the access patterns from your application, as described:

- Performance of lookups using a unique hash index is likely to be improved by adding data nodes.

- Performance of scans against user-defined partitioning is likely to be improved by adding data nodes, because such scans access only a certain data node.

- Performance of scans without user-defined partitioning, which return many rows, is likely to be improved by adding data nodes, because such scans are performed in parallel on all data nodes.

- Performance of scans without user-defined partitioning, which return just a few rows, is unlikely to be improved by adding data nodes, because all nodes must be involved to return just a few rows. This type of operation causes serious overhead. So, adding data nodes may make the performance worse.

On the other hand, performance is often improved by just adding extra SQL node and spreading loads among them. SQL node can be a bottleneck, because it consumes lots of CPU resources. Parsing, optimizing, and executing queries are CPU-intensive workloads. If the performance of the data nodes is high, many SQL nodes can be required to fully utilize the potential of data nodes.

Using NoSQL API in Conjunction with SQL

If the response of simple queries is important, consider using a NoSQL API instead of SQL. It can achieve much quicker response times and much higher throughput than SQL. In MySQL NDB Cluster, it is possible to access the same data from different APIs, such as memcached, NDB API, and ClusterJ.

Writing applications using only NoSQL can be very difficult, because the NoSQL API is a low-level API with very little overhead. Mixing SQL and NoSQL can achieve a good balance between development efficiency and performance.

Summary

This chapter discussed the key points to improving the performance at the system level and at the application development level. Performance is always the most significant issue for database application development, because any application without sufficient performance is useless.

When using MySQL NDB Cluster, the underlying system must be configured properly, and MySQL NDB Cluster must be configured so that it can utilize the computer resources efficiently. The configuration of the CPU is especially important, because the load of MySQL NDB Cluster is CPU intensive, except for the I/O required for checkpointing and disk data tables related to I/O.

The way to write queries is also an important issue with database applications. Since database management systems have their own characteristics, it is important to understand what the database system is good at. MySQL NDB Cluster has various optimization algorithms and functionalities, as discussed in this chapter. When you face a performance problem, review this chapter and find a way to improve it.

Index

▦ D, E

Get the eBook for only $5!

Why limit yourself?

With most of our titles available in both PDF and ePUB format, you can access your content wherever and however you wish—on your PC, phone, tablet, or reader.

Since you've purchased this print book, we are happy to offer you the eBook for just $5.

To learn more, go to http://www.apress.com/companion or contact support@apress.com.

Apress®

Printed in the United States
By Bookmasters